He who lives to see two or three generations is like a man who sits some time in the conjurer's booth at a fair, and witnesses the performance twice or thrice in succession. The tricks were meant to be seen only once; and when they are no longer a novelty and cease to deceive, their effect is gone.

Arthur Schopenhauer, "On the Sufferings of the World"

THE MAN
BEHIND THE MICROCHIP

Robert Noyce and the Invention of Silicon Valley

LESLIE BERLIN

OXFORD
UNIVERSITY PRESS

2005

OXFORD
UNIVERSITY PRESS

Oxford University Press, Inc., publishes works that
further Oxford University's objective of excellence
in research, scholarship, and education.

Oxford   New York
Auckland   Cape Town   Dar es Salaam   Hong Kong   Karachi
Kuala Lumpur   Madrid   Melbourne   Mexico City   Nairobi
New Delhi   Shanghai   Taipei   Toronto

With offices in
Argentina   Austria   Brazil   Chile   Czech Republic   France   Greece
Guatemala   Hungary   Italy   Japan   Poland   Portugal   Singapore
South Korea   Switzerland   Thailand   Turkey   Ukraine   Vietnam

Copyright © 2005 by Leslie Berlin

Published by Oxford University Press, Inc.
198 Madison Avenue, New York, NY 10016
www.oup.com

Oxford is a registered trademark of Oxford University Press

Library of Congress Cataloging-in-Publication Data
Berlin, Leslie, 1969–
   The man behind the microchip : Robert Noyce and the invention of Silicon Valley /
Leslie Berlin.
      p.   cm.
   Includes bibliographical references and index.
   ISBN-13: 978-0-19-516343-8
   ISBN-10: 0-19-516343-5 (alk. paper)
1. Noyce, Robert N., 1927– . 2. Electronics engineers—United States—Biography.
3. Santa Clara Valley (Santa Clara County, Calif.)—History. I. Title.
TK7807.N69B47   2005
621.381'092—dc22   2004065494

9 8 7 6 5 4 3 2 1
Printed in the United States of America
on acid-free paper

To Rick, Corbin, and Lily
My beloved ones

Contents

Acknowledgments

One reason it took me several years to write this book was that before I could even start, I needed to create my own archive. Noyce's papers were not collected—he freely admitted he was "very sloppy in record-keeping"—and many important documents in the history of Silicon Valley have been lost, forgotten, or (I was dismayed to learn) destroyed. In the process of copying or gathering materials from basements and archives around the country, I have been fortunate to encounter more than a hundred people who were willing to share their documents and their memories of Noyce and the early days of the Silicon Valley semiconductor industry. The names of those generous people appear in Appendix A; to each of them, I am endlessly grateful. In addition, I would like to express particular gratitude to the following people who met with me multiple times or shared useful documents with me: Julius Blank, Roger Borovoy, Warren Buffett, Maryles and Mar Dell Casto, Ted Hoff, Paul Hwoschinsky, Steve Jobs, Jean Jones, Jim Lafferty, Jay Last, Christophe Lécuyer, Regis McKenna, Gordon Moore, Adam Noyce, Bill Noyce, Gaylord Noyce, Penny Noyce, Polly Noyce, Ralph Noyce, Karl Pedersen, Evan Ramstad, T. R. Reid, Daniel Seligson, Robert Smith, Charlie Sporck, Bob and Donna Teresi, and Bud Wheelon. Donald Noyce, Robert Noyce's older brother, was an amateur historian and—thank goodness—an inveterate packrat. Before he died quite unexpectedly in November 2004, he shared his collection of family memorabilia with me, a gift that contributed immeasurably to the early chapters of *The Man Behind the Microchip*.

Ann Bowers deserves special thanks of her own. This biography has been an entirely independent undertaking, but it would not be the book it is without her support. She sat through many hours of interviews, helped me contact key players in Bob Noyce's life, and granted me access to boxes of papers and photos—all without imposing any limitations of any kind on my research or writing.

In addition, the following experts merit thanks for their guidance: Polly Armstrong, Maggie Kimball, Henry Lowood, and Christy Smith at the Stanford Special Collections; Tim Dietz and Annie Fitzpatrick at Dietz and Associates; Leslie Gowan Armbruster at the Ford Motor Company archives, Ford Motor Company; Mickey Munley and Catherine Rod at Grinnell College; Daryl Hatano at the Semiconductor Industry Association (SIA); Marilyn Redmond at SEMATECH; John Clark at National Semiconductor; and the incomparable Rachel Stewart at the Intel archives and museum. The book also benefited from materials made available to me at the following archives and repositories: the Center for History of Physics, American Institute for Physics; the California History Center, De Anza College; the Electrochemical Society; the Grinnell Room, Stewart Public Library, Grinnell, Iowa; the Hewlett-Packard archives, Hewlett-Packard Corporation; the IEEE History Center Oral History Collection; the Libra Foundation, Portland, Maine; the Institute Archives and Special Collections, MIT Libraries; the MIT University Physics Department; the Pacific Studies Center, Mountain View, California; and the Stanford News Service.

Many thanks to members of the Stanford biographers seminar; to Alex Kline; to two anonymous readers selected by Oxford University Press; to Liz Borgwardt, David Jeffries, and Ron Newburgh, who read early chapter drafts; to Jose Arreola, a friend and physicist who spent more than an hour talking to me about Noyce's doctoral dissertation; to David M. Kennedy, whose review of the manuscript did more to improve it than he will ever know; and to Ross Bassett, not only a fantastic reader but also the author of an excellent work of semiconductor history.

My editor at Oxford, Susan Ferber, always asked the right questions and pushed me just as much as I needed. Donald Lamm, my agent, has helped me through every step of this process. My parents, Steve Berlin and Vera Berlin, and my sisters Jessica and Loren have been endlessly inquisitive and supportive.

The Life Member's Fellowship in Electrical History from the IEEE and a Franklin Research Grant from the American Philosophical Society supported the research for *The Man Behind the Microchip*; grants from the Andrew P. Mellon Foundation, the Charles Babbage Institute, and Stanford University funded earlier research for my doctoral dissertation, some of which has been incorporated into this book.

A special thanks to the History Department at Stanford University, where I have worked for the past two years as a visiting scholar in the Program in the History and Philosophy of Science and Technology. Two professors in the department—Tim Lenoir and David M. Kennedy—have been thinking with me about Robert Noyce since 1997, when they began advising my dissertation on Noyce's career. I have long considered Tim and David mentors and am now honored to count them among my friends, as well.

In addition, I am immensely grateful to the staff of Discovery Children's House, as well as to two wonderful young women—Michelle Casady and Megan Baldwin—who cared for my children for the hours each week that I devoted to research and writing.

The final thanks—and the word seems so inadequate—goes to my husband, Rick Dodd, the great love of my life and my partner in every possible way. From tutoring me on the finer points of semiconductor electronics, to running to the copy store, to reading the manuscript at midnight, to making the kids' breakfasts the next morning, he did everything possible to ensure that this book had the best chance of success.

THE MAN BEHIND THE MICROCHIP

Introduction

B ob Noyce took me under his wing," Apple Computer founder Steve Jobs explains. "I was young, in my twenties. He was in his early fifties. He tried to give me the lay of the land, give me a perspective that I could only partially understand." Jobs continues, "You can't really understand what is going on now unless you understand what came before."[1]

Before Intel and Google, before Microsoft and dot-coms and Apple and Cisco and Sun and Pixar and stock-option millionaires and startup widows and billionaire venture capitalists, there was a group of eight young men—six of them with PhDs, none of them over 32—who disliked their boss and decided to start their own transistor company. It was 1957. Leading the group of eight was an Iowa-born physicist named Robert Noyce, a minister's son and former champion diver, with a doctorate from MIT and a mind so quick (and a way with the ladies so effortless) that his graduate-school friends called him "Rapid Robert." Over the next decade, Noyce managed the company, called Fairchild Semiconductor, by teaching himself business skills as he went along. By 1967, Fairchild had 11,000 employees and $12 million in profits.

Before the Internet and the World Wide Web and cell phones and personal digital assistants and laptop computers and desktop computers and pocket calculators and digital watches and pacemakers and ATMs and cruise control and digital cameras and motion detectors and video games— before all these, and the electronic heart of all these, is a tiny device called an integrated circuit. The inventor of the first practical integrated circuit, in 1959, was Robert Noyce. It was one of 17 patents awarded to him.

In 1968, Noyce and his Fairchild co-founder Gordon Moore launched their own new venture, a tiny memory company they called Intel. Noyce's leadership of Intel—six years as president, five as board chair, and nine as a director—helped create a company that was roughly twice as profitable as its competitors and that today stands as the largest producer of semiconductor chips in the world.

1

But Noyce believed "big is bad"—or if not downright bad, at least not as much fun as small companies in which "everyone works much harder and cooperates more." When he left daily management at Intel in 1975, he turned his attention to the next generation of high-tech entrepreneurs. This is how he met Jobs. This is how he came to serve on the boards of a half dozen startup companies and informally provide seed money to many more. He did not think that all these companies would succeed—he filed his paperwork for several of them in shoe boxes that he kept in his closet—but he strongly believed that by investing, he was doing his part, as he put it, to "restock the stream I've fished from."[2]

Noyce was constitutionally unable to sit on the sidelines of any operation with which he was involved. He once called his invention of the integrated circuit "a challenge to the future," and turning away from the television interviewer, he stared straight into the camera to speak directly to the viewers: "Now let's see if you can top that one," he said, flashing a smile. At a father-son baseball game, which the dads traditionally allowed the boys to win, Noyce hit the very first pitch out of the park. "My poor father couldn't help himself," recalls his daughter Penny, who was in the stands that day. "He always threw himself entirely into the activity at hand—in whatever he did, he tried to excel."[3]

Robert Noyce's favorite ski jacket featured a patch that declared "no guts, no glory." It was a fitting motto for a man who flew his own planes, chartered a helicopter to drop him on mountaintops so he could ski down through the trees, rode a motorcycle through the streets of Bali in the middle of a thunderstorm, and once leapt with his skis off a 25-foot ledge into deep powder, exultant because he "had never jumped off a cliff into that much snow." His powers of persuasion were legendary. In 1963, he convinced the notoriously conservative board of one of his companies to start the semiconductor industry's first offshore manufacturing facility—at a site that was then completely under water, soon to be reclaimed from the bay by the government of Hong Kong. He talked a carload of traveling companions into joining him for a dip in a brackish Tibetan river, murky and, just a bit upstream, filled with crocodiles. He inspired in nearly everyone whom he encountered a sense that the future had no limits, and that together they could, as he liked to say, "Go off and do something wonderful." Recalls Intel's former chief counsel, "He was like the pied piper. If Bob wanted you to do something, you did it."[4]

Like so many others who spend their lives in the limelight, Noyce was an intensely private man. "He was the only person I can think of who was both aloof and charming," says Intel chairman Andy Grove. "I don't know how Bob kept you away, but you just didn't know anything about him. And this is the guy who would go down on one knee to adjust my skis, put my chains on, when I was a nobody."[5]

To be sure, Noyce's was not a simple personality. A small-town boy suspicious of large bureaucracies, he built two companies that between them employed tens of thousands of people, and he spent many years working through the maze of federal politics after he helped launch the Semiconductor Industry Association, today one of the nation's most effective lobbying organizations. He was a preacher's son who rejected organized religion, an outstanding athlete who chainsmoked, and an intensely competitive man who was greatly concerned that people like him. He was worth tens of millions and owned several planes and houses but nonetheless somehow maintained a "just folks" sort of charm: you half expected him to kick the ground and mutter "aw shucks, you guys," when his hometown declared "Bob Noyce Day" or an elite engineering group named him the first recipient of an award many called the Nobel Prize for Engineering. Recalls Warren Buffett, who served on a college board with Noyce for several years, "Everybody liked Bob. He was an extraordinarily smart guy who didn't need to let you know he was that smart. He could be your neighbor, but with lots of machinery in his head."[6]

It is easy to imagine Noyce, tuxedoed, smiling shyly, and desperately wanting a cigarette, in October 2000, when, had he lived, he undoubtedly would have shared the Nobel Prize for Physics awarded to his integrated circuit co-inventor, Jack Kilby. Amazingly, this is the second Nobel Prize that Noyce might rightfully have won. The first was in 1973, when a Japanese physicist named Leo Esaki was one of three recipients of the physics prize. Esaki was cited for his pathbreaking work on the tunnel diode, a device that provided the first physical evidence that tunneling, a foundational postulate of quantum mechanics, was more than an intriguing theoretical concept. Noyce had written a complete description of the tunnel diode nearly a year and a half before Esaki published his work in 1958. The two men's research was thus happening almost simultaneously on opposite sides of the Pacific. Noyce had not published his ideas, however, because his boss, the Nobel laureate William Shockley, discouraged him from pursuing them.

Beginnings fascinated Noyce. He could imagine things few others could see. In 1965, when push-button telephones were brand new and state-of-the-art computers still filled entire rooms, Noyce predicted that the integrated circuit would lead to "portable telephones, personal paging systems, and palm-sized TVs." His sense of near-limitless possibility led Noyce to pursue technical hunches that his colleagues believed were dead ends. (Often his peers were right, but occasionally, spectacularly, they were wrong.) Ideas fell from Noyce like leaves from a tree. For his work to be successful, he had to be surrounded by people who could follow up on his thoughts, filter them, and attend to the detail-work of running a company, because almost as soon as Noyce mentioned an idea, he had left it behind in order to explore another one. Noyce's peripatetic mental style could be maddening at times. Andy Grove likens it to "a butterfly hopping from thought to thought. Unfinished sentences, unfinished thoughts: you really had to be on your toes to follow him."[7]

Noyce was forever pushing people to take their own ideas beyond where they believed they could go. "That's all you've got?" he'd ask. "Have you thought about . . ." An exchange of this sort left Noyce's colleagues and employees feeling as though his blue eyes had bored right through their skulls to discover some potential buried inside themselves or their ideas that they had not known existed. It was exhilarating and a bit frightening. "If you weren't intimidated by Bob Noyce, you'd never be intimidated by anybody," recalls Jim Lafferty, Noyce's friend and fellow pilot. "Here is this guy who is so capable in everything he does, and here you are trying to stumble through life and make it look respectable, and now you're trying to keep up with him. And nobody can keep up with him."[8]

Indeed, Noyce can sound too good to be true. He was a brilliant, wealthy, generous, greatly beloved man gifted with enormous vision. But to leave a description of Noyce here would be to sell him short. He was not a super-hero. He could be indecisive and would do almost anything to avoid confrontation, a trait that kept him from making difficult decisions and taking tough actions. His resolute focus on the future, his persistent gaze beyond the horizon, left him blind to many details and uninterested in the mundane minutiae of corporate management. This lack of attention had real consequences. He recoiled from strong emotions and would rather pretend a problem did not exist than address it head on. For many years, his personal life was difficult, and he was not entirely without fault in this area.

But these elements of Noyce's character make him more of a man, not less. And to watch him come to recognize—and then devise means of working around—his own shortcomings, particularly as a manager, is to observe an exceptionally creative mind in action.

NOYCE'S INNER CIRCLE included the best-known players in Silicon Valley—Andy Grove and Gordon Moore of Intel, Arthur Rock and Eugene Kleiner of venture capital fame, Steve Jobs of Apple, William Shockley, co-inventor of the transistor—as well as the inventors of the planar process (which made it possible to mass produce complex microelectronic devices) and the microprocessor. Some of the lesser-known Silicon Valley pioneers who worked with Noyce hold their own interest: among them are a monomaniacal genius, a Swiss with two doctorates, an aristocratic refugee from Nazi terror, and the son of a New York cabbie who really wanted to run a bed-and-breakfast. Most of the people who worked with Noyce admired him—some loved him—but a few resented his notoriety, which they felt obscured their own contributions. "Credit floats up" was the only comment one would offer about his former boss.

Together these men built a network of specialized equipment providers, high-caliber technical trade schools and engineering programs, and tech-savvy financial, public relations, and legal support services that helped to transform the once rural Santa Clara Valley into a high-tech business machine called Silicon Valley. When Noyce arrived in the San Francisco Bay Area in April 1956, electronics was the fastest growing industry in the region, with government defense contracts and sales to the military accounting for well over half the business. But the plum, cherry, and apricot trees that had once anchored the valley's economy still dotted the landscape. Twenty years later, the orchards were gone, government purchases accounted for less than a quarter of integrated circuit sales, and the electronics industry that had been suckled on government work was now sustained by a complex private network founded on a culture of high-stakes risk. Noyce's career offers an ideal window into how this happened.

That Noyce and his contemporaries changed their world is only half the story. Their lives bear the marks of the monumental social, political, technical, and economic shifts that reshaped America in the second half of the twentieth century. When Noyce went west, he joined the massive postwar migration to California. His industry, launched in the torrent of defense spending and creative panic triggered by a tiny beeping satellite that the Soviets had lofted into orbit in 1957, placed itself at the center of the debate over industrial policy in the 1980s. Semiconductors also catalyzed the high-tech bubble in the 1990s.

Little more than a dozen years ago, the *San Jose Mercury News* declared Noyce the Thomas Edison *and* the Henry Ford of Silicon Valley. He received the National Medal of Science from President Carter and the National Medal of Technology from President Reagan. Noyce was featured in hundreds of newspaper and magazine articles. Peter Jennings profiled him as "the person of the week" on ABC. CBS anchor Charles Osgood called Noyce "the man who changed the world." Tom Wolfe, who knew a hero when he saw one, wrote about Noyce in a 1983 *Esquire* article that ran next to pieces on other "American Originals," including Jackie Robinson, John F. Kennedy, Betty Friedan, Walt Disney, and Elvis Presley. Futurist George Gilder called Robert Noyce "undoubtedly the most important American of the postwar era," while Isaac Asimov went even further by hailing the invention of the integrated circuit as "the most important moment since man emerged as a life form."[9]

And yet until now the story of Robert Noyce has not been told in full. "High-tech history' is almost an oxymoron," Noyce once said. "Our major activity is to make yesterday's 'gee-whiz!' mundane today." Writing the history of a man, an industry, and a place that consider self-obsolescence the pinnacle of success is not easy. Companies routinely shred their paper-work, and those items not destroyed by corporate fiat are consigned to wastebaskets and dumpsters by employees unable to imagine that the world might one day be as interested in their past as these technologists are in the future. It is only now that the one-time young Turks of the semiconductor industry are entering their seventies and eighties that they have begun to look backward, and remember.

Noyce did not live to look back. In 1990, at age 62, and just weeks after informing the board of SEMATECH—a two-year-old, billion-dollar, manu-facturing consortium jointly funded by 14 semiconductor companies and the Department of Defense—that he planned to leave his job as the consortium's founding CEO, Noyce succumbed to a heart attack. Three thousand people attended memorial services for him. President George H. W. Bush phoned Noyce's widow to offer his personal condolences.

And yet even Noyce, the man who always looked forward, acknowledged that "roots are important." His core had been shaped by his Depression-era boyhood in the small town of Grinnell, Iowa, and by his birth into a family with deep Midwestern roots and a tradition of its men serving as teachers, ministers, or both. Noyce knew that his high-flying, high-tech adult self had its source in the Iowa boy who pedaled flat-rate annual snow-shoveling contracts to his neighbors and who spent every spare minute building mo-torized sleds and the town's best model airplanes. Surely the shape of the future electronics entrepreneur can be divined in 12-year-old Bobby Noyce's comment from a long-forgotten journal: "My hobby is handicraft," he wrote in 1939. "I like this hobby because it is useful. You can make things cheaply that are worth a lot."[10]

I

Adrenaline and Gasoline

Ask nearly anyone who lived in Grinnell, Iowa, during the 1940s and 1950s what they remember about Bob Noyce, and the answer is bound to involve a glider. In the summer of 1940, Noyce, who was then 12, built a boy-sized aircraft with his 14-year-old brother, Gaylord. This glider has attained mythic proportions among native Grinnellians, some of whom claim to have seen one of the Noyce brothers take flight from the roof of the Grinnell College stables, from the bleachers at the college stadium, from a large open window on the third floor of the Noyce home. The most dramatic story involves Gaylord and Bob convincing their seven-year-old brother to climb in the glider, which the older boys then tied to the bumper of a car that took off at top speed.

For Bob Noyce, the glider was "an all-time high" in "my long career of making things"—or so he claimed at 17. He had built a radio from scratch and motorized his sled by welding a propeller and an engine from an old Briggs and Stratton washing machine to the back of it. When the winter weather grew bitter and his hands cracked from one too many cold mornings delivering the *Des Moines Register* through the quiet streets of Grinnell, he had wired a car headlight to a battery that he found at the dump. Early risers could watch him precariously balance his way along his route, morning papers over his shoulder, warm headlight in his hands, ten-pound battery perched in the wire basket on his handlebars. He filled a scrapbook with *Popular Science* plans for constructing various ship models, a bed, a contraption that worked like a windsurfer but was used on ice, a skate sharpener, a xylophone, and a "half-horsepower sidewalk roadster."[1]

But always, his passion was flight. On summer evenings, he and Gaylord built balloons from wrapping paper and wire, lit oily rags underneath and watched their creations rise into the night skies like so many moons before drifting into a farmer's field when the rags burned out. They built innumerable balsa-wood model airplanes, the parts forever littering the window sills and steps of their house, to their mother's great displeasure. Bob

Noyce could spend weeks on a plane, perfecting the design, fine tuning the motor, and hunting it through the tall weeds that dotted the fields around town. But when a plane was shopworn, he showed no remorse. Grandly, boldly, he lit it on fire and sailed it from a window.[2]

When Bob Noyce was 11, he and a neighbor rode their bikes to a pasture where Grinnell's first barnstormer was giving 15-minute trips in his new Ford tri-motor for a dollar per ride. Noyce and his friend spent the day craning their necks upward, and when the line for rides had dwindled, the two boys convinced the ticket seller to let them share a seat. Perched on the edge of his half of the seat, Noyce watched the ground fall away, and soon he could see the Congregational Church where his family worshipped every Sunday and Grinnell College, where his oldest brother Don attended classes and his father, a minister, worked for the regional Congregationalist offices. Bob found his house, a modest one on a well-kept lot, just across the street from the college. And after they landed, after the two boys pedaled furiously home for dinner, after Noyce washed up and bowed his head for grace, he told his parents nothing of his great adventure. Keeping it secret made it that much more exciting.[3]

Bob Noyce was almost certainly remembering this flight when he proposed to Gaylord that they make their own glider. Bob had long ago proven himself the mastermind of mischief in their home, the daredevil forever pulling Gay, who would one day become a minister and who was already a very good boy, into impish hijinks. The two boys designed the glider themselves, working from their experience building model planes and from an illustration that they found in the *Book of Knowledge*, a multivolume encyclopedia that their parents kept deliberately accessible on a low shelf in the living room bookcase.

The brothers pooled their combined savings of $4.53 to buy materials and sent word to their neighborhood pals that a great invention was under construction. Soon the friends were helping too. Bob Smith, whose father owned a furniture store that regularly received rolls of carpet wound around bamboo spindles, provided sticks for the frame. Charlotte Matthews, the only girl on their block of 17 boys, sewed the cheese cloth to cover the wings. When the Noyce brothers declared the glider finished, it stood some four feet tall, and its wings stretched nearly 18 feet from tip to tip. Constructed largely from $1' \times 2'$ pine boards, it had neither wheels nor skids and ran entirely on boy power.[4]

The pilot moved and steered the plane by standing amidship in an opening, holding up the frame with his two hands, and running as fast as he could. "We succeeded in running and jumping to get a little lift as experienced by the pilot," Gaylord recalls. "In running off a mound about four or five feet high, we got more." This was not good enough for Bob. Together he and Gaylord convinced their neighbor Jerry Strong, newly possessed of a driver's license and the keys to his father's car, to hitch the glider to the auto's bumper. Jerry was instructed to drive down Park Street fast enough to launch the glider and keep it aloft. The experiment, which in no way involved a seven-year-old brother, proved more terrifying than effective.[5]

Still this was not sufficiently thrilling for Bob Noyce. He and Jerry Strong decided to try, as Noyce put it a few years later, "to jump off the roof of a barn and live." The barn in question was in Merrill Park, just across the empty fields and asparagus patch behind the Noyces' house. Word spread through town, and the *Grinnell Herald* sent a photographer.[6]

Bob clambered up to the barn's roof and a few other boys handed him the glider, which weighed about 25 pounds. Bob then took a deep breath, thrust his sturdy body against the glider's frame . . . and jumped. Then, for one second, two, three, young Bob Noyce was flying. He hit the ground almost immediately, but as he proudly reported in a college admissions essay a few years later, "We did [it]!" Even the boys' mother, who privately thought her sons' fascination with airplanes a bit frivolous, was impressed. "It was all their idea," Harriet Noyce later recalled with emphasis, *"but I made the paste."*[7]

IT WAS UNDOUBTEDLY FROM HIS MOTHER Harriet that Noyce inherited his love of adventure. Growing up in suburban Chicago, the daughter and granddaughter of Congregationalist ministers, Harriet Norton had dreamed of work as a missionary—perhaps the most daring path available to church-going young women of her age. She could imagine herself in China, where her mother's alma mater Oberlin had established a mission school. Harriet would have made a good missionary. She was fearless, quick witted, studious, and voluble, with an opinion on nearly every subject and a habit of narrating her thoughts aloud so that she seemed never to stop talking. She often said that she liked to "do a lot and do it well." When she left home to attend Oberlin at the age of 17, it was with scarcely a backwards glance.[8]

In 1920, when Harriet was wrapping up her sociology major, her brother introduced her to Ralph Noyce, a shy, quiet man just finishing his studies at Oberlin's Graduate School of Theology. The soon-to-be Reverend Noyce, slight and barely over five-and-a-half feet tall in his Sunday shoes, was 28 years old, a veteran of the Great War. He had been raised in the northeast corner of Nebraska, where his father, an ordained Congregationalist minister, preached and ran a dairy. A careful, soft-spoken man, Ralph Noyce loved philosophy and fancied himself more an intellectual than a religious leader. He studied ancient Greek and Latin at Doane College and collected images of the Madonna on which he could discourse in the manner of an art historian.

The church centered their courtship, which is not to say that it dictated their beliefs. No Congregationalist creed or formalized set of rituals defined the religion, and the individual churches for the most part operated independently, with no bishop or synod above them. Instead, the religion offered Harriet Norton and Ralph Noyce a common language and set of values: tolerance, respect for education, egalitarianism, and a belief in an unmediated relationship between God and His earthly servants. As Harriet put it, she and Ralph shared the same dream: "to be Christian leaders, in the best sense . . . equip[ped with] a concern for the needy, [and] an attitude towards people as equals, sacred in some way."[9]

But Harriet, always independent and strong willed, insisted on working for a year after college before she would marry. She taught high-school Latin and English near her parents' home and proved to her own satisfaction that she was capable of caring for herself. As soon as the school year ended, on June 20, 1922, Harriet Norton and Ralph Noyce were married. Her father performed the service; his assisted.

After a short honeymoon, the young couple arrived in Denmark, Iowa, a town of about 250 in the southeasternmost corner of the state. The Denmark church was small but prestigious: the oldest Congregational church west of the Mississippi, it was crowned with a 250-foot spire visible from farms miles away. The families on those farms were Ralph Noyce's parishioners, and they braved icy country roads in the winter and sweltering heat in the summer to hear Ralph speak to them from his well-annotated outlines on subjects such as "Christian Optimism."[10]

Ralph and Harriet Noyce lived in the parsonage. With housing expenses covered by the church, his $1,500 annual salary could provide small indulgences such as barbershop haircuts, a secondhand car, and hospital births for Donald Sterling Noyce, who arrived in May 1923, and Gaylord Brewster Noyce, born in July 1926.[11]

When Harriet discovered that a third child would arrive around Thanksgiving 1927, she and Ralph decided that their family could benefit from an increase in pay and a move to a larger community. Ralph learned of an opening at the church in Atlantic, Iowa, a town roughly triple the size of Denmark and a few hours' ride west on the Burlington and Rock Island railroad. He arranged to "candidate" for the job, and when he was offered the position at a salary nearly twice his current pay, he agreed to start as soon as the new baby was born.

Meanwhile, Harriet prepared for the arrival of her third child. A friend came to help Ralph with the boys and, at the suggestion of her doctor, Harriet took a room near the hospital in Burlington, 18 miles from home. She told her mother, her in-laws, and her friends that after two boys, she desperately wanted a little girl. Hedging her bets, she did not even pick out a boy's name. On December 12, 1927, the Noyces' third son arrived in a flash, beating his doctor to the delivery room. "Congratulations, and my sincere sympathy," read a letter from Ralph's brother. "Too bad he was a *he*." Harriet rallied soon enough, however. The healthy baby boy was named Robert, to be called Bobby.[12]

WHEN BOBBY WAS SIX WEEKS OLD, the Noyce family arrived in Atlantic. The church had 200 active members and a study for Ralph, who spent most days there, meeting with parishioners and clipping articles from *Life*, *Literary Digest*, and *Christian Century* for sermon fodder. Harriet found kindred spirits among a group of church women who organized Chautauqua-style study sessions for themselves. The two older Noyce boys—Don, who was nearly five, and almost-two-year-old Gaylord—delighted in the sanctuary's opera-style seats, which provided hours of slamming and clambering fun.

The parsonage in which the Noyce family lived was not only owned by the church, it was furnished and decorated by the Ladies Auxiliary, which meant that Ralph and Harriet were never comfortable changing things to suit their taste. Harriet ran the vacation bible school, headed the makeshift kitchens on church-sponsored camping trips, witnessed marriage licenses, oversaw the Ladies Auxiliary, and whispered forgotten lines from backstage at Christmas pageants.

For the boys, there were hymns and prayers most evenings at home, as well as Sunday services, Sunday school, and Sunday supper. Reverend Noyce devoted his ministry to the children of the church, and he assumed his own sons would participate in the classes, retreats, church youth group meetings, and Christmas plays he organized. Moreover, if no one volunteered to lead these activities, the Noyce brothers were expected to do so. And though neither Harriet nor Ralph emphasized them, the boys also had to contend with the intangible responsibilities of being a preacher's child: their behavior reflected not only on themselves, but on their father, their religion, and maybe even on God.

Ralph Noyce was a constant presence in his sons' lives. He often worked at home, in a room lined with his books in Greek and Latin. Even when he was spending his day at the church, he walked the three blocks to the parsonage at noon to eat with his wife and sons. The boys knew not to disturb Dad on Saturdays, when he finished his sermons, but otherwise, he was usually available. Bob Noyce's earliest childhood memory involves beating his father at Ping Pong and feeling absolutely devastated when his mother's reaction to this thrilling news was a distracted "Wasn't that nice of Daddy to let you win?"

Even at age five, Noyce was offended by the notion of intentionally losing at anything. "That's not the game," he sulked to his mother. "If you're going to play, play to win!"[13]

THE RAPIDLY DEEPENING agricultural depression fully descended upon Atlantic in 1932, when farm prices and income hit record lows. By 1935, a bushel of wheat still fetched only 20 percent of its 1919 price, and at ten cents a bushel, the most efficient use for corn was to burn it to save the need for coal. Farm foreclosures were common. A drought plagued the countryside. The Atlantic bank failed in February 1933, shortly before the birth of the Noyces' fourth son, Ralph Harold, taking with it the amount Reverend Noyce had borrowed against his government life insurance policy to cover hospital expenses.[14]

Ralph's church began "adopting" needy families, with one member paying the way to statewide Congregationalist conferences, another sewing school clothes, and the Noyces regularly inviting small children to play with Gaylord and Bobby while the parents did what work they could. The parsonage became a regular stopping point for hoboes. Harriet could almost always manage to offer them a sandwich and a glass of milk, or sometimes a short stint of labor in exchange for a meal and a spot to sleep in an unused chicken coop.

Although the Noyce family was initially blessed with a steady income and reliable housing, they too soon felt the pinch of the Depression. In 1932, the trustees closed Ralph's beloved church office to save the expenses of heat and a telephone. (They gave Ralph the telephone handset, which he and his boys promptly wired to ring in the study he set up at home—no easy feat at the time.) Ralph's salary, officially $2,400 annually, plummeted. In 1934, he was paid only $1,200. By mid-1935, the church was five months in arrears; often he was given a wagonload of corncobs or a ham in lieu of remuneration. The family found itself dipping into the GI life insurance benefits of Harriet's younger brother Don, who had died of meningitis shortly after introducing Harriet and Ralph. This money, now pressed into service for daily expenses, had been earmarked for investments and college savings.

The strain was too much. After eight years of service, Ralph preached his last sermon in Atlantic on October 25, 1936. The family strapped a Halloween pumpkin to the bumper of their old Ford and began a drive across the state to Decorah, in the northeastern corner of Iowa that had not suffered as badly from drought. The Noyces hoped the church in a less depressed area could meet its commitments to its minister, but within months of the family's arrival, Ralph's approach to religion had rankled several prominent congregants. Ralph was a humanitarian and an intellectual—Bobby was unsure if his father believed in an afterlife—who felt a minister, first and foremost, should be a listener, "someone to tell things to." The congregation wanted a bit more fire and brimstone, and so, less than two years after they came to Decorah, the Noyces were on the move once more, this time to Webster City, 65 miles north of Des Moines, a town roughly the size of Atlantic. Bobby was ten years old.[15]

Ralph's work and his relationship with his sons changed significantly with this move. The Webster City job was not a parish ministry but an administrative post with the Iowa Congregational Conference, the umbrella organization for the churches in the state. As associate superintendent, Ralph planned and ran meetings, filled in for absent ministers, and directed youth education programs throughout Iowa. In a single year, Ralph drove more than 25,000 miles of twisting rural roads and addressed 110 different audiences. His boys felt lucky if he made it home for Sunday dinner once every six weeks.[16]

Harriet called these the years of "Mothering with a Daddy on the Road." She was fiercely devoted to her boys, playing anagram games with them, listening to their troubles (always taking their side), and keeping watch over their friends and their homework. She schooled her sons in manners and social niceties, cautioning them again and again to speak only in ways that were "kind, necessary, and honest." It could not have been an easy time for her. Don developed asthma so debilitating that he could attend school only in the mornings. Bobby and Gaylord's early interest in science progressed from digging up earthworms, to taxidermy experiments with cats and saltpeter, to chemistry disasters involving nitrogen tri-iodide and exploding houseflies. Harriet nonetheless found this period strangely liberating. "I felt the sense of belonging as a person of worth for myself," she said, "and not just as the minister's wife."[17]

Webster City proved yet another temporary stop. Barely a year after their arrival, the boys were told they would be moving at the end of the school year. Their father's job had been transferred to the campus of Grinnell College, site of the state conference's headquarters. Ralph and Harriet had secretly been hoping for this outcome ever since Ralph accepted the Webster City job. Grinnell College offered all children of local ministers, regardless of denomination, a scholarship equivalent to roughly one-third the cost of tuition. For parents expecting to send three boys to college in the next five years, this was an attractive offer indeed. For the boys themselves, it meant yet another new school and another new set of friends, with no guarantee the family would stay any more than a year or two.

GRINNELL, at least for Bobby, became home in a way no other town had been. He had moved three times in the four years before he came to Grinnell, but he would stay in this town from the age of 12 until he graduated from college. Grinnell had 6,000 residents and 21 churches when the Noyces moved into a white Victorian they rented at the corner of Tenth and Park in the spring of 1940. The neighborhood, which abutted the college campus to the east and the city limits to the north, teemed with children—children tearing down the streets on bikes, or rushing in the front door when their mothers rang the cow bells they kept on the porch to call them home for dinner. Parents worked as teachers or lawyers, or they owned one of the town's small businesses: the lumber yard or funeral home or feed shop. These people had felt the impact of the Depression but had not suffered inordinately during the past few years. Nearly everyone was white, and nearly everyone, whether or not they went to church, was Christian. The Noyces set up housekeeping quickly, and Ralph resumed his traveling, though at a somewhat reduced intensity.[18]

Grinnell sat in the middle of prime Iowa farmland. Scarcely a decade after the fiery Congregationalist minister Josiah Grinnell founded his namesake village in 1853 (choosing the site because it was rumored to become the crossing point of Iowa's main East-West and North-South railroads), homesteading farmers had cleared every tree within a three-mile radius of the town's borders. When the Noyces arrived nearly a century later, soybean, corn, and livestock flourished in the farmland that ringed the city limits. Farmers were a regular part of daily life and an essential part of the town's economy. Men drove to Grinnell for feed and fertilizer. The women sold their produce and handmade soaps at the market. Their children came to school in yellow buses paid for by the county.

How his own brain stacked up against his older brothers' caused Bobby Noyce no small measure of worry as he prepared to start eighth grade in Grinnell. Harriet and Ralph Noyce expected their boys to be excellent students. Not only were Harriet and Ralph college graduates, but all four of their parents had also graduated college—a remarkable fact given that, at the end of the nineteenth century, less than 2 percent of the population received a university education. The boys' great-great-grandfather Reuben Gaylord had helped found Grinnell College in 1846, one of some 20 "prairie colleges" founded by Congregationalists in the mid-nineteenth century.[19]

Noyce's eldest brother Don set a blistering academic pace. Despite multiple moves and asthma-related absences, he managed to graduate second in his high school class and earn a generous merit-based scholarship at Grinnell College before the family left Webster City. Gaylord, just starting high school when the family moved to Grinnell, was poised to extend the family's intellectual honor. At 15, with a lean build and an unruly cowlick, he was a model student, polite and handsome with a near-perfect grade point average. He would graduate as valedictorian and would one day be nominated for a Rhodes scholarship, like his father before him. Bobby Noyce, on the other hand, was short, stocky, and sullen at 12. He brought home report cards marred with the occasional B, usually appearing in penmanship or conduct. He would delay doing his schoolwork until the last possible instant.[20]

He was three months into his freshman year at Grinnell High when Principal Cranny called a special assembly for all 400 students. It was the day after the Japanese bombed Pearl Harbor. Cranny told the students that President Roosevelt had just delivered a speech declaring December 7 "a day which will live in infamy" and requesting that Congress "accept the state of war Japan had thrust upon the United States." Some of the boys whispered excitedly. Most of the students were subdued by the thought of the brothers they had at home or by their own proximity to draft age. No one knew exactly what war meant for the town of Grinnell, Iowa, but everyone knew what it meant for 18-year-old boys.[21]

Within months, the government had rationed rubber, meat, coffee, and gasoline. Nearly 2,000 men arrived on the campus of Grinnell College to participate in military training programs. The *Grinnell Herald Register* exhorted townfolk and farmers to bring iron, rubber, aluminum, copper, brass, and burlap to the World War One cannon in Central Park. The 250-ton take, along with a 500-pound fire bell that was lowered from the tower where it had hung for decades, was towed off for scrap. Druggists donated quinine to the government for war use. A group of 53 Grinnell women made sweaters, stockings, blankets, and clothes for refugee infants in England. The federal government issued a "Call to (F)arms!" urging farmers to "keep 'em eating" by upping production by ten percent; the county's farms were to expected to produce 2.2 million dozen eggs, nearly 10,000 acres of soybeans, and more than 66 million pounds of milk in 1942.[22]

Noyce and his classmates felt the effects of the war every day. On Tuesday mornings, teachers sold ten-cent stamps that could be pasted into a book and traded in for a war bond. The Grinnell High School newspaper carried stories of graduates in the war, and the yearbook began with a sobering series of photos featuring very young men in uniform who would never return for their reunions. Bobby volunteered for the civil air patrol, which was on alert during blackout drills. He and Gaylord compiled, annotated, and laboriously typed booklets of war poetry. Farm kids, whose parents were allowed unlimited gasoline for their tractors, suddenly found themselves uncommonly popular. Did they want to go to the football game, and by the way, would they mind driving?

In many ways, though, life for Bobby Noyce proceeded in much the same way as it might have without the war. Midway through high school, he started calling himself Bob. He played the oboe in the band—Gaylord was on bassoon—and proudly labeled the band photo in his freshman annual "STATE WINNERS SINCE '39!" Afternoons were filled with taffypulls, hayrides, play rehearsals, parties, and listening to Tom Mix, Jack Armstrong, and Little Orphan Annie on the radio. Noyce spent his share of time at Candyland, the soda fountain on Fourth Street, eyeing the girls in wool skirts and bobby socks crammed together in the high-backed booths.

Bob Noyce also worked nearly 20 hours each week beginning in very early adolescence. He threw the *Des Moines Register* on porches in the mornings before school, and he worked almost every afternoon either at Bates Flower Shop downtown, where he arranged flowers and corsages, or at the post office, where he delivered special orders on his bike. He developed a flat-rate annual snow shoveling contract that he would offer his neighbors— and then he would hope for mild weather. These jobs were his primary source of spending money. He later said he felt no particular deprivation as a child, but finances were tight in the Noyce household.

Reverend Noyce's employment was precarious. Shortly after the family moved to Grinnell, he suffered a mild cerebral hemorrhage that damaged his short-term memory and left him partially blind. Harriet did not want to assume the debt they would need to buy a home, which meant that nearly every year, the family moved to a new house.

"Harriet had her hands full," recalled a Grinnell neighbor. "Those boys, especially Bob, were into devilment." Noyce would show up at neighbors' houses, his pockets full of wires and clips, and ask to borrow the 220-volt outlet for the kitchen range so he could try to build the electrical arc *Popular Science* claimed was capable of burning a hole through steel. He started smoking cigarettes. He and his friends enjoyed tipping over outhouses on the nearby farms, though attacks of conscience often sent them back to the scene of the crime, swearing and sweating in the stench as they righted the wooden building. They shot firecrackers off the slides at Merrill Park and from the roof of Gates Hall on the college campus. And while his older brothers' commitments to Congregationalism deepened in high school, Bob began spending less and less time at the old stone church at the corner of Fourth and Broad.[23]

At 16, Noyce was one of the select few in his class to have a car at his disposal, a '39 Plymouth that belonged to his mother but that she rarely drove. (His father put the miles on the old family Ford.) Noyce was not beyond sneaking off to a farm and siphoning a bit of precious gasoline from the tank of an unprotected tractor. He drove like a man possessed, taking ditches at 40 miles per hour and racing his friends down Sixth Avenue, one of the town's two main drags. "It seemed like he was always in a hurry to get somewhere," one of his friends observed. "And he got there."[24]

By the time Noyce was a junior in high school, "all the girls were crazy about [him]," recalls one of his classmates. "They though he was the most handsome thing on the face of the earth." The quick lopsided smile, the good manners and fine family, the wavy hair high on his forehead, the dash of rapscallion—it made for an appealing combination. He was not tall, only 5'8", but his childhood pudginess had hardened into muscle, and he had acquired a visible confidence in his body. "He was probably the most physically graceful man I've ever met. Just walking across the lawn . . . on a horse, even driving a car," recalls Marianne Standing, Noyce's steady girl-friend for several years of high school. Marianne was the glamour girl of the class of '45: a gorgeous brunette with smoky eyes, a biting wit, a penchant for unfiltered cigarettes—and, most shocking of all, a divorced mother. Harriet Noyce, who thought Marianne "had a gift for trouble, learned from playing one divorced parent against the other," made sure the family sang hymns after dinner whenever she joined them for a meal.[25]

His high-spirited antics did not keep Noyce from practicing his oboe, doing his homework (and sometimes his friends' homework, too), or maintaining a reputation among teachers as a "very fine boy." The yearbook called him "the Quiz Kid of our class, the guy who has the answers to all the questions." He maintained a straight-A record in high school and demonstrated an astonishingly intuitive sense for science and math, never earning less than 96 percent in either subject. Although he spent much of the first semester of high school physics dismantling and rebuilding a watch under his desk during lectures—he had the audacity to use a jeweler's loupe when the teacher's back was turned—he nonetheless aced every test.[26]

Harriet may not have known about the watch or Noyce's other antics, but she well understood that high-school physics bored Bob and that he would create his own special brand of challenge in the absence of more appropriate alternatives. This was especially true after Gaylord, who had always moderated Bob's tendencies towards excess, had left home in 1944 for the navy's V-12 officer training program. Gaylord had read about the Nazis' concentration camps and decided this war was a moral imperative. Bob admired his brother's ideals, but Gaylord's departure left him bereft and even more restless than usual.[27]

Desperate for a productive time-filler for Bob, Harriet Noyce took it upon herself to pay a call on Mr. Grant Gale, the physics professor at Grinnell College. The Noyces and the Gales attended church together, and Bob or his brothers went to the Gales every few weeks to help with babysitting, snow shoveling, repairing the lawn mower, or installing screens on the windows.[28]

In her characteristically straightforward way, Harriet asked Gale to let Bob join his introductory physics course. After verifying that a few other high school students had taken an occasional course at Grinnell College over the years, Gale agreed to let Noyce enroll when the second semester began in January 1945. As it was, his classes were unusually small, since nearly every physics major on the campus had been drafted.

In this introductory course, Gale focused on demonstrating the relevance of physics to daily life. He eschewed note taking—"that's what textbooks are for"—in favor of real-life demonstrations. With what force did the snowball he hurled against the side of the science building hit the bricks? Why did a skater spin faster when she pulled her arms in to her side? Why could you fill a drinking straw with water, seal the top with your finger, and lift the straw without spilling the water? How could you prove your answers to these questions? His stock of homilies was legendary. "Have the courage of your convictions," he would urge a student hesitating to guess an answer. "Be brave." When a student with real promise began to ramble, Gale would gently admonish, "If you can't define it in one sentence, you probably don't understand it."[29]

Noyce was the only male in the class of 14, a position to which he did not object. While Gale lectured, Noyce would lean back in his chair, listening carefully and occasionally volunteering comments. "[Gale's] interest was infectious," Noyce later recalled. "I caught the disease." At the lab tables, Noyce was eager and thorough, despite being somewhat preoccupied with flirting with his lab partners, who despite his best efforts, treated him like a kid brother. At the semester's end, Noyce had earned the highest grade in the course. [30]

MUCH TO HIS RELIEF—"it's almost become a family tradition now," he explained—Bob Noyce was named valedictorian of his high school class. The honor surprised several of his friends, who knew Noyce was a good student, but not that good. They knew he took a class at the college, but not that he was the best student in the room; that he shoveled walks, but not that he had developed an elaborate contract system to entice clients. Noyce did not try or need to hide such facts from his friends. They simply never would have expected such things from him, the buddy one of them described as "bright but common."[31]

He spent the summer after graduation taking classes at Miami University of Ohio where Gaylord was undergoing his officer training. Noyce arrived at Miami a bit cocky from his end-of-year accomplishments. He told his math instructor that he was "getting a nice bit of review out of her course, even though [he] didn't attend classes."[32]

Alone with his brother, Noyce's world began telescoping far beyond rural Iowa. He saw his first opera, Verdi's *Aida*, and was transfixed. He stayed up late talking with Gaylord and his friends about the atomic bomb that had recently devastated Hiroshima and Nagasaki. He hitchhiked 200 miles to Gallipolis, Ohio, to visit Marianne Standing. He listened attentively to Gaylord's stories about his trip to New York City, and swamped with the admixture of envy and insecurity that was his typical response to any of his brothers' accomplishments, wrote to his parents: "So Gay has seen the Statue of Liberty, huh! Some day I may get to. I hope. I'd better stop dreaming."[33]

He began swimming for an hour every day and after watching three Miami divers flipping and twisting through the air, he decided he wanted to dive, too. "After landing flat on my back only twice, I perfected the technique," he reported to his family. "Before I went home, I did both a half and a full gainer off the ten-foot board—Whoopee!" [34]

He met with similar academic success. At the end of the summer, the head of the Physics Department made him a job offer: if Noyce would enroll in the fall, the department would place him on the faculty payroll and employ him as a lab assistant, a position traditionally reserved for graduate students. He would be expected to grade papers, teach a few class sessions, and explain experiments to other students—all while he was a freshman. The invitation pierced Noyce's veneer of academic nonchalance. "My front teeth almost fell out," he proudly wrote to his parents, sounding like the 17-year-old he was. [35]

Noyce was slowly gathering experiences that would anchor his adult approach to life, which was not so much an approach as a headlong rush into any challenge with the unshakable assumption that he would emerge not only successful, but triumphant. If joining a college physics course as a high school senior meant finishing first in the class or getting an offer to teach, if dating meant snagging the most desirable girl in the school for your steady, and learning to dive meant turning full back flips off the platform's edge within hours of climbing the board for the first time— well, why wouldn't you come to think you could do almost anything?

Noyce was tempted by the offer to teach at Miami but worried he might be just "another insignificant student" on the large campus. If, on the other hand, he attended Grinnell College, he would face no possibility of insignificance. He had already won the same prestigious scholarship earlier awarded to his brother Don. The college president, Samuel Stevens, was a family friend who personally congratulated Bob on his acceptance to Grinnell with a note that inadvertently encapsulated the best and worst aspects of life as a Noyce boy: "Your brothers before you have performed in a distinguished manner. You seem to have the ability to perform equally well. We expect great things from you." At the end of the summer, Noyce decided to return to Grinnell for college. [36]

Once on the Grinnell campus, Noyce hurled himself into a frenzy of activity. In addition to a full course load, he stuffed his waking hours with nightly bridge games, chorus practice, yearbook staff meetings, play rehearsals, and attendance at dozens of lectures and musical performances. Noyce starred in a campus radio melodrama that his parents, to their great delight, could pick up on a neighbor's radio set. He approached dating with the same gusto that characterized everything he did. In his spare time, he plowed through the recently issued Smyth report on the atomic bomb, fascinated by the details of its technical development. [37]

The GI Bill and the end of the war meant that the campus now teemed with veterans, but Noyce drew most of his friends from a more traditional group of freshmen—boys and girls just graduated from high school, most from churchgoing Iowa families that could afford to pay what was then one of the highest tuitions in the state. He immediately assumed a leadership role among this group, usually managing to convince even the most studious to take a break for a sandwich or a stroll past the girls' dorms. "He never pushed himself forward at all," recalled one of Noyce's college roommates. "But why not follow him?"[38]

Noyce's father once wrote that in the same way toddlers thrive on juice and milk, Bob thrived on "adrenaline and gasoline."[39]

THE INTENSITY THAT NOYCE BROUGHT to his extracurricular activities extended to the classroom. He challenged himself to derive every formula he used in physics class rather than simply accepting the formulas written on the board as accurate. This was not easy work, even for Noyce, who declared himself "elated" after deriving the formula for determining the viscosity of a liquid. His electronics professor had him write his own exam and requested his help designing the circuits for his airplane models. His calculus professor asked him to teach a class based on the independent investigations Noyce had conducted into De Moivre's theorem for calculating complex numbers. These academic accomplishments earned Noyce an invitation to join the campus honorary society and inspired a heartfelt note from his father, who wrote, "You won't know till you have a son in college doing as good and grand work there as you are in Grinnell[,] how much satisfaction we are getting from reports of your good work."[40]

Such praise did not lessen Noyce's constant comparison of himself to his brothers. When Gaylord was named to Phi Beta Kappa after only five semesters of college, Bob's congratulations were tempered with doubt. "I'm just sorry that I've got such brothers to follow," he wrote. "When and if I get the same, it will just be another key in the family." As if to prove his own worth, he proceeded to describe in great detail how Grant Gale had asked him to help build an apparatus to study expansion and compression of metals.[41]

Money was always an issue. "$5 in the bank, $4 in my pocket" was the state of his finances soon after his arrival at Grinnell. Noyce worked several jobs—go-fer in the campus post office (until a returning vet asked for the work), lifeguard during Sunday afternoon free swims, assistant in Grant Gale's lab—but pleas for cash, accompanied by detailed accounts of where his last installment went, dominated many of his letters to his parents. Harriet Noyce, who never forgot that Bob once used his $19 savings to buy a pair of saddle shoes and a sweater rather than a bond during the war, thought him a spendthrift, particularly when it came to clothes and girls. She asked repeatedly about expenditures she found suspicious, including a check to an unnamed woman, whom Noyce, in great frustration, explained was simply the bank clerk who cashed the check, not a cause for worry.[42]

In the second semester of his freshman year, Noyce decided he wanted a varsity letter from Grinnell. His small stature and lack of experience would handicap him in most sports, but he thought he had a shot in diving. The Grinnell College pool was primitive, a wood-frame building over a concrete hole and a wooden deck. The roof was so low that divers would have undoubtedly hit their heads on it had a ten-foot by twelve-foot hole not been cut into the area directly over the diving board and the roof raised some eight feet in this one spot. From the outside, this "diving well" looked a bit like a widow's walk eight feet above the main roofline. Inside, a diver looking up from the board would have had the sense of peering up a short, broad chimney. When the team practiced, people in the pool or on the deck would see the diver leave the board, disappear into the chimney (where he would twist, flip, and turn) and then reappear shortly before he hit the water. The diving well was nerve wracking, but it gave an advantage to Grinnell divers. If they could dive up a chimney, everything else was pretty simple.[43]

Every night before he fell asleep, Noyce would mentally rehearse each of his dives in slow motion until he could see himself executing them perfectly. He called this habit "envisioning myself at the next level," and he carried it with him throughout his life. In his mind's eye, he could always see himself achieving something more.[44]

Two years after joining the diving team, Noyce won the 1948 Midwest Conference Diving Championship in Rockford, Illinois, defeating divers from Beloit, Carleton, Knox, and Monmouth colleges. He proceeded undefeated through the next season, when he lost the conference championship by two points. His parents were in the audience for this 1949 championship, and he worried that they were disappointed by his performance.[45]

LIKE OTHER UNMARRIED STUDENTS at Grinnell, Noyce had been assigned to a residence hall in which he was to live for all four years of school. The halls functioned much like fraternities, complete with internal house governments and athletic, academic, and social competition with other houses. Every spring and fall, each hall hosted a party. In their zeal to create the most spectacular party—the better the celebration, the larger the pool of potential dates—residents often enhanced the décor with a few bales of hay or a stack of lumber "borrowed" from unsuspecting farmers or townfolk.

Noyce lived in Clark Hall, which decided upon a Hawaiian luau theme for its spring house party a few weeks before the end of his junior year. Since Noyce knew the town of Grinnell especially well, he was assigned the task of liberating a young pig to be roasted upon a realistic looking spit.[46]

Noyce accepted the assignment but most likely gave it little thought. He was contending with the direst news of his young life. His girlfriend was pregnant. He was the father. She was going to have an abortion.

Whether Noyce encouraged her to have the operation, whether he offered to marry the young woman, how they paid for the procedure—these are all mysteries. What is known, however, is that Noyce was in an extremely agitated state the night he and a partner in crime downed a few drinks and set off to steal the pig for the luau.[47]

They walked across the golf course behind campus, grabbed a suckling pig, and ran with it back to Clark Hall. His housemates decided to butcher the piglet in a third-floor shower. A frantically squealing animal, intoxicated young men with knives—the ruckus was such that students all over campus immediately knew something untoward was happening in Clark Hall. The administration, however, did not hear about it until the next day, when Noyce and his housemate repented and returned to the farm with an offer to pay for the pig, whose absence had not yet been noticed.

It quickly became apparent that Noyce had not chosen a good farm to target. The farmer was the mayor of Grinnell, a no-nonsense man given to motivating his constituents through mild intimidation. He wanted to press charges. The college's dean of personnel, a recently retired army colonel, was also inclined towards the harshest punishment possible; a few months later, he would expel another of Gale's advisees for swearing at his house-mother. Since the farm was outside the city limits, the county sheriff was called in.[48]

Noyce's previous exploits—tipping outhouses, lighting illegal fireworks—had been dismissed as boys-will-be-boys tomfoolery. Stealing a pig was a different matter entirely. It crossed the line Noyce had skirted throughout his high school years, for as the letter the dean sent home to Ralph and Harriet Noyce explained, "In the agricultural state of Iowa, stealing a do-mestic animal is a felony which carries a minimum penalty of a year in prison and a fine of one thousand dollars." A prize pig could easily sell for $1,000, nearly three times Noyce's annual college tuition.[49]

Grant Gale and Grinnell College president Stevens were in a frenzy. Even without a criminal conviction, expulsion alone would have meant the end of the boys' education. In 1948 no school would have accepted a student expelled from another, and Gale in particular could not bear the prospect of "losing Bob." The two college representatives, both longtime residents of Grinnell and friends of the Noyces, brokered a compromise in which the college would compensate the farmer for his pig, and no charges would be pressed. The boys would be allowed to finish the few remaining days of their junior year but were suspended for the first semester of their senior year—exiled not only from the college, but from the town of Grinnell as well.

After his sentence was handed down, Noyce fled. He hitchhiked to Sandwich, Illinois, where his parents and youngest brother had moved af-ter Reverend Noyce had been asked to leave his job at the Congregational Conference. Bob Noyce returned to his parents a chastened soul, convinced he had brought disgrace on himself and his family. It must have come as a relief to discover that Harriet and Ralph Noyce were angrier at the farmer than at him. Reverend Noyce decried those "who are more concerned with hogs than they are with the problems of adolescence and youth's efforts to find it[s] place in this terribly uncertain world that we adults are presenting to them." He wrote an angry letter to the dean of men that pointedly concluded: "the rest of us will have to be the more ready to accept youth's offer of repentance and desire for forgiveness even if Iowa hog farmers do not see it that way." Bob urged his father not to mail the letter, which he thought criticized college's handling of his case, but his father sent it anyway.[50]

NOYCE DECIDED to spend his semester's expulsion working as a clerk in the actuarial department of the Equitable Life Insurance Company in Manhattan, where his math professor helped him secure a position. Noyce could imagine himself as an actuary after college: the days immersed in numbers and the paycheck steady and generous enough to permit some fun in the evenings. To become an actuary, however, he would need to pass the five-part actuarial exam before he returned to Grinnell and his frantic pace of life there. The exam was notoriously difficult and assumed several graduate-level math courses that Noyce had not taken. He nonetheless signed up to take the exam.

As soon as Noyce left for Manhattan, his mother, whose inchoate fears about Bob had been confirmed by the pig heist, began worrying about him with fresh vigor. She criticized his choice of roommate (whom she knew vaguely and thought drank too much), reminded him to visit his brother Don, who was completing a PhD in chemistry at Columbia, and carefully scrutinized his every letter for any mention of church, which he appeared to have attended with some regularity for several weeks as he was settling in.

Noyce reported to work in a ten-dollar suit he had bought from a friend and spent hours at his desk, one of scores of young men with a penchant for numbers and a need for cash. "I have been working on settlement option mortality," he wrote his parents. "From the looks of things, the annuitant table which is being used is now quite outdated. . . ." He soon found the work unceasingly, unbearably dull, the tedium relieved only by the fact that female clerks outnumbered male by a ratio of ten to one. Noyce lived for the nights and weekends, when he spent nearly every cent he earned on plays, films, museum exhibits, and evenings with young women he met at the office. He befriended flat-broke producers, playwrights, and artists—the kind of folks that people in Grinnell might have called unsavory. He was busy but not particularly happy, suffering, he said, from "the loneliness which often overtakes you here in the middle of the largest city on earth."[51]

The suspension gave Noyce time to think about his future. He had taken sufficient extra credits in his first three years that he could return to Grinnell and graduate with his class in the spring of 1949. Noyce tried to join the air force, but when he learned he could not serve as a fighter pilot because he was color blind, he swore to avoid military service all together. He then considered that if he passed the actuarial exam—his math professor had suggested a few textbooks to read in preparation—he might try to find a job in California, where he had always wanted to live. Grant Gale wrote to suggest he apply to the doctoral program in physics at MIT. Noyce did.

When he returned to Grinnell in February 1949, Noyce immediately resumed the back-to-back schedule of working, diving, studying, singing, acting, and dating that had filled his earlier college days. A few weeks into the semester, he received a letter notifying him that he had passed the actuarial exam. His family's relief was almost palpable. "Congratulations high dive brain child!" read a Western Union telegram from a family friend. "Make no small plans." The Equitable offered him a permanent job at more than $80 per week, a sum tempting enough that Noyce thought it might overcome his dislike of actuarial work.[52]

Meanwhile, in his physics class, Grant Gale had begun talking about a device so unusual and potentially revolutionary that Gale's description of it struck Noyce "like an atom bomb." Noyce later explained, "I couldn't grasp how it worked—or why it worked—immediately, but that it worked . . ." His voice trailed off.[53]

It was called a transistor. A mere half-inch long, it could amplify electrical signals, a feat that had previously been accomplished only by much larger, and very fragile, vacuum tubes. These vacuum tubes were everywhere in postwar America, amplifying small currents to pull in radio and television stations, transmit telephone signals, operate hearing aids, and vibrate the cones of loudspeakers to produce sound. Vacuum tubes also enabled Noyce to control his model airplanes.[54]

The transistor promised to accomplish the same tasks—but with one essential difference. It amplified signals through a solid crystal of germanium, not through a vacuum. For years, scientists had theorized that it would be possible to amplify current through solids, thereby avoiding the high power consumption and heat generated by vacuum tubes. But no one had been able to do it until the transistor. "It was really a rather astonishing revelation that could get amplification without a vacuum," Noyce recalled. He decided the transistor was "a phenomenally new and wonderful thing, [a glimpse] as to what might happen in electronics in the future."[55]

The transistor was invented at Bell Labs, in Murray Hill, New Jersey, in 1947. Bell Labs was the research arm of AT&T and the nation's premier electronics research laboratory. Its scientists, several of whom would

go on to win the Nobel Prize, were probably the best electronics researchers in the world.

Bell Labs was normally a somewhat staid place, but when the transistor's
inventors Walter Brattain and John Bardeen first demonstrated their device to the lab's senior management at the end of 1947, the researchers
were almost giddy. One history of the event explains, "They hooked up a
microphone to one end of their invention and a loudspeaker to the other.
One by one, the men picked up the microphone and whispered 'hello'; the
loudspeaker at the other end of the circuit shouted 'HELLO!'" William
Shockley, a physicist who supervised Brattain and Bardeen and whom Bell
Labs quickly named a co-inventor of the transistor, later used the occasion
to recall another auspicious moment in Bell Labs history: "Hearing speech
amplified by the transistor," he said, "was in the tradition of Alexander
Graham Bell's famous, 'Mr. Watson, come here, I want you.'"[56]

Six months after this dramatic demonstration, Bell Labs announced
the transistor's invention not in the pages of a technical journal, but at a
press conference in downtown Manhattan, not far from where Noyce was
then calculating annuities at the Equitable.

Noyce, however, did not learn about the transistor's invention while
he was in New York. With automatic transmissions, frozen foods, the electric clothes dryer, and the Polaroid camera just coming on the market,
Americans had little interest in the esoteric transistor, which had no obvious
consumer application. In most American homes, vacuum-tube-powered radios encased in wooden cabinets occupied places of honor. The *New York
Times*, the only paper in which Noyce might have read of the transistor's
invention, buried the story on page 46, allotting it four paragraphs at the
end of a "News of the Radio" column headlined with the promise, "New
Shows on CBS Will Replace 'Radio Theatre' During the Summer."[57]

Military researchers, who had witnessed a demonstration of the device
a week before the public press conference, had a very different reaction. A
military press release declared that the device "could take a great load off
the ground soldier's back." The statement was literal. Historians estimate
that the heavy batteries used to power the vacuum tubes in standard-issue
"walkie-talkie" radio telephone sets accounted for almost 40 percent of a
set's weight. After considering and rejecting a plan to classify the transistor, representatives from the armed services were the first to request samples
from Bell Labs.[58]

Among those next requesting "a couple of transistors" was Grant Gale,
who had read and understood the significance of the short *Times* story,
which he immediately posted on the bulletin board outside the physics
classroom at Grinnell. Gale felt almost personally connected to the transistor. One of the inventors, John Bardeen, had attended the University of

Wisconsin with Gale and grown up with Gale's wife. The head of research at Bell Labs, Oliver Buckley, was a Grinnell graduate and the father of two current students. Buckley regularly sent Gale castoff equipment and spare copies of technical reports from Bell Labs, and it was to him that Gale mailed his request for transistors.[59]

Buckley did not have any devices to spare, but he did send Gale copies of several technical monographs that Bell Labs had written on the transistor. These monographs formed the basis of Noyce's initial exposure to the device. No textbooks addressed transistors, and (although prevailing mythology claims otherwise) Bell Labs did not ship Gale a transistor until after Noyce graduated. Together Gale and Noyce, who was far more interested in the transistor than any other student, pored over the Bell Labs monographs: "The Transistor and Related Experiments," "Positive Holes and the Transistor," "Physical Principles Involved in Transistor Action," "Some Contributions to Transistor Electronics."[60]

Through these monographs, Noyce learned that the secret to the transistor lay in the unusual properties of elements called semiconductors. The conductivity of semiconductors falls in between that of metals (which conduct electricity freely) and insulators (which do not conduct electricity at all). Moreover, a semiconductor's conductivity can be changed. Apply a certain stimulus to a semiconductor—light, voltage, or temperature—and it becomes a conductor. Change the stimulus, and the semiconductor can be made into an insulator. In electrical terms, it is equivalent to turning copper into glass instantaneously.[61]

Semiconductors can be doped or modified to come in two varieties. N-type semiconductors have an electron (negative charge) that is only loosely bound to its atom and is thus free to move around, thereby conducting electricity. P-type semiconductors have the positive virtual-equivalent of the electron, called a hole, that is only loosely bound to its atom and thus free to move around. If P- and N-type semiconductors make contact—at a point called a junction—something remarkable happens: a few electrons flow from the N-type area, across the junction, and into the P-type area. A voltage applied to the junction will accelerate the trickle of electrons into a rush. But reverse the voltage and essentially no electrons at all can flow across the junction. Bell Labs hoped to use these properties of semiconductors to create a device that would serve as an electrical switch.

At Bell Labs, Walter Brattain and John Bardeen built their transistor from a strip of an N-type semiconductor called germanium. They suspended a plastic triangle, point-down, above the germanium strip. A thin gold contact ran down each side of the triangle, with less than two-thousandths of an inch between the contacts at the point. The scientists carefully positioned the triangle so that the gold contacts just touched the surface of the germanium. Then they introduced a tiny current into the germanium via a thin wire. If they "wriggled [the wire] just right," the device could amplify current 100-fold.[62]

It is impressive that Noyce, at 21, was able to understand the Bell Labs transistor monographs describing these events. The reports had been written by PhD scientists for senior electronics researchers, not for undergraduates. Yet Gale insists that when it came to transistors, "it would be a gross overstatement to suggest that I taught Bob much. . . . We learned about them together."[63]

The information that Noyce absorbed about the transistor in his last months at Grinnell inspired him. When he was accepted at MIT with a partial scholarship, he told Gale that he hoped to focus his studies on the movement of electrons through solids. [64]

Noyce graduated from Grinnell College with a double major in math and physics and a Phi Beta Kappa key. He also received a signal honor from his classmates: the Brown Derby Prize, which recognized "the senior man who earned the best grades with the least amount of work"—or as Noyce preferred to explain to his parents, the recipient was the "man who gets the best returns on the time spent studying."[65]

2

Rapid Robert

The decision to attend MIT was an enormous gamble for Noyce. He could not afford it. The $400-per-semester scholarship he received from the Physics Department was enough to cover tuition, but provided nothing toward the remaining $735 the university estimated would be needed for books and room and board. Noyce's parents were unable to be of much assistance, and Bob did not want to ask his maternal grandmother, who had loaned him money in college, for more. He needed to earn as much as he could in the summer before leaving for graduate school. This meant living with his parents in Sandwich and working long, sweaty days at a construction site, where he was badly burned on his back and hands after carrying wood that had been treated with the volatile preservative creosote. Even before this injury, Noyce had always hated this sort of labor. Most of his high school and college classmates worked every summer baling hay or detasseling corn, but Noyce and a close friend had spent the summers after their first and second years of college tending bar and waiting tables at the Century Country Club north of New York City. There Noyce had been shocked and more than a little impressed to learn that his customers regularly paid $25 for a dinner and $2,000 to rent a tiny home on the water.[1]

The contrast between those country club summers and the blazing toil of the summer of 1949 left Noyce cursing a world in which a Phi Beta Kappa physics major could earn more with his muscles than with his mind. It also led him to a decision. He would not do this again. He would so impress the Physics Department powers-that-be that within a year they would give him the graduate-school equivalent of a free ride: a research fellowship that not only covered tuition but also paid $122.50 every month.[2]

WHEN NOYCE parked his beat-up Ford in Cambridge in September 1949, he encountered a world dramatically different from Grinnell College. Where Grinnell had been a self-contained red-brick universe safely tucked in the middle of cornfields, in the middle of a state, in the middle of the country,

MIT was an urban campus—three miles from downtown Boston, a short train ride to New York—run by men eager to extend its reach beyond the traditional limits of the academy. MIT professors helped develop the radar technology that saved American planes, and they helped build the atomic bomb that devastated Japan. MIT faculty served on presidential commissions and in the boardrooms of the nation's most powerful corporations.

The "military-industrial complex" would not be named until a dozen years after Noyce entered graduate school, but it was well under construction at MIT in the fall of 1949. During the Second World War, MIT received $117 million in federal research contracts from the Office of Scientific Research and Development—by far the most money awarded to any American university during the war. A few weeks after Noyce started classes, the Soviets exploded their first atomic bomb, and the monumental threat this implied would help ensure a steady flow of federal defense dollars to MIT researchers throughout the Cold War.

The MIT physics building sat near the middle of campus. In its basement were multiple subterranean corridors, some of which branched off into dimly lit classrooms, all part of the vast network of tunnels that linked MIT buildings to each other. This underground universe was a place apart, filled with miles of exposed overhead pipes, thousands of tools to build all sorts of scientific equipment, giant machines that occupied entire rooms, and clusters of young men working together over tables covered with instruments. This part of the Physics Department, in other words, resembled the world's greatest basement workshop—and what, Noyce might have asked himself, could be better than that?[3]

The Physics Department had undergone dramatic changes during the past two decades. Before 1930, the department had focused on teaching physics to engineers. Then in 1930, MIT's president Karl Compton recruited a young professor named John Clarke Slater to build a research program in physics that would rival any in the world. Slater was an impressive man: a leading proponent of quantum theory, a top student of a Nobel Prize winner, a pioneer in the electromagnetic theory behind radar, and a prolific author who churned out dozens of articles while also writing a textbook or other weighty tome roughly every three years. (Such accomplishments led to his election to the National Academy of Sciences at the age of 31.) His youthful, almost prissy, appearance—his face full-cheeked, his brown hair thick and parted carefully at the side—led more than one person to mistake him for an undergraduate, but no one made that mistake more than once. Slater had a glare that could petrify and an overall presence that one student called "remote and austere, with all the warmth of an emotional iceberg."[4]

Armed with a generous grant from the MIT president, Slater spent the decades of the 1930s and 1940s tightening graduation standards, raising faculty salaries, and loosening departmental controls over faculty research. The wartime combination of increased federal funds and a pool of top-notch European physicists eager to emigrate worked to Slater's advantage. By the time Noyce came to campus, some of the best-known physicists in the world— nuclear physicists Herman Feshbach and Victor Weisskopf, microwave physicist Nathaniel Frank, acoustics and operations research pioneer Philip Morse—were members of the faculty. The department was also home to the most famous graduate student in America, Murray Gell-Mann, who had arrived a year before Noyce. A prodigy who taught himself calculus at age seven and began studying physics at Yale just a few weeks shy of his fifteenth birthday, Gell-Mann would emerge with his PhD in quantum theory after only two years in the program. He was one of two students in graduate school with Noyce who would one day win the Nobel Prize for Physics.

It was an intimidating place by any standard, and presumably even more so for a student from a two-man Physics Department led by someone who did not even have a PhD. "I had come from a protected home and sort of sailed through college, never worrying too much about getting the work done," recalled one of the few students in Noyce's cohort who arrived with a similar background. "Then I got to MIT and bam! I was with the best of the bunch, 800 miles from home.... It was incredibly difficult." Grant Gale certainly worried whether he had adequately prepared Noyce for the academic rigors of the nation's premier scientific university. He wrote to the head of the department, asking for periodic updates on MIT's "reaction to Mr. Noyce and to the training which he has had."[5]

If Noyce, who soon learned that most of his classmates came to MIT with teaching fellowships in hand, had begun to wonder whether he belonged in Cambridge, his first months on campus could not have helped matters. Most students lived in the Graduate House at the corner of Massachusetts Avenue and the Charles River—a five-minute walk from the physics building and the center of graduate student social life—but the monthly $78 room-and-board fee was too dear for Noyce, who instead shared an apartment in a slightly seedy part of Cambridge with a friend from his semester as an actuary. A month into the school year, Noyce took the first set of required exams, which were designed to assess a student's knowledge of physics and determine in which subjects, if any, he needed to do remedial coursework. He did so badly on the first test that he refused to tell his parents his grade and even asked his current girlfriend to stay away for the weekend, presumably because he needed to study.[6]

At the end of the exam period, Philip Morse, who oversaw registration in the department, marked Noyce's background "deficient" in several areas and required him to take the two-semester undergraduate introduction to theoretical physics as well as advanced undergraduate courses in electronics and experimental physics. "My only observation for comfort," Noyce told his parents, "is that everyone I talked to did at least as badly as I did."[7]

This was not exactly true. Noyce entered MIT at a distinct educational, as well as financial, disadvantage relative to many of his classmates. Consider, for example, Alfred "Bud" Wheelon, who was just 19 years old when he came to MIT with a freshly minted engineering degree from Stanford. Wheelon's mentor in California had been Frederick Terman, Stanford's ambitious dean of engineering who had himself earned his PhD at MIT under Vannevar Bush (the founding director of President Roosevelt's Office of Scientific Research and Development). When Terman decided that Stanford could not provide Wheelon a sufficiently challenging graduate education, he made a few calls. "This guy is great," Terman told his colleagues at MIT. "Fix him up." MIT enticed Wheelon with a teaching assistantship. When it came time for the entrance exams, he passed every one easily.[8]

Noyce admitted to his parents that "life looks unpleasant in spots," but he tried to put the best spin possible on the challenges he faced. He was glad he did not have a research fellowship, he said. It would just slow him down. His goal, Noyce reminded them and himself, was to get through this stage of his life as quickly as possible—a philosophy that had served as his guiding force since childhood.[9]

The bravado he displayed in letters to his parents was harder to maintain in person. He sought comfort in his hometown friends. The Strong brothers, neighbors from Grinnell who had helped with the glider, were both in Cambridge, one studying architecture, the other in law school at Harvard. His brother Gaylord was in New Haven, and Noyce spent several days with him and his new wife Dotey. The visit was filled with good home-cooked dinners and interesting conversation. When he returned to Cambridge, his own life struck him as so bleak that for one of the few times in his life, Bob Noyce openly questioned what he was doing: "The whole of [the visit to Gaylord] served to point out to me how misdirected I am. These people have some worthwhile goals in life. It doesn't seem to me that I have. I keep hoping that I will get wrapped up enough in physics to forget this. Anyway, my materialistic interests flew out the window until I got back here and started to wonder how I was to stay alive."[10]

AT MIT, few of Noyce's classmates sensed his despair. He had fallen in with what his mother undoubtedly would have called "a nice group of boys." George Clark, a Harvard graduate from a well-to-do Chicago family, was studying cosmic rays and would spend his career at MIT teaching physics. Another friend was Henry Stroke, a Jewish refugee from Hungary who, as a teenager, had escaped first to Paris and then to Spain before being brought to New Jersey by the Quakers in 1943. Stroke, too, would become a professor. Maurice Newstein, who seemed to know Noyce better than anyone else at MIT, was a sharp-tongued young man from New Jersey who had grown up too poor to own a bicycle and who was financing his education through the GI Bill. Newstein would spend years in industry before joining the academy himself.

The four friends focused on surviving their first year classes. Noyce took five, not including the undergraduate courses he was required to attend as a "listener." Like everyone else in the department, he took Philip Morse's Theoretical Physics course, which included problems so elaborate that the students claimed—only half jokingly—that they ought to receive an automatic master's degree for each one answered correctly. Noyce's Thermodynamics and Statistics course was hardly any better: the class average on the first exam was 29 out of 100, and the textbook, written by professors Slater and Frank, was bitterly known as "Slaughter and Flunk" by the students making their way through it. Noyce also took a Modern Algebra course in the math department.[11]

The two-semester Quantum Theory of Matter course taught by the imperious John Slater was one of Noyce's favorites. Slater would enter the room on the last ring of the bell announcing the start of class. After quickly greeting the students, he would distribute the blue sheets of notes he had typed up the night before—they would soon be published in a book that became one of the field's foundational texts—and walk briskly to the front of the room. Slater then turned his back on the class, faced the blackboard, and began to lecture in ringing, complete paragraphs, his precise script snaking its chalky way across the board. The lecture would continue in this manner— occasionally punctuated by Slater's calling out a question (still not turning around)—until his writing reached the lower right-hand corner of the board. At that point, Slater would tuck any loose end of the discussion neatly into the conclusion of his talk, and turn to face the students. "That will be all for today, gentlemen," he invariably concluded—mere seconds before the dismissal bell rang. This happened at every lecture.[12]

The subjects covered in Slater's remarkable performance included quantum mechanics, simple systems, and thermal dynamics in the first semester, and then in the second—finally—solid-state physics: the study of how electrons move in solids. The field was founded on the quantum mechanics in which Slater was expert, and its most exciting practical application, of course, was the transistor that had captivated Noyce in Gale's Grinnell classroom. Noyce had an intuitive sense about solid-state physics that impressed even his most well prepared MIT classmates. He could answer almost any question Slater posed with alacrity.

Noyce's fifth course was Electronics, taught by a pale-eyed, strong-jawed experimental physicist named Wayne Nottingham. He was MIT's primary expert in a field called "physical electronics," which explored the movement of electrons through solids, vacuums, and gases. Like most experimental physicists, and like Noyce himself, Nottingham possessed a God-given talent for tinkering. Nottingham was forever building equipment that he could not find elsewhere. His most significant contribution to the field was the Nottingham gauge, which measured the pressure in vacuums electronically.

Although Nottingham had made his reputation in the study of electrons in vacuums, he and his students followed the developments in solid-state physics from ringside seats at the Seminar on Physical Electronics, a conference Nottingham organized every year at MIT. The seminar was extremely informal—presentations had no time limits, and panelists were warned that they would not so much be addressing specific subjects as "introducing topics for discussion"—but it nonetheless attracted some of the nation's top solid-state electronics researchers. In Noyce's first year at MIT, the seminar included a panel specifically on transistors and several on semiconductors. One of the speakers was John Bardeen, one of the three inventors of the transistor at Bell Labs.[13]

The Physical Electronics seminar might well have been Noyce's only direct instruction on the topic that year, for MIT had yet to incorporate the transistor into its formal curriculum. Nottingham's Electronics class, for example, did not mention the device at all in 1949. The transistor was a new technology, and it had very real problems. It was hard to build a functional point-contact transistor; indeed, simply replicating the Bell team's results was difficult. Vacuum tubes, by contrast, were entering their heyday: they were far cheaper and more stable than ever before. No one—certainly not Nottingham—saw any evidence to indicate that the point-contact transistor would be in a position to replace tubes for a long, long time.[14]

OVER THE COURSE of his first semester at MIT, Noyce developed tactics to compensate for his deficits in undergraduate science classes. He learned how to study, something he had hardly bothered with in college, where he had chosen his math and physics double major because it offered "the path of least resistance" for him. Indeed, one reason he had enjoyed his science classes at Grinnell, he said, was that unlike courses such as history, in which "you had to study because you had to know the answer going into the exam," in his science classes, he could "always come up with the answer" simply by deriving it from his existing knowledge of "basic scientific principles." This approach simply did not work when he arrived at MIT, where his knowledge of those basic principles lagged that of his classmates so dramatically. For perhaps the first time in his life, he had to make a concerted effort to acquire scientific knowledge.[15]

But after those first difficult weeks spent cramming new information into his head, Noyce began to relax. Once he had brought his knowledge base to the point that it equaled his classmates,' he found he could once again improvise and derive his way into solutions. Indeed, after his first semester, he passed every course he took at MIT with honors.[16]

His classmates first began to take note of his quick mind during the impromptu study sessions that convened nearly every night in the Graduate House. (Noyce had to drive there from his apartment and then drive home in the early hours of the morning.) Most nights Noyce could be found in a group of three or four students, his cigarette aglow and his chair tilted back so far that he occasionally toppled over. Noyce relied on a stock of shortcuts to stay focused and drill through to a problem's solution. In calculus, for example, the symbol for derivative is a lowercase "d." Partial derivatives are represented by a rounded lowercase "d" (∂), which had a tendency, when dawn was breaking, to look remarkably similar to a lowercase d. Instead of saying "take the derivative (or partial deriviative) of X," which was how everyone else read problems aloud, Noyce invented a verbal notation that simultaneously reduced confusion and sped up the reading. "Dee X," he would say, rather than "take the derivative of X"; he used "die" for partial derivative. It was a small thing, but little timesavers like this enabled him to solve problems faster than almost anyone else—and this was fast company. His friends soon nicknamed him "Rapid Robert."[17]

Bud Wheelon, the gifted Stanford graduate, was shocked to learn that Rapid Robert did not have an assistantship and was living in penury. Wheelon, who would one day run technical operations for the CIA at the height of the Cold War, was already a man of action at age 20. He scheduled an appointment with Professor John Slater who, he freely admitted, scared him to death. At the appointed time, Wheelon appeared at Slater's office in coat and tie. "I know it's not any of my business," he said, "but I'm convinced one of the two smartest people here [Gell-Mann being the other] is without any assistance. He's really struggling and might leave." Wheelon ventured that so many students had research assistantships that the department should be able to fund one more for Noyce.[18]

Slater listened carefully and then flashed what Wheelon called a "microsecond smile." The reply was short: "You're right. It's none of your business." Wheelon was dismissed and the conversation was never mentioned again.

Within weeks, however, the department awarded Noyce a teaching fellowship, plus a $240 "staff award" effective when school resumed after the holiday break. Slater, who certainly was familiar with Noyce's newly outstanding academic performance, might well have been planning to increase Noyce's financial aid at the end of the semester, even without Wheelon's intercession. But then again, he might not have had such plans. It is impossible to know. Bud Wheelon never told Noyce what he did on his behalf.[19]

The struggles over financial assistance reveal something about Noyce's talents—that they could inspire such action is impressive—and his temperament, which kept him from lobbying on his own behalf. After all, Noyce could have gone to Slater himself, either to plead for more money or to demand that Slater increase his funding since he had proven himself one of the top students in the department.

Noyce was constitutionally incapable of either of these approaches. He hated to ask for help, and he always avoided confrontation if he could. Typical was the occasion when Noyce was involved in a traffic accident in downtown Cambridge. The two drivers climbed out of their cars, their voices rising as they surveyed the damage. As Maurice Newstein, whom Noyce had dropped off at a corner just moments before the accident, headed back towards the scene, he was surprised to see Noyce suddenly back away from the other driver and return to his own car. When he realized that Newstein had witnessed the exchange, Noyce seemed embarrassed—not about losing his temper but about backing down. "He thought he should have stood up to the guy," Newstein said. Noyce worried about looking like a coward to his friend, but even that was preferable to a direct confrontation. Years later he would tell his daughter, "Nothing good ever came from being angry."[20]

THE TEACHING ASSISTANTSHIP liberated Noyce. He moved to the Graduate House, where he roomed with his friends Newstein and Clark. His finances in order, he quickly immersed himself in a whirlwind schedule that recalled his college days. Cambridge was a mecca for young, mostly single, men and women attending schools up and down the Eastern Seaboard. Handbills posted around town advertised football games, hockey tournaments, crew regattas, formal dances, socials, and parties—many of which Noyce attended. He organized a clambake at Wingaersheik Beach, off Cape Ann. He was there for MIT's infamous "raining beer" party of 1950 during which a room full of physics graduate students was drenched in suds when the hosts, unable to determine how to tap the keg they bought, decided to drill into it with a corkscrew. He performed in several musicals, landing the lead in at least one, which his brother Gaylord attended. Sitting in the audience, Gaylord recalls, he understood something important about his brother for the first time. Bob's confidence and charisma—not his innate talent—enabled him to "pass himself off as an expert" performer. "His tone wasn't that great or accurate," Gaylord explains, "but there he was, singing a lead."[21]

Bob Noyce's tone could not have been *too* off, however. He auditioned for and joined Boston's Chorus Pro Musica, one of the top choral groups in the country. Membership entailed weekly two-and-a-half-hour rehearsals, plus several performances each year. Noyce was a baritone and enjoyed singing a wide range of music: not just traditional favorites like the Haydn Mass (which the chorus performed each year in the New England Conservatory's Jordan Hall), but also more modern pieces such as Randall Thompson's "Alleluja"—a slow, meditative work based on the single word. In short order, Noyce began working his way through the female choral singers, dating one after the other. "He was smooth as silk," recalls a friend from chorus who also attended MIT. "All the girls, wherever he went, were always very interested."[22]

"[Noyce] was a physical specimen," explains his friend Maurice Newstein. "He was built like a bodybuilder." Noyce swam almost daily and had a prizefighter's well-defined physique. An ongoing parade of extremely attractive women appeared with Noyce at the front doors of the various houses he shared with Newstein and Clark during their four years at MIT. Noyce at several times seemed quite serious about a particular girl, but for whatever reason—he kept such matters to himself—the relationships inevitably ended.[23]

In addition to their good looks, the women tended to share a certain attitude, a shell of East Coast urban sophistication that Noyce found irresistible. Clark, who came from a socially prominent family, and Newstein, who says he tried to project a "cocky" personality, also fit this description. His friends surmised that Noyce harbored deep within himself a fear that he would be seen as a Midwestern hayseed. Perhaps by associating with sophisticates, he might absorb a bit of élan himself. No one could ever accuse Noyce of pretending to be something he was not—his MIT colleagues invariably described him with terms such as "ordinary," "easy to talk to," "never put on airs," or "down to earth"—but occasionally his friends would feel him studying them almost as if they were a lesson he had yet to fully master.[24]

Noyce took his friends' strengths as a personal challenge. His roommate George Clark, for example, was an amateur astronomer who kept in his room a six-inch parabolic telescope mirror that he had ground and polished by hand in high school. Although Noyce knew nothing about astronomy, he managed to turn the mirror into a working telescope with only a little direction from Clark. In another instance, Noyce watched with avid attention while Clark made a new mirror, carefully grinding a handful of grit between two pieces of glass—one slightly convex, one slightly concave—until, after a good interval of grinding and rotating the glass, the curvature of the two pieces began to approximate a sphere. At this point, the glass could be covered with a reflective coating and installed in a telescope. Noyce decided grinding mirrors was unnecessarily labor intensive. He took it upon himself to outfit a phonograph machine with a wooden handle and built, in effect, an automatic mirror grinder, where one lens rotated on the spinning turntable, and the other was held in place by the handle. He jerry-rigged a workable model, but lost interest shortly after it was finished.[25]

Maurice Newstein was a talented amateur painter, and so Noyce decided that he, too, wanted to try painting. True to form, Noyce determined that the key element he needed to inspire painterly greatness was not a class, but a model. He managed to convince a young woman—possibly his girlfriend—to model in bra and panties for him, Newstein, and a few others. It was all very discreet, and nothing untoward happened, but the experience was far more memorable for its participants than any painting Bob Noyce ever managed to produce.[26]

Noyce also found time to fly the model airplane his parents sent from home, and to play a great deal of bridge, often late into the night. He applied for a Fulbright award to study in France, a country he chose because he wanted to see Europe, he could speak a bit of French—his maternal grandmother had taught him enough to complete his language requirement at Grinnell—and he calculated that he would be more likely to win a posting to France than to any English-speaking country. He won the award but declined it in favor of finishing his studies as soon as possible. Rapid Robert indeed.[27]

AT THE END OF NOYCE'S FIRST YEAR of graduate school, Nathaniel Frank (of "Slaughter and Flunk" fame) replied to Grant Gale's letter requesting information about Noyce's performance:

> Mr. Noyce has been an outstanding student in all respects. . . . We are sufficiently impressed with his potential that we have nominated him for a Shell Fellowship in physics for the next academic year, and he has received this fellowship.
> You are to be congratulated on the excellence of the training which he has had, and we look forward to an outstanding performance by Mr. Noyce.[28]

Grant Gale kept this letter for the rest of his life.

The Shell Fellowship, which provided $1,200 per year, plus tuition, meant that Noyce would not have to worry about finances for his second year of school. After that, he was virtually guaranteed a research assistantship in his adviser's lab. "When I came here this fall, I was hoping something like this might work out," he told his parents. "It seems that my optomism [sic] was somewhat justified."[29]

After a summer in Boston working for Sylvania, Noyce began his second year with a semester of course work followed by oral examinations. These he passed in May 1951. He briefly worked as a consultant with an optics company on whose board Nottingham served, and Noyce also began working on cathodes and vacuum tubes as a research assistant in the Physical

Electronics group at MIT's Research Laboratory of Electronics (RLE). He audited a Solid-State Physics course at Harvard because he had already taken every relevant MIT class. But the bulk of Noyce's attention shifted to selecting an adviser and starting the research for his PhD dissertation.[30]

Nottingham was the obvious choice for an adviser. Noyce knew that he wanted to do experimental, not theoretical research. ("He admired people who *did* things," says Newstein.) He also knew that he wanted to write a thesis somehow relevant to the transistor, and Nottingham's work was as close as MIT got to experimental research on the topic. By 1951, half the questions on his Electronics exam involved transistors, and several of his advisees were writing dissertations that addressed the basic physics of the device, albeit indirectly.

Moreover, Noyce liked Nottingham, who oozed bonhomie and practically bounced when he walked. Nottingham owned a rustic ski home in Rindge, New Hampshire, at the foot of Mount Monadnoc, and he did everything he could to spend his winters there, often inviting small groups of graduate students north for "working ski trips." In exchange for skiing and lodging privileges, Nottingham required his visitors to help chop wood or work on the rope tow he had designed. In the evenings, he would mix martinis with the special gin he kept in deep freeze in his basement.

During one of his trips to Nottingham's house, Noyce learned to ski. Perhaps it would be more accurate to say that he began skiing at this time— no one remembers Noyce in the skis-awry-falling-down-the-mountain stage that plagues most beginners. Skiing shares with diving an exhilarating sense of abandoning the body to gravity, of tightly controlling physical form while hurtling through space. Noyce apparently started on the intermediate runs, on the assumption that since he would end up there soon enough, why not just skip the bunny slopes and aim high? Noyce's passion for skiing soon ran so strong that by his third winter in Boston, he worried it might interfere with completing his studies. "I still see some possibility of getting out [of graduate school] sometime this winter," he wrote near Thanksgiving, 1952, "but I think that I will have to introduce a 'no thesis-no ski' rule to do so."[31]

Nottingham's personality and physicality appealed to Noyce, who had a profound distrust of people he thought overly cerebral. (He once described a professor's mind as "perverted . . . too much wrapped up in his own field and closed to anything else. . . . [He] will sit in silence rather than talk about anything but math.") Noyce knew that he needed to consider more than just a personality match when choosing an adviser, however. An adviser's reputation spilled over to his students, and Nottingham's name did not hold the same power as Slater's or Weisskopf's. Moreover, Noyce worried that the equipment in Nottingham's lab was "archaic" and that the professor himself "kn[ew] no theory, only how to do an experiment better than anyone else."[32]

In the end, however, the desire to write on solid-state electronics outweighed all other considerations. Noyce asked Nottingham to advise a dissertation to be called "A Photoelectric Investigation of Surface States on Insulators." Since early in the twentieth century, physicists had known they could study the movement of electrons in a solid by shining a light on the material. The light would excite the electrons within the bulk of the material, and as electrons made transitions from one area (called an energy band) within the material to another, they either absorbed or emitted a minute amount of energy that could be measured. These photoelectric measurements would indicate where and at what density within the solid the electrons congregated, and also how they moved under the stimulus of light.

By the end of the Second World War, the photoelectric findings had given scientists a relatively good understanding of electrons inside solids. Inside a crystal, for example, every atom is firmly connected to every other. One might picture a neighborhood in which houses (atoms) are connected to each other by a clearly defined pattern of walkways that radiate from the front, back, and side yards of each house. Any electron wanting to move from one house to another needs to stick to the established pathways.[33]

But what about the last row of houses in the neighborhood, the houses at the "surface" of the neighborhood, so to speak? These atoms have no back-door neighbors to connect to, no paths from their back yards for an electron to follow. Any electrons that made it out the back door of these houses would encounter a no man's land where the yard ends and whatever-comes-next begins. The "surface states" that Noyce proposed to investigate can be thought of as this area where the end of the neighborhood meets the whatever-comes-next. In this surface state, electrons liberated from the established paths would not be as predictable as their counterparts in the interior of the neighborhood (the bulk of the solid). The electrons in the surface state would have a lot of room to move about, and in these wide open spaces they might even meet a few foreign intruders.

Surface states remained an area of great confusion in the early 1950s. What quantum mechanical laws governed the behavior of electrons in the surface state? How many could squeeze into this space at one time? What could move an electron in or out of the surface state? How did the presence of impurities on the surface of a material affect its electrical properties? On the most fundamental level, for most materials, the existence of these "surface states" had yet to be demonstrated at all. Noyce wanted to see if they existed in two particular insulators: quartz and magnesium oxide.

Noyce's interest in surface states came directly out of the Bell Labs transistor research. The point-contact transistor did its most important work at the surface of the germanium, specifically at that point on the surface where the gold wires contacted the P-N junction. The device had been developed in the course of investigations into surface states in semiconductors; all three inventors wrote papers on the subject. For a while, Bell had even referred to its transistor research by the code name "Surface States Project."

The connection between the transistor and Noyce's proposed surface-state research on insulators was tenuous at best, however. The Bell Labs surface-state research concerned semiconductors, not the insulators that Noyce proposed to study. Moreover, transistor research had taken a turn away from surface states in the years between the device's invention at the end of 1947 and Noyce's proposal in 1951. William Shockley, the leader of the Bell Labs transistor group, had invented a completely different type of device, called a junction transistor, a few weeks after the patents on the point-contact transistor were filed. The junction transistor did its work not on the surface, but in the middle of the semiconductor, which is where its P-N junction was located—picture a microscopically thin layer of N-type peanut butter between two P-type pieces of bread. This junction transistor, made public in July 1951, was more reliable, more easily produced, and capable of amplifying signals nearly a million times more efficiently than its point-contact predecessor. It was a marvelous device, but it had nothing to do with surface states.[34]

Noyce undoubtedly knew about the shift away from surface states in transistor research. In fact, William Shockley spoke at a departmental tea around the time Noyce was writing his proposal. Noyce nonetheless understood that he needed to devise a thesis project that he could complete and that Nottingham could advise. Moreover, scientists continued to debate the merits of point-contact versus junction transistors. In any case, surface states were still a worthwhile subject of study, and investigating them would still enable Noyce to research the electrons, holes, quantum mechanics, and other topics he would need to understand if he wanted to work with transistors after he graduated.

The project Noyce set for himself—to measure the presence of electrons at the surface of quartz and magnesium oxide—is today absolutely trivial, the near-instantaneous work of a $600 digital electrometer. In the early 1950s, however, Noyce found obtaining this information to be an ordeal that lasted more than a year.

He needed perfectly clean samples, since impurities on the surface could cause confusing readings that would render his data useless. This meant he needed to conduct the experiment in a vacuum, where not even gas or oxygen could contaminate the sample. Noyce, like many of Nottingham's students who were also conducting research that needed to run at high vacuum, built his experiment in a glass vessel that he hooked to a vacuum pump. The whole apparatus was then put into an oven and cooked at as high a temperature as the glass could withstand. As Noyce's work progressed, the lab table assigned to him gradually disappeared beneath a layer of glass vessels, glass jars, glass tubes, glass pipes, and glass nozzles that he was using or had used at various points in his work. The other tables in the room looked the same way. The overall effect to the untrained eye was of a workshop belonging to a glassblower gone mad.

"Oh, Noyce had a hell of a time," chuckles one physicist who reviewed Noyce's doctoral work some 50 years after its publication. Noyce needed to heat his sample to about 1,000° C, but it took him several tries to find a sufficiently powerful heating device. He tried two different light sources before finding a third that was bright enough to generate a measurable current. Twice the samples he was using shattered in the process of trying to clean them. Another time, a short developed between the heater and a back electrode, rendering the sample unusable. Each of these failures meant completely reconstructing the experiment from the beginning: requesting new equipment from the glassblowers who worked with Nottingham (or occasionally, if the job was easy enough, blowing his own glass), building the experiment inside this new equipment, pumping it out, and re-calibrating his instruments.[35]

The instruments presented their own problems. The Compton electrometer Noyce had planned to use to conduct his measurements proved insufficiently sensitive, so he switched to a vibrating-reed electrometer, a higher-performing device that he needed to teach himself how to use. He soon discovered, though, that the device was so sensitive and the currents he wanted to measure so small that he was detecting interference from stray fields in the lab. He tried wrapping the leads to the electrometer with polystyrene to reduce interference, but this did not help. Finally he discovered that if he rid the experimental apparatus of any insulators other than two—the sample he was studying and the glass press of the vacuum tube—he could cut the interference from stray electric fields to nearly zero simply by slightly altering the relative positions of the tube and the electrometer from time to time. This was not an ideal solution, however, because every change of position entailed a wait of several hours while the background currents settled down.

Noyce's work was interrupted when he suffered a bad spiral fracture of the humerus from falling hard on his right elbow while practicing his ski jumping near Nottingham's property. Noyce was in traction for two weeks—and in agony because a nerve just above his elbow was pinched between two pieces of bone. Gaylord, Maurice Newstein, and George Clark came up from Boston to drive Noyce to Hanover, where the doctors at Dartmouth surgically removed a piece of bone. Then a blood clot set in. By the time he was fully recovered and back at MIT, Noyce had lost almost two months of work. His arm would bother him for the rest of his life.[36]

By the summer of 1953, his dissertation was nearly finished. In the end, it had proven a bit of a disappointment. Noyce had not been able to find evidence of surface states in the insulators he studied. To make matters worse, he had to admit he did not know whether his results meant that surface states did not exist in these materials or simply that his experimental methodology had been poor. The one consolation came from the work with magnesium oxide. He had managed to characterize its electrical properties, and the 11 curves he drew to demonstrate his findings were a small but real contribution to knowledge in his field.

The most important lesson that Noyce learned from his dissertation could not easily be translated onto paper. He had developed outstanding laboratory skills as a solid-state experimental physicist. His early false starts had taught him how to prepare materials and how to keep them from contamination. He also understood photoelectric emissions, electrons, holes, quantum states, and the physical properties of solids.

His knowledge and skills attracted offers to conduct research at Bell Labs at a starting salary of $7,500. IBM offered him a similar research position at $7,300 annual pay. Noyce spurned both these prestigious offers to accept a job at Philco, a Philadelphia-based company best known as a manufacturer of radios and televisions, for $6,900. Although Philco had 25,000 employees, only 30 worked in its semiconductor research group. Noyce liked the idea of working at a small company—perhaps, he thought, because he had grown up in a small town—and he also believed "[Philco] needed me very, very badly. They literally did not know what they were doing. I would be a necessary cog in that machine [whereas] in those larger, better-funded research organizations, I wasn't going to have an essential role." Noyce privately felt that the lack of a top-notch research team at Philco meant that he would have better opportunities to make a name for himself there than at either IBM or Bell Labs.[37]

Meantime, he had to file the dissertation, a daunting task. In 1953, the MIT Physics Department required five pristine copies of the document, which meant a new set of carbon papers for each of Noyce's 79 pages. A single typographical error, and the entire page was ruined. Noyce also hand-drew 22 figures included in the dissertation.

IN AUGUST 1953, a few weeks before Noyce was slated to submit the dissertation, he placed an unprecedented person-to-person call to his father. As Harriet Noyce recalled it, the conversation was remarkably brief:

"This is Bob, at Ephraim, Wisconsin. Will you marry us, Dad?"
"You and who?"[38]

THE GIRL WAS NAMED BETTY BOTTOMLEY, Noyce said. They were already en route from Boston, and they wanted to be married within the week.

Bob Noyce had met Betty Bottomley while performing in a musical at Tufts College, for which Bottomley was the costume designer. (Noyce had accompanied a girlfriend to auditions for the play and ended up with a role himself.) Betty Bottomley was 22, small and slight, with short blonde curls that hugged her head. Bad eczema that left her skin flaky and bumpy kept her from conventional prettiness, but Noyce had not been drawn to her by her looks. Ever since high school, he had liked a woman to have a touch of acid in her heart and a "tounge [sic] as sharp as a razor," as he once put it. Betty Bottomley certainly fit this description. A sickly child, asthmatic and unathletic in a family that spent a good deal of its time skiing and sailing, she had developed a slicing wit and an ability to comment on any situation with a jaw-dropping combination of humor and venom. She reminded more than one person of Dorothy Parker. Even her own family joked somewhat uneasily about the need to "sharpen our wits" when Betty was around. She seemed every inch the East Coast sophisticate that Noyce found attractive.[39]

Betty Bottomley's mother called her "a little human dynamo." In raw energy, impulsivity, and strength of will, she was every inch Bob Noyce's equal. She had graduated Tufts with a degree in English in 1952 and had spent the next year taking a graduate writing course, working in the public relations office of her alma mater, and writing for a literary magazine in addition to designing and sewing costumes for the Gilbert and Sullivan society. In her spare time, she enjoyed working complex word puzzles she found in magazines such as the *Atlantic*. She had also recently broken up with a boyfriend of several years, as Noyce made it his business to learn in relatively short order.[40]

By the end of the play's short run in May, the two were a couple. Three months later, Betty was typing Bob's thesis for him. The shared sense of camaraderie and stress must have been exhilarating. The relationship certainly felt special to Betty, who brought Bob to meet her parents at their home near Providence, Rhode Island. She often invited groups of friends to stay, but inviting just one was unusual. Her parents noticed immediately.

Betty's family had more in common with the men Bob had served as a waiter at the Century Country Club than with the Noyces. Frank Bottomley was a vice president at the Sealall manufacturing company. Helen MacLaren Bottomley had raised four children (Betty was the youngest) while serving on committees at her club and volunteering at a school for handicapped boys from broken homes. The Bottomleys owned a large sailboat and spent so much time on the waters around their yacht club that they often said they might as well live in Narragansett Bay itself.

For all their wealth—which was not truly substantial but may have seemed so to Noyce—the Bottomleys were unpretentious. Frank Bottomley, who had emigrated from England and left school after eighth grade, considered himself a glorified draftsman. Helen Bottomley had let the wind and sun weather her face and the simple braids she wound around her head each morning. She called the luncheons she organized at the club "production lines for the entertainment committee." Noyce's final assessment: the Bottomleys were the sort who joined a yacht club for the sailing, not for the society connections. He approved of this attitude.[41]

The Bottomleys liked how Bob helped Frank work on the boat, and they appreciated the eagerness with which he joined them around the piano to sing Gilbert and Sullivan tunes from memory. He was "pretty much all one could ask for" her parents told Betty, fully aware that their opinions would hold little sway over her. As Helen Bottomley once put it, weariness and pride equally evident in her voice, Betty "has made her own decisions for a long time."[42]

THIS ONE-WEEK NOTICE for an impending marriage was a bit much, even for Bob, whose impulsivity and lack of communication were legendary in his family. Both Don and Gaylord had introduced their future wives to the Noyces before proposing, of course, but Ralph and Harriet Noyce had never even heard of Betty Bottomley. Bob dated so many women that he had long ago stopped mentioning them in an effort to escape the inevitable deluge of questions from his mother. Indeed, he wrote home quite infrequently by the end of graduate school, perhaps only a few times per year, and then only to report truly dramatic news—that he had broken his arm, or won an award.

What was Bob Noyce thinking? To be sure, it was quite common for men to marry within months of finishing their PhDs. While there were good reasons for the timing—post-graduate jobs, income, and location often were not settled until a few months before graduation—dorm wisdom also warned that the light at the end of the tunnel had an unfortunate habit of bathing the nearest female in an idealized glow.

The prospect of heading off to a new place for a new job without any companionship undoubtedly led to a few hastily proffered proposals, but Noyce would have welcomed a completely unfettered beginning after graduate school. Although he was only 25 years old, he had already developed a habit of mentally tying up one part of his life, shelving it, and never looking back. Shortly after coming to MIT, he admitted to his mother that he wanted, more than anything else, to "be free." He had almost nothing to do with his childhood friends after he graduated Grinnell High School. He rarely communicated with college buddies after those first few months in Cambridge when he had actively sought them out as an antidote to the academic and financial demands of MIT. After he left graduate school, none of his colleagues, including the ones he lived with for years, would see or hear from him more than a handful of times in the next four decades.[43]

Even Gaylord, his beloved older brother, felt the effects of Bob's need for constant new starts. The two brothers drifted apart as the years passed. "Old friends and family can slow you down," Gaylord pointed out. "There are birthdays to remember, letters to write, and calls to accept even if you don't want to talk. Bob was not the type to slow down for much of anything."[44]

Why then would Noyce marry Betty Bottomley, whom he had known only three months? Betty told her friends that it had been a spur-of-the-moment decision, but again, this seems an unlikely explanation. Noyce was impulsive, but he was shrewd when it mattered. He would not have married on a whim. Years later Bob told his daughter that he and Betty had feared she was pregnant in the summer of 1953. He did not want another abortion on his conscience. It is unclear whether Betty was pregnant and miscarried, or whether the fears were unfounded, but the couple bore no children for 15 months after the wedding.[45]

Harriet Noyce worked herself into such a frenzy over the prospect of hosting a wedding and entertaining the wealthy Bottomleys that she had no time to worry about the marriage itself. "I felt it simply could not be true," she later wrote. "Maybe he had on'y said 'will you marry us' without saying 'this week.'" Betty and Bob wanted a simple ceremony, but the logistics were daunting nonetheless. Harriet and Ralph had moved to Richmond, Illinois, only a few months before—Reverend Noyce had taken another new job—and they were not yet at home in the community. To make matters worse, the family car was broken. Harriet ordered a wedding cake from the local grocery store, dressed a chicken herself, and called on friends from Sandwich to bake rolls, play the wedding march, house the Bottomleys (who were arriving in four days), and decorate the sanctuary with pink and white gladiolas donated by Ralph's congregation.[46]

She prayed that the Bottomleys would not turn up their noses at her work. "It really is easier for 'big' folks like them to make the adjustment here than for us to do it there," she explained to her mother. "I just tried to tell them this was what we could do for the children in lieu of a wedding present." If Harriet resented the demands Bob had placed on her so suddenly, she never let him know it, though it was during these few days that she swore for the only time anyone could ever remember—a tiny "darn" escaped her lips when the chicken salad threatened not to turn out the way she wanted.[47]

Betty Bottomley met her future in-laws in the throes of an asthma attack. Florid and wheezing, she was not the sophisticated Easterner the family had expected from Bob's description of his fiancée. When she had recovered a bit, she and Bob rode off on Ralph Harold's bicycle—Betty perched in the handle bars—for blood tests that were quickly handed off to a family friend who knew someone in the public health office in Chicago who would expedite the lab work. Bob, who had been informed that the suit he brought—the only one he owned—was too threadbare for a groom, borrowed a truck to buy a new one. Gaylord and Dotey had arrived a few days earlier for one of their regular visits to his parents; Gay, who, like Bob, had worked at the florist shop in Grinnell, offered to make the bride's bouquet and groom's boutonnière.

Bob and Betty seemed happy together. Bob was proud of his fiancée and treated her with a tenderness his family had never seen, touching her often and gently brushing her hair. But he and Betty could also be flamboyantly combative. They enjoyed verbally jousting with each other in what seemed to some family members to be a flagrant attempt to show off their agile minds.

After a few days' observation, Harriet decided Betty was "all right for Bob." She liked that Betty had not wanted "all the fuss" of a social wedding, and commented approvingly on her "nice poise and gaity [sic]." She reassured herself that "Bob is pretty fine and grown up, and we can trust his decision." Ralph Noyce said Betty Bottomley would make "a fine and loving daughter-in-law" and spoke of the "joy" he felt in the marriage of these "young people trained, educated, mature, [and] with such brilliant minds and so many interests." Though one younger family member found Betty surprisingly "cool," this was chalked up to nerves. She was, after all, meeting her future family only a few days before she committed to spending a lifetime with them.[48]

On the morning of the ceremony, Bob wore his new gray suit, and Betty wore a simple blue dress and a triple strand of pearls. Ralph Noyce was visibly moved by the young couple reciting their vows from memory, holding hands and looking seriously into each other's faces before their 20 guests, almost all of whom were family or intimate friends of Ralph and Harriet. Bob's only friends to attend were his roommates of four years, George Clark and Maurice Newstein. Betty does not appear to have invited anyone other than her parents and siblings. She, like her husband, knew many people but counted few among them good friends.

At Harriet's reception, the Bottomleys declared themselves positively "overwhelmed" that the Noyces and their close friends could create such a lovely gathering with so little notice. Harriet crowed to her mother, "It wouldn't have happened so soon among their friends . . . some of whom they admit are definitely snooty."[49]

On the afternoon of August 26, 1953, several hours after the reception ended, Dr. and Mrs. Robert Norton Noyce left for a week's honeymoon at Harriet's family cottage on the shores of Crystal Lake near Traverse City, Michigan. From there they would head to Philadelphia, where Bob was slated to begin his job at Philco. "It's a good enough salary so that he plans to pay off his debts to you," Harriet wrote to her mother, "and a little to us. They really say lots of nice things about Bob."[50]

BOB AND BETTY NOYCE started their life together in a two-room apartment in Elkins Park, about 20 minutes north of Philco's Philadelphia headquarters. Theirs was the quintessential 1950s marriage. Every morning at 8:00 Noyce met his carpool— the three other riders were also researchers in the transistor division at Philco—in the corner of the apartment parking lot. While he was at work, Betty spent her days keeping house, cooking, sewing, grocery shopping, and painting for a class she was taking. They would have dinner together when Noyce arrived home around 6:00. In the evenings, Noyce either finished up his Philco work or pieced together his model airplanes while Betty read or occasionally went off "Scrabbling" with a friend who lived in the apartment next door. Sometimes Bob would give her a bridge lesson. They both enjoyed entertaining and often invited friends for an evening. They had lived in Philadelphia for only a month when they learned their first child would arrive in the summer of 1954.

Work for Noyce was less peaceful but no less pleasant than his time at home. Noyce had joined Philco at an exciting time for its transistor researchers. The four men in Noyce's carpool represented nearly 15 percent of the company's transistor research staff. Until quite recently transistors had been a sideline business for Philco, an experiment in backwards integration: transistors were essential components in radios and would clearly play a role in televisions in the future. Even more important, Philco coveted the military market for transistors. The company had worked under Defense Department contract for decades—its combined WWII contracts for fuses, radar equipment, radios, vacuum tubes, and storage batteries amounted to more than $150 million—and when Noyce arrived in 1953, the company was overhauling its military production facilities with the assistance of a $40 million line of V-loan revolving credit guaranteed by the United States Navy.[51]

When Philco launched its program to develop a proprietary transistor in 1950, Bill Bradley, the 40-year-old head of research within the applied physics group, was tapped to lead the effort. An advanced formal education in transistors did not exist—witness Noyce's cobbled-together efforts at MIT—and so Bradley hired an eclectic group of men (and one woman) for the research division: a few Physics PhDs, several electrical engineers, many self-taught engineers and technicians, and a sprinkling of fresh-faced college kids with science degrees. Experience was education's equal for a company less interested in a theoretically intriguing transistor than in a sellable transistor, a device that would be, in the words of Philco's vice president of research, a "useful member of society." Because markets were as important as science at Philco, Noyce's group conducted research on applications at the same time as the basic scientific investigations.[52]

The first important invention to emerge from the transistor group was a germanium device they called the "surface-barrier transistor." A variation on the point-contact transistor, the Philco device somehow managed to side-step the Bell Labs patents. Philco announced the invention of the surface-barrier transistor in December 1953, at a special meeting attended by representatives of the Department of Defense and the Institute of Radio Engineers (IRE), the premier professional organization for electronics researchers. "The surface-barrier transistor is the most important advance in electronics since discovery of the point-contact transistor," asserted Philco's head of Research and Engineering. It operated at higher frequencies and consumed less power than other transistors, which meant it would be more stable than competing devices. The key innovation behind the transistor was a new method of processing germanium that Philco thought "promised transistor mass production" in the very near future. Reliable mass production was the holy grail of the industry in the early 1950s, when devices were still produced in small batches in a slow and painstaking process. The IRE devoted 50 pages in its *Proceedings* to technical articles by the Philco staff that covered the theory behind the device, the production methods used to produce it, and its market applications.[53]

The timing of the announcement and articles, roughly three months after Noyce's arrival at the company, must have thrilled him. He had wanted to be a large fish in a small pond, and now, just weeks after his arrival, the eyes of the entire transistor world were focused on the tiny Philco pond. And just as he had hoped, Noyce could contribute in significant ways from the beginning. As its name implied, the surface-barrier transistor did its work on the surface of the germanium. It thus correlated well with Noyce's expertise in surface states, and he had no trouble jumping into the effort midstream.[54]

The key Philco production innovation was a method of etching and electroplating germanium by shooting two jets of liquid indium salt at either side of a sliver of the semiconductor. Noyce's first assignment was to help develop a way to determine when it was time to stop etching and start electroplating. This was not the fundamental physics he had studied at MIT. It was immediately practical and obviously relevant to a specific problem—more engineering than physics in some ways. This was an ideal assignment for someone who valued, above all, doing something useful. Noyce suggested measuring the base width of the transistor by shining a beam of light on it. As the base width of transistor decreased, the intensity of the light would increase. When the light indicated that the base width had been etched to the appropriate thinness, the electroplating process could begin. Philco adopted this approach with some success, and the innovation served as the basis of Noyce's first patent. Within months, Noyce was co-authoring the basic paper on surface-barrier transistor theory, which, when it was completed in 1955, the company considered too important to publish in the open literature.[55]

Noyce's immediate boss, Carlo Bocciarelli, was a swarthy, rotund, former artist who had no use for traditional ways of doing business. He spoke three languages in addition to his native Italian and knotted a rope through the buttonholes in his pants instead of wearing a belt. Bocciarelli openly ogled the attractive women who worked throughout the company as secretaries and production workers. He particularly admired the bottle blondes, whose bleached hair he called "a promising indication of a will-ingness to please." Noyce followed his boss's example enough to eschew both coat and tie. He also enjoyed the women at Philco and was happy that several of them happened to be named Betty. "When I talked in my sleep [at home]," he explained later, "it was fine."[56]

Noyce liked Bocciarelli, but it was Bill Bradley, the head of the transis-tor program, whom he considered a professional mentor. Bradley was roughly a dozen years older than Noyce. He held a bachelor's degree in electrical engineering, and had spent the Second World War at the MIT Rad Lab before joining Philco. He loved music—particularly medieval singing—and as a boy had started an "association for the advancement of science" con-sisting entirely of friends who wanted to experiment with chemicals and build firecrackers and rockets. Bradley held several patents in television and transistor production techniques, and he could offer an apparently endless stream of ideas and potential research routes to anyone who would listen. Noyce, who called Bradley a "white noise source" with a buried but valuable "useful signal," found his mentor's relentless there-must-be-a-way attitude extremely encouraging.[57]

When he was temporarily given management responsibility for a small group of researchers in the spring of 1954, Noyce adopted Bradley's ap-proach, always encouraging and explaining, always ready with a new idea to try if the original one threatened to fail. One man who worked for Noyce during this period recalled him as "very easy to talk to, very helpful, and very different from a typical manager." Noyce only expressed impatience when dealing with people he considered intellectually slow. He did every-thing he could to avoid them, and when that failed, he would sit so immo-bilized as they spoke that one could almost see a cartoon thought bubble over his head: "Why am I forced to sit through this?"[58]

ABOUT A YEAR AND A HALF into his work, Noyce's feelings about Philco began to change. The company had trumpeted that its techniques would usher in an era of automated transistor production, but in the year that had passed since that announcement, Philco had been unable to move the tran-sistors out of development and into production at the Landsdale, Pennsyl-vania, facility that had once made vacuum tubes. Although the company claimed that its patented etching and plating techniques allowed for "the highest mechanical precision yet attained in machining germanium," the transistors that emerged from the Landsdale facility were leaky and unreliable. Noyce was one of several researchers brought in to try to improve the yield, or percentage of usable transistors to emerge from the production process. He was part of a team that built a device that used a scanning electron beam to monitor voltage differences on the surface of the transistor. The crude technology did pinpoint the location of the problems, but tweaking the production line proved time consuming and expensive. Meanwhile, other problems had emerged, most troubling among them the fact that even when the transistors worked, their delay before starting was too long for military purposes.[59]

Adding to Noyce's frustration with his job was his increasing involvement with Defense Department bureaucracy. Although Philco's primary backing for its transistor research came from the Bureau of Ships branch of the navy, which wanted the devices for its Sidewinder missile, most of Noyce's work before 1955 had fallen outside the navy contract and was funded by Philco's in-house commercial research and development budget. In early 1955, however, Philco decided it could not afford to fund its own research. The company was in trouble. Earnings dropped by two-thirds from 1953 to 1954, when a strike closed down two key plants and the federal government sued Philco, charging antitrust activities in its relationships with distributors. The net effect of this turmoil for Noyce was that the transistor group began working exclusively under government contract. "It seems that Philco is not yet really convinced that research pays for itself in the long run," Noyce bitterly reported to his family.[60]

Noyce could not believe the "bullshit, waste, make-work, and lack of incentive" he faced in his research measuring the channels in P- and N-semiconductors under an air force transistor contract. The nature of his work was uncertain from one funding cycle to the next. He had to complete a time card and to file monthly and quarterly reports on his small research group's progress. He particularly loathed the reporting requirements and would never write his reports on time, much to the frustration of the nearly half-dozen writers whose sole job at Philco was to oversee reporting compliance in the transistor group. Finally, Joe Chapline, who managed the writers, began preparing his own version of Noyce's reports, complete with imaginary "good news." His ultimatum: correct the fictitious reports or sign them. Noyce, of course, corrected them. Chapline had to resort to this ruse for nearly every report Noyce was required to submit, and he had to use it on a few other researchers, as well.[61]

Meetings with military planners, purchasing agents, and technical experts filled Noyce's days. He went to Dayton, Ohio, to consult with military engineers at Wright Field and to Fort Monmouth, New Jersey, to discuss an army contract. The meetings to review "proper procedure" and the reporting requirements, not to mention the strikers yelling outside his window and the indirect insult of effectively being told by his company that his work was not important enough to fund—all of this kept Noyce from "doing good science," as he liked to say. To make matters worse, he thought he was doing "a lousy job" managing other researchers at Philco. Management, he said, was a chore that "took time away from useful work."[62]

Betty Noyce was also miserable. She and Bob both worried that he might be drafted. She delighted in her son Billy, who was born in July 1954, but she found life as "Mrs. Noyce" stifling. She spent her days at home or at a neighbor's with the baby. She and Bob still entertained, and they spent long hours making home movies of Billy together, but Betty nonetheless found herself without adult companionship more than she would like. Bob sang in an oratorio choir at a local church one evening per week. He thought nothing of announcing that he would be gone for an entire Saturday—taking the car with him at 4:30 in the morning—to watch a model airplane meet. The meetings with the military and trips to Landsdale meant Bob was often absent, and Betty found herself increasingly resentful of the travel. "Bob has got to go up to Boston on business either this Friday or Mon. He gave me my choice which day he should go—I don't know if this is an invitation to come along … or if I was just consulted on when I'd most like to be alone," she wrote to her family. When Bob took out the suitcase, little Billy would burst into tears. When Noyce was home, he liked to sequester himself in a corner of the living room, where he was trying to build a transistorized organ with the help of a book loaned to him by another Philco employee with a penchant for music. ("What will they think of next?" Betty muttered to herself.)[63]

Noyce's co-workers suspected that his marriage was not happy. "Noyce never talked about his wife," recalled one. "He never mentioned an anniversary, or her birthday, or what she liked to do." Concurred another, "The only time I ever saw her was when I came over once to help with a window air conditioning unit. Bob seemed to have kept her in the back."[64]

Through all her troubles, Betty maintained her wit. She signed her letters to Ralph and Harriet (she had assumed the writing duties): "B, B, b, & 1/2 b," for Bob, Betty, Billy, and the baby due a few months after Billy turned one. She consoled herself with dreams of dramatic change. She wanted to buy a home, a nice old place with a big yard for the children. She imagined a summer cottage on Cape Cod or in New Hampshire, where she could take the children or meet her family when Bob was away. Such reveries were pure fantasy. The roughly $300 the Noyces spent to rent and heat their little apartment each month could only buy a house they did not want: a downtown Philadelphia rowhouse, which Betty declared "revolting," or a bungalow in Levittown, a "homogenized suburbia" Betty admitted herself "too snobbish" to enjoy, though Bob liked the development quite a bit.[65]

When Westinghouse called with an offer to join the Pittsburgh-based transistor group at an immediate 25 percent raise, plus a guaranteed annual 10 percent raise for each of the two years thereafter, Noyce was tempted. They could buy a house in a nice neighborhood near Carnegie Tech, and the work sounded more interesting than what he was doing at Philco. Philco countered with an offer to meet the raises and make the management position permanent. The company also dangled the possibility of a transfer to Landsdale, where Betty, who reminded Bob it was time to "start thinking of a permanent site for ourselves," thought they could buy "a little house and a big yard." Bob wrestled with the decision for a week before deciding one morning at 2 AM to stay at Philco.[66]

In August 1955, Noyce noted, "My current assets are: household furnishings of a four-room apartment, a car valued at $700 with a lien of $232, about $300 cash on hand, stocks and savings of about $650, and a $20,000 life insurance policy two years in force with a cash value of $260. My current liabilities, other than monthly household running expenses of about $400, are debts to the extent of $500. My wife and children [a baby was due in October] live with me and are wholly dependent on me for their support." How dramatically his life had changed.[67]

In December, the draft board sent Noyce a belated twenty-eighth birthday present in the form of an "indefinite postponement of induction." He would not need to worry about the draft. The new baby, a girl called Penny, had arrived safely. The little apartment looked downright cheerful with her mobile suspended from the ceiling and the philodendron Betty had decorated as a makeshift Christmas tree propped against the rabbit-ears FM antenna. But the military work continued, and the move to Landsdale never materialized. When the calendar turned to 1956, Bob knew he wanted nothing more than "to walk away [from Philco] and start over again somewhere else."[68]

On January 19, 1956, Noyce answered his ringing telephone. The man at the other end of the line greeted him with two words: "Shockley here." William Shockley, one of the inventors of the transistor, assumed Noyce knew who he was, and he was right. "It was like picking up the phone and talking to God," Noyce recalled later. "He was absolutely the most important person in semiconductor electronics." And he wanted Noyce to work for him—in California.[69]

3

Apprenticeship

William Shockley held more than 50 patents for electronic devices and by one estimate was personally responsible for nearly "half the worthwhile ideas in solid-state electronics" in the field's first dozen years. Lanky and lean, with a wide forehead that began overtaking his hairline when he was still in his twenties, he was a direct descendent of Mayflower Puritans. Educated at California Institute of Technology and MIT—where he received his PhD in Physics in 1936—Shockley was a technical genius whose work ethic recalled that of his ancestors. During the Second World War, while working in the navy's Anti-Submarine Warfare Operations Group, he developed systems that quadrupled the number of successful American attacks on German subs. He was a pack rat and a vigorous note taker who filled notebook after notebook with cryptic, penciled records of the day's events. He was also a showman and amateur magician who had been known to pause in the middle of delivering a scientific paper to conjure a bouquet of flowers from the lectern. His colleagues sometimes wondered if he slept. When his wife Jean fell ill with uterine cancer in 1953, Shockley, then overseeing a team at Bell Labs, launched an intensive one-man research effort into the disease, analyzing her lab slides at home, annotating complex medical articles, and writing to doctors around the world.[1]

Shockley had left Bell Labs in 1954, roughly the same time Noyce began work at Philco. It was not an amicable parting. The inspiring story of the "three inventors of the transistor" that Bell Labs had circulated around the world in 1948 whitewashed a nasty internecine conflict within the solid-state group. The point-contact transistor, the world's first transistor, had been invented by Brattain and Bardeen without assistance or blessing from Shockley, who was their boss. Indeed, Shockley, nearly apoplectic with jealousy, had marked the transistor's discovery by calling the inventors into his office to tell them, his voice rising with every word, that since the point-contact transistor built on some of his own early ideas, he could write a patent "on the whole damn thing." When Brattain responded, "Oh hell,

Shockley! There's enough glory in this for everyone," Shockley took his argument to the Bell Labs patent attorneys. In the course of investigating his claim, the attorneys discovered that the ideas he said were the foundation of the transistor might not be so original, after all. The safe route was not to include Shockley's name on the patent application.[2]

Even before receiving this personally devastating news, Shockley had begun an effort to develop a transistor on his own. Within days of hearing of Bardeen and Brattain's invention, he cloistered himself in a hotel room in Chicago (where he was attending a conference), thinking and writing furiously. A patentable device eluded him, but he kept his musings to himself, fearful that if he shared them with Brattain and Bardeen, he might have to list them as co-inventors of whatever device he planned to bring into being by sheer force of intellect and will. In mid-January, Shockley's secret stewing paid off, when he realized that a Bell Labs colleague's research findings meant that the ideas he had mapped out in his Chicago hotel room could be fused into a workable device: the sandwich-like junction transistor. It may be spite's greatest contribution to American science.

The conflict with Brattain and Bardeen—which only widened when Bell Labs decreed that any picture of "the inventors of the transistor" must include Shockley—represented merely one in a string of battles and hard feelings between Shockley and his colleagues. By 1951, Bell Labs senior management could no longer ignore complaints about Shockley's prickly personality, especially after Brattain and Bardeen told the head of the Physical Research Department that they no longer wanted to report to Shockley. Within days, the department was reorganized, with most of Shockley's old transistor group shifted to someone else.

His career clearly beginning to stall, Shockley took a sabbatical. After a year spent teaching at his alma mater Cal Tech and another in Washington, D.C., where he headed the Pentagon's Weapons Systems Evaluations Group (a cadre of civilian scientists and engineers charged with advising the military on the weapons planning process), Shockley was desperate for a change. He divorced Jean, whose life he had fought so valiantly to save only the year before. He moved to California.[3]

And he decided to start a transistor company. He foresaw a day when transistors would power everything from airplanes to televisions, and he felt confident that Bell Labs and its manufacturing arm, Western Electric, which viewed the transistor as little more than a potential replacement for vacuum tubes in the telephone grid, would offer little competition. He spent most of the summer of 1955 in conversations with Raytheon, Texas Instruments, and Laurence Rockefeller, trying to secure half-a-million dollars to launch a transistor operation. After promising starts, all of these efforts stalled.[4]

In August 1955, however, Shockley found a willing source of financial support in millionaire Arnold Beckman, a fellow graduate of Cal Tech with whom Shockley had become reacquainted during a black-tie dinner at the Los Angeles Chamber of Commerce the previous February. A professor of analytical chemistry whose military bearing and bald pate recalled Dwight Eisenhower, Beckman had successfully made the leap to industry that Shockley longed to make as well.

Beckman Instrument's first product had been a pH meter that could electronically measure the acidity of oranges. It soon found a number of industrial uses in water treatment plants, plating and anodizing operations, and paper factories. The company's other major products included a helical potentiometer, used in the nose of proximity-fuse missiles, and an ultracentrifuge employed in the first successful separation of the polio virus. Headquartered in a low-slung, attractive glass-and-steel building in Fullerton, California, Beckman Instruments had offices in a dozen sites in the United States, Canada, and Germany.

Beckman Instruments was flush in 1955. With more than 2,000 employees, sales of more than $21 million, and profits in excess of $1.3 million, the company was in its second consecutive record-breaking year and had acquired two small firms within a few months. Since the firm was already organized into multiple autonomous divisions, each with its own general manager and complete operating organization, adding another independent business unit was relatively easy.[5]

As befitted a former scientist, Arnold Beckman was deeply committed to research and development, the heading under which he classed Shockley's work. Beckman Instruments regularly reinvested at least 8 percent of sales in R&D, a move its founder called "insurance against obsolescence." In the mid-1950s, when improved data-processing methods and advances in semiconductor technology seemed likely to shape the future of Beckman's military and industrial markets, Arnold Beckman decided he wanted a stake in the basic research in both fields. Accordingly, in early 1955, Beckman Instruments launched an expensive R&D effort to investigate optimal methods of digitally interpreting data. Shockley's proposed transistor efforts would give Beckman Instruments a leading position in semiconductor research.[6]

The negotiations between Shockley and Beckman were quick and friendly. Beckman Instruments would fund the operation, but Shockley would have complete managerial control. As a director and president of the new division, he would receive an annual salary of $30,000 and options to purchase 4,000 shares of Beckman Instruments stock. Beckman and Shockley estimated first-year costs at $300,000, including a $25,000 payment to Bell Labs to license patent rights for the transistor. On September 3, 1955, they signed an agreement to "engage promptly and vigorously in activities related to semiconductors." They predicted that within a year the new Shockley Semiconductor division would generate monthly sales of $30,000.[7]

Beckman would like to have situated the semiconductor operation in Fullerton or at least in the greater Los Angeles area, but Shockley wanted to start the company further north—in the San Francisco Bay Area. He had grown up in Palo Alto, near the Stanford University campus, and his mother, whom he adored with a devotion that unnerved some of his acquaintances, still lived there. He was an avid mountain climber and outdoorsman, and the topographical diversity of the Bay Area intrigued him. Palo Alto still had the feel of the semirural college town Shockley recalled from his boyhood. Wood-shingled houses dominated the oldest neighborhoods near the small downtown built around University Avenue, a street that was called Palm Drive at the entrance to the Stanford campus. Slightly farther south, where the houses took on a distinctly Mediterranean cast, walnut and olive trees lined the wide boulevards named for famous poets and local families. A half mile beyond, south of Oregon Avenue, lay scattered dairy farms. Palo Alto had one telephone exchange and shared a municipal court judge with the neighboring town of Mountain View.[8]

The once quaint rural town was rapidly becoming a small city in 1955. Between 1950 and 1960, its population more than doubled, from 25,000 to 52,000, and its acreage tripled. Developers and builders, who had opened housing tracts among the dairy farms at a rate of three per year since the end of the war, enticed returning veterans and young families to the area with two- and three-bedroom bungalows that sold for roughly $9,000—monthly payments of only $60, advertisements touted—and included a guaranteed "six or more bearing-fruit trees" to each 6,000 square-foot lot. Do-it-yourself shops and hardware stores sprung up around town, including at the Stanford Shopping Center, an upscale mall that opened in 1956, the same year as the town's first golf course. To accommodate the area's families, Palo Alto built 15 public schools between 1948 and 1956.[9]

Several successful technical companies had gotten their start in Palo Alto, and Shockley undoubtedly would have welcomed the opportunity to associate himself with this auspicious entrepreneurial history. A hotbed of radio and microwave research in the first decades of the century, the town was home to Federal Telegraph's manufacturing plant and 626-foot transmitting tower until 1932, when the Depression-plagued company consolidated its operations in New Jersey. Electronics giant Hewlett-Packard was founded in a Palo Alto garage in 1939. In 1948, two scientists affiliated with Stanford's Physics Department started Varian Associates to commercialize innovations that they believed would prove useful in radar technology. By 1950, traffic from the industrial districts a few miles south of town was so heavy that locals were lobbying to expand the narrow Bayshore Freeway (nicknamed "Bloody Bayshore") to four lanes.

A concerted effort by Stanford University accelerated Palo Alto's trend towards electronics industrialization in the 1950s. Frederick Terman, professor of engineering (later dean and provost) at Stanford, wanted the university to serve as the center of what he called a "community of technical scholars"—a web of academic and industrial researchers that would work together to advance "sophisticated technologies." Terman envisioned a symbiotic relationship in which technically oriented companies would support advanced research at Stanford while at the same time benefiting from a supply of well-educated graduates and professors interested in consulting work. He encouraged students and faculty—most notably William Hewlett, David Packard, and the Varian brothers—to start their own companies, rather than travel back East to work for established ones. He pioneered an innovative "Honors Cooperative Program" that allowed employees of local electronics firms to work part-time towards advanced degrees. Shortly after endowment-poor Stanford opened a research park in 1953 in an effort to raise funds, Terman began wooing "smokeless industries" whose work would be relevant to the university's academic programs. He even alerted highly placed contacts at the Defense Department to the existence of local firms that might be logical contracting choices.[10]

When Terman learned of Shockley's hopes to locate in Palo Alto— the two men belonged to several of the same professional societies—he wrote to him with assurances that the university "would heartily welcome this activity in the Stanford area, and I believe that its location here would be mutually advantageous." Terman had been contemplating how to increase Stanford's participation in the semiconductor field for several years. He told Shockley that Stanford had recently hired its first faculty member who specialized in semiconductors, and that other prominent Stanford professors were already incorporating transistors into their coursework. He suggested that Shockley might find the Honors Cooperative Program a useful recruiting tool and spoke glowingly of the 200 potential employees enrolled in graduate electrical engineering courses at Stanford. He concluded, "It is an exciting business to observe the University and the technical community grow cooperatively to the benefit of both. We hope that you will see your way clear to participate in it."[11]

After sending his letter, Terman contacted the local Chamber of Commerce on Shockley's behalf (though without disclosing Shockley's identity) and secured a list of appropriate industrial sites and knowledgeable real estate agents that he forwarded to Shockley. He offered occasional use of "the facilities of the University" and planned to name Shockley to the unpaid but prestigious post of university lecturer. Even for Terman, the courtship was unusually intense. He was excited by the knowledge that "Shockley-Beckman [are] playing for big stakes."[12]

Terman's overtures and the proximity to Stanford may well have served to make Arnold Beckman more comfortable with a Palo Alto site for the semiconductor operation. It is unlikely, however, that such attractions held much sway with Shockley, whose location plans were driven almost entirely by personal concerns. Having Stanford and Frederick Terman nearby was a nice bonus—and Shockley certainly mentioned it in recruiting workers to his company—but he wanted to come to Northern California regardless.

Shockley had devised a unique plan to staff his company based on research he had conducted during his spare time while serving in the navy. Detailed analysis of scientific papers written by researchers at some of the nation's most prestigious labs—including the nuclear weapons facility at Los Alamos—had convinced Shockley that every person had a "mental temperature" that could be objectively determined through a series of tests and evaluations of written work. The brighter the mind, the higher the temperature. Theorizing that "a mere doubling of mental temperature may jump a man's scientific creativity a hundredfold, like a heat-triggered chemical reaction," Shockley was determined to staff his company with the hottest minds in the world.[13]

After his attempts to recruit Bell Lab scientists failed—his reputation preceded him—Shockley spent the end of 1955 phoning colleagues at other leading research labs and technical firms around the country, asking their assistance in finding the top young men with expertise for the various positions he sought to fill. He wanted to reproduce the division of labor at Bell Labs. To do so, he needed to hire several experimental and theoretical physicists, as well as chemists, metallurgists, and electrical and mechanical engineers.

First to join Shockley were Smoot Horsley, a clean-cut, mild-mannered, 40-year-old physicist from Motorola with extensive semiconductor experience; and Dean Knapic, an engineer who had worked at Western Electric and whom Shockley hired to head up production. Beckman Instruments proudly included a photo of the three men in its 1956 annual report, along with a comment from Arnold Beckman that could have been penned by Shockley himself: "In research there is no substitute for superiority."[14]

In October 1955, Shockley flew to Pittsburgh to hunt for hot minds at a semiconductor symposium sponsored by the Electrochemical Society. The symposium had been a last-minute addition to the regular meeting agenda, tacked on by the conference organizers. After receiving so many papers on the burgeoning new semiconductor field, they decided to sponsor a series of ten-minute presentations on the topic over the course of a single day.[15]

The meeting was the typical technical conference, with multiple sessions running simultaneously, luncheons in the grand ballroom of the stately William Penn hotel, conference-sponsored scenic drives and sightseeing, and a full "ladies program" of get-acquainted coffees, fashion shows, and shopping excursions for the wives. Shockley did not allow himself to be distracted from his primary mission. He spent his time attending lectures, assessing candidates, and grilling professors at the University of Pittsburgh about their most promising students. He wrote page after page of impressions in a small green memoranda book that fit in his pocket.

On October 10, Shockley noted, "Noyce—Philco; has talked sense about surface transistor." Bob Noyce had presented a paper on "Observations of Channel Formation on N- and P-Type Semiconductors" at the last Electrochemical Society conference. The subject of his talk this time is unknown—the semiconductor session was assembled so quickly that the paper abstracts were not included in the main program—but back at Philco, Noyce was investigating the well-known "punch-through" problem in which the electric field extends through the whole width of the base, which makes the base disappear electrically and causes the transistor to malfunction. His ten-minute talk at the October conference likely concerned this topic. Shockley quickly decided that Noyce was the only scientist worth pursuing at Philco.[16]

Three months passed before Shockley—busy finding a building, outfitting a lab, pursuing other recruits, and finalizing arrangements with Beckman—called Noyce in Philadelphia. By that time, the famous physicist knew what sort of work would appeal to the young researchers he wanted to attract. Shockley Semiconductor would conduct the finest scientific research, he promised, with an aim towards building a saleable, profitable product. A job at the company would be an opportunity to work not only with him, but also with the finest rising men in the business, on one of the most exciting technologies to appear in the field of physics for decades, the transistor. ("Is your future brighter in another electronics job?" he reminded himself to ask.) It was also a chance to come to California.[17]

Certainly, the company's location appealed to Bob Noyce. From his earliest years of shoveling snow through Iowa's frigid winters, he had fantasized about the Golden State's towering mountains and sunny beaches. "All Iowans think California is heaven," he once said. His brother Don's recent move to Berkeley for a job in the university's Chemistry Department only added to the region's attractions. Noyce frankly told Shockley that he had been considering leaving Philco and would love to move to California—especially if it meant a chance to engage in basic research again. Privately, he swore that he would not miss an opportunity to work for William Shockley: "Getting that job," he told himself, meant he would "definitely be playing in the big leagues." The call from Shockley had also gotten his competitive juices flowing. "I sort of wanted to see if I could stand up in that league of competition," he later admitted.[18]

Betty Noyce was less excited. However wonderful the professional opportunity for Bob, the essential feature of the Shockley job in Betty's mind was its location in California. Her family's ties to New England ran deep. She had a network of friends there. Her parents were only a few hours away. The prospect of moving two children under the age of 18 months to the other side of the country, where she knew no one, did not appeal to her. Noyce's promise that they would buy a nice house in the San Francisco Bay Area, which at the time was more affordable than Philadelphia, swayed her—but not entirely. She agreed only to a two-year trial period in California. He promised that if she was not happy at the end of two years, they would head back east.[19]

Before Shockley would bring Noyce to California for an interview, he asked him to report to the offices of McMurry-Hamstra, a New York psychological testing firm, for evaluation. Noyce spent an entire day in Manhattan, where he completed a standard IQ test, described ink blots, and played word association games. The testers also asked a question specially devised by Shockley to gauge creative thinking: 127 people enter an elimination tennis tournament. Since it's an odd number, one player must draw a bye in the first round. How many matches must be played to determine a winner?[20]

The standard approach to solving this question would be to chug through a multistep process of division and addition. (Pair the 126 people into 63 matches. Add to those 63 winners the player who drew the bye, and then split this group into 32 new matches, which would yield 16 winners, etc.) Shockley was looking for a much simpler sort of solution, one that Noyce gave him. There is only one winner, so 126 people have to be eliminated. Since a person can only be eliminated through a match, it must take 126 matches to come up with a winner. Q.E.D.

Shockley required this extensive testing of every one of his top-level recruits. Few of them thought it strange. Indeed, several had undergone similar aptitude testing for other employers, and one had even taken a college course on "Testing Evaluation for Employees." What did strike the young men as unusual, at least in retrospect, was the overt attempt to gauge personality. As one of them put it, "They spent, I think, too much effort on whether I liked my mother or not." At one point, the testers showed the recruit a line drawing of a man with clenched fists standing at the foot of a bed in which a woman lay with her eyes shut. How would you describe this scene, the testers wanted to know. Had the man just killed the woman? Was he worried that she was ill? Was she sleeping? Was he angry at her?[21]

Why Shockley required this psychological evaluation is a bit of an open question. He had recently fallen in love with a nurse who taught at a psychiatric facility, and this relationship deepened his already keen interest in the workings of the human mind. Perhaps he felt that if there were a way to gain insight into his employees' personalities and access to their innermost thoughts, why not do it? Such knowledge might help him match scientists for personal compatibility and maintain harmony in the lab.

Noyce completed the tests to the satisfaction of the McMurry-Hamstra evaluators, and quickly accepted Shockley's offer to fly him and Betty to San Francisco for an on-site interview. On February 23, 1956, Bob and Betty Noyce left the frigid East Coast on a red-eye flight to San Francisco. They touched down at 6 AM to one of the Bay Area's beautiful Indian summer days. Bob insisted that they find a house near the lab before lunch— "First things first," he would later recall—and only then did he go to his interview. He got the job.[22]

SHOCKLEY ASSEMBLED a team quickly. Vic Jones, a young PhD from Berkeley who specialized in plasma and nuclear physics, moved across the Bay in March. A Welshman with bushy eyebrows and boyish good looks, Jones was so genial and unassuming that the regulars at his favorite pub had no idea he was a scientist with a PhD. Shockley hired Jay Last, a rangy 26 year old who looked too young to drive, out of the new solid state physics program at MIT before he even completed his doctorate. Campus rumor held that no one built thinner crystals than Last, who was very proud of his "damn steady hands." A call to Lawrence Livermore Labs led Shockley to Gordon Moore, a quiet 27-year-old physical chemist at the Johns Hopkins Applied Physics Lab who had been born in a small farm town on the Northern California coast and raised only a few miles north of Palo Alto. Dean Knapic hired two young men whom he worked with in production at Western Electric: Julius Blank, a portly mechanical engineer with a heavy New York accent who thought the job might be "an adventure"; and Eugene Kleiner, a well-born Viennese refugee from Nazi terror and an expert tool builder.[23]

A professor at MIT referred Shockley to a PhD metallurgist named Sheldon Roberts, who had developed an interest in silicon and wanted to leave his job at Dow Chemical. When Jean Hoerni, a Swiss theoretical physicist with two doctorates, called Shockley looking for a job at Bell Labs, Shockley lured him to his own company. Vic Grinich, tall and thin with curly hair he wore longer than the fashionable buzz cuts, responded to a want ad that Shockley had written in code and published in a scientific journal to screen out insufficiently intelligent applicants. Grinich came from the Stanford Research Institute, where he had tried to use grown-junction transistors to drive a color television. (He managed to get the video portion functioning, but never got the audio to work.)[24]

Only a handful of the roughly 20 men who came to Shockley Semiconductor in the first half of 1956 had passed their thirtieth birthdays. A few had worked in private corporations, but most had either recently received their doctorates or had been employed exclusively in academic or government labs. Almost no one had worked directly with semiconductors, which were still considered esoteric devices. Many of the researchers, such as Gordon Moore—who had been so frustrated by his government-funded research that he once calculated the taxpayers' cost-per-word he published—were drawn to Shockley by the prospect of "actually making a product and selling it." The chance to live in California excited them all. In every case, however, the biggest attraction was Shockley himself.[25]

Shockley planned to unify this hodgepodge of expertise under his own technical leadership. He made it clear to his young team that he would assign them to projects of his own choosing to be done as he directed. "You would be able to discuss your way, your thoughts about how you might do it," recalls one former employee, "but at the end of the time, [Shockley's] view was that unless your thoughts were better than his, you'd do it his way."[26]

SHOCKLEY DID HIS BEST for the young men. He flew them and their wives to California at a time when flying was still relatively uncommon. He put them up at the nicest hotel in town, Rickey's, a wood-paneled beauty of an inn with sumptuous landscaping. He hired them at salaries of better than $800 per month—substantially higher than they had been making in their other jobs. He recommended a real estate agent—his aunt—who could help the men and their young families settle into their new homes. He even apologized for the weather when an unusual cold snap meant that several recruits, who arrived in March with bathing suits in hand, instead found icicles on the fountains outside their hotel room doors.[27]

A critical mass of employees had arrived by mid-April, and Shockley arranged a welcoming party. Noyce, then in his last weeks at Philco, was determined to attend, even though it meant driving across the country in his four-year-old Chevy, its back seat covered with suitcases. As was often the case with him, he ran behind schedule—so far behind in fact, that he had only gotten as far as Salt Lake City by the morning of the festivities. It was raining when he left Utah and positively pouring when he got to the Bay Area. One of the windshield wipers had given out, and he had smoked without stopping to keep himself awake. By the time he found the party, at 10 PM, the celebration was well under way. His appearance made an indelible impression on another recruit:

> He hadn't shaved, he looked like he'd been living in his suit for a week— and he was thirsty. There was a big goddamn bowl of martinis on the table there. Noyce picks up the goddamn bowl, and starts drinking [from] it. Then he passes out. I said to myself, "this is going to be a whole lot of fun."[28]

Meanwhile, Shockley was feeling no pain himself. He spent the latter part of the evening dancing the tango with a rose in his teeth.[29]

SHOCKLEY MADE TWO KEY TECHNICAL DECISIONS when he started his company. First, he would build transistors from silicon, rather than from germanium, which was then the preferred semiconductor substrate. Shockley had been an early advocate of silicon, dashing off a letter outlining its benefits within weeks of learning, in March 1955, that researchers at Bell Labs had successfully grown silicon crystals as pure as germanium crystals. Although its higher melting point makes silicon more reactive and therefore harder to work with than germanium, silicon (the basic ingredient in sand) is the second-most abundant element on earth, after oxygen. Even more important, unlike germanium devices, which often leaked and had a debilitating tendency to malfunction at high temperatures or in high humidity, silicon devices would function reliably in almost any environment, hot or cold, wet or dry. Since the world's largest potential transistor buyer, the Department of Defense, was willing to pay top dollar for stable equipment, silicon transistors seemed to promise financial success.[30]

The second critical decision was to build transistors using the new doping process called diffusion, recently developed at Bell Labs. In the diffusion process, a semiconductor is cooked in a furnace containing appropriate impurities (called "dopants") that then seep into the silicon in much the same way that hickory flavor seeps into meat cooked in a barbecue pit. Diffusion resulted in the best-defined P- and N-regions of any method then available, which in turn meant that diffused transistors ought to be faster and capable of operating at a higher frequency than other devices. The process was important and new enough that Shockley had sent Noyce and Gordon Moore to a Bell Labs seminar to learn more about it.[31]

The company set to work in a converted Quonset hut at 391 South San Antonio Road, in the heart of an industrial district-cum-shopping center—the nearest neighbor was a Sears store—roughly five miles south of Stanford and footsteps across the Palo Alto border into Mountain View. The building, which one observer likened to an auto-parts warehouse, had insufficient gas and power for a laboratory's needs, and privately Shockley's new employees worried about whether or not their boss would outfit the lab appropriately. Their concerns proved unfounded. Shockley bought good scientific apparatus and tools, though he certainly did not bother with any sort of investment in aesthetics, since he planned to move the offices and labs to the Stanford Industrial Park, where Beckman was building a facility, in the fall of 1956.[32]

The entirety of Shockley Semiconductor Laboratories was housed in a single room. Lab tables ringed the perimeter, and a big desk was planted smack in the middle. Here sat the business manager, who in the beginning was Shockley himself—tangible proof that business stood at the heart of the operation. One corner of the hut served as a modest machine shop for building models and equipment. Semiconductor manufacture was far too new to have generated standard, off-the-shelf equipment.[33]

FROM THE MOMENT he stepped through the doorway of the Quonset hut, Bob Noyce was in a position of leadership at the lab, simply because he, unlike most of the other new hires, was an experienced transistor researcher. His work at Philco and his long-standing interest in transistors gave him an understanding of the most current theories about semiconductors and practical experience in working with the devices. He had an almost intuitive notion of how things should work in a semiconductor lab. One Shockley employee recalled Noyce building a clean vacuum pump without drawings—blowing the glass himself. Noyce also had clear ideas about how the technology could potentially develop in the future. "In his mind, he could see where it was all going," observed another co-worker.[34]

Within weeks of his arrival at Shockley, Noyce was heading up a team that included six members of the senior scientific staff, all of them PhDs. He also helped with recruiting, set salaries for incoming technical employees, and escorted prominent visitors through the lab. When Shockley wanted to estimate how many crystals the company should be able to process per month, he asked Noyce about Philco's run rate. When he wanted suggestions on technical journals the company should receive, he asked Noyce to gather the information. Shockley also noted several suggestions from Noyce about the diffusion process in his early days at the company.[35]

To his peers, Noyce was approachable in a laid-back way. "He was somebody you went over to and said, 'What do you think about this?'" recalled Vic Jones. "He had a very quiet leadership style, a gee-whiz-aw-shucks-farmboy approach that was very attractive." Noyce taught without condescension. For example, rather than simply handing orders to the technician in charge of photoresists—the light-sensitive liquid used in the process of transferring a semiconductor pattern onto a wafer—Noyce was likely to chat with him about the types of lenses that would be used in conjunction with the resists. Such information would not only result in better photoresists, it would teach the resists man a little bit about a part of the development process that perhaps he had not known before. Many of Noyce's peers felt that they learned more from him than they did from Shockley.[36]

The only other employee with knowledge and experience equivalent to Noyce was Smoot Horsley, the first man hired. Horsley was a decade older than the rest of the staff, and while they came to work in shirtsleeves—Noyce once even showed up in shorts—Horsley preferred the thin dark ties and white shirts he had worn for his mission work for the Mormon church. Horsley was intensely loyal to Shockley, and the young scientists saw him as an extension of the boss, not as a peer. Behind his back, they called him "Smooth Horsley."

Noyce was also quite close to Shockley. The men would swim together and occasionally go for drinks. Shockley's new wife, the psychological nurse, had become friendly with Betty and regularly stopped by the Noyces' home to chat or to play with the children while their mother ran errands or worked on the creative writing she still enjoyed. Several employees thought that Noyce's was the only opinion in the lab that mattered to their boss, who viewed the Iowan, with his quick mind and love of performing, as a youthful incarnation of himself.[37]

SHOCKLEY SET THE YOUNG MEN TO WORK according to their specific fields of expertise. Sheldon Roberts organized an analytical laboratory so he could better understand the properties of silicon. Others joined him in an effort to grow pure crystals. Julius Blank and Eugene Kleiner worked with Dean Knapic, lathing and jigging many of the lab's rigs and measuring devices in-house. (They sent their simplest designs to local machinists.) They also built the crystal puller used to grow the silicon ingots. Jean Hoerni calculated diffusion curves, theorizing for how long, and at what temperatures and concentrations, different impurities should be diffused into the surface of the semiconductor. Gordon Moore empirically tested Hoerni's theories in furnaces he had helped to build.

Bob Noyce led a group focused on transistors, paying special attention to the work and results Bell Labs had reported on the diffusion process. Noyce had ample opportunity to do the collaborative good science he loved, preparing highly technical papers with his colleagues on topics such as "Carrier Generation and Recombination in the Space-Charge Region of a P-N Junction," and "Localized Radiation Damage as a Source for Interstitials or Vacancies."

On August 14, 1956, Noyce noted an idea for a "negative resistance diode" in his lab notebook. With most diodes, the current flow increases with increases in voltage—the more voltage applied to the device, the more current passes through it. Noyce, however, made a startling prediction. He imagined doping a semiconductor with roughly a thousand times more impurities than was standard. When the voltage applied to this heavily doped diode increased from zero, Noyce predicted, current would also initially increase (as in any other diode). But, he said, as the voltage increased even further, "current must drop" because the high impurity density would make it possible not only for electrons, but also for holes, to transfer across the P-N junction—a phenomenon called tunneling. If one continued to increase the voltage through this period of "negative resistance," Noyce theorized, the amount of current passing through the device would begin to rise, and the diode would resume normal behavior.[38]

Noyce's musings about a negative resistance diode excited him. They indicated that an important concept of quantum mechanics—"tunneling," which existed only as a theoretical postulate—could be demonstrated in a simple P-N junction. If one thinks of conduction electrons in a semiconductor as balls bouncing against a wall (a wall built from an insulator or other potential barrier), quantum tunneling would predict that every once in a while, a ball would not bounce off the wall but would instead tunnel right through it.[39]

Noyce brought his lab book entry to Shockley, fully expecting him to be impressed. Instead, "the boss showed no interest in the idea." The lab was not equipped to do anything profitable with Noyce's thoughts, and besides, Shockley did not like his employees to chart their own investigative paths. Disappointed, Noyce closed his lab book and "went on to other projects." He later commented that this exchange with Shockley taught him that "the message of 'no interest' is certainly a powerful demotivator.'"[40]

Noyce may have given up his ideas about a negative resistance diode, but the device soon reappeared in his life. On January 15, 1958, almost exactly 17 months after Noyce noted his ideas, a Japanese scientist named Leo Esaki published an article in the prestigious *Physical Review* describing the same negative resistance diode. The article caused quite a sensation in the electronics community. The audience for Esaki's presentation at an international physics conference was filled to overflowing.[41]

After reading the Esaki article, Noyce found his friend Gordon Moore. Noyce's lab book pages and Esaki's foundational paper are strikingly similar—they use almost identical illustrations, for example. There was, however, one important difference. Noyce predicted the drop in current (the evidence of tunneling) would occur. Esaki, who actually built a device to demonstrate his ideas, showed that it would. This difference is crucial—many good ideas die en route from the mind to the lab bench—and it is almost certainly a direct result of William Shockley's discouraging comments to Noyce, who was an experimentalist at heart, in 1956. Noyce was irritated, primarily with himself for not pursuing his ideas even after Shockley dismissed them. "If I had gone one step further," he told Moore, "I would have done it." In 1973, Leo Esaki shared the Nobel Prize for physics for his work on the negative-resistance, or tunnel, diode.[42]

None of Noyce's colleagues aside from Moore knew about Noyce's near-miss on the tunnel diode, but they had seen ample evidence of his advanced understanding of semiconductor physics, which Moore describes as "an equivalent amount of knowledge as the rest of us combined." Noyce filed for four patents while he worked at Shockley; two of these patents listed William Shockley himself as Noyce's co-inventor. When Shockley asked the staff to rank its senior members in terms of technical leadership, Noyce emerged as the top choice.[43]

SHOCKLEY'S MANAGERIAL METHODS came as somewhat of a surprise to his employees. He had been careful to test his recruits for compatibility with each other, but no one had tested them for compatibility with their boss. Shockley spent hours in the machine shop telling Kleiner and Blank how to build the equipment, even going so far, in one case, as to redesign the bolts Kleiner wanted to use on the crystal puller used to grow silicon ingots. He sent Hoerni to work alone in an apartment near the lab, ostensibly because he did not want him distracted, but more likely because he felt threatened by the brilliant young theoretician with his clipped accent and pair of doctorates. Angry and lonely, Hoerni managed to talk his way back into the Quonset hut after only a few days' banishment.[44]

The work preoccupying the hot minds was fundamental. Physics, chemistry, optics, thermodynamics, fluid mechanics: every one of these disciplines had to work in concert to build a functional semiconductor device. Many of the basic properties of silicon were still not well understood. How did heat diffuse off a specific point? What happens if silicon is bombarded with atoms of argon? No one knew how to build production quantities of silicon transistors. What type of furnace would work best? How best to measure the thickness of the layers etched on the silicon in the manufacturing process? How efficient were semiconductors with melting temperatures lower than silicon's?

Answers to these questions would serve as the foundation for transistor manufacture throughout the world, for Shockley was not the only man to see the future in diffused silicon transistors. Indeed, by the time Shockley Semiconductor Labs began operation, researchers at Bell Labs, Texas Instruments, and Philco were already exploring the same issues that preoccupied the Shockley team. Closer to home, Hewlett-Packard had one man working in a similar vein. "We used to go back and forth with [silicon] ingots, like borrowing cups of sugar from one another," laughs Julius Blank. "The blind leading the blind."[45]

Although there was some official reporting structure at Shockley, in reality, everyone worked with everyone else in the cavernous room, constantly comparing results and asking for feedback. What about this way of doing things? Do you see anything wrong? If I build a furnace, what do you want it to do? Any ideas about why I might have gotten this result from this experiment? It was a welcome change for Noyce, who was accustomed to the formal management hierarchy and equipment requisitioning procedures that Philco had adopted as part of its military contract work. At one point over lunch with his friend Julius Blank, Noyce started sketching out his ideas for a piece of equipment he wished he had. "I need a bell jar. . . . I want to expose the contacts . . ." Nothing more specific than that. A few days later, Blank handed him a rough model. "We just got through talking here!" Noyce shook his head in astonishment. "If we wanted the same thing at Philco, it would have taken six months!"[46]

The scientists arranged informal technical seminars for themselves, each man familiarizing the others with his particular field of expertise. Shockley gave them each a copy of the textbook he had written, which was universally acknowledged as the world's best semiconductor physics text. Shockley himself was an excellent teacher, regularly cutting to the heart of a problem in less time than it took other people to formulate it. "Shockley has this marvelous ability of going all the way back to first principles and making the right simplifying assumptions so you can wade through the mathematics and do it relatively simply," Noyce explained in 1982. "If you were going to try to put wave equations down for every electron in a solid material, you would be in such a mess you couldn't ever do anything. So you have to find representations that are manageable." Shockley's physical intuition was so great that his employees claimed that he could actually see electrons. He could speak on even the most technical topic with remarkable clarity. His best-known book on semiconductor theory, for example, starts by comparing the movement of electrons to cars looking for a parking space in a full garage.[47]

The young men got to work by 9:00 and generally left around 6:30. At lunch time, groups of three or four would head for a burger at Kirk's, the nearby greasy spoon, or if they were lucky, Shockley might take them to his favorite waiters-and-menus restaurant, the Black Forest, in his green Jaguar convertible. Several of the men shared an interest in hiking and mountain climbing. Their wives and children had become friends. In general, it was a happy time.[48]

THE MORNING of Thursday, November 1, 1956, found the lab abuzz with excitement. Shortly after seven that morning, William Shockley had received a phone call notifying him that he, along with his Bell Labs colleagues Walter Brattain and John Bardeen, had won the Nobel Prize for Physics for their invention of the transistor. The workday began with champagne toasts to Shockley, who had not yet come into the lab. No matter. The young men were as much celebrating their own good fortune at working with a Nobel Prizewinner as they were happy for their boss. The award confirmed everything they had told themselves before they joined the company. They were indeed playing in the big leagues. Arnold Beckman, who certainly was feeling the same way, flew up from Southern California to offer his congratulations in person.[49]

Later that day, Shockley interrupted the rounds of interviews, telegrams (he received more than 200), and phone calls to take his staff—now 40 or 50 strong—to the restaurant at Rickey's, the hotel where many of them had stayed during their job interviews. It was a luncheon in high style:

white tablecloths, flowers, and candles graced the tables, while the heavy curtains lining the walls muffled the group's animated chatter. After coffee, several of the men assembled around Shockley, who was seated at the head of one of the tables. A flashbulb popped. The oft-reprinted photo sparkles with raised wine glasses and grinning young men in open-neck shirts all but patting their beaming boss on the back. Noyce, standing in square-jawed profile at the center of the picture, is strikingly handsome, his wineglass held carefully to avoid blocking the camera's view of his own or his neighbor's face. You can almost hear strains of "For He's a Jolly Good Fellow" rising from the blurred background of the black-and-white snapshot.

A month later, Shockley left for the award ceremonies in Stockholm, accompanied by his mother and wife Emmy. He arrived a day after Brattain and Bardeen, who had flown together with their families and spent a celebratory night on the airplane catching up and exchanging stories of what happened when they got the news. Brattain had been greeted by a standing ovation when he reported for work at Bell Labs. Bardeen had been so surprised by the call from Sweden that he had dropped the pan of eggs he was cooking for breakfast.[50]

The award ceremony was a glorious affair. Men in white tie and women in formal gowns rose to their feet in Stockholm's elegant concert hall as King Gustav VI Adolph presented each man with his award. Bardeen, Brattain, and Shockley each gave a short talk. While the other laureates limited their comments to science, Shockley ended his with plugs for his own prescience—he had predicted a great future for "transistor electronics" as early as 1950, he reminded his audience—and for his "new organization in California."[51]

Shortly after midnight, when Shockley and his wife wandered into the elegant bar at the Grand Hotel, they saw Brattain and Bardeen already sharing a drink. Though the scientists had scarcely spoken to Shockley for more than five years, the occasion was too special to nurse old grudges. They invited him to join them.[52]

SHOCKLEY RETURNED FROM STOCKHOLM at the end of December in spirits so high they verged on egomania in the eyes of his staff. He gathered the lab for a little speech. He said that when he received the Nobel Prize, he had felt like Churchill. He added, as an aside, that it was "about time" his contributions were appropriately recognized. At first the young scientists thought he was making a joke. He was quite serious.[53]

Shockley's behavior had grown increasingly erratic in the months leading up to his Nobel Prize. He had never been an easy man to like, even when he was trying to be likeable. When he gave a raise to Jay Last, the youngest scientist, for example, he did so with the admonishment that Last never should have agreed to work for the $675 he had previously been earning. "Jay, that will teach you never to sell yourself out cheap again." Shockley seemed not to trust his hand-picked team. He infuriated Noyce by calling Bell Labs to double-check his interpretations of data. "Am I really needed here?" Noyce asked himself. "If he can call friends at Bell Labs and get answers to the same questions that I [am] trying to answer in the laboratory, my presence here isn't that important."[54]

Shockley strongly adhered to a belief that in almost every aspect of life, there could be but one winner—and he wanted to be it. He had himself listed as a co-presenter and co-author on every one of the papers given by his employees at the elite American Physical Society conference in December 1956. Lunchtime workouts in the Stanford pool were always races for Shockley, who pushed himself to exhaustion if it appeared another man was swimming faster or farther. He once told an employee that although many people could write a paper together, patents should officially list only one inventor because "there's only one light bulb to go on in somebody's head. . . . The other [people] are mere helpers." He nonetheless listed himself as a co-inventor on his employees' most significant patent applications.[55]

Shockley would attack people when they made mistakes—"reduce them almost to tears," in the words of one former employee. One man who worked with Shockley in a different context described his behavior thus: "He could be helpful, but you had to go through a ritual humiliation first." Where'd you go to school? Are you sure that you actually went to school? How could you not know something like this? In one instance, Shockley publicly fired a secretary who had not made travel arrangements in the manner he had specified. The other employees were horrified.[56]

In the months after the Nobel Prize ceremony, recalls Jay Last, Shockley's behavior deteriorated to the point that the lab came to resemble "a big psychiatric institute." When he wanted people to leave the building, Shockley would quote T. S. Eliot's "Love Song of J. Alfred Prufrock" ("Let us go then, you and I . . .") rather than simply announcing an end to the day. When a secretary cut her hand on a tiny piece of metal protruding from her door, Shockley convinced himself that it was deliberate sabotage. He informed the lab that he planned to hire a private investigator and that they would all need to undergo lie detector tests to find the culprit. Sheldon Roberts spent the better part of a week proving to Shockley, with the help of a microscope, that the offending object was simply a thumbtack that had lost its protective plastic head.[57]

Jay Last, for one, thought things were becoming intolerable. He and Hoerni found working with Shockley so frustrating that nearly every weekend they would drive south for hours and hike, mile after mile, complaining and "kicking Joshua trees" to vent their frustrations. Last had observed that Noyce's relationship with Shockley seemed strong, and one day he described to Noyce his own troubles with the boss and asked for advice. Noyce could not offer much in the way of concrete suggestions to improve the situation, but Last left feeling that at least he had unburdened himself of his concerns. The next day, Shockley barreled up to him and began shouting: "What the hell did you say to Noyce?" Last was shocked. "Bob said he thought [telling Shockley] was 'the best way to handle it.' It sure wasn't best for me."[58]

Shockley's abrasive style, with its increasingly frequent dips into irrationality, was only one stress facing the young men working for him. "There was always this business about 'how would Shockley respond to this?'" explains Vic Jones. Every idea, every potentially exciting new process—it all had to meet with Shockley's approval, or it could not go further. The young scientists found themselves putting the brakes on their own ideas in anticipation of Shockley's disapproval. It did not help that Shockley was a night owl who did some of his best work over cocktails and expected his favorites, including Noyce, to join him at the bars.

To make matters worse, far from raking in the profits and churning out the products that Shockley and Beckman had anticipated when they drafted their business agreement, Shockley Semiconductor was losing money and had yet to sell anything. By contrast, the data-processing research that Beckman Instruments funded at roughly the same time as Shockley Semiconductor had already yielded a prototype system and orders from leading firms such as Dupont, Westinghouse, General Electric, and General Motors.[59]

The nub of the problem was simple. As a former employee put it, "Shockley ran the company for the benefit of his personality and his image, not for pure economic pay." Succeeding as a businessman meant foregoing interesting explorations of basic physical phenomena for the more mundane task of building a usable product, but Shockley feared losing his status as one of the world's leading solid-state physicists. One raised eyebrow from a scientific colleague or a few comments to the effect that he had not been publishing much lately, and Shockley would completely reorient his company, telling his employees to stop whatever they were doing and start writing up their findings for presentation at the next prestigious scientific meeting. If, in the course of one of these periods of intense work on basic science, someone from outside the company asked what was happening on the business front, Shockley was likely to reverse course again and throw the company into a flurry of product-oriented activity.[60]

Further adding to the troubles was Shockley's obsession with a device he had conceived while still at Bell Labs, the "four-layer diode"—a diode that, as its name implies, has one more layer of diffused semiconductor than a transistor. Shockley hypothesized a semiconductor diffused in four alternating layers doped P and N could do the work not only of a transistor, but also of a resistor. It would also be faster and cheaper than either conventional diodes or germanium transistors. Shockley was quite certain that Western Electric would want to buy thousands of these four-layer diodes to replace the hundreds of thousands of mechanical relays that switched and connected calls across the telephone grid, and he imagined that computer companies would be interested in the product, too. Shortly after his return from the Nobel Prize ceremonies, Shockley pulled a half-dozen senior scientists off the silicon transistor project to work on the four-layer diode.[61]

The four-layer-diode was ingenious in theory; it could, indeed, perform all the functions of a transistor (which amplifies current), a resistor (which restricts the flow of current), and a diode (which allows current to flow in one direction but not in the other). The problem arose in production: the four-layer diode was fabulously difficult to build and proved impossible to manufacture in quantity. Several of the young men at Shockley privately suspected that the diode's greatest appeal for its inventor was that he had patented it alone.[62]

Noyce's group suggested that the company should focus on the less cutting-edge, but more practical, transistor, or at the very least, that they should perfect transistors before moving on to the trickier diodes. Noyce, Moore, Last, and Hoerni had already overcome some of the major hurdles blocking production of the diffused silicon transistor, and researchers at Bell Labs and elsewhere were making similarly quick progress. The young scientists were convinced that they could not only build the diffused silicon transistors they thought they had been hired to build—they could also sell them. Even without sophisticated research to back them up (there was no marketing or business development group at Shockley), they knew in their guts, as Gordon Moore put it, that "there'd be plenty of market" for diffused silicon transistors. Transistors were increasingly common in hearing aids and radios, and the military, of course, would pay a small fortune for the reliable silicon transistor the group was sure they could build. Beckman's own data-processing system already used primitive germanium transistors; in fact, for more than six months, Noyce had spent one day each month with the data systems operation, consulting with them on the problems they encountered in their use of the devices.[63]

Shockley was unmoved. He set up a team of five to work on the four-layer diode, assigned them to a different building, and put himself in charge of the effort. This sent a clear signal about the company's future direction: research and development of a device that even Arnold Beckman called "a novel, special-purpose diode." When other divisions of Beckman Instruments declined the opportunity to use four-layer diodes in their applications, Shockley was not disturbed. He simply extended similar offers to

IBM, to little effect. He would pursue his four-layer diode for years. It was his white whale.[64]

Meantime, Noyce's group took matters into their own hands. They decided that when Shockley was not at the lab—he traveled frequently and for weeks at a time, especially after becoming a Nobel laureate—they would work on transistors in the manner they chose. When he got back, they would do as he told them.

Throughout the first half of 1957, the group focused on building a type of diffused silicon transistor called a "mesa" transistor. Mesa transistors, so named because under magnification they resemble the flat-peaked land masses of the Southwest, represented a solid breakthrough in semiconductor technology because they could be produced by masking, diffusing, and etching on only one side of the silicon. Mesa transistors were built in a three-step process pioneered by Bell Labs. First, dopants were diffused beneath the surface of a slice of silicon. Next, a drop of canuba wax was deposited on top of the wafer. Finally, the entire surface was doused with a strong acid, which etched away the top layer, except where the wax drop protected it. This transistor could be attached to other devices via two wires, which were affixed to the now-flat-topped wax droplet.[65]

The scientists organized their work along the lines Shockley had originally specified for them. Noyce set the general direction. His collaborative style provided an important alternative to William Shockley's fierce competitiveness. The young men worried about impressing Shockley, but they were comfortable making mistakes around Noyce. "Bob you could talk to and not expect to blow up," explains Vic Jones. "You didn't get any *sturm und drang* from Bob."[66]

Last focused on polishing the wafers and put his steady hands to work applying the tiny droplets of wax to the surface of the transistor. Hoerni and Moore took charge of diffusion. In relatively short order, the group found themselves producing rudimentary transistors. Noyce, the other members of the group assumed, had gotten Shockley's official approval—or at least had not been explicitly forbidden—to undertake the work, but none of them inquired too closely. Certainly they knew that when Noyce filed for a patent for one part of the process to build the transistor, Shockley's name was listed—before Noyce's, of course—as a co-inventor.[67]

Despite these successes, Shockley's micromanagement and obsession with the four-layer diode, as well as the start-and-stop, covert nature of the transistor work, combined to make the atmosphere in the lab nearly unbearable for the scientists working with Noyce. Their academic training rewarded open inquiry and placed a high value on the professional opinions of senior people in the field. The sense that William Shockley considered their work if not second-class, then certainly of secondary importance, offended their views of themselves as elite researchers.

Arnold Beckman was frustrated for other reasons. Beckman Instruments was facing a difficult year. Net income was dropping precipitously—the company would earn scarcely $200,000 in 1957 and would lose money in 1958—due to substantial losses on government contracts, an industry-wide recession, and what Beckman obliquely referred to as "certain inadequacies in internal organization and controls."[68]

In May 1957, Beckman convened a meeting of senior research and development managers from every division of his company. Shockley and Horsley attended on behalf of Shockley Semiconductor. R&D costs were spiraling out of control, Beckman told them, and were projected to reach nearly 14 percent of sales by 1958 if they continued unchecked. The meeting seemed designed specifically to rein in Shockley. Every division but his offered presentations on the screening methods, development schedules, and procedures they used to evaluate proposed projects and bring them to completion. Shockley had no such formal methods; all such decisions rested on his personal whim. Beckman proposed a list of eight "dangers to be guarded against in development work." Shockley had fallen victim to every danger, but two in particular seemed targeted at his efforts: "6. Using boys for men's jobs" and "8. Failure to regularly assay progress of development programs objectively. It is important to recognize dead horses and bury them."[69]

Beckman decided it was time to pay a visit to Mountain View and speak directly with Shockley's research staff. He laid out his concerns and suggested several cost-saving measures, all of which were familiar to Shockley from the earlier meeting but nonetheless enraged him. Shockley jumped to his feet and announced that if Beckman did not like the way he was running his business, he would pick up his team and find another backer.[70]

The outburst astounded the scientists on Shockley's staff. Already Vic Jones, frustrated with "spending so much unproductive time on putting out fires and trying to keep Shockley from doing awful things," had left, with Shockley's blessing, to teach at Harvard. Several other employees were considering departures, and no one had any illusions about what it was like to work for Shockley. He would never be able to inspire even his senior staff—much less the entire company—to follow him to another venture. "The situation was such that some drastic action was called for," Noyce wrote his parents a few days after the confrontation, "or we could all pack our bags and leave." Shortly after this meeting, Noyce, Kleiner, Hoerni, Grinich, Roberts, Moore, and Last went to lunch at the Black Forest. When one of them began running through the often-repeated litany of complaints about Shockley, Grinich, the son of a lumberman and never one to put things delicately, began to shout. "Look, goddammit! We either have to do something about this or stop talking about it!"[71]

Beckman needed to know that Shockley's threats were hollow, the group decided. They had always admired Beckman, a scientists' scientist who had made it big, and he seemed genuinely interested in their opinions. Gordon Moore was chosen to make the phone call. The others clustered nearby as he dialed and asked, his voice quaking with anxiety, for an appointment to meet with Beckman in private.[72]

NOYCE WROTE to his parents shortly after the call was made. Beckman "had gone far enough into Shockley's background to be fully aware of the possibility of this sort of turn," he explained. Beckman flew in from Southern California and met with the young scientists in a private room at a fine restaurant. The group told Beckman that Shockley was not a leader, but a "disruptive force" in the efforts to build silicon transistors. He was technically terrific, but his outbursts and unpredictability were destroying the group once so eager to work with him. "Beckman assured us that he would support the staff rather than Shockley in a showdown, if indeed some arrangement could be found which seemed to have a reasonable chance of success," Noyce told his parents. The next week was occupied with what Noyce called "secret evening meetings of the staff, discussing the problem and thrashing out what we thought was the best solution." At the end of May, they again met secretly with Beckman to suggest that he "try to get Shockley to accept an academic position, removing him from contact with the laboratory on a day-to-day basis, but consulting with us if he so desired." Sympathetic to their complaints, concerned about the welfare of his company, and committed to finding a solution, Beckman took Shockley to dinner tell him about the discontent at the lab.[73]

The news devastated Shockley. He knew that Last was unhappy and, of course, that Jones had left, but overall, he thought things were progressing just fine. He saw himself as his employees' benevolent-but-firm leader, teaching them the basics of his field, correcting their mistakes, paying them well, and offering them the opportunity to coauthor papers with a Nobel Prize winner. If he had been a bit harsh, it was because he was the intellectual equivalent of a boot camp drill sergeant, harassing his recruits for their own good. After his dinner with Beckman, Shockley went straight to bed.[74]

The next morning he called Bob Noyce into his office. Shockley's notes from this meeting appear in a spiral-bound notebook dated 23 May–10 June 1957, on the front of which he has scrawled, as if to remind himself. "Try to work it out for the benefit of everyone," "Like you did at meeting, listening."

The lab, Noyce told Shockley, was a family, and at this point, it was having "family troubles." Noyce was "very factual," noted Shockley, and the young man stressed that he was not disputing any facts with his boss, but rather was bringing to him a "different viewpoint." Noyce was not particularly ready to walk out the door, but he was worried that almost everyone else in the organization was profoundly discontented. Shockley consistently angered and abused his staff, Noyce told him. "If a man has not spurs," Shockley wrote to himself poetically, "criticism really hurts." Noyce reminded Shockley that the team was "doing [its] best with [its] ability," and assured him that they were not thirsting for blood. "We are not out to get Bill—hope you can see," was Noyce's message, as interpreted by Shockley.[75]

The staff was "a little disappointed on the technical situation," Noyce mentioned diplomatically, presumably in reference to the four-layer diode, and he stressed that the decision to go to Beckman had been an act of courage tinged with desperation. "Felt they couldn't talk to W=S [Shockley's shorthand reference to himself]." "A few had tried. Would be fired," Shockley wrote, adding, "It took a lot of doing to go behind my back."

Finally Noyce said that his colleagues believed there was "no feeling of stability in the lab." He spoke of "whims" and "individual reactions" and said something that made Shockley understand "instability due to Bill [himself]." And then, just as it seemed Shockley might begin to see "W=S" as the source of his problems, he added two additional points to the ones made by Noyce. "12. Rex Sittner is sales mgr of Motorola. 13. Always thought it a mistake not to offer Rex [a job]." The problem, in other words, was not Shockley. The problem was the people working for him.

Shockley, Beckman, and the scientific staff met in various combinations in the final weeks of May 1957. At one point, Shockley brought with him a man whom he did not identify; Noyce was convinced this was a psychiatrist Shockley hired to analyze the staff from afar. Again and again, Noyce was the intermediary. Shockley thought Noyce was on his side. The scientists, with the possible exception of Last, thought he was on theirs. Through Noyce, the dissidents suggested to Shockley that he forego management for an advisory role. Shockley detested this idea. "Non directing position is not effective," he wrote in outlining his thoughts on potential solutions. "If this is the intention, let's work out terminations starting now." He promised that he would provide his team "increased security and work satisfaction," and sought to forestall any mass resignations by suggesting that no one be allowed to go off the Beckman payroll for six months.[76]

He contemplated a new organizational structure, with Noyce not only heading R&D, but also managing the lab. He sketched out a different plan, in which work was administered through a team of four, including Noyce, with Noyce also serving as an "independent authority." Ultimately, Shockley decided not to grant Noyce independent authority—or even the job as manager. He believed, as he told Arnold Beckman, that Noyce was good technically, but not an "aggressive leader." He lacked what Shockley called "push," by which he probably meant that Noyce did not drive his employees as hard as Shockley thought he should.[77]

Shockley's assessment of Noyce's managerial shortcomings would ultimately prove to hold some truth, but at the time, his decision to bring in an unnamed "mature and experienced manager for non-technical, non-policy decisions" seemed conclusive proof that he was unwilling to give his employees, including Noyce, any power whatsoever. Some have suggested that if Shockley had named Noyce manager, the company might have never faced the problems it did, but that seems unlikely. Whatever Noyce's pull with Shockley, it almost certainly could not have swayed him from the four-layer diode project—and this project, as much as interpersonal conflict, fed the young scientists' dissatisfaction.

While Beckman hunted for his mature manager, he and Shockley arranged a managing committee made up of Noyce, Smoot Horsley (then heading the four-layer diode project), and two others. Shockley could overrule any decisions made by the committee, but "decisions and proposals [would be] a matter of record." It was a tenuous compromise; enough to keep the company from falling apart, but not enough to push it past the crisis.[78]

The interim management committee lasted less than a month, at which point Beckman abruptly reversed his previous support of shared management and declared that Shockley was in charge. The reasons behind this reversal are unclear, but it seems that someone at Bell Labs or at Stanford told Beckman that undercutting Shockley's authority would irredeemably damage the Nobel laureate's reputation. Did Beckman really believe that the scientific efforts of a group of young unknowns were more valuable than the contributions of William Shockley?[79]

Beckman tapped Maurice Hanafin, who had proved an able administrator in Beckman Instrument's Spinco centrifuge division, to serve as a buffer between Shockley and his employees. Noyce, given charge of R&D with seven senior staff, reported directly to Hanafin. "He is a very good man ... and the chances of things cooling down are much improved by his presence," Noyce told his parents. Horsley, who led the four-layer diode project with five senior staff, and Knapic, who oversaw engineering and production with three senior staff, also reported to Hanafin.[80]

At this point, Noyce declared himself "more confident of the eventual success of the venture than I have been since I arrived"—a confidence that inspired him to buy the biggest, most modern refrigerator he could find. It was a gift of sorts for Betty, who, in the last weeks of her third pregnancy in as many years, admitted "the larger box ought to simplify housekeeping and childcare immensely."[81]

Noyce's optimism was not shared by the group of disaffected scientists. At a staff meeting Hanafin convened shortly after his arrival, he was pelted with exceedingly direct questions about "future technical decision making and where it would reside." When, no matter how they put the question, Hanafin responded that Shockley was the ultimate decision maker, the atmosphere in the room turned ugly.[82]

Most of the group that had met with Beckman felt that they were right back where they started. Shockley was in charge; production was given short shrift (research and development work received four times the senior staff and nearly twice the funding of engineering and production); and the four-layer diode project was alive and well. Shockley had succeeded in making the leadership of the lab into yet another competition with only one possible winner, and Beckman had cast his lot with Shockley. The young scientists had, as Moore put it, "grossly overestimated our power." They felt they had no choice but to leave.[83]

Julius Blank, Victor Grinich, Jean Hoerni, Eugene Kleiner, Jay Last, Gordon Moore, and Sheldon Roberts (all but two of whom reported to Noyce under the new management structure) were absolutely determined to go. Last, Hoerni, and Roberts were the ringleaders. Last already had another job offer, but he told the others that he would rather continue working with them. By mid-June, the group of seven had resolved to resign en masse.[84]

They wanted Noyce to join them, but he was not particularly interested. Unlike the group of seven, Noyce had a managerial title and employees who reported to him. He was Shockley's favorite, and he thought that Hanafin might solve some of the problems the others perceived as intractable. Moreover, Noyce had joined Shockley with the expectation that he would spend his career there, and he felt he had a moral and professional obligation to make the company successful. "He was the son of a minister and he was not any purer than the rest of us," one Shockley dissident recalled, "but sometimes he worried, what would his father think, or what would God think, of what he was doing. Was it disloyal or not?" Noyce also had a brand-new baby at home, a little girl named Polly who had been born during the rounds of meetings among Shockley, Beckman, and the unhappy scientists. It was not the right time to contemplate a move.[85]

The group could certainly leave without Noyce. Where to go was another question, however. Easiest would be for them to peel off, one by one, to be hired by one of the electronics firms popping up along the East Coast or in Southern California. The easy route was unappealing, however. The seven young men liked working together. They respected each other's minds and enjoyed bouncing ideas around. They also had a sense that, given their deliberately complementary skills—Shockley had chosen wisely—they were more valuable as a group than separately.

Was it even possible to stay together? The Shockley dissidents were unsure. The work they wanted to do was much too risky and research intensive for traditional bank financing, and venture capital did not exist.

The only way that the young men could envision staying together was to try to get hired as a group and convince the corporation that hired them to set up a semiconductor division.

They set about exploring their options while keeping up appearances at Shockley. Quite early on, Eugene Kleiner suggested that they write a letter to an investment firm where his father had an account. Hayden, Stone, and Company was a small firm, but it had a solid reputation among New York investment banks, and it had recently arranged the financing for General Transistor, the first publicly held independent transistor firm and a manufacturer of germanium devices. Perhaps the bankers could help find a company to hire the group en masse. The other six men agreed to this plan.

Kleiner composed a letter to the person in charge of his father's account. "We have an experienced and well-diversified group of men with background in the fields of physics, electronics, engineering, metallurgy, and chemistry," he wrote. With $750,000 to cover salaries and expenses, "we believe that we could get a company into the semiconductor business within three months." Kleiner continued, "The initial product would be a line of silicon diffused transistors of unusual design applicable to the production of both high frequency and high power devices. It should be pointed out that the complicated techniques for producing these semiconductors have already been worked out in detail by this group of people and are not restricted by any obligation to the present organization." The young men felt they knew as much as anyone in the world about building transistors. Between them, they had done everything from basic scientific research to ordering supplies, to building equipment, to overseeing small-scale production runs.[86]

They admitted they had already done much of the work—"at a cost of over a million dollars"—necessary to bring their new employer into the semiconductor business. They also said they expected to hire several highly trained technicians from Shockley Semiconductor Labs. Privately they may have discussed whether or not importing techniques learned and people trained at Shockley might constitute some sort of intellectual property theft, but they decided the techniques were common practice, and the potential hires would always have the option of staying with Shockley's operation.

The group had two pressing concerns. First, they needed to obtain a $25,000 license from Western Electric to cover Bell Labs' semiconductor patents—a cost they factored into their projected expenses. Second, they admitted they needed "good management," for no one within the group "ha[d] ambitions as a manager at the top level." Kleiner's letter promised that despite the management vacuum, "the horizontal ties in the group are strong and adequate technical leadership is present within it."[87]

The account manager to whom the letter was addressed had left Hayden, Stone, so the missive was passed around the office until it landed on the desk of a newly minted Harvard MBA, Arthur Rock, who describes himself as the investment firm's version of a "resident scientific guru." Rock, a native of Rochester, New York—his father had owned a candy store— had a runner's build and an unusually intense manner for someone who was barely 30. He had been a professional investor since the day he left Harvard. He read the letter carefully. The seven men sounded inexperienced but promising. The letter's strongest selling point, in Rock's estimation, was "the fact that Shockley had chosen them"—for as Rock well knew from his research on the transistor business, "[Shockley] had the choice of almost anyone in the country."[88]

Adding to his interest were the early reports out of the General Transistor financing, which looked extremely promising. Rock knew that his boss, Alfred "Bud" Coyle, was interested in making similar investments. Rock showed Coyle the letter and said that he thought it was worth the price of a plane ticket to visit the seven scientists in California.[89]

A few weeks later, in late June, Coyle, Rock, and the seven Shockley scientists were seated around a dinner table in San Francisco. After a bit of probing, Rock decided that the seven men, all about his age, were "pretty good guys." He and Coyle were prepared to help the group—but not in finding a company to hire them and start a new division. The bankers urged the scientists to consider asking a firm to finance an entirely new business along the lines detailed in Kleiner's letter. Rock and Coyle further suggested they seek more than $1 million, not the $750,000 the group thought they needed.[90]

The conversation fired the young men's imaginations. Picture what they could do with $1 million and no Shockley to thwart their efforts! Starting something on their own would also mean that they could stay in the Bay Area. That would make it easier to attract the people they had met at Shockley and other local companies. It would also make them happy personally. They had all grown deeply attached to their new home, with its glorious weather and easy driving distance to mountains, ocean, and San Francisco.[91]

There was, however, one problem. As the group had itself admitted in its letter, they lacked a manager. Coyle and Rock were concerned they might "have a little problem selling this thing" to other bankers at the firm without being able to point to a clear leader among the Shockley defectors. The seven told the bankers about Noyce: "We have a leader, but he feels a lot of obligation to Shockley. He ha[s] a title that we don't have, and he is also a very sharp guy. He is not going to give away the store."[92]

At Rock's and Coyle's urging, they decided to try again to convince Noyce to join them. Sheldon Roberts spent a long evening on the phone with Noyce, telling him about the meeting with the bankers, trying to convince him that the group could stay together, do something exciting, and even make money. At one point Roberts told Noyce that Shockley was playing him for a fool by giving him titles but little real authority. He pointed out that the group's departure would eviscerate Shockley Semiconductor—only the four-layer diode effort would remain intact. Noyce waffled. One minute he would sound like he was ready to join the seven; the next, he was (in Moore's words) "chickening out." He was concerned that his fellow technologists might have mistaken the bankers' excitement at the prospect of a fast commission for a genuine belief that the young group could build a viable company. He wanted absolute assurance that the seven were going to leave and that they had a realistic chance of launching a successful transistor operation. He was not going to stake his career on high hopes and friendly feelings.[93]

At last Noyce agreed to come to the next meeting with Coyle and Rock, scheduled for the following morning. "I have looked back on my two primary reasons for coming out here—to work with Shockley and to come to the west coast [sic]," he explained to his parents. "The importance of the first has been considerably diminished, primarily by recent experience, but also by finding out that the great aren't much better than the average. And the second can be maintained otherwise, in a different situation."[94]

At the appointed time, the men converged in the driveway of Vic Grinich's house. Several of them were surprised to see Noyce: "I looked in the back seat and there was Bob," recalled Julius Blank. "'Nice to have you here,' I said. He replied in that deep voice of his, 'Nice to be here.'" Half the group squeezed shoulder to shoulder in the Roberts family's station wagon, the rest in another car. Excited and nervous, they headed up the Peninsula to the Clift Hotel in San Francisco.[95]

They met Arthur Rock and Bud Coyle in the Redwood Room of the historic hotel. Noyce made an immediate impression on Arthur Rock, who sensed he was *primus inter pares* (first among equals). As bright and competent as the other seven, Noyce also exuded a confidence and charm that Rock had not sensed in the rest of the group. "What came through was that he was some kind of a leader and they looked up to him," says Rock. "He became the spokesperson." One of the other dissidents put things a bit more directly: Noyce, he said, "swung from being recalcitrant to becoming the big talker. The rest of us did not have anything to say after that point."[96]

The eight Shockley men and two bankers agreed they would start their own company. Coyle, a ruddy-faced Irishman with a fondness for ceremony, pulled out ten newly minted one-dollar bills and laid them carefully on the table. "Each of us should sign every bill," he said. These dollar bills covered with signatures, the bankers told the eight young scientists, were their contracts with each other.[97]

4

Breakaway

Days later, the group of eight and Arthur Rock reviewed copies of the *Wall Street Journal* and lists of firms traded on the New York Stock Exchange, circling the names of companies that might, maybe, be interested in backing them. If a company made capacitors, batteries, resistors—anything that even hinted at an interest in electronics—the young men considered it fair game. Soon Rock had written some 30-odd names on his legal pad. Included were computer manufacturer Sperry Rand, adding-machine giant Burroughs, National Cash Register, and consumer electronics giant Magnavox, as well as companies such as General Mills and United Shoe that might want to use transistors when they upgraded their manufacturing processes. Rock promised that when he got back to New York, he would start calling around.[1]

Meanwhile, the group should continue their work at Shockley and keep their thoughts on future good fortune. That was not hard to do. The oldest, Kleiner, was 32, and the rest were under 30. Most had young children. They lived in one of the fastest-growing, most beautiful spots in a country more prosperous than ever before in its history. The very soil beneath their feet was so fertile that every spring Noyce hosed down his seven budding plum trees to avoid a summertime deluge of fruit. In such a place, it was not difficult to focus on the future.[2]

The group of eight was working at the heart of one of the most exciting and patriotic industries in Cold War America: electronics, glamour girl of the space age. At the beginning of the decade, space travel had been only a fantasy; now, in 1957, both the Soviets and the Americans had announced imminent completion of rockets that could orbit the Earth. Such sophisticated technology relied on the smallest, fastest, most reliable electronics available—and that meant transistors. Already in 1957, more than 3.5 million transistors had been produced, an increase of 175 percent over the previous year's output. Transistor sales had zoomed 105 percent to $7.1 million in that same one-year period. In the six years after Bell Labs

Bobby Noyce between his two older brothers, Don (left) and Gaylord (right), who clasp their hands in prayer. Courtesy Don Noyce.

Noyce, about age 12, with his oboe. Family photos.

Bob (left) and Gaylord (right) with their dog Piglet and the bikes they used for their paper route. Family photos.

Bob, age 12, and Gaylord, age 14, proudly display the glider they built in the summer of 1945. Bob would soon attempt to take off from the roof of this garage. Family photos.

Bob and Gaylord run at top speed to launch their glider. Family photos.

A teenage Bob Noyce with one of the model planes he loved to build. Family photos.

Noyce, 20 years old and a conference diving champion, prepares to dive for his school, Grinnell College. Courtesy Don Noyce

Grant Gale, Noyce's college physics teacher who introduced him to the transistor. Courtesy Grinnell College Archives.

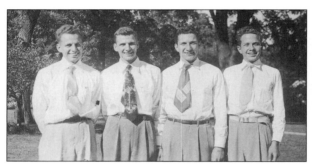

The four Noyce brothers—Don, Gaylord, Bob, and Ralph—in 1950. Family photos.

Bob Noyce and Betty Bottomley and their parents on the couple's wedding day in 1953. Left to right: Reverend Ralph Noyce, Betty Bottomley Noyce, Harriet Noyce, Frank Bottomley, Bob Noyce, and Helen Bottomley. Courtesy George Clark.

Noyce's four children smile from the steps of their new home around Christmas, 1962. Family photos.

The employees of Shockley Semiconductor Laboratory celebrate the award of the 1956 Nobel Prize for Physics to their boss William Shockley for his invention of the transistor. Shockley sits at the head of the table. Noyce stands behind him and to the left, holding a wine glass. Jay Last stands in the far right corner of the shot. Seated at the table are Gordon Moore and Sheldon Roberts. Courtesy Intel Corp.

William Shockley. Receiving a call from Shockley in 1955, Noyce said, was like "talking to God." Photo by Chuck Painter, Courtesy Stanford News Service.

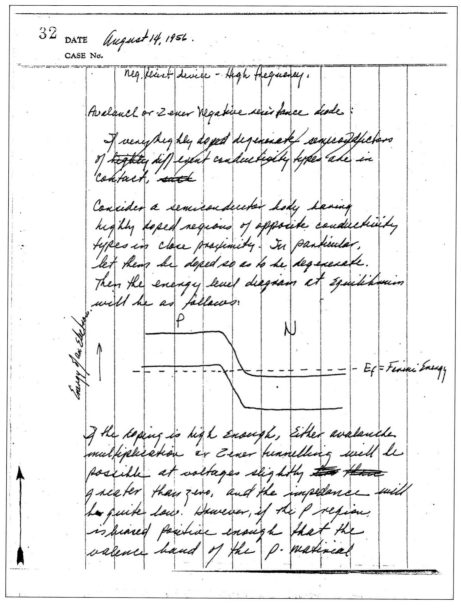

neg. fluit device - High frequency.

Avalanch or Zener Negative resistance diode:

If very highly doped degenerate semiconductors of tightly different conductivity types are in contact, ~~and~~

Consider a semiconductor body having highly doped regions of opposite conductivity types in close proximity. In particular, let them be doped so as to be degenerate. Then the energy level diagram at Equilibrium will be as follows:

If the doping is high enough, either avalanche multiplication or Zener tunnelling will be possible at voltages slightly ~~the the~~ greater than zero, and the impedance will be quite low. However, if the p region is biased positive enough that the valence band of the p· material

Here and facing page: In these unknown notebook pages, dated August 14, 1956, Noyce gives a full description of a tunnel diode, a device that demonstrated a key theory of quantum mechanics. The man who published the first paper on the device, Leo Esaki, was awarded the 1973 Nobel Prize for Physics for his work.

lies below the conduction band of the
n material, both tunneling and avalanche
will be impossible. Tunneling will be
forbidden because it must occur between
states of the same energy, and under
the condition stated above, there are no
allowed states of a common energy in the
majority carrier bands. Avalanche
cannot occur because an electron or hole
falling over the potential drop cannot pick
up energy equal to that necessary to
create a hole-electron pair. Consequently,
the current must drop as the applied bias
is increased. Finally at higher
biases, the normal diode forward
characteristic will be observed.

R. N. Noyce   August 14, 1956

The eight future founders of Fairchild Semiconductor and the two bankers who pledged to help them find financing signed this dollar bill as their contract with each other. Courtesy Julius Blank.

The eight founders of Fairchild Semiconductor pose in the California sunshine shortly after starting their company in the fall of 1957. Noyce sits front and center, his arm slung over the back of his chair. Seated clockwise from Noyce are Jean Hoerni, Julius Blank, Victor Grinich, Eugene Kleiner, Gordon Moore, C. Sheldon Roberts, and Jay Last. Courtesy Julius Blank.

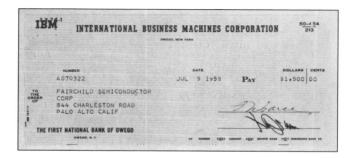

This check is an early installment on Fairchild Semiconductor's first sale: 100 transistors, sold to IBM for $150 apiece. Equivalent transistors today cost less than a hundred-thousandth of a penny. Family photos.

began licensing the rights to the device, some dozen new transistor firms emerged from within Bell Labs, Hughes Aircraft, Motorola, and RCA. These companies all sold to the same customers, the United States military and its subcontractors, the only organizations with sufficient financial resources and incentive to buy complex state-of-the-art electronics.[3]

The coterie of eight also planned to target the military market, but the group differed from other young transistor entrepreneurs in its large size, particularly relative to the size of the Shockley operation from which it came, and in its funding plan. Fully half of the senior scientific staff, and almost 15 percent (one in eight) of Shockley's entire workforce had signed the one-dollar-bill contracts. By contrast, firms such as Transitron or Philco had been started by one or two rebels from firms with hundreds of employees.

Most of the transistor entrepreneurs had been backed by family money or other private capital resources. Arthur Rock at Hayden, Stone soon came to appreciate why. Every company he approached on behalf of the group of eight turned the idea down flat, without even asking to meet the men involved. Some firms may have found the pith of the letter—please give a million dollars to a group of men between the ages of 28 and 32 who think they are great and cannot abide working for a Nobel Prize winner—unpalatable. Even if a firm thought the proposal was interesting in theory, no standard operating procedure existed for the company-within-a-company undertaking Rock and Coyle recommended. What accounting procedures would be used? How could the funding firm allow this group of unknown young men to run their own operation, according to criteria of their own devising, and not permit other employees the same autonomy? In the 1950s, with its ethos of conformity, this smacked of unseemly preferential treatment.[4]

Undaunted, Bud Coyle mentioned the scientists to playboy-millionaire-inventor Sherman Fairchild. A meticulous man in his sixties, Fairchild was a bon vivant who frequented New York's posh 21 Club and wore "a fresh pretty girl every few days like a new boutonniere," according to *Fortune*. His father had preceded Tom Watson as the chief executive of the company that would become International Business Machines, and thanks to the vagaries of inheritance (Tom Watson had several children, while George Fairchild had only Sherman), he was the largest shareholder in IBM.[5]

Fairchild liked to invent and to build companies around his inventions. He developed an efficient method of lighting tennis courts and started a tennis-court company. Fairchild Recording Equipment Corporation sold several audio products of his design. His biggest companies, Fairchild Aviation and Fairchild Camera and Instrument, manufactured and sold planes and aerial cameras for which he held important patents.

Sherman Fairchild was not involved with day-to-day operations at his companies, but he suggested to the senior management at Fairchild Camera and Instrument that it might explore the prospects of the West Coast technologists. Headquartered in Syosset, New York, with roughly $23 million in assets, Fairchild Camera and Instrument was a company in transition in the third quarter of 1957. Sales were a satisfactory $43 million, but profits hovered at a negligible $267,000, and the company was suffering from administrative bloat. Sherman Fairchild had recently tapped 37-year-old John Carter, a burly, ruddy-faced vice president at Corning Glass, to assume the reins at the firm.

A 250-pound, cigar-chomping man who looked every inch the fat-cat capitalist, Carter was uneasy with Camera and Instrument's focus on defense work, which accounted for 80 percent of profits. His discomfort was confirmed in the third quarter of 1957, when Camera and Instrument began receiving only partial payments on its invoices submitted to federal agencies, thanks to austerity measures recently instituted by the government. Carter immediately slashed administration by 22 percent and sold off several unprofitable divisions. He felt acquisitions offered the easiest entrée into commercial and industrial markets and convinced the board of Camera and Instrument to acquire a small teletype company in the summer of 1957.[6]

Semiconductors were a logical choice for the expansion-minded company. The devices were increasingly making their way into the very missiles, satellites, radiation circuits, and reconnaissance computers that used Fairchild Camera and Instrument's products. In the industrial markets Carter coveted, automobile manufacturers, oil refiners, and tobacco producers either already used semiconductors in their automated operations and testing functions, or were actively looking into how to do so. Camera and Instrument had closely studied the possibility of entering the semiconductor field about six months before Coyle contacted Fairchild, but the company feared the large capital investments and years of basic research that semiconductor work would require. Acquisition would circumvent the problem, CEO John Carter decided, but no promising firm had surfaced until the group from Shockley. As Noyce put it, Fairchild management was "primed and eager to go along if [the Shockley defectors'] ideas seemed practical."[7]

Carter charged Camera and Instrument executive vice president Richard Hodgson with investigating the West Coast group of eight. A Bay Area native and Stanford graduate who had worked at MIT and Paramount Pictures, Hodgson had been hired by Fairchild with the mandate "to get the company into electronics." Hodgson was a likeable and technically capable man whom one Fairchild Semiconductor founder described as "just the right personality to work with us."[8]

Hodgson was eager to meet the California group, who were still working for Shockley at the time, but Sherman Fairchild first insisted that Hodgson personally contact Arnold Beckman to let Shockley's backer know what was happening and to confirm that he would not stand in the way of unfolding events. Beckman took the high road, assuring Hodgson that "there's never going to be a problem from me against Fairchild for taking this group away." Hodgson then flew out to visit with the would-be Shockley defectors and the men from Hayden, Stone. The group of eight, the bankers, and Hodgson talked in general terms about what the group could do and what they wanted in terms of funding and support.[9]

Hodgson left the meeting satisfied enough to invite Eugene Kleiner and Bob Noyce to Fairchild Camera and Instrument's Syosset headquarters. The two flew to New York in late August, with the purpose, as Noyce wrote his parents, "of selling the group [to Sherman Fairchild] and settling the principle of the financing arrangements." Noyce was impressed with Sherman Fairchild and with his enormous townhouse in Manhattan, which offered commanding views of the city through windows Fairchild had specially outfitted with a gadget he designed to open and shut the blinds electronically.[10]

IMMEDIATELY UPON NOYCE'S AND KLEINER'S RETURN to California, Richard Hodgson flew to San Francisco to begin formal negotiations with the eight scientists and Rock and Coyle at the offices of a law firm hired by the bankers. The negotiations proceeded along a friendly and predictable path. The Shockley defectors, fresh from 30-odd "no-thank-yous," felt that they were in no position to drive a hard bargain, but Arthur Rock and Bud Coyle, who had a good sense of the type of arrangement they sought, ensured the young men were not fleeced.[11]

After the discussion ended, Richard Hodgson took the group to celebrate at the St. Francis, a classic San Francisco hotel on Union Square. Dressed in his New York business suit and a fine hat, Hodgson looked a bit like a Mafioso as he approached the maitre d'. "Hodgson is the name, reservation for nine," he said gruffly. The maitre d' looked at his reservation book and then called over another tuxedoed man who shuffled through pages, increasingly discomfited. After a whispered conference, the pair looked up. "I'm sorry sir, we cannot find the reservation."

Hodgson began to fume and fuss, showing a side the young men had not seen before. He muttered under his breath, "How many times did I tell her to make the reservation . . ."

The restaurant staff looked nervous: "We'll make up a table for you right away, sir."

In short order, the group was escorted to a fine corner table. As soon as they were alone, Hodgson began to laugh. "Works every time."[12]

WHILE NOYCE AND HIS PEERS CELEBRATED, his parents worried the deal might be "shaky." What did he know about this Fairchild, or these bankers, for that matter? Noyce hastened to reassure them. "We [have] over a million dollars guaranteed which will keep us going for about 18 months without any income from sales," he wrote, adding "we have acting as our agents in this one of the ten largest investment banking houses in the country." He had paid close attention during the negotiations and declared the entire process "a very interesting education for me!" His excitement was palpable: "The agreement will be signed in a couple of weeks, and shortly therafter [sic] The California Transistor Corporation will spring into being, with yours truly as Director of R & D."[13]

For all his bravado and talk of large sums of money, Noyce had no savings. This proved a problem when Rock and Coyle told the group of eight that they each needed to pay $500 for an ownership stake in the new company. Noyce asked his parents to inquire if his grandmother, the only member of the family with financial reserves, could lend him the money. He promised to repay her with interest.

THE DEAL WITH FAIRCHILD Camera and Instrument now imminent, the eight men needed to break the news to William Shockley, who suspected— perhaps Beckman had called him after his conversation with Hodgson?— that a group of employees planned to leave. Shockley began summoning his researchers to his office one at a time, probing them for information about a brewing insurrection. Gordon Moore was the second man called— the first was not among the group—and he told Shockley he might as well stop questioning people because Moore was leaving and so was nearly everyone else in the R&D lab. The news devastated Shockley, who left the building a few minutes later.

Moore found himself surprisingly saddened by Shockley's obvious dismay. To be sure, Shockley was a martinet who browbeat his young employees and who knew nothing about running a business. And yet he was an excellent teacher. Before joining Shockley, the group of eight had, between them, three years of transistor experience — and all that experience resided in Bob Noyce. None of them had ever worked with silicon. After less than 18 months with Shockley, however, the eight were sufficiently competent to start a company that within the space of a decade sold hundreds of millions of dollars of silicon semiconductor devices. To be sure, these extremely bright young men learned from day-to-day immersion in the technology and the literature surrounding it. They gleaned much from each other in their makeshift seminars and daily professional banter. But they also learned from Shockley, who may not have been an easy man to work for, but who had an uncanny ability to suggest experiments and simplify complex ideas.[14]

Maturity and distance have even brought a new perspective on some of Shockley's management techniques. He, for example, refused to hire technicians for manufacturing. Production, he said, was so important that he wanted his top technical men to serve on a "PhD production line" to build the devices themselves. This production line has been cited as evidence of Shockley's fondness for humiliating his employees with work that was far below their training, but the kernel of his demand—the notion that precise production techniques lie at the heart of successful semiconductor manufacturing—is today universally accepted. In the 1960s and 1970s, moreover, a variant of the PhD production line was a standard troubleshooting method in the industry: engineers would personally walk chips through the production process in a "hand-carried run" to determine the root of production problems.[15]

Given this influence, it is in some sense sad that Shockley never reaped the benefits of his vision, never made a success of his company staffed by carefully chosen young men who in the beginning had been overjoyed to be working for a bonafide genius and overeager to please him. Shortly after learning that the group would be leaving, Shockley set to work on a terse statement to the press. The departure of the eight would have "no real effect on the Shockley Lab," he told a reporter from *Electronic News*. He subsequently flew to Munich, where he hired a passel of German scientists accustomed to a relationship with their academic advisers that more closely approximated Shockley's hierarchical management style. He moved his operation to the Stanford Industrial Park, where it went through several permutations, but never turned a profit.[16]

Shockley followed the fortunes of his former employees with masochistic attention, at one point even hiring an informant to provide him with details on the production methods used at their new company. He also sought to protect his firm's intellectual property by filing for patents on several of the ideas the defectors had written in their Shockley lab notebooks. He wanted to be sure the licensing fees and credit for their work came to Shockley Semiconductor. After the group left, Shockley filed four patent applications that listed Noyce as the inventor.[17]

In 1963 Shockley left industry to join the faculty of the Stanford Electrical Engineering Department, where he taught for the next two decades. As he aged, bitterness and paranoia came to dominate his once-brilliant mind. He became an outspoken eugenicist who donated his sperm with the stipulation it be supplied only to women who were members of Mensa. While his protégés achieved his goals of earning millions of dollars and seeing their names in the business press, Shockley rarely left his Stanford home, where he wrote articles on the intellectual inferiority of blacks to whites and the need to institute birth-control measures for people with low IQ scores. Small wonder Shockley has been called the Moses of Silicon Valley—he brought people to the Promised Land but was himself denied entrance.[18]

Before the group officially departed, Arnold Beckman called them into a conference room. Looking sad and reading from notes clearly drafted by

an attorney, he reminded them of the rules surrounding confidential information and suggested they try to find work in fields unrelated to semiconductors "to avoid complications." Jay Last took careful notes:

> Beckman feels that our leaving in this manner is a disloyal act. The right
> of the individual to change employment is different from a planned con-
> certed action. [Ours] is an act of conspiracy, prejudicial to the employer.
> We should consider the effect of our actions on employer and on re-
> maining employees.
>   This is a great financial loss [for Beckman]. We are not living up to
> the spirit of [our] employment contract. We have given an implied promise
> that we would come out and make the operations successful. We are
> running away because the going has gotten tough. We haven't thought
> things through clearly, because we are young and because of the emo-
> tion-charged atmosphere. The cost to Beckman is a million bucks down
> the drain.
>   . . . Beckman feels as if a good friend has stabbed him in the back. . . .
> Our new sponsor is not ethical.
>   We should consider the community reaction. This will be looked
> on as a shameful act.[19]

At precisely the same time that Noyce was abandoning an established
firm backed by a known industrialist for a brand-new operation run by him
and his friends, expenses in the Noyce household were rising. Billy had
just started nursery school, and Penny would begin soon, too. There were
payments due on the luxurious refrigerator Bob had bought for Betty when
he thought the situation at Shockley looked promising. Betty, who already
found herself in tears over money, was further rattled when Mrs. Shockley
came for one last visit, staying only long enough to ask, "How could you
possibly do this without telling me?" before sweeping out the door. "Mr.
and Mrs. Shockley don't like us any more," Billy told his younger sisters.[20]

William Shockley never forgave Noyce for his "betrayal." Years after
Fairchild was a success, when the two men encountered each other at an
industry dinner, Shockley said only two words—"Hello, Bob"—before turning his back and walking away.[21]

ON SEPTEMBER 19, 1957, the Shockley defectors, representatives from
Fairchild Camera and Instrument, and Bud Coyle and Arthur Rock met to
sign papers establishing Fairchild Semiconductor Corporation. The firm
incorporated with 1,325 shares of stock. Hayden, Stone owned 225 shares,
purchased for $5 per share. Each of the founders—including Noyce, whose
grandmother provided the money—owned 100 shares, purchased at the
same price. Three hundred shares were held in reserve for key managers
yet to be hired. Camera and Instrument agreed to loan Semiconductor a
total of $1.38 million over a period of 18 months. In exchange, Camera
and Instrument controlled the company through a voting trust. The par-

ent firm received an option to buy all of Fairchild Semiconductor's stock for $3 million at any point before Fairchild Semiconductor had three successive years of net earnings greater than $300,000 per year. If Camera and Instrument waited more than three years but bought within seven years, the company would have to pay $5 million for Fairchild Semiconductor. It was, as one founder put it, "a very good deal for both sides."[22]

Arthur Rock's and Bud Coyle's work in the establishment of Fairchild Semiconductor in many ways presaged the role of venture capitalists in future Silicon Valley startup operations, even though the term "venture capital" did not yet exist. The bankers helped the young technologists develop a business strategy, determine their funding requirements, and find investors. In return, Coyle's and Rock's firm took both a financial stake in the new company and a board seat from which they could influence the outcome of their investment. Coyle and Rock found only one investor to back only one company, whereas modern venture capitalists organize a pool of outside investors to back a number of startups of the financiers' choosing, but the Northern California roots of venture capital—the pairing of brains and dollars—were established with the founding of Fairchild Semiconductor.

After the signing, the entire group went to Rickey's for a celebration. The flowing champagne and rousing toasts recalled the festivities, held in the same room less than a year before, surrounding Shockley's Nobel Prize. The focus now, however, was on the future, as Richard Hodgson firmly reminded them when he leaned in close and whispered loudly enough for them all to hear, "I hope to hell you guys know what you're doing. Because if you don't, I'm going to lose my job."[23]

EVEN BEFORE THE PAPERS HAD BEEN SIGNED, Hodgson, who had been named chair of Fairchild Semiconductor, had asked Noyce to serve as general manager of the new company. Since Hodgson and the rest of the Camera and Instrument executive team would remain in New York, the general manager would organize Semiconductor's launch and manage operations thereafter. The general manager would also serve as Semiconductor's public face and its link to Camera and Instrument management.

Noyce was tempted, but he feared himself ill prepared to oversee an entire company. Moreover, the prospect of having the final say over the many employees he could imagine one day working for Fairchild Semiconductor frightened him. He was, in a very real sense, afraid of his own ability to influence people—a fear with roots in a domestic incident that occurred shortly before he left Philadelphia. A refrigerator salesman had convinced him and Betty to try an icebox for a free week-long trial, promising no obligation and no problems should they decide not to keep it. At

the end of the week, when the salesman appeared at their front door, saying "of course you want to buy the refrigerator," Noyce told him they had
decided they did not want it, and he should take it back.

"No? Was there a problem?"

"No. We just don't want it."

The salesman seemed distraught, "But you must, you see the features . . ."

"I'm not buying it. Take it back."

After a few more minutes of this, the man loaded the refrigerator on
his truck and left. Several days later, Noyce read in the paper that the salesman had killed himself. Noyce could not shake his sense of responsibility
for the suicide and vowed to avoid other situations in which saying "no"
might drive someone to such distress.[24]

Noyce did not share this story with Hodgson, of course. He simply
told him that he would prefer heading R&D to running the company. At
least in the lab, Noyce thought to himself, the right answers can be found
in a book.

Hodgson accepted Noyce's choice but nonetheless treated him as the
de facto general manager while conducting the search for a permanent
hire. Hodgson communicated almost exclusively through Noyce and advanced him $3,000 "to cover necessary expenditures in setting up the semi-
conductor operation until such time as the Corporation is formally
organized." Through Noyce, Hodgson offered the new company use of
Camera and Instrument's surplus shop equipment and assured the founders
that Fairchild Semiconductor employees would be covered under the larger
company's benefits. Noyce earned more than the other founders, and he
alone among them held a seat on the board of Fairchild Semiconductor
(though not on Camera and Instrument's board).[25]

The press release issued by Fairchild Camera and Instrument referred
to "Noyce and his seven researchers." It quoted Noyce at length but referred to the other seven founders simply as "associated with Dr. Noyce in
the founding of the new company." The attention to Noyce did not go
unnoticed. Although most of the founders recognized that they had invited Noyce to join them explicitly to lead and provide credibility for the
group, others—particularly Last, Hoerni, and Roberts, who catalyzed the
defection from Shockley—found it hard to sit in the shadow of a man who
had joined the operation at the last possible moment. "Bob was more of a
politician than we were," complained one. The problem, according to another founder, was simple: "If [Noyce] climbed in the boat, he would always be captain." When Jay Last took charge of typing up the employee
list, he put all the founders in alphabetical order—except Noyce, whom he
deliberately put at the end of the list as a reminder of who had, and who
had not, started this all.[26]

Excitement and anticipation usually overrode jealousy, however. Until they could find a building, they worked in each other's houses, planning, talking to suppliers, trying to find an office, and making lists of the employees at Shockley whom they would like to join Fairchild Semiconductor. A small group of founders was working in Vic Grinich's garage when news broke that the Soviets had launched the world's first orbiting satellite, a small, beeping ball called Sputnik whose signal Noyce and other amateur radio buffs could hear on their home sets. Sputnik would prove a godsend to the young men's fortunes, for it sent the United States military, already investigating the uses of silicon transistors, into a frenzy for smaller, higher-performing electronic components for missiles and satellites. On that October 4, though, the Sputnik announcement brought only anxiety to the founders of the country's newest electronics firm. If the Soviets could launch a satellite into orbit, they could loft a nuclear warhead and aim it at an American city. As media reactions climbed towards hysteria, President Eisenhower announced that an American satellite would circle the earth by year's end. The space race began in earnest.[27]

THE SAME MONTH, Fairchild Semiconductor signed a two-year, $42,000 lease on a building at 844 Charleston Road (later named a California historic landmark, thanks to the activities that transpired there). The building, little more than a 15,000-square-foot empty shell, sat near the southern border of Palo Alto, not far from Shockley Labs. The space seemed huge to the young men, who had turned down a building twice the size because they were certain they could never fill it. They worked hard to rein in their excitement as they began moving into the facility in November 1957. One minute they would be horsing around the building like kids, or installing the cabinets Jay Last had bought at Sears, and the next they were talking to plumbers and electricians about their water and power needs or carefully moving lab tables and equipment from one area to another until they settled on the configuration they thought best.[28]

The search for a general manager led the founders to Tom Bay, a former physics professor who had also worked as a sales manager for Fairchild Camera and Instrument in the early 1950s. A handsome, hard-drinking sophisticate, Bay was dapper, witty, and smart, down to his wing-tipped toes. Although it had been years since he worked with Hodgson, Bay's competence and obvious intelligence had impressed the Fairchild executive enough to recommend the group of eight consider him for their general manager—a puzzling suggestion since Bay was the first to admit that he "didn't know bupkis about transistors." Clearly, though, Noyce, who interviewed him, thought Bay would have no trouble learning about the tiny devices. Bay was granted a small bit of stock and joined Fairchild Semiconductor in December 1957, as the head of marketing.[29]

INCIDENTS IN THE NEXT FEW WEEKS portended the importance of Fairchild Semiconductor to its parent company's future. In January 1958, Camera and Instrument received word that the US Air Force had cancelled the company's contract developing B-58 bomber reconnaissance cameras. This contract, which once provided the firm with more than half of its sales, had fallen victim to the military's new desire for digital electronic reconnaissance systems. "Photo reconnaissance systems as we know it is [sic] a thing of the past," Carter told the board.[30]

The drive for digital electronics that spelled Fairchild Camera and Instrument's loss was Fairchild Semiconductor's gain. In the past year, the air force had begun shifting its major contractors away from systems based on analog computers—which suffered from easily blown vacuum tubes and a multiplicity of moving parts—towards all-digital systems, which were faster and more accurate than their analog counterparts. The air force had further begun requiring the use of silicon transistors (which, unlike germanium devices, could withstand high temperatures and avionic jostling) in the digital computers for its missiles and airplanes.[31]

Shortly after Camera and Instrument lost the B-58 camera contract, Fairchild Semiconductor marketing manager Tom Bay came across an article detailing the difficulties that IBM's Federal Systems Division faced in its efforts to build a navigational computer for the B-70, a long-range strategic bomber nicknamed "the manned missile." When he read that IBM's most pressing problem was its lack of a silicon transistor for the computer, Bay, who was familiar with guidance systems, thought immediately of Sherman Fairchild's connection to IBM. Sensing opportunity, Bay and Hodgson convinced Sherman Fairchild to arrange for Bay and Noyce to meet with the IBM engineers working on the B-70 computer in Owego, New York.

IBM wanted a transistor that could withstand high temperatures and that could switch quickly. Bay recalls the specs called for a device that could switch 150 milliamps with 60-volt capability at 50 megacycles—faster than any silicon transistor then on the market and faster than many germanium devices, as well. Moreover, IBM wanted 100 of them. Noyce listened intently to the engineers and then said simply, "Sure. We can do that." Noyce's confidence—or was it bluffing?—both impressed and surprised Tom Bay, who at the time noted that "Bob is so articulate, no one questions [him]." Their three-month-old company had yet to build even a single basic transistor, and here was Noyce coolly promising 100 state-of-the-art devices, with "never a doubt in his mind that we could do it," as far as Bay could see. Perhaps Noyce counted the fact that Fairchild Semiconductor had not built any other transistors a benefit—no established standards, practices, equipment, or training meant nothing to undo or retool for the IBM device. They could, in effect, build the company around IBM's needs.[32]

Noyce's assurances did not overcome the IBM engineers' immediate doubts about Fairchild Semiconductor, a complete unknown distinguished in the industry only by the rebellious history of its founders. Although IBM had no real alternative supplier to Fairchild (the best approximation of the device they needed, a Texas Instruments component, had failed in testing), it took a private meeting among Sherman Fairchild, Dick Hodgson, and IBM chief Thomas Watson, Jr.—a meeting with a singular theme: your largest shareholder has invested more than $1 million in these men, so you should trust them—to persuade the IBM Federal Systems engineers to take a chance on Fairchild Semiconductor. By February 1958, the young men had an order for 100 silicon transistors. IBM agreed to pay $150 for each transistor, this at a time when basic germanium devices were selling for less than $5. Fairchild Semiconductor was in business.[33]

THE IBM ORDER made Fairchild Semiconductor. IBM left little to chance, carefully specifying not only the device's electrical parameters, but also the packaging and testing procedures the young company should use in manufacturing the transistors. Noyce and the other scientists at Fairchild Semiconductor agreed they could only achieve the sort of reliability and speed that IBM wanted if they built double-diffused silicon transistors: devices, that is, built out of silicon and with two P-N junctions. They would build mesa transistors like the ones they had worked on at Shockley Semiconductor. The only question was whether the transistors should be diffused PNP or NPN. The group decided to split the company in two and try to build both devices, with Gordon Moore heading the NPN effort and Jean Hoerni leading the drive on a PNP device.[34]

With semiconductor manufacturing still in its infancy, the Fairchild Semiconductor men "had to develop our own equipment as we developed the processes," as Gordon Moore put it. They had done this type of work at Shockley and could quickly assume responsibility for their areas of expertise. Sheldon Roberts, section head for materials processing and metallurgy, took charge of growing the silicon ingots, slicing them into "wafers" approximately the size of a dime, and polishing them until they gleamed like mirrors. Ultimately, dozens of transistors would be etched onto each wafer, but first the silicon needed to be diffused—doped with impurities in high-temperature furnaces so that some areas of the silicon wafer were P-type and others N-type. Gordon Moore and Jean Hoerni oversaw the diffusion process, with Hoerni taking charge of the theory (determining how long to diffuse the wafers and at what temperature) and Moore overseeing the practical necessities of building the furnaces. Moore's needs were so specialized, and the pickings so thin, that he ultimately had to order the elements he needed from a company in Sweden and design and build the furnaces himself.[35]

Once the silicon was properly diffused, it was time to start differentiating the individual transistors. This was done through a process called photolithography, an area that Noyce and Jay Last led together at Fairchild. The two men created a pattern that showed where every transistor would appear on the wafer, how the current would pass through the transistors, and where the transistors would be attached to the canisters that would then be plugged into the IBM system. This pattern would then be shrunk hundreds of times in succession until it was so small that multiple copies could be lined up side by side on a small glass plate called a mask. When Noyce needed to build the camera that would reduce the pattern, he went to a photography store in San Francisco, where he rummaged through a bin of 16-mm movie camera lenses until he found three that, while not flawless, could be aligned in such a way that the errors on them did not affect the process of shrinking the pattern. This cobbled-together machine became the prototype of the step-and-repeat cameras used throughout the industry.[36]

To transfer the patterns on the mask to the silicon, Noyce and Last needed to coat the surface of the silicon with a light-sensitive resin. Eastman Kodak had developed a resin (for use in printed circuit boards) whose chemical composition Noyce and Last could modify to meet their needs. After this resin, called "photoresist," was applied to the wafer, the mask was placed on the coated wafer. Then the wafer and mask were exposed to light, acid, and a dopant that added one more P-N junction to the surface of the silicon wafer while also etching away areas that had not been covered by the photoresist. These processes happened over the surface of the entire wafer, so that all the transistors were processed simultaneously, rather than one at a time.[37]

Once the silicon wafers emerged from the photoresist process, the transistors needed to be cut apart and tested. Not every device that started production worked by the end. Out of 100 transistors on a wafer, for example, the number of working devices (called a "yield") would be somewhere between 10 and 50. Yields were low because contamination of any sort ruined the electrical characteristics of the device—and contamination was rampant, despite plastic sheeting and other rudimentary attempts to keep the lab clean. Moreover, even a slight change in the moisture in the room or a bit too much dust could cause a device to fail.[38]

Victor Grinich, who also helped to define product applications and evaluation protocols for new devices, took charge of testing. Julius Blank designed the manufacturing facililty (called the "fab") and ran plant engineering in collaboration with Eugene Kleiner, who was also responsible for general administration since he had known a banker. Blank and Kleiner also supervised the women (invariably called "girls") who cut the transistors apart, wired them into canisters, and packaged the finished product for shipment to customers. Women were hired for these jobs because it was believed that their small hands and well-developed fine-motor skills would ideally suit work with tiny devices and small wires—and they could be paid less than men.[39]

For the founders, it was a very egalitarian arrangement. "Noyce was the technical head of the lab, and that was it for organizational structure," according to one founder. "The rest of us were pretty much on equal footing. Everybody wore as many hats as possible."[40]

The group began quietly recruiting from Shockley Semiconductor Labs. Capable Shockley employees knew that if they read the *Palo Alto Times* carefully, they would at some point see their current job description listed in the classified advertisements. "Fairchild Semiconductor did everything but put our names on the ads," recalls one employee. Soon Harry Sello, who worked at Shockley, joined, as did Dave Allison, who came to work on the NPN transistor, and C. T. Sah, a gifted physicist. A small contingent of technicians also came to Fairchild from Shockley.[41]

A general manager joined the company in February 1958. Ed Baldwin was a former paratrooper who had managed the diode operations at Hughes, a major military subcontractor and one of the nation's leading producers of silicon semiconductors. In addition to his experience in precisely the markets Fairchild Semiconductor targeted, Baldwin had a PhD in Physics and a presence as compact and sturdy as a cannon. The eight founders offered him a stake in the company equivalent to their own—$500 for 100 shares—but he did not accept. Privately Baldwin was lobbying Hodgson for stock, arguing that his managerial position justified his having a larger stake in the company than did the founders. Soon some dozen engineers from Hughes, most of them specialists in manufacturing—the eight founders' weak point—were on the Fairchild Semiconductor payroll.[42]

Baldwin's job was not easy. After an initial $50,000 loan, Camera and Instrument transferred funds to Semiconductor only to reimburse properly documented expenses, in effect keeping Baldwin and his team on an allowance. Although this did provide a workable method of cost accounting for the parent firm, it also created a burdensome layer of bureaucracy for Fairchild Semiconductor.[43]

Baldwin's slogan could have been "Think Big and Focus." He told the eight founders that they needed to develop an organizational chart. They needed to begin planning—immediately—for a much bigger manufacturing facility, even though they had yet to build a product. They should separate engineering from manufacturing, and both of them from Research and Development. This was not a radical suggestion; inasmuch as there were traditional operating procedures for an industry as young as semiconductors, these sorts of divisions would qualify. Baldwin did not particularly admire the founders' abilities to perform multiple jobs. "Do one thing and do it well," he told Noyce. Baldwin wanted an instrumentation expert to build the test equipment and the preproduction engineering to be over-seen by someone who had actually put products into production in the past. When Tom Bay told him that he thought Fairchild Semiconductor might have $15 million in revenues in five years, Baldwin ordered him to "shoot ten times that high."[44]

Despite his contributions, Baldwin was always outside the founding group. The rapport the eight of them shared was dynamic and imperme-able. They worked together ten or twelve hours each day, not counting the trips to Rupert's Bar, where they liked to go for drinks in the evening. They often found themselves standing in a circle when they were together, their shoulders nearly touching, each man holding one conversation with the man on his left and a different one with the man on his right (and perhaps a third with someone across the circle). Noyce loved these mo-ments, loved the buzz of talk and the smell of the cigarettes many of them held between their lips. If he reached in his pocket for a smoke and discov-ered an empty pack, he would crumple the wrapper, toss it on the ground, grab a cigarette out of his neighbor's pocket (without asking and almost without looking), pound it on his leg, and pop it in his mouth so the guy from whom he took it could light it. Were it filtered, Noyce would grumble something about sissies. All the while, he and the other fellows would main-tain their end of two or three conversations.[45]

A formal photo from the founding period hints at this rapport. The eight founders sit around a table under a flower-print, fringed umbrella. They are seated in a circle with Noyce, as always, front and center. They all wear suits—most of them owned only one—and ties, which give them a serious air, as do the papers and books strewn across the table. But every man wears a smile big enough to be called a grin. They are clearly having the time of their lives.

By May of 1958, the NPN transistor Moore's team had built for IBM was ready to move into production. By early summer, Fairchild Semicon-ductor had delivered its promised 100 devices to Owego, New York. Though he was not one for sentiment, Noyce kept the check stub from the transaction for the rest of his life. In August, Fairchild Semiconductor brought its NPN transistor to Wescon, the six-year-old trade show spon-sored by the West Coast Electronics Manufacturers Association. There the company's founders, several of whom presented papers together, were elated to learn that theirs was the only double-diffused silicon transistor available on the open market. "We scooped the industry!" Noyce whooped to a group of Fairchild employees a few days after the show ended. "No-body [is] ready to put something like this on the market ... [and there is] no prospect of anybody getting in our way in the immediate future." In-deed, Fairchild kept its monopoly on the device for over a year.[46]

5

Invention

The infancy of Fairchild Semiconductor undoubtedly ranks as the most
intellectually fertile time of Noyce's life. Seven of his 17 patents, including his most important, for the integrated circuit, date from the 18
months after the company was launched, when Noyce served as the director of R&D and oversaw Fairchild's research efforts. During this time, he
focused as much attention as possible on his own scientific work. He spoke
at technical conferences on topics such as "Switching Time Calculations
for Diffused Base Transistors." His mind was so filled with ideas that sometimes he would rise in the middle of the night to write them down while
Betty and the children slept. In the office, he kept careful lab notebooks in
which he adopted a highly didactic tone—"let us look at the following structure," "we may set these criteria"—almost as if he were lecturing to himself in page after page of notes, charts, figures, and oscilloscope readings.
Sometimes he scrawled complex mathematical equations over entire pages;
at other points he slowed down long enough to draw up a "plan of calculation" before launching into the math.[1]

Truth be told, though, the brutally methodical labor of science—the
careful working and recording of one's way through experiment after experiment, each one only slightly different from the iteration that preceded
it—interested Noyce far less than the moments when a new idea came to
him. At his core, Noyce was an almost compulsive idea generator, a mental
perpetual motion machine. Thomas Edison famously declared genius to
be 99 percent perspiration and 1 percent inspiration, but Noyce preferred
to spend as much time as possible in the inspiration stage.

Some scientists do their creative work by starting small and building
up. When William Shockley wanted to invent, for example, he liked to
pull out every publication he could find in the relevant fields. He would
then spread the patents and papers across his desk and try to make novel
connections among them or to identify potentially fruitful areas that had
not yet been investigated by other researchers.[2]

This assembly line inventiveness was not for Noyce. Unlike Shockley, he never sat down and told himself he needed to invent something before he could stand up again. His approach, Noyce once told a friend, was to know the science cold and then "forget about it." He did not slog or grind his way to ideas; he felt they just came to him. When he heard Picasso's famous line about artistic creativity—"I do not seek; I find"—Noyce said that he invented in the same way.[3]

Noyce's creativity often required a kick start, usually in the form of a practical question from a colleague. Once his attention was engaged, Noyce did not start small, and he did not turn to journals or patent files for ideas. Instead, he tried to "think about the fundamentals of the physics"—as big a starting point as possible—and he refused to ask himself whether or not an idea ought to work according to the most current research in the field. In his opinion, there were only two relevant questions in the earliest stages of scientific innovation: "Why won't this work?" and "What fundamental laws will it violate?" If an idea seemed within the realm of physical possibility, then Noyce deemed it worthy of exploration—conventional wisdom on the topic be damned.[4]

Noyce's try-anything approach, by no means unusual among technically or mathematically gifted thinkers, meant he consistently generated ideas that seemed implausible, more flashes of intuition than products of careful science. Often these ideas proved dead ends, but occasionally they were brilliant. No one knew this better than Gordon Moore, Noyce's second in command at the lab, and a deft screener of what he called "Bob's many ideas, some of them good." Moore excelled at the perspiration work of science, which made him an ideal creative complement to Noyce.[5]

One of the most memorable examples of Noyce's inspiration working thanks to Moore's perspiration came in 1958, when Moore, who was working on the IBM transistor, was searching for a way to use a single metal to make contacts to both the P- and N-type silicon at the surface of the transistor. (Contacts were little dots of metal to which the wires that connected the transistor to its canister were attached.) Western Electric had experimented with using two different metals for contacts—aluminum on the P-type silicon and silver on the N-type—but their process was so complicated, and their yields so dismal, that Moore wanted something better for Fairchild.

He began talking things over with Noyce, who surprised him by suggesting he try using aluminum to make the contacts to *both* the P- and N-type silicon. In the semiconductor industry of the late 1950s, this was a nearly preposterous suggestion. Everyone knew that aluminum acts as a P-type impurity, which means that while it makes an ideal contact for P-type silicon, it is a terrible choice for contacts to N-type silicon. In fact, aluminum contacts to N-type silicon tended to add another P-N junction to the transistor, rendering it useless. Of all the people at Fairchild, Noyce, the most experienced, should have known better.[6]

Noyce was unswayed, insisting that if Moore used a new process developed by their colleague Jean Hoerni, then aluminum should work as a contact for N-type silicon as well as P-type. Noyce knew more than Moore about the surface of semiconductors, which was where the connection would be made, and the Hoerni process looked promising. Since Moore was running out of alternatives, he decided to try using aluminum as the only contact metal, even though, he recalls, "all the conventional wisdom said it wouldn't work."[7]

What happened next perfectly illustrates Noyce's approach to invention. He left his idea in Moore's hands and moved on to something new. He began sketching ideas for a semiconductor switching device and for a scanning device that could "serve in many of the same applications in which an electron beam device is used, such as display, camera tubes, beam switching, amplifiers of the traveling wave variety, etc." He patented both of these ideas.[8]

Meanwhile, Moore sweated out the details of the aluminum contact process, laboring alone and in occasional consultation with Noyce, Jean Hoerni, and Sheldon Roberts. Every time one problem seemed solved with the aluminum contacts, another arose. Wires connected to the contacts fell off indiscriminately. The junctions (the meeting points of the P- and N-type regions) began leaking a tiny bit of current in the wrong direction. The metal pulled away from the silicon. Noyce was a willing consultant to Moore in these travails. He tried to imagine how the pulling-away problem could be turned into an asset, and he suggested that Moore try plating the back of the transistor with nickel to solve the leaking junction problems. But it was the big idea—why not try aluminum?!—not the details of making that idea work ("reducing the idea to practice," in scientific parlance) that Noyce cared about.[9]

Moore's work paid off on May 2, 1958, when he could finally report that "pure Al[uminum] works very well on N-P-Ns in all respects." The combination of aluminum contacts and nickel plating yielded transistors with hard junctions and contacts large enough to minimize spreading resistance but not so large that they shorted across the junctions. Noyce and Moore filed for a joint patent on the process. It was one of the most significant early patents at Fairchild Semiconductor, since aluminum became the standard metal for contacts in the semiconductor industry.[10]

In this case, as in many others, the Fairchild researchers did not understand precisely why this innovation worked. In an academic environment or at Bell Labs, which was the research arm of a regulated monopoly, this question would have been paramount. At Fairchild Semiconductor, however, why something worked was far less important than the fact that it did. In a newborn company with only one customer of any significance (IBM), pursuing science for its own sake was an ill-afforded luxury. Thus early research at Fairchild Semiconductor was almost all process oriented, with building a saleable product the fundamental goal of the research lab. Noyce and several of the other researchers directly refer to the IBM specifications in their scientific lab books, giving as much weight to performance targets as they did to the science they needed to reach those targets. Noyce, who believed that "the only thing that's technologically exciting is something that has a need for it," was the ideal man to oversee this work in the lab.[11]

Of the seven patents Noyce filed in his first 18 months at Fairchild, the best known is #2,981,877 for "Semiconductor Device-and-Lead Structure." Fairchild called the product developed on the basis of this patent, which Noyce filed in 1959, a "monolithic integrated circuit." Years later, John Bardeen, co-inventor of the transistor, would call it an invention "as important as the wheel." The integrated circuit made electronic devices smaller, faster, and cheaper than ever before. Every modern computer, microwave, airplane, traffic light, missile, telephone, ATM, and automobile in use today has at its center direct descendants of the integrated circuit Noyce sketched in his device-and-lead patent application.[12]

An integrated circuit is a complete electronic circuit built on a chip of silicon small enough to be carried off by an ant. Every electronic circuit is actually an interconnected series of discrete components that serve specific functions—resistors to control current, diodes to block it, transistors to amplify it. When these discrete components are strung together, the resulting circuit can do anything from adding millions of numbers to sensing when coffee is done brewing. Before the integrated circuit, these components were attached to each other one at a time, by hand, in a process fraught with errors and failures. With the integrated circuit, by contrast, the components could be printed and connected to each other simultaneously in a reliable process that resulted in a complete circuit no larger than any one of the components taken individually.

In the 1950s, semiconductor firms manufactured hundreds of identical discrete components (transistors, for example) side by side on a silicon wafer. All these companies used a process similar to the one Fairchild Semiconductor employed to build its mesa transistors. Before the integrated circuit, the last step of the production process was a painstaking assembly line affair. Hundreds of women attired in identical lab coats sat side by side hunched over high-powered microscopes that magnified the wafer so that the women could slice apart individual components and attach leads and wires to them using tiny tweezers. The individual components were then tested, packaged, and shipped to customers. The customers would then reconnect various components to each other to configure a circuit.

Noyce, along with everyone else in the electronics industry, knew that this method of cutting apart components only to reassemble them later was inefficient. The ideal procedure would be somehow to connect the components to each other at the same time that they were built. Knowing this and doing it were two very different exercises, however. Under a microscope, the metal wires used for interconnecting discrete components, while thinner than a human hair, nonetheless resembled huge logs capable of flattening a component's delicate architecture. No one could figure out how to deposit this metal on the surface of the semiconductor wafer in amounts small enough not to short out the circuit, but large enough to connect the components to a package, power source, and other devices. This is why the "girls" made the interconnections by hand, after the components had been safely cut from the wafer.

This cumbersome method of interconnecting components posed an additional problem: even if the components were themselves reliable, an accomplishment one could never take for granted, bad interconnections could render a circuit useless. Each component could be attached to many others, which meant that as the number of components in a circuit grew, the number of interconnections grew exponentially, until a circuit board could come to resemble a nesting ground for tiny wire-quilled hedgehogs. Circuits in the 1950s regularly consisted of hundreds, or even thousands, of discrete components, and people were predicting that the demand for "space-age electronics" would soon push the numbers of components into the hundreds of thousands, and the numbers of interconnections into the millions.

Although the women in the lab were chosen for their dexterity, it was physically impossible for anyone to solder millions of connections perfectly. This meant that given a big enough system with enough interconnections, even if every component in a system had a reliability of *better than 99 percent*, failure was statistically possible within the first two minutes of operation. The interconnections, often shorthanded the "tyranny of numbers," were the industry's Achilles' heel. If the problem could not be resolved, real progress in electronics would grind to a halt.[13]

The military desperately wanted to end the tyranny of numbers. One air force-sponsored effort tried to synthesize, atom by atom, a single piece of solid metal to achieve a complete circuit function. Another tried to build the wiring right into the discrete components and then snap the components together like a child's plastic pop-beads. Neither effort proved commercially viable, nor did attempts to build tiny electron tubes or to grow a complete circuit with little or no wiring needed to interconnect the components. By the end of the 1950s, at least 20 companies, ranging from small component makers to huge equipment manufacturers, were on a quest to find a solution to the interconnections problem.[14]

Neither Bob Noyce nor anyone else at Fairchild Semiconductor set out with a grand plan to resolve the tyranny of numbers, though the integrated circuit accomplished precisely that. The course of events that led to the Fairchild integrated circuit is murky at best. Discoveries and ideas wind past each other and double back. Noyce's involvement with the integrated circuit changed dramatically halfway through, when he was named general manager and left his lab bench, essentially forever. And the fame that the moniker "inventor of the integrated circuit" brought to Noyce left some other contributors to the invention resentful. The lawyers who defended Noyce's patent, and the cutthroat pricing strategies that Fairchild adopted to ensure that their circuit became the industry standard, are also woven into the "invention" of the integrated circuit. This much is certain: the integrated circuit rests on the planar process invented by Jean Hoerni—no planar, no integrated circuit—and that invention, like so many at Fairchild, came in an effort to solve an immediately pressing practical problem.

In late 1958, several of Fairchild's mesa transistors were returned to the company after random catastrophic failures. Tests in the lab soon revealed that it took nothing more than a sharp tap of a pencil against the side of a Fairchild transistor to make it stop working. The problem did not affect every transistor, but reliability was the single most important selling point of the Fairchild transistor, and so R&D had to solve the tap problem—immediately.

It is hard to appreciate how crude the techniques and analytical tools available to the Fairchild researchers were at this stage. Troubleshooting the tap problem meant taking a transistor, tapping it ten times with a pencil, recording whether it failed, pounding it on the table ten times, again recording results, and then finally opening up the failed transistors, at which point the diagnoses would read something like this from Gordon Moore's notebook: "They each showed a fleck of crud (it looked like yellow metal) on the top edge of the mesa."[15]

Eventually a skilled technician determined that during the process of sealing the cans, a tiny piece of metal was flaking off, bouncing about within the can, and eventually shorting out the transistor. Before he made this discovery, however, a few key lab employees launched a pull-everything-out-of-your-hats effort to solve the tap problem. Jean Hoerni began once again considering a subject that he had first begun to explore with Noyce and Moore at Shockley: how to protect a transistor's junctions without contaminating them. The question had clearly preoccupied Hoerni since the very earliest days of Fairchild Semiconductor; in December 1957, when the company was scarcely two months old, Hoerni had proposed that "the building up of an oxide layer . . . on the surface of the transistor . . . will protect the otherwise exposed junctions from contamination and possible electrical leakage due to subsequent handling, cleaning, [and] canning of the device." This was unusual thinking for the time. Most people thought that the oxides that grew naturally on the clean surface of a semiconductor needed to be washed away so they would not trap impurities between the oxide and the silicon. Hoerni instead wondered if the oxide might *protect* the surface—even from impurities as gargantuan and menacing as a rogue sliver of metal. About six months after Hoerni's journal entry, several Fairchild researchers attended a conference where they learned that a group at Bell Labs had demonstrated that an oxide layer indeed could stabilize the surface of the semiconductor.[16]

At the end of Hoerni's December 1957 entry, Noyce wrote "read and understood," added the date, and signed his name. Scientists regularly asked their peers to "witness" their most important work in this way. In the future, the witnessed signature could help to document when precisely a researcher had first noted his ideas—an essential element for any patent application. But although Noyce understood Hoerni's ideas and almost certainly knew of the Bell Labs oxide findings, neither he nor anyone else in the lab paid any special attention to Hoerni's thoughts on oxide layers. Instead, the lab team focused on the IBM transistor and the other transistors and diodes that followed it. Solving the problems that led directly to more sales and building products that would make money was far more important than optimizing the Fairchild transistor process to an ideal level, which is what the oxide layer aimed to do. If it weren't terribly broke, the Fairchild men saw no reason to fix it.

The tap problem, however, made it apparent that the Fairchild process *was* broken, or at least, that it was producing breakable transistors. For three weeks in January 1959, Hoerni thought about nothing but oxide layers. Imagine a cake that somehow grows its own icing. The surface of the cake is analogous to the surface of the semiconductor; the icing is similar to the oxide layer. Bell Labs had shown that the oxide icing would protect the surface. Now Hoerni wanted to develop a way to grow a perfectly consistent icing and then work between it and the cake—right at the all-important surface of the semiconductor, the same area that had interested Noyce ever since his dissertation research. Hoerni needed either to lift up the icing or drill through it to get down to the surface of the cake.

After what he described as an "epiphany" in the shower one morning, Hoerni realized that he ought to be able to use a mask to create an oxide layer over the entire wafer and then engrave a precisely located "window" in the oxide through which impurities could be diffused to form the base. At the same time as this first diffusion, another layer of oxide could be grown on the surface of the silicon. Then another window, another diffusion (this time to form the emitter junction), and another new layer of oxide. On January 14, 1959, Hoerni wrote out a two-page patent disclosure of this process. The next week he wrote another disclosure on a closely related process. Noyce witnessed this second disclosure and almost assuredly saw the first, as well.[17]

During these same remarkable weeks of January 1959, Noyce began sketching out his ideas about the integrated circuit, which he classed under the heading, "Methods of Isolating Multiple Devices." He wrote, "In many applications now it would be desirable to make multiple devices on a single piece of silicon in order to be able to make interconnections between devices as part of the manufacturing process, and thus reduce size, weight, etc., as well as cost per active element." Noyce imagined making an adder circuit from diodes and included thoughts on using P-N junctions to isolate components from each other so they would not interfere with one another's electrical characteristics. (The work of Kurt Lehovec at Sprague had introduced Noyce to the possibility of using junctions to isolate devices.) Noyce included among the "important features" of such a circuit "use of the SiO_2 [silicon dioxide] layer as an insulator to isolate contact strips from the underlying silicon" and "protection of junction at the surface with an oxide layer." Noyce also refers to "impurities diffused through the holes in the oxide."[18]

Noyce's thoughts on the integrated circuit are thus directly and inextricably linked to Hoerni's oxide work. In essence, Noyce was imagining that Hoerni's process would make it theoretically possible to drop a relatively large bit of metal onto the surface of the semiconductor wafer, on top of the tiny holes etched in the icing. If done properly, precisely the right amount of metal would touch the silicon in precisely the right place, and any of the metal that happened to "overhang" the hole would benignly sit on top of the icing, unable to affect the rest of the circuit.[19]

"I don't have any recollection of a 'Boom! There it is!' light bulb going off," Noyce later said of his ideas. Instead, he conceived of the integrated circuit in an iterative method he described thus: "[I thought,] let's see, if we could do this, we can do that. If we can do that, then we can do this. [It was] a logical sequence. If I hit a wall, I'd back up and then find a path, conceptually, all the way through to the end. [Once you have that path], you can come back and start refining, thinking in little steps that will take you there. Once you get to the point that you can see the top of the mountain, then you know you can get there."[20]

After noting his ideas in his lab notebook, Noyce did . . . nothing. He showed the entry to no one—he did not even have it witnessed—and failed to mention it not only to Hoerni, on whose ideas it leaned so heavily, but also to any other co-worker in the lab. Twenty-five years later, Noyce explained his inaction thus: "We were still a brand new company ... worried about basic survival. That meant getting transistors out the door. The integrated circuit seemed interesting, it was something that might make you some money somewhere down the road, but that was not a period when you had a lot of time for it." This comment offers a compelling reason for why Noyce did not push the lab to work on his ideas, but it does not offer any insight into why he did not at least mention their existence. Perhaps Noyce considered his entry as some form of theoretical doodling—recall that when he made his lab book entry, Hoerni's process was simply an intriguing idea. There had been no evidence that it would actually work. And if it had not worked, Noyce's integrated circuit ideas would have been moot.[21]

Several members of the founding group offer their own provocative explanation for Noyce's silence: the idea was too obvious to bother mentioning. *Of course*, you would want to try to interconnect components over the oxide layer if the oxide layer stabilized the surface of a semiconductor. The idea was positively self-evident.[22]

That Noyce's notebook entry served to codify what virtually everyone in the lab would have said had they thought about it does not diminish the importance of his work. Anyone walking through a display of modern art has privately thought, "I could have done that." Perhaps, but the relevant point is that we did not. The artist did.

JUST SIX WEEKS AFTER Noyce made his integrated circuit notebook entry, Ed Baldwin, the general manager found through the *Wall Street Journal*, announced that he was decamping to form his own semiconductor operation, which would operate as a wholly owned subsidiary of a larger firm, Rheem Manufacturing. Baldwin had probably not planned to leave in March, but Richard Hodgson, who had gotten word of Baldwin's talks with Rheem, flew out to Mountain View and summarily fired him with the immortal words, "I wish you lots of luck—all of it bad." Baldwin did not leave alone. He took with him eight senior Fairchild operations people, including five key engineers, and a process manual detailing how to build Fairchild's mesa transistors. Shortly after his departure, Baldwin met with an employee of William Shockley who wanted to gather more details on Fairchild Semiconductor's operations and their possible link to Shockley Labs.[23]

The Fairchild Semiconductor founders, who felt the sting of having done unto them what they had done unto Shockley, recognized that Baldwin's departure was "a disaster" for the company, not yet two years old. Baldwin had functioned as the firm's de facto CEO, coordinating technical, manufacturing, and business operations, and serving as the official emissary to the parent company—an exquisitely important role at a time when Semiconductor was still receiving its monthly "allowance" from Camera and Instrument.[24]

Noyce was the obvious choice to replace Baldwin. "God, he was head and shoulders above anybody in the business," recalls Tom Bay. "By this time, we'd met most of them." If Noyce were general manager, Moore could more than ably manage R&D, Bay had marketing under control, and Kleiner and Blank knew manufacturing. Furthermore, as Bay put it, "everybody had still reported what they did to Bob" even when Baldwin had been around. Noyce not only knew more than anyone else about what was happening at Fairchild, but he also had a flair for corporate politics and a patience for dealing with nontechnical people that the other founders lacked (and that a few founders found downright distasteful). This skill would be particularly important in working with John Carter and the other Camera and Instrument executives.[25]

As he had a year before, Noyce again resisted the move into management. He had no manufacturing experience, no financial experience, no sense of even rudimentary business tools such as balance sheets and profit-and-loss statements, and no desire to leave the lab, where he was on an inventive roll and "felt sure of [him]self." He had not changed his managerial approach since his days at Shockley: he still displayed the same tendency to make suggestions ("why don't you try" or "have you considered") rather than to issue commands, and he offered the same impression that he was not really in charge of the other men so much as simply happening to do a bit of administrative work in addition to his bench work. He led the weekly lab meeting, but to all outward appearances, the meetings ran themselves. He reviewed monthly progress reports from each of the half dozen research groups and determined which innovations were sufficiently novel and potentially lucrative enough to merit the $1,500 in attorney's fees and hours of work necessary to patent them. But he did all of this in such close consultation with his subordinates that they felt they worked with him, not for him.[26]

In the lab, Noyce had trusted people to fulfill their commitments, and he rarely followed up in a systematic way to confirm that promised work was actually delivered. "If you're looking at a long-term research program, in general, the people that are doing it [the research] are in the best position to evaluate it, not the people that are supervising it," he said. "The people that are supervising it are more dependent on their ability to judge people than they are dependent on their ability to judge the work that is going on." Noyce believed that most people, given enough freedom, will choose to do the right thing. This message had been etched in his mind by his father and was further reinforced during his semester's banishment at the Equitable insurance company while in college. He had spent his days absorbed in actuarial tables, but he thought he noticed that the people who bought the most life insurance tended to die younger than the actuarial data predicted they should have. Noyce interpreted this to mean that somehow people just instinctively knew the right things to do and should be left alone to do them.[27]

Such faith in his fellow man, which he maintained throughout his life, led Noyce to give his employees free rein. This approach worked particularly well in the Fairchild lab because the people reporting to him—the other Fairchild founders and a few choice newly hired employees—neither needed nor wanted to be told exactly what to do or how to do it. Indeed, Noyce was "a very good supervisor of technical people," according to Jean Hoerni, precisely *because* he was "casual" and "didn't interfere" with his researchers' work. Creative freedom and collaboration, which proved crucial to the young company's technical success, blossomed under Noyce's laissez-faire management of the lab.[28]

Even when he was managing the lab, however, Noyce thought of himself as a scientist, not a businessman. "I could direct the work and see that it was channeled properly, so there wasn't any great personal trauma involved in that switch [from scientist to head of R&D]. The switch from directing a research program into directing a complete commercial program, however, was quite a traumatic one." He added, "It was with a great deal of fear of inadequacy, if I can put it that way, that I got into [an] administrative role"—so much fear, in fact, that he would agree only to a six-month trial run as general manager, after which he planned to return to the lab.[29]

During this trial period, Noyce oversaw the introduction of seven new transistors, the building of a new diode plant in Santa Rosa that quintupled the company's manufacturing space, and a ten-fold increase in the size of the employee base, which reached 1,260 at the end of 1959. The R&D operation alone was now as big as the entire company had been only a year before. He also approved the filing of two lawsuits: one charged Rheem with theft of trade secrets; the other, against Baldwin personally, alleged a "breach of confidential relationship." Both suits were settled out of court.[30]

Beyond his work on internal Semiconductor matters, Noyce served as the company's public face. He met with representatives from Japanese electronics firms in town for a conference. He granted interviews and made presentations to the financial community in San Francisco and in New York. He attended several meetings in Syosset and declared "being in on major actions before they were taken" to be "good for my ego."[31]

As general manager, Noyce tried to track the activities in the lab as closely as he could. Back in R&D, Jean Hoerni had spent the six weeks after his January 1959 patent disclosures attempting to translate his intriguing ideas about oxide layers into silicon reality. He asked Jay Last, with whom he shared an office, to build the extra masks he needed to coat transistors with a layer of silicon dioxide. On March 12, one week after Baldwin left, Hoerni invited several people to join him for a dramatic demonstration of his oxide ideas. On his lab table lay a transistor made with the oxide icing and not yet in its canister. Under a microscope, this transistor looked dramatically different from the mesa devices the group had been building. There were no elevated surfaces in Hoerni's transistor; it was flat, with all the electrically active regions terminating in the same plane. Its shape resembled a bull's-eye with one part of the outer ring pulled out a bit to make room for a wire—almost like a teardrop.[32]

Eying the assembled group, Hoerni spat directly on the device he, Last, and their technicians had spent weeks building. Heresy! Transistors were handled with tweezers in rooms as clean as possible. This transistor, however, weathered its nasty baptism with no ill effects, as an attached oscilloscope confirmed. This was remarkable. Any device hardy enough to survive saliva directly on its surface could undoubtedly withstand a pencil tap on its canister. The buzz that arose from the assembled group was surprisingly matter of fact: is this transistor a fluke, or can we make a million of them? Because if we can make a million, then we can bypass this tap problem completely—and Baldwin's stolen process manual will describe how to build a soon-to-be-obsolete product.

A mightily impressed Noyce likened Hoerni's oxide layer to "building a transistor inside a cocoon of silicon dioxide so that it never gets contaminated. It's like setting up your jungle operating room. You put the patient inside a plastic bag and you operate inside of that, and you don't have all the flies of the jungle sitting on the wound." Gordon Moore, the new head of R&D, was more wary. A new process with another masking layer—that would not be easy to implement. Yields would definitely be lower than for mesa devices. Once again, where Noyce admired the inspiration, Moore foresaw the perspiration.[33]

Hoerni's jungle transistor clearly merited a patent. Two, in fact: one for the bullseye structure and one for the process to build it. It also needed a name. Fairchild Camera and Instrument vice president Richard Hodgson, who immediately came to Mountain View to see the device, suggested calling the nearly flat transistor and the process that produced it "planar." He wanted to copyright the name, but Noyce disagreed, explaining that he thought Fairchild would get more advertising value if the industry adopted "planar" as a generic descriptor while Fairchild advertising stressed that the process was invented there. Hodgson deferred to Noyce's opinion.[34]

What happened next is unclear. Something motivated Noyce to dust off his integrated circuit notebook entry in March 1959. The precipitating event may have been Texas Instrument's announcement, in mid-March, of a breakthrough in "Solid Circuits," which purported to be an entire circuit on a single semiconductor chip—precisely what Noyce had described in his notebook entry.

In the fall of 1958, a young Texas Instruments researcher named Jack Kilby set out to build an integrated circuit. By early 1959, he had built a complete circuit on a single germanium substrate. Kilby's circuit was meticulously hand assembled with a network of gold wires connecting the components to each other. The wires precluded the device from being manufacturable in any quantity, a fact of which Kilby was well aware, but his was undoubtedly an integrated circuit of sorts. As soon as the patent work was filed, Texas Instruments proudly announced its invention.

It is not hard to imagine this announcement triggering Noyce's competitive ire. He thought the Texas Instruments circuit was cumbersome— "not aesthetic" was his description, a fairly harsh criticism in a technical world that values elegant, clean solutions to messy problems. Noyce's notebook entry, by contrast, was highly "aesthetic." It required no wires to interconnect components on the chip; it eliminated much of the tweezers' work of connecting chips to each other by hand; and it took advantage of the planar process, one of the most elegant breakthroughs in semiconductor history. Gordon Moore remembers that Noyce called a meeting specifically to discuss the Fairchild response to the Texas Instruments circuit, and that it was during this meting that Noyce introduced his ideas about integrated circuits. No one else remembers the meeting, however, and no record of it survives.[35]

A second version of events holds that shortly after Hoerni demonstrated the planar process, Fairchild's patent attorney asked Noyce and a few key technical men to think as broadly as possible about how the process could be used, so that the patent could be written to cover the greatest number of potential applications. This seems the most likely explanation for Noyce's having resurrected his integrated circuit ideas in March. Good patent attorneys often make these sorts of requests of their clients, and the timing, with Noyce's integrated circuit work coming to light almost immediately on the heels of the successful planar demonstration, makes sense. Moreover, if the attorney's request were the motivation, it would offer a key explanation for why Noyce's version of the integrated circuit ultimately proved so successful. Noyce was not trying to solve an abstract problem. He was completing a specific task: determine a practical and profitable way to use the planar process. Motivation is often underplayed in discussions of invention—the unintended consequences of technological innovation are often of most interest to researchers—but in the case of the integrated circuit, motivation mattered.

Whereas Kilby at Texas Instruments asked "how can I build an integrated circuit?" Noyce wondered "how can this planar process be used?" (Noyce: "I was trying to solve a production problem. I wasn't trying to make an integrated circuit.") Noyce was thus focused on production from the beginning; with this intellectual launch pad, it would have been difficult for him to consider seriously any device that could not have been mass produced. He also thought about selling the device from the moment he conceived of it; his notebook entry considers "cost per active element."

For his entire life, Noyce saw the integrated circuit as essentially a process breakthrough, not a scientific achievement. His children loved to tease him about his most famous invention—when would he get his Nobel Prize for it? His answer was always the same, always tinged with his disdain for abstract theory, and invariably delivered with a smile: "They don't give Nobel Prizes for engineering or real work."[36]

Noyce filed his integrated circuit patent on July 30, 1959. The "principal objects" of the device, according to the patent, were "to provide improved device-and-lead structures for making electrical connections to the various semiconductor regions; to make unitary circuit structures more compact and more easily fabricated in small sizes than has heretofore been feasible; and to facilitate the inclusion of numerous semiconductor devices within a single body of material." The patent application also included a figure that contained within it all the basic elements of the modern complex microchips. Noyce later said that the mother of this particular invention was not necessity, but laziness, that he conceived of the integrated circuit simply because he did not "want to go through all that work [of interconnecting components by hand]."[37]

It is not unusual for an invention to appear in two different places almost simultaneously, as happened with Kilby and Noyce. Indeed, Noyce always maintained, "There is no doubt in my mind that if the invention hadn't arisen at Fairchild it would have arisen elsewhere in the very near future. It was an idea whose time had come, where the technology had developed to the point where it was viable." Noyce's design was founded on existing, mainstream efforts in the industry—and that was part of its appeal. Relative to manufacturing a new element or growing a device atom by atom (as attempted in the defense-sponsored efforts) Noyce's design was easy to build.[38]

Noyce liked to say that the real impetus for the integrated circuit came from the realization not that it would be desirable to put all these devices on one chip, but that it was possible to do so. "Both of these are necessary. You've got to realize that it would be desirable to reach a given goal, and then you've got to have a method of getting to that goal before you can really . . . jump in with both feet and start dumping the effort into it." In his plan to use the planar process to build integrated circuits, Noyce moved Fairchild from theoretical wouldn't-it-be-nice musings to a practical we-can-do-this launch pad.[39]

In 1965, Noyce said that he could "recall very vividly" that at the end of 1959 he "call[ed] a group of technical people together and [said], 'Look this [integrated circuit] is possible [using the planar process]. Now, let's explore every possible way that we could do it besides this way.'" He continued, "From there on out, we laid out a program to go ahead and do it. It was a very conscious decision at that point." This may be the meeting that

Moore recalls in connection with the announcement of the Texas Instruments circuit. Whether the "go ahead and do it" message was transmitted in this single formal meeting or instead through a series of informal conversations, the key point is that the message was sent and it was Noyce who sent it.[40]

The man who bore the brunt of moving the integrated circuit to the third stage, from "it's possible" to "it's finished," was Jay Last. Noyce kick-started Last's interest in July of 1959, when he wandered into the R&D lab and told Last that he thought Texas Instruments would make much ado about its integrated "solid circuits" at an important industry conference called Wescon, held every August. Noyce said that he wanted Fairchild to demonstrate some sort of integrated device at Wescon, too. It was far too early to try to build any sort of complex integrated circuit using the ideas Noyce had outlined in his patent. Instead, Noyce wanted a "show the flag" circuit, a bulwark against Texas Instrument's claims to primacy in the field of integrated electronics.

Last cobbled together a basic flip-flop circuit by putting four transistors on a ceramic plate, making resistors from pencil graphite, interconnecting everything with wires, and putting the plate into a transistor package about a half inch in diameter. This item demonstrated the fundamental concept behind integrated circuits—a complete circuit in a single package—but no one at Fairchild considered it a potential product or even particularly interesting. It was a defensive marketing measure suggested by Noyce and developed and built by Last.[41]

Immediately after Wescon, Last began work in earnest on what he called "microcircuits." He hired Lionel Kattner, who had worked at Texas Instruments, and Jim Nall, who had just won a Defense Department award for fabricating microminiature circuits. Two researchers from other parts of Fairchild—Bob Norman and Isy Haas—also joined Last's group. The team mounted a ferocious campaign to try to build microcircuits. Noyce's patent did not provide much guidance. His patent said that it ought to be possible to build integrated circuits using isolation techniques and the planar process. It did not, however, say how to do it. That was what Last's group needed to figure out. Yes, it ought to be possible to isolate devices with extra junctions, but what did that mean? Did you do it by diffusion, and if so, for how long, and using which chemicals? Did you do it by etching an isolating groove through the back side of the wafer through to the oxide on the front and fill the groove with some sort of inert isolating material? (Last patented this idea.) Did you need to build transistors optimized for use on integrated circuits, or could you use the transistors developed for other purposes? What type of metal would you use to interconnect the components on the chip?

As general manager, Noyce's primary contribution to the microcircuits group was continuing to fund its research and to encourage its researchers. Several employees, including Isy Haas, who worked on the microcircuits team, felt that Noyce was instrumental in Fairchild's decision to pursue work on the integrated circuit, even in the face of opposition from within the company. And there was stiff opposition. Tom Bay and the marketing department worried that integrated circuits would cannibalize transistor and diode sales. Last's boss, Gordon Moore, expected the device would not be a significant product for many years. Most straightforward calculations would have predicted yields on integrated circuits so abysmal as to render it impossible to make money from the business.[42]

Moreover, the integrated circuit was almost prohibitively expensive. A simple gate made with an early integrated circuit would have cost about $150, while another device, identical in function but built with discrete components, might have been $3. Only customers with extreme constraints on size and weight and no limits on cost—in other words, the United States military—would willingly pay such prices. Every additional pound added to the weight of a rocket required an additional ton of fuel to launch it into space. Reducing the payload weight by even a few ounces in this scenario was thus easily worth thousands of dollars to the military.[43]

Despite opposition within the company, Noyce kept the integrated circuits group alive with the quiet support of Moore, who believed the integrated circuit was an "interesting and exciting" advanced research project. Noyce did not feel especially connected to the integrated circuit, but he did believe that creative laboratories were duty-bound to allow a researcher to "go ahead and pursue [ideas] until either he does get somewhere or he proves to himself that he can't get anywhere."[44]

Perhaps the singular experience of Noyce's six-month trial run as general manager came in September, when Fairchild Camera and Instrument exercised its option to acquire all outstanding capital stock of Fairchild Semiconductor. In just the previous nine months, Fairchild Semiconductor had sold $6.5 million worth of its high-speed silicon devices, each of which cost 13 cents to build, for $1.50 apiece—an 87 percent profit margin. John Carter estimated that revenues would triple in the next year and wanted those profits for the Camera and Instrument balance sheet.[45]

On September 24, 1959, Noyce received a Western Union telegram informing him that in a tax-free stock swap, the shares of Fairchild Semiconductor had been exchanged for 19,901 shares of Camera and Instrument stock (with value equal to the $3 million purchase price agreed upon two years earlier). These roughly 20,000 shares were split among the eight founders and Hayden, Stone, the investment bank that had brokered the original deal.[46]

Noyce flipped over the telegram and did some quick math. He, like each of the other founders, now owned stock worth roughly $300,000. He could pay off his debts from school and reimburse his grandmother the $500 she loaned him to start Fairchild Semiconductor. He could replace the Chevy that had made the trek from Philadelphia and was now in such bad shape that his co-founders asked him to park it in the back lot "because it ruins the look of the building to have it parked in front." He and Betty began talking about buying a new house, and they paid for Noyce's parents to travel to Europe. Arthur Rock and Bud Coyle threw a party at Trader Vic's for the founders and their wives. After dinner, Rock gave each of the men an 18-karat gold money clip festooned with a golden horseshoe.[47]

When he called his parents with the news, Noyce did not quite manage to contain his excitement, although he very much wanted to sound casual about his new wealth. Noyce had not originally thought Fairchild would make him rich—as Jay Last put it in a letter home to his parents shortly after the company was launched, "our motivation for going into this is the chance to be our own bosses and to do a job the way we think it should be done, rather than the financial aspects." But the realization that he could indeed become wealthy dawned on Noyce quite early at Fairchild and was, of course, quite welcome. Once the money came, however, it also opened a tiny area of disquiet for him. To put in $500 and two years later emerge with $300,000 did not seem real. The reward seemed too much for the effort.[48]

The acquisition by Camera and Instrument gave Noyce the final confidence boost he needed to accept the general manager's position permanently. At a press conference at the Waldorf Astoria in New York announcing the changes, he answered questions with ease despite being, at 32, the youngest man on the dais by at nearly a quarter century. He privately told Richard Hodgson that he enjoyed the power of the general manager's position—"People used to do things I asked to be cooperative; now they do it because I tell them to do it"—and he reveled in the diverse work the job required: "It's a very satisfying thing, particularly coming from a place [R&D] where you're looking at a narrow field. . . . [S]uddenly you're sitting in a balloon looking down from branch to branch and . . . for the first time you can see the whole."[49]

Noyce had definite ideas about the type of company he wanted Fairchild Semiconductor to become. "We're not ever going to screw a customer," he warned a candidate for a marketing position. "We are going to run Fairchild in an honest way." Noyce went on to explain, by way of example, that Fairchild planned to charge the same amount of money for two different transistor products, even though one was a significantly higher performance device than the other. His reasoning? The yields out of the manufacturing process were roughly equal for the two transistors, so the higher-performance device was no more costly for Fairchild to build than its lower-performance cousin. When the candidate pointed out that demand, not yield, should drive pricing, and that Fairchild could get more money for the higher-performance device, Noyce nearly growled in response: "That's just the sort of shady practice we're talking about [avoiding]!" Noyce's yield-based pricing system prevailed only until large stockpiles of the lower-performance transistor began building up in the shipping area, at which point prices on the more desirable transistor were raised.[50]

Shortly after he became general manager, Noyce asked Jack Yelverton, an MBA whom Eugene Kleiner had hired to write job descriptions and establish salary guidelines, to help him clarify his thoughts about "what makes a good company" and codify them into policy. When Yelverton began talking to him about recruiting, or wage and salary administration, Noyce waved him away with a dismissive "you're the guy who went to business school. You figure that out." It soon became apparent to Yelverton that what Noyce wanted was not nitty-gritty detail on specific personnel issues, but a sweeping "anthropological approach" to company building, a conscious effort to develop what today is called "corporate culture."[51]

Noyce's top objective was to keep Fairchild from becoming Shockley Semiconductor Labs, a place he called "the model of what not to do." Over the course of about three weeks, Noyce explained to Yelverton how he loathed Shockley's mind games, his top-down approach to management, and his habit of playing one employee off another. Most pernicious of all, in Noyce's opinion, was Shockley's love of keeping secrets. Noyce wanted Fairchild to be as open as possible. He wanted "to tell the story as it really is," rather than let rumors run rampant. He and Yelverton talked about one employee lunch room with "no class distinctions"—just a big space with rows of tables. They talked about orientation sessions where every new employee could meet Noyce and the heads of the various departments. Noyce urged Yelverton to devise ways to encourage "frank and earnest expression" because above all, Noyce wanted to lead not through command-and-control methods but by inspiring the "voluntary cooperation of motivated people." Such philosophy echoed the egalitarian teaching of his Congregationalist boyhood.

Noyce's was an unusual approach to management, particularly since the "girls" in the fab, whose work would be classed as "unskilled labor," comprised the fastest-growing group of employees in the company. Noyce well understood that the success of Fairchild Semiconductor would depend in no small measure on the precision and rigor of its manufacturing facility. He thought, however, that the best way to achieve the necessary level of discipline was not to clamp down on the lowest-paid workers but to open up as much as possible. Fab employees had to complete very specific tasks quickly and in a highly routinized manner, but Noyce wanted instructions for these workers to go beyond describing what to do to explaining how each job in the assembly process related to the others. He wanted Fairchild employees at every level to be able to eat with their bosses. He wanted the company to produce an employee newsletter with real data about performance and technology, and he wanted to organize small meetings in which he could personally tell each employee how his or her work contributed to the firm's success.

Noyce and Yelverton felt that these "ethically right" actions would also improve the company's bottom line by increasing employees' identification with Fairchild and consequently reducing turnover, which posed enormous problems. Building a semiconductor device in the late 1950s and early 1960s was as much an art as a science. Even for well-paid and highly sought-after circuit designers and engineers, there were few formal courses and little knowledge that was not best gained directly through a process of trial and error, supervised, however informally, by someone who had already successfully built semiconductor devices. Operators would check a device's "doneness" as they would a cake: looking at color and returning it to the furnace for a few more minutes if it seemed necessary. Work in the fab required dexterity and eye-hand coordination that invariably improved with practice. A single lead welder, for example, would weld more than 5,000 microscopic wires every week. An experienced workforce throughout the company meant lower production costs and better, more reliable products.[52]

Treating employees right—particularly in the manufacturing fab—also helped to keep workers out of unions and unions out of Fairchild. By the early 1960s, organized labor had begun casting covetous eyes towards the semiconductor industry's lowest-paid workers, who seemed perfect candidates for unionization. They worked at highly repetitive tasks for little money and were subject to tight discipline. Recalls one woman who worked on the line at this time: "We could not wear pants to work. We had to wear skirts or dresses under the green nylon smocks Fairchild gave us. Other than two short breaks and one half-hour lunch break, we couldn't stand up during the time [we were on the line] for any reason. You even had to raise your hand and get permission to use the bathroom. Sometimes girls would say they had a headache just to get a break."[53]

But this same employee felt strongly that Fairchild had been a "good place to work." She had health insurance and paid vacation days. When production began to ramp up, Fairchild offered its assemblers a deal: if they committed to reporting to the fab every Saturday, the company would guarantee them work—at time-and-a-half pay. The company had no problem finding people eager to participate in the program.

The Mountain View fab ran a series of breakfast meetings for production employees and managers. Foremen could participate in formal management-training classes taught by Fairchild executives. Another Fairchild plant held a weekly "coffee-conversation meeting" in which a manager invited six assembly-line workers for "cookies, coffee, and conversation."[54]

Paid holidays and overtime, ongoing training sessions, medical care—such personnel practices matched or bettered those usually won through union negotiations. An hour spent chatting and sharing coffee with your boss's boss humanized the white-collar workers and blurred the traditionally sharp line between "labor" and "management." When in 1962 a union attempted to organize Fairchild production workers, it was voted down. The result must have pleased Noyce. The strikes he witnessed when he worked at Philco had left a bad taste in his mouth, and he also thought that collective bargaining by definition undermined individual striving. He believed that it was far better to let a person rise on the basis of talent rather than due to seniority or some other bureaucratic requirement.

Noyce asked human resources chief Yelverton and a young man named Jerry Levine whom Noyce had hired to handle "special assignments," to codify some of the ideas they had been discussing in a policy and procedures book. Much within this book was non-negotiable: the nitty-gritty around signature and approval requirements or reporting relationships, for example. Any work for the military was subject to its own special procedures, and every step in the fab was likewise spelled out in excruciating detail. For other areas, though, Yelverton and Levine consulted with all the department and section heads, hoping to devise "something that worked smoothly and that the people who were subject to it helped to create," in Levine's words. They also talked to managers from Hewlett-Packard, Eitel-McCullough, Varian, and a few other established and progressive-minded local technology companies about how to balance the tension between freedom and discipline.

NOYCE'S MANAGERIAL INSTINCTS might sound idealistic, but humanitarian values were deeply ingrained in all the Noyce boys. In the first years of the 1960s, Ralph was finishing college; Don was a chemistry professor at Berkeley; and Gaylord, now a professor at Wesleyan University (soon to move to Yale Divinity School), had joined the Freedom Rides against segregation, gotten himself arrested in the deep South with several other riders, and was in the process of appealing his case to the Supreme Court, which would later rule in the riders' favor. Bob Noyce took great pride in Gaylord's bravery and ideals, bragging about him to his children and eagerly introducing himself as "Gaylord's brother" when he once happened to meet Martin Luther King, Jr., on an airplane.[55]

In general, the early 1960s were a decidedly heady time for Noyce. The company he managed was growing at a rate of 100 employees per month and selling millions of dollars worth of semiconductors each year. He had eight patent applications on their way to being granted. By the end of 1960, Fairchild had announced the earliest successful tests of a mass-producible integrated circuit, which would be sold under the name "Micrologic." At 33, Noyce had more money than he or anyone else in his family had ever possessed, more money than he could ever imagine spending. And he had no real failures to make him cautious.

He began traveling the world as part of his work. In March, 1960, he spent two weeks in England and Central Europe exploring possibilities for penetrating the European transistor market. Betty joined him on this trip, but not on his three-week jaunt to Japan in June to discuss potential licensing agreements with Japanese firms. The Japanese trip was Noyce's first encounter with a radically different culture, and he enjoyed everything about the country, from its "delicious raw fish" to its orderly streets. He left reassured that the Japanese semiconductor industry significantly trailed the American. Japanese germanium transistors were comparable to a midgrade American device, but he felt the island nation was years behind in silicon. Since he thought Japan was essentially a factory for churning out devices built on ideas licensed from American firms, Noyce saw no harm in licensing select Fairchild technology to a few Japanese companies.[56]

In September, life continued to smile on Noyce as he and Betty welcomed their fourth child, a girl named Margaret. Shortly thereafter, they bought a nice but not ostentatious French-style house in Los Altos Hills with lovely views, a bedroom for each child, and a backyard big enough for a horse. Noyce "felt a little guilty about buying the house" and imagined his parents would disapprove of such an "extravagant" purchase. In general, he thought, men of his age "financially outperformed their parents, which leaves them a little bit estranged from their parents."[57]

Despite this miasma of intergenerational tension, Noyce enjoyed having a bit of money for the first time in his life. He could afford to send his older children to the private school Betty selected for them. On weekends, the family could drive to the mountains around Lake Tahoe, where he taught the children to ski, making his way down the hill with one of them wedged between his legs. Noyce bought a one-third share in a Ryan airplane. He could not legally fly it because he did not have a pilot's license, but one of his co-owners, a Fairchild employee and former Navy pilot, gave Noyce lessons on the sly until Betty told him she did not want to be left a widow with young children.[58]

A strict division of labor marked life in the Noyce home. Bob was responsible for income gathering and large fix-it projects. Betty had full charge of the children and the house. She maintained very high expectations of her children. Betty thought Bob's family a bit crass—his mother dunked her bread in her soup, which appalled Betty—and she sought to counter this influence. The Noyce children had chores and music lessons and extremely good manners from very early ages. Betty wanted them to read well before kindergarten, and they did.

Bob's most significant contribution to the children's early upbringing was to pull them from all religious education when Billy, the oldest, was seven. Noyce thought that the Bible stories and miracles that the children learned about in Sunday School were "not the truth," and that Billy and Penny were too young to appreciate metaphor, which was how Noyce tended to view religious teachings. The family never attended religious services after 1961 unless they were visiting Bob's parents. Noyce did not talk much about religion, though he did on one occasion point out the entrepreneurial and motivational messages latent in the Christmas story, which he appreciated not as a miraculous tale of a virgin birth but as a reminder that "one event, or one man, can substantially change the course of history." In general, he thought that religion kept people from achieving all they could in this life by focusing their attention on the rewards they could expect in the life to come.[59]

With his young family, rising income, high education, and new home, Noyce was an avatar of the changes sweeping the San Francisco Bay Area at the end of the 1950s. More than 3,000 people moved into Santa Clara County every month. Some came explicitly for opportunities in the electronics industry. Others were drawn to the Bay Area by Stanford and Berkeley or by jobs at Lockheed, Admiral, or Kaiser Industries, among the area's largest employers. Almost everyone made the trek for the same reasons that had attracted Noyce five years before: the weather, the proximity to the mountains and the oceans, the easy access to San Francisco, and the near-mythic allure of the Golden State. Because the immigrants to the areas closest to Noyce's home tended to be young and nearly as well schooled as he was, Noyce could watch his neighborhood and the towns around him grow younger, wealthier, and better educated with each passing month.[60]

Even the buildings were edgy, new, modern, and built on idealism. In towns up and down the Peninsula, Joseph Eichler, a liberal developer who lobbied against discriminatory housing practices, was building airy community centers surrounded by affordable, high-concept homes with open floor plans, flat roofs, glass atriums, and radiant heat. IBM's new facility in San Jose, designed by modernist architect John S. Bolles to encourage workers' contemplative activity, was 63,000 square feet of steel and floor-to-ceiling windows with views of the lushly landscaped grounds, banded with a frieze of rectangular yellow, brown, and gray ceramic tiles.[61]

The year 1960 marked the first time that electronics sales on the Peninsula surpassed $500 million. Of the firms engaged in this now half-billion-dollar business, nearly two-thirds were less than a decade old. A test equipment company was born in Palo Alto, a printed circuit firm in Menlo Park. A new Palo Alto-based technical services operation designed and fabbed prototype components, while a crystal-growing facility in Mountain View (founded by another refugee from Shockley) specialized in the manufacture of pure silicon ingots. The number of tenants in the Stanford Industrial Park increased sixfold in five years.[62]

The concentration of firms benefited Fairchild Semiconductor, which could use the mass spectrometer at Lockheed and ask the Bay Area Pollution Control Lab to perform a series of important experiments on silicon oxide. Fairchild could have a Menlo Park firm deliver de-mineralized water, purified to the precise standards the lab required for washing components and mixing chemicals. They could have lenses ground at a company a few miles down the road. It was hard to believe that only two years before, Moore needed to build his own furnaces and Noyce had to scrounge for photolithography lenses at a camera shop.[63]

Sweeping developments unrelated to electronics also benefited Fairchild Semiconductor and Bob Noyce. The increasing mechanization of agriculture in California freed up thousands of low-skilled workers for work in electronics assembly plants. An aggressive state-sponsored infrastructure-building spree changed zoning regulations and installed a network of roads and sewer pipes to attract people and industry to California. In the two decades after the end of the Second World War, the state of California also established its consolidated system of 9 universities, 19 colleges, and 106 community colleges, which could provide an educated workforce for high-tech industry.[64]

Noyce had never before felt as at home in a place as he did in this patch of California, where so much was new, and life changed so quickly. With the dashing John F. Kennedy just elected in Washington, not just this state but the entire country, Noyce thought, seemed full of possibility and promise. He felt, he said, as if the "world were [his] oyster." It was a time when he truly believed "you could do anything you wanted."[65]

NOT EVERYONE AT FAIRCHILD was as happy as Noyce. His move to general manager and Moore's accompanying promotion to lead R&D elevated these two founders above the other six in the corporate hierarchy. Only Vic Grinich, who was named associate director of R&D, held a management position even approaching the level of responsibility accorded Noyce and Moore. Marketing, another key part of the company, was under the control of Tom Bay, who was not one of the founders. Charlie Sporck, a blunt-talking pillar of a man who joined Fairchild from General Electric in 1959, had leap-frogged both Eugene Kleiner and Julius Blank for the top manufacturing position. Several of the founders chafed under the new stratification and resented feeling, as Jay Last put it, like "just another employee working in a research lab for somebody else."[66]

Every founder, regardless of his position in the new management order, noticed that Fairchild Semiconductor was slipping from his grasp as it contributed an ever-increasing portion of the profits of Fairchild Camera and Instrument. Within the boundaries of Fairchild Semiconductor, Noyce and the men who worked for him determined how to allocate resources, whom to hire, which customers to pursue, which products to build, and when to introduce them. But the Fairchild founders had no influence over some of the biggest decisions affecting their company because Fairchild Semiconductor now belonged to Camera and Instrument and had no representative on the parent company's board. John Carter controlled the size of the Semiconductor budget. He determined how its profits were used and whether or not its employees should be granted options on Fairchild stock. Stock options were a particularly sensitive area. Noyce wanted them for senior scientists, engineers, and managers, at the very least; Sherman Fairchild, schooled in the East Coast, big company, gold-watch-on-your-thirtieth-anniversary-with-the-firm approach to benefits, considered stock options "creeping socialism."[67]

The Fairchild founders could only watch with dismay as John Carter, misinterpreting the success of the Semiconductor acquisition as evidence of his own ability to rescue struggling technical businesses, expanded Camera and Instrument's operations almost willy-nilly. Profits from Semiconductor were not reinvested in the division or shared with its employees; instead, they went to buy a cathode tube company and a firm that manufactured offset printing presses and other printing supplies. In short order, Camera and Instrument expanded into space research, oscilloscopes, office equipment, home movie cameras, and stamp machines.[68]

What was hardest for the men who started Fairchild to swallow was that Sherman Fairchild owned roughly 100 times more stock than any founder. Camera and Instrument CEO John Carter owned nearly twice as much stock as did the group of eight combined.[69]

BY THIS POINT, Noyce's attention was focused almost entirely outside the lab. The new diode plant was slated to open in March 1961. Noyce gave a great deal of thought to the job responsibilities of plant manager ("o[ver-head] control, run prod[uction] show, marketing liaison, [good] relations [with headquarters]") and personally interviewed every potential candidate for the job. At the same time, Noyce was trying to convince IBM to buy more Fairchild products. He orchestrated an elaborate meeting with IBM to feature Fairchild in the best possible light. There would be a presentation on the integrated circuit, another on the lab, and a third, by Charlie Sporck, to emphasize that Fairchild was an up-and-coming volume manufacturer ("running 3 M[illion devices]/yr [with] capacity of 25 M[illion]/ yr"). Noyce would close with a discussion of Fairchild as a trustworthy supplier: we are "not guilty of talking about non-existent products," he planned to say. "Others will copy [us]—always have." All this planning came to naught; aside from its purchase of Fairchild's first 100 transistors, IBM was never an exceptionally important customer for Fairchild.[70]

Meanwhile, a senior Camera and Instrument executive had heard that Noyce and Hodgson wanted Semiconductor someday to gain a foothold in the European market. The Camera and Instrument man happened to know the uncle of an executive at Italian business machine giant Olivetti. Olivetti had just started a joint venture called Societa Generale Semiconduttori (SGS) with Telettra, a young microwave company. SGS built germanium transistors and silicon diodes and rectifiers in a modern glass-fronted factory located in a northeastern suburb of Milan. If Fairchild took a stake in SGS, the joint venture would build and sell Fairchild silicon planar transistors, as well. Fairchild Semiconductor would not need to put up any capital or divert significant resources away from United States markets, which were far larger than the fledgling European demand. In fact, all the American firm needed to do was teach the Europeans how to build silicon planar transistors. In exchange, the Americans would have exclusive rights to sell SGS germanium transistors in the United States.[71]

Noyce and Bay liked the idea of penetrating the European market with no capital outlay, but they were unsure it merited trading their proprietary state-of-the-art knowledge about the most exciting development to emerge from Fairchild labs. They did not officially object to the plan, however, and the next thing they knew, Fairchild Camera and Instrument had signed the papers to establish the joint venture.

In very short order, Noyce found SGS a big headache for which even the trips to Italy could not compensate. Fairchild was obligated to send several top production people across the Atlantic to teach SGS engineers how to build silicon planar transistors—a loss Fairchild felt keenly. The SGS venture probably gave Fairchild a two-year lead in the European market relative to what the company could have achieved on its own, but Noyce and Hodgson, who served as directors of the joint-venture, had difficulty influencing decision making at SGS because representatives from the two Italian companies tended to vote together—and against Fairchild— on many issues before the board.

Also preoccupying Noyce were nearly $8 million in military subcontracts with Autonetics, a division of North American Aviation, which was an associate prime contractor to the air force on the Minuteman intercontinental ballistic missile. Autonetics expected to use roughly 1,000 Fairchild mesa transistors on the missile contract and required Fairchild to establish a Reliability Evaluation Division (at a cost of nearly $1 million to Fairchild) that would demonstrate the reliability of the NPN transistors. This special reliability division of the company, which would be administered entirely separately from the rest of Fairchild, needed to accumulate 150 million hours of data on how the company's transistors performed under stresses similar to those the devices would face in a missile shot. Noyce was trying to convince Autonetics to accept planar transistors instead of the mesa transistors originally specified, since he expected planar yields would soon match mesa yields and thus saw no reason to continue making mesa transistors given the greater reliability of the planar devices.[72]

OF ALL THE DISCONTENTED FOUNDERS at Fairchild Semiconductor, none was more disillusioned than Jay Last. He thought Fairchild Semiconductor was giving the product on which he worked—the integrated circuit—short shrift. At the end of 1960, Gordon Moore had told him that he planned sizable cuts in the integrated circuits group. Indeed, the only significant personnel reductions in the R&D budget issued in mid-January, 1961, come from the "microcircuitry" group. It was at about this same time that Moore announced at an R&D staff meeting: "OK, we've done integrated circuits. What's next?" Last, on the other hand, felt their work had barely started.[73]

Jay Last also recalls a general staff meeting in November 1960, at which Tom Bay suggested that the integrated circuit project be scaled back or shut down "since Last has already pissed away a million dollars on it." That estimate was probably exaggerated by a factor of two, and divisions other than Last's were spending money on integrated circuits—Bay himself had approved advertising, sample giveaways, and trade-show marketing for the integrated circuit—but Last says that no one came to his defense. Noyce, who was running the meeting, remained silent. His unwritten policy was to allow people to thrash out their disagreements without his intervening. An employee once broke his wrist banging on a table to make a point during one of Noyce's staff meetings.[74]

Last stood up, announced he was taking a leave of absence—effective immediately—and walked out. He got as far from Fairchild as he easily could, traveling across the country to deliver a series of talks at his alma mater, MIT.

At this point, Arthur Rock, the young banker who had helped with the initial Fairchild funding, re-entered the life of the company. Rock had recently left New York and Hayden, Stone, drawn to California by the "energetic scientists forming around Stanford." Rock and a partner, Tom Davis, a former vice president of the Kern County Land Company who oversaw Kern's investments, had just started a private investment company and raised a $5 million fund with plans to back new electronics companies. Almost all of this money came from Rock's friends in the East Coast financial community, but he also invited the eight Fairchild founders to invest. Six agreed to do so immediately, but Noyce and Gordon Moore felt their positions required them to ask Camera and Instrument's permission before investing. Camera and Instrument immediately forbade them from participating, citing potential conflict of interest. No one noted it at the time, but Davis and Rock were launching the first venture capital fund on the West Coast.[75]

Rock had become a close friend to Jay Last and so knew of Last's longstanding dissatisfactions at Fairchild. Rock had also made the acquaintance of Henry Singleton, a PhD engineer who had left his research job at Litton Industries two years before to start a high-tech conglomerate he called Teledyne. Singleton wanted to start a division of Teledyne to develop advanced semiconductor devices for military applications. In other words, he wanted to start an integrated circuits company.

Rock, who would become one of the nation's top corporate matchmakers, had spent the past few months urging Last, who wanted to oversee an operation devoted entirely to integrated circuits, to call Singleton. Rock had also asked Singleton to contact Last, but neither man wanted to make the first call. Finally, on the very day of the Fairchild Christmas gift exchange—somehow Last, who hated this sort of thing, had been roped into playing Santa—Rock called to say that he had Singleton waiting by the phone, and Last had better call him right now.

After a short conversation, Last and Singleton agreed to meet in person. Jay Last said he would bring Jean Hoerni to the meeting. Hoerni, who saw no hope for advancement at Fairchild with the R&D director's slot now filled by Moore, was also eager to try something new. He and Last drove to southern California—Hoerni hated to fly—and on the last day of 1960, they donned their best suits ("negotiating suits," they called them) and met with Singleton and his co-founder George Kozmetsky at the Teledyne office in West Los Angeles. The meeting lasted several hours and ended well enough that Last and Hoerni left feeling fairly certain they would go to work for Singleton. Restless with adrenalin, they drove far out into the East Mojave, where they had planned a New Year's Day climb in the Old Woman Mountains. They arrived at their campsite just before the calendar flipped to 1961 and stood together under the star-pricked sky, shouting and honking the car horn to welcome the new year and its new opportunities.[76]

Back in Mountain View a few days later, Last had second thoughts. He felt a deeper connection to Fairchild than he had known. He called Noyce to ask him about the future of integrated circuits at the company. Noyce put him off. He still had not found a manager for the new diode plant opening in less than a month. Moreover, the general manager of SGS was in town for the next few days. Noyce hoped a relationship with the Italian executive would give him some leverage at the joint venture. Could Last wait until later in the week to talk?

The question gave Last the answer he needed. In February 1961, he, Hoerni, and Sheldon Roberts (who long ago had told Last and Hoerni that he would leave Fairchild if the right opportunity arose) resigned from Fairchild to start the Amelco division of Teledyne.

The departure of three founders opened the floodgates at Fairchild. In the next few months, a key researcher left to join Amelco. The integrated circuits development team departed *en masse* to Sunnyvale, where they, along with personnel expert Jack Yelverton, started an all-integrated-circuits company called Signetics with $1 million in start-up funds from three investment banks (White Weld, Lehman Brothers, and Goldman Sachs). Another integrated circuits company, Molectro, spun out, as did an operation, started by Gordon Moore's assistant, to build furnaces for semiconductor firms. Moore, with the dry wit he showed only to his closest associates, told Noyce, "If the personnel expansion rate of the last few weeks is maintained, instead of achieving a 60 percent expansion, we are likely to end up with about 60 percent of the personnel."[77]

Eugene Kleiner's departure, in January 1962, left only half the founding team at Fairchild Semiconductor. The group of eight worked together as a group only one more time, and then not by choice. On Christmas Eve 1963, every founder received a registered letter at his home. The IRS had billed each of them nearly $250,000 in back taxes and penalties related to the acquisition of Fairchild Semiconductor by Camera and Instrument. Together the group of eight hired a top-notch legal team to contest the charges. ("I'm glad these fees are deductible," said Last. "I'm glad they are divisible," Moore shot back.) The case was settled out of court to the founders' satisfaction, but not before giving them all a good scare.[78]

The acquisition had caught the attention of the IRS because it seemed somehow *wrong* in 1959 for a young scientist to make more than a quarter-million dollars in a year and a half. This prospect, however, struck the men who left Fairchild Semiconductor in 1961 as not only fair but also potentially reproducible. If they started their own companies, they could run them and hold the majority of stock. Contrast this with their situation at Fairchild, where they had no managerial control, no prospect of moving into senior management, and no significant stake in the company, even though some of these men had been instrumental in its success. To stay on as an employee or to start something new as a founder was a choice between a twice-monthly paycheck and a potential fortune, between what one person who left called "just a job" and "a taste of blood."[79]

Why stay? The market certainly said to go. In 1958, electronics stocks had risen twice as fast as the Dow Jones industrial average; one year later, their value increased another 50 percent. Across the country, new semiconductor firms were spinning out of old. In Southern California, Microsemiconductors spun out of Pacific Semiconductors. In New York,

Silicon Transistor filed suit against an unnamed firm started by its own former employees. Diotran Pacific emerged from Electroglass in Palo Alto, and Melpar sued a group of employees for starting a firm called Scope in Virginia. One estimate holds that by the end of 1961, between 150 and 200 semiconductor operations had emerged from the handful of companies that had existed in the mid-1950s.[80]

Indeed, the frenzy for electronics was so great in 1960 and 1961 that new companies could raise capital on terms similar to those enjoyed by established firms. The Securities and Exchange Commission even felt obliged to issue a warning to consumers about "improper practices in the issuance and sale of space-age stocks." One newspaper reported that brokers were willing to float an issue for almost any company managed by "a bright electrical engineer under 40 years of age."[81]

The people who worked with integrated circuits at Fairchild had an additional motivation for leaving. Moving the Micrologic (integrated circuit) line from R&D to manufacturing—a process that was haltingly progressing at the time of the spinouts in 1961—had revealed a chasm between these two key parts of the company that could easily be exploited. In the broadest terms, a device passed through three distinct stages from concept to product. First, the R&D division determined the feasibility of a certain design, or else discovered a primary effect that might have some commercial value. In the development stage, which is where Last's team worked, slivers of silicon were doped, etched, and otherwise tinkered with until a successful prototype, and then a small batch of devices, could be produced.

The transition from development to the third stage, manufacturing, was in some sense the trickiest part of getting a semiconductor device to market. In manufacturing, several thousand devices were produced every week in a cavernous fab manned by dozens of "girls"—quite a different undertaking from the development stage, in which fewer than 1,000 devices were churned out over several weeks' time in a controlled laboratory setting.

A strangely mystical aura surrounded the move from development to manufacturing. The fact that a device worked in development did not automatically mean that it could be reliably manufactured in mass quantities. Problems appeared in the fab that simply had not existed in the lab. Sometimes the problems would disappear for no apparent reason, only to suddenly reappear. Solutions that worked one time might not work the next. Many elements of semiconductor manufacturing were so poorly understood that the problems encountered were given colorful names, such as "Purple Plague" and "Red Death." Scientists routinely referred to "black magic" and "witches' brew" in describing their process techniques. At Semiconductor, the appearance of one problem after another in transferring a device or technique to manufacturing was so common that, at one point,

Moore was happy to tell Noyce, "No new significant problems have arisen, which is a kind of progress."[82]

By 1961, Fairchild Semiconductor's R&D and manufacturing operations were not just in different buildings, but in different towns: R&D had moved to Palo Alto, and the manufacturing fab was in Mountain View. The tensions between the two sites ran so deep that Moore confided to Noyce that "our transfer procedure is plagued by meetings that must be attended by everyone to protect their positions." Moore and the R&D team resented these delays because every day that the Micrologic elements were not coming out of manufacturing was another day that the development pilot line was occupied with building Micrologic devices instead of moving on to new work. Manufacturing, of course, felt that they were doing all they could to move things along, and they complained that R&D was unwilling to send anyone to Mountain View to help manufacturing get through process troubles.[83]

In later years, Noyce would try to ease the tensions between development and manufacturing. He pulled his staff together to tackle agendas like this one:

Communication lines—how can these be shortened? Decisions must be made!
Reaction time—why are we doing so poorly?
What are problems on transferring new products?
   a. Enough R&D
   b. Enough factory effort[84]

But in 1961, before the first exodus from Fairchild Semiconductor, Noyce seems to have done little to bridge the divide between his development and manufacturing groups. Perhaps he considered this gap and its attendant tensions to be a normal part of the semiconductor business. After all, Bell Labs, the granddaddy of the semiconductor industry, had no manufacturing division at all. Manufacturing was done at a separate, though organizationally related, company: Western Electric. Perhaps Noyce thought that Fairchild would outgrow these difficulties when Charlie Sporck settled into his new job at the helm of manufacturing, or perhaps Noyce wanted to let Sporck and Moore fix the problems themselves, or perhaps Noyce was too distracted with affairs in Italy, Syosset, and elsewhere to pay attention to such nitty-gritty conflicts.

Whatever the reason for the development-manufacturing divide's persistence, the companies that spun out of Semiconductor used it to their own advantage. If Fairchild could not manage to build the products it developed, then the development teams would launch their own companies to build them—and try to make a bit of money in the process.

For nearly a year, when every month seemed to bring the announcement of another new spin-off or another key player's defection, Noyce seemed a bit stunned. Hurt, too, particularly when his fellow founders left. Noyce had occasionally joined Hoerni, Roberts, Last, and Art Rock on weekend climbs or hikes in the Yosemite back country—excursions so physically draining that the men had to help each other out of the car when they got home. Now three of these men had left, with the assistance of the fourth. Nonetheless, when Noyce could push his personal feelings aside, he could appreciate the siren song of wealth and managerial control. He maintained a philosophical attitude and managed a smile and good wishes for anyone who said they were leaving. He also warned them, his tone always friendly, not to recruit too aggressively from the Fairchild ranks. He would rather not take his friends and former employees to court, he said.[85]

Noyce's sadness at his colleagues' departures was certainly eased by the fantastic performance of Fairchild Semiconductor throughout 1961. In that single year, Semiconductor doubled both its share of the world semiconductor market and the size of its product line. Largely on the strength of Semiconductor's growth, Fairchild Camera and Instrument boasted record highs in both profits ($6 million) and sales ($101.5 million), its share price soared, and the stock split two for one for the second time in two years. By the end of 1962, sales were up another 10 percent, profits 14 percent, and some 3,000 people worked for the Semiconductor division.[86]

6

A Strange Little Upstart

Noyce once said that "the job of the manager is an enabling, not a directive job … coaching, and not direction, is the first quality of leadership now. Get the barriers out of the way to let people do the things they do well." He had adopted this approach when he ran the lab, and as general manager, he continued it. He wrote personal notes to researchers whose work impressed him. He poked his head into employees' offices to thank them for their work—and said it sincerely enough that one man so complimented compared the experience to "a hundred percent raise." Many of the elements of Noyce's managerial style trickled through the ranks. Supervisors tended to give the people who worked for them a job and let them do it themselves, with little guidance and often little systematic follow-through to check on progress.[1]

Noyce's disdain of hierarchy, present since he assumed the reins as general manager in 1959, was thoroughly imprinted upon the company within five years. A visitor in 1964 described the "lack of adornments" in the Fairchild building, the "informal feel to the place [with] offices nowhere near as plush as you'd find at a Motorola, where [the CEO's] office was about four times the size of Noyce's office." Noyce would wander through the main Semiconductor building, admiring aloud the family photos that employees had on their desks. He would stop to talk to anyone about anything and knew many details of his employees' personal lives. Noyce liked to gather a group of informed people in a room, listen to their opinions, and ideally, get a broad acceptance on the next steps before he made a decision. His staff—a small group of managers—met weekly over cocktails at Chez Yvonne, a local restaurant. This was in sharp contrast to meetings in other parts of the Camera and Instrument organization, which were held not to make joint decisions but to pass commands from John Carter down to his subordinates. Although the visitor in 1964 viewed the casual atmosphere at Fairchild Semiconductor as evidence of "a lack of professionalism"— "they seem to be playing at going into this. The professional management type of idea just isn't there"— for Noyce, with his egalitarian notions, it was a point of pride.[2]

The Fairchild company newsletter once listed the comments made so often by company managers that they had become signature taglines. Sporck's "executive expression" was a bearish harrumph; Bay's was a distracted mmmhmmm. For Noyce, the comment was, "Well, what's new and exciting today?" Noyce forever looked to the future and its technical promise. In 1965, for example, he told a gathering of financial analysts that he expected one day to see integrated circuits inside of "portable telephones, personal paging systems, and palm-sized TVs." Around the same time, he predicted that "the time will come when every industry will have its electronics shop just the way it has its machine shop right now." At the end of the 1960s, Noyce enjoyed thinking about how he might build thin tiny television screens that could flip down over a pair of glasses for easy viewing. Kennedy's call for Americans to land on the moon thrilled Noyce, who eagerly talked with anyone who would listen about how solid-state devices would best be deployed in the moon shot. He was a lifelong devotee of space travel who, well after it became commonplace to push beyond the confines of the earth's atmosphere, regularly erased his own television interviews to make room for video recordings of various liftoffs.[3]

Noyce's focus on the future and innovation appealed to the creative instincts of many Fairchild Semiconductor employees and permeated the company. To be sure, in the mid-1960s, Fairchild Semiconductor was not a typical semiconductor company. Andy Grove, who joined in 1963, once described Fairchild as "a strange little upstart," a phrase that captures the essence of the organization. Noyce's unorthodox management style was just one innovation launched at Fairchild. In the lab, informal company policy allowed "PhDs to play with their 'toys' [ideas] for about a year" before expecting results. If an idea appealed to a researcher—for whatever reason—he was free to pursue it. This rather loose definition of relevance led Fairchild researchers to develop roughly one-sixth of all major integrated circuit innovations during the technology's first two decades.[4]

Divisions outside of R&D were likewise highly innovative under Noyce's leadership. In 1964, Semiconductor replaced the industry's traditional product-based marketing structure with an application-based selling approach. Instead of a diode or transistor sales manager, for example, Fairchild would have an entertainment-consumer market manager or a military market manager. Each product was shipped with a technical manual that was so much more informative and detailed than any competitor's that the manuals, written by Fairchild engineers, became products themselves. In 1961, Fairchild announced that its semiconductor products would be available not only through distributors (who sold on commission and represented the traditional sales channel) but also via individual representatives who would buy products outright and sell them at a profit. These stocking representatives in effect became a secondary sales force for Semiconductor. In 1967, the company broadcast one of the world's first "infomercials"— a half-hour "Briefing on Integrated Circuits," designed to update and entertain engineers with chipper discussions and colorful illustrations of the state of the art in integrated circuits.[5]

Ever since Fairchild's inception, the focus on innovation had led the company to reject most direct government contract work. Of course, Noyce knew that without the government—specifically, the Department of Defense— Fairchild Semiconductor would not exist. In the company's first two years, direct government purchases accounted for 35 percent of Fairchild Semiconductor's sales, and well over half of the company's products eventually found their way into government hands. The multimillion-dollar Minuteman contract for transistors cemented the company's success, and the vast majority of Fairchild Semiconductor's other early customers were aerospace firms buying products to use in their own government contract work. In 1960, 80 percent of Fairchild's transistors went to military uses, and fully 100 percent of the company's early integrated circuits were used in defense functions as well. The company worked closely with military contractors in designing and building its products. Even by the mid-1960s, when Fairchild Semiconductor assiduously courted the industrial and commercial markets, its products nonetheless could also be found in surveillance radar and transmitters for space vehicles; in Polaris, Minuteman, and Advent missiles; and in the MAGIC airborne inertial guidance computer, as well as the MARTAC missile-control computer.[6]

Though Noyce welcomed the government as a customer and appreciated that federal mandates—such as one issued in April 1964, that required all televisions be equipped with UHF tuners, a law that effectively forced the introduction of transistors into every television in the United States— could benefit Fairchild Semiconductor, he believed there was something "almost unethical" about using government contract money to fund R&D projects. "Government funding of R&D has a deadening effect upon the incentives of the people," he explained to a visitor in 1964. "They know that [their work] is for the government, that it is supported by government dollars, that there is a lot of waste. This is not the way to get creative, innovative work done." He added, "The best way to get something done is to have enough confidence in yourself and your men to do it yourselves."[7]

Noyce also resented that the proposal requests issued by the government were "written as if everyone who bid was a crook," complaining to his son, who was only a boy, that "it's not enough to say they want a certain result; they specify every test to be run, every result they want to see." The bureaucracy this represented—and required in the bidding company— seemed wasteful to Noyce, and he also worried that such specificity limited a lab's creative flexibility to explore the "interesting slop" that might unexpectedly emerge in the midst of research. "A young organization, especially in the electronics industry has to be fast moving," he explained in 1964. "It runs into problems with the unilateral direction mandated by government work." By this point, the company was relatively well established, and Noyce reminisced, "We were a hard, young, hungry group. [Our attitude was] 'We don't give a damn what [money] you have [to offer], buddy. We're going to do this ourselves.'" Gordon Moore shared Noyce's beliefs. Consequently, while other firms in the early 1960s used government contracting as the primary source of R&D funding, less than 10 percent of business at Fairchild was contracted directly by the government in 1963. "And we like it that way," Noyce hastened to tell a reporter.[8]

In the early 1960s, Fairchild began to internationalize its business. Before 1965, with only a few exceptions (among them, SGS, the Fairchild-Olivetti-Telettra joint venture), the United States semiconductor industry researched, developed, manufactured, assembled, tested, and marketed every semiconductor from a location on American soil. Fairchild broke the mold. In May 1962, Noyce's assistant Jerry Levine, who had a penchant for travel and a nose for business, cashed in three years' accumulated vacation days and paid his own way to Hong Kong because he thought Fairchild should consider building an assembly plant there. Levine had been talking about this for months. Labor costs were low in Asia—$1 a day was considered a good wage—and the workforce was certainly capable of assembling and packaging low-performance transistors destined for the entertainment market, which did not have the exacting standards of the military or computer markets.

Nearly everyone who heard Levine's idea thought he was crazy to imagine that Fairchild could send nearly finished semiconductor devices 5,000 miles across the ocean, teach people from a vastly different culture how to assemble and package them, and then ship the devices back to California for testing. Noyce, on the other hand, did not see why Levine's idea should not work. American transistor radios had been fabricated in the Philippines and India for years, and the Bay Area electronics firm Ampex had a successful, small, low-skilled assembly operation in Hong Kong. "Space in Hong Kong. I should work out responsibilities for organization of o[ver]seas operation." Noyce wrote to himself after his meeting with Levine. "My ball," he added, meaning that he needed to take the next step.[9]

Noyce knew that paychecks for people who assembled and tested Fairchild's products were the single largest source of the company's expenses. Texas Instruments and Motorola had both automated chunks of their low-skilled test and assembly processes to cut costs, but a brief experiment with a "semi-automatic assembly line" at a Fairchild transistor plant in 1960 had convinced both Noyce and manufacturing head Sporck that the upfront costs of automation were daunting, and the payoff uncertain since production processes changed so quickly that machines installed one year might need to be retooled the next. One month after Levine's initial trip to Hong Kong, Noyce asked Sporck and Julius Blank, who served as facilities manager, to visit Hong Kong themselves. Sporck and Blank returned to California convinced that Levine's idea was worth trying. Hong Kong offered the three key features of a good plant location: low wages, low building costs, and a large potential workforce of women whose small fingers and dexterity were considered critical for assembly work. Adding to the attraction were special tariff regulations allowing companies that shipped components overseas for assembly to re-import them into the United States for testing and distribution under a special "low-value-added" duty.[10]

Convincing the Camera and Instrument board to go along with the idea was another matter entirely. Noyce and Richard Hodgson, who also met with Levine, formally proposed a Hong Kong assembly plant at the January 1964 directors' meeting and were "practically thrown out of the board room," as Hodgson put it. Hong Kong was undergoing massive development in the early 1960s, and the site proposed for a new semiconductor facility was then completely under water—soon to be reclaimed from the bay by the government. Objections about risk and cost and the untrainability of the women in Hong Kong were aired. Noyce and Hodgson persisted, reiterating the tax benefits and precedents in other industries. The board ultimately agreed to a small-scale experiment.[11]

Beginning in mid-1965, Fairchild shipped silicon wafers from Mountain View to a Hong Kong plant that would produce 100,000 planar transistors per week with the help of a staff of about 12 technical and 135 production employees, each of whom was paid one dollar per day—less than their American counterparts earned in an hour. Later, when wages in Hong Kong neared $2 per day, Semiconductor added production facilities in Korea, where the daily wage was 80 cents.[12]

The Hong Kong facility was the first in a string of some half-dozen offshore assembly plants for Fairchild. By 1965, Fairchild had facilities in five countries—Italy (SGS), Hong Kong, England (an SGS plant in London), Australia (a small lab near Melbourne), and the United States. By 1968, Fairchild employed some 4,000 people in 145,000 square feet of plant space outside the United States—40 times more people and 11 times more building space than five years earlier. More impressive, production output at Semiconductor's overseas facilities had jumped some 500 times in five years.[13]

Other major semiconductor firms, including Motorola, Philco-Ford, Signetics, Transitron, and Raytheon, quickly imitated the offshore move. In less than half a decade, the American semiconductor industry went multinational. By 1974, the 32 semiconductor firms that together represented 75 percent of American production had 69 assembly plants in other countries.[14]

The Hong Kong plant offers a perfect example of how Noyce encouraged innovation and built a culture at Fairchild that welcomed the novel thought or unusual solution. He was not directly responsible for this particular idea, but he gave an employee both the freedom to pursue it and the promise of a thoroughly engaged audience when he wanted to discuss it. Once Noyce believed in the idea himself, he pushed it up the corporate hierarchy with little concern for how foolish it might have sounded or made him appear. Later, the once-crazy idea became standard operating procedure for the entire industry.

The management culture Noyce inspired provided rich sustenance for the young, bright, self-motivated types that Semiconductor courted so feverishly. For these men, fresh out of school and eager to make their mark, the freedom to do their jobs in the way that they believed best was a fantastic reward. To have Noyce, the head of the company, listen carefully to their ideas was exciting in itself.

As a manager, Noyce remained calm in the face of potential disasters that had others panicking. "I remember we lost the process at the diode plant," said one employee. "We simply lost it. I mean, it's like all of a sudden the bread came out of the oven and it was all flat. It just didn't work any more. . . . I said to Bob, 'My god, this is terrifying. Oh my god, we're going die.' He said, 'Oh no. We'll figure it out.' . . . He was completely relaxed about it; it was wonderful [and] calming to me." Noyce could also be brutally competitive—he reputedly sought out the Shockley booth at an industry tradeshow so that he could tell his former boss, "We [Semiconductor] are going to bury you"—but for people on his team, that was an asset.[15]

Noyce's greatest strength as a manager was that he gave people confidence in themselves. Partly this came from the undeniable evidence of his own success—a technical man who made it big on the strength of raw intelligence and unusual ideas—and partly this derived from the potent combination of responsibility and support that he offered his employees. For many of the young men at Semiconductor, Noyce was the guiding light he had himself sought in Shockley many years before.

THE MID-1960s were a time of feverish work for Noyce. In September and October, 1965, for example, he held separate meetings with representatives from seven electronics companies, one magazine, three brokerage houses, and one military subcontractor. He also spent ten days in Japan and two more in Syosset. He recorded far fewer internal meetings, presumably because several were standing commitments and more were informal unscheduled gatherings in corridors and conference rooms. He did note a staff meeting on alternate Mondays, several meetings with both Bay and Sporck, and two with Moore and Grinich on patent protection issues. Noyce spoke to technical audiences and to financial analysts, at the inaugurations of plant sites—Fairchild opened nine between 1960 and 1967— and to two junior achievement groups.[16]

By this time, Noyce was well known within the industry. His children remember him waking them at 6:30 in the morning to watch him in his first television appearance, a debut so fleeting that no one recalls its context. Whatever the audience, Noyce's demeanor in his talks was invariably calm, benignant, and irreproachably informed. At home, though, he sweated over his speeches, and on the rare occasions when his children saw him speak, they noted their father's foot tapping or knee jiggling behind the lectern even while, to the audience, he appeared to be casually leaning against it.

In four years, he made 13 trips out of the country—mainly to Europe for SGS and to Hong Kong and Japan. Roger Borovoy, Noyce's friend and Fairchild's lead counsel, asked Noyce to join in any Japanese licensing negotiations. Noyce drove a hard bargain—one note to himself says "ask for 10% [of licensing royalties], settle for 7"—but Borovoy believed Fairchild "could get much more out of the Japanese if I had Noyce with me. . . . Noyce is God in Japan." Between 1964 and 1967, Noyce went to Japan every year, most often in connection with NEC, the firm to which Fairchild had granted exclusive Japanese licensing rights to Fairchild planar and integrated circuit patents. In 1963, Noyce and Borovoy negotiated the contract. The 1965 visit seems a goodwill gesture. In 1966, Noyce helped NEC defend its exclusive integrated circuit license. When Fairchild's Japanese licenses expired in 1981, they had generated in excess of $100 million dollars for the company.[17]

Among the most pressing of Noyce's concerns during the first half of the 1960s was how to keep his employees motivated. The pace of companies spinning off from Fairchild had hardly abated since the horrible year of 1961, when half the founding team left. By 1965, at least seven companies had been started by people who had left Fairchild—so many that people collectively shorthanded the spinout firms the "Fairchildren." "I'm concerned now with how to copy the original incentive idea that motivated the original eight [of us]," Noyce said in 1964. "We wanted to leave [Shockley] for professional reasons but soon discovered that [we] could become very, very wealthy by leaving, and that became its own motivation." With management in Syosset still refusing any broad granting of stock options and controlling the overall budget of the semiconductor division, Noyce felt his hands were tied.[18]

Noyce also turned his attention again to the integrated circuit, though by now his interest had shifted from the technical aspects of the device to its business implications and its place in the electronics market. An air force experiment had dramatically demonstrated the efficiency and performance capabilities of integrated circuits when the military branch compared two experimental computers from Texas Instruments. One computer contained 8,500 separate discrete components, the other 587 integrated circuits. The integrated-circuit machine performed as well as the discrete model 150 times its size and almost 50 times its weight.[19]

Fairchild had introduced its first commercial integrated circuit, a flip-flop (the basic storage element in computer logic), at an industry convention in New York in March 1961. Throughout that convention, Fairchild had conducted seminars twice daily in the ballroom of the St. Moritz Hotel, strictly limiting attendance to a select group of attendees who had been carefully screened for potential ties to rival firms. Fairchild announced that this circuit was just the beginning; five other members of the "Micrologic family" were in the works, and together the six devices were all anyone would need to build an entire computer logic system.[20]

Computers had been an important market for Fairchild ever since its first sale to IBM in 1957. At that time, computers were still a novelty. The general public received its introduction to the computer in 1952, when CBS television used a UNIVAC 1 machine to predict the outcome of the presidential election. In 1954, a corporation bought the first computer to be used for business (rather than purely scientific) applications. Analysts marked the occasion by predicting that only about 100 corporations worldwide would ever need a computer. In the ensuing years, demand for the machines grew rapidly. To take but one example, in 1956, the federal government had a total of 90 computers. Ten years later, it would have 7,575 machines and a computer budget of $115 million.[21]

In the earliest years of the 1960s, computers were hulking machines, called "mainframes," with various tape drives, consoles, 900-pound hard drives (with a measly two megabytes of memory), and storage devices that together took up entire rooms. The invention of the transistor had shown the way to marginally smaller and significantly more reliable machines driven by silicon, not vacuum tubes. The integrated circuit would accelerate this trend.

Fairchild's 1961 Micrologic introduction generated enormous interest among computer experts and others. The Fairchild booth was jammed throughout the show. The Micrologic devices graced the cover of the daily paper issued at the conference, the *New York Times* ran two articles on Micrologic, and the leading semiconductor industry journal ran five more. Within weeks of the introduction, Philco, which had been in discussions with Fairchild about acquiring a license for planar transistors, began lobbying for an integrated circuit patent instead. Noyce and his patent attorney had one word reply: "tough." It was planar or nothing. Fairchild was not yet ready to permit anyone else to build its newest innovation.[22]

The reaction was gratifying but did not translate into widespread adoption. By the end of 1961, Fairchild had sold fewer than $500,000 of its Micrologic devices, which were priced at about $100 apiece. Texas Instruments, the only other major supplier, was having such problems selling integrated circuits that it cut prices from $435 to $76 in 90 days. The move had little effect.[23]

Customers' objections to integrated circuit technology abounded. The devices were extremely expensive relative to discrete components—up to 50 times the cost for comparable performance, albeit in a smaller package. Many engineers, designers, and purchasing agents working for Fairchild's customers feared that integrated circuits would put them out of work. For decades, these customers had designed the circuits they needed from off-the-shelf transistors, resistors, and capacitors that they bought from manufacturers like Fairchild. Now Noyce wanted to move the Fairchild integrated circuit team into designing and building standard circuits that would be sold to customers as a *fait accompli*. If the integrated circuit manufacturers designed and built the circuits themselves, what would the engineers at the customer companies do? Moreover, why would a design engineer with a quarter-century's experience want to buy circuits designed by 30-year-old employee of a semiconductor manufacturing firm? And furthermore, while silicon was ideal for transistors, there were better materials for making the resistors and capacitors that would be built into the integrated circuit. Making these other components out of silicon might degrade the overall performance of the circuits.[24]

As late as the spring of 1963, most manufacturers believed that integrated circuits would not be commercially viable for some time, telling visitors to their booths at an industry trade show that "these items would remain on the R&D level until a breakthrough occurs in technology and until designs are vastly perfected."[25]

But Noyce was excited by the prospects for this cutting-edge technology. In October 1961, he called the microcircuit "the most important 'Fairchild First' [the in-house term for invention] to date." One year later, Noyce was asking for "more effort on µckts [microcircuits]" at his staff meetings. The next month, it was "µckts must be here!" A brief flurry of customer interest in 1962 proved little more than a frustration because Fairchild could not build circuits in any real quantity. "Inventory on all [Micrologic] short," Noyce wrote with great irritation in May 1962, "13K [orders] backlog." He worried that Signetics, the company started by the former Fairchild integrated circuit team, might be first in line to meet customer demand if it ever materialized in any serious way. He hoped to "find evidence of Signetics infringement [of Fairchild patents]," presumably so Fairchild could send them a nasty "cease and desist" letter and keep the integrated circuits market for itself.[26]

By the end of 1962, Noyce had to admit that the integrated circuit had thus far had "less than a 10 percent effect on our conventional sales." He called his staff together on a weekend to discuss "how to get more effort on micro ckts [circuits]."[27]

Fairchild worked hard in the early years following the integrated circuit's introduction to overcome customers' objections to the device. To give customers some sense of control, the company (as well as others, such as Motorola) permitted buyers essentially to custom design the circuits using methods very similar to what had been standard operating procedure for discrete components. To counter concern about reliability, Fairchild stepped up its in-house testing methods and advertised the strenuous conditions under which the integrated circuits had already been proven to perform. The company also participated in several widely publicized reliability tests sponsored by the federal government, including experiments for the Apollo project. Fairchild advertised that the high up-front costs of integrated circuits might be recouped in reduced costs for space (up to a 95 percent reduction), design and assembly (up to a 90 percent reduction), and power (up to 75 percent reduction). Fairchild even designed its integrated circuit packages to make the devices look and feel like discrete components.[28]

The need to crack the commercial market became more acute after 1962, when Defense Secretary Robert McNamara instituted changes in military procurement and cost-cutting measures that began shrinking the defense market for integrated circuits. (The military would move from buying 100 percent of integrated circuits produced in 1962 to 55 percent of those made in 1965.) Meanwhile, Signetics, the early Fairchild spinoff, began to have some success in the high-end commercial market, which provided equal doses of hope and fear to Fairchild.[29]

"The selling of new ideas is really an engineering problem," Noyce once said. To him it was obvious that despite their other purported concerns about the integrated circuit, customers' primary objection to the new technology was its cost. Had not every other issue been handled? Nor would a glitzier marketing program turn more customers to the integrated circuit. The buyers were extremely technically sophisticated. If their technical objections had been met and they still were not buying, the problem had to be the price tag.[30]

Accordingly, in the spring of 1964, Noyce made a little-discussed but absolutely critical decision. Fairchild would sell its low-end flip-flop integrated circuits for less than it would cost a customer to buy the individual components and connect them himself, and less than it was costing Fairchild to build the device. Gordon Moore calls this move "Bob's unheralded contribution to the semiconductor industry," and it shocked most competitors into a frigid "no comment" until they made the decision to match prices. When a Fairchild distributor asked Noyce if combining the function of several transistors on one integrated circuit and then selling that integrated circuit for less than any one of the individual transistors was a sure path to corporate suicide, Noyce simply smiled in a way that made it clear he did not think so.[31]

In effect, Noyce was betting Fairchild's bottom line against two hunches. He suspected that if integrated circuits could make their way into the market, customers would prefer them to discrete components and would begin designing their products around the new devices. He also calculated that as Fairchild built more and more circuits, experience curves and economies of scale would enable the company eventually to build the circuits for so little that it would be possible to make a profit even on the seemingly ridiculously low price. Gordon Moore has said that Noyce's decision to lower prices to stimulate demand so that the production volumes could grow and the cost of production be decreased accordingly was as important an "invention" for the industry as the integrated circuit itself. "It established a new technology for the semiconductor industry [that holds true] to today," he explained. "Whenever there's a problem, you lower the price. That was as revolutionary a concept to people within Fairchild as it was to the customers."[32]

To explain how volume can more than make up for price cuts, Noyce liked to use a book-printing analogy. The first copy of a book, taken by itself, is extremely expensive because the printer must buy equipment, typeset, proof, and otherwise ready the document for printing. Once the process is in place, however, every additional copy is relatively cheap because the investment in materials and equipment for the original printing is fixed. Moreover, the more copies made, the lower the per-copy price, since the original investment can be amortized over more items. Noyce was betting that once Fairchild artificially lowered the price for integrated circuits, the resulting demand would be so high that his "per-copy price" would actually fall below the price they charged.[33]

"I doubt if Noyce was very sure [price cuts were] the best way," Gordon Moore says, but Noyce was never one to shy away from a calculated risk. Fairchild was already infamous for its aggressive pricing, and integrated circuit prices were already falling in the spring of 1964. Noyce had an intimate familiarity with the realities of the experience curve. Between 1959 and 1962, for example, Fairchild's production of its LPHF transistor line increased 660-fold, with costs only quintupling. The price of the transistor fell by 90 percent, yet revenue grew ten-fold and profits tripled. Noyce suspected something similar could happen with integrated circuits if only he could convince customers to buy them.[34]

There was nothing graceful or subtle in the price-cutting approach; it was, instead, an attempt to develop the market and reduce costs by means of brute force. This brazen play for market share leapfrogged Fairchild to the top position in number of circuits sold each year. At the same time, the entire market for integrated circuits took off. In early 1964, industry-wide integrated circuit sales for 1966 were projected to reach $58 million, or 8 million units at an average cost of $7.25 a unit. Within a year of the Fairchild-triggered price drop, estimates had been upped more than 150 percent, to $157 million annually—remarkable growth, given that the average price per unit had dropped.[35]

LESS THAN A YEAR after the dramatic price cuts, the market had so expanded that Fairchild received a single order (for half-a-million circuits) that was equivalent to 20 percent of the entire industry's output of circuits for the previous year. One year later, in 1966, computer manufacturer Burroughs placed an order with Fairchild for 20 million integrated circuits. By this time, the circuits had begun pulling in radio stations on stereo receivers and amplifying sound in state-of-the-art hearing aids.[36]

The integrated circuit had also come to play a key role in the burgeoning commercial market for computers. In 1964, IBM introduced the revolutionary "System/360 family" of six different-sized computers. To research, develop, build, and market the System/360 series, IBM spent $5 billion, more than twice what it cost the United States government to develop the atomic bomb. The System/360 machines, designed to share software and peripherals such as printers and tape drives, were meant to be "the only computers anyone would need"—and this standardized system ushered in the rapid-fire proliferation of computers in business and government offices around the world. "Electronic Girl Fridays" (as one contemporary characterized computers) calculated payrolls, figured mortgage payments for loan companies, kept track of inventory and utility uses, and processed billing records. By 1967, some 95 percent of all banks in the United States would use computers to handle their checking accounts.[37]

Many of these new machines were "minicomputers," smaller machines that used integrated circuit technology to offer mainframe-competitive computing power at a fraction the size and cost of mainframes. The most popular of the minicomputers was an offering from DEC called a PDP-8, which was the size of several refrigerators and cost about $18,000. In 1966, there were 3,600 minicomputers in use worldwide, all of them dependent, to no small degree, on integrated circuit technology.[38]

As the demand for integrated circuits grew, the lawyers for Fairchild and Texas Instruments continued their fight in the patent courts. In 1964, the patent office interference board split its decision on who owned the patent to the integrated circuit, awarding 4 of 5 claims to Texas Instruments' inventor Jack Kilby. Both sides appealed the ruling, but they also recognized that it meant each company needed a license from the other in order to manufacture integrated circuits. In the summer of 1966, Noyce,

Hodgson, and Fairchild counsel Borovoy met with Texas Instruments president Mark Shepherd and counsel Matt Mims. The group agreed that each company would grant the other licenses. They further decided that any other company that wanted to build integrated circuits would need to negotiate separate licenses from Texas Instruments and Fairchild. With these agreements, each side acknowledged the other's claim to some part of the invention of the integrated circuit.

In October, Noyce and Kilby shared the prestigious Ballantine Medal of the Franklin Institute, presented to them "for their significant and essential contributions to the development of integrated circuits." The citation noted, "The full extent of the [integrated circuit] revolution is not yet in sight: for a dream, the dream of doing things with electronic motion alone, has come true, and the coming to fruition of dreams is a rare event and full of implications difficult to comprehend completely."[39]

Many at Fairchild objected that Kilby's device was not a monolithic integrated circuit at all. In Texas, meanwhile, there was grumbling about Noyce having done nothing more than adapt Kilby's idea for industrial use. A few people who had helped bring the integrated circuit to life at Fairchild wondered how it had happened that once again, Noyce seemed to get all the credit from their company. Why was Noyce's interconnection patent any more important than Hoerni's planar process or Last's isolation work or Isy Haas's patient attempts to build the ideal transistor for use in integrated circuits? Absent any of these, the integrated circuit would never have emerged from the Fairchild lab. Moreover, Noyce had almost nothing to do with building the device, since he moved to the general manager's position even before the patent was filed. His designation as the lone inventor of the integrated circuit from Fairchild struck several of his early laboratory co-workers as arbitrary. Noyce himself freely admitted that his insight "was a question of having these rather vague concepts of insulators, of isolation, of interconnection . . . so that you drew on your bag of tricks to combine these elements to make the integrated circuit. There was no huge lightbulb flashing."[40]

On the most simplistic level, Texas Instruments, not Noyce or Fairchild, was responsible for Noyce, and not someone else at Fairchild, being named co-inventor of the integrated circuit with Kilby. It was Texas Instruments, after all, that claimed that Noyce's patent for interconnecting devices infringed upon Jack Kilby's application for a patent that covered putting more than one device on a single substrate. Once this interference was filed, the Fairchild claim to any part of a potentially enormously valuable product rested on Noyce and his January 1959, lab notebook entry. Noyce did not lobby to be the Fairchild representative in the integrated circuit debacle with Texas Instruments. The opposition drafted Noyce, and then his own organization devoted huge amounts of time and money to ensuring he prevailed.

Moreover, if nearly any invention is examined closely enough, it almost immediately becomes apparent that the innovation was not the product of a single mind, even if it is attributed to one. Invention is best understood as a team effort, with the person ultimately called "inventor" occupying much the same space as the pitcher who has just had a perfect game. The outfielders might have caught a dozen fly balls, the first baseman might have nearly broken his neck to step on the bag an instant before the runner, the catcher might have called for pitches perfectly calibrated to each batter's weakness, but the record books note only that the pitcher threw a perfect game.

So it had been at Fairchild all those years before. The lab team played beautifully, and Noyce never hesitated to admit that his ideas about integrated circuits relied heavily on ideas that were "in the air" in 1958 and 1959. Without Hoerni, without Moore, without Kurt Lehovec at Sprague, Noyce never would have imagined the integrated circuit in the way he did. Without Last or the development team that decamped to start Signetics, Noyce's ideas would never have become marketable products. People all around the country were experimenting with integrated circuits in 1958 and 1959, but no one could offer a practical way to build the devices. That is what the ideas Noyce scribbled in his patent notebook in January 1959, provided. In the same way that the great beauty of Noyce's integrated circuit was its simplified interconnections between existing components, so too did the elegance of his insight lie in its interconnection of ideas already in play. His notebook entry was but one piece of the puzzle, but it was an essential piece, the one that comes at the critical time and slides easily into place—the one that reveals how all the other parts of the picture fit together.

BY THE MIDDLE OF THE 1960s, Fairchild was one of the fastest-growing companies in the United States. In the first ten months of 1965, Camera and Instrument's share price ballooned 447 percent, shooting from 27 to 144, with a 50-point growth in the month of October alone. This was the fastest rise of any stock listed on the New York Stock Exchange at the time. Sales and profits hit another record high. IBM bought the rights to the planar process in a lucrative cross-license deal so important to Noyce that on the first day of the negotiation he blocked his calendar with a giant "IBM" that he wrote, circled, *and* underlined in black, felt-tip pen. (Nearly every other entry is in pencil.) By year's end, only established industry giants Texas Instruments and Motorola manufactured more semiconductor devices per year than did Fairchild. Fairchild facilities ran throughout the night. Salesmen were encouraged *not* to move to their territories so their families would not distract them from the business of selling.[41]

For Noyce, the energy and growth were incredibly seductive. Piloting Fairchild through its acceleration, Noyce told a friend, was a bit like riding a fast horse—that same combination of exhilaration and fear and teetering on the edge of losing control but never quite doing so. He was a success because the company was a success, and it had triumphed because he had triumphed.[42]

AS THE SECOND HALF of the 1960s opened, however, shadows began to form within Fairchild Semiconductor. A two-tiered market for semiconductors had emerged: at one end were mature products available at very low prices, manufactured in very high quantities, and with very low margins. These devices were often used in the entertainment market—as parts for radios, for example—and sold for less than a nickel apiece. On the other end were new devices, technically superior to the old, which were manufactured in smaller runs and sold at higher profits. These devices were used in military applications and also in the burgeoning computer market. Most firms in the young industry, including Semiconductor, served both ends of the market. As a result, the companies needed to function simultaneously as sophisticated research organizations and as mass manufacturer. In 1965, for example, Fairchild sold its integrated circuits of a sort called complementary-transistor logic (CTL) in quantities of a half-million units or more.[43]

At the same time that Fairchild was shipping hundreds of thousands of devices each week, it maintained essentially the same organizational structure it had developed as a tiny startup operation. All manufacturing reported to a manufacturing manager, all engineering to an engineering manager, all design to a design manager. As the gap between development and manufacturing revealed, the different divisions of the company did not readily coordinate operations. There were no product managers to ensure that a product moved efficiently from conception through shipping. The only person with responsibility for more than one division was Noyce himself, and his managerial style did not lend itself to the sort of detailed coordination the company needed.[44]

Adding to the troubles was Noyce's promotion to vice president of Camera and Instrument, an assignment that extended his authority to a new instrumentation division, headquartered in Clifton, New Jersey, which sold semiconductor test equipment. Noyce tapped Sporck to become Semiconductor's new general manager and asked marketing head Tom Bay to run the instrumentation division. With this move, the two men, whose skills had complemented each other's and Noyce's so well, were separated, leaving a vacuum within day-to-day management at Semiconductor.

Between the monthly managers' meetings in Syosset and the requirements of the instrumentation division, Noyce began to split his time in half between the Fairchild Semiconductor offices and Camera and Instrument headquarters in New York. Betty Noyce declared this the perfect reason to move back east. The state of California had begun building a new freeway near their house. Already several fields of mustard and apricot had been plowed under, and the construction noise was drowning out the sound of a brook Betty used to hear from the yard. She dreaded the prospect of seeing and hearing traffic every minute of her life. Bob offered to enclose their property behind a wall.[45]

The freeway, in any case, was simply one in a string of justifications Betty offered for leaving the state. Everything Bob liked about California— the fast pace, the constant change, the opportunity to become wealthy without a family name or pedigree, the relentless drive to perform—she hated. She preferred a life where change was incremental, where people lived in homes that had belonged to their families for generations, and where everyone knew his or her proper place. Bob refused to move, despite his promise, sworn when they first arrived in California, that they would leave if Betty wanted.

As their tenth anniversary approached, it was apparent that Bob and Betty Noyce were fundamentally incompatible. Bob tended to like most people he met; Betty had different standards. Bob always rushed to buy any new technology, any new bit of stereo equipment or electronic gadgetry. Betty collected antiques and enjoyed the old-fashioned craft of quilting. Betty barreled her way through obstacles with sarcasm and intimidation; Bob's approach, as described by Gordon Moore, was to "spend two hours trying to convince someone about the way something ought to be done, rather than [taking] the two minutes in which he could tell them [to do it]." Betty's depiction of a party at Charlie Sporck's house, which she sent to her son Bill in 1963, highlights a few of the differences between the couple: "Da [Bob] went swimming, as did most of the men but very few of the ladies, and did some nice diving and joined in a game of water polo. After he got out and got dressed again, three of the men threw him back in the pool, considering it a very funny joke. They in turn were thrown in by others, which made me want very much to come home, but Da put his clothes in the dryer and was good as new in half an hour, and appeared not to be angry. He's a very good sport!"[46]

Bob and Betty did still occasionally enjoy each other's company. They tiled a wall of their kitchen in a pattern they designed together. They took the children camping in the Sierras and made matching jackets for the entire family. They tried to top each other's Tom Swifties. (Betty: "'My birthday is today,' Tom said presently." Bob: "'We're all out of pineapple juice,' Tom said dolefully." Betty: "'This is our very best ground meat,' Tom said off-handedly.") Every Christmas, they invited all the children they knew to join in an informal orchestra that Bob conducted at a party in their home. When Bob broke a leg skiing and a friend sent him a collection of single socks to wear, he and Betty spent hours sewing sock puppets and naming them. The puppet with a laurel-leaf crown was Sockrates. The tie-dyed sock with string hair was Sockadelic. They made Socko and Vanzetti, Sam the Sockeye Salmon, Sockajawea, and a "sockreligious" puppet from a black stocking to which Betty attached a white clerical collar. To add to the amusement, Betty labeled the socks and had the children hide them in the neighbor's house.[47]

Such fun was too rare. Even when he was not at work or traveling for his job, Bob spent as much time as he could away from home. Every Wednesday, the 12-voice madrigal group that he directed met for rehearsals. He helped Charlie Sporck build his barbeque grill. He took Billy to help tune the carillon at Stanford and to fly model airplanes in a field. He scheduled weekend meetings.

He pushed Betty to buy a ski cottage at Lake Tahoe. "A thousand times he picked us up from a snowbank, dusted us off, and led us up the mountain, the four of us in our matching orange jackets," recalled his daughter Penny. "He did this until we could share his exhilaration." At the end of a day of skiing, he would have the children wait for him while he took one last run, at top speed, just for himself. Betty, meanwhile, would spend the day in the cabin. She liked the mountains more than she liked skiing, and she always felt like an "innkeeper" at Tahoe, biding her time until the family returned and she fed them hot cocoa and dinner.[48]

Bob assembled collections of Fairchild equipment to send to Grant Gale for use in his classes. He further extended his commitment to Grinnell College in 1963, when at the age of 35, he joined the board of trustees. The trusteeship took him to his alma mater for a few days every four months. His fellow trustees fondly called their youngest member "Boy Noyce" when they thought he could not hear them.

Even when he was at home, Noyce sequestered himself in the basement. Here he built an organ, a harpsichord, many model airplanes, a microwave oven. The basement was his refuge, an underground lab for a scientist who no longer did much science, a place where, as his son put it, Noyce could "work on something that doesn't fight back." Betty suspected he was avoiding her.[49]

He was. Betty Noyce's standards of behavior were so high, and her methods of reinforcement so verbally combative—she yelled at and even taunted the children—that Bob worried she was damaging the children's psyches. The children's memories of their "Da," by contrast, are generally tender—his coming to check on them at night, the glow of his cigarette scarcely visible in the dark; his placing their cold mittened hands under his shirt and jacket as they rode the ski lift. He encouraged, and occasionally re-directed, their sense of adventure. When 13-year-old Penny wanted to skydive, for example, he introduced her to a man swathed head to toe in bandages. "This skydiver had a bit of trouble with his parachute," Noyce explained. Then he offered to pay for hang-gliding lessons. "It worked," Penny said later. "I was diverted"—but still soaring through the sky. To be sure, Noyce tried to imbue the children with his own competitive nature. He never understood why they did not want to race for the swim team at the country club or to show their horses competitively. He made elaborate offers related to grades and money, proposing for example, "I'll pay you 40 cents for each A, an A– is neutral, and you pay me $1 for every B"—and then encouraged the children to counter with offers geared to their anticipated report cards.[50]

"He wanted children who were empowered," recalled one of them. "She wanted children who behaved properly."[51]

Whatever Bob thought of Betty's childrearing tactics, he respected the division of labor in the household. He intervened with the children only occasionally and then in only the most passive of ways. When their three-year old, who had been sent from the table for unacceptable behavior, kept returning to provoke Betty's anger, Bob stood up, and without chastising the child or asking Betty to stop yelling, he blocked the door with a chair so the little one could not come in. Then he sat down and resumed eating in silence. Another time, a child had problems keeping her left hand in her lap. Every time her hand approached the table, her mother would slap her wrist. Finally Bob stood up, pulled off his belt, and strapped his daughter's left hand to her chair. For this the daughter was grateful. She could not move her hand, so she could not be slapped.

Betty Noyce was in a difficult situation. Wives were seen as an extension of their husbands for most of the 1960s. Indeed, not much had changed since 1953, when William Shockley had dismissed a potential recruit with a jotted notation in his notebook that he "did not want a man whose wife was annoyed about it all." In 1966, the leading electronics newsletter, which Bob almost certainly read, noted that "American corporations are adopting the practice of taking a careful look at [a man's wife]" and went on to describe "the ideal executive wife" as "a kind of glorified Girl Scout" who not only performed "the standard wifely duties" but also "provides the emotional and psychological balm to relieve the pressures on her tension-ridden husband."[52]

Betty Noyce did not accede willingly to this role. Even when she tried her best to appear demure and self-effacing, she did not succeed. She told a reporter, for example, that "I fear I neglect my housekeeping as a result of all the books I read." In other words, she was not a glorified Girl Scout; she was an intellectual. She also refused to think of herself as an object for display and regularly ran her errands with a head full of wet hair and attired in a sartorial style one friend affectionately described as "not bag-lady, but close."[53]

Betty Noyce resented the situation in which she found herself: a Tufts-educated woman with four small children, a husband who was never home, and a life in a place she detested, far from the place she loved. She disliked cooking—"meals should not take longer to cook than to eat," she often said—and she asked Richard Hodgson, in front of Bob, "Why is it, if we're so damn rich, that I'm still washing dishes?" Moreover, she considered herself Bob's intellectual equal and hated appearing as his appendage at social functions, which she avoided as much as she could.[54]

She found an intellectual outlet in volunteer work. She helped to establish a library in Los Altos and chaired a fundraiser for the San Francisco educational television station. This work allowed her to exert considerable leverage in support of causes that mattered to her—but on a schedule that enabled her to be home for her children. Betty Noyce also wrote, always using a pseudonym, but she was never published. And she created beautiful needlepoint art and quilts, several of which elaborately chronicled the family's activities.

She suspected that her husband was unfaithful. Bob Noyce functioned in a testosterone-drenched world in which all of his equals were men and every woman a subordinate. "The business ran on alcohol and playing around," recalls Jay Last. Noyce's trips to Japan included female entertainment. Salesmen openly joked about buxom blonds in noisy conference halls. At the end of an announcement that a pre-production line was changing buildings, a Fairchild newsletter could note that "all the R&D men will miss the smiling faces of the beautiful young girls in the 4200 line." Noyce was powerful, attractive, unhappy at home, a risk taker who believed in grabbing as much from life as he could, and in regular contact with the "girls" who not only worked on assembly lines and behind reception desks but who also joined the scientists and engineers for drinks after work. He probably did have casual affairs.[55]

Noyce knew that he was becoming "a stranger to [his] own family." He said he envied "people out in the machine shop who could go home at night and sleep with no concern." He was appalled to discover that the longer he stayed at Fairchild, the less he had any interest in anything except business. "What are you as a person when that happens?" he asked. Then he answered his own question: "You're nothing."[56]

MATTERS ONLY WORSENED at the office. While Noyce split his attention between Semiconductor and the instrumentation division, new Semiconductor general manager Charlie Sporck reorganized the firm along the product-manager model made famous by Procter and Gamble. He designated several product managers, all of them engineers, to coordinate production of their specific devices. The reorganization did not fully decentralize the Semiconductor operation, since marketing and central production control (which determined the volumes of devices to be manufactured) maintained centralized operations. Nonetheless, it was a significant change from the organization structure under Noyce.[57]

The changes came too late. By the end of 1966, Fairchild began to miss its promised deliveries, at times meeting only about one-third of its customer commitments. At the same time, the company failed to market new products developed in R&D because the transfer from development to manufacturing was so inefficient that the devices were never manufactured in volume. Indeed, Semiconductor's difficulties in bringing its own inventions to market were so renowned that they generated an oft-repeated industry one-liner: "The first parts coming out of Fairchild R&D were probably made in Sunnyvale." Sunnyvale was home to Signetics.[58]

By the end of 1966, Semiconductor's festering troubles had become apparent even to outsiders. In the fourth quarter, Camera and Instrument's profits dropped below those of the third quarter. Although the parent company publicly blamed the semiconductor division, Wall Street was not fooled. One vice president of Kidder, Peabody spoke for many in the investment community when he said, "If I could just buy the semiconductor division, I might do it, but I can't see paying a premium for Fairchild's management and all the uninteresting stuff you have to take with semiconductors."[59]

At the urging of Camera and Instrument, Semiconductor initiated "FAIRCHILD 71," a five-year planning tool and the launch pad for "a concentrated program of process cost reduction and mechanization [that] established definitive guidelines for expansion." A command to reduce costs infuriated the Semiconductor employees. For years, their division had been more profitable than the company as a whole, with other parts of the company losing money and serving as net drains from the Semiconductor bottom line. And even though Noyce now served as a vice president, the Semiconductor division still did not have a formal representative on the parent company's board. Although another vice president of the corporation served as a director, Noyce did not.[60]

In March 1967, over drinks at Chez Yvonne, a disgusted Charlie Sporck told Noyce that he was leaving to take the job of CEO at the moribund National Semiconductor. Leaving with him were several key integrated circuits men. For months Sporck had been complaining about how hard it was to attract new engineers to Fairchild when competing firms could match a Fairchild salary and offer about 1,000 stock options. Sporck further resented that Camera and Instrument was "throwing away in various directions" money made by the sweat of his brow at Semiconductor. Moreover, he recalls watching the rising fortunes of Semiconductor's spin-offs and wondering, "Why don't I do that sort of thing?" Why not indeed? Sporck

had long thought that he would run a bed-and-breakfast in his native up-
state New York after he left Fairchild, but the offer from National Semiconductor was too attractive. Noyce did not even bother trying to convince
Sporck to stay at Fairchild. He understood his friend's frustrations.[61]

Sporck's departure was personally very painful for Noyce, who leaned
heavily on his strong second-in-command. "I suppose I essentially cried
when he left," Noyce said. "You know, working with people that you're
fond of, then having them break apart, was I would almost say devastating." Noyce asked Gordon Moore, the head of R&D, to serve as general
manager. Moore had kept the laboratory functioning smoothly throughout its dramatic growth. He had required every group within R&D to update him on their activities with a brief weekly progress report. The
technicians had begun their own series of reports that covered issues ranging from the importance of flushing the pipes to the relative merits of
paper towels versus filter paper for drying wafers.[62]

Moore declined the general manager's job. "The rest of the company
[other than R&D] was a mess, and I didn't know what to do about it," he
later explained. Noyce then named Tom Bay, his former marketing lieu-
tenant, as general manager of Semiconductor, a move that did not ease the
company's troubles.[63]

A disquieting uncertainty settled over Fairchild Semiconductor in the
months after Sporck's defection. No one knew who was staying and who
was secretly hatching plans to go when at the end of March 1967, Noyce
and patent counsel Roger Borovoy, along with their wives and Noyce's
assistant Paul Hwoschinsky, traveled to Vienna to negotiate a licensing
agreement. When the Noyces and Borovoys realized that the next day was
April Fools', they decided to play a joke on Hwoschinsky. Noyce called
Tom Bay in California and asked him to send a telegram. The two couples
had carefully worked out the wording:

> Paul. Have just learned that [two senior Semiconductor managers] are
> leaving for National and have reason to believe that Bob Noyce plans to
> join them. Delicately probe his intentions and report back. Urgent. Tom.

Bay agreed to send the telegram immediately, and the group, eagerly an-
ticipating the next morning's foolery, went to sleep.

When they assembled for breakfast, Hwoschinsky looked miserable.
It was clear he had been up all night. Recalls Brenda Borovoy, "Our scheme
had worked perfectly, and Betty, my husband and I glanced at each other
conspiratorially, waiting for the fun to begin. No sooner had Paul cleared
his throat, however, than Bob blurted out, 'It's a joke.' We felt cheated.
How could he? But Bob Noyce, in the face of someone so troubled, could
only be Bob—a nice, honest, and fundamentally good human being."[64]

The merriment in Europe was a welcome break for Noyce. "I just felt that things were falling apart," Noyce would later say of the months following Sporck's departure. Noyce knew that there was no way he could keep high-caliber employees at Semiconductor much longer: the offers from outside were simply "too enticing" and the situation at Semiconductor too dismal.[65]

Noyce was a highly creative man who by 1967 found himself functioning in an almost purely reactive mode: fighting lawsuits, assimilating acquisitions he did not want in the first place, and wrestling with Camera and Instrument management over stock options. His notes from meetings in Syosset deal almost exclusively with administrative details that Noyce would have found mind-numbing: accounts receivable, advertising budgets, organization charts, breakdown of overhead costs, and ongoing personnel issues. At one point, he wrote to himself, "Try to get East Coast out!"—apparently, managers in Syosset were trying to dictate precisely how many people should be assigned to each group within Semiconductor.[66]

Noyce had no respect for senior Camera and Instrument management other than Hodgson. Noyce often told the story of waking up in Syosset to a snowstorm so severe that he could not find a cab to take him to his meeting at Camera and Instrument headquarters. He walked to the building, muttering and cursing to himself the whole way, only to discover that no one else was coming. He had managed to make it from the other side of the continent, but the men who ran Camera and Instrument could not be troubled to attempt the trip of several miles from their homes. Noyce had no use for these people.

By the late 1960s, Noyce was not only alienated from his bosses, he was also out of touch with the innovative, technical side of Semiconductor in which he had taken such pride a decade before. Although he continued to receive copies of all the reports from R&D, this was simply acquiring scientific knowledge, not contributing to it. And while he brought his lab notebook with him to the general manager's office, he did not write an entry in it for nearly three years—and then he wrote only at very scattered intervals. He missed doing science, and even after Semiconductor had grown to tens of thousands of employees, even after it had been years since he sat at a lab bench, Noyce would tell his family that he was "going to the lab" when he left for work each day. "After growing up with a baby, you don't like to abandon it," he ruefully told a reporter about the Fairchild lab. "You'd rather keep in touch, to stay aware of what's going on, but there is less and less time to do this and more and more time that must be spent worrying about other kinds of problems—people, organization, production, marketing, and all the rest of what makes an industry rather than what makes a science." It was no doubt around this time that Noyce, who was nearing 40, began to consider leaving Semiconductor.[67]

While Noyce plotted privately, he urged Camera and Instrument to take steps to soften the blow of Sporck's departure for the rest of the employees—some of whom he knew were wavering—at Semiconductor. Camera and Instrument finally took decisive action. Noyce was given a seat on the board, and shortly thereafter, the directors pushed through a vast democratization of the stock-option plan, authorizing 300,000 additional shares for options. The stock-option committee, which had met only sporadically in the past, began meeting monthly to distribute options. Almost 100 employees, many of them middle managers at Semiconductor, received new option grants. About half of these employees had never before held options. For the other half, the new grant more than doubled their total holdings.[68]

In any case, it was all too late to stanch what had become a hemorrhaging of employees from Semiconductor. Six months after Sporck's departure, some 35 people had left to join him at National. Employees began fleeing Semiconductor from almost every possible exit door. "Suddenly," wrote *Business Week*, "every semiconductor company in the Bay area was able to hire Fairchild professional people."[69]

Semiconductor's fortunes plummeted quickly. In late March 1967, the company announced that several production difficulties had been overcome, but the announcement went largely unnoticed in a tide of bad news. An unanticipated drop in consumer demand throughout the industry meant many customers no longer needed the devices they had ordered. In October, Semiconductor, for only the third time in its ten year history, reported monthly losses.[70]

Due in large measure to Semiconductor's slipping performance, Camera and Instrument's earnings for the third quarter of 1967 were a paltry $137,000—down a staggering 95.5 percent from the preceding year's third-quarter profit of $3 million, and a worse performance than an already leery Wall Street had expected. With the company barely breaking even, the stock price slid to 52 from 92 at the beginning of the year.[71]

In the wake of the appalling third-quarter earnings report, the board of Camera and Instrument ousted the company's high-living CEO, John Carter, and asked Richard Hodgson, the man who first lured the Shockley defectors to Fairchild, to add CEO to his title of president. In 1981, a reporter claimed that Noyce had forced the change of leadership and that in 1967, shortly after Carter's departure, Noyce had proudly told the journalist, "When you set out to kill the king, you'd better kill him *dead*." Noyce's purported intervention seems plausible. With its Semiconductor golden goose so clearly in trouble, and Noyce now a member of the Camera and Instrument board, it is likely that the board would follow his suggestions about how to remedy the crisis. And Noyce undoubtedly would have suggested that Hodgson replace Carter.[72]

Whatever its genesis, Hodgson's elevation to CEO did not generate immediate effects, of course. By year's end, Camera and Instrument, admitting that the semiconductor division accounted for well over half the company's sales, reported a $7.7 million loss. Some $4 million of this were write-offs, but the remaining $3.5 million trail of red ink compared to a profit the previous year of more than $12 million. The company described the results as "a deliberate attempt to group all losses and take the beating at one time."[73]

Just weeks into the new year, it became apparent to Noyce that his fellow Camera and Instrument board members were losing patience with Hodgson's leadership. If Hodgson were to be ousted, no one Noyce respected would remain in the executive suite. Noyce needed to consider his options. He decided to pay a visit to Gordon Moore.

"I'm thinking of leaving Fairchild," Noyce told Moore in the offhanded tone he so often used to announce big news. Perhaps, Noyce said, he would try to start a company to build computer memory chips out of integrated circuits. What did Moore think? Noyce would love to have him as his cofounder of a new company. If he left, would Moore join him?[74]

Noyce must have known the idea of building semiconductor-based memory devices would appeal to Moore. Just a few months before, in fact, Moore had told Noyce that he thought semiconductor memories were "one of the first ideas I've seen in a long time that you could probably start a company on." The computer market was growing dramatically. In the past two years, the number of minicomputers had increased fivefold. Noyce and Moore knew this market well; some estimates contend that by 1968, Fairchild held 80 percent of the computer market for integrated circuits. Meanwhile, the semiconductor industry's progress in squeezing ever more devices onto a circuit meant that soon it would be possible to build an integrated circuit complex enough to be practical for computer memories. Fairchild itself had brought to market two-bit flip-flop chips that could perform memory-like functions. IBM, by far the world's dominant computer manufacturer, announced that it had begun researching semiconductor memories with the intent to use them as the primary memory in future IBM computers.[75]

It seemed to Moore that Noyce's proposal that they start a company together in January, 1968, was another one of his boss's why-not mind flashes—a big idea that Noyce, as was so often his wont, needed Moore to help determine whether or not to take further. Moore told Noyce that while he still believed in the future of computer memories, he liked his job in the Fairchild lab. He was insulated from the Syosset politics, and he ran the finest commercial research operation in the industry. Moore said that he was not ready to leave Fairchild. Noyce made no effort to change Moore's mind.

A month after Noyce floated his proposal to Moore, the Camera and Instrument board stripped Hodgson of power and told him to report to an "office of the chief executive," which consisted of four Camera and Instrument directors: Noyce, Walter Burke (Sherman Fairchild's personal investment advisor), Joseph B. Wharton (a financial and tax consultant), and Sherman Fairchild himself.

Meanwhile, the board announced a search for a permanent CEO. Everyone at Semiconductor, in the industry, and on Wall Street expected Noyce, the logical internal candidate, to be named CEO. Noyce was under consideration for the top spot, but he was surprised to learn that the board felt that while he might "be considered as presidential material someday," he was not ready now, at age 40. The decision left Noyce, in Moore's words, "kind of ticked off": "kind of" only because Noyce probably did not want the job. But he certainly wanted it offered to him. The slight, coupled with the ousting of Hodgson, confirmed Noyce's long-held suspicions that the Camera and Instrument board had absolutely no idea of what they were doing, and no appreciation of the fact that for years Semiconductor had been the tail wagging the corporate dog.[76]

According to one version of events, an irritated Noyce went to Sherman Fairchild and resigned in person, but the chairman (who by now was on the verge of panic) asked Noyce to stay on long enough to find a replacement CEO. Noyce offered his own suggestion for the position—C. Lester Hogan, the general manager of the powerhouse semiconductor division at Fairchild's arch rival, Motorola—and even arranged a meeting between Camera and Instrument director Walter Burke and Hogan. Hogan, however, had no interest in the position. Motorola's Phoenix-based semiconductor operation was already bigger than Fairchild's, and it was not encumbered with aerial cameras and printing supplies. Sherman Fairchild flew down to Arizona in an attempt to change Hogan's mind. Hogan demurred. Finally Noyce flew to Phoenix and spoke frankly about the company and his own reasons for leaving. He urged Hogan to reconsider the job.[77]

Hogan ultimately negotiated a compensation package from Fairchild Camera and Instrument so extraordinary—an estimated $120,000 annual salary, plus 10,000 shares of stock and an interest-free loan to buy options on another 90,000 more—that it was reputedly immortalized as a distinct unit of measure, the "Hogan." (As in, "That guy can't be worth more than half a Hogan.") He brought with him to Fairchild every senior manager from Motorola's semiconductor operation, save one. He even convinced Camera and Instrument to move the corporate headquarters to the Bay Area—tangible evidence of the pivotal role of the Semiconductor division in the corporation. Even given the spectacular deal he finessed, Hogan insists, "I wouldn't have gone if Bob Noyce [had not encouraged me]. I had great respect for Bob Noyce and he's a great salesman."[78]

Noyce formally resigned from Fairchild on June 25, 1968. He included with his brief formal letter of resignation a heartfelt two-page missive addressed to Sherman Fairchild, which Fairchild read aloud at the July board meeting. "As [the company] has grown larger and larger, I have enjoyed my daily work less and less," Noyce explained. "Perhaps this is partly because I grew up in a small town, enjoying all the personal relationships of a small town. Now we employ twice the total population of my largest 'home town.'"[79]

Noyce wrote that he wanted to find or start a smaller company, a place where he could "get close to advanced technology again" and enjoy "more personal creative work in building a new product, a new technology, and a new organization." Again and again he expressed the desire for a professional home nearly completely opposite from Fairchild Semiconductor: not a mass manufacturer, but a "small company which is trying to develop some product or technology which no one has yet done"; not a division of a diversified large organization but a place that would "stay independent (and small)." He acknowledged that "the limited resources of any small company will be a handicap" but claimed to "have no large scale ideas."[80]

Noyce placed a good measure of blame for Semiconductor's troubles on the management of Fairchild Camera and Instrument. "The necessary overall sense of direction and leadership have been lacking," he wrote. "It's not enough to say simply that our objective is to grow and make a profit—everyone is trying to do that." He told Sherman Fairchild that the parent company had grown erratically and irresponsibly, that it had denied Semiconductor the incentives it needed to keep employees; that it "lacked interdivisional awareness, support, and cooperation"; and—most "disabling" and "dishearten[ing]" of all—that it had commandeered Semiconductor's profits to carry other divisions, rather than plowing the monies back into the division. "I believe this has caused our difficulties," he said. He was characteristically careful never once to name a specific person or group of people whom he would hold personally responsible, but it is clear that the culprits, in his mind, are John Carter and the board of Camera and Instrument.[81]

"I accept whatever part of the responsibility is mine," Noyce continued. And he must indeed bear some responsibility for the decline of Fairchild Semiconductor. The very geniality and openness to new ideas that contributed to Noyce's success as a leader and entrepreneur hampered his ability to manage a large organization. As a manager, Gordon Moore recalled, "Bob really thought that the logic of his arguments was the [only] tool he needed to make the organization work." Recalled Harry Sello, who worked at Shockley and Fairchild, "He was too nice to too many people." As Charlie Sporck put it, "You could get him to say yes on something and then the next guy who came in could get him to say yes too, and that was Bob."[82]

Noyce's manner of offering general directives rather than following up on specific process details was ideal for supervising highly creative technical work—indeed, it was the source of his success as the head of R&D—but this management style did not translate well to large, multifaceted organizations. Moreover, Noyce's and Semiconductor's focus on innovation, which had served the company so well in its early years, proved debilitating as the firm matured. It contributed to a culture that privileged research over manufacturing and disdained such routine but important work as knowing inventory levels or the status of an order. As business historian Alfred Chandler has so aptly put it, "Fairchild's problem was that it produced entrepreneurs, not products."[83]

Noyce had long had his own secret doubts about his management ability, and he certainly held himself partially responsible for Semiconductor's fall from grace. He once said that by leaving Semiconductor he "gave up and tried again." He later elaborated: "One thing I learned at Fairchild ... is that I don't run large organizations well. I don't have the discipline to do that, have the follow through. . . . My interests and skills are in a different place, that's all. It's getting people together to do something, but that only works for me in a smaller group."[84]

7

Startup

The news of Noyce's departure from Fairchild took Wall Street investors and nearly everyone in the semiconductor business by surprise. Rumors rushed in to fill the vacuum created by uncertainty: Hogan would spin off Semiconductor as its own company separate from Camera and Instrument. No, Semiconductor would merge with Hughes Aircraft—no, with Jay Last's semiconductor group at Teledyne; no, with Signetics. Charlie Sporck would return to run Fairchild; no, Noyce planned to join Sporck at National to build a new semiconductor powerhouse; no, Noyce was going it alone. The trade press promoted the saga of Fairchild Semiconductor like a particularly juicy soap opera: "the industry has devoured each chapter in the exciting story—readers wonder, 'What's going to happen next?' while they anxiously await the latest report."[1]

"Bob is having a harrowing time, but will come out all right in the long run," Betty wrote shortly after Noyce left Fairchild. The day his departure was publicly announced, telephones began ringing at the Noyce house even before the sun had risen, when one East Coast recruiter, forgetting the three-hour time difference, placed a call at the very start of the work day—and startled Noyce out of bed at five in the morning. A firm in New York City offered "to back you financially in another electronics company which you would head." A Southern California investment group promised to "commit ourselves to no less than $200,000 towards any venture you are heading." Noyce fielded calls from Fairchild employees and competitors, reporters, headhunters, bankers, and well-wishers.[2]

Most people assumed Noyce had turned down the CEO job, rather than having not had it offered to him. Noyce did little to dispel this impression, and he tried to keep his plans for the future from the press, acknowledging only that he would not have enjoyed "pushing more and more paper" at Fairchild. Sherman Fairchild also hewed to this version of events. When asked why Noyce was not the company's new CEO, Fairchild said,

"I don't think he likes management. He has been cooperating with us, but he prefers a technical atmosphere."[3]

In all the hubbub surrounding Noyce's resignation, another departure went "practically unobserved," according to its overlooked subject. Gordon Moore, head of the lab at Fairchild, resigned on July 3, 1968, a date he always remembered because payroll refused to compensate him for the Independence Day holiday. The press may not have paid attention, but the timing of his resignation—one week after Noyce's departure—was no mere coincidence. In May, Noyce, undaunted by Moore's previous lack of interest in starting a company, had tried again. This time Noyce had been much more definitive. He had been passed over for the CEO's job, and he was not going to work for someone new at Fairchild. He was leaving at the end of June. He had talked to Arthur Rock, who after a bit of ribbing—"It's about time!"—had said that if Noyce and Moore kicked in some of their own money to seed a new semiconductor operation, they "wouldn't have any trouble" securing enough additional capital to launch the firm.[4]

Now what did Moore think about joining him?

Moore paused. He strongly believed in the potential of semiconductor memories. He did not want to take his chances on a new boss. And although he and Noyce were not particularly close outside of the office—while Noyce pursued flying and daredevil skiing, Moore enjoyed quiet early morning fishing trips and, as one friend affectionately put it, "weekends spent painting the windows"—they had worked together productively for more than a decade, thanks to their remarkably complementary skills. Where Noyce saw the big picture, Moore could discern detail. Where Noyce had honed his abilities to construct strong connections between Fairchild and various outside constituencies (the press, the board, customers, suppliers), Moore had become an expert leader within the company itself. Noyce rarely set foot in the lab after 1965, but Moore had an intensely loyal following in R&D, which he led with a light hand and a quiet, laid-back style that recalled Noyce's approach but added the extra layer of deliberation and moderation that Moore brought to everything he did.[5]

And for all their apparent differences, Noyce and Moore shared one key trait—a burning competitive desire to *do* something extraordinarily well. To be sure, this drive was harder to discern in Moore than in Noyce, but it was there nonetheless. "Gordon loves fishing, but he doesn't do it for relaxation or mediation," explains one friend. "He does it because he wants to get the fish."[6]

Moore agreed to leave Fairchild and launch a new venture with Noyce.

What would Noyce have done if Moore had said no? It is difficult to imagine Noyce starting a company alone. The experiences at Fairchild—particularly Sporck's departure—had taught him the importance of having a strong team around him. Moreover, without Moore, Noyce would have had difficulty attracting the top Fairchild scientists he wanted for the backbone of a new organization.

Had Moore not agreed to join him, Noyce might have involved himself in some form of venture capital. By the end of the 1960s, more than two dozen venture capital firms had sprung up in the San Francisco Bay Area, many of them targeting the semiconductor industry. In Rock, Noyce knew the single most important player in this vibrant new financial community. Venture work would also have appealed to Noyce's love of starting new things, and he possessed the financial reserves to make a material difference in new firms. Indeed, even before Noyce left Fairchild, he had begun to do a bit of informal investing on his own, giving young entrepreneurs small sums of money and accepting the occasional board seat in their companies.

Noyce and Moore had begun brainstorming together in Noyce's study at home for nearly a month before they officially resigned. During these weeks, a few intimates joined the effort. Andy Grove, a physicist who by his own description "worshipped" Gordon Moore, had invited himself to join Moore in "whatever you're planning to do" within seconds of Moore's telling him he was leaving Fairchild. Moore had not even had time to mention the company's plans or Noyce's participation, much less officially offer Grove a job—something Grove is not sure Moore planned to do. Grove possessed not only expertise in a new semiconductor process called MOS, but also a surfeit of ambition, a fastidious eye for detail, and a take-no-bullshit attitude that had catapulted him to assistant director of R&D. Grove, in turn, suggested the addition of Les Vadasz to the team. Vadasz was an engineer in charge of big chunk of Fairchild's integrated circuit development and another expert in MOS. When he resigned from Fairchild, the human resources manager, instead of trying to convince him to stay, asked how he could join Noyce and Moore, too. Grove also brought in Gene Flath, a former manufacturing foreman at Fairchild who had managed the proprietary integrated circuits group.[7]

Noyce invited Bob Graham, the marketing expert who had argued for demand-based pricing in his job interview, to join the new company. Graham was in Noyce's study on the evening after Senator Robert Kennedy was murdered in Los Angeles. Noyce thought the tragedy, following on the heels of Martin Luther King, Jr.'s assassination, proved that "instead of drawing the people closer together for the mutual good, our society seems to be polarizing itself into antagonistic groups, each with little regard for the rights of the other." The notion of a "mutual good," the achievement of which was the ultimate goal of society, could have come straight from a sermon by Reverend Ralph Noyce. In Bob Noyce's case, the message served as a call to action. No one knew how long he had allotted on this planet. After Robert Kennedy's death, Noyce was more determined than ever to *carpe diem*.[8]

GROVE ALONE among the group planning to leave Fairchild with Noyce and Moore had serious doubts about its leadership. He did not like Bob Noyce. Grove, who had attended two of Noyce's staff meetings, was shocked to see how Noyce let "people bite into each other like rabid dogs" around the conference table: "Bob just sat there [at his meetings]. . . . He wore a pained expression and a slight, somewhat inappropriate smile. His look said either 'Children, would you please behave,' or 'I want to be anywhere but here'—or some combination of the two." Noyce's refusal to take charge irritated Grove, who had, by the time he was 20 years old, hidden in a cellar to elude the Nazis, fled the Communist takeover of Hungary, and crossed the Atlantic to the United States, where, a few years later, he graduated first in his engineering class at City University of New York despite having begun his coursework without knowing how to say "horizontal" or "vertical" in English. Grove had little respect for a man who, in his estimation, "did not argue [but] just suffered." For his part, Noyce probably expected to have little to do with Grove, who was slated to head R&D and report to Moore.[9]

Noyce and Moore officially incorporated NM Electronics on July 18, 1968, with Rock as board chair, Noyce as president, and Moore as executive vice president. "We don't care who has what title," Noyce told his son. "[Titles] are mainly useful for helping the people outside the company figure out what you do." Both Noyce and Moore considered themselves partners and peers. "It's very comfortable to have someone on essentially the same level to discuss problems with," Moore explained in 1994. "He and I had worked together so long, we were very comfortable doing that." The incorporation was a much more subdued affair than the ceremonial dollar-bill signing that Bud Coyle had choreographed to launch Fairchild Semiconductor. Neither Noyce, nor Moore, nor Rock assigned great value to symbolism or ceremony. They signed only legally required papers, which one of the attorneys hired to help with the incorporation then submitted to the secretary of state. Then they got to work.[10]

The new company was incorporated with two million shares of authorized capital stock. Noyce and Moore had considered investing $500,000 apiece—but then, Moore says, "We both kind of gulped at that [much money]." Half that amount, a quarter of a million dollars apiece, was much more tolerable, though it still represented a sizable portion of their personal wealth, nearly all of which, in Noyce's case, was concentrated in Fairchild stock. Noyce's $30,000 annual salary represented a 66 percent cut from his Fairchild pay, but he fully expected his stock holdings in the new firm would cover the shortfall.[11]

Noyce and Moore each bought 245,000 shares in their new company at $1 per share, and Rock bought 10,000 at the same price. Of the half-million dollars thus raised, Moore and Noyce expected to spend $200,000 on equipment and improvements to whatever building they leased. Another $100,000 would go to R&D expenses, with the balance earmarked for working capital. Noyce and Rock also secured a $1.5 million loan to keep the company afloat until Rock could line up private investors. Noyce could not resist bragging to his mother that the company could secure this sort of money largely on the strength of his name, an idea she found almost impossible to believe.[12]

THE SEMICONDUCTOR INDUSTRY was in the midst of a near-ecstatic flurry of entrepreneurial activity at the end of the 1960s. NM Electronics was just one of two dozen semiconductor companies launched in 1968 and 1969. Thirteen of these startups were founded in the Santa Clara Valley, and of these thirteen, eight were begun by refugees from Fairchild Semiconductor, and several had been financed with venture capital. Silicon suppliers reported a 40 percent increase in business between mid-1968 and mid-1969.[13]

In October 1969, *Business Week*, as part of a special report on semiconductors, commissioned a cartoon that captured the spirit of the times. "The semiconductor industry is in a greater frenzy than ever before as companies vie for a slice of the lucrative market," read the caption. At the far left of the drawing stands the headquarters of "Integrated Circuits, Inc.," a low-slung building with a madly whirling revolving door, dozens of employees bumping into each other on every floor, and still other employees tossing a computer out a window. People who can't fit in or out the revolving door (it's quite full) are climbing into the building through windows, or else using the windows to jump to the ground and run to other integrated circuit companies. A man is being plucked from a wall by an automatic arm attached to the shell of a yet-to-be-built building that has a sign plastered to its side: "Roll Your Own Integrated Circuits." There's a shop called "Frontier IC," a lean-to marked "Overnite Integrated Circuits Co.," and an operation the size of a hot dog stand that calls itself "Instant IC Co."

Meanwhile, in the far right corner of the drawing, salesmen are at battle. "Want a beam-leaded MSI Flip-Flop Chip in MOS-Compatible DLT off-the-shelf for $2.14 the unit at 10,000K?" one asks. "That went out back in July!" counters another. "We'll give you . . ." Business-suited people run back and forth; a helicopter emblazoned "Sky Hook Integrated Circuits, Inc." pulls employees from rooftops and chop-chop-chops them through the sky; heavy technical equipment is hauled up the sides of buildings.

The cartoon people look a little addled but perfectly happy. The comic depicts chaos to its readers, but for the folks in the picture, the scene is darn near heaven.[14]

Startup fever ran so high that the major industry trade show in 1969 offered several sessions on management problems, starting companies, and talking with venture capitalists. Attendance at a session called "New Company Start-ups: The Engineer Becomes Entrepreneur" broke all previous records, with nearly 1,000 people either squeezed into the conference room (many sat on the floor or stood in the back) or watching the closed-circuit television broadcast on a stifling August afternoon.[15]

Just as the industry's high hopes for integrated circuits had launched the earlier gaggle of startup companies, the 1968–1969 generation was inspired by a belief that semiconductors were on the cusp of another dramatic technological breakthrough. In 1965, Gordon Moore had pointed out that every 18 months, the number of transistors on an integrated circuit doubled. If this trend predicted by "Moore's Law" continued, the day was not far off when integrated circuits could be orders of magnitude more complex than their counterparts just a few years ago. Already Moore's own R&D group at Fairchild had fit a once-unthinkable 1,024 transistors onto a single circuit. In 1968, this circuit was little more than a lab curiosity, but the general consensus held that circuits with more than 1,000 components integrated together—so-called Large Scale Integrated circuits—should be physically possible to mass produce by 1970.[16]

This era of Large Scale Integration (LSI) would usher in integrated circuits that could not only perform their current functions more quickly and cheaply than ever before but could also do things that had previously been considered too complex or expensive for semiconductors, such as serve as memories for computers or as control drivers for heavy machinery. LSI also promised a boost for a semiconductor company's bottom line because a single chip integrating thousands of functions could drastically cut the cost-per-function while still commanding top prices in the market. Noyce predicted that the economic impact of LSI would eventually rival that of the integrated circuit itself.[17]

Most of the new semiconductor companies formed at the end of the 1960s, including Noyce and Moore's startup, were begun in hopes of bringing LSI circuits to market before anyone else. Noyce and Moore, in fact, had settled on computer memories as a first product not primarily because the computer market was growing—although that was a welcome reality—but because memories would be the easiest types of LSI circuits to build. Memories consist of row upon row of identical transistors, laid out in a gridlike pattern that was far easier to design and manufacture than the mazes of gates and leads used in logic circuits. Moreover, the regular layout pattern cut down on the interconnection and packaging costs that often represented the most expensive and complicated parts of a circuit. In Moore's words, LSI was a "technology looking for applications" in 1968. Which is to say: if LSI technology was going to work anywhere, it would work first in memories. If it worked in memories, Noyce and Moore could anticipate an ever-growing market of computer makers ready to buy.[18]

"I KEEP REALIZING that today your office is at home for the present," wrote Noyce's mother Harriet in July of 1968. She no doubt imagined it quite a come-down from an executive suite at Fairchild Camera and Instrument. "What a lot of thinking about the future and dreaming and playing with a lot of ideas you must have done already. It is a courageous step." In her inimitable fashion she added, "Well, we have no conception how you organize a start. I hope that it is exciting to you and in some way exhilarating, and that you don't feel pushed or hurried into organizing a company before you are ready."[19]

Noyce was more than ready. He threw himself into the launch of this new company with a professional enthusiasm he had not felt for years. He talked to bankers, attorneys, journalists, realtors, equipment suppliers, possible board members, architects, insurance agents, and potential customers. He met several times with his personal accountant. He was happy handling almost any aspect of the company, from drawing up a business plan ("planning, cash flow, how big a hole[?] Cap Equip, People, Revenue, Guess of balance sheet"), to re-immersing himself in technical discussions, to meeting with a fellow who organized softball teams for a popular corporate league, to typing documents and securing tax identification numbers for the new venture.[20]

People from Fairchild were continually resurfacing at this stage, and not just among the inner circle in Noyce's study. When Noyce and Moore found a building they thought might work to house offices and a fab, Julius Blank, still at Fairchild, dropped by to help them evaluate the site. Noyce's contact at the semiconductor company vacating the facility was Dave Beadling, who had once headed Fairchild's work on the Minuteman missile. The company for which Beadling now worked, the semiconductor division of Union Carbide, had been started by Jean Hoerni after he left Jay Last and Amelco-Teledyne. In July and August alone, Noyce noted meetings with a dozen current or former Fairchild employees, most of them looking for jobs. Chances are high that meetings with many other Fairchild people went unrecorded.

The West Coast semiconductor industry was still so small that it seemed as if nearly everyone in a professional position knew everyone else—often from having worked together at Fairchild. Jay Last's Amelco-Teledyne rented space from Ed Baldwin's Rheem, a company later bought by Raytheon, yet another Fairchild spin-off, which years later would hook up with former Fairchild CEO John Carter, who had started his own new company. The industry watering holes—Rudy's, the Wagon Wheel, Dinah's, Chez Yvonne, the Velvet Turtle—were as busy as ever, and the fact that two guys no longer worked at the same company did not keep them from grabbing a table and discussing subjects that would have given corporate attorneys fits. Raiding became a high art, for as Noyce put it, "the schools weren't turning out anyone that knew anything about [semi-conductors, and] consequently the only source of knowledgeable people were the companies that were already working in the field." It seemed people had a greater sense of loyalty to the industry itself than to any particular company.[21]

A key part of Noyce's early work at NM Electronics involved convincing the most capable engineers, technicians, and scientists he knew to join the company. "We are only going to hire perfect people," Noyce told his oldest children one summer afternoon. "A small bunch of people who know what they are doing can accomplish much more than a big group of people who don't know what they are doing." When Noyce attended the Fall Joint Computer Conference in San Francisco he was nearly overrun by men wanting jobs and asking questions. At one point during the conference, he apparently had meetings scheduled with so many Fairchild employees that he simply noted in his datebook, "Fairchild Circus."[22]

Within a month of launching NM Electronics, Noyce was on the East Coast, recruiting for his new venture. "He was like the Pied Piper," recalled Roger Borovoy, attorney at both Fairchild and Intel. "If Bob wants you to come, you come." Early recruiting advertisements requested that applicants "please drop a note with qualifications to Bob Noyce" adding oh-so-casually, "he is still doing our personnel work."[23]

Noyce also hunted for new talent at Stanford. Jim Angell, a friend from MIT and Philco who now taught in the university's engineering department, invited Noyce to address his students. Noyce also told Angell that he was looking for "a good circuits guy who also knows [computer] systems." Noyce needed someone familiar with computers to help determine the most desirable features of semiconductor memories. Angell, himself a systems expert, suggested that he join the company, but Noyce refused to consider pulling him from academics. He had a great respect for teachers and thought Angell was one of the best he had ever seen. And so Angell suggested that Noyce talk to one of the postdoctoral fellows in the department, a young man so gifted with computers that Angell swore he could tell whether a program was running properly by the rhythm of the lights on the display.[24]

Ted Hoff, who would soon be known around the world as the inventor of the microprocessor, came for a job interview at Noyce's study shortly after Noyce and Moore incorporated their company. Hoff had heard rumors about Noyce, the most persistent of which claimed that Fairchild had made him "a millionaire or close to it." One look at Noyce's house was enough to convince Hoff of the rumor's veracity. "If you're in academia and you do something good, you get a nice pat on the back," Hoff thought, as he made his way to Noyce's front door. "When you're in industry and you do something good, people throw money."[25]

Noyce led Hoff to the study and then asked him the central question of the interview: what did he think would be the next big area for semiconductors? Hoff immediately answered "memories," though he had no idea that this was the area Noyce and Moore sought to target. Hoff then asked Noyce if the world really needed another semiconductor company. Several of the Fairchildren had failed rather spectacularly, and Hoff wanted to know why this venture would not follow suit.[26]

Noyce had asked himself the same question. He had briefly wondered if he and Moore were too old—Moore at 39, Noyce at 40—to start a company. Moreover, as much as Noyce longed to "get close to advanced technology again," he was concerned that perhaps he had "been away [from the lab] too long" to jump back into the game. After a bit of thought, however, he had decided that his and Moore's age, if reconsidered as experience, was an asset. As he put it, "the semiconductor business hadn't existed longer than we'd been in it. There wasn't anybody who knew the business better than we did." Noyce was also confident that Moore's familiarity with state-of-the-art advances in the technology more than compensated for his own relative lack of knowledge. And although he was almost loath to admit it, the contacts and skills Noyce had acquired in his managerial work at Fairchild had their own value. Besides, if for some reason this new firm faltered, Noyce figured he and Moore could sell it to a computer company.[27]

In fact, Noyce told Hoff at his job interview, even if the company was not a runaway hit, the founders and early employees could expect to "do quite well," thanks to the stock options they would all hold. After consulting an attorney to find out what, exactly, a stock option was and whether it was potentially valuable, Hoff decided to join Noyce's and Moore's team in the nebulously defined position of "manager of applications research." His reasoning? "I felt I was young enough that this wouldn't be my last job opportunity. If this panned out, great. If not, there would be other opportunities." Hoff may have been too young to know it at the time, but this cavalier attitude was a direct outgrowth of Noyce, Moore, and their six cofounders' decision to depart Shockley a little more than a decade before. In 1957, Arnold Beckman could seriously call leaving an established company for a more attractive alternative "disloyal" and "shameful." Now it was routine.[28]

By the time Hoff and Noyce talked, summer vacation had begun, and the Noyce children, who had not yet left with their mother for their annual summer pilgrimage to the East Coast, were everywhere—in the house, in the yard, swinging on the rope over the pond, or chasing after the pony, who forever seemed to be nudging her gate open and cantering down the street. Added to these distractions was a near-constant stream of visitors and ceaseless ringing of the telephone. When it got to be too much for Noyce and Moore, they would wander through their neighborhood—they lived close to each other in Los Altos—or even commandeer a neighbor's porch in hopes of finding a quiet place to talk and think.[29]

Noyce and Moore spent a good deal of time considering a name for the company. Noyce wanted a moniker that was "sort of sexy," a criteria not met by NM Electronics, nor by Moore-Noyce, an early contender that suffered from the problem of sounding like "more noise"—not an ideal association for an electronics operation. Noyce and Moore considered various combinations of California, Electronic, Computer, and Technology. When none of these choices were available—at least four had recently been taken by other new companies—Noyce and Moore drafted a list of some 20 other possibilities, including "Electronic Solid [S]tate Computer Technology" (abbreviated to "Esscotek"), "Electronic Computer" (abbreviated to "Tronicom"), and "Integrated Electronics" (abbreviated to "Intel").[30]

Noyce liked "Intel," which he felt met the "sort of sexy" criteria because it "implied other things, rather than just another company"— precisely what other things remains unclear, although the association with "intelligence" was obvious. The attorneys found a few other "Intels," including a hotel supply chain in Ohio and an International Television Company in New York, but there were no conflicts that could not be resolved by buying out a license. The new company would be called Intel.[31]

IF NOYCE AND MOORE had a third co-founder in the launch of Intel, it was financier Arthur Rock, who had been urging Noyce to leave Fairchild long before Noyce actually decided to do it. When he began working on the Intel launch, Rock's partnership with Tom Davis had just dissolved, under the terms of its own contract and with great success. Investments made with the first $3 million of the fund (the other $2 million were never invested) were now, seven years later, worth nearly $100 million, thanks in large measure to stakes in Teledyne and Scientific Data Systems, an early scientific computer company. Over the years, Rock had focused on investments in technology, but he considered his real expertise to be identifying good teams with the ability to change their industries and the desire to generate large profits. "The man has to have a killer instinct," Rock said. "He has to know where the game is—on the bottom line." Noyce personally thought that Rock's own competitive intensity accounted for much of the success of the companies he funded. "The main thing is," Noyce explained, "Art likes to win." Noyce, who also hated to lose, admired and worked well with Rock.[32]

The two men spoke daily in the first weeks and months of Intel's existence. Rock had decided to fund the company by selling 500,000 shares in it at $5 apiece. The formal investment vehicle would be $2.5 million of convertible debentures. Convertible debentures, which Rock had used in other funding situations, are a sophisticated IOU. Investors are treated like creditors and are paid interest on their loan—though Intel waived such payments—until the investors convert the debt into equity (stock). If the company went under, the early investors were at the end of the line of creditors. If, on the other hand, Intel proved successful, the first-round investors would together own half the company.[33]

Noyce and Moore wanted any potential investor to know that the company intended to fund both a stock option plan and a stock purchase plan for employees. The founders believed that stock ownership was the best guarantee of both loyalty and innovation. Noyce thought profit sharing encouraged employees to stick with safe products already proven to generate a profit, however small. Owning stock, on the other hand, gave employees an incentive to pursue high-risk, high-reward, next-generation products—precisely the attitude Intel hoped to foster.[34]

Noyce had celebrated his freedom from Sherman Fairchild's muttered curses about "creeping socialism" by beginning to outline stock-option and stock-purchase plans for Intel within days of leaving Fairchild. Rock also strongly supported a generous distribution of stock options. Scientific Data Systems, the biggest hit of his career thus far, had given options to almost all employees.[35]

The dissolution of Fairchild convinced Noyce, Moore, and Rock to design a stock-option plan that discouraged employee defections. "There are too many millionaires who did nothing for their company except leave after a short period of time," Rock noted before proposing that Intel reserve for itself the "option to purchase stock of an employee who quits the company or is fired within a short period of time." Rock also suggested that Intel "wait four to eight weeks before granting any stock options," just to be safe in the churning market for semiconductor expertise. Such practices, which became industry standards, were important additions to the standard incremental vesting procedure already in use at Fairchild and other companies.[36]

Intel set aside options for 100,000 shares to be granted to key employees at a price of $5 per share. On the first day of 1969, a stock-purchase plan went into effect allowing full-time exempt employees to take up to 10 percent of their pay in Intel stock, at the same $5-per-share price through payroll deductions. For at least the first year of Intel's existence, every eligible employee in the company elected to participate in the stock-purchase plan. By the end of 1968, options on 64,700 shares had been granted, and Intel had reserved an additional 25,000 shares for employee purchase.[37]

Noyce spent a good part of the end of July working with Rock to identify potential investors. Intel was too risky for banks, pension funds, and insurance companies who had to abide by the "prudent man" rule of investing, and so Noyce and Rock targeted individuals. Noyce personally received several unsolicited offers of "financial assistance" equivalent to hundreds of thousands of dollars, but he, Rock, and Moore decided to limit the investor pool to people they knew well. They invited each of the other six Fairchild founders, as well as Dick Hodgson and Arthur Rock's old investment firm Hayden, Stone (now chaired by Bud Coyle), to invest up to $100,000 each. Two associates of Rock's—Max Palevsky (the founder of Scientific Data Systems) and Rock's business school classmate Fayez Sarofim—were included on the investors' list, as was Paul Cook, the CEO of Raychem who had recently offered Noyce and Moore the opportunity to start their company as a subsidiary of the materials sciences firm. Noyce suggested also including the Rockefeller investment group, whose manager he knew through Grinnell contacts, and Gerard Currie, who had cofounded a successful young firm called Data Tech that used Fairchild circuits in boards sold to the military. Noyce was a director of Data Tech and an early investor in the company. Noyce also considered inviting Sherman Fairchild to invest, but Rock or Moore must have objected, because Fairchild did not make the short list.[38]

Noyce also wanted Grinnell College, whose board of trustees he had chaired for the past two years, to have a chance to invest. A few years earlier, Joseph Rosenfield, a wealthy Des Moines financier who served on the Grinnell board, had told him that the college would want a stake in any new venture that Noyce started. When Rock began lining up investors for Intel, Rosenfield and another trustee, neither of whom knew technology, each wrote $100,000 checks on Grinnell's behalf. The college endowment invested another $100,000. The trustees, who hoped the investment in Noyce's company would add $10 million to the college's endowment, planned to donate the stock to the college if Intel were successful but to eat the losses if the company failed. Even Warren Buffett, who joined the Grinnell board shortly before the decision to invest in Intel was made, was willing to abandon one of his fundamental rules of investing—only put money into things you understand—in this particular instance. As Buffett put it, "We were betting on the jockey, not the horse."[39]

In case an investor had questions, Rock had Noyce draw up a business plan, which Noyce did by typing up three pages, the meat of which said that Intel was going to try to build semiconductors "not of the types of integrated circuits now on the market" and that Intel "will seek to extend the technology to higher levels of integration." The word "memory" never appeared in the plan. "Frankly," said Noyce, "we didn't want people to know what we were going to be doing. We thought it would attract too many competitors too soon."[40]

What the plan did or did not say was irrelevant in any case. Not a single investor asked to see it. "People had known Bob and were kind of lined up to invest in the company," explains Rock. Fewer than 48 hours elapsed between the moment Rock began formally calling investors and the moment every dollar needed had been committed. While Rock concedes that raising $2.5 million in two days was an "exceptional" feat in 1968, he makes it clear that had the search been launched in an age of email and cell phones, the response would have been even swifter. "Back then," he explains, "people had to return calls."[41]

Many more people wanted to invest than were given a chance to do so. Thanks to a news story that printed Noyce's and Moore's home addresses, Betty Moore received several calls at the house from people who wanted to put money into her husband's company, even though the callers had no idea what it would do. For years after Intel's founding, Noyce was approached by "keenly disappointed" friends wanting to know why they hadn't been invited to invest. He told them Rock had been in charge of financing the launch.[42]

Rock, never an emotionally expressive man, demonstrated his own excitement about Intel by augmenting his original $10,000 purchase by another $300,000. This made him the firm's single largest investor after the founders. Years later, after he had funded dozens of successful companies (including Apple Computer) that together were valued at billions of dollars, Rock averred, "Intel is probably the only company I ever invested in that I was absolutely, 100 percent sure would be a success—because of Moore and Noyce."[43]

THE EASE WITH WHICH INTEL WAS LAUNCHED offers quite a contrast with the frustrating attempt, just 11 years earlier, to fund Fairchild Semiconductor. The founders' track records can be credited for some of the difference. Noyce and Moore had built and run a company that grew into a $150 million enterprise, third biggest in its industry. Arthur Rock, too, had developed a reputation for picking winners. His imprimatur meant a great deal.

As important, however, was timing. The American economy was booming—and the electronics industry was soaring. As the war in Vietnam escalated to once-unthinkable levels, the military spent record amounts on electronics. The industrial and consumer markets were also vibrant. Two months before Noyce and Moore launched Intel, failures of companies in the electronics industry dropped to record lows, with manufacturers failing on average only one-third as often as they had five years earlier. The industry was mature enough to have developed a network of suppliers, employees, lawyers, advertising firms, and other service providers familiar with semiconductors. At the same time, the microelectronics field was still new enough to support fresh entrants. It was, said one magazine, "the Age of Electro-Aquarius."[44]

This ideal moment would not last long, however. *Business Week* declared 1969 "the last year to start an integrated circuit operation . . . and make it big," in light of increasing competition and rising capital costs. In that same year, Congress increased the maximum tax on long-term capital gains from 28 to 49 percent—a move aimed at getting a piece of the venture-capital pie for Uncle Sam and one that had the unintended effect of devastating the venture capital industry. By 1970, many people familiar with the industry believed the semiconductor market was fully saturated.[45]

In the summer of 1968, however, life was so good for most electronics companies that firms up and down the Pacific Coast, flush with success, feeling generous, and hungry for employees, trained "young people from disadvantaged minorities" and "hard-core unemployed" as part of President Johnson's War-on-Poverty programs. In Europe, student protests turned violent. In Chicago, police clubbed Vietnam War protesters at the Democratic National Convention, while in Washington, the United States Army, citing the "large number of civil disturbances" around the country, began construction on an "emergency action headquarters" anchored by a series of computers running on integrated circuit technology and designed to coordinate military action at as many as 25 domestic "hot spots" simultaneously. But in the electronics labs and fabs dotting the San Francisco Peninsula, it was a time of unbridled optimism.[46]

Noyce and Moore were among the most optimistic. They knew that Intel would lose money until production got up to speed, but their business plan assumed only two years of losses. In effect, Noyce and Moore were saying that in 730 days their company would design a circuit, build a production line, produce in mass quantities a technology that had never before gone beyond lab prototyping, and then sell enough of those circuits to turn a profit. The plan has Noyce's fingerprints all over it. Looking back 30 years later, Moore said the agenda was "more aggressive than I had ever planned on."[47]

IN EARLY AUGUST, Noyce left the exhilaration and furor of the Intel startup to spend two weeks with his family, who had passed almost the entire summer in Maine. Noyce joined them in time to close on a house they bought on the coast near Bremen, about an hour-and-a-half north of Portland. The house was modest, but the property was fantastic, nearly 30 pristine acres that ended in a promontory jutting into the Atlantic. From the porch of their new summer home, the Noyces could see only ocean, sky, and the small islands dotting Muscongus Bay.[48]

The house was a concession to Betty, who had wanted Bob to start Intel in Boston. The region around Boston's Route 128 had become a center of high-tech manufacturing when the Santa Clara Valley was still best known for plums. When Intel was started, more high-technology workers could be found in the minicomputer companies clustered along Route 128 than in the low-slung semiconductor buildings on the Peninsula. Noyce had briefly considered a move east at least seriously enough to ask Dick

Hodgson, on whom he had come to rely as a mentor, what he thought of the idea. Hodgson immediately shot it down. "The whole concept of Intel is built around Fairchild, and your reputation and the people [on the Peninsula]. What's Boston got to offer compared to this?"[49]

And so, the Maine cottage. Noyce, of course, could not sit on the porch and watch the days meander by. He called back to California. He built a dock, bought several boats, made multiple trips into town for provisions and tools, met the neighbors, tried to swim in the ocean, and sailed with the family, the sun beating on his back and shoulders while Betty, who disliked getting wet, sat carefully in her life vest.

Betty Noyce, at long last and at least for those two weeks on "her side" of the continent, was happy. She had wanted a home on the East Coast for so many years that even her mother-in-law, with whom Betty preferred to share nothing, knew of her dream. "So Betty's home on the coast is a reality," wrote Harriet, who thought such luxuries mildly sinful, in a letter to Bob. Harriet rather unfairly believed that Betty had made Bob overly interested in money, and she left unsaid what she clearly was thinking: now maybe she'll give you some peace.[50]

Shortly after Noyce returned from Maine, Intel began moving into the Union Carbide building, a 30,000-square-foot manufacturing facility at 365 Middlefield Road in Mountain View, not far from the original Fairchild Semiconductor headquarters. The building was a distinctly Spartan arrangement: even the offices of the "high muckety-mucks" (as Noyce laughingly referred to the management team) were rooms appointed with furniture cast off from the previous occupant. These offices, which lined the front of the building, were so small and crammed together that Noyce estimated that nobody was ever more than 20 steps away from another person—close enough to call meetings by hollering. It was quite a change from Noyce's office at Fairchild, which Syosset management had insisted on having professionally decorated by an interior designer. The arrangement of the offices of Intel perfectly reflected the roles that the young company's executives would play. Noyce sat nearest the front door. R&D director Grove sat closest to the middle of the building, near the research area. Moore's office was between these two.[51]

Intel's first official communications center was a long table with three telephones (each with its own number) lined up across the top. The corporate "cafeteria" was a bare room with about six tables, a couple dozen chairs, a few vending machines, a bulletin board, and a sink with a rack behind it for coffee cups.[52]

Union Carbide had not entirely moved out of the fab area in the back of the building that Intel intended to upgrade and use as its own manufacturing facility. Old Union Carbide equipment punctuated the cavernous space at odd angles and in random locations. Pipes poked from the ceiling.

Wires drooped from the walls. The tile floor had more holes than tiles. Below the floor, things got even worse. The sewer pipe running out to the street had been completely eaten away by the acids Union Carbide had washed down the sinks.[53]

It was either a disaster or an opportunity. Gene Flath decided the disarray gave him carte blanche to choose precisely where and how to build the fab that Intel needed. He began drawing up a plan. When Wescon, the annual trade show for which almost a decade earlier Noyce had asked Last to demonstrate a rudimentary integrated circuit, opened in Los Angeles, Flath attended, "with the equivalent of a checkbook" in hand. Flath went straight to the suppliers and equipment manufacturers' booths at Wescon and proceeded to order equipment for the Intel fab right off the show floor: "I'll have one of those, two of those, three of these." A bank of furnaces, an evaporator, a lithography machine. The astonished salesmen, far more used to wooing and haggling that could stretch weeks, were writing makeshift purchase orders on the backs of random sheets of paper.[54]

When it came time for the first Intel Christmas party, the company was still small enough that all 30 employees and their spouses could fit into Gordon Moore's living room, where they drank themselves silly on a sweet, fruity Boston Fish House Punch brewed with a potency only a chemist like Moore could devise. Gordon and Betty Moore rarely hosted parties, but Betty Noyce had already announced at an earlier and smaller gathering that she was never again planning to engage in the sort of business socializing that had been expected of her at Fairchild. Her announcement had struck many as rude, but Betty had always found superficial conversation—particularly with those who knew her only as "Bob's wife"—stressful. In her own mind, she was simply exercising her prerogative, as the wife of the man who made the rules, not to put herself into that situation again.[55]

Every one of the 30 employees who celebrated that December night was technically oriented with the exception of a Controller, a receptionist, and a senior secretary from Fairchild, Jean Jones, who agreed to help out after being promised that she would only need to work part-time. Several of the newest hires—Hoff from Stanford, Dick Bohn from Sylvania, Skip Fehr from Texas Instruments, and Bob O'Hare from ITT—had not personally known the Intel founders, but had jumped at the opportunity to work with them for the same reason Noyce and Moore had wanted to work for Shockley. "They were absolutely the gods of the industry," explained one early employee, using language almost identical to Noyce's claim that the first call from Shockley was like hearing from God. Minor deities though Noyce and Moore might be, they did not have the final word on hiring. Andy Grove had the power to veto any technical hire.[56]

A move to Intel was not an immediately lucrative proposition. Intel engineers were brought over at an average salary of $1,000 per month, plus options on 1,000 shares. This package was competitive, but not spectacular—Noyce and Moore knew, in the words of one early employee, that Intel "really had, frankly, a lot of sex appeal." This employee recalls being impressed with the team and the "technical challenge" they were pursuing: "These guys seemed to be holding the challenge in their hands and steering the future."[57]

IF NOYCE HAD WANTED Fairchild to be the anti-Shockley, then Intel was the anti-Fairchild. The decision to structure Intel as what Noyce called "a two-headed monster," with power split evenly between him and Gordon Moore, was a direct result of Noyce's having confronted his own managerial limitations at Fairchild. Intel's board of directors, which included Rock, Noyce, Moore, Richard Hodgson, and senior executives from several computer companies who could bring a customer's perspective to board deliberations, was an intentional response to Noyce's experiences with the Fairchild trustees who had been unburdened with any knowledge of semiconductors.[58]

The ghost of Fairchild cast long shadows over technical day-to-day operations at Intel, as well. Because the difficulties in transferring devices from development to manufacturing at Fairchild were legion, the Intel founders completely erased the distinctions between the two divisions. Where other companies had one line for developing prototypes and another for mass-production runs, Intel had a single line. Processes developed in R&D were tested and fine-tuned with the same equipment used for commercial manufacturing. By "co-locating" development and manufacturing in this way, Moore and Noyce hoped to ensure that Intel did not waste its time developing high-concept devices that could not be built. Noyce and Moore further ensured the integration of R&D and manufacturing when they gave overall responsibility for production to Andy Grove, who had a theoretical and research background.

Noyce and Moore decided to orient Intel 180-degrees away from Fairchild in product mix. Where Fairchild built huge volumes of relatively easy-to-manufacture, low-margin chips and engaged in the price cutting and trench warfare that this approach necessitated, Intel would be tightly focused on being first to market with state-of-the-art devices that could command high prices and generate high profits that could be plowed back into R&D. By the time other firms entered the market and drove prices down, Intel would pull from its quiver a next-generation device that would once again command high prices until other companies could join the fray and the cycle would begin again.[59]

Secrecy was essential for Noyce and Moore's plan to work. Intel scientists did not give talks that could benefit competitors. They did not publish technical papers. This, too, was in direct opposition to the culture at

Fairchild, and at most semiconductor companies and research labs, where PhDs openly discussed their findings at conferences or in print. The only currency in the Fairchild lab had been scientific prestige, but at Intel, the researchers had stock, which they knew would be worthless if they spread secrets around town.

On a more philosophical level, too, Noyce wanted Intel to be the anti-Fairchild. Fairchild, he said, had come to be managed by "group think," which killed innovation. He admitted that his personal drive for consensus was partially responsible for "group think," which he defined this way: "any decision to go along with a new product innovation had to pass through a narrow gate. A single negative vote could kill a project, and one positive vote was worth approximately zero." He wondered aloud if he would do better to champion a policy in which "a single 'yes' could initiate action."[60]

Where Fairchild had lumbered in the last few years, Noyce and Moore wanted Intel to race. "Use money to buy time because money is cheaper than time," Noyce told Gene Flath, who had, of course, put this philosophy into practice when he bought equipment off the trade show floor. In the white-hot semiconductor industry of the late 1960s, being first to market would put Intel in the position of what Gordon Moore called "a rifleman who shoots at a blank wall, finds the bullet hole, and then paints the target around it." The first company in the market always hits the bull's-eye because that company can draw the target around its own shot. Any late arrivals find the target already in place, the market defined by someone else.[61]

"ALL WE [HAVE] TO DO is reduce the cost [of semiconductor memories] by a factor of one hundred," Noyce enjoyed reminding his employees in the first few months of Intel's existence. The problem was not that a competitor was selling semiconductor memories far cheaper than Intel. The problem was that the existing storage technology for computers, an electromagnetic arrangement called "magnetic core memory," sold for about 4 percent of what most people expected semiconductor memories would cost. Noyce wanted to get the cost of semiconductor memory down to about a penny per bit—even less than the cost of comparable core storage.[62]

Magnetic core memories resembled stacks of tiny square tennis racket heads strung with wire instead of cat gut. Iron donuts, each about the size of a pinhead, sat at every intersection of two pieces of wire. Currents sent through the wires could polarize the little doughnut in a particular direction—magnetized or not—to represent a binary one or zero. In other words, each donut could store one bit of information, which was transmitted to the computer through a series of transistors. Magnetic core memories were reliable, cheap, and perfectly adequate for the storage needs of late-1960s computers. Even with the relatively limited computer market of that era, core memories had netted hundreds of thousands of dollars in royalties for MIT, which held the patent.[63]

Magnetic cores had their shortcomings, however, and in these Noyce and Moore had seen a potential foothold for Intel. Cores were not a particularly fast means of storing data. The computer's electronic pulses had to travel along about 10 square feet of wire to store 1,000 bits (zeroes or ones) of information. This traveling distance slowed processing, and as computers became more powerful and their storage needs grew, the wait to process and access data would become increasingly unacceptable. Moreover, the core memories were built by hand. Every one of those iron donuts was individually strung on a wire by a woman in a factory, most likely in Asia. Noyce and Moore knew that this labor-intensive means of production was not sustainable for a computer market growing exponentially, just as they had known a decade earlier that hand-wired discrete components could not serve the exploding market for space-age electronics.[64]

Moore and Noyce also knew that the problems with cores were irrelevant to most computer engineers, who did not spend time thinking about how they would build their machines ten years in the future. These engineers cared that their computers work *now*, and so the cost advantages of semiconductor memory would have to be overwhelming before the engineers would consider abandoning the clunky, but reliable, magnetic cores. A sense of déjà vu may have again struck Noyce and Moore, who faced a similar obstacle when they initially brought the integrated circuit to market. Noyce, the architect of Fairchild's decision to sell integrated circuits below cost to get a foothold in the discrete components market, was betting a similar strategy would work for semiconductor memories. Hence the mantra: "all we have to do is reduce the cost."

But, of course, that was not all they had to do. First they had to build the memories. A group consisting of Noyce, Moore, Grove, Hoff, Graham, and occasionally two or three others, had begun developing formal product plans in August 1968. They decided to take a three-pronged approach. Dick Bohn, a mercurial, brilliant, intense researcher from Sylvania who held several key patents in the bipolar field, would lead the effort to build a bipolar memory device. This would be a very fast chip that would drive other memory devices in a computer. Bipolar techniques had been around since the earliest days of Fairchild, and building them was as close to rote as anything in the semiconductor industry. But no one had squeezed as many transistors on a bipolar circuit as Intel proposed to do.[65]

Andy Grove and Les Vadasz would open up a second line of attack by trying to build a memory built with a much newer technique called MOS (metal-oxide-silicon). It takes fewer steps to build MOS integrated circuits than bipolar circuits, and MOS devices could be much more densely packed with transistors, which made them the logical choice for complex chips.

That, at least, was the theory. In reality, MOS devices were slower, more temperamental, and even more dependent on "black magic" than other semiconductor devices. MOS circuits had yet to be produced in volume and existed primarily as lab curiosities. Here Intel planned to start slow, building a small memory targeted to serve functions too simple for cores.[66]

A third group attempted to assemble four small memory chips into a single module that would function as a large-but-cheap memory. This memory was called the "multichip" or sometimes the "flip chip" because it was turned over, front to back, in the assembly process. The flip chip intrigued Noyce, not the least because it offered the possibility of eliminating one bonding step from the process of building memory chips. He focused his lab efforts on the die attacher that picked up the chip, placed it into a package, and slightly pressed down on the chip to attach it to the package. It was not easy to build a machine that did not crush or crack the chip at some point during this process.[67]

Noyce and Moore developed the three-pronged attack on the assumption that if one approach did not work out, maybe another one would. Moreover, the bipolar and MOS approaches could share many techniques and facilities, which meant that the company's effort, when it came to buying equipment and developing operating procedures for growing crystals, cutting wafers, maintaining cleanliness, and the like, was not as fractured as might appear on first blush. If, in the best-case scenario, more than one process yielded success, each was targeted to serve a different market and to work in tandem with the other processes.[68]

Noyce spent more time in the lab during the first year at Intel than he had in the previous eight years at Fairchild, yet he offered no insights that approached the level of his integrated circuit ideas and no far-out suggestions that worked in the way he anticipated—though he did have one idea, for using blown diodes to make a type of memory device, that eventually led Ted Hoff to a related patent. Noyce's work on the flip-chip bonder was more a shop-class than physics-lab type of job. As he had feared, Noyce had indeed been gone from the lab too long to make a meaningful technical contribution.[69]

But his technical instincts were still excellent. "His questions were so perceptive," recalls Ted Hoff. "No matter how deep you went, he was right there, always caught up and then racing ahead. It is kind of a shame he was so successful as a businessman that it kept him away from the technical side." Says Les Vadasz, "He challenged you at the time. Why can't we do this? How come we do this? What about this? . . . He really pushed you to push yourself. If you were talking about a 512-bit memory, [Noyce would ask] why not 1K? If you'd say this speed, he'd say, why not this speed? He just pushed and pushed and pushed. Even though he may not have known the details about the area he was pushing, he had enough conceptual understanding that he pushed you to the point where you had to question your own basis for why you're coming up with a conclusion. I think that had an impact on all of us."[70]

To be "pushed" by Noyce in this way was not an altogether pleasant experience. It was a bit like being peeled, coolly and efficiently stripped down, layer by layer, until Noyce reached what he considered the heart of the matter. The person whom Noyce "pushed" would leave the conversation strangely invigorated by a sense that he had sloughed off all superfluous accretions of conservative thinking and conventional wisdom—and that he could now do what Noyce had somehow convinced him it was possible to do.

After observing William Shockley's methods of using simplifying assumptions to speed up his company's research, Noyce had come to believe that scientists could approach their work in two very different ways. Researchers could adopt the "pretty" approach, in which they devote a great deal of time and effort to developing a technique or machine that will allow them to test their ideas with exact measurements that yield final definitive answers. Or a researcher could try the "quick and dirty" way, moving forward with an idea as soon as a rather rudimentary test indicates it will probably work. Noyce believed that the quick-and-dirty method generated "90 percent of the answer in 10 percent of the time." He disdained the pretty method as "a bit like telling a soccer player never to kick the ball until you have an ideal shot all carefully lined up and know exactly how hard to kick the ball. Ninety minutes may be over before you locate that opportunity."[71]

The quick-and-dirty research method, which Moore nicknamed "the Noyce principle of minimum information," prevailed at Intel, which was, like its founders, forever in a hurry. Even at Intel speed, it took five or six man-years to design a new circuit. And there was another benefit to operating on the Noyce principle, according to Moore. The company produced few spin-offs "because it does not generate a lot more ideas than it can use."[72]

Andy Grove was the ideal man to implement the Noyce principle of minimum information. Noyce, who called him "the whip," once told a friend that one of the many reasons he was happy to have Grove at Intel was that "it is tough for me to do the hard things, but it's not tough for Andy." To succeed with Grove, an early employee recalled, one needed, above all, "to do something. . . . No soul-searching, no thumb twiddling. [Grove was] keeping it moving, Hannibal through the Alps, keep the elephants moving, don't let them go down on their knees."[73]

Grove quickly moved from directing the lab to overseeing all aspects of research and manufacturing as manager of operations. He tracked everything, trusted nothing and no one, yelled and cursed to get his point across, frustrated others to the point that they yelled and cursed to get their points across, and insisted that people state—often in writing—exactly what they were going to do and when. And always, always, Grove followed up to confirm people kept their commitments. In later years, he would require all employees in his area of responsibility who arrived at work after 8 AM to sign a "Late List," which was then circulated to managers and supervisors. He once called a plan to test Intel's finished, ready-to-ship product with the rigorous high-temperature, high-voltage procedures that most companies used only for the first batches of chips "the best thing since the Pill."[74]

He could not have been more different from Noyce. Their divergent approaches caused more irritation for Grove than for Noyce. Grove, a linear thinker, found it hard to follow Noyce's thinking, which reminded him of "a butterfly hopping from thought to thought." Occasionally these ideas were intriguing enough to distract Grove from the work he had set for himself, but even more maddeningly, they would distract his employees, whom Grove would occasionally find had launched themselves on a tangent to chase down one of Noyce's more tantalizing mind flashes. For his part, Noyce had little problems with the differences between his and Grove's approaches to business. Noyce believed that for a company to be successful, it "must keep the vision of product and direction very narrow, while keeping the peripheral vision of market forces affecting the business very broad." Noyce would provide the necessary wide ranging vision and Grove would provide the equally necessary precision focus.

In truth, Grove and Noyce had little to do with each other in the earliest days of Intel. Noyce was outside of the office as much as he was in it, talking to the press, potential customers and investors, and job candidates. One executive hired in January 1970 says, "I don't think I talked to, or even met, Bob for months. He was always just whipping through." Most of Noyce's direct reports soon found surrogate bosses to whom they could turn for daily feedback. "I guess I officially reported to Bob," mused one such employee, "but I really reported to Andy and Gordon." Explained another, "Nobody actually reported to Bob. Nominally some people did report to both Bob and Gordon, but Gordon was always on the scene, and Bob was never there."[75]

With Noyce turning his attention outward, Grove focused on the inner workings of Intel, the essential minutiae of day-to-day operations. Moore bridged the gap between the two, weighing Noyce's signals from the outside against research in the field and Grove's reports from the inside. One person familiar with the trio described their roles this way: "Noyce would say, 'Some day we will use semiconductors to perform [some outrageous job].' Then Moore would say, 'To do that, we would need to transcend technical problems Y and Z.' And Grove would say, 'That means we'll need to get however-many-more engineers and increase yields by X percent and plant space by Y feet.' Their strengths just balanced each other so well." Their roles, in many peoples' opinions, could be described even more succinctly: Mr. Outside (Noyce), Mr. Inside (Moore), and Mr. Implementation (Grove).[76]

Intel meant something different for Grove than it did for Moore or for Noyce, who once said he started Intel, in part, to see "whether [we] could do it again; whether [Fairchild's success] was just plain dumb luck the first time around." Noyce and Moore had already proven their worth at Fairchild. Intel represented Grove's chance to do the same. Grove has said that the months he spent watching Fairchild R&D's "outstanding work" languish in the purgatory between development and manufacturing "fill[ed] me with self doubts to the point that I was wondering if the work we were doing was as good as I thought it was." In his last year at Fairchild, Grove had been convinced that the Simon and Garfunkel hit song "Faking It" was directed at him.[77]

Grove and marketing manager Bob Graham were at constant loggerheads. Grove thought Graham was trying to do his job—every day, Graham went down to the room where the designers worked to "check on the progress of the product"—and besides, Grove had "almost no use" for marketing. Grove figured that if Intel built an excellent product (his responsibility, thank you very much) the customers would not need too much convincing to buy it.[78]

For his part, Graham thought Grove, a research scientist until a few months before, did not know enough about manufacturing to be running operations. It further incensed Graham that Grove paid no attention to his explanations of customers' expectations for Intel products. Graham also thought that for someone who had "no use" for marketing, Grove spent a great deal of time nitpicking the wording on Graham's proposed advertisements and press releases.[79]

The real problem between Graham and Grove was far more fundamental than their fine-pointed accusations, however. Only one of these two men could be the second-in-command to the founders. Too much was at stake for both Graham and Grove for them to tolerate each other's presence in the company for long. Within months of Intel's founding, the enmity between these top two lieutenants threatened to poison relationships throughout the company.[80]

8

Takeoff

The first three years that Noyce spent at Intel were among the most exhilarating of his career. He enjoyed his return to the jack-of-all-trades he had been in the early days of Fairchild. He regularly sat in on technical reviews, led the weekly executive staff meeting and a product planning session every two weeks, helped a technician build a tool she thought would make her work easier, met with promising recruits, mopped the floor when a pipe broke, and delivered a number of lectures at technical and business conferences on topics such as "What Happened to LSI?" He and Moore set aside one lunch hour each week to eat with small groups of employees, and a morning every month to talk to industry analysts.

Noyce's interactions with potential customers in the first months of Intel's existence revolved around determining market needs. He spoke with senior managers at Burroughs, Honeywell, and Univac, firms interested in semiconductor memories for the computers they were building, and at Memorex, whose executive vice president, Jim Guzy, had recently joined the Intel board. Occasionally Noyce would explain what Intel was trying to build and ask for suggestions for improving their technical plan. That Noyce believed the need for feedback overrode the risk that a customer might share Intel's plans with competitors is perfectly consistent with his instinctive trust in people and his determination to build products that people would actually buy.[1]

The steady stream of phone calls Noyce had fielded from his study at home became a constant rush of visitors to his Mountain View office. As Grove recalls it, "nobody in the industry would move from a job, or start a company, or do much of anything, without paying homage to Bob and getting his blessing. On top of this, there were customers, bankers, directors, people connected with the financing. . . . It was funny. All these people in suits, coming and going. Noyce was the 'go-to person' of the day."[2]

Even his family picked up on his excitement. Noyce would at times bring the children with him to the office on weekends. He put license

In September 1961, Stanford provost Frederick Terman joined Noyce and Fairchild Semiconductor research head Gordon Moore in breaking ground for the company's new Research and Development building. Family photos.

The other Fairchild founders look at Noyce, who poses near equipment in the production area. Courtesy Julius Blank.

Above: Noyce in 1959, explaining Fairchild Semiconductor's breakthrough planar process to John Carter, CEO of the firm's parent company. Carter knew almost nothing about semiconductors. Family photos.

Left: Noyce in about 1962, shortly after Fairchild began selling its integrated circuit. Courtesy Grinnell College Archives.

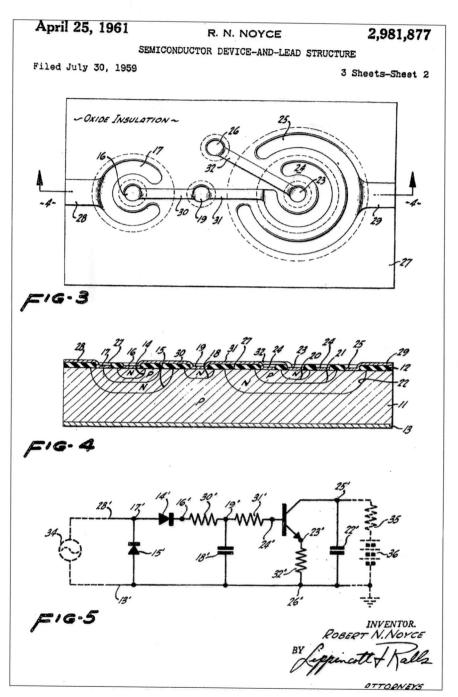

Several key illustrations from Noyce's integrated circuit patent.

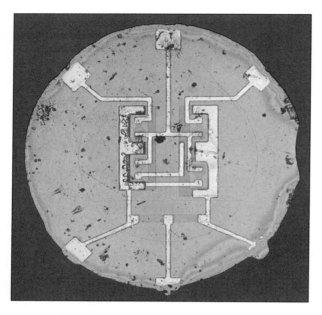

The first integrated circuit available as a monolithic chip, Fairchild's 1961 resistor-transistor logic (RTL) flip flop. Courtesy Fairchild Semiconductor.

A Fairchild Semiconductor employee in May 1963 uses a microscope to package chips in the gold "headers" lying in the tray to her right. She is wearing a hairnet and gloves in a company-mandated effort to reduce contamination of the devices in production. Visible in the background is a man supervising the women (always called "girls") at work. Courtesy Department of Special Collections, Stanford University Libraries.

Bob Noyce and manufacturing head Charlie Sporck speak to employees at Fairchild's Portland, Maine facility. A casual style was a hallmark of Noyce's approach to management. Courtesy Fairchild Semiconductor.

Walker's Wagon Wheel was one of several famous after-hours meeting places for semiconductor engineers and other workers. Some firms' lawyers, concerned corporate secrets might be spilled over drinks, explicitly discouraged employees from frequenting the Wagon Wheel. Photo by Carolyn Caddes. Courtesy Carolyn Caddes and the Department of Special Collections, Stanford University Libraries.

Brenda and Roger Borovoy, Betty and Bob Noyce, and Paul Hwoschinsky (in fake mustache and pipe) in Vienna for a licensing deal, pose near a sign they think would amuse their friend Charlie Sporck, who had just left Fairchild for National Semiconductor. Family photos.

Left: Noyce was 41 and happy to be back in the lab at his new startup, Intel, when this photo was taken in 1969. Courtesy Intel Corp.

Below: Nearly the entire staff of the young Intel poses in front of the company's first building. The tall man in glasses behind Moore is Ted Hoff. To the right of Hoff is Andy Grove, and two people to the left (in the tweed jacket) is Les Vadasz. Courtesy Intel Corp.

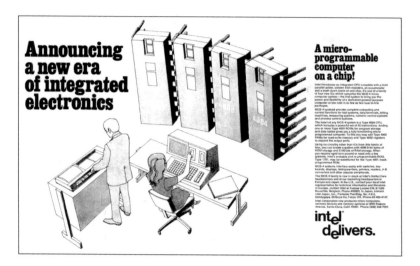

Above: This advertisement for Intel's first microprocessor generated enormous interest within the technical community. Noyce was a driving force behind the microprocessor at Intel. Courtesy Intel Corp.

Right: A pensive or tense moment at Intel in the mid-1970s. Courtesy Intel Corp.

Intel co-founders Bob Noyce and Gordon Moore with Andy Grove, who rose quickly to join them in the "Office of the President," pose before a chip layout in 1978. Courtesy Intel Corp.

Noyce leading his madrigal group at a Renaissance Faire, 1971. Photo by Jefferson Cotton, Courtesy Jefferson Cotton.

Noyce with Ted Hoff, inventor of the microprocessor, in Noyce's Intel cubicle, probably in the late 1970s. Courtesy Regis McKenna.

plates that read "INTEL" on his new car, a white Cougar. One memorable day, the entire family helped to cut rubylith, the red cellophane-like
sheets that operators laid over a paper design of a circuit and cut according
to the paper pattern. (The rubylith would then be shrunk to the proper
size and used to make the mask for the circuit.) The children—now young
adolescents—enjoyed a fine few hours wielding exacto knives and "helping
Da," who was also hard at work over the light table, along with Betty. At
dinner, Noyce would often talk about Intel's struggles and successes, and
the children felt enough a part of the company that Penny burst into a
neighbor's house shouting "They made one, they made one!" after her
father told her that Intel's first memory chip had been successfully tested.[3]

Toward the end of 1969, Noyce and Rock began to talk about taking
Intel public, going so far as to split the stock four for seven in an attempt to
get the price per share in the $20–$30 range most investors preferred. Both
men, however, had significant concerns that taking a young company public
would mean subjecting it to stockholders' demands for short-term profits
at a time when Intel needed to invest for long-term growth. Noyce had
another worry. He thought that the public's voracious appetite for semiconductor issues would unrealistically inflate the firm's market cap, and
thereby sever any clear connection between the employees' work and the
value of the company. "A company worth $5 million could be bid up on
the market by unsophisticated bidders to $50 million," he explained. If the
value of the company did not "follow the real progress of its growth," Noyce
said, "the value of the employees' stock options would not correspond to
their performance." In other words, he worried that employees would find
it demoralizing to get rich from a stock bubble.[4]

The funding also boosted Noyce's confidence in the company's future. He bought his own plane, a single-engine Pegasus, shortly after passing his pilot's exam in 1969. He approached flying with an uncharacteristic
seriousness and deliberation, always thoroughly examining the plane before climbing in the cockpit and not touching alcohol for at least 24 hours
before he was scheduled to take off. In the air, too, he was surprisingly
careful. "It was an interesting transformation," recalls Gordon Moore.

Rock and Noyce managed to arrange a second round of private financing in 1969, and then a third in 1970, at prices that rivaled market
rates without introducing the hassles of public ownership. Noyce worked
closely with Rock to identify and entice investors sophisticated enough to
understand the risks they were taking and the need for patience. He attended meeting after meeting with banks, financiers, current investors
wanting to increase their participation, and new investors, most of them
again personal acquaintances of Noyce, Rock, or Moore. These second
and third rounds of funding brought another $2.2 million into Intel.[5]

"Driving with [Noyce] in a car was like taking my life in my hands—he didn't pay much attention to his driving. But flying in his airplane: boy, he was nothing but business."[6]

By this time, almost no trace remained of the Bob Noyce who had turned down a general manager's job at Fairchild because he feared he might fail. Where Noyce had been almost apologetic about not being a particularly good details manager when he left Fairchild, by the time Intel was two years old, he was nearly defiant. "I don't get my kicks out of seeing things run at the highest level of efficiency with the greatest degree of control," he said. "Control immediately means a loss of personal freedom for either the people in the factory or, as far as that goes, for the management. Once you've set down the ground rules for return on investment or earnings before taxes, you're suddenly cut off from some of the choices you could have made. . . . I guess what I'm saying is that the venture part of management[,] rather than the control part of management[,] is more fun for me." He added a bit pointedly: "This 'immature' management has been much more successful than the mature management that tried to get into the [semiconductor] business."[7]

INTEL INTRODUCED ITS FIRST PRODUCT, a 64-bit random access memory (RAM) in May 1969. This was the bipolar device from the group run by Bohn, and its development had proven far easier than Intel could have imagined. The memory was also easy for competitors to build, however, which meant that Texas Instruments and Fairchild introduced their own 64-bit memories at nearly the same time as Intel. As a result, the bipolar RAM generated little more than what one person called a "revenue trickle" for Intel in 1969.[8]

At the other end of the spectrum was the multichip memory effort. Intel had no problem building the individual memory chips but could not reliably attach them to their ceramic base. Moreover, yields were terrible, power dissipation was high, Intel could not determine how to test the devices efficiently, and it was difficult to imagine ever shrinking the package enough to make it appealing to customers. When Gordon Moore tried to test an almost-finished device for shock resistance by dropping it, nearly every chip popped off the ceramic base and clattered across the ground.[9]

Clearly the MOS device would make or break the company. If the three-pronged effort was, as Gordon Moore liked to put it, "like Goldilocks," with the multichip memory too hard to build and the bipolar memory so easy that anyone could do it, the MOS device needed to prove itself "just right"—easy for Intel to build and hard for everyone else.

It certainly was not easy to build. Vadasz and Grove were trying to make MOS transistors that would have silicon, rather than metal, gates. At Fairchild, Grove and Vadasz had been members of a research team following up on intriguing Bell Labs research that indicated that silicon gates might reduce the risk of contamination and improve the yields in MOS devices. The Fairchild research was underway when Grove and Vadasz left the company and resurfaced trying to build silicon-gate MOS devices for Intel.

In March 1969, Fairchild requested that Noyce meet with the company's general counsel for an informal deposition to determine whether or not Fairchild had grounds to sue Intel for violations of trade secrets related to the silicon gate process, or for corporate raiding. Although the deposition was informal and friendly—both of the Fairchild attorneys were social friends of the Noyces, and one later came to work for Intel—the stakes were high. At Fairchild, Les Hogan wanted to discourage future spinouts, and suing a startup as prominent as Intel would both prove he was serious and could also slow down a company that, while no threat at the present, might become one later. For his part, Noyce insisted that Intel's silicon gate work represented not stolen intellectual property, but "evolutionary improvements" on efforts "discussed by researchers in other locations, but . . . never really brought into production."[10]

Fairchild never filed a suit against Intel. An intellectual property case would have been hard to prove, since Fairchild research had not gone much beyond confirming the Bell Labs findings, and since no lab books, process manuals, or masks were missing from Fairchild. Moreover, researchers at several companies other than Fairchild and Intel were also pursuing silicon gate research. A raiding suit offered even less hope for success for Fairchild. The company had hired more than 60 Motorola employees devoted to Hogan in the past year, which meant Fairchild was itself the defendant in a raiding suit brought by Motorola. The Fairchild attorneys would have been hard pressed to explain why they were in any position to charge another firm with questionable practices on this front.

Moreover, as Fairchild counsel Roger Borovoy, who thought they might have had a case, explains with a sigh, neither he nor anyone else at Fairchild relished the prospect of suing Noyce: "We just said, 'The hell with it.' There was no way Sherman Fairchild, who was still active, would sue Bob Noyce. . . . All the up Sherman ever had was from Bob Noyce. Bob Noyce made Fairchild. So why screw around with this [talk of a suit] any more?"[11]

Grove, Vadasz, and the MOS team in the Intel lab found the notion that they might be significantly benefiting from Fairchild's silicon gate research laughable. Recall the difference between lab work and production. Fairchild's work had never left the lab. There were no transistors rolling off the lines with silicon gates at Fairchild and certainly no integrated circuits. The MOS team that went to Intel did indeed owe all their knowledge about silicon gates to their experiences at Fairchild, but it took them a year to translate this familiarity with a theory into a reality etched in silicon. An Intel progress report from November 1968, claims that the process is "off and limping." Recalls one employee, "It was a little bit like peeling an onion. Every time we would fix a problem, we'd uncover another one. I was afraid the last layer was going to be nothing. For all we knew, the silicon gate process was no good." About this same time, Grove wrote of the MOS effort: "Results: one day ho, the next day hum."[12]

Intel produced its first working silicon-gate MOS memory in March 1969, just days after Noyce's deposition. The MOS team called the company into the cafeteria to share several bottles of champagne. Noyce, however, did not attend the celebration. He was in a hospital in Aspen, where he had broken his leg in five places when he fell while skiing. When Moore called to tell him about the working MOS circuit, Noyce called it "the best news that I've ever gotten" and was immediately swamped with guilt for not having been at Intel when the milestone was met.[13]

NOYCE ALWAYS MAINTAINED that the "genesis" for any successful thinking about semiconductor products "must not be 'we have this product, how do we get rid of it?' but 'this is a critical product.'" The technology itself interested Noyce less than the *need* for the technology, a distinction that he explained thus: "A company must go out and find what the customer wants. Where is the need? Where is the opening? . . . The need is not for, say, half a million ¼-inch drill bits. The need is that there are ten million ¼-inch holes that need to be drilled." Even if a customer thinks he needs a drill bit, it was Intel's job, in Noyce's estimation, to recognize that the real need was to make a hole, and then to find the best way to make it.[14]

The most storied example of Intel's commitment to this approach is the company's development of the microprocessor—the so-called computer on a chip—in 1969 and 1970. The legends surrounding the microprocessor are many, and the reality is especially hard to pinpoint because almost none of the original documentation—drawings, progress reports, contracts, communications among people at Intel or between Intel and the companies that used the microprocessor—survives. In other words, any account depends a great deal on the memories of the participants.[15]

A dependence on human recall, particularly of events more than 35 years old, is always risky. It is particularly so in this case because the stakes are so high. The microprocessor is one of the most important inventions of the twentieth century. Every computer and piece of "smart electronics" on the planet depends on microprocessor technology, as do many things not considered particularly intelligent, such as internal combustion engines and automobile brakes. Microprocessors are a multi-billion-dollar industry. The devices have also made Intel the world's dominant semiconductor company, which makes receiving credit for it within the company a particularly appealing prize.

The combination of high stakes and little original information has led to a not-unexpected result, namely that in the same way that everyone of a certain age seems to recall voting for Kennedy in the 1960 presidential election even though Nixon almost won that contest, nearly everyone involved with Intel's work on the microprocessor remembers himself as playing a crucial role in developing and promoting the device, even though the company abandoned its development for several months, considered it unimportant enough to assign the rights to someone else, and then, after securing these rights back to Intel, almost did not market the microprocessor at all.

And then, of course, there are dozens of people who never worked at Intel who can make legitimate claims on the invention of the microprocessor. Bill Davidow, who oversaw microprocessor marketing at Intel and who himself had some strong technical ideas on the subject, has said, only partly in jest, that there are 500 inventors of the microprocessor. Fairchild, IBM, Signetics, Four-Phase, and RCA were also working on microprocessor-like devices at the same time Intel was tackling the project. Intel filed for its first patent in 1973, but a small company called Microcomputer had filed for a patent on a general logic device in 1970, and Texas Instruments applied for a patent on a microprocessor-like device in 1971.[16]

In the same way that ideas about interconnecting components were "in the air" for years before Noyce and Kilby independently demonstrated their integrated circuits, so too were ideas about a general-purpose logic device "in the air" for years before anyone at Intel began working on what would come to be called microprocessors. "This is a funny deal with the microprocessor," explains Gordon Moore. "There was no real invention [in a technical sense]. The breakthrough was a recognition that it was finally possible to do what everyone had been saying we would some day be able to do."[17]

In the midst of all this confusion and uncertainty, one fact emerges with surprising clarity—Bob Noyce was absolutely essential to the microprocessor's development and success at Intel. He encouraged its development; he lobbied for its introduction; he dreamed of its future importance; he promoted it tirelessly within the company and to customers. The operations manager (Grove), the key inventor (Hoff), and the board chair (Rock), have each independently said, in one way or another that "the microprocessor would not have happened at Intel if it had not been for Bob."[18]

INTEL'S MICROPROCESSOR STORY opens in the spring of 1969, around the time that Moore called Noyce in Aspen to tell him that the MOS team had a working silicon-gate memory. A manager from a Japanese calculator company called Busicom, which was planning to build a family of high-performance calculators, contacted either Bob Graham or Noyce to ask if

Intel, which had a small business building custom chips designed by customers, would like to manufacture the chip set that would run the calculator. Calculator companies around the world were seeking out semiconductor companies to build the chips for their machines, and Noyce said that Intel was nearly the only manufacturer left who had not already agreed to work with a calculator company. It made sense for Intel, young and unknown, and Busicom, ten years older but still not well established, to work together.[19]

Tadashi Sasaki, a senior manager with Japanese electronics giant Sharp, explains that it was he, not serendipity, that brought Intel and Busicom together. Sasaki says he had long felt great gratitude to Fairchild and Bob Noyce because the planar and integrated circuit research published by Fairchild had contributed to Sasaki's own professional success. Sasaki had also been intrigued by an idea one of his researchers had proposed in 1968—that it would one day be possible to build an entire calculator on a single chip. Sasaki says that Noyce and Graham visited him at the end of 1968 trying to drum up business for Intel, but that Sharp's existing contracts made it impossible to give even a small order to Intel. Sasaki says he then tried to help Noyce by arranging a dinner that included Sasaki, Noyce, Graham, and Yoshio Kojima, president of Busicom and a university classmate of Sasaki's. Sasaki also funneled roughly 40 million yen to Busicom, with the stipulation that it be used in a contract to Intel to build a calculator on a chip.[20]

Noyce's datebooks do not note any meeting with Sasaki or Sharp, but it seems likely that he did travel to Japan around this time. Intel established a sales office in the country in 1969, and Noyce's prestige among the Japanese made him the logical person to have facilitated the process. Several people who traveled with Noyce to Japan have commented on how greatly he was admired there. Roger Borovoy described Noyce as "a god" to the Japanese. Ed Gelbach, Intel's second marketing vice president, recalls being "in awe" of Noyce's influence in the young Japanese electronics industry. "[Japanese executives] would come up to him and say, 'we designed this [Intel chip into our product] just because of you, Dr. Noyce.' In Japan, [Noyce] had single handedly the most significant impact on getting Intel parts designed in." There is thus no reason to doubt Sasaki's feelings about Noyce. His encouraging Busicom to contact Intel also seems plausible. "Busicom kind of appeared out of the blue," Moore recalls.[21]

It is certain, however, that Busicom did not request that Intel build a calculator on a single chip. In fact, where the standard calculator used about six chips, each with 600–1000 transistors, Busicom, which was designing a particularly complex calculator, wanted a set of a dozen specialized chips with 3,000 to 5,000 transistors each. Busicom planned to send a team of engineers to Intel to design the chips on-site and would pay Intel $100,000 to manufacture its calculator chip sets. Busicom expected to pay Intel about

$50 for each set manufactured and promised to buy at least 60,000 of them. Intel agreed to this arrangement.[22]

Three Busicom engineers arrived in California towards the end of June, and by the first week of July, they were a fixture in the Intel building. Noyce asked Ted Hoff, Intel's resident computer expert, to serve as the official liaison to the Busicom team. No one, including Noyce, expected that the Busicom project would require much attention from Hoff. The idea was simply for the Busicom team to have someone specific to whom they could turn with questions or requests for assistance.

"I had no design responsibilities for the project, but soon I was sticking my nose where it didn't belong," recalls Hoff. "Normally you wouldn't do that, but [Intel] was a start-up company, and a lot of us had hopes for its financial success, so I didn't want to let major effort go into something disastrous."[23]

In short order, Hoff, "kind of shocked at how complex this was," became convinced that it would be impossible to build the chips at the agreed-upon price. And the more he thought about it, the more strongly he believed that he knew a better way to build the calculator Busicom wanted.[24]

Busicom was requesting a number of logic chips—the chips that manipulate data rather than just storing it—each of which could do precisely one thing: one chip performed calculations, another controlled the printing, a third handled the display, and so on. Hoff thought that instead of using specialized logic chips, Intel could build a single, general-purpose logic chip that in effect would be a rudimentary computer programmed to act like a calculator. The secret would be to simplify the instruction set for this chip, which came to be called a microprocessor, by offloading as many of the instructions as possible to a memory chip—and memory chips, of course, were Intel's specialty.[25]

To Hoff his ideas seemed irrefutably right. But when he tried to convert the Busicom team to his vision, they showed no interest. "The detail was not so good," recalled Masatoshi Shima, a member of the Busicom team. Shima cited the plan's "lack of system concept, lack of decimal operations, lack of interface to the keyboard, lack of real-time control, and so on."[26]

Frustrated, Hoff went to Noyce. "I think we can do something to simplify this," Hoff said. "I know this can be done. It can be made to emulate a computer." Hoff sketched out his thoughts, which would have required only one microprocessor and three other chips (two memories and a shift register). Noyce, who never would have claimed to know anything about computers, kept pushing Hoff, asking question after question, all of them so basic that Noyce was almost apologizing for his lack of knowledge. "Um, can you tell me the functions of a computer operating system?" What did it mean, precisely, to build a computer that acted like a calculator? What was it, exactly, that the chip would need to do? It was the same Socratic method of forcing people to "argue ourselves into some smart things," as Vadasz put it, that had worked so well in the lab.[27]

At the end of the conversation, Noyce told Hoff, "Why don't you go ahead and pursue those ideas? It's always nice to have a backup position."[28]

With this single seemingly casual remark, Noyce directed someone who did not officially report to him (Hoff says he nonetheless "tended to report to Noyce") to do something that was not in his job description—something that ran counter, in fact, to what the customer's representatives wanted—at a time when the company had yet to generate revenue and when its key technical employees could ill-afford distractions. And Noyce did this simply because he thought Hoff's ideas were intriguing. That is one take on Noyce's telling Hoff to go ahead. It would have been Andy Grove's take at the time.

A second interpretation would look like this: Noyce told Hoff to pursue his ideas precisely *because* Hoff was so important to the company. At Shockley, Noyce had seen how a boss's lack of interest stunted Noyce's own work, cut the company off from important ideas, and devastated his young researchers' commitment to the firm. He was not going to risk doing the same thing to Hoff.

The first interpretation certainly has merit. Even Noyce would have admitted in 1969 that work on the Busicom chip was orthogonal to Intel's primary business of building semiconductor memories. And that business was not going particularly well. The excited call Moore placed to Noyce's Aspen hospital bed was a bit premature. For several months afterwards, yields on the silicon-gate MOS memory hovered around two working chips per wafer, less than 10 percent of what the company thought it needed to be successful. Every time even a single good memory came off the line, the silicon-gate MOS team announced it over the company intercom. The MOS chip underwent nearly 20 design changes. The engineers and designers altered the brand of bottled water they used. They varied the acid dips. They reverse engineered a competing chip from a company called Mostek, which had spun out of Texas Instruments. They hung a rubber chicken over an evaporator to serve as a good-luck talisman.[29]

The breakthrough came in late 1969, when someone changed the formula of the acid dip yet again. Suddenly the yield went from two chips per wafer to 25. The employee in charge of sorting good dice from bad started yelling, "Holy hell, look what's going on here!" People came pouring out of their offices, urging the MOS team to test another wafer, and then another. When it was ascertained that the key change was the acid dip, an employee recalled, "Les [Vadasz] was so excited he started jumping up and down and yelling, 'It's a *soo*per dip,' with his Hungarian accent, 'It's a *soo*per dip, it's a *soo*per dip,' over and over again. Someone heard him and went back and marked the container of acid, 'Super Dip.' So even though it wasn't a precise chemical formula, for over a year that container just sat there with that label 'Super Dip' on it."[30]

In September 1969, Intel introduced its MOS chip, a 256-bit memory called the 1101. It was not the "just right" solution Intel had hoped for. The chip proved too slow and, priced from 20 to 60 cents per bit (depending on the quantity purchased), too expensive to replace cores, which cost about four cents per bit, as a mainframe memory. Even when Intel reduced its initial price on the part by 75 percent, sales were sluggish. Only when Intel applied the basic MOS structure to shift registers, an already established market, did silicon-gate technology make a profit, albeit a small one, for the company. But this me-too business was not what Noyce and Moore had planned for Intel, nor was it a strategy for extended long-term growth.[31]

Meanwhile, Ted Hoff had been working on the novel general-purpose logic chip for Busicom. He did this in the time not spent on his "real" job managing applications research. Outside of the MOS team, with whom Hoff, who had not previously designed an MOS circuit, needed to consult fairly regularly, Noyce was his main contact on the Busicom project. ("He was always very encouraging, always very helpful, always had an idea," Hoff recalls.) Moore was also intrigued by Hoff's vision, though he admits "my enthusiasm may not [have been] so obvious at times." In late August, an engineer named Stan Mazor began helping Hoff with the processor chip. With Mazor on board, the two men completed a block drawing of the architecture within two weeks. Throughout this time, the Busicom engineers were working on their own design.[32]

In August, Noyce sent a note to Busicom president Yoshio Kojima, warning him that the "complexity of the circuits for this machine" meant that there was "no possibility that we could manufacture these units for $50/kit, even for the simplest kit." If Intel built the calculator set according to Busicom's design, Noyce estimated that the final cost per kit would be around $300. (He hastened to add, "I do not criticize the design of the . . . calculator.") Noyce ended with a question: "Is it reasonable to proceed with this development on the basis of this design, or should the project be abandoned?" Kojima must have immediately responded that he wanted to continue some sort of relationship, because on September 16, Bob Graham followed up by letter, again emphasizing the complexity of the Busicom chip set and ending with a proposal: why not try a different design, an Intel design, in fact?[33]

In October 1969, a pair of Busicom executives came to Intel to decide which chip set to pursue—Hoff and Mazor's or the Busicom engineers'. The Intel design required four chips, with about 1,900 transistors on the most complicated chip, at a cost of roughly $155 per kit. The Busicom design would cost twice that and require 12 to 15 chips with about 2,000 transistors each. The Busicom executives chose the Intel design with its general-purpose logic chip over their own engineers' designs—a decision Ted Hoff declared "a bit of a coup."[34]

The Busicom team returned to Japan. But it was February 1970, before the agreement between the two companies was formally signed. From October to February, Hoff turned his attention to a contract for a central processor for Control Terminal Corporation, and no one at Intel was designated to lead the work on the Busicom chip set. Perhaps it is not surprising that the chip set lingered untended, since both Noyce and Hoff, the two men within Intel most excited by it, enjoyed coming up with ideas more than implementing them. In March 1970, a Busicom executive sent a gently worded letter to Noyce wondering why he had heard nothing about their calculator chip set. He requested an update and specific signs of progress.[35]

The letter got results. Intel hired Frederico Faggin, an MOS process expert from Fairchild, to work on the Busicom chips. Faggin immediately began refining Hoff's architecture and implementing the design into silicon, working in close consultation with the Busicom engineers, who had flown back across the Pacific to assist with the effort.

Noyce also went into Andy Grove's office and sat down on the corner of his desk, a move that immediately raised Grove's suspicions. Any time Noyce affected a faux-casual air, Grove knew he was not going to like the message. Noyce looked at Grove more from the corner of his eyes than face-on. "We're starting another project," Noyce said with a little laugh. Grove remembers thinking, "Go away, go away, we don't have time for this." What kind of company started new projects when its very survival was at stake?[36]

Intel was indeed struggling. One internal company timeline shorthands the first months of 1970 with the phrase, "Management Near Panic." The next-generation silicon-gate MOS device was proving as difficult to build as the 1101, even though almost everyone in the company had been assigned to work on it, and even though Intel was collaborating with computer manufacturer Honeywell to increase its chances of building a MOS memory with desirable features. At the end of the second quarter, Intel laid off about 20 people and reined in the most ambitious of their expansion plans—"probably a more painful task for Noyce than for Moore," explained one contemporary account.[37]

The energy and optimism that ended the 1960s had cratered under their own weight, leaving only surplus inventory and employees without work to do. Headlines on a single page of an industry newsletter in July 1970 read "Raytheon Profits Off in Quarter," "GT&E Quarter Net Slumps; Sylvania Nosedives 63%," "Itek Earnings Skid 30.5% for Quarter." The year 1970 threatened to end with Intel almost $2 million in the red.[38]

Arthur Rock felt a sense of urgency—even impending disaster—about Intel that he was not certain the management and directors shared. "Rock was quite comfortable making [the situation] sound quite severe and bad in order to make people be more realistic," recalled one board member. "Noyce and Moore weren't good penny-pinching, pencil-pushing types. Rock was a fiend of that sort." Intel needed a source of significant revenue, Rock said—and quickly. They needed to put the next-generation silicon-gate MOS memory into production, even if it was not perfect. In October, Intel officially introduced the 1103, its second memory chip built using the silicon gate process, with a full-page ad blaring, "THE END: Cores lose Price War to New Chip." The 1103 held four times more data than the 1101. It was also the first semiconductor memory that could be made in volume and thus the first that could really challenge cores on price.[39]

To be sure, the device was far from perfect. Among the 1103's many failings known to Intel was the fact that, in Andy Grove's words, "under certain adverse conditions the thing just couldn't remember"—a problem for a memory. Some 1103s failed when they were shaken. A few developed moisture inside the glass used to seal them. Often no one knew why the devices would stop working. The problems inspired Ted Hoff to write a 28-page memo explaining the 1103's operation and quirks.[40]

Andy Grove had nightmares that boxes and boxes of 1103s would be returned to the company for defects—and would ruin Intel entirely. Gordon Moore, on the other hand, wondered if, in some perverse way, the 1103's problems made it easier to convince customers to use the device. Engineers who specialized in core memories recognized analogs in the 1103. Both suffered from voltage and pattern sensitivity, which means that their performance was affected by other nearby electronic devices. The 1103 "refreshed itself" every thousandth of a second, an operation that regularly caused problems; cores did something similar called "destructive read." "All these things made the 1103 more challenging and less threatening to engineers [at customer companies]," Moore explains. "We did not plan it to happen this way, but I think that if [the 1103] had been perfect out of the box, we would have had a lot more resistance [to it] from our customers."[41]

Even with its problems, the 1103 represented a real technical breakthrough. As Steve Jobs once said, when the light bulb was invented, people did not complain that it was too dim. A firm called Microsystems International Limited (MIL), the manufacturing arm of Bell Canada, approached Intel about serving as a "second source" on the 1103. Customers recognized that building state-of-the art semiconductors was a temperamental business, and so no customer was willing to leave an important order in the hands of only one supplier. They wanted an officially sanctioned alternative source of product.[42]

Noyce told MIL that if the company wanted to second source 1103s, all it had to do was "pay us our net worth and we'll all teach you what we know." This is essentially the arrangement to which MIL agreed. In exchange for

$1.5 million (roughly Intel's net worth at the time), plus royalties on MIL sales until the end of 1972, Intel would provide the know-how, technical information, and licenses necessary to produce 1103s. Intel would also send a team to Ottawa to help MIL set up a fab to build the devices. If the new MIL fab met certain production goals, another $500,000 would be transferred from MIL to Intel. Noyce told Intel's investors that "[MIL's] payments under the agreement will substantially improve our already good cash position, [and] the implied endorsement of our process excellence will also be a valuable marketing aid for us." Noyce later said that the MIL deal was one of his favorites of his career because "it's not every day you get a chance to double your net worth."[43]

Operations manager Andy Grove, whom Noyce had not consulted on the second source plan, was irate when he learned of it. "We were seeing one or two [working] dies per wafer of 1103s. It's hard to describe what shit we were in with that product. [This MIL deal meant] I would have to improve yields without a manufacturing manager or chief technologist," both of whom would be part of the team transferring technology to Ottawa. Grove, who could not believe Noyce would even consider such a proposal, had tried several times to dissuade him from this plan of action. When spring turned to summer, and the deal seemed imminent, Grove tried again. He went into Noyce's office and found him there, talking with Moore. Grove immediately began arguing against the plan "as aggressively as I was capable—which was very." He insisted that Intel could not increase the 1103 yield, maintain the fab, satisfy customers, and find new prospects with half the staff in Canada. "This will be the death of Intel!" he yelled at one point. "We'll get the $1.5 million, and then we'll sink."[44]

Noyce waited until Grove finished. Then he looked at the younger man, his eyes hard. "We have decided to do this," Noyce said slowly. "You need to put your energies into figuring out how to do this." Grove could bluster all he wanted, but Noyce ran Intel at this stage. Grove left, as he put it, "with my tail between my legs." The MIL deal was inked in July, and at the very end of 1970, Intel received its first payment from the Canadian firm— $500,000—which lowered Intel's losses for the year to $1 million.[45]

In the end, the arrangement with MIL could not have gone better if Intel had scripted it. The initial technology transfer was successful enough to earn Intel the $500,000 incentive bonus and allow the transfer team to return home in the spring of 1971. Intel paid for the transfer team members and their wives to fly to Hawaii for a three-day party. Noyce arrived in time to share a fancy dinner of chateaubriand and copious volumes of liquor with the celebrants at the Kauai Surf Hotel. After a few hours listening to the jazz band, he joined a group stripping to their undershorts for a quick swim at the beach. Noyce threw himself headfirst into the water with characteristic vigor—only to discover the tide had gone out. He emerged from the shallow waters covered in scrapes, cursing and laughing.[46]

The dive in the ocean is vintage Noyce. He was trying, as he always did, to be "just one of the guys." Any sort of hierarchy—but particularly one that placed him at the top—made him nervous. He once said that what he loved about madrigal singing was its blend of multiple voices into one, with no single voice dominating: "Your part depends on [the others' and] it always supports the others." When asked in social situations about his profession, he would say that he was a physicist. At Intel, Noyce spoke of "hierarchy power" and "knowledge power" and firmly believed that when it came to technical decisions, the word of the person with the most knowledge ought to trump the opinion of the one with the higher title. Intel board meetings were not the typical two-hour drone of rubber-stamp motions and resolutions. Noyce insisted that operating managers present to the board—both to keep the directors informed and to teach the operating staff how to field tough questions and make compelling arguments.[47]

When an early employee wanted to see Intel's organization chart, Noyce drew an X in the middle of a circle, and then drew seven more Xs along the perimeter of the circle. As the amazed employee looked on, Noyce proceeded to connect the center X to each of the other Xs in the system so the drawing resembled a wagon wheel. The X in the center, said Noyce, was the employee asking the question. He added, the other seven Xs "are me, Gordon, Andy, Les [Vadasz], Bob [Graham], Gene [Flath] and other people you'll be dealing with." Noyce's point was that he expected a reciprocal relationship between all employees—from the center to the perimeter, and back again—and that formal reporting structures and hierarchies were largely irrelevant.[48]

"You never heard him say, 'I did this, I did that,'" recalls Judy Vadasz, who is married to Les. "It was always, '*we* did this.'" Intel's far-reaching stock-option plan can be seen as a reflection of Noyce's democratic tendencies, which were also shared by Moore. The founders' beliefs on this matter further led them to refuse to set aside parking spaces for executives, and to decide, when Intel moved to a new building in the mid-1970s, that everyone—including the founders—should work in essentially identical cubicles.[49]

A FEW MONTHS AFTER STARTING INTEL, Noyce told a reporter, "One of the reasons I wanted to set up this two-headed monster is so that either Gordon or I can feel free to take off without severe guilt feelings about leaving a job undone behind us." Noyce "took off" to lead Wednesday evening rehearsals for his madrigal group. He permitted himself long weekends away from Intel during the ski season and a week-long family vacation. He and Betty sold the ski cottage she disliked. Instead they began an annual tradition of renting the entire lodge at Alpine Meadows near Lake Tahoe for several days every winter and inviting nearly two dozen people to join them. Noyce also served on the boards of three startups—including Eugene Kleiner's short-lived company, Cybercom, which designed and manufactured computer peripherals such as printers and display terminals—each of which held monthly meetings.[50]

In 1967, Noyce was a founding director of Coherent Radiation, a company that developed and manufactured lasers for use in scientific instruments and as machine tools in industrial applications. Noyce had learned about the company from Charles B. Smith, an associate with the investment arm of the Rockefeller family, who were willing to invest in the company if Smith could find a "man on the West Coast to keep an eye on things."[51]

After meeting with one of the company's founders, Jim Hobart, Noyce agreed join the Coherent board. He also purchased roughly 22,500 shares of stock for about $1.40 per share. "I'm not sure why Noyce wanted to come on board," admits Hobart. "Maybe he just wanted to try something different [from semiconductors]."

As an experienced entrepreneur, Noyce served as a stabilizing force at Coherent. "Noyce's biggest contribution to the company," Hobart recalls, "was [to say], 'Let's not be emotional. Let's figure this out. Let's discuss it, debate it, think about it.'" Noyce also pushed Hobart to use stock options as an incentive tool. Hobart had already planned to distribute options to all technical employees, but Noyce promoted their use even more aggressively. He thought that Hobart should use what Noyce called an "evergreen" program— one that he would implement at Intel—in which employees are given a new options grant every year in an effort to keep the staff loyal to the company.

When Coherent Radiation went public in May, 1970, Noyce made roughly $250,000. He held onto his stock and served on the board for another 13 years.

Noyce also served on the board of Four-Phase Systems, a Fairchild spinout founded by the leader of Fairchild's MOS circuit design group, Lee Boysel. Four-Phase aimed to build an MOS-based computer with solid-state memory and a logic chip built from silicon. Intel, too, of course, was building solid-state memory and logic chips. But neither Noyce nor Boysel saw any potential conflict of interest in Noyce's decision to serve as a director of Four-Phase. Boysel's company was not going to sell any components at all—only finished computers—and so would not compete with Intel in any market.

Noyce invested about $50,000 in Four-Phase. His was one of several fairly small investments by individuals; the major backer, Corning Glass (which had also backed Fairchild spinout Signetics) invested $500,000. Noyce most likely did not have high hopes that Four-Phase could accomplish the goals Boysel laid out for the company, but Noyce enjoyed involving himself with operations risky enough to sound almost audacious. He was also fascinated by the Four-Phase computer effort, and it may have been his early exposure to Boysel's ideas about general-purpose logic chips that made him so receptive to Hoff's thoughts on the subject.[52]

THE BOARD THAT MATTERED MOST to Noyce netted him no income and met in Grinnell, Iowa. Four or six times each year, Noyce traveled to Grinnell College, where he was completing his fourth, and final, year as board chair in 1970. He loved this job. One of his nephews attended the college, and Noyce always stopped by his dormitory to talk to the students and "get a sense of the place." Noyce led the Grinnell trustees meetings with the same air of apparent nonchalance he brought to all his meetings, seemingly more interested in understanding his colleagues' ideas than in expressing his own. And yet the questions he asked had a way of bringing people around to his point of view, one of the college presidents recalled. "Somehow they usually reached the conclusions Bob wanted them to reach. You just never had a sense he was leading them there."[53]

In May 1970, Noyce received a call from Grinnell College president Glenn Leggett. At Kent State University in Ohio, members of the National Guard, called in by the governor in response to massive campus protests against the war in Vietnam and the invasion of Cambodia, had killed four unarmed students and wounded nine others. Leggett told Noyce that the Grinnell campus was in an uproar unlike any in its history—and its recent history was the sort that inspired an FBI report stating "this College has a widespread reputation in the Midwest as being of the ultra-liberal type." In 1968, Grinnell students had protested a Marine recruiter's visit by transforming the campus into a makeshift military graveyard, complete with hundreds of crosses dotting the lawns. In 1969, a representative from *Playboy*, on campus in connection with a new policy allowing opposite-sex visits in the dormitories, had been greeted by ten naked students carrying signs reading, "*Playboy* is a Money Changer in the Temple of the Body"— a protest Noyce attributed to "outside agitators." Grinnell had also seen near-continual anti-war protests for the past year.[54]

But nothing had prepared the administration for the reaction to Kent State. Students from universities all over Iowa began to congregate at Grinnell, many of them "big city kids," as Leggett put it. Leggett received threats of "violent action" planned to erupt on campus. The student body sent a resolution to the faculty, which was meeting in special session, declaring the Kent State atrocity an "act of official repression" both "immoral" and "irrational." The faculty voted to suspend classes for two days, a move that left hundreds of agitated students with time to stage impromptu teach-ins and protests. Adding to the sense of barely contained chaos was the physical condition of the campus: the buildings and grounds employees had been on strike since mid-April, and vandals had overturned furniture in department lounges, defaced the library walls, and dumped garbage on the lawns. As Leggett put it, "The temperature was rising every minute of every day after Kent State."[55]

Leggett wanted to know how Noyce, as chair of the board of trustees, felt about the school shutting down for the safety of the students. Noyce told Leggett, "We [trustees] don't know anything about what the students will do. That's your problem. Do what you can about it, and we will support you."[56]

On May 14, Leggett asked Noyce to come to Grinnell immediately. He had decided to cancel not only classes but also the commencement exercises and reunions scheduled for two days hence. Many parents and alumni—and some students, as well—were furious. The people in town, a fair portion of whose income came from serving families and alumni attending these functions, were even angrier.

For three days, straight through the would-be commencement weekend, Noyce sat in the living room of Grinnell House, the campus home of a dozen Grinnell College presidents and now used primarily for entertaining distinguished guests. Cigarette always in hand, Noyce talked to anyone who came in to register a complaint or get more information. Or, to be more precise, Noyce characteristically listened more than he talked.

Noyce felt that the events at Kent State were tragically predictable, the near-inevitable outcome of mixing young angry students with young armed troops and high tensions. Privately, and in discussion with other trustees, Noyce worried that Grinnell was pandering to its students, overly sensitive to every individual psyche and interest. The faculty had dropped nearly all graduation requirements as part of what was called "a pioneering adventure into free and open curricular territory." Student athletes had begun refusing to compete because they "didn't believe in competition." Noyce thought this was all absurd. Students had to learn that the world did not always accommodate every whim. He was concerned that Grinnell was failing in its educational responsibility to teach students how to succeed. A few years after Kent State and the events at Grinnell, Gordon Moore said of the team at Intel, "We are really the revolutionaries in the world today—not the kids with the long hair and beards who were wrecking the schools a few years ago." Noyce undoubtedly would have agreed.[57]

Noyce, of course, shared none of these thoughts with the parents, alumni, students, and community members who came to speak to him at Grinnell House. Among this crowd, Noyce was more sponge than speaker—his gaze always focused on the person talking, his head cocked in deliberation and understanding. President Leggett has always felt that Noyce, with his calm demeanor and longstanding affiliations with both the town and the college, helped to defuse a potentially explosive situation.

BACK AT INTEL, Noyce focused a good deal of his energy on trying to build Intel's credibility. Most potential customers at this point were large computer companies comfortable working with established suppliers like Texas Instruments, Motorola, or Fairchild. The plethora of little startups nipping at these big players' heels did not impress executives accustomed to more mature suppliers. Noyce offered Intel's best tool for standing out from the other upstarts. "It helped that Noyce could come in having run Fairchild, with that understanding and experience," explains Intel's marketing vice president. "We were the only [young company] that maybe could count, and Bob [did that]." Customers gave Intel a chance in part because they believed Noyce when he said that this little operation could perform. In some sense, he could play the same role for Intel that Sherman Fairchild had played for Noyce and his seven Fairchild Semiconductor co-founders when Mr. Fairchild vouched for them with IBM. "Nobody else could have done that [made Intel a credible alternative to big suppliers]," the vice president averred. "Andy couldn't have done that. I couldn't do it and didn't do it. Bob did it."[58]

In early February 1971, Noyce spent two weeks in Japan encouraging Japanese firms to design the 1103 into their products. The island nation would come to account for about 15 percent of Intel's 1972 sales. During his visit to Japan, Noyce spent a day at Busicom, the calculator manufacturer for whom Hoff had developed the microprocessor. Noyce must have been feeling good about the project. Frederico Faggin had proven an inspired hire. Only nine months after he joined Intel, Faggin produced working samples of the entire calculator set—a remarkable accomplishment. Busicom president Kojima, too, must have been pleased with the progress on the chip set. But he had a new issue on his mind. The calculator market was proving more competitive than expected. Even though Busicom was only beginning to receive shipments from Intel, Kojima wanted Intel to reduce their prices.[59]

When Noyce returned to California, he asked Hoff what Intel's top priorities should be if a chance arose to re-negotiate the Busicom contract. Hoff was insistent: "If you can't get any other concession, just get the right to sell to other people." Frederico Faggin recalls making the same request to Noyce. Busicom cared about the microprocessor only as a calculator, but Noyce, Moore, and the technical men behind the chip saw that it could just as easily be programmed to do other things. A programmable, general-purpose logic device, Noyce thought, could be the "standard 2-by-4 or

6-penny nail" in the electronics industry. As things stood now, engineers at computer companies designed every plank and nail equivalent used in their systems.[60]

Shortly after Busicom chose Hoff's architecture for their calculator, Noyce had quietly begun his own private version of market research on "a general purpose way of programming logic." (The term microprocessor had not yet come into use.) When he visited customers who were requesting custom circuits for certain simple logic functions, Noyce made sure at some point to ask, in an offhanded way, why the customer did not just buy a computer and program it to do the task. The answer was always the same: I could do that, but it's too expensive. This research further reinforced Noyce's own hunch that the microprocessor could be used in dozens of potential applications—not only in computers, but also in areas largely untouched by microelectronics, such as cars and home appliances—if the price was right.[61]

Hoff believes that Noyce was almost alone among senior management in his excitement about the microprocessor in 1969 and 1970. Moore insists that although "Hoff thinks it was Noyce who kept that from being killed, [there was] no way that project was going to be killed! The microprocessor was an example of exactly the kind of product that we were looking for for the next generation." Andy Grove wanted the microprocessor to go away. Bob Graham felt the company already had enough to do just selling memory chips. How could they sell microprocessors? And why would they want to, since Graham estimated Intel could expect to sell, at best, 2,000 units per year? It would just be a big distraction with little potential for income.[62]

Perhaps this opposition explains why Noyce did not act immediately on the Busicom request to renegotiate prices. He certainly had other things on his mind. In June, the company was scheduled to move into a new building on a 26-acre abandoned pear orchard in Santa Clara, about ten miles south of the original Mountain View headquarters. The building had been under construction for more than a year and represented the first step in a $15–$20 million office and fab complex that Intel expected would eventually occupy nearly 400,000 square feet. The shareholders meeting was scheduled for April, and before that, Noyce planned to attend an electronics research meeting sponsored by the IEEE in New York and then leave for a packed ten-day trip to Europe. In Paris, he planned to speak on "microcircuits" to about 100 people, roughly one-third of whom were potential customers, one-third competitors, and one-third potential investors. In Brussels, he would meet with the head of Intel's first European sales office. Noyce and Bob Graham, who joined him for part of the trip, also met with potential customers and distributors to promote the 1103 and Intel's other products.[63]

Hoff, who accompanied Noyce on this trip, treasures one memory from it. "When I came down for breakfast one morning, I met [the Intel Europe sales manager]. He looked like he had been run over by a train. It seems that Bob had wanted to stay up talking and drinking, and the salesman made the mistake of trying to keep up with him. Just as I was wondering what condition Bob was going to be in, he came downstairs as fresh and chipper as anything. And the salesmen are the ones who are supposed to be the ones who can do all the drinking and such!"[64]

As soon as Noyce returned from Europe, Moore left town for a week. These sorts of oscillating schedules were not at all unusual in the early years at Intel. As long as the other was home to "mind the store," both Noyce and Moore were comfortable going away.

Throughout the spring and summer of 1971, Noyce was also preparing for Intel's initial public offering of stock, slated for the fall. The 1103 was beginning to look like a breakaway success. It had met and then passed Noyce's penny-a-bit target and every major computer mainframe manufacturer other than IBM (which used proprietary devices) had committed to the product or had the 1103 in prototype. This news helped position Intel as a promising upstart bursting with potential—investors' favorite type of company. Noyce and Rock also wanted to take Intel public because they felt that it was time to give the employees, the earliest of whom had seen the value of their stock options nearly quintuple, a chance to sell some of the stock on the public market. Plus, Intel could use the cash. The move to the new building generated losses of more than $400,000 for July and August, and while September was looking more promising, Noyce warned employees that "one robin doesn't make a spring, and the competitive situation remains severe."[65]

In preparation for the IPO, Noyce consulted with attorneys and bankers, reviewed drafts of the prospectus, met with auditors, signed the certificates necessary for the offering, wrote explanatory letters to employees and current investors, invited employees to buy stock in the offering as "friends of the company," and met dozens of times with Rock and with executives from C. E. Unterberg, Towbin, the investment bank that was underwriting the offering. By August, most of Noyce's days included at least one IPO-related appointment.[66]

SEC rules for public offerings required Intel to cancel the stock-purchase plan set up at the company's establishment. Noyce dreamed of replacing this plan with options packages that would be distributed to every employee, "including janitors." He worried, though, if people with limited educations could understand what a stock option was and how volatile the markets could be. He and Moore finally decided that once a plan could be developed that met SEC guidelines for publicly held companies, Intel should re-institute a stock-purchase plan, rather than options, for nonprofessional employees. Under this plan, which was implemented in 1972, every employee would be allowed to take up to 10 percent of base pay in Intel stock, which could be bought at 15 percent below market rates. The stock purchase plan met Noyce and Moore's goals of giving employees a stake in the company without requiring the sophisticated financial knowledge associated with stock options.[67]

Adding to Noyce's workload were the tensions between Graham and Grove, which reached a breaking point in the summer of 1971. In May, Grove had marched into Moore's office and told him that he thought he might need to leave Intel because, as he later put it, "it was far too painful for me to continue to do what I needed to do at work *and* fight Bob Graham." Faced with this news, Moore had begun to fiddle with a paper clip on his desk—a sure sign of stress to those who know him. Bob Graham was a close personal friend of Moore's. They often fished together.[68]

Grove left Moore's office worried that his boss was not going to do anything, but Moore almost immediately walked over to Noyce's office and shut the door. Shortly thereafter, Noyce began interviewing candidates for the marketing job. Although Noyce and Grove had very different approaches to management at Intel, Noyce had grown to like Grove—and more importantly, to appreciate his value to the company. Noyce saw what had happened at Fairchild when his detail-man Sporck left. He could not let that happen again.

By June, Noyce had found a marketing candidate who impressed him and who he thought could work with Grove: Ed Gelbach, a luxuriously mustachioed, straight-talking, technically trained, number crunching marketing expert from Texas Instruments. Just to be safe, Noyce and Moore insisted that Grove interview Gelbach before they offered him a job. Grove came away so impressed by Gelbach that he not only approved his hiring but also began growing his own mustache. Gelbach immediately demonstrated his negotiation skills by securing a very rich stock-options package for himself.[69]

With Gelbach on deck and Moore away on a fishing trip—a planned absence that "just made it a lot easier for me," Moore says—Noyce walked into Bob Graham's office in early July and sat down. "Shit," Noyce said, cutting straight to the point. "We have an incompatible situation here, and you're going to have to go." When Graham called home to tell his wife that he had lost his job, all she said was, "Thank God." The battles with Grove had been destroying them all.[70]

Graham was probably the first person that Noyce personally fired, a remarkable situation given that Noyce had been a senior manager for more than a decade. Firing Graham must have been excruciating for Noyce, who thought he was smart and good with customers. At Fairchild, those feelings, coupled with Noyce's own dislike of personal confrontation, would have been reasons enough to keep Graham on board. But Noyce had learned his lesson. He needed the Grove "whip" at Intel. "What that must have taken for Noyce to do," Grove mused aloud years later. "It must have been like cutting out his liver."[71]

ED GELBACH'S ARRIVAL AT INTEL had an immediate effect on the company's approach to the processor chip in the Busicom calculator set. Texas Instruments, Gelbach's previous employer, was trying to build a general-purpose logic chip, and Gelbach, like Noyce and Hoff, saw the promise in the devices. He absolutely thought Intel needed to find a way to get the rights to the microprocessor they were building for Busicom.

Gelbach's enthusiasm refocused Noyce's thoughts on the device. Within a week of Gelbach's arrival, Noyce began jotting down ideas about microprocessors in the thin, black-covered record book he carried with him nearly all the time. The pages are peppered with ideas that ranged far beyond calculators: "point of sale—inventory control," "concept for data retrieval," "electronic checkout," "Supermarket—3 mkts [markets]—1. hardware, 2. processing of data for mgmt [management], 3. market research data from volatile base." He imagined customers who might be interested in microprocessors: "NCR, Litton, RCA, Pitney Bowes, AC Nielson, Time Inc." He could picture the devices used in "traffic control—stop lights" or in "gas pumps."[72]

In August, Noyce requested that Intel's general counsel investigate "exclusivity" issues related to the microprocessor. This is probably when the process of negotiating the rights to the microprocessor back to Intel began in earnest. Noyce met with Mr. Kojima in Japan on September 21, most likely the date that the negotiations, which were quite casual, were finalized. "The Japanese don't use lawyers for these kinds of negotiations; the Americans tend to," Noyce explained later. "So [Busicom] had a guy ... who was just writing down the terms of what we agreed on, sitting there talking in the office; very nice simple agreements. . . . It was just simply writing down, 'You agree to do this, we agree to do that.'" When the discussions concluded, Intel had secured the right to sell the chip for non-calculator applications. Around this time, concerns about a potential conflict of interest led Noyce to resign from the board of Four-Phase, the company building a computer around a general-purpose logic chip.[73]

Intel did not, however, immediately exercise its right to market the microprocessor. Noyce told Hoff, "We have a tiger by the tail, but we're just not ready to announce the product. We're not ready to make a decision." At this point, Noyce and Moore were not concerned about whether a market existed for a microprocessor device, but they were unsure whether this particular microprocessor was, in Noyce's words, "adequate to serve that market. Should we wait to get something better?" A few board members feared that the microprocessor might push the company into the systems business. Intel, like most other semiconductor companies, sold individual circuits that customers would plug into systems of their own design. But this four-chip microprocessor family Hoff had designed was already a system in itself. Some board members worried that a move to market the microprocessor would put Intel in the position of competing with its own customers, a fear that echoed those faced by Fairchild Semiconductor when it introduced the integrated circuit. Noyce had begun Intel with the expectation that the day would come when semiconductor companies would also build the computer systems that used their circuits—that is, in fact, one reason why Noyce hired Hoff, with his expertise in computer systems—but this was far from a universally accepted opinion.[74]

When Noyce finished explaining to Hoff that he was not certain Intel would bring the microprocessor to market any time soon, Hoff was almost beside himself. "Every time you delay [a public announcement of the microprocessor], you *are* making a decision!" he said. "You're making a decision not to announce. Someone is going to beat us to it. We're going to lose this opportunity."[75]

In the end, the few board members' objections had no hope of succeeding against the force of the support Noyce, Moore, and Gelbach—as well as Arthur Rock—expressed for this new device. (Grove says, "Microprocessors meant nothing to me. I was living and dying on two points of yields in memory.") It was probably October when Intel decided to market the microprocessor.[76]

Yet the microprocessor was far from the most important item on Noyce's agenda in the fall of 1971. On October 13, the company went public, offering nearly 300,000 shares at $23.50 apiece. This was not a large slice of the company. Early employees and directors of Intel held a combined 2.2 million shares (after stock splits), for which they had paid an average of $4.04. The offering was a smashing success: oversubscribed and immediately raising nearly $7 million for Intel.[77]

Noyce had flown to New York for the IPO, and he spent most of this first day as head of the publicly traded Intel walking the city, stopping every few hours at a pay telephone to call Arthur Rock for the latest word on how Intel was trading.

Walking with Noyce among the skyscrapers of Manhattan was Barbara Maness, a mask designer in Intel's MOS group. Maness was 28 and attractive, with long, straw-colored hair and clear blue eyes. She was employee number 43 at Intel. She and Noyce had been engaged in an affair since the summer of 1969, when Noyce, his wife and children in Maine for three months, invited Maness to dinner.[78]

As a mask designer, Maness was among the most highly compensated women at Intel. Masks are the detailed blueprints for any type of integrated circuit. In the late 1960s, they regularly consisted of thousands of squares, Xs, dashed lines, dotted lines, fat lines, thin lines—each color-coded and hand-drawn as small as possible, and each symbolizing a transistor or a diode or particular type of connection among the components in a circuit. Engineers had traditionally drawn their own masks, but in 1966, Fairchild had decided to teach a select group of women how to translate the engineers' plans into mask designs.

In 1966, Maness worked for Fairchild as a die attacher on the swing shift. (She did not know Noyce at Fairchild.) She was recently divorced from a man who provided no support for her three young children. She lived near the freeway in what she described as a "bad part of San Jose," in a mobile home that was the only option available to her because most apartment landlords did not want to rent to single mothers. She existed in a state of permanent exhaustion, getting off work at midnight, picking up her children at a sitter's in the wee hours of the morning, and sleeping only a few hours before the children awoke and needed her. When one of the Fairchild engineers suggested that she try to win a spot in the inaugural mask-design class, she jumped at the chance for a bigger paycheck and more reasonable hours. She took the required tests and was one of six women admitted to the class. She left Fairchild for Intel only because the engineer with whom she worked most closely had accepted a job at Intel and asked her to work for him there.

Maness's presence in Noyce's life was an open secret at Intel, where many people considered Betty's announcement that she was going to live in Maine for the summers "an open invitation for Bob to find another woman." Extramarital affairs, while always considered a bit shady, were common enough to have generated their own lexicon. The women were called "girlfriends." The couples were "dating." Noyce and Maness regularly spent time with other semiconductor executives and their girlfriends.[79]

Barbara Maness was every bit as bright as Betty Noyce but, unlike Betty, she was also young, adventurous, undemanding, and unquestionably devoted. Noyce enjoyed doing with her things he never could have done with his wife. He could talk with her at length about Intel and the technical aspects of its products. She happily joined him to sail in Hawaii, to ski in Aspen, and to watch the Independence Day fireworks from the copilot's seat of his plane as they flew down the California coast. Noyce paid for Maness to take flying lessons—"If something happens to me, I want you to know how to land the plane"—which she adored. He kept a collapsible motorcycle in the back of his plane, and he and Maness would often ride to remote locations after they landed. Then they would backpack for hours, sometimes above the snow line. Later they would unwind with cups of "Purple Jesus"—grape Tang and vodka—that Noyce chilled in the snow pack.

Maness was entirely self-sufficient. While singlehandedly raising three children, she also managed to save enough to buy a parcel of land in the Santa Cruz Mountains, where she intended to build a home. Noyce found her independence attractive. "You'll do well," he told her admiringly, "and I'll just stand by and watch."

One of Noyce's favorite parts of their illicit romance was the element he called "intrigue." Always a risk taker, he reveled in bringing his family and Maness into close proximity with each other. He paid for Maness's children to attend sleep-away camp so that she could live in his house with him for the summers while his family was away. He enjoyed having Maness with him when he talked to Betty on the phone. When his daughter's dog had puppies, Noyce asked Maness to come to the house to buy one from Betty, posing as a random Intel employee who had read about their sale on a company bulletin board. Maness was "scared to death," but she did it. It would not be surprising if Maness had designed the mask that the Noyce family followed when they came to Intel to cut rubylith.

Noyce played the same sorts of games at work. When Intel bought a block of tickets for a play, he obtained a pair and gave one to Maness, whom he dropped off a few blocks from the theater. She sat next to an empty seat until the lights went down, at which point he ducked in and joined her. Immediately before the lights came up again, he left. On a business trip, he made a show of buying a stunning pearl necklace in front of a colleague who would be almost certain to see it around Maness's neck at the company Christmas party. He had Maness accompany him to a dinner with an important visitor to Intel, and the next morning went out of his way to lead this man past Maness as she worked on her design. This notion of "pulling one over on people" delighted him to no end. For her part, Maness generally kept quiet. "I was very protective of him," she explains. "I didn't go bragging about."[80]

Walking through the streets of New York City on the day his company went public, Noyce made sure to take Maness to the Statue of Liberty, the very place he had only dreamed of seeing he was a teenager in Grinnell. Now he was here, an important man with a beauty at his side—and his last phone call to Rock informed him that he was also a millionaire ten times over.[81]

ALMOST IMMEDIATELY UPON HIS return to California, Noyce began lessons for certification as a jet pilot. He kept detailed notes in his daily calendar: "Watch—at 5000 flatten to get 500'min—level air plane and check horizon—at 65% power for cruise 5-7 speed altitude and main[tain] for 500 and 1000—hi speed. . . ." He also began shopping for small jets and attending meetings of the Aircraft Owners and Pilots Association. At home, the Noyces' family life registered few visible changes after the IPO. Noyce worried that it was "tough to teach values" when a family had great sums of money. "It's much easier to be raised with a father who is poor—[because] you have to hustle—than it is with a father who is wealthy," he told a friend. He and Betty kept knowledge of the family's financial situation hidden from the children as much as possible.[82]

Almost exactly a month after the IPO, on November 15, 1971, Intel announced its microprocessor with a bold advertisement proclaiming the arrival of "a new era of integrated electronics—a micro-programmable computer on a chip!" More than 5,000 people wrote to the address at the bottom of the advertisement, requesting more information—the most dramatic response to a product announcement Intel had ever experienced. Noyce was attending the Fall Joint Computer Conference in Las Vegas at the time of the announcement, and he almost certainly helped to staff the Intel suite, which was soon overrun with customers wanting to know more about "this computer on a chip thing."[83]

To use the microprocessor, customers had to change their thinking. Before the microprocessor, designers at Intel's customer firms built their systems by configuring individual integrated circuits, each with a different dedicated function, on a board. Changing the system required changing the physical arrangement of the integrated circuits, or hardware. Intel's new microprocessor systems required something very different—changes made not by moving physical objects, but by reprogramming the instructions stored in program memory. The microprocessor, in other words, brought software to the semiconductor industry. In doing so, it placed new demands on customers, most of whom were experienced hardware designers unfamiliar with using computer programs to solve their systems problems.[84]

Regis McKenna, a marketing and public relations expert hired by Intel late in 1971, summarized the problems facing Intel's microprocessors thus: "You couldn't promote the things [if] people didn't know what they were." The challenges faced on this front were daunting enough that Gelbach set up an independent microprocessor marketing operation, separate from the rest of the marketing division. The company developed voluminous written technical documentation for the 4004—the owner's manual alone ran well over 100 pages at a time when other Intel chips were boxed with only a ten-page data sheet. Intel shipped more manuals for the 4004 than actual processors. "There were just lots of people who wanted to read about microprocessors, independent of whether they were buying any," explained Bill Davidow, whom Gelbach had hired to run microprocessor marketing.[85]

Intel developed and marketed hardware tools to facilitate programming the microprocessor. The EPROM, a specialized read-only memory chip, could be programmed electrically and erased with ultraviolet light, which made it possible to reprogram the microprocessor very easily. Development aids, marketed under the name "Intellec," were hardware simulation environments, simple single-board versions of a computer with all the proper circuitry to emulate the functioning of a central processor. A designer could use this development aid in prototype before committing to a specific microprocessor program. The EPROM and Intellec systems functioned as software but looked like the hardware familiar to designers.

Intel also sponsored a series of technical seminars on the microprocessor as part of the ongoing attempt to "lower the confrontation level with the engineers," as Davidow puts it. Senior Intel engineers led seminars at a bruising rate in 1971 and 1972. A typical schedule found them one day in Connecticut, the next in New Jersey, the next in Philadelphia, the next in Rochester, and then, after a weekend of rest, in Minneapolis, Chicago, Ann Arbor, Houston, and Dallas. These meetings were as helpful to the presenters, who received pointed commentary on the processors' architecture and performance, as they were to the audience.[86]

Most of the early microcprocessors were used as control devices, not in computers. An applications book that Regis McKenna developed in 1972 to explain "how people use microprocessors" included an airport "marijuana sniffer" to find illlicit drugs in luggage, a device to flush all the commodes in a bank of toilets simultaneously to save water, blood analyzers, traffic light controllers, simple testers, and machine tool controls. When Gelbach presented this list to the board, one director turned to him and asked, "Don't you have any customers you could be proud of?"[87]

NOYCE SPENT MUCH OF THE END OF 1971 trying to placate customers who had bought large numbers of 1103s and were frustrated by the device's problems. Mike Markkula, who joined Intel's marketing group in 1969, recalls how Noyce often defused problems: "Bob was just so straightforward and didn't try to sweep things under the carpet. He'd say, 'We know what the problem is. We're fixing it. Here's when we'll get it fixed. We're doing everything humanly possible to meet your requirements—and yeah, we goofed up.' You know, when you're that honest and that straightforward, it's hard [for the customer] to continue to be angry." Markkula saw Noyce use this approach several times with Burroughs, which was using the temperamental 1103s in one of its computers. "Without Bob's interaction on many occasions, that relationship would have died," Markkula says. "There was no way that we could keep the whole thing together without his help. [Noyce] would say, 'Okay, what do you want me to tell these guys?' And we'd give him all the background, all the scoop, and he would go [talk to them]. And he was really good at it." Concurs Roger Borovoy, "If you have a disgruntled customer, the best thing you can do is send Noyce. First of all, he's an instant sponge. Sits down with whomever, the marketing guy or whatever, and instantly absorbs every detail in his head in ten minutes. And then he goes out there and beautifully massages [the details], and he knows everything, and it looks like Noyce—this great god Noyce—is intimately involved in this customer's problem."[88]

Noyce was proud of his ability to calm hostile customers, but his favorite part of his job was what he called the "missionary work ... to spread the word about microprocessors." He certainly adopted a bit of a religious zeal about the microprocessor-driven world-to-come and was happy to talk about it in the most unlikely places. In 1972, he and Betty surprised his parents with a fiftieth anniversary tour of San Francisco that included the entire extended family. The Noyce clan was riding in a bus Bob and Betty had chartered when Noyce made his way to the front and faced his seated family. "Everybody," he said, "I want you to see this." He held up a silicon wafer about three inches in diameter and printed with microprocessors. "This is going to change the world. It's going to revolutionize your home. In your own house," he continued, clearly caught up in the moment, "you'll all have computers. You will have access to all sorts of information. You won't need money any more. Everything will happen electronically." He carefully handed the wafer to the person nearest to him and sat back down. At least one person on the bus, the fiancée of Noyce's nephew, was surprised by her would-be uncle's showboating and appalled at the arrogance she thought it implied. She remembers thinking, "This guy really thinks he can see the future. This will never happen."[89]

The skepticism expressed by Noyce's soon-to-be niece was an only slightly exaggerated version of the response Intel's microprocessor provoked in many people who heard Noyce speak about it. Noyce's early rounds of "missionary work" can best be understood as preparing the soil of public opinion for the planting of the microprocessor. The ground was hard, and the debris to be cleared away was thick. Computers in 1971 had shrunk from room-sized million-dollar behemoths to refrigerator-sized units costing tens of thousands of dollars. But Noyce was trying to make people understand that a computer could be as small as a few chips you could hold in your hand. Bill Davidow, who joined Intel in 1973 as head of microprocessor marketing, says that in most customers' minds, "the microprocessor was just a toy, and [computers] were these massive machines with massive amounts of storage. And here was Noyce predicting that someday this [microprocessor] would be the central processor for everything. That was a big step."[90]

Several people remember a talk Noyce gave to a general business audience in 1970 in which he was asked, "Well, let's just say my [IBM] 360 computer could be as small as you say. What if it fell through a crack in the floor?" Noyce's quick response—"You wouldn't care. It would just cost a few dollars to replace it"—sparked more than a few disbelieving laughs.

Ted Hoff recalls a similarly unconvinced audience member asking him about microprocessor repairs—where would you take the chip to have it fixed, and would they do it under a microscope? Hoff explained that you would just throw away the chip and buy a new one.[91]

"It was a battle of opinion," Noyce once said of Intel's bid to foster the microprocessor market. The battle only heightened when several other companies introduced their own microprocessors in 1972.[92]

In an attempt to raise senior executives' awareness of the microprocessor, Noyce visited high-level managers at customers that he and Davidow thought might one day become major accounts. This was not particularly easy work. It required promoting a vision of the future that corresponded in only the most tenuous ways to the realities of the available technology. When Noyce suggested to a team of General Motors executives that the company might one day use computers to control the fuel consumption of engines or nonskid brakes, the managers were unconvinced. The last time they had installed computer-controlled, antilock brake equipment in one of their concept cars, the computer had cost nearly twice as much as the car and taken up nearly all of the trunk space. If they filled the trunk of a car with these computers Noyce was promoting, where would the drivers store their grocery bags?[93]

In other words, the GM executives found it nearly impossible to believe that a slice of silicon could do the work of a computer—and in 1971, Noyce almost certainly told them, their skepticism was well grounded. No one would want the 4004 controlling the brakes in production cars; the device was too slow and too rudimentary for general use. And its successor, the 8008 (introduced in April 1972), was not much better.[94]

But Noyce was not trying to sell 4004s or 8008s to General Motors. He was starting conversations that he expected would only bear fruit years later. He knew he was contending with entrenched ways of thinking and years-long design cycles. He felt confident that by the time these customers were prepared to experiment with microprocessors, the technology would have caught up to his visions for it. As indeed it did. It was 1974 when automobile manufacturers held their first Conference on Automobile Electronics and around this same date that microprocessors began to make their way into production vehicles. But in 1972, GM would only allow Intel to install a 4004 to serve as a controller for the nonskid brake system in its concept car. Noyce, true to form, celebrated their installation by donning a helmet and racing the car around and around the steeply banked GM track.[95]

9

The Edge of What's Barely Possible

A ndy Grove spent much of 1972 worrying. In February he wrote, "We are not doing well at all! Momentum broken, refresh [problem with the 1103] still with us, bipolar yield still (or again) nowhere!" He kept detailed tabs on Intel's competition, noting that the 4,000 1103s ordered by Texas Instruments were not going to their computer group, and announcing how many semiconductor memories had been shipped by TI-spinout Mostek in a given quarter. In December, he was concerned because the comments offered at the executive meeting to review the operations plan he laid out for 1973 were "brief, between long periods of silence and sighs."[1]

Noyce, on the other hand, took a wider view and liked what he saw for most of 1972. Intel was building about 100,000 1103s each year and still could not keep up with demand. By year's end, the 1103 was the best-selling memory chip in the world. It was so terribly difficult to reverse engineer that Intel had almost no competitors, outside of its official second source MIL, for more than a year. When Intel increased the size of its wafers and MIL tried to follow suit, the Canadian company lost the process entirely. This left Intel with a near-monopoly on the 1103. Effectively all of Intel's $23.4 million revenue in 1972 came from sales of this one device.[2]

A tentative foray into building complete memory systems for customers was proving very profitable. The microprocessor had brought Intel hundreds of new customers, most of them small firms with small orders, but the trend nonetheless augured well for the future. Noyce expected that once Intel could build a more powerful microprocessor, the market would take off. And Intel had that processor under development. The company was building new facilities on the Santa Clara campus, a fab in Livermore, California, and an assembly operation in Penang, Malaysia. Noyce was considering adding an on-site day care center to the Santa Clara campus as a way to attract the largely female workforce for the fabs, but a series of informal discussions he held with various Intel employees never really went anywhere.[3]

In July, Intel acquired a six-man digital watch company called Microma for roughly $2 million. Noyce and Moore predicted that in the next five years, some 200 million digital watches would be sold around the world. Every one of them would require elements in which either Microma or Intel was expert: liquid crystal displays, detailed assembly, and a type of MOS chip called CMOS. Intel, true to its unwritten policies, was going to try to capture this market before it attracted attention from anyone else. Noyce expected Intel would, in the next few years, sell some $20 million in watch modules, 20 percent of which would go into Microma watches. The rest would be sold to other watch manufacturers.[4]

In November, Noyce invited one of the Grinnell trustees, Sam Rosenthal, to tour the new fab and independently assess the merits of the college's investment. "Boy Noyce showed [us] through the plant at Santa Clara," Rosenthal wrote to his fellow trustees, using their affectionate nickname for Noyce. "It was a most interesting and baffling experience for me. Interesting, because it is a most complicated and ingenious manufacturing process[,] and baffling, because I didn't understand very much of it, though Bob did his best to inform me." Rosenthal was astonished by the manufacturing facilities, parts of which, he said, "reminded me of a hospital operating room, for the employees were dressed in white outfits and hats [to avoid contaminating the chips], but their feet were not protected." His conclusion: "I was most impressed by the plant and the manufacturing process. [Noyce] is as optimistic as ever about business."[5]

By December of 1972, Noyce's optimism had proven well founded. Intel was entirely debt free and had more than doubled revenues and tripled profits. Just one year later, when Intel's fifth anniversary coincided with a boom in the industry, the company's revenues and profits again tripled, and so, too, did the number of its employees and its manufacturing space. Intel's pretax profit margin was a remarkable 40 percent (25 percent after tax).[6]

Behind the scenes, Noyce worked carefully to ensure Intel's financial figures looked good to Wall Street. In 1973, for example, Intel's profits were so high that the company accelerated its research, starting work on projects originally slated for 1974, in hopes of reducing its net income. "Bob [is] very anxious that the earnings not fluctuate erratically up and down and that each quarter make a favorable showing with both the preceding quarter and [the] corresponding quarter of a year ago," reported Grinnell trustee Joe Rosenfield.[7]

He added that Noyce had suggested that Grinnell might want to sell some of its Intel stock, while the price it could command was so high. Noyce had himself sold a bit of his stock to buy a small jet shortly after passing his flight test on Valentine's Day, 1972. Rosenfield disagreed with Noyce's suggestion to sell and believed, in fact, that Noyce had made it only because he felt a deep "responsibility to the College" to be a bit conservative. Warren Buffett agreed: "While you know much more about electronic widgets than I," he wrote to Rosenfield, "Intel seems to me to be the best vehicle we have, or are likely to have, to gain a quantum jump in our endowment." The board decided to keep their position intact.[8]

When Intel's stock split three for two in April, Noyce was bombarded with questions from many of the company's 1,000 employees about the effects of the split on their options. He wrote a careful letter, beginning "just to put your minds at rest," explaining the split's implications to this group still largely unfamiliar with the stock options they had nonetheless come to value greatly. By the end of 1973, Intel was worth more than $160 million, and Moore was saying that the only thing that might limit its growth in the future was its ability to hire enough engineers and scientists.[9]

Noyce, always the "receiver of messages from the outside," had another concern—not a nagging, panic-inducing worry, but a bit of unpleasant noise that registered on the periphery of his radar screen. In October, OPEC had embargoed exports of oil in the wake of the Yom Kippur War in Israel. Within weeks, the state of California had declared the need to ration electricity and announced plans to ask industrial customers to cut their power consumption to levels 10 percent below those of the corresponding month a year earlier. If the voluntary 10-percent plan did not work, then the utilities companies might resort to rolling blackouts to conserve power.

The prospect of rolling blackouts alarmed Noyce, who readily admitted that the semiconductor industry had designed its processes and equipment "assum[ing] that petrochemicals were free and available and that power was free and available." The average wafer fab used 30 times as much electricity as a commercial office building of the same size, and consumed large quantities of xylene, acetone, and disopropyl alcohol, all petrochemical derivatives.[10]

Immediately upon learning of the state's plans, Noyce had Intel start conservation and recycling efforts in-house. He had the company contribute to a political action committee organized by WEMA, a trade association of West Coast electronics manufacturers. He also joined a contingent of semiconductor executives testifying before the California Public Utilities Commission in December 1973. Noyce told the commissioners that the fast-growing industry needed more, not less, power—and he pointedly reminded them that during the past year, the semiconductor industry accounted for an estimated 40 percent of Santa Clara County's employment growth. During his presentation, he offered the commissioners a variety of doomsday scenarios: 40 percent layoffs if Intel was forced to slow production to last year's levels, poisonous gases escaping into the atmosphere if the fabs could not use their ventilation systems due to unannounced power shutdowns, a million dollars' worth of product lost in less than an hour if electricity were shut off unexpectedly. "After a third power blackout," he said, "we'd quit and close the factory." Noyce and the other electronics executives pushed for passage of a bill that would prohibit blackouts and grant electronics companies a high priority in the state-wide hierarchy of users. The bill failed.[11]

The energy crisis worried Noyce more for its long-term implications about the semiconductor industry's relationship with the government than for its potential immediate effects on Intel. He had always been sensitive to the need to work in tandem with the government. In 1970 he said, "This really is a controlled society, controlled out of Washington, and if you're trying to steer around in all the traffic out there, you'd better listen to what the cop is telling people. Go with the tide, not against it. If a company is in the right business at the right time, then the whole society sweeps it along [—] if it is truly providing some useful service to the society. If it's not, it's going to be fighting everybody in sight all the way, and eventually will fail."[12]

What Noyce had not sufficiently understood until the mid-1970s, however, was that the government traffic cop could decide to block a street midway through rush hour. The threatened electricity rationing awakened him to the reality that he and Moore and everyone else at Intel could build the best possible product and in any number of ways "truly provide some useful service to society"—but ultimately, the government had the power to render such efforts moot. "I think all of us are getting into the position where government is affecting our lives more and more," Noyce groused to a reporter from an industry trade journal after his testimony. "The things that we used to think were the basic prerequisites of business have been taken over by the government."[13]

All in all, however, Noyce said he was ending 1973 feeling "very optimistic." On New Year's Eve 1974, he proudly told a reporter that Intel was forever "teetering on the edge of what's barely possible." Assuming the energy issue could be resolved, he said, "electronic applications appear to be unlimited."[14]

Noyce had other reasons to feel cheerful. By 1973, his Intel holdings alone—he and Moore each still owned 16 percent of Intel's stock—were valued at $26 million. By the middle of 1974, they were worth double that.[15]

He and Betty anonymously built a new library for the town near their summer home and gave large sums to libraries and educational television in California. Noyce helped with an effort to build a bank in low-income East Palo Alto. He was acutely aware of his own privileged position, which he did not ascribe simply to the blessings of an unusually capable mind. When one of his children wondered aloud whether her successes came from her own skills or from her status as his daughter, he asked, "Do you think I could do what I've done if I had been black or a woman?" The notion that skin color, poverty, or gender deprived people of their potential annoyed him. He felt committed to Grinnell in no small measure because it had not permitted his family's lack of resources to keep him from an education. He was no radical, but he served on the board of Big Brothers and Big Sisters, and he always took particular pride in a fab that Fairchild built on a Native American reservation in New Mexico, which for a time in the mid-1960s made the company, with 300 Navajo employees, the largest nongovernmental employer of Native Americans in the United States. His actions on what might loosely be termed the "social justice" front bring to mind his comments about good managers "getting the barriers out of the way to let people do the things they do well."[16]

In 1973, Noyce involved himself with the most unusual of his charitable efforts. He learned that the Audubon Society had developed a plan to reinvigorate Maine's nearly extinct population of puffins by flying chicks from Newfoundland to Eastern Egg Island, where it was hoped they would mature to build a colony. The project seemed tailor-made for Noyce. He could see Eastern Egg Island from his home. The plan to resurrect the puffin colony was risky but feasible—Noyce's preferred type of operation. No one knew if the puffins could even survive an airplane flight, much less establish themselves in a new location, but it seemed possible. Helping the Audubon Society would also provide Noyce with an excuse to fly, for what the group really needed was a private plane to transport an Audubon team to Newfoundland and then fly the team and a few chicks back to Maine.

Noyce was thrilled to offer his new jet and himself as a pilot. True to form, he also asked to join the researchers as they made their way along the 150-foot cliff that jutted over the ocean and served as a home to more than 300 puffins. The Audubon team and Noyce spent several hours searching for puffin chicks in burrows dug by the adult birds, all the while dodging attacks by screaming great black-back gulls protecting their own nests in the cliff's ledges.

The puffin airlift to Maine proved a success, and Noyce again volunteered his services in 1974 (when 54 puffin chicks were moved). He paid for the plane flights for the next two years, as well. After this, the colony was well established, and Noyce turned his attentions elsewhere.[17]

Bob and Betty maintained their reluctance to discuss the family wealth with their children. If they dined out, which they did quite infrequently, Noyce tended to order the lowest-priced dinner specials. Betty Noyce did not indulge in clothes or shopping sprees. Neither of them drove luxury cars. Even when Noyce's net worth approached $100 million, he once walked several blocks to buy a box of colored pencils at a grocery store to avoid paying what he considered exorbitant prices at a specialty art supplier. He did not think this at all incongruous behavior for someone who bought airplanes with nary a second thought. The young Noyces were paid a pittance for chores, and if they complained, Noyce would say, "You do a little work for a little money. You need to do a lot of work for a lot of money."[18]

But Bob and Betty were also quietly preparing their heirs for the responsibility that came with great wealth. They set up a trust to serve as an educational vehicle for the children, who were all now teenagers and who personally reviewed grant applications and determined which projects to fund. The young Noyces were more than up to the task. Bill was on his way to Dartmouth college after a high school career that included a top ranking in a statewide physics exam. Penny had been named one of the "outstanding high school students of English in the country" and was off to France to improve her fluency in *la belle langue*. Polly was bright, beautiful, and vivacious. Margaret was feisty and daring, on the cusp of adolescence. To all of them Noyce said the same thing: "Money can be used to do lots of things: it can be spent, it can be used to make more money, or it can build a future."[19]

NOYCE BEGAN TO GARNER ATTENTION from the general press in the early 1970s, when journalists started writing about California's "Silicon Valley." The name, which had first appeared in January 1971, in an *Electronic News* article, was far from ubiquitous, but whether the cluster of electronics firms on the San Francisco Peninsula was called "Silicon Valley," "Semiconductor Country," "California's Route 128," or "California's great breeding ground for industry," the national business press was beginning to take notice of it and of Noyce. In the early 1970s, *Business Week* and *Fortune* articles on the Peninsula's semiconductor companies prominently featured Intel, and by extension, Noyce and Moore.[20]

Noyce's speaking schedule also began to reflect a more general sort of attention. Most of his speeches were addressed to technical gatherings or analysts who specialized in the semiconductor industry, but he also keynoted a conference on innovation and shared a stage at the Iowa Academy of Science with Paul Ehrlich, author of *The Population Explosion*. Whenever he had the opportunity, Noyce talked about the microprocessor. Most of the devices were still used only in traffic lights, elevators, butcher scales, and other relatively rudimentary control functions, but in 1973 Noyce predicted that of all the electronics technology available anywhere in the world, "the thing that we will see make the most difference will be the extension of the microcomputer [microprocessor] into just about everything." Two years before, he had been even more specific about how the microprocessor would change things: "Control gadgetry of the future will permit a housewife to tell her oven to cook a roast rare rather than at a specific temperature—and it will. The motorist will direct his auto to travel at 55 miles an hour. A subscriber will remind his telephone he will be at the neighbors and calls will be transferred there." His son, after hearing one speech at MIT in 1973, said his father was most animated "when he got to predictions of new market areas: cars, calculators, watches, telephones." After the talk, Bill wrote to his sisters, "[Da and I] stayed up till about midnight talking about such things as Fermat's last theorem."[21]

All in all, Noyce cut a rather dashing figure, especially for a press used to less charisma from the technical sector. Reported one particularly fawning account: "Dr. Noyce finds time for skiing at Squaw Valley and sailing off the Maine Coast. 'We have six boats—if you want to count the row boat—one for each member of the family,' he says." In a similar vein came this comment from a newspaper aimed at engineers and managers in the electronics industry: "In many ways, Dr. Robert N. Noyce is just what every parent hopes his technically talented son will become: a thoroughly nice guy, technically brilliant (he holds more than a dozen patents), who raises four bright kids and becomes a success in business."[22]

Much was cracking beneath the veneer of unqualified success, however. Microma, Intel's digital-watch acquisition, was proving problematic, less for technical reasons than for its forcing Intel to contend with a commercial product for the first time. Noyce, Moore, Gelbach, and Grove found themselves discussing not yields and bits but gift boxes, watch bands, store displays, and jewelers' kits. Radio Shack put out a digital watch under the name Micronta, which confused customers. And the watches themselves were far from reliable. The Board of Directors meetings began by collecting those of the directors' watches that needed to be repaired. Even Noyce's brother Don, who was thrilled by the prospect of seeing his first digital watch, privately told his children that the display on "Uncle Bob's new kind of watch" was almost impossible to read.[23]

Closer to home, Penny had been hospitalized for asthma attacks so severe she landed in the intensive care ward. (Bob and Betty, unable to break their two-pack-a-day habits, refrained from smoking in her bedroom.) Her father was so worried about her, Penny wrote in 1972, that "I'm convinced that if I made the simplest request, a motorcade of Intel underlings would arrive at utmost speed." One of Noyce's planes, a twin-engine Cessna that he enrolled in a small charter service at the San Jose airport, crashed in Nevada and killed all four men who had been leasing it for the day. Noyce was not at fault, but he sold the plane shortly after it was returned to him.[24]

Moreover, the general tenor of the youth movement sweeping the United States made Noyce uneasy. Bill was growing his hair to his shoulders, and his letters from college referred to spending the night with his girlfriend. The Vietnam War had cast a shadow over the image of the once-glamorous technical industries. For Noyce, who was accustomed to people considering his work "worthwhile and important," this change was difficult. During and immediately after the war, Noyce later recalled, technology suddenly became an evil thing that "made napalm, burned babies, and polluted the environment." At his talk with Ehrlich, for example, Noyce had been angry and hurt to realize that most of the students in the audience considered himself and his colleagues in technology-based industries "bad people." He explained a few years later, "That's what scared me. [We were] bad compared to Paul Ehrlich, who was essentially arguing we should have zero progress from here on out. . . . How ridiculous can you be?"[25]

"I think my father really lost his compass [in the 1970s]," Penny Noyce has said. "It was a time of such change everywhere, such liberalization, such a relaxing of rules." Ten years later, Noyce said of this period in his life, "I didn't like myself the way I was." He said that he tried to "switch" by, among other unspecified things, growing a Gelbach-style mustache, but "it didn't help at all."[26]

Betty had begun spending more and more time on the East Coast, no longer returning to California when the school year began. Instead, she would stay in Maine from the end of May through the end of October. She felt that Bob's work and Intel's rising star further chained her to the second-class status of "Mrs. Robert Noyce" in California. She might have dealt with this by following some of her friends who were taking tentative steps into employment outside the home. Eugene Kleiner's wife Rose was heading back to school for a graduate degree. But Betty felt very strongly that "only bad mothers weren't home for their children." She would never have strayed from her own expectations of her proper place.[27]

A second alternative for Betty Noyce might have been to adopt the attitude assumed by many of the wives of senior Intel executives. Judy Vadasz said of the early years of Intel, "It was kind of like the war effort. You stayed home and did your thing so the warriors could go and build a temple." Judy Vadasz, Eva Grove, and other young "Intel wives" shared common ground in their young children, frequently absent husbands, and new-found wealth. They would often get together during the day, but they rarely complained to each other about their role in the Intel "war effort." They saw themselves as "a part of something big," Vadasz said. "Your part was, I guess, sacrificing your husband, your kid's father."[28]

Betty Noyce, however, had little in common with these women. She was a decade their senior. Her children were leaving the house, not starting elementary school. She had already been through the instant-wealth phenomenon. Moreover, she most definitely would not have found solace in the image of tending the hearth while Bob fought the battles. "There was too much executive ability in my family," explained Penny Noyce. "[My mother] was good at bossing people around and organizing them." Betty's friends were people whom she had known for decades, back when Bob was "just another husband always carrying a briefcase," as one confidante described him. These friends tended to view Bob as "a normal human being and not a genius" and Betty as a bit of a whirling dervish, always doing everything at a level far beyond the necessary. When the public television station held an auction, Betty wrote the catalog copy in beautiful, literate prose that took her hours to compose. Her needlepoint and quilts had become increasingly elaborate and detailed—several would eventually hang in a museum. She was, nonetheless, miserable in Bob's shadow in California. She often found herself yelling or crying as the days passed.[29]

She had long suspected Noyce was having a serious affair. When she and Bob went out together, the tension between them was palpable. It was not uncommon for each of them to go through an entire pack of cigarettes after dinner. Their refusal to accommodate their differences was astonishing. Betty thought her husband's need for stimulation and change bordered on pathological. He either had so little regard for or paid so little attention to her love of things old and traditional that he gave her a birthday gift of a bright orange and very high-tech Mazda rotary car—one of the first to come off the line. She, of course, hated it. He, in turn, was angered by her rejection.[30]

About this time, Noyce and a friend took a walk alone after eating dinner with Noyce's family. Staring straight ahead, Noyce said, almost to himself, "Boy, sometimes it's simpler to get on a plane to New York than to come home." He later told his daughter that he used to sit in the Intel parking lot for five or ten minutes every evening, idling the motor and wishing there was somewhere he could go that was not the house on Loyola Drive.[31]

He accelerated the risk in his relationship with Maness—rapidly committing "marital suicide," as one daughter put it. He would deliberately leave items belonging to Maness's children in his car, where Betty was almost certain to find them. In the spring of 1973, Noyce went out to dinner– Betty was in Maine—and instructed Maness to climb in through his open bedroom window and meet him in bed. It was here that one of his children discovered them.

THE UNDENIABLE EVIDENCE OF BOB'S TRANSGRESSIONS and of the deplorable state of the Noyces' marriage blew the family apart. The oldest daughters escaped to Ivy League colleges. The youngest was sent to a boarding school on the East Coast. Nineteen-year-old Bill announced his intention to marry within the year, a declaration that propelled Noyce, who clearly feared Bill would relive his own mistakes, to write an unusually heartfelt letter to his son. He told Bill not to marry to "shut out competition," that he was looking for a security in marriage that he would never be able to find, that living together unmarried was preferable to a hasty match, that his son should feel no obligation to support his fiancée while she finished school, and that, in general, he was not sure any young person was ready for the responsibility of marriage. To which Bill, who more than 30 years later remains happily married to his teenage love, rather acidly replied, "I'm not afraid of the responsibility of marriage; is there that much you know about it that I can't envision?"[32]

In general, Noyce dealt with the crisis by giving and giving to his children, each gift soaked with guilt and an unspoken plea to forgive him. A child asked for money; he sent a check for twice the request. Another wrote, "I am overwhelmed, awed, a little frightened by the way you people keep giving me things. You don't have to do that, you know." Another asked that Noyce restrict his gifts to a tuition check. "I'm not ungrateful," this child wrote. "I just want to prove to myself that I'm worth something."[33]

Betty's reaction to Bob's affair came in stages, which she detailed in a remarkable letter to her mother written in April 1974, but never sent. Of course she insisted that Bob end the affair, which he did, over the telephone, almost immediately. Maness was heartbroken but not too surprised. She thought Noyce had been losing interest even before they were discovered. Perhaps that was why, at least unconsciously, he had proposed such a dangerous liaison in the first place. Getting caught would simultaneously end two relationships without his actively needing to terminate either one himself.[34]

Betty Noyce had consulted a divorce lawyer within days of learning about her husband's affair. The attorney told her that he would be happy to work with her, but suggested that she first "try for a reconciliation." Her emotions were complicated. She felt confident that Bob had ended the relationship, but she was nonetheless jealous of his memory of it, which she believed he was protecting by refusing to share details of it with her or the marriage counselor they had begun seeing. "[Bob] refuses to discuss his relationship with Barbara because he wants to cherish his reminiscences and keep her image inviolate, and because he feels it's nobody's business anyway," she wrote. "[It is Bob's] same old 'Let's not talk about it because I don't want to' lordly attitude, often expressed by his saying, 'it's all in the past let's forget it'—a statement he makes in almost the same breath in which he belabors me for having been short-tempered or remiss in the culinary department, or with some such historical gripe."

She wrote, "I've swallowed my pride and postponed (and maybe cancelled) many of my own wishes in order to be both women to him." Just a few lines later, however, she is enraged again, furious that Bob clearly thought she bore some responsibility for the affair because he felt "abandoned" and "deserted" when his family went to Maine every summer. Betty suspected that Bob felt no such thing, that "he was not really convinced that he was an innocent victim of my mistreatment but was nonetheless egotistically able to say to himself, 'I'll tell her that she's to blame, if she ever catches me at it.'" She added, "He can't see very clearly that, because his lying made *him* feel bad, he cherished a constant sense of grievance against me—a dissatisfaction which made my slightest shortcoming a serious flaw, to his way of thinking (flaws serving as strikes against me in his mental scoring of Barbara vs. Betty, of course!)."

When Betty told Bob that she had scheduled another appointment with a divorce lawyer in April 1974, he grew angry. Harriet and Ralph Noyce had impressed upon their sons that "divorce was wrong—a scandal, not just a personal pain." But very soon Noyce's fury at the prospect of a divorce began to recede, according to Betty, who declared him "(inexplicably?) easy and affectionate in the two and a half days since [learning of the appointment]." This was, after all, what he wanted, even if he had not yet admitted it to himself.[35]

While Noyce's marriage was disintegrating and his children spinning away from him, his work life was proving to be an unqualified success. At almost precisely the moment Betty wrote to her mother, Noyce announced Intel's first-quarter performance for 1974, which was record setting in almost every possible way. Net income for this quarter alone was equivalent to 72 percent of the total profits for the previous year. Intel was growing so quickly that 60 percent of its plant space and 70 percent of its employees had joined the company in the last year. The technical progress had been equally rapid: a silicon transistor that cost $20 when Fairchild introduced it in 1959 now could be bought (inside an 1103) for less than one-tenth of a penny. The second quarter, incredibly, would be even brighter: almost 20 percent profit margins and quarterly net income of $6.7 million.[36]

In April, the stock again split three for two—bringing Noyce's total holdings to nearly a million shares. Intel was shipping 1103s at a rate of a billion bits per month. In that same month, the company introduced the 8080, the third-generation microprocessor. It offered about ten times the performance of its predecessors and retailed for $360. Finally here was a chip powerful enough to go beyond rudimentary control functions into true computing. Digital Equipment Company (DEC) announced it would use the 8080 in its computers. Other companies had brought another 18 microprocessors to market, but by 1975 the 8080 had become the defining standard for its class in the same way that the 1103 had done for 1K semiconductor memories.[37]

Back in the Noyce household, Bob and Betty muddled their way through fights and counseling sessions for more than a year after the discovery of Bob's affair. The end came in the summer of 1974. Bob decided to spend several weeks in Maine with Betty. He may have planned to try hard for a reconciliation. Betty joined him when he flew the Audubon team to Newfoundland to gather more puffin chicks, and he in turn skipped the cliffside adventures in order to accompany Betty on a tour of the historic town of St. John's.[38]

But it was not a summer of moonlit walks or heartfelt conversation. When friends came up to visit towards the end of the summer, they entered a scene one described as "outright warfare between Bob and Betty." The visitor recalled one night in particular: "All evening long, Betty was hammering at Bob. He was just bowing his head and taking it, but some switch must have flipped in his mind that night, because the next morning he announced that he wanted a divorce. Betty was stunned." The friends made a hasty exit, and Bob left with them. As quickly as he could, he returned to the safety of his Intel office.[39]

Noyce knew divorce would have significant financial implications for him. Because California was a community-property state, the couple's assets were automatically split 50-50. But determining those assets would prove a challenge. Noyce had never bothered to have an accountant draw up a personal balance sheet.

He asked his assistant from Fairchild, Paul Hwoschinsky, to try to calculate the total value of the Noyces' holdings. Hwoschinsky had long specialized in finance, and he possessed an unusual combination of character traits. He had an MBA from Harvard and had taught Noyce about accounting and finance when they were both at Fairchild. At the same time that he was a successful businessman, Hwoschinsky also studied yoga and was in the vanguard of New Age thinking. He would one day write a bestselling book called *True Wealth* to remind readers that "money is just one part of a total system that produces a feeling of well-being. The challenge is earning money to live life rather than living life to earn money."[40]

Hwoschinsky was also one of the few people who actively fought against falling under Noyce's spell. "If you walk off a cliff, everyone else will follow you," Hwoshinsky once told Noyce. "But I will not." When his boss looked startled, Hwoschinsky continued, "What I'm saying to you is that your charisma is scary. Use it wisely." Hwoschinsky suspects that Noyce asked him to determine his assets—and later, to administer the Noyce children's trusts—precisely because he knew that Hwoschinsky could remain objective in situations that had the potential to be quite emotionally fraught.[41]

Hwoschinsky agreed to help Noyce determine his assets. "By far the bulk of it was Intel stock," Hwoschinsky recalls. "But there were also the properties in California and Maine and the Noyce Air Force [Bob's planes]." When the settlement agreement was signed, Bob got the house in California, Betty got the Maine estate, and the Intel stock was split down the middle, with Bob and Betty each receiving roughly a half-million shares worth nearly $25 million.[42]

At some point while Hwoschinsky was doing his calculations, Noyce rather sheepishly handed him a shoe box. "What's this?" Hwoschinsky asked.[43]

"Just some little companies."

Hwoschinsky opened the box. It was filled nearly to the lid with IOUs and legal paperwork granting Noyce shares in various young companies in which he had invested. "Noyce could not just let his money sit," Hwoschinsky explains. "He wanted to use it to stir up new adventures. He was in all sorts of little deals with people whom he had met socially. He just loved doing projects, loved people."

If an entrepreneur asked Noyce for money for a project that struck him as interesting, practical, and not technically impossible, he would usually agree to help. "He was a very generous person," explains Intel's Les Vadasz. "He did not have money worries, and . . . even if his heart wasn't in [an investment], he probably felt, 'Well, so what? There's some upside.' He didn't take it so seriously."[44]

The type of private investing in which Noyce engaged is today called "angel investing" in high-technology circles. It took root in the United Sates in the 1930s, when wealthy benefactors such as Laurence Rockefeller helped their protégés to start new companies. Angel investing appeared in Silicon Valley around the time William Shockley started his company. By the early 1960s, for example, a dozen Hewlett-Packard executives set up a business-based "drinking club." Each man promised to keep his door and ears open to electronics entrepreneurs and paid monthly "dues" of about $100. At the monthly "meeting," held at one or another fellow's home, the group would share a few drinks, and anyone who had heard of an exciting investment opportunity would talk about it. The group would then decide how much, if any, of their pooled money to invest in the company. After a half-dozen years, this little drinking group—which adopted the name "Page Mill Partners"—split roughly $30 million in profits.[45]

Such returns were far beyond those of Noyce's shoe box startups, Hwoschinsky soon learned. Paperwork from Advanced Micro Devices (AMD)—a successful company started by Fairchild salesman Jerry Sanders in which Noyce had invested a small amount—was stuffed in the box, but otherwise, Hwoschinsky had never heard of most of these operations, whose names are at this point lost to history. He had to determine the value of Noyce's holdings and how much they had appreciated, based on some of the sloppiest record keeping he had ever seen.

He grabbed a random sheet of paper from the box. "Noyce, how much did you pay for this stock?"

"$16.95 a share."

"How do you remember? Do you have a canceled check?"

"Paul, it was $16.95."

Hwoschinsky tracked down every entrepreneur whose name appeared in the box. When he met with the entrepreneur, Hwoschinsky also double-checked Noyce's recollection of the price he paid for the stock against the founder's paper work. Always, Noyce's numbers were right. "He was a bloody elephant," says Hwoschinsky. "I've never seen anything like it. He could remember anything and everything."

"Every now and again," Hwoschinsky reminisces, "I'd get another call: 'Uh, Paul? I found another shoe box.'"

THE NOYCES OFFICIALLY BEGAN LIVING ON OPPOSITE COASTS in September. "Da is a little sad, but he seems resolved," Penny wrote to her mother, an apt description of Noyce's emotional state. At a dinner with his parents, brothers, and a few other relatives shortly after the decision to split from Betty, he started talking in a quiet, vulnerable tone no one in the family had heard before. His own parents and grandparents would never have gotten themselves into the situation in which he found himself, Noyce said. He was concerned about the effects of this marriage and its dissolution on his children. Already his youngest daughter was forced to choose which parent would attend parents' weekend at her school. "Nothing else I've done matters," he said, "because I've failed as a parent." He had spent his life finding problems he could solve in innovative ways. This one he could not solve—he had helped to create it, in fact—and he worried that his children would pay the price for his failure.[46]

Adding to his woes was the situation at Intel, which had changed dramatically. Over the course of three months, the semiconductor industry had fallen apart. Some portion of the excellent results Intel and its competitors had posted for the first half of the year could be traced to customers' stockpiling semiconductor memories in the wake of concerns about the energy crisis. But by the middle of the third quarter, with the world economy beginning to spiral into recession and demand for electronics dropping rapidly, these customers had no need to buy more semiconductors.

IN JULY 1974, the share price of Intel stock fell 30 percent—from 63½ to 44½—overnight. When Noyce arrived at work on the day after the precipitous drop, he learned that several Intel employees who had exercised their options when the price was in the sixties had not been able to sell their stock before the price drop due to inefficiencies in the option-exercising process. This struck Noyce as profoundly unfair. The employees would be short by one-third not because they timed the market wrong but because the elaborate stock-option protocol required by the SEC had delayed their sale. He wondered if it was possible to change the system.[47]

Converting stock options to cash in the mid-1970s was a drawn-out, tedious process. At Intel, for example, employees first went to the on-site options desk to submit a form and a check for an amount equivalent to their strike price times the number of shares they were selling. An employee exercising an option to sell 1,000 shares with a $5 strike price, for example, would hand in a $5,000 check. Intel employees who did this in early July 1974, when the stock was at 63½, expected to receive $63,500 from the sale (1,000 shares at $63.50), thereby clearing a profit of $58,500 ($63,500, less the $5,000 paid to exercise the options).

But submitting the form and check did not immediately sell the stock. The sale would be completed only when the employee signed the back of a paper stock certificate. These certificates were held by Intel's transfer agent, Wells Fargo Bank in San Francisco, which did not release them until it had cashed the check. A week could easily pass between the time the employee exercised the options at Intel and the time he or she received the stock certificate and, by signing it, sold the stock. The sale was processed at the price on the day the certificate was signed, *not* at the price on the day the option was exercised.

In general, the weeklong delay while paperwork traveled among Intel, Wells Fargo, and the employee was not problematic. But when the stock dropped 30 percent overnight, that delay would have cost the employee in the example above nearly $20,000. Of course, an employee could choose to exercise and hold the stock until the price recovered, but anyone who needed the money immediately was out of luck.

Noyce soon was on the phone with his broker, Bob Harrington of Dean Witter. "We had five execs who exercised options in the last week but haven't been able to sell the stock yet [because they had not received the certificates]," Noyce explained. "Two of these guys were planning on using the money for down payments on houses. Now the stock is down nearly one-third, and escrow is closing. Do you have any ideas about how we might help these guys?"

Harrington could sympathize. To drum up business for his brokerage services, he had begun broadcasting stock reports every morning on a local Silicon Valley radio station. Many people had told him that they never missed his 7:57 "semiconductor report." They sat in their cars, listening attentively and mentally calculating how much their stock was worth that day.

Harrington was always surprised at how *real* the stock seemed to his listeners with stock options. If a man held options on 50,000 shares in a company and Harrington reported that company trading at $20 per share, then by golly, the person considered himself a millionaire! Never mind that this fellow's options might not be fully vested, or that he might not have the cash to pay the upfront costs of exercising shares, or that prices might drop and leave him with nothing. People thought of themselves as already possessing the money that was theirs only if everything went according to the most optimistic scenario. Although the Intel executives Noyce mentioned to Harrington were certainly more sophisticated investors than many of his listeners, Harrington knew that for them, too, it must have been a blow to find themselves 30 percent short. Harrington told Noyce that he would check with the legal department and get back to him.

Not more than an hour later, Dean Witter's securities attorney told Harrington that the brokerage house could do nothing about this situation, although Intel could offer loans to its employees to cover the shortfall.

But Harrington had an idea: if there were some way to sell stock immediately upon exercising, no one would ever get caught in this bind again. If an employee exercising options could sign a note promising to turn over the paper stock certificate just as soon as it was in his or her physical possession, could that promissory note itself not serve as the temporary equivalent of the signed stock certificate? And why stop there? If a promissory note could stand in for a stock certificate, why couldn't it stand in for a check? Why not simply add a line to the promissory note directing that the cost of exercising the options be deducted from the proceeds of the sale? This way an employee would not need to have large amounts of cash on hand in order to exercise options.

In the scheme Harrington imagined, the employee in the above example would not submit the $5,000 check to Intel. He would not need to wait to receive the stock certificate before selling his stock. Instead, as soon as he signed a promissory note, his options would be exercised, his stock would be sold, and the $5,000 needed to exercise the options would be automatically deducted from his $63,500 payout. In other words, he would sign the promissory note and almost immediately receive the $58,500 coming to him.

Harrington contacted a law firm, and together they secured an "assurance of no action" from the Securities and Exchange Commission. In effect, the SEC said that if a company wanted to assume the liability of accepting promissory notes in the place of checks or stock certificates, a firm could do so, as long as it provided notice of these actions in its annual report.

Harrington told Noyce that he planned to start an "Option Exercise—Immediate Sale" program for corporate clients. Intel signed up for the service, and within a few months Intel's finance vice president was reporting that "virtually all" of the Intel employees exercising options used the "1-day stock buy/sell turnaround."[48]

Harrington had hoped to keep the program proprietary, but the idea was too good. It spread rapidly through Dean Witter and then around the country. "That program made life easier for tens of thousands of people," Harrington explains, "and the seed for it came from Bob Noyce asking a simple question: 'Isn't there a better way?'"[49]

The same-day sales innovation was one of very few bright spots in Noyce's life in the second half of 1974. While his marriage was suffering its death throes in Maine, semiconductor companies in California began laying off workers. In July alone, 50 people lost their jobs at Intersil, Signetics laid off 100 workers, and AMI cut 230 jobs. In an attempt to avoid layoffs at Intel, Moore and Grove—with Noyce's assent—decided to close two production facilities for a week before both July 4th and Labor Day, temporarily furloughing 600 employees, who were granted only half their normal pay.[50]

Such efforts could not save Intel's bottom line. The memory market had essentially disappeared in the recession. The Microma watch business was well on its way to disaster and would post losses of more than 1.5 million pretax dollars in 1974—nearly double the hit projected by the executive team at the beginning of the year. Intel's 4K RAM was so late that the company began second-sourcing a competitor's product. The only bright spots were the memory systems and microprocessor businesses, whose sales had increased both quarters, but these were too small to have a significant effect on overall results. Intel's total sales dropped 5 percent in the third quarter—earnings slipped 48 percent—and would fall another 9 percent in the fourth. Although the company did better than many of its competitors—AMD's $2.4 million net income in 1974 evaporated into a $2.5 million loss in 1975; Signetics went from $10 million profits to $4 million losses; and Mostek fell from $4 million profits to $1.2 million losses—a 48 percent fall in profits was a devastating performance for a company accustomed to tripling its revenues annually.[51]

In October, Noyce signed his name to one of the most difficult letters of his career. "To all Intel Employees," he wrote. "Continued reduced business conditions have made it necessary for us to have a reduction in our work force today. . . . We have tried to avoid such reductions in force by instituting transfers of people within the Company into areas which have not been seriously affected by the economy. We hoped that our overhead reduction in August and periodic reduced work weeks would be sufficient to cope with the slackening product demand until the economy recovered. This was based upon the hope that business would be improving by now. Unfortunately, it is not."[52]

With this letter, signed two days before his legal separation from Betty, Noyce terminated roughly 30 percent of Intel's 2,500 employees, most of them in production. He found the move profoundly upsetting and miserably confided in a friend, "For a few goddamned points on Wall Street, we have to ruin peoples' lives."[53]

His letter to employees promised, "When business does improve, our first action will be to recall employees affected by this cut," but he did not anticipate any changes for at least six months. He told a meeting of the New York Society of Security Analysts that Intel was bracing for more layoffs as well as "tremendous price attrition." When Thanksgiving came, Intel again closed part of its operations—and did not pay workers—during the long weekend. Hewlett-Packard, Fairchild, National, Signetics, and AMI did the same, some of them also furloughing employees for the week between Christmas and New Year's.[54]

By the end of 1974, nearly 20 percent of the semiconductor industry's blue-collar workers in Silicon Valley had been laid off. The industry's job losses and involuntary and unpaid sabbaticals sparked a protest by about 125 production workers and supportive college students outside the annual Western Electronics Manufacturing Association (WEMA) meeting at which Noyce received the 1974 WEMA medal of achievement—granted "to those who have made most significant contributions to the advancement of electronics." The citation called Noyce "a dominant force in the development of the semiconductor industry on the San Francisco Peninsula," but the protesters outside the meeting had other thoughts about him. Among the signs reading "No Short Work Week!" "Fairchild Workers Unite!" and "70,000 Electronics Workers Say No Vacations Without Pay!" was one wishing "Indigestion to Noyce from Intel Workers." This was the last thing he needed at the end of the horrible fourth quarter of 1974.[55]

SHORTLY AFTER DECIDING THE LAYOFFS WERE NECESSARY, Noyce told Moore that he wanted to leave his position as Intel's president. Arthur Rock conjectures that the layoffs were the final stress that led Noyce to leave daily management at Intel, but Moore had seen signs of Noyce's desire for a change even during the glorious first and second quarters of the year. Early in 1974, Noyce told Moore that he had suggested to Charlie Sporck that they merge National and Intel. "It was not unusual for him to talk to people about things without consulting me first," Moore later explained, without apparent rancor. Moore agreed to meet with Sporck but ultimately decided that he would "like to try running Intel for a while" rather than merging forces with National.[56]

Moore and Noyce agreed that if Noyce left, Andy Grove should be promoted so that he and Moore could run Intel as a team, continuing the tradition set by the founders. Grove had been pushing for more responsibility for several years. Explained Intel director Richard Hodgson, "Andy Grove wanted more and more and more—in a good way. You just couldn't contain him." Gordon Moore, who liked to say that "Andy had gotten over his PhD," was certain that if Noyce moved to board chair and Moore stepped in as president and CEO, Grove would make an excellent executive vice president. Already he had moved beyond simply implementing the founders' plans to refining, supplementing, and even convincing Moore and Noyce to change them. Grove had arrived at Intel a scientist, rapidly transformed himself into an operations manager, and would no doubt be capable in a general management role.[57]

In fact, the attention to hard data and formal processes that one associates with Grove had been ascendant in the company for at least a year, ever since the success of the 1103 had made Intel's success dependent upon the ability to manufacture this device in quantity. Beginning in 1972, agendas for the weekly staff meetings, which were once open-ended, ran on a five-week cycle that addressed a different set of topics each week—"1. Bookings, shipments, organization, personnel; 2. Prior months' performance (financial, unit sales and revenue, production to finished goods, business indicators); 3. Key customers [the only subject Noyce underlined] and new activities; 4. Pricing review/Cost reports, new and old product scheduling and pricing; 5. General."[58]

As early as 1972, says Gelbach, "Bob gave advice but Andy and Gordon ran it." Another employee explains that although from the outside it appeared "Bob was running the company," it only took a few weeks at Intel to "discover that Andy was running the company."[59]

This arrangement—Noyce giving counsel and Moore and Grove managing—was formalized in the fall of 1974, when Noyce and Moore asked Grove to join them for lunch at an out-of-the way restaurant in Sunnyvale. "I don't think I can spend so much time on Intel," Noyce said to Grove. "How can we get you ready for more responsibility?" Forever unflappable, Grove paused only an instant before he answered, "You can give me the job."[60]

In December, Intel announced that come April 1975, Grove would move into Moore's position of executive vice president, Moore would take Noyce's president/CEO slot, and Noyce would become board chair, replacing Arthur Rock, who would move to vice chairman. Noyce and Grove planned to meet for lunch nearly every Friday between October and April to ease the transition. Press coverage of the changes focused on Noyce and on Grove, who was less well known than the founders and could be easily slotted into the role of brilliant *enfant terrible*. As was so often the case, Moore did not get the attention he deserved.[61]

NOYCE HAD BEEN AN IDEAL FOUNDING PRESIDENT for Intel because he was, at his core, what Moore called "a wild expansionist." The jobs Noyce enjoyed and excelled at—plotting a new product, brainstorming new ideas, establishing a market from thin air—meshed perfectly with Intel's needs as a young company. He loved, he said, leading a company "walking the thin line next to the cliff of disaster," his eyes always scanning for the next opportunity.[62]

Noyce led by knowing where he wanted to go and assuming someone else would figure out how to get there. When asked in 1983 if Intel had developed a long-range plan in its first few years of operation, he spoke of "our five year goal, one that we talked about a great deal, to do $50 million [in sales]." This, of course, was not a plan, not a step-by-step approach bristling with incremental target goals and detailed thinking. But in Noyce's mind, achieving the goal *was* the plan.[63]

Explains Roger Borovoy, chief counsel at both Fairchild and Intel: "Noyce's idea of planning was to yell, 'Let's take the hill!'" and then so inspire his troops with his own charisma and intelligence that they all began running behind him, no one exactly sure of his responsibilities, but everyone heading in the same general direction with the same general end in mind. Noyce and Moore spotted the semiconductor memory hill and led the company to the top of it. Next they spotted the microprocessor hill in the ideas Hoff had sketched, and then the digital watch hill, and flanks of the company rushed to secure those, too.[64]

Shortly before he decided to resign as president, Noyce tried to stake out one more hill for Intel: the personal computer business. In late 1974, a young Albuquerque, New Mexico, company called MITS announced it would soon begin selling a build-your-own-computer kit, which ran on an Intel 8080 microprocessor. These "Altair" machines were among the world's first personal computers. Although they were quite rudimentary—anyone using them needed to know how to use a soldering iron—they offered the processing power of a $20,000 minicomputer at a cost of only $5,000. Less sophisticated Altair computer kits would sell for as little as $500.

Noyce must have learned about the Altair in early 1974, when Intel agreed to provide the processor. At this same time, Intel was building microprocessor development systems that made it easy for customers to debug the software they wrote for the microprocessor. These development systems in effect functioned as rudimentary computers. They could be programmed to simulate any number of environments, from controlling a lathe to running a cash register.

"Bob looked at the Altair, looked at the microprocessor development system, and [saw something very similar]," said Andy Grove. His imagination fired, Noyce sat down with Ed Gelbach, and, in Grove's words, "they began marching along, heading into the personal computer business." Gelbach developed a "great display" and hung mocked-up print advertisements for this "fully functional $300 computer" on his wall.[65]

The personal computer, however rudimentary, fascinated Noyce. He bought one for his son Bill, a computer buff who along with his high school friends had programmed a timeshare PDP-8 minicomputer to serve as a computer dating service. "You'll never guess what this is, so I'll tell you," Bill Noyce wrote excitedly to his grandmother shortly after receiving his own machine. "Actually, it's just a very quiet typewriter. When you type on the keyboard, letters appear on the screen." Recalls Bill, "[My dad] didn't think that a bunch of big computers in the middle of university classrooms or back rooms of banks would make much of a change in the world. But with computers in the hands of the people, changes were not anticipatable.

He used to talk about how when electricity was used only to drive existing motors—the big motor in a mill, for example—it didn't do much to change society. But when the fractional horsepower motor was put into people's hands [in the form of sewing machines, electric fans, and power tools], there was a real change."[66]

At a staff meeting in 1974, Noyce casually began a sentence with the phrase, "Now that we are in the computer business." Gordon Moore looked surprised, and as he listened further, something almost unheard of occurred: Moore became positively furious. "I thought he was going to either faint or hit me," recalls Gelbach. His lips thin and almost white from pressing them together, Moore finally managed to speak. "Ours is not—repeat after me—a general purpose microcomputer." Where Noyce saw the possibility of Intel becoming a major computer manufacturer, Moore saw the far more likely possibility of Intel becoming a failed computer manufacturer. He needed to look no further than Microma (which ultimately cost Intel $15 million before it was sold in 1977) to appreciate the risks of attacking an entirely unknown consumer market.[67]

Noyce did not argue with Moore, although a few months later he did tell a *Fortune* interviewer, "only half in jest," that Intel was "the world's largest computer manufacturer." Gelbach pulled the advertisements off the wall and repositioned the "computer on a board" as a design aid. Moore was probably right. Intel had enough to do without trying to take on the major computer manufacturers of the world.[68]

But the Altair episode may have given Noyce yet another indication that Intel had left its youth forever. "The entrepreneurial phase is not entirely over," Noyce said when he announced his move to board chair, "but the emphasis is shifting to control." At age six, Intel was the world's leading manufacturer of semiconductor memories and the sixth largest semiconductor company in the world. It did not need to be capturing new hills. It needed to build on the hills already occupied. That meant manufacturing in massive quantities and making incremental improvements in existing technologies.[69]

What Intel needed going forward was not the courage to take great leaps ahead but the discipline to take orderly steps in a controlled fashion. Not leadership by "gut feel" or what Noyce called "personal contact" but management by hard, cold numbers. It needed not Noyce but Andy Grove, who in 1974 said he hoped to model Intel on McDonalds. The hamburger chain, Grove said, had taken standardization to a level that Intel would do well to copy. Intel needed to start thinking of itself as a maker of "high technology jelly beans" as uniform, standard, and predictable as the products served in clamshell boxes and paper wrappers emblazoned with the golden arches. Someone even mocked up a hamburger box emblazoned with "McIntel" for Grove. He kept it on his desk.[70]

Noyce knew that "control" was important work. But he did not want to do it. The press release announcing Noyce, Moore, and Grove's new positions at Intel had included an assurance that even as board chair, "Noyce will continue to take an active role in the operating management of the company." But Andy Grove has said that once the men were established in their new jobs, "Bob practically disappeared."[71]

FOR ONCE IN HIS LIFE, Noyce needed a break. He had laid off one-third of his employees. His family had disintegrated. The value of his stock had plummeted. He had ended an affair with a woman for whom he had once cared deeply. He spent most of the early part of 1975 regrouping, traveling nearly constantly, usually for Intel and almost always extending his stay beyond the end of his business commitments. He spent two weeks in Europe, a week in Greece, another in Israel (where Intel had a small operation), and ten days in Japan. He skied in Aspen several times and in the Bugaboos ("the camp for aging athletes," he called it) where a helicopter dropped him on the mountaintops to schluss his way down, a transponder clipped to his jacket in case he got lost in the snow.

One of the places Noyce visited in his world travels was quite unlikely: Crete, Nebraska, population 4,500. Shortly after the Noyces announced their decision to divorce, Bob decided to donate $50,000 to his father's alma mater, Doane College in Crete. He and his brothers told their father to expect a big surprise at his sixtieth reunion, to be held in May 1975.[72]

When the appointed weekend arrived, Noyce, who was in Japan, arranged for his friend and flight instructor Jim Lafferty to fly the senior Noyces and Bob's oldest brother Don from Oakland, California, where they were now living, to Crete in Bob's new plane. Gaylord and Ralph would meet their parents in Nebraska. Bob would do his best to fly in from Tokyo in time to make the dinner banquet announcing that thanks to Bob's generosity, a small campus chapel would now be designated the Noyce Chapel in Reverend Noyce's honor.[73]

The weekend was the highlight of 81-year-old Ralph Noyce's life. Jim Lafferty flew him and Harriet to Nebraska in their son's jet. "It is as comfortable for us passengers as a commercial plane," Harriet wrote, proudly adding that the airport attendant in Crete said it was the largest plane ever to land there. When Reverend Noyce learned of the chapel's new name, when he listened to Gaylord speak on the topic "Small is Beautiful" at the dedication, when he saw his four grown sons sitting shoulder to shoulder in the pews, he was overcome. "I just don't know how in the world to let you know how deeply it moves me," he wrote to Bob. "I don't know how a son could honor a father more."[74]

Even with all the excitement of that weekend, for Harriet Noyce "Bob's arrival [minutes before the banquet announcing the chapel dedication] was the high moment." She explained, "The plane that Bob had boarded in Tokyo after a week's business trip had arrived in San Francisco on time. He had caught the only plane to Omaha that could possibly give him time to fly his own plane back from Omaha to Crete. The tight schedule had worked out. It seemed nothing short of a miracle that the impossible had come true." She added, "I find myself crying and blowing my nose here alone as I record the moment, choked up now as I never was during the whole momentous weekend itself."

For Harriet, the Noyce chapel was more than a generous gift. It was a sign that her jet-setting, millionaire, soon-to-be-divorced son had not entirely forgotten his roots in the church and in the Midwest. It was an affirmation that even though he had strayed, he honored his father and his upbringing. The Noyce Chapel offered her hope that maybe, just maybe, the prodigal might return.

10

Renewal

At the end of her notes about the weekend at Doane College, Harriet Noyce wrote, "As we left the airport, son Bob was at one telephone booth making a date for Ann to meet him for dinner." Ann was Ann Bowers, Intel's head of personnel, and one of the only female executives in the semiconductor industry. She was 37 (ten years younger than Noyce) and physically small, with a quick mind and blunt manner of speaking that lent her a distinctly assertive air. She would become Noyce's second wife.

Bowers had grown up in Oakmont, Pennsylvania, a small blue-collar town outside of Pittsburgh whose economy was anchored by a paint factory and a rolling mill. Her mother had been born in Oakmont, and her father, a patent attorney for aluminum production giant Alcoa, agreed to live there because it was located midway between Alcoa's headquarters and its R&D labs. Bowers's educated family and her own reserved demeanor left her feeling rather out of place for most of her childhood. She was a bookish girl, but the town's one high school, which focused on vocational education, never required its students to write anything longer than a paragraph. She lived for the summers, when she spent weeks with family friends near Long Island Sound. There she learned how to sail and swim and play accompaniments on the piano while the family matriarch sang dramatic scales in a throaty contralto voice.

In 1955, Bowers left Oakmont for Cornell, from which she graduated four years later with a double major in English and Psychology. When it came time to choose a career, Bowers decided to apply for a position as a management trainee at Macy's. She liked fashion, but more importantly, she had noticed that retail was one of the few businesses in which women wielded any real authority. At her job interview, she made it clear that she would only accept a job in California, where she had wanted to live ever since she took a quick visit to the West Coast as a high-school senior. She went to San Francisco in 1959 to work at the Macy's store on Union Square.

A few years later, she moved to the Peninsula to head personnel at the store opening in the new Stanford Shopping Center in Palo Alto.

The Macy's jobs were followed by a two-year stint as a teacher at an economically depressed high school in San Jose—"I was tired of White Flower Days [monthly sales at Macy's] and got caught up in the idea of civic good"—and three years as the head of personnel at a small laser and medical equipment startup company.[1]

In 1969, Bowers learned that Intel was preparing to hire its first personnel manager. "I didn't really know a lot about Intel," she says. "Bob Noyce and Gordon Moore meant nothing to me." But several colleagues encouraged her to apply, as did a friend, who told her that she had once worked with Bob Noyce, "and he was wonderful."

The first interview, with Intel finance chief John Cobb, went well enough to lead to a second. During this meeting, Bowers had the gall to tell Cobb, who was also slated to be her supervisor, that she wanted to report either to Gordon Moore or to Bob Noyce—"by that point, I had done some research, and [learned that] they were the ones to work for"—not to him. After a bit of negotiation, Intel agreed to change the reporting structure, and Bowers accepted the position. "My father," she recalls, "almost lost it when he heard I was going changing jobs again. You just did not do this where I came from." Within a few weeks on the job, Bowers learned, as would so many after her, that although she nominally reported to Noyce and Moore, she in fact reported to Grove." This was fine with her. She found Grove to be a good boss.

In her first four years at Intel, the company grew from 200 to 2,500 employees. As head of personnel, Bowers not only recruited many of these workers but also ensured they received competitive benefit and salary packages, useful training, and meaningful performance reviews. She arranged seminars to teach new employees about stock options. Her office was often the first stop for people unhappy with their bosses or subordinates. She worked closely with Grove, who approached his management duties with characteristic rigor. He wanted to develop a highly disciplined, measurement-based corporate culture at Intel and read a management book every weekend for hints and ideas. He usually arrived on Mondays eager to put his newly acquired ideas into practice. The week following his study of *Management by Intimidation* was particularly memorable for Bowers.

Bowers also oversaw the small layoff at Intel in 1971 and the big one in 1974. She never managed to harden herself to this most difficult part of her job. During both layoff periods she developed canker sores so severe that it hurt to talk.

The strength of Bowers's intelligence and the steel in her spine attracted Noyce almost immediately. Even while he was married to Betty Noyce and seeing Barbara Maness, he had several times asked Bowers to join him for drinks after business meetings. At one point, he arranged for his secretary to seat Bowers next to him at a corporate event. Bowers knew she was being pursued, but she refused to take the bait. "He was married, and he was my nominal boss," she explains. "I wanted nothing to do with this." Bowers also knew about Noyce's affair with Maness. An employee had confidentially asked Bowers if she could do anything to end the relationship, which the employee feared would have negative repercussions for the company. Bowers had declined to intercede, but her knowledge of the affair made her even less susceptible to Noyce's advances.

Which is not to say that she found Noyce unappealing. "I always found him phenomenally attractive. He had this aura. It was undefinable but very tangible. And it was very hard not to be affected by it—men were as well as women." She continues, "I had never met anybody like that. I don't know any movie stars, but maybe some of them have that same kind of aura. He had a way of looking right at you, like he's looking right *into* you, like he really cared about you."

The first time they spoke at any length, Noyce interrupted their conversation about Intel to ask Bowers, "How did you get to be the way you are?" When she looked startled, he added, "I have a daughter, and I'd like her to be like you." Bowers was taken aback—"I remember thinking, 'You don't even know me; how can you ask me that?'"—but she was also flattered by his interest. Later she began to notice other things about Noyce. "He was a physical being, you could tell by the way he moved. When he was sitting down, with his swimmers' shoulders, he seemed much bigger than he was. I always was surprised when he stood up. He should have been six feet tall." But she kept her distance from him. "If we were in a group and people started to amble off," she laughs, "I would be sure to amble off, too."

In the fall of 1974, around the time Bob and Betty Noyce officially separated, Noyce invited Bowers to join a group of Intel employees heading to dinner at the Nut Tree, a popular restaurant about a half-hour's drive north. Since this was a group activity, Bowers decided to join in. After dinner, however, she was irritated to learn that a mixup with the carpools meant that she would need to ride home with Noyce, alone. She climbed into his Cougar and immediately scooted as close to the passenger-side door as she could comfortably sit.

As they headed down the Peninsula towards Bowers's house, Noyce started talking in the casual tone that everyone at Intel knew signaled an important statement. "I presume you know that I'm getting a divorce," he said. Bowers had not known. She tried to appear nonplussed by the news, but a little voice inside her head said, "Well. That changes everything."

Ten months later, Noyce proposed to Bowers on the terrace of a restaurant in Athens. They had talked about Noyce's affair, and Bowers was confident it would not happen again. She had spent Sunday dinner with his parents and felt welcome. Even the two Noyce children whom she met seemed grudgingly accepting of her. And yet, Noyce's proposal—a month before his divorce was finalized—surprised Bowers. She had briefly been married once before and would have felt happy just to live with Noyce. But he thought it would be best for his children if he were married, rather than living in proverbial sin, and after she thought about it a bit, she decided he was right.

A few days after Bowers tearfully agreed to marry Noyce, she offered him a proposal of her own. He wanted her to get a pilot's license so they could fly together. She said that she would do it if he quit smoking. And she made a pledge to herself: when it was clear to her that he truly had kicked the habit for good, she would change her last name to Noyce.

He promised that he would try to give up cigarettes. Bowers began flying lessons. Noyce puffed on. When Bowers became a licensed pilot, he was still a smoker. He knew he ought to quit. When he skied a particularly challenging run or tried to speed up the laps he swam every morning, he felt his lungs straining. The surgeon general had been slapping warning labels on his cigarette packs since 1965. Noyce tried buying low tar or low nicotine cigarettes, but he would always break off their filters or just smoke more. A friend who worked in a hospital pointedly showed Noyce a piece of a diseased lung that had belonged to a smoker. "That's amazing," Noyce said, staring at the holes where the alveoli should have been. But still he smoked his Camels. Bowers forbid him to smoke in the house. He moved to the porch. She tried what she called "the Chinese water torture" approach to the topic, gently bringing it up time and again. No effect. She tried yelling. No better. She arranged for him to meet with a Stanford doctor who was an expert in nicotine addiction. Noyce left the meeting with an intellectual appreciation for the complexity of his addiction and a desire for a cigarette. Bowers even considered refusing to fly with Noyce— after all, he had not held up his end of their deal—but she enjoyed it too much to give it up, and besides, she knew her boycott almost certainly would have no effect on his smoking.

The closest Noyce came to quitting was a few years after his marriage, when a group of his ski buddies issued what Bowers called "a man's challenge": "If you quit, we'll pay for you to ski with us in the Bugaboos. But we don't think you can do it." Noyce immediately stubbed out his cigarette. He did not pick up another one for nearly a year. Just as Bowers began to think about changing her name, Noyce bummed a cigarette in a parking lot and immediately returned to his smokestack ways. He had to pay his own way to the Bugaboos that year.

Smoking somehow steadied Noyce. At times when he was forced to sit still—on the telephone, in a meeting, on a commercial jetliner—the rituals of smoking (banging the pack on a table, selecting a cigarette, putting it between his lips, lighting it with one hand cupped around the flame, inhaling deeply) gave him something to do. When he was worried or angry, he smoked almost constantly, lighting a new cigarette from the stub of the one still in his mouth. At other times, he reveled in the sensual pleasures of smoking. He could recall the advertising slogan for Lucky Strike cigarettes—"so round, so firm, so fully packed"—decades after it had been retired. Several people, including one of Noyce's daughters, have conjectured that somewhere deep within himself, Noyce thought that he was immortal. From the moment he leapt with his glider from the roof of a Grinnell barn, Noyce never stopped at the edge of a precipice but instead ran, at full speed, right over the edge and into the unknown. This had been his approach with ideas, with companies, with skiing, with driving, with women, and with inventing. How on earth could something as mundane and trivial as a cigarette kill someone like him?[2]

WHEN BETTY NOYCE FIRST LEARNED of Bob's plans to marry Ann Bowers, she reacted with her characteristic biting wit. She told him that this move would make her the largest "single" stockholder in Intel. To be sure, Wall Street watched Betty Noyce's actions quite closely. In 1976, when the stock of nearly every other semiconductor company was rising, Intel's temporarily fell on rumors that she planned to sell 100,000 shares.[3]

Once permanently settled in Maine and out from Bob's shadow, Betty Noyce put her half of the Intel money to good use. She developed a dynamic, entrepreneurial, low-profile approach to what she called "catalytic philanthropy," starting a bank, rescuing a floundering bakery, underwriting one-third of the cost of a children's hospital, restoring several buildings, and launching a market in downtown Portland. When she wanted to donate $1 million to Maine Public Broadcasting, she did not simply write a check. She built five houses (thereby employing dozens of people) and donated the money from the homes' sales. At the time of her death in 1996, the $75 million she had given to the people of her adopted state ranked her among the most generous philanthropists in Maine's history.[4]

Bob and Betty Noyce's divorce was final on August 12, 1975. Noyce and Ann Bowers were married 11 weeks later, on November 27, Thanksgiving Day and Bowers's 38th birthday, at Noyce's home. Until that time, they had kept their relationship a secret from nearly everyone at work. Their families, who had no idea Noyce and Bowers were even engaged, thought they were simply coming to Thanksgiving dinner on the day of the wedding. After the meal, Bowers opened two boxes. Each held a bouquet, one for her and another for her five-year-old niece, who would serve as a flower girl.

"Why do you think we have these?" Bowers asked the little girl.

The child's eyes grew wide. "Because someone is getting married?"

Noyce and Bowers looked at each other. "That would be us," Noyce said.

The dinner guests began shrieking. Harriet Noyce started to cry because Bob's father, who had suffered a debilitating stroke, was unable to perform the ceremony. The minister, who had hidden himself in a closet, stepped forward to marry the couple in a ceremony from which Bowers had excised every reference to God. "Bob agreed to that. Neither of us could decide about God," Bowers says. "I remember Bob saying, 'Some people who believe in God are good, and some people who believe in God are not good. So where does that leave you?' He had [also] looked around and decided that religion is responsible for a lot of trouble in the world." Noyce, always pushing against the limits of accepted knowledge, told Bowers that what bothered him most about organized religions was that "people don't think in churches."

But for all his insistence that "an ethical life is what really matters," Noyce did not want a secular wedding. When his brother Gaylord could not fly in to perform the service, Noyce said, "Well, we'll have to find a minister here." There was no thought of a civil ceremony.

On the Monday after her wedding, Bowers went to see Andy Grove. "Bob and I got married on Thursday," she said. "I think I should resign." Grove disagreed. She had been at Intel almost since its founding. Anyone would be able to see that she had not gotten her job through nepotism. "Anyone can see that now," Bowers corrected him. "But in a year or two, this will start to look very bad for Intel." Still Grove protested. "Let Bob resign," he suggested. He was not at all joking.[5]

In the end, Bowers agreed that she would stay at Intel long enough to hire and train her replacement. Finding someone took until April. In May, just when Bowers was ready to leave, Gordon Moore asked her not to go—at least not yet—because a union was attempting to organize Intel's workers.

In the first week of May, the International Union of Operating Engineers Local 39 filed a petition seeking a representation election for the janitorial staff at Intel's Santa Clara headquarters. The National Labor Relations Board soon dismissed the petition with an explanation that "the union has failed to demonstrate to the NLRB that a sufficient number of [Intel] employees in an appropriate bargaining unit desired representation by this union." But Intel could not breathe easy. On June 4, the International Brotherhood of Teamsters, Local #296, filed a petition seeking representation of certain Intel "warehousemen, drivers, shipping and receiving clerks, TWX operators, PBX operators, and mail service personnel."[6]

Moore's letter announcing the Teamsters' efforts read, in part: "In case you have any questions regarding the position of Intel's management with respect to union representation of any of our employees, I would like to reiterate it. Union representation of any group of employees would have a serious impact on all of Intel's operations. We wish to continue to seek development and growth opportunities for each employee through the growth of Intel. This goal can best be achieved if each individual continues to be free to communicate directly with anyone else in the company to solve problems or to seek help or information." This is a muted version of Moore's strong anti-union sentiments, which were shared by nearly all of Intel's senior management, including Noyce.

The Intel team was not alone in their beliefs. In 1973, WEMA, an industry association to which Intel belonged and in which Noyce actively participated, offered a two-day seminar for "companies that are non-union and wish to remain so." Led by an attorney who specialized in labor law, the seminar featured a simulated union organizing drive, so participants could practice making decisions in realistic scenarios. WEMA (which changed its name to the American Electronics Association [AEA] in 1977) also provided legal aid to companies facing union drives and furthermore served as a highly efficient clearinghouse for information about union activity throughout the electronics industry. As one union organizer explained, "Whenever organizers passed [out] leaflets in one plant, a copy of the leaflet would be on the desk of every human resources director in the Valley within two or three days."[7]

Conventional wisdom within the semiconductor industry held that no matter how rich a company's wages and benefits package, it would cost 25 percent more to operate the business with a union in house. A strike in April 1968, by 5,000 workers at Ampex, Lenkurt Electric, and Dalmo-Victor—the only three unionized electronics (not semiconductor) companies in Silicon Valley—reinforced the prevailing bias against unions. The work stoppage stretched more than a week. Had this lacuna hit a company in the fast-moving semiconductor industry, it would have put the firm at a significant competitive disadvantage.[8]

Intel had long employed many of the same preemptive personnel tactics that had kept unions at bay at Fairchild. Hourly workers at Intel had health care, dental care, paid vacations, and sick leave. They could buy Intel stock at a reduced price. The company also held meetings each month at which supervisors answered questions from employees, either asked in person or submitted anonymously in writing. Such practices, common in Silicon Valley semiconductor firms since the early Fairchild days, were widely encouraged by the AEA, one of whose representatives warned, "The way to thwart unions is to make them unnecessary. And the way you do that is to think as though you really had a union in the plant."[9]

Intel had union-thwarting personnel policies on the books, but policy and practice diverged in 1975 and 1976, when the industry pulled out of the 1974 downturn and Intel resumed its dramatic growth. By the second quarter of 1976, when the unionization efforts began, demand for Intel's latest-generation memory devices exceeded production capacity. This led the company to open a new fab near Portland, Oregon and a testing facility in Santa Cruz, California, while also beginning construction on an assembly plant in Barbados, West Indies. At the same time, Intel was hiring at a furious rate. More than 1,250 new employees joined the company in the last half of 1975—a rate better than 200 each month. This breakneck growth continued into 1976, which saw another 2,700 employees join the company.

In the midst of all this activity, everyone at Intel felt pressured to put in ever-longer hours, and even Andy Grove did not notice that a foreman at one of Intel's facilities had given every employee identical merit increases. This was anathema. Intel always awarded performance-based increases. The company said this policy rewarded individual effort; the labor movement claimed its primary effect was to discourage collective thinking of any sort among workers.

In any case, Intel's failure to follow its own policies led someone at the company either to contact the Teamsters or to listen carefully when approached by them. "I felt we brought the unionization problem on ourselves," Bowers explains. "If we had followed our own policies, it never would have happened."

The timing of Intel's misstep coincided with a spike in union-organizing activity throughout Silicon Valley. In 1974, the United Electrical Workers (UE) created an organizing committee specifically to target the Silicon Valley labor force. Many in the labor movement thought that workers might be more open to collective bargaining after the massive 1974 layoffs, especially if someone pointed out to them that with every passing year, more semiconductor production jobs moved offshore.

A worker's sense of insecurity may have been heightened by the increasingly austere and antiseptic nature of semiconductor production work. Even Intel's head of manufacturing, Gene Flath, admits that semiconductor fabs had become increasingly "scary places to work" by the mid-1970s. Intel's Fab 3, completed at Livermore, California, in April 1973, was twice the size of its predecessors and specifically designed to be "a big 1103 machine." Every surface in its $2 million, 10,000-square-foot clean room gleamed, and hanging on many walls were huge warning signs reading CAUTION or ACID. Here Intel employees, who had once worn lab coats that they embroidered and shortened into minidresses, were required, for the first time, to don head-to-toe "bunny suits" with hats, goggles, long sleeves, pants, and gloves. They were forbidden to wear makeup. The suits and scrubbed faces were designed less to protect the workers than to keep the manufacturing climate uncontaminated—even a wayward flake of human skin or mascara caused problems.[10]

In part because experienced fab technicians thought the bunny suits were unnecessary, Fab 3 was deliberately staffed with people with little experience in the industry. Recalls one early employee, hired at age 16 for $2.30 per hour: "We were just petrified because this was such a big job, such an important job, and it was so scary in the clean room. Everything was crammed so closely together. The aisles were very narrow. . . . Everything was under yellow lights, and we were petrified."[11]

Intel found that a number of its new employees were quitting after only a few days on the job because, as Flath put it, "they were just so nervous they'd go home and shake at night because they [hadn't known] what they were going to get into." The strangeness of the clean room that terrified workers gave union organizers hope. Indeed, the most significant unionizing effort Intel faced was at Fab 3 the late 1970s.[12]

But that effort failed, too, as did every other attempt to unionize the semiconductor industry in the late 1970s and early 1980s. Union organizers in these years were swimming against the tide. Between 1970 and 1988, the percentage of California workers represented by a union dropped from 36 percent to 22 percent. By the end of the 1970s, nearly three-quarters of semiconductor production workers were women and almost half were members of minority ethnic groups (mostly Hispanic or Asian). Neither women nor minorities had traditionally joined unions in large numbers. Moreover, as soon as the industry's fortunes improved, this workforce proved so mobile—in 1979, turnover rates among Silicon Valley assembly workers topped 50 percent annually—that it was difficult to organize.[13]

A month after he announced the Teamsters' request to hold an election at Intel, Moore informed employees that the union had withdrawn its petition, presumably because its leaders decided that Intel workers would not support a union at the company. "Our non-union status is the direct result of your choice as Intel employees to have open and free communication and to solve our problems together, without outside intervention," Moore reminded his employees. "We want to keep it that way."[14]

A few weeks after the union scare passed, Ann Bowers quietly left Intel. She soon established a human-resources consulting business. She also cofounded the California Electronics Association—an organization that helped small electronics companies to develop personnel policies, find insurance, contract with credit unions, and train their employees.

Noyce, meanwhile, continued to spend a good bit of his time at the company. Even Gordon Moore says Andy Grove's comment about Noyce "practically disappearing" is "too strong." Noyce chaired board meetings every month, work that required regular check-ins with Moore and Grove. He attended executive staff meetings whenever he was in town. He maintained an office at Intel's new headquarters building in which all offices were cubicles. He in short order found himself pulled into meetings at the company so often that he also commandeered an office at Bowers's consulting firm "so I can get something done." (He soon missed Intel too much, however, and returned to his cubicle there.) He attended Intel sales meetings and plant openings. He stood as the company's spokesman at conferences, particularly those having to do with the microprocessor or automotive electronics. He built customer relationships by speaking to General Electric managers on "new electronics" and to Monsanto executives on "managing innovation." He made many presentations to analysts, including an important talk to the New York Society of Security Analysts on Intel's tenth anniversary. Noyce also continued the high-level negotiations with customers that had been his specialty as CEO.[15]

Intel employees who encountered Noyce in the halls during these years found their interactions with him as stimulating as ever. "I remember I ran into Noyce [in about 1976]," recalls one employee, who at the time was working on a special memory device (called an EPROM) that was one of Intel's best sellers. "I said to Noyce, 'I'll bet you can't sleep at night knowing that [I am] in charge of the [EPROM], which is a third of your profit.' He looked at me and he said, 'Yes, I can; I can't think of a better guy to run the thing.' And that made me feel good. I said, 'Yes, maybe he's right.'"[16]

AS BOARD CHAIR, however, Noyce did have more time to devote to interests outside Intel than had been the case when he was president. One of these interests was investing in young startup companies. Noyce liked the notion of reseeding the soil that had produced Intel and the other Fairchildren.

Noyce had done a small bit of seat-of-the-pants investing while he was at Fairchild, but in 1973, he decided to establish his own small investment business with Paul Hwoschinsky, who soon would also help him with the financial aspects of the divorce from Betty. "I've been doing a lot of venture stuff personally, out of my back pocket, and it's not working," Noyce had said, referring to the shoebox startups. "If you'll start this investment partnership with me, I'll put up the money and pay you a small salary [to manage it]. You'll get a percentage of any money we make. I'll eat the losses."[17]

After a bit more discussion, Hwoschinsky agreed to oversee Noyce's angel investing through a partnership that Hwoschinsky suggested they call the Callanish Fund. Callanish is the name of a Stonehenge-like structure in Scotland that some believe represents an ancient use of binary logic.

Noyce established the Callanish Fund with about $1 million. Hwoschinsky rented an office on Sand Hill Road for $70 per month. The office held nothing more than a desk and chair, but it was the Sand Hill Road address that was important. Over the past few years, Sand Hill Road office complexes, a stone's throw away from a major highway but nestled among lovely trees atop one of the highest hills rimming Silicon Valley, had become the epicenter of the region's venture capital industry, which by 1975 included some 150 firms.

Among the Callanish Fund's new neighbors was Eugene Kleiner, who in 1972 partnered with an engineer-turned-Harvard-MBA named Tom Perkins to launch a venture capital company called Kleiner Perkins. Kleiner's experiences at Fairchild had convinced him that it was best for entrepreneurs to remain independent for as long as they could. And after seeing the returns Davis and Rock achieved after seven years of supporting independent entrepreneurs—Kleiner had worked as a consultant to Rock's venture capital business—Kleiner was convinced that he could make a decent amount of money as a venture capitalist. The early 1970s were a funders' market: the increase in the capital gains tax had scared away many casual investors but not significantly shrunk the pool of entrepreneurs looking for funding.

The first Kleiner Perkins fund was $8 million, half of which came from Henry Hillman, a Pittsburgh steel magnate, and half from various limited partners, Noyce most likely among them. These limited partners were simply sources of money. The firm's managing partners—in this case, Kleiner and Perkins—chose the companies in which to invest the fund's assets (provided by the limited partners) and decided how much to allocate to each company. In exchange for this work, the general partners earned what is called a "carry"—a fixed percentage of the fund's overall returns.[18]

In much the same way that Arthur Rock had helped Noyce and Moore incorporate Intel and draw up a business plan, Kleiner Perkins sought to go beyond the traditional investor's approach that Eugene Kleiner once described as "putting in money and then hoping for the best." Kleiner Perkins and the other Silicon Valley venture capital firms that soon followed its example recruited on behalf of the companies they supported (called "portfolio companies"), helped the firms contract for accounting and legal work, facilitated introductions to potential customers, and sponsored networking events in which the CEOs of various portfolio companies could discuss common problems and concerns. Kleiner Perkins also developed business ideas in-house with the assistance of "entrepreneurs in residence" or "business incubation" divisions. These ideas were then spun into portfolio companies in which the venture capitalists invested.[19]

Kleiner Perkins's first $8 million fund returned more than 40 times over. Today, Kleiner Perkins Caufield and Byers is the world's premier venture capital firm, with assets worth more than $1 billion under management.[20]

NOYCE PLAYED NO ROLE in deciding where other venture capitalists invested his money, but his own investment decisions for the Callanish Fund were guided by a philosophy that his partner Hwoschinsky summarized as "That's an impossible task. Let's do it." Noyce liked to say, "You can only lose 100 percent, but the multiples on the up side are fantastic." In some sense, Hwoschinsky's most important job was to protect Noyce—who did want to make money—from his own "let's do it" instincts.[21]

Callanish's first significant investment, in 1974, was roughly $50,000 to support a physicist and a businessman who believed that they could use computers to find underwater oil reserves. Several large companies had already plunged millions of dollars into this "measurement well drilling" effort without success. This alarmed Hwoschinsky, but Noyce was impressed by two pages of simultaneous equations that the physicist, Norman MacLeod, showed him to explain why his ideas ought to work. Hwoschinsky rated MacLeod Labs "an eleven" on a one-to-ten scale of risk; Noyce gave it a six, and Callanish funded it. Noyce had little to do with the operation after this influx of dollars, but Hwoschinsky helped the founders weather a rough period and then sell MacLeod Labs to oil services giant Core Labs. The transaction netted Hwoschinsky, who eventually bought Noyce's stake in the company, a good profit.[22]

Callanish supported an eclectic congeries of small companies: computer software companies Siderial and Dynabyte; Compumotor, a software company for stepper motors; Benz, a project to convert a wheel chair into a street vehicle; Nortron, the first machine that balanced automobile tires using microprocessors. Callanish also backed Sonoma-Cutrer winery in Napa and for a brief time owned the second-largest peach orchard in California, which had valuable riparian rights to the Tolumne River. Through Callanish, Noyce invested in a salmon fishery near Santa Cruz in which Gordon Moore also had a stake. Almost every Callanish investment was small—no more than about $50,000—and targeted to move an idea from a paper proposal to a commercial reality. Noyce rarely invested beyond this "seed stage"; it was helping to start something new that he loved best. The Callanish Fund was not a success on the scale of a Kleiner Perkins, but it was profitable, and it satisfied Noyce's hunger for new ideas and novel approaches.

But one investment particularly captivated Noyce: Caere (pronounced "care"), the company that built OmniPage, the first successful software for computer scanners. Noyce was involved with the firm so intensely and for so long—it existed for 13 years before it went public, leading Noyce, rather ruefully, to call it "the world's oldest startup"—that some described it as "Noyce's *other* company," after Fairchild and Intel.[23]

In 1974, Brian Elfman, the founder and president of Caere (which was then called TypeReader), contacted the Callanish Fund. Elfman wanted seed money to build a hand-held wand that would operate much like the bar-code scanners that today can be found throughout the world. The TypeReader wand, however, would not need specially coded lines to function; instead, it could electronically read simple alphanumeric text—typing, for all intents and purposes. Elfman believed that this wand would greatly simplify inventory control and sales tracking.

Noyce was intrigued, less by Elfman's vision for inventory control than by the broad concept of type recognition. Noyce had long thought that until the tedious and error-prone task of typing data into computers was eliminated, the machines would never achieve their potential for speed, efficiency, accuracy, or power. The TypeReader product offered a way around the keyboard. Noyce invested $30,000. His interest was sufficiently piqued that he also accepted a seat on the TypeReader board.

The company struggled technically. Every month, Noyce invested another small amount of money so that TypeReader could continue to operate. After a year passed with little technical progress, the board, on Noyce's recommendation, hired a new president and two top-flight engineers from Fairchild.

The personnel changes helped the company, which by now had changed its name to Caere, to hit several key milestones. By the end of 1976, J. C. Penney had agreed to test the scanning wands in select stores. This progress enabled Caere to raise a $10 million round of venture financing. Noyce, who was now board chair, invested another $130,000 in this round and also convinced several of his friends in venture capital and at Grinnell College to invest.[24]

When Caere shipped its first product in 1977, the company fully expected the market for its handheld scanner to ramp up quickly. They soon discovered, however, that the scanner was too temperamental to be useful. It could accurately read the numbers and letters on a tag only if the clerk held the wand in precisely the right way.

Caere quickly retooled the scanner as a bar-code reader. The device now worked well—it is a far less complex thing to read a series of lines than text—but the bar-code reader market was already mature and dominated by a few huge companies such as Hewlett-Packard, IBM, and Recognition Equipment Incorporated.

Caere chugged along, never making more than a small profit. Noyce took to arriving early for board meetings so he could talk to the Caere employees, especially the engineers and technical managers. He enjoyed asking them to update him on their progress and problems, and he never hesitated to offer technical suggestions of his own. It is unlikely that his ideas proved particularly useful, but the morale boost that the Caere employees received from Noyce's attention was substantial. To have the founder of one of the Valley's most successful companies and chairman of the Caere board take an interest in one's work was heady stuff indeed.

In 1979, Caere's president left and Noyce decided that the company should not rush into hiring a replacement. He wanted to wait for the right candidate, and in the meantime, he would manage the company himself in tandem with Bob Teresi, Caere's vice president of finance. On one of their first days as co-presidents, Noyce called Teresi into the office that Noyce had begun using at Caere. Noyce asked, "What do you think we should do?"

Teresi thought the company's future in the highly competitive scanner market looked bleak. He said, "I think we should let it go, file for bankruptcy."

"No way," Noyce said emphatically. "We have people [about 30 employees]. We need to keep it open. We have a responsibility to the employees and their families."

Noyce then took out his checkbook and ripped out a check. "Pay to the order of Caere Corp.," he wrote. Then he signed his name. He left the rest of the check blank and handed it to Teresi. "Don't write it for more than a million dollars," Noyce said. "That's all I have in that account."[25]

Teresi held on to the check but did not cash it. After roughly nine months as co-presidents, Teresi and Noyce hired a new CEO, Jim Dutton. One of Dutton's first questions to Noyce was the obvious one. "Why are you screwing around with Caere? You could be doing anything."

Noyce's response came quickly. "It's kind of my way of just paying back the system," he said. By which he meant: it was how he reinvigorated the environment that had made his own success possible. "Besides," Noyce added, "I know that if we can figure out how to make this work, it's a useful technology. It will save people a lot of work."[26]

Shortly after Dutton joined Caere, he and CFO Teresi decided that the time had come to cash Noyce's blank check. The two of them sat together for a long time, trying to determine what numbers to write in the space above Noyce's signature. "The funny thing was that because Bob trusted us to use our judgment and not take more than we needed, it somehow put pressure on us to take less than we would have asked for," Dutton explains. "We knew he had not offered that money in a cavalier way, and we wanted to be damn sure to live up to his trust." Finally Teresi filled in six figures—Dutton guesses it was probably between $250,000 and $350,000—and deposited the check into Caere's account. That was enough to keep the company going a while longer. Meanwhile, Noyce told no one, not even his investment partner Hwoschinsky, what he had done.[27]

IN 1976, 28 INDEPENDENT SECURITIES ANALYSTS named Intel "Electronics Company of the Year." A candid photograph from the awards presentation shows Noyce receiving the commemorative plaque and sharing a hearty handshake with the presenter. Grove stands next to Noyce, beaming a full-wattage grin straight into the lens of the photographer's camera. On Noyce's other side is Gordon Moore, but he is hardly visible, his body half-way out of the frame.[28]

The photograph perfectly encapsulates the popular perception of the relative importance of the three men to Intel's success. Noyce deserves the accolades, Grove is at the center of the action, and Moore does something inscrutable in the margins. This image, of course, was entirely inaccurate. The few sheets of correspondence that survive from the mid-1970s make it clear that Moore ran Intel after Noyce became board chair. Moore had the final say on products, acquisitions, growth, pricing, and budgets. Moore was the one planning board meetings, writing to potential partners ("I propose that it would be sufficient if the exchange consisted of the following . . ."), directing senior staff ("would you two please look at what would be involved"), defining essential problems ("you should concentrate on the most important advantages and disadvantages and educate us with respect to the economics"), articulating Intel's approach to growth ("Intel is not a loose conglomerate that is interested in acquisitions because they are antidilutive; rather we are an operating company and are interested in large developing markets that utilize our technological base"), and informing employees about major changes ("Ann Bowers, Intel's Personnel Manager since the company's formation, has announced her intention to resign"). And Grove, meanwhile, was "amplifying" Moore's direction. "I tend to see things in delicate shades of gray," Moore explained, but Grove honed in on the black or white aspects of a decision and made sure Intel took action. By all rights, the attention paid to Noyce when he was president of Intel should have shifted to Moore, and possibly to Grove, after 1975.[29]

But it did not. Indeed, in the years after Noyce became board chair, his visibility and prestige as one of Intel's founders continued to grow even as his direct involvement with the company was shrinking. This apparent contradiction can be explained in simple terms of time and inclination. Because Moore was consumed with the day-to-day running of the company, and because he was far more reserved than Noyce, he did not mind functioning as Intel's stealth CEO. In dozens of interviews that Moore has granted over the past four decades, only once did he make any comment indicating even the slightest resentment of Noyce's visibility. He told an interviewer in an aside that Noyce's "personality was so outstanding that people kind of gave him credit for everything that happened." But almost immediately, Moore added, "Bob was truly an unusual guy—an exceptional intellect, an amazing personality—people like that don't come along very often."[30]

In contrast to Moore, Noyce had time to grant interviews and speak to various organizations that wanted to understand the secret to Intel's success. He generally enjoyed the exposure, and he and Moore agreed that it was important to keep Intel in the public eye. Every favorable article served as an invitation to potential investors, employees, and customers and a reminder to existing investors, employees, and customers that their decision to affiliate with Intel had been wise.

Regis McKenna, whose agency handled public relations for Intel, believed that the best way to get a company in the news was to put a human face on it. "What really differentiates a business [in the eyes of the public]," he said, "is people. . . . The idea of infusing personalities into this started back very, very, very early." Noyce—father of a critical invention, humble millionaire, Midwestern preacher's boy made good—possessed ideal characteristics to "infuse" into the public's sense of Intel.[31]

Moreover, Noyce's soft-spoken, thoughtful communications style was very persuasive—as he well knew himself. When his broker Bob Harrington, himself a minor radio personality, complimented Noyce on his "tremendous delivery," Noyce, looking a bit embarrassed, admitted, "Yeah, I know. I was just born this way. The way I talk, the way I think—it has just worked really well for me in my life so far."[32]

In 1976, McKenna arranged for Noyce to appear on the cover of *Business Week*, leaning over a chess board, under the headline "New Leaders in Semiconductors—Intel's Robert N. Noyce, Masterminding a Radical Change in Technology." The article compared Intel and National Semiconductor—on the inside cover flap, Noyce's good friend Charlie Sporck was playing black to Noyce's white. The *Business Week* article introduced smiling "youthful-looking semiconductor pioneer" Noyce to the general business reader as "the innovator-entrepreneur" of the industry and Intel's "most articulate spokesman." Later that year, Noyce was the subject of a *New York Times* profile.[33]

At this point, nearly all of the $6 billion semiconductor business depended on integrated circuits very similar to the planar-based device Noyce had conceptualized at Fairchild. As the importance of this invention grew increasingly obvious, the scientific community began to bestow important honors on Noyce. In 1978, he received the Medal of Honor from the Institute of Electrical and Electronics Engineers (IEEE) "for his contributions to the silicon integrated circuit, a cornerstone of modern electronics." A distinguished member of the IEEE wrote to Noyce, "It is rare that a truly revolutionary major invention, the direction of the development of the invention, and its successful exploitation in the marketplace are the work of a single individual. You deserve, far beyond most winners, this highest honor of the IEEE."[34]

At the White House in 1979, President Carter presented Noyce the National Medal of Science, the highest award granted for scientific achievement in the United States. Noyce was one of 20 recipients that year; sharing the stage with him were such luminaries as quantum physicist Richard Feynman, DNA pioneer Arthur Kornberg, and nuclear physicist (and Noyce's one-time MIT professor) Victor Weisskopf.

Ann Bowers wrote in her 1978 Christmas letter that "all of this [recognition] has made [Noyce] much in demand as a speaker. He seems to be a

model of entrepreneurial endeavor." The National Association of Manufacturers recognized his "distinguished contribution to the well-being of
mankind through scientific research and development." He also received a
Corporate Leadership Award from MIT and keynoted the Institute's alumni
conference on "the management of innovation." He began the talk with a
description of his own career choices, which he claimed had never been
particularly daring. "The entrepreneur as a pin-striped John Wayne blazing economic frontiers is a Hollywood myth," he said. "There is risk [in
entrepreneurship], but it is usually a calculated risk, and what you leave
behind is not usually worth looking over your shoulder for." When he left
Shockley for Fairchild or Fairchild for Intel, he said, "The only risk was
that I wouldn't meet the goals I had set myself. I always knew I could go
out and get a job." This is a slightly revisionist version of his thoughts—he
had never worried about getting another job; he had simply assumed he
would not fail—but perhaps the young Noyce seemed a bit too brazenly
self-confident from the perspective of his 50-year-old self. At the end of
his talk, Noyce emphasized that "innovation feeds on success" and suggested that the best way to encourage innovation is "to be confident of
success and to reward it generously." He cited Intel's stock-option plan as
an example of this philosophy in action.[35]

By the early 1980s, Noyce had been featured in *Business Week*, the *Economist*, *Forbes*, *Fortune*, *National Geographic*, the *New York Times*, *Time*, and
the *Wall Street Journal*, as well as many electronics-related publications.
Noyce's story was the paradigmatic tale of high-tech industry and of Silicon Valley in the eyes of many. The title of Tom Wolfe's 1983 *Esquire*
profile of Noyce, "The Tinkerings of Robert Noyce: How the Sun Rose
on Silicon Valley," might have been a bit more openly hagiographic than
some of the other articles, but it captures their general tone. In November
1983, the town of Grinnell declared "Robert Norton Noyce Day." The
proclamation described Noyce as "a man from Grinnell who has gone on
to high professional accomplishment and enterprise but who has never
forgotten the upbringing and education he received here." When Noyce
was asked how he felt about being known as "the father of Silicon Valley,"
he ducked his head, grinned, and answered, "a little humble, a little proud.
What can I say? I love the term."[36]

When *San Francisco Chronicle* reporter Herb Caen admitted in 1979
that he "had let another year go by without learning what a semiconductor
is," his readers wrote to him, not to describe the device or the physics
behind it, but to describe Noyce. "Several people hasten to tell me about
Robert Noyce of Los Altos, who not only pioneered the blamed thing [the
integrated circuit], he founded Fairchild Semiconductor and Intel Corp.
($600 million in ten years) and, to boot, is a pilot and champion skier. Not

only that! He has just become one of only 130 people in U.S. history to receive the National Science Medal. . . . Sure." Caen's readers, in other words, thought Noyce was all the layman needed to know about semiconductors. And Caen thought he sounded too good to be true.[37]

And in fact, Noyce's public success and accolades were once again shadowed by personal difficulties. Two of his children, now young adults, were struggling with drug problems. In 1976, one of the young Noyces was diagnosed with bipolar disorder and hospitalized. A few months later, one of Noyce's daughters was hit by a car while walking across a street near Noyce's home. She lay in a coma for six weeks with an open head injury. Rehabilitation was slow and difficult.

Aside from an initial flare of anger, during which he mercilessly grilled one of his children's doctors on his credentials, Noyce dealt with the crises using the same strangely passive denial tactics that had enabled him to weather his early difficulties with Betty. "He absolutely did not want to connect on anything that was emotionally difficult," recalls Ann Bowers, who says that during this period she found herself sympathizing with Betty Noyce for the only time in her life. Noyce's behavior when Bowers wanted to talk with him about the family's problems reminded her of a toddler sticking his fingers in his ears and singing, "I can't hear you." He would disappear for hours into the basement or onto the tennis court behind their house. It got to the point that Bowers found herself trying to trap him—in the car, or at a restaurant—so he might be forced to bring his creativity, influence, and brainpower to bear on the situation.

But if life got too tense at home, Noyce would leave town. There was always a speech that could be given, a customer who needed wooing, a sales meeting that required inspiration, or an interview that might be granted. "My father was good at everything," one of his daughters once said, "except, maybe, human interaction."[38]

Betty Noyce was no more willing than Bob to become involved. At one crisis point she explained that she would not cancel a scheduled vacation to the Bahamas because "[the ill person] is in the hospital, so what good would I do anyway?" It fell to Noyce's healthy adult children and Ann Bowers to find the best treatment programs and therapists and to confer with school officials, doctors, and other medical experts.

Noyce found it emotionally impossible to cope with the pain that his children were suffering. He no doubt felt at least partially responsible for it. Their troubles seemed to confirm his fear that the wages of his sins would be visited upon his children. In 1979, Noyce was invited to dinner at the home of an entrepreneur whose company the Callanish Fund had supported. After the dishes had been cleared and the children sent to bed, Noyce listened as the company founder explained that some day, if the business did well, he would like to move his family into a bigger, nicer house. Noyce looked up at him and said very quietly, "You've got a nice family. I screwed up mine. Just stay where you are." Twenty-five years and a successful company later, the entrepreneur has not moved.[39]

PUBLIC RELATIONS CONSULTANT Regis McKenna insists that Noyce did not actively seek opportunities to promote himself, that Noyce considered granting interviews and garnering publicity to be part of his job at Intel. It does appear that Noyce had little interest in fame. While others resented, on his behalf, that he had to share credit for the integrated circuit with TI's Jack Kilby, Noyce never had a problem with it. When Leo Esaki won the Nobel Prize in 1973 for his work on the tunnel diode, Noyce apparently told no one that he, too, had conceived of the device, and at the same time as Esaki. When, a decade later, Noyce did mention his tunnel diode work, he dismissed it with "I didn't miss much [by not publishing my research]; the work had already been done elsewhere."

Whether or not Noyce wanted to occupy the center of the Intel spotlight, one man sorely resented his apparently permanent claim to it. Shortly after his *New York Times* profile appeared, Noyce called Regis McKenna. "Andy [Grove] feels like Gordon and I get all the credit [for Intel]," Noyce said, sounding a little worried. "We have got to make Andy more visible, and we've got to give him more credit." McKenna called the reporter who wrote the *Times* profile of Noyce. Grove, McKenna pointed out, had an outstanding story of his own. His was the much-cherished tale of an immigrant who comes to America and through education and diligent self-application, rises to business success. Six months after the Noyce profile appeared, the same reporter wrote a half-page feature article on Grove, Intel's "high technology jelly bean ace," for the Sunday *New York Times.* "That article launched Andy," McKenna recalls with satisfaction.[40]

Noyce may not have actively pursued public accolades and attention, but he thoroughly enjoyed them. "He liked being looked at and being the center of attention," explains Ann Bowers. "There was a showoff side to Bob." Almost anyone who knew Noyce well has a story of him deliberately drawing attention to himself. Charlie Sporck recalls Noyce putting on "a hell of a diving show" at a hotel pool. Richard Hodgson remembers that Noyce once insisted on wearing a bright yellow jacket—which commemorated his having downhill skied some 100,000 feet in deep powder—throughout a luncheon at Hodgson's home. Later Noyce admitted that although he had almost overheated, he had noticed another guest wearing a jacket from a successful climb of K2 (the second highest peak in the world). Noyce said that he "was not going to have a K2 jacket take precedence over a hundred-thousand-foot [jacket]." Jim Lafferty, Noyce's sometime flight instructor said simply, "He liked being special at everything he did."[41]

Harry Sello, a Fairchild employee who hosted a public television show
called *This Week in Science*, recalls the day in the late 1960s when he invited
Noyce to appear as his guest on the show. Sello had planned to have Noyce
look at a transistor through a microscope while he, Sello, looked through
another microscope and described what they were seeing for viewers, who
could see the magnified image on their screens. Events transpired differently, however:

> [Noyce] walked over and he stepped in front of me. And I'm the damn
> lead on the show! He cut my lines. He upstaged me all over the place. He
> said, "Let me show it to you," and all of a sudden Noyce's voice comes
> on and we're looking at the same [microscopic] pictures [while] he ex-
> plains it. After he looked up, I made a crack about, "Do you see why he's
> president of the organization and I'm not?" He burst out laughing.

Sello stressed that Noyce did not deliberately steal the limelight. "That's
just how he was."[42]

When Tom Wolfe's glowing *Esquire* article appeared, Noyce was impressed that Wolfe "got it pretty much right," despite having spoken to
him only for a few minutes. Noyce sent a copy of the article to his mother,
who promptly wrote to her sisters-in-law, "Tom Wolfe of *The Right Stuff*
book chose to write up Bob and the miracle chip. He [Bob] was given
twenty pages, and Jackie Onassis [profiled in the same issue] got two pages
by another, dull, author." Several people at Intel honored the publication
of the Wolfe article with a "pictorial salute to our man of the year." They
superimposed Noyce's face on several risqué pictures in *Playgirl* magazine
and captioned every image with one or another of Wolfe's most histrionic
lines—"He seemed to enjoy finding new ways to hang his hide over the
edge" or "Hey, it's your ass." Then they gave the magazine to Noyce. He
loved it.[43]

NOYCE'S PUBLIC IMAGE was particularly compelling for a nation just beginning to emerge from the difficult years of the 1970s. The OPEC oil em-
bargo and ensuing energy crisis in the middle of the decade were followed
by double-digit inflation and a combination of high prices and record mort-
gage rates that put homeownership beyond the means of many. In November 1979, 70 American embassy employees were taken hostage in Iran
and held for 444 days.

Against this bleak backdrop, Noyce and the semiconductor-based, high-
technology economy of Silicon Valley shone like beacons. While other
sectors suffered, worldwide electronics sales increased at an annual rate of
15 percent between 1968 and 1978, to a whopping $140 billion. Some
experts predicted sales of $500 billion by 1988. Semiconductors did even
better, growing at an estimated 18 percent annual rate. While more than

1.5 million American manufacturing workers lost their jobs, high technology employment in the San Francisco Bay Area grew 77 percent from 1974 to 1980, with Santa Clara County (the county whose boundaries most closely match those of Silicon Valley), gaining an impressive 83,000 jobs in the sector. In 1979, the "help wanted" section of the *San Jose Mercury News* listed more than 60 pages of advertisements for technical personnel. Per capita personal income growth in Santa Clara County outpaced the rest of California by more than 10 percent.[44]

According to some calculations, Silicon Valley produced more millionaires in the decade of the 1970s than anywhere else in the country at any time in history. Between 1975 and 1983, more than 1,000 companies— some of them fantastically successful—were launched in Silicon Valley. In 1983, the chairman of the American Stock Exchange was excited enough about young high-technology firms that he told *Time* magazine, "If there is any hope for our economy, it rests with these people. They are the most challenging, irreverent bunch around."[45]

The chairman's comments appeared in an issue of *Time* whose cover featured a soft-focus picture of Apple Computer co-founder Steve Jobs under the headline, "Striking it Rich: America's Risk Takers." Jobs was 26 years old and worth nearly $150 million. He was the most visible member of a new generation of electronics entrepreneurs—young men (a new generation, but the dominance of men remained a constant) building companies whose products relied on semiconductor technology. Noyce once said that "small entrepreneurs depend totally upon the infrastructure that is— has been—established . . . so that they can use those tools, those techniques, and go off and do something specialized." This certainly was true of Apple Computer, which was financed by men associated with Fairchild and Intel and staffed with many people from Hewlett-Packard and Intel.[46]

Apple had gotten its start in 1976, when 19-year-old Jobs convinced his friend Steve Wozniak, who had developed a personal computer in his garage, to start a business with him. The two showed their computer to venture capitalist Don Valentine (a former Fairchild salesman), who suggested they contact Mike Markkula, recently retired (at age 34) from his job in Intel's marketing group. Markkula, who had long dreamed of something like a personal computer—as a teenager, he had built a "programmable electronic sliderule"—invested $91,000 in the company. In exchange, he received a one-third ownership stake in Apple.[47]

One of Markkula's first calls on behalf of Apple was to Noyce. "I want you to be aware of this," Markkula said. "I'd like to present to the [Intel] board." Noyce gave his approval and on the appointed day, Markkula and Steve Wozniak gave a presentation about the personal computer, an Apple II on hand for demonstration purposes. "If you want to participate in this in some way, say so," Markkula told the board. "If you don't, fine. But this is something you should have in front of your consciousness." Intel had not given much thought to the personal computer since Moore squelched Noyce and Gelbach's plans to go head to head with Altair. The board listened politely and asked a few questions, but no one proposed a relationship between Intel and Apple that went beyond Intel's possibly providing the microprocessor for Apple Computers. "Nothing else was really in Intel's best interest," Markkula acknowledges.[48]

But Arthur Rock had paid careful attention to Markkula and Wozniak's presentation. A few days later, he called Markkula's office. "I want to talk to these guys," Rock said. After attending a small computer hobbyists' convention and noticing many more people crowded around the Apple booth than any other, Rock decided to invest $60,000 in the company. He also brought in Henry Singleton of Teledyne, who invested $108,000.

In 1977, Regis McKenna, who handled Intel's public relations, began working with Apple. He hosted a party, one of whose key objectives was to introduce Ann Bowers, who was building her consulting business, to Steve Jobs, who McKenna thought needed to hire a human-resources expert. Jobs did not make a good impression on Bowers. He was a 22-year-old, self-described "college drop in," with a stringy beard and long hair. He attended McKenna's dinner party in scruffy jeans, a t-shirt, Birkenstock sandals, and a morning coat. But he was interesting enough to talk to, and soon Bowers found herself engrossed in what she called "all Steve's schemes," only half of which she thought were even remotely feasible. Clearly this was a company that needed her help. She agreed to consult for Apple.[49]

A few months into her consulting work, Bowers learned that Steve Wozniak wanted to sell some of his founders' stock for $13 a share. She bought it from him. "Bob thought I was nuts," she recalls. Noyce did not try to stop her from investing—they had long ago agreed that she could do what she liked with her money, and he could do the same with his—but he could not take Jobs and Wozniak seriously. Even Arthur Rock admits, "Steve Jobs and Steve Wozniak weren't very appealing people in those days." Wozniak was the telephone-era's version of a hacker—he used a small box that emitted electronic tones to call around the world for free—and Steve Jobs's ungroomed appearance was offputting to Noyce. In his day, Noyce, too, had worked outside the corporate mainstream, with his company hopping and his attempts to democratize Fairchild's corporate culture. But even Noyce, who had dared to wear shirt sleeves in the office, wore a coat and tie to meetings. He respected protocol. He always had cut his hair short, and he did not wear sandals beyond the pool deck.[50]

Besides, Noyce asked Bowers with perhaps a touch of jealousy, what made this hippie company worth $13 a share? Yes, Noyce was convinced that personal computers would one day be a huge market. But he was equally convinced that Jobs and Wozniak were not the men to lead that market. This was especially true after Bowers brought home her first Apple in 1978, and she and Noyce spent much of the weekend on the phone to Mike Mark-kula trying to set it up properly. The Apple machine did not strike Noyce as the groundbreaking technical breakthrough necessary to bring computing power to the common man.

But over time, Noyce's feelings about Apple began to change. This was due, in no small measure, to Steve Jobs, who deliberately sought out Noyce as a mentor. (Jobs also asked Jerry Sanders and Andy Grove if he could take them to lunch every quarter and "pick your brain.") "Steve would regularly appear at our house on his motorcycle," Bowers recalls. "Soon he and Bob were disappearing into the basement, talking about projects." Noyce decided Jobs was immature but extremely bright and a lot of fun. In 1979, Noyce invited Jobs to fly with him in his Seabee, a World War II–era plane that could land on either water or land. After landing on a lake, Noyce pulled a wrong lever, inadvertently locking the wheels. It was not until he tried to land the plane on a runway that he realized there was a problem. Immediately upon hitting the ground, the Seabee leapt forward and nearly flipped. Jobs watched with mounting panic as Noyce furiously tried to bring the plane under control while sparks shot past the windows. "As this was happening," Jobs recalls, "I was picturing the headline: 'Bob Noyce and Steve Jobs Killed in Fiery Plane Crash.' It was only due to his excellent piloting that we survived. It was really close."[51]

Bowers says that Noyce treated Jobs "like a kid, but not in a patronizing way. He would let him come and go, crash in the corner. We would feed him and bring him along to events and to ski in Aspen." Noyce answered Jobs's phone calls—which invariably began with "I've been thinking about what you said" or "I have an idea"—even when they came at midnight. At some point he confided to Bowers, "If he calls late again, I'm going to kill him," but still he answered the phone.

Jobs agrees that his relationship with Noyce was almost more filial than professional. "The things I remember about Bob are the personal things," he says. "I remember him teaching me how to ski better. And he was very interested in—fascinated by—the personal computer, and we talked a lot about that." Jobs thought that "Bob was the soul of Intel," and Jobs wanted, he said, "to smell that second wonderful era of the valley, the semiconductor companies leading into the computer."[52]

What did Noyce get out of the relationship? Jobs surmises, "Apple was probably the first Silicon Valley company that was widely known as a lifestyle company, the first that made a broad consumer product—and here I was, twenty-five [years old]. And for Bob, it was a bit of 'What?! Who is this guy? What's going on here?' It was just a little strange for him. Bob might have been a little curious."

Apple went public in December of 1980 at $22 a share. The offering netted Apple more than $100 million, roughly 14 times the proceeds Intel received from its IPO.[53]

Noyce had a front-row seat for all that transpired at Apple. Not only was he one of Jobs's mentors and Markkula's friends, but in August of 1980, Ann Bowers joined the company as the human resources vice president. Apple burst with the young-company spirit and hunger that Noyce adored, and every once in a while, Noyce would, as Markkula put it, "come over to Apple and just hang around. Go in the lab and talk to the guys about what they were doing." Years later, when Noyce was testifying before Congress against a "national industrial policy" administered by the federal government, he would refer to his experience with Apple to bolster his point. "If *I* can't pick the technological winners," he said, "how can we expect the U.S. government to do so?"

LIKE APPLE, many of the successful Silicon Valley companies formed in the 1970s were built around microelectronics, and by extension, around Noyce's integrated circuit. In 1974, James Treybig started Tandem Computer, a company that made nearly fail-safe minicomputers by linking 16 processors and programming them to back each other up in case of failure. Tandem's primary backer was Kleiner Perkins, where Treybig had worked before starting the company. The company went public in 1980—Noyce's broker Bob Harrington arranged for employees to participate in his same-day stock-sale program—and within three years had a book value of $1 billion. (It was sold to Compaq computer in 1997 for $3 billion.)[54]

Video game maker Atari was started on $500 in 1972 and within three years was among the most recognized names in American business. Several of its more complex games ran on Intel microprocessors. The home version of Atari's video-tennis game Pong was the bestselling Christmas gift of 1975, and the Atari 2600, introduced in 1976, ushered in the era of video console games, in which a person could purchase any number of games on cartridges that plugged into hardware connected to a television set. In 1977, Warner Communications purchased Atari for $28 million.[55]

Genentech, one of the world's first biotech companies, was started in 1976 by a San Francisco–based biochemist at the urging of a Kleiner Perkins partner. The company was the first to produce a human protein in a microorganism and among the earliest groups to clone human insulin and human growth hormone. The anticipation surrounding Genentech's public offering in 1980 was so great that in a single hour during the first day of trading, the company's share price shot from $35 to $88. In 2004, Genentech had a $57 billion market capitalization.[56]

In the same way that these companies built on the previous generation's technical advances, they also took advantage of the network of suppliers, venture capitalists, equipment vendors, specialized law and public relations firms, contract fabs (that would build chips designed elsewhere), and customers that had sprung up in the past decade to support high-tech entrepreneurs in Silicon Valley. By 1983, more than 3,000 small consulting firms in Santa Clara County provided new companies with startup expertise and continuing help over the early years of operation. Many of the chip designers, glass blowers, fab houses, and die cutters that catered to Silicon Valley high-tech entrepreneurs were themselves small privately held firms. This "supply chain," most often mentioned for its support of small companies, is itself an entrepreneurial phenomenon.[57]

Wealthy investors, many of whom had made their fortunes at small high-technology companies, perpetuated the success-breeds-success cycle through formal venture capital funds and "angel investments" such as Noyce's funding of the shoebox startups or his Callanish fund investments— or the $30 million drinking club, which Noyce joined sometime in the 1970s.[58]

Local educational institutions committed to meeting the needs of nearby industry helped to replenish the pool of talent from which Silicon Valley firms drew their employees. Universities such as Stanford, Berkeley, and San Jose State trained engineers and offered relevant coursework in their business schools. Foothill College in Los Altos offered an A.S. degree in semiconductor processing and a program for electronics technicians. Stanford developed a distance-learning program that allowed engineers at select local high-tech firms to take Stanford courses, for credit, via television.[59]

Real estate developers and city planners also formed an important part of the entrepreneurial support system. Developers were clearing orchards south down the Valley as fast as they could, hurriedly constructing low-slung buildings to house new companies. "It is likely that [non-high-tech] growth will be inhibited by both economic factors and policy decisions. High technology firms will be strong competitors for the best available sites," noted an independent study of the Valley in 1982. "The prestige and 'clean' image of the electronics industry will favorably influence planning and zoning decisions in many cases." By the mid-1980s, Andy Grove was calling Silicon Valley a "business machine," implying that the region churned out companies the way that Intel churned out chips.[60]

Zoning laws, venture capital companies, and course offerings—unrelated as they may seem—were predicated on a common assumption in Silicon Valley: that high-tech entrepreneurship was the best way to assure personal and regional vitality. Venture capitalists on Sand Hill Road, entrepreneurs in their garages or plotting defections in their low-walled cubicles, planners in City Hall, and students picking their way through course offerings made decisions based on a faith that the cycle of success would continue to perpetuate itself, that the innovations would continue to flow and the markets to develop and grow.

At the heart of this assumption stands the entrepreneur. As Noyce once put it, "Look around Silicon Valley and see who the heroes are. They aren't lawyers, nor are they even so much the financiers. They're the guys who start companies." Silicon Valley could not function without the abiding faith that entrepreneurs will continue to succeed.[61]

And for many, Noyce was the paradigmatic entrepreneur at the center of the story. His financial success directly benefited the entrepreneurs whose companies he funded, but the *stories* about Noyce's success indirectly inspired many more. One entrepreneur put it this way: "Why do we love this dynamic environment? I'll tell you why. Because we have seen what Steve Jobs, Bob Noyce, Nolan Bushnell [founder of Atari], and many others have done, and we know it can and will happen many times again." In other words, if they could do it, why couldn't he? Such rationale functioned as a self-fulfilling prophecy in Silicon Valley, propelling the region forward on a self-perpetuating cycle of entrepreneurship and wealth.[62]

Noyce once happily explained that with semiconductors, "Everything gets better simultaneously, without any tradeoffs. As they get smaller, devices also get faster, use less power, are more reliable, and cost less per function to produce." The industry, he said, was "a violation of Murphy's Law." To be sure, established semiconductor companies flourished in the late 1970s boom in Silicon Valley. Profits at Charlie Sporck's National Semiconductor were $34 million in 1979—more than double its 1975 performance. At AMD, Jerry Sanders' operation in which Noyce had invested a small bit of seed money, profits grew tenfold over the same period, to $11 million. At the end of the decade, the top 12 American semiconductor firms claimed 80 percent of the world market.[63]

Intel's growth was most dramatic of all. In 1979, the company's profits were $78 million, quadruple the 1975 performance and nearly 40 times 1972 profits. The company had been the largest supplier of semiconductor memory components in the world since 1976. The stock had split five times between 1973 and 1979. The company celebrated its tenth anniversary in 1978 with an extravagant party at San Francisco's Cow Palace that included a casino with play money and two discotheques. The highlight of the festivities was the announcement that Intel would give every one of its employees one share of stock for every year of service. This amounted to a distribution of more than 10,000 shares with a combined value that surpassed $560,000.[64]

In May 1979, Intel debuted on the *Fortune* 500 at number 486. By this time, every dollar that Noyce invested when the company began in 1968 was worth $600. The stock he had bought at the founding for $245,000 was now, 11 years later, worth $147 million.

With stories about spectacular successes at Intel, Apple, and Tandem Computers crossing the media wires at the end of the 1970s, it is no wonder that Silicon Valley came to represent an innovative, wealthy, daring, successful, world-leading America that some had begun to fear might have disappeared forever in the difficult middle years of the decade. Indeed, stories cast the region as a reincarnation of the most "American" place imaginable, the mythic West, legendary birthplace of freedom and rugged individualism. Many accounts called Silicon Valley entrepreneurs "cowboys" and "pioneers." These men had staked out new territory where they could build egalitarian, antibureaucratic companies in the same way that Americans a century earlier had headed to the frontier to escape the confines of a stultified Eastern culture. Noyce himself used the same vernacular when he described large-scale integration as "a broad and fertile plain, . . . more or less virgin territory . . . less verdant today, but it will support a large herd still." The daughter of a displaced Santa Clara County orchardist wrote (in a rather poignantly titled book *Passing Farms, Enduring Values*) that although the Old West was gone, its spirit endured in men like Bob Noyce. "Thanks, in part, to Noyce, today's Santa Clara County has a reputation for egalitarian management," she wrote. "He has been credited with establishing the style that is the hallmark of the new corporate culture: open shirts, casual clothes, interaction on a first-name basis. He has also helped to show the way for employees to become owners very much as farm laborers used to become landed farmers."[65]

In his 1983 State of the Union address, President Reagan, who regularly used images of the American West as shorthand for freedom, independence, and small government, praised Silicon Valley's "pioneers of tomorrow": "Surely as America's pioneer spirit made us the industrial giant of the 20th century, the same pioneer spirit today is opening up on another vast front of opportunity, the frontier of high technology." A week later, in a speech before a Washington, D.C. conference on high-technology public policy, Noyce quoted Reagan and added, "I wish I'd said that."[66]

11

Political Entrepreneurship

By the end of 1979, Intel employed twice as many people as lived in Grinnell, Iowa, when Noyce was growing up. The company had a dozen major facilities in seven countries and roughly twice that number of sales offices. The dramatic growth led Noyce, Moore, and Grove to decide they would again shuffle jobs and assume new positions at Intel. The president/CEO job occupied by Moore would be split. Grove would become president, Moore would retain the title of CEO but also serve as board chair, and Noyce would leave the chairmanship to become vice-chairman of the corporation. In effect, this meant that Grove would run the company with Moore in close consultation.[1]

This second round of management musical chairs was significant for Noyce because it left him, for the first time, without an official leadership role at Intel. His status as a founder would always give him some measure of special influence within the company. He would still be brought in when Intel needed to access a high-level executive at a key account or to close a particularly important deal. In 1985, for example, he presented to IBM as part of an effort to convince the company to use Intel's newest microprocessor in its personal computer. But as vice-chairman, Noyce no longer felt obligated—or entitled—to "watch the store," as he put it.[2]

With the move to vice-chair, the Intel-centered phase of Noyce's career effectively ended. Throughout the 1980s, he spent so little time at Intel—his one-time secretary estimates he was there no more than twice a week—that an April Fool's edition of the company newsletter ran an article in 1983 under the headline, "Rare Bob Noyce Sighting Reported." By this time, Noyce's divorce and his decisions to sell some of his Intel holdings either to make purchases or to support startup companies had left him with less than half the amount of stock than was owned by his co-founder Gordon Moore, who had sold very little. At the company's blowout twentieth anniversary celebration in 1988 (for which Intel hired a professional stage troupe of 50 people to perform a 90-minute musical tribute to the company), Andy Grove was celebrated as one of the company's "three founders," while Noyce was referred to rather lamely as "the physicist" in the showstopping "Grove, Noyce, and Moore" number that called Moore "the chairman" and Grove "the president." In some Intel annual reports after 1979, Noyce's name appears only in the list of directors on the last page. Around this time Noyce privately admitted, "It's so hard to get off the stage."[3]

A poem he composed in honor of a friend's fortieth birthday in 1980 makes it clear that Noyce wrestled with the possibility that he might grow irrelevant as he aged. "Now's the only time to be," he wrote rather stiltedly to his friend, whose nickname was Bougin:

> Time should come, my dear Bougin
> 	At least for those mortal men
> To act one's age, and gone's the day
> 	One stops to get "Chip chip hooray."
>
> Saving for advancing years,
> 	Shouting down the gnawing fears
> Of missing something here on earth
> 	Because of time's increasing dearth.
>
> [. . .]
>
> Challange [sic] snowy slopes so steep
> 	Plunge through the waves of ocean deep
> Aerobic dance, and hit the ball
> 	Jet the world and see it all.
>
> This is the way the world should age
> This is the way the world should age
> THIS IS THE WAY THE WORLD SHOULD AGE
> Just with a BANG, not a whimper.[4]

Determined to age "with a BANG," Noyce built himself a new stage when he stepped down from the Intel chairmanship. The late 1970s marked the opening of a new phase of his career—one spent not in the service of any specific company, but in the service of the industry itself. During these years, and throughout the 1980s, the American semiconductor industry found its worldwide supremacy challenged—and nearly toppled—for the first time. The challengers were Japanese firms, and leading the American response became the defining animus of Noyce's work.

For decades, American semiconductor companies had sustained among themselves a tenuous balance between cooperation and competition. Many of the CEOs in the industry served together on the executive board of trade association WEMA's semiconductor group, which Noyce chaired.

Others had worked together—and for Noyce—at Fairchild. When they left Fairchild to run competitor firms, they stole each others' employees, copied each others' products, and occasionally sued each other, but much of this aggression was akin to flashes of sibling rivalry among brothers who had come of professional age side by side and had grown wealthy and influential together.

The chumminess of the American semiconductor industry was the subject of a self-parodying skit in 1971. The show, called "Oh Say, Can I.C.?," concluded with a "Friendship Finale" that featured Sporck, Sanders, Noyce, and executives from Texas Instruments, Motorola, Signetics, and Intersil (or perhaps actors playing these executives) singing about their support for each other—"If you ever lose your shirt, I'll be hurt"—and their "friendship, friendship, just a perfect blendship." Every one of these singing executives, of course, wanted his company to beat the others—and each did what he could to ensure his triumph. But they all could take comfort in knowing that if their company was not number one in the world at any given time, at least one of their brothers' firms was.[5]

This all changed in the late 1970s, when Japanese semiconductor firms began selling chips that were less expensive and at least as high-quality as American devices. At the same time that the Japanese chips were being sold in the United States, the large and ever-growing Japanese market was almost completely closed to imports, which meant that American firms could not attempt to make up their losses by selling in their rivals' territory. The appearance of competitive Japanese chips raised the stakes for American firms. Suddenly the consequences of not winning were much higher than they had ever been. In 1974, for example, American firms had supplied nearly all of the world's demand for 4K DRAMs (memory chips). But by 1979, 35 percent of the next generation (16K) chip was supplied by Japanese firms, and three years later, the Japanese share of the DRAM market surpassed that of the United States. It was no longer a given that one's brother firm would lead the world.[6]

Noyce and his fellow semiconductor executives worried that ripple effects from losses in the DRAM market could threaten the entire American industry. The DRAM was what the industry called a "technology driver"—a relatively simple chip produced in such large quantities that it enabled the manufacturers to hone skills that they could then apply to the production of more complex devices. In other words, fewer 16K DRAM chips produced by Americans in 1979 would mean less efficient production of other, more profitable chips in 1981. "Capturing the 16K market is like taking the top of a hill," explained AMD founder Jerry Sanders. "Once you have it, all you have to do is shoot down."[7]

Americans in other industries had learned in the most painful way possible not to underestimate the Japanese. Although "made in Japan" was once synonymous with shoddy workmanship, after World War II, the Japanese had developed into world-class manufacturers and business leaders. By 1985, Nippon Steel outproduced U.S. Steel, and a Japanese bank (Dai-Ichi Kangyo) was the world's largest. Japanese televisions had driven American products out of the market. America's trade deficit with the island nation ballooned to $40.7 billion—almost 40 times the deficit just one decade earlier. As the 1980s drew to a close, 68 percent of Americans named Japan as the number one threat to the nation's future.[8]

As early as 1978, Noyce was warning that historians might someday note that "in addition to originating and nurturing a vibrant semiconductor industry, the United States also lost it—the same way we have lost the steel industry and the TV market—to foreign competition." In just the previous eight years, 19 United States semiconductor firms had been partially or entirely purchased by foreign investors.[9]

The prospect that the industry he had helped to launch might soon die on American shores absolutely infuriated Noyce. He certainly was not a racist—he pushed for eased immigration laws, praised the "brilliant minds from places like India and the Orient which have made such major contributions to high technology," and had been as harsh in his criticism of European semiconductor firms when Europe had a protected market as he was of the Japanese—but his comments about the Japanese could be spiked with uncharacteristic racial nastiness and hyperbole. He told *Fortune* magazine that the Japanese were "out to slit our throats," a comment that he later admitted got him "almost thrown out of Japan," and he warned that "the time to throw up a block to a karate chop is before it lands." When a Japanese semiconductor executive referred to United States firms as "boutique semiconductor companies" (thus implying that Japanese firms were more efficient manufacturers), Noyce started yelling at him—highly unusual behavior for a man so shy of confrontation that his nickname was "Dr. Nice." When as a joke, one of Noyce's friends made him a cake covered with paper Japanese flags, Noyce pulled out his cigarette lighter and burned every one of them.[10]

He was not alone in his feelings. In 1977, Noyce, Fairchild president Wilfred Corrigan, AMD president Jerry Sanders, National Semiconductor president Charlie Sporck, and Motorola vice president John Welty decided to join forces to counter the threat to their industry. Three of these men had worked together at Fairchild, and all five had known each other for nearly a decade. This group founded the Semiconductor Industry Association (SIA) with plans to harness the industry's cooperative spirit and innovative thinking in the service of what one founder described as the SIA's "essential task": "slow down what the Japanese government is doing in support of its industry, and speed up what our government [is doing]."[11]

The two governments' approaches were indeed quite different. Where the Americans had taken a fairly laissez-faire approach to fostering business development, Japan's Liberal Democratic Party, which had governed the island nation since the mid-1950s, actively fostered the country's industrial sector. This meant importing raw materials—Japan had almost none—and exporting high-value-added finished products manufactured from those materials.

Until 1980, Japan's Ministry of International Trade and Industry (MITI) held exclusive power to grant import and export licenses. In the 1950s and 1960s, MITI focused on two export industries: automobiles and steel. The government offered companies in these industries low-interest loans and developed national policies to shut established foreign (usually European and American) competitors out of the domestic Japanese auto and steel markets. This government-sponsored protection and support enabled the target industries to prosper, and eventually, to challenge the very European and American competitors once excluded from the Japanese market. As the steel and automobile industries strengthened in the 1970s, the Japanese government used many of the same policies to support consumer electronics and the semiconductors that made them work.

Partially as a result of their governments' approaches, the Japanese and American semiconductor industries were structurally quite different from each other. The prototypical Silicon Valley semiconductor firm in the 1980s was the independent, "merchant" producer, which manufactured chips for end users other than itself (although Texas Instruments, IBM, and Motorola were vertically integrated companies). Merchant companies often got their start as entrepreneurial ventures; depended on continuous technological innovation and mass production; and before the 1980s, had traditionally regarded the government's proper role to be that of an eager customer with very deep pockets.

In sharp contrast to this model, the Japanese semiconductor industry consisted of six huge, vertically integrated electronics firms (Nippon Electric, Fujitsu, Hitachi, Toshiba, Mitsubishi Electric, and Oki Electric Industry), which had been developed with direct assistance from the government for the express purpose of growing Japan's high-technology sector. These firms manufactured not only chips, but also the electronic equipment—such as computers or VCRs—that used the chips. In fact, in 1979, only 7 percent of the companies' combined revenues were derived from semiconductor sales.[12]

The Japanese government conferred substantial benefits on these semiconductor firms, imposing tight restrictions on foreign imports from competing manufacturers, subsidizing and organizing national research projects, developing programs designed to funnel talented students into fields such as engineering, and permitting a flexible application of antitrust laws. Equally important was the signal that such government actions sent to the Japanese banking community. Japanese banks, many of whose directors also served on the boards of the electronics companies, were willing to make loans to companies in such clearly "favored industries," despite the firms' debt ratios, which would have been considered astronomical by American standards. As a result, Japanese semiconductor firms found it much easier to obtain capital than did American companies.[13]

The difference in access to capital launched the Semiconductor Industry Association's first serious lobbying push. In February of 1978, Noyce, who headed the SIA's Trade Policy committee and would serve as chair of the organization's board, traveled to Washington, D.C. on behalf of the SIA to testify before a United States Senate Committee on Small Business about the need to lower the capital gains tax, which stood at 49 percent in 1978. The fact that nearly half of any capital gains would go to the federal government had contributed to a general drying up of venture capital, and less available capital put American high-tech businesses at a competitive disadvantage relative to the Japanese. Many other business groups—including the American Electronics Association (formerly WEMA), which had invited Noyce to testify—had their own reasons for wanting the capital gains tax lowered and vigorously lobbied for a reduction.

Their efforts paid off. At the end of 1978, the Carter administration reduced the tax to 28 percent. The lower capital gains tax—coupled with nearly contemporaneous changes easing the "prudent man" rules that had restricted pension funds' abilities to invest with venture capitalists—had dramatic effects. By one estimate, within 18 months of the changes, the amount of money flowing into professionally managed venture capital companies each year shot from $50 million to nearly $1 billion.[14]

But the decline of the American semiconductor industry relative to the Japanese did not slow. Indeed, just as the SIA had feared, the American share of the worldwide semiconductor market began to slip in areas other than DRAMs. The Japanese began cutting prices so dramatically that Intel, accustomed to dropping prices approximately 30 percent every year, found itself forced to cut the price of its 16K EPROM, once the company's cash cow, by 90 percent in just 18 months. The American industry was convinced that the Japanese were "dumping" their chips on the American market—selling them well below the cost of production—and then planning to raise prices once their foothold in the American market was established. The situation was desperate enough that Intel furloughed 2,000 employees and in 1982 allowed IBM to acquire a 12 percent interest in the company in exchange for $250 million. Other companies suffered as well. From 1981 to 1982, AMD's net income fell by two-thirds, and National

Semiconductor went from a $52 million annual profit to losses of $11 million. Around this time, Noyce started an SIA meeting with an offer to "lead the group in prayer."[15]

EXCEPT FOR A BRIEF UPSWING IN PROFITS in 1983 and 1984, things just got worse. The Japanese market continued to be closed to foreign sellers: United States firms manufactured less than 10 percent of the chips sold in Japan, whereas in other export markets, American-made devices accounted for about one-third of the chips sold. Meanwhile the share of the total market for semiconductor devices supplied by Japanese manufacturers continued to rise until, in 1985, the once-unthinkable happened: Japan's share of the *total* world market for semiconductor devices surpassed that of the United States.[16]

Noyce estimated that between 1984 and 1986, the American semiconductor industry lost $2 billion in earnings and 27,000 jobs. In that same period, 13 percent of the electronics jobs in Silicon Valley disappeared. Adding insult to injury, the Japanese electronics giant Fujitsu began maneuvering to take over 80 percent of Fairchild, the granddaddy of Silicon Valley semiconductor firms. Fairchild was already owned by a foreign company— French conglomerate Schlumberger had bought it in 1979—but the prospect of Japanese ownership led the *San Jose Mercury News* to lament, "The transaction seems to tell us, in one quick message, how far we've fallen and what we're up against." Industry leaders, including Noyce, briefly discussed some sort of united opposition to the deal, but abandoned the idea in light of antitrust concerns. One well-known semiconductor analyst, when asked about the potential sale, could do little more than shake his head and mutter disgustedly, "Talk about the world being turned upside down."[17]

The phrase captured the overriding sense of the times. America was accustomed to dominating high-tech industry, but in many markets the country now lagged in second place. The semiconductor industry had seemed impervious to the recessionary forces of the 1970s, but now it was sucked into the vortex.

In one of the more shocking reversals, Gordon Moore and Andy Grove recommended to the Intel board of directors that the company leave the DRAM memory business altogether in 1985. A DRAM memory—the 1103—had been Intel's first best-selling product. DRAMs had brought the firm from a two-man startup to the *Fortune* 500. But now the product line was acting as a net drain on profits from other areas of Intel's business, particularly microprocessors, because Intel had to price the memories so cheaply. Andy Grove recalls "going to see Gordon [Moore] and asking him what a new management would do if we were replaced. The answer was clear: get out of DRAMs. So, I suggested to Gordon that we go through the revolving door, come back in, and just do it ourselves."[18]

Arthur Rock calls the vote to abandon memories in order to focus Intel's attention on the microprocessors once considered only a sideline business "the most gut-wrenching decision I've ever made as a board member." But Noyce had no second thoughts about approving Moore and Grove's decision. "He thought the Japanese were already beating the heck out of memories," recalls Ann Bowers. "He hoped microprocessors would offer a way out." By the end of the decade, seven of the nine American DRAM manufacturers had left the business.[19]

And still the problems persisted. In 1986, for the first time since it went public in 1971, Intel lost money—$173 million. AMD, declaring the year the worst in the company's history, lost $37 million. National lost $143 million. Even after cutting 7,200 jobs (28 percent of the employee base), Intel was still in such trouble that several times its senior managers met in Noyce's living room to discuss a topic no one wanted to contemplate: "how to shut down Intel, if it comes to that." An April Fool's edition of the company newsletter offered its own suggestion in a cover story headlined "Japanese Buy Intel: Grove Named Shogun." Explained one SIA executive, "It's hard for someone who did not live through it to imagine how bad things were. We had really begun to think that the American semiconductor industry might cease to exist, [having been] erased by Japanese competition."[20]

NOR WAS IT ONLY THE AMERICAN SEMICONDUCTOR INDUSTRY that was in trouble. Noyce was convinced that everywhere he looked in the United States he saw signs of "the decline of the empire." The federal government was running record deficits, Americans were saving less and spending more than at any time in history, the country was importing more than it exported, and math and science literacy among American students was declining with every passing year. "Can you name a field in which the U.S. is not falling behind now, one in which the U.S. is increasing its market share? We're in a death spiral." Noyce told a reporter. He predicted that Silicon Valley might one day become "a wasteland," one of many around the country. "What would you call Detroit?" he asked. "We could easily become that." To make matters worse, Noyce believed that the gloom overhanging the industry was dangerous in and of itself. He was convinced, he said, that "optimism is an essential ingredient for innovation. How else can the individual welcome change over security, adventure over staying in a safe place?"[21]

IF FREEING UP THE FLOW OF CAPITAL had not helped, and dropping unprofitable products and cutting jobs had not worked either, perhaps the answer to America's economic woes lay in adopting a homegrown version of the Japanese government's industrial policy targeting a few select industries. Noyce did not think so. He said that the government should "target entrepreneurs" in every field and not single out any particular industry for support. His voice was one of many engaged in the American debate over industrial policy. In one camp were those—generally supporters of President Ronald Reagan—who argued that the correct response to the Japanese threat was a redoubling of current supply-side efforts to revitalize the American economy: reduce regulatory burdens and capital gains taxes; create incentives for long-term investment; and increase government expenditures, generally through military spending. According to this argument, the most useful step that the American government could take was a flying leap out of industry's way. Government should give more by taking away—via taxes and regulation—less.[22]

Leading the opposing camp were Democrats who argued that the Reaganites' traditional means of stimulating the economy had already proven futile against the Japanese. The Republicans' supply-side approach had led America into this problem in the first place, according to Reaganomics' opponents: previously unimagined deficits had pushed up interest rates, thereby increasing the value of the dollar to the point that foreign manufacturers could easily undersell their American competitors anywhere in the world, including in the United States.[23]

Hewing to the philosophy that if you can't beat an enemy, you should join him, many Democrats suggested that the United States government follow Japan's lead and play a more active role in fostering its industrial sector. "It is time to moderate the national habit of blanket legislation and broad policy strokes with more attention to the 'micro' requirements of individual sectors, industries and firms," argued Senator Adlai Stevenson III. "The United States is the only industrial country which does not attempt to do this and rejects 'industrial policy' in any systematic sense." In 1983 as part of the LaFalce Plan, House Democrats called for a new Bank for Industrial Competitiveness, capitalized with $8.5 billion in federal funds, which would "make and guarantee loans to older industries in need of modernization and to innovative businesses having trouble getting started."[24]

Much more than money was at stake in this debate over industrial policy. At issue was the country's understanding of itself as a stronghold of free-market, laissez-faire capitalism. Republicans couched their arguments in language calculated to strike fear into a nation historically suspicious of federal power: did Americans really want *more* government meddling in industry affairs? Did voters really believe that Washington bureaucrats should have the power to determine the "proper" focus for the American economy? (In a strangely self-defeating slap at industrial policy advocates, Republican congressman Dan Lundgren of California alleged that "Supporters of industrial policy have never been able to demonstrate that the 'best and the brightest' are in Washington and . . . can do a better job [than is currently the case] of making the economic decisions affecting our lives.")[25]

Industrial policy advocates, on the other hand, claimed that laissez-faire ideals were hollow and that the United States had a *de facto* industrial policy, administered largely by the Department of Defense. For decades, the federal government, in the guise of defense contracts, had supported research and development in specific target industries such as electronics and aerospace. Moreover, as recently as 1983, the federal government had purchased, largely for military use, more than half of all aircraft, radio, and TV communications equipment; a quarter of all engineering and scientific instruments; and a third of all electron tubes manufactured in the United States. In the words of one industrial policy advocate: "If Japan's industrial policy has been implemented by ... MITI and for purposes of economic defense, then America's industrial policy (to the extent that it already has one) has been implemented by the Department of Defense and for purposes of its own military defense and that of the free world."[26]

AS POLITICIANS ACROSS THE COUNTRY formed joint government-industry committees to study the proper role of government in the economy, Silicon Valley businessmen and SIA members, including Noyce, played prominent roles. President Reagan established a Commission on Industrial Competitiveness, chaired by Hewlett-Packard president John Young (another member of the Page Mill drinking and investment club), on which Noyce served. A select committee of prominent Democrats—including businessmen, labor leaders, and Senators—formed a special "Industrial Policy Study Group," and one group of young Democrats, led by Gary Hart, Tim Wirth, and Michael Dukakis, pushed so hard for high-tech industries to be the focus of the party's industrial policies that the young men came to be known as "Atari Democrats." In Sacramento, Governor Jerry Brown established and chaired a California Commission on Industrial Innovation. Charlie Sporck, along with Apple Computer's Steve Jobs, served on Brown's commission, but Noyce declined to join, despite multiple requests from the governor himself.[27]

High-tech executives were highly sought for these committees because the politicians believed information-based technologies represented the nation's economic future. No politician wanted to be caught designing policies around the needs of the declining heavy industries. The Brown commission spoke for many when it said, "Our former policy goals of a strong economy built on heavy industry and cheap energy are no longer appropriate for an age marked by national economic sluggishness, fierce international competition and emerging third world nations reclaiming their resources. . . . We must look to a new 'post-industrial' economy built around relatively resource-efficient information technologies and innovation."[28]

The debate over industrial policy and the politicians' high hopes for high tech informed the SIA's second round of lobbying on the issue of

Japanese competition. Although Noyce freely admitted behind closed doors at an SIA conference that "we are attempting to influence our national strategy," the organization was in a delicate situation. The SIA had to encourage President Reagan to consider actions that on first blush appeared departures from his much-ballyhooed free market, small government ideals and more in line with some of the Atari Democrats' calls for industrial policy. At the same time, the SIA had to convince Democrats to support the semiconductor industry—perhaps over the heavy industries that employed many members of the Democrats' most reliable constituencies.[29]

The SIA also needed to take into account the semiconductor industry's reputation as the last bastion of do-it-yourself, up-by-the-bootstraps American individualism—exemplars of treasured American values, and the polar opposite of the Japanese. This linking of the semiconductor industry with "American values" was so pervasive that one newspaper article attributed the industry's problems with Japan to differences in national culture: "One is a nation of immigrants, the other a homogenous society of isolationists. One values adventure, innovation, and debate; the other security, conformity, and harmony." How, on the one hand, could the SIA take the seemingly quintessential Japanese step of asking for increased government involvement in their industry—and at the same time stay on the right side of adventure, innovation, and individualism? How, in short, could the semiconductor industry ask for government help without seeming un-American?[30]

IN JUNE 1985, THE SIA LAUNCHED a two-pronged campaign to accomplish two goals: open the Japanese market, which the SIA argued was closed to foreign chip imports; and end what the SIA alleged were Japanese firms selling chips below the cost of production. To achieve the first goal, the SIA filed a petition with the United States Trade Representative for relief under Section 301 of the Trade Act of 1974, the section that authorizes the president to penalize countries that deny United States products fair access to their markets. Three months later, Intel, National Semiconductor, and Advanced Micro Devices—working in close cooperation with the SIA— began work on the second goal by filing an antidumping case pertaining to 64K EPROMs. The SIA had considered filing its Section 301 petition and lawsuits much earlier but waited until Clyde Prestowitz, a former colleague of SIA's lead attorney, joined the Reagan administration as counselor for Japan affairs for the secretary of commerce. This personal connection encouraged a favorable reception for the SIA's agenda.[31]

The SIA planned its strategy with great care, working in close consultation with the Washington law firm of Dewey, Ballantine, Bushby, Palmer & Wood, chosen largely for its international trade expert, Alan W. Wolff, who had been deputy United States trade representative in the Carter administration. The SIA did not have a Political Action Committee to donate money to candidates, but member firms—including Intel—formed PACs that together donated some $350,000 to national political candidates during the mid-1980s. The SIA also strategically expanded its membership base to include small companies that built specialty chips; major chip buyers such as Hewlett-Packard; and large captive producers of chips, such as IBM, which build chips primarily for use in their own products. Some of these new members, whose primary concern was maintaining reasonable prices and flexible supplies, might potentially oppose SIA initiatives that would result in higher overall chip prices. By bringing these companies into the tent, SIA could solicit their opinions and cultivate their support before initiatives were made public. Finally, to make its message as appealing as possible, the SIA consulted regularly with public relations expert Regis McKenna. The SIA also devoted at least one board meeting, which Noyce attended, to a discussion of the organization's "image—what are we trying to accomplish."[32]

The SIA rounded up a cluster of allies known informally as the Congressional Semiconductor Support Group. This group of 20—Democrats and Republicans, senators and representatives from states including California, Missouri, Florida, and Pennsylvania—made calls to the White House and met with cabinet officials to express support for the SIA's requests. Another 180 federal representatives and senators sent letters, drafted by SIA general counsel Alan W. Wolff, to people in the executive branch. Both senators from California worked hard to support the SIA's position.[33]

The SIA used the executives who ran its member companies as a "platoon" of CEOs that could be sent to Washington, D.C. to lobby on behalf of the semiconductor industry. This was an unusual and highly successful innovation. Other trade associations had at times pressed well-known executives into lobbying duty on particularly critical issues, but most day-to-day industry lobbying was the purview of paid professionals based in the nation's capital. The small SIA staff worked closely with its general counsel to draft articles and position papers and to brief the executives on the political nuances and stakes at play in specific issues.

In 1985 and 1986, the SIA sent so many executives to the nation's capital that United States trade representative Clayton Yeutter told an SIA meeting, "We joked in Washington that many of you were becoming permanent fixtures." An academic study concluded, "Direct lobbying by top company executives is the most effective tactic adopted by the SIA." SIA co-founder Charlie Sporck called it "*the* secret to the SIA's success."[34]

Politicians and political appointees in Washington were indeed impressed that the semiconductor industry's leaders, who had for so long disdained government "interference" in their business, were willing to dirty their hands with lobbying. Counselor for Japan affairs Prestowitz wrote that "appealing to Washington was not easy for these men and the others like them in the industry who embodied the ideals of the American dream.

Coming from modest, even poor, backgrounds, they had succeeded through initiative, inspiration, and perspiration, in founding an industry widely seen as the key to the twenty-first century. They had done it on their own as lone riders without government help—indeed, sometimes in the face of government harassment."[35]

Most prominent among the "lone riders" for the SIA was Bob Noyce. He "is something of a legend in the electronics world," wrote the *Harvard Business Review*. "The Washington establishment wanted to get to know him as much as he wanted to develop political contacts." Counselor Prestowitz put it this way: "Noyce is one of our guys, and if anyone can hack it, he can." Noyce's mere appearance at a congressional hearing sent a compelling message: the semiconductor industry is in such trouble that even Noyce—the embodiment of entrepreneurial spirit—is willing to swallow his pride and ask for help.[36]

Noyce possessed the time, confidence, political savvy, and credibility necessary for any successful lobbying campaign. And he pointed to another reason he was so effective—he was wealthy. "I found that money gave you power, that your opinion was more highly valued in Washington if you were rich. [Money] was a way of keeping score. It was a way of keeping track of who had contributed [to society] and who had not, and consequently [if you were a politician], who you should listen to and who you should not."[37]

Promoting the SIA agenda was, in some sense, another one of the high-level sales jobs at which Noyce excelled. And in this case, he passionately believed in the "product." It must have frustrated him to consider that American semiconductor companies, so money-hungry and so supremely confident of their technological edge in the 1960s and 1970s, had inadvertently helped to create their own Japanese competitors when they sold them early licenses to key American patents. And Fairchild had led the way, charging for the rights to the Noyce integrated circuit patent a royalty of 4.5 cents on every dollar the Japanese makers earned on chips— and effectively handing them blueprints that represented years of advanced research at Fairchild.[38]

Throughout his career, Noyce had enjoyed an unusually close relationship with Japanese semiconductor executives and researchers. He hosted delegations of Japanese visitors at Fairchild and later at Intel, and he had been flattered by the respect accorded to him when he visited the island nation. "Bob was a very trusting person," Ann Bowers explains. "You had to practically punch him in the nose to have him think there was something untoward happening. You can imagine how he felt when he realized that all those years that he had been hosting the Japanese guys, they had been trying to get [American] secrets."[39]

As part of his campaign to save the American semiconductor industry, Noyce raised money for several political candidates and encouraged the formation of a Government Affairs Committee at Intel. He estimated that he spent nearly half his time in Washington, D.C. in the mid-1980s. There he met informally (for various meals and coffees) with senators, congressional representatives, and people from the Democratic National Committee. Recalls Tom Campbell, who first worked with Noyce on an effort to discourage frivolous shareholder lawsuits and then served as a United States representative from the district that included much of Silicon Valley, "He really helped me to see the importance of letting invention happen—letting people take a risk. It is important to create a system in which people are free to innovate, create, be bold. [Noyce believed in] empowerment, rather than in the government directly helping out."[40]

Noyce also testified multiple times before Congress, at one point identifying himself as speaking "as a representative of all high-tech industry." He began working with a speechwriter in the early 1980s. Jim Jarrett, now Intel's vice president of legal and government affairs, was a newly hired public relations manager in 1980 when he began helping Noyce on his presentations and occasional articles. The two men had an easygoing relationship: Noyce would talk to Jarrett about his ideas and what he wanted to say, and then Jarrett, after conducting a bit of research, would draft a talk, which Noyce would edit—usually quite lightly. Together Noyce and Jarrett developed a plug-and-play system of speech building in which they would craft various "modules," each ranging from one to a half-dozen paragraphs, and each centered around a different theme or slide. These modules could be assembled in any number of ways and linked with customized transitions tailored to a specific audience.[41]

Jarrett recalls that Noyce never seemed entirely comfortable when he delivered his talks, even though he would regularly ad-lib and appeared from the audience to be quite at ease. "He wasn't a great speaker from an oratorical style standpoint, but he had so much charisma that it really overrode his moderate ability as an orator," explains Jarrett, in a remark that recalls Gaylord Noyce's explanation of how his brother always managed to land lead singing parts with only a better-than-average voice. Jarrett continues, "His presence was the really the thing that mattered. He did not have a Baptist-preacher approach. [His] was a thoughtful, kind of modestly presented style. He was just being himself." When Noyce spoke, his body, tone, pace, and intonation all sent the same message to the listener: this talk is not about me; it's about the points I'm making.[42]

By this time, Noyce had learned to keep his emotions under control in public presentations. There were no more "karate chop" or "slit our throats" comments after 1978. But in private, he was still very upset. The depth of his feelings gave his lobbying efforts a compelling fervor and passion. His message in his testimony built on three points—economic vitality, fair play, and national security—that the SIA had identified as key to building support for their goals of opening the Japanese market and stopping chip dumping.

The importance of the semiconductor industry to the United States economy was Noyce's favorite topic in the early 1980s. He wrote more than a dozen speeches on the subject and delivered many of them more than once. He told the National Governors' Association that Intel alone had paid over $245 million in taxes in its first 13 years of business and estimated this was a tenth of the amount contributed by the industry as a whole. Repeating an often-used SIA line, he told the House Ways and Means Committee that "the American semiconductor industry provides the 'crude oil,' or fundamental technology, for the electronics industry." He told the *Los Angeles Times*, "Semiconductors are in everything from automobiles to aircraft. Our sales are an index to the state of the economy."[43]

Always most comfortable with quantifiable claims, at one point he calculated the "'social surplus' which has been returned to the society by the semiconductor industry" to be more than $120 billion. Noyce's calculations were hard to follow, but his basic argument was this: because semiconductors' cost-per-function fell so dramatically with each new generation of chips, customers could greatly improve productivity over time at relatively little cost. The "$120 billion social surplus" was the difference between (on the one hand) the theoretical costs of such productivity improvements if chip prices had not historically fallen so precipitously and (on the other hand) the actual costs to consumers. This "windfall," Noyce contended, "can be used to further the other goals of society."[44]

Noyce repeatedly stressed the link between the semiconductor industry and the emerging "information economy." He told the Department of Commerce that "half of the country's work force is now dealing with information rather than goods" and that the semiconductor industry was "fundamental to the new information age." He promised that the new information technologies would improve workplace efficiency "even more than the mechanical age enhanced the output of manual labor in the last century."[45]

Noyce further sought to stress that the semiconductor industry was not seeking protectionist legislation: the Section 301 petition focused on gaining access to Japan's market, rather than closing off America's market to Japanese imports. As Noyce liked to say, "America has a concern for fair play, for having the rules of the game the same for all participants."[46]

While Noyce was making these points, the SIA was making a third: a weak American semiconductor industry posed a significant security risk. Superior weapons technology depends on superior electronics, which in turn depend on state-of-the-art semiconductors. If the United States semiconductor industry could not stay on the technological cutting edge, the American military would be forced to use, perhaps even to depend upon, foreign sources for key electronics components. These foreign sources might dry up in wartime, and they might be supplying the Soviet Union as well as the United States, potentially compromising American security by passing along information about her technology to her most dangerous military rival.[47]

IN THE SPRING OF 1986, the SIA's efforts began to bear fruit. After a year of inquiry, the International Trade Administration issued a preliminary determination that several Japanese companies were selling EPROM chips in the United States at less than the cost of production. In August, President Reagan signed the United States–Japan Semiconductor Agreement, which required Japan to "open" its semiconductor market, with the unstated goal of foreign firms gaining 20 percent market share within five years. The agreement also curbed alleged Japanese dumping of chips by mandating a "fair market value" at which semiconductors should be sold not just in the United States, but throughout the world. These were unprecedented steps, taken against a military ally, to extend United States government jurisdiction into a private-sector business on a global scale. A few months later, the Reagan administration determined that Japan was violating the accord and imposed 100 percent tariffs on $300 million of Japanese imports—the first such penalties against an ally since World War Two.[48]

That this outcome was engineered by an organization that was less than a decade old, staffed by fewer than a dozen people, and represented fewer than 40 member companies whose workforces were concentrated in only three states (California, Texas, and Arizona) is astonishing. In some sense, the SIA should be considered yet another remarkably successful startup, co-founded by Noyce and his peers. By mid-1989, a survey of government officials, paid for by several large computer companies contemplating the formation of their own SIA-like association, found the SIA to be the "most effective" of eight electronics industry trade groups because of its "clarity of purpose" and "constructive agenda."[49]

A further measure of the semiconductor industry's influence in the nation's capital was the outcome of the proposed Fujitsu purchase of Fairchild. When news of the pending sale broke in 1987, Defense Secretary Caspar Weinberger, Commerce Secretary Malcolm Baldrige, and several congressmen voiced their opposition, citing security concerns. The president of Fairchild's parent company Schlumberger charged his American competitors—Noyce in particular—with orchestrating the government's objections, but while Noyce publicly called the purchase a "lousy deal," he insisted that he never directly passed on his opinion to the Pentagon or the Department of Commerce. When Fujitsu rescinded its offer, citing "political controversy," Charlie Sporck acquired the company as part of a move to expand operations at his Silicon Valley-headquartered National Semiconductor. The world, it seemed, was once again turned right-side-up.[50]

By August 1987, many American semiconductor firms had returned to profitability, selling more chips at comparatively healthier prices than ever before. One year later, Gordon Moore declared it "a great time at Intel." But it is unclear how much credit for this improvement should go to the trade agreement and sanctions (the remaining antidumping sanctions were lifted in November 1987) for which Noyce and the SIA worked so hard. The decision to cede the memory market to Japan, while agonizing when it was made, seemed prescient by the early 1990s. American companies' focus on more design-intensive products such as microprocessors coincided with strong growth in the personal computer and other logic-driven industries. At the same time, countries such as South Korea entered the commodity memory business and intensified price wars and cost cutting in that market. The rise of Japanese memory manufacturers thus forced American firms out of a business dependent on slim margins and manufacturing muscle and into much more profitable work building research-intensive products for which demand was growing exponentially.

Time was another important factor behind the American industry's recovery. After all, in the decades before the mid-1980s recession, the industry had emerged from several two- or three-year downturns without trade agreements to help it on its way. Or perhaps the weaker dollar—which made Japanese products more expensive for United States consumers—was the most important source of the industry's rosy balance sheets. In any case, in 1987, even Noyce said that he could not attribute the "general pickup in business" to "the trade agreement or anything else," conceding only that "the cessation of dumping has helped our profitability."[51]

WHILE HE WAS LOBBYING on behalf of the SIA, Noyce could not stop himself from thinking beyond his particular industry. His field of vision had been expanding ever since he left the lab bench with its technical problems visible only under a microscope. He had moved on to think about organizing a laboratory, then a division of a company, then a company in its entirety, and next an industry that encompassed many different companies. Now he pushed his thoughts to include the entire high-technology base of the American economy. "Economics and societies are the laboratories that define the problems thinkers solve and on which entrepreneurs capitalize," he explained. "The role of the individual as thinker or prophet, as scientist or engineer, as entrepreneur or advocate, is not be minimized. Yet these roles can thrive only in conducive social and insutrial environments."[52]

In 1985, Noyce wrote to Grant Gale, "I am spending more time trying to figure out the causes for the economic malaise we are experiencing in the U.S. There must be something I'm missing, for I am beginning to think that I do understand the cause." America had allowed its K–12 schools to decline, its college-level science and engineering classes to dwindle, and its immigration laws to force foreign students to leave the country after graduation, thereby depriving the nation of a valuable workforce. He thought that America's "emphasis on consuming, not saving" had led to disaster: "our national savings rate is the worst in the industrial world, our corporations are starved for capital, our trade deficit is enormous, and our trading partners are buying our national assets," Noyce claimed.[53]

"We have [already] taken the politically easy road" to try to improve things, Noyce told Gale, "and the wise road seems impossible politically. Things like cutting consumption and saving for tomorrow." Politically impossible or not, Noyce wanted to try to build momentum for the measures he believed would "cure" the American economy. He thought the capital gains tax should be dropped entirely to encourage investment. He believed R&D tax credits should be expanded. At one point he seemed to flirt with the notion of a consumption-based tax to replace income taxes. He said, "Microelectronics is giving us the opportunity to ask ourselves what we want for our society—five cars in every garage, [or] a stimulating intellectual environment, better medical care?" He thought that most Americans, with their abysmal savings rates and their laissez-faire attitudes towards the federal deficit, were consistently answering this question irresponsibly. He was willing to risk sounding "old fashioned," he said, to encourage the United States to return to the "first principles" responsible for his own success: "Work hard, save your money, get an education, try to get ahead."[54]

Noyce promoted these ideas as a member of President Reagan's competitiveness commission and in speeches before the National Governor's Association and Congress. He also sought to act on his beliefs, particularly when it came to improving the educational system. In 1982, he became a regent of the University of California. He endowed the Donald Sterling Noyce Prize for Excellence in Undergraduate Teaching (in honor of his brother) to recognize outstanding science instruction at the flagship Berkeley campus. He led the fundraising drive for the Grant O. Gale Observatory at Grinnell College.

Noyce averred, "The collective individualism of Americans will continue to provide opportunity for investment, profit, and individual accomplishment." His work with young entrepreneurs, which only increased in the 1980s, can be understood as an effort to reinforce these bonds of "collective individualism" that had supported him as a young man. In 1982, he joined the board of a company that planned to build a magnetic recording technology that could offer a potential order of magnitude improvement in density while working faster and costing less than any competitive product. The company, called Censtor, did not prove successful. Noyce also

Noyce and Apple Computer co-founder Steve Jobs at a dinner for Governor Jerry Brown. Jobs is one of many entrepreneurs who count Noyce among their major influences. Courtesy Regis McKenna.

Noyce addresses Japanese engineers during a visit to Tokyo Electric Company (TEC) Okito in October 1978. Noyce enjoyed an unusually close relationship with Japanese semiconductor executives for many years, although he became greatly concerned that their firms might drive American companies out of business. Family photos.

President Jimmy Carter awards Noyce the National Medal of Science in 1980.
Family photos.

Noyce celebrates his fiftieth birthday dressed as Superman. His wife Ann Bowers, whom
he married in 1975, surprised him with the costume. Family photos.

President Ronald Reagan awards Noyce the National Medal of Technology in 1988. Courtesy Intel Corp.

Noyce speaks at a campus of the University of California. (His wife says he never spoke at Davis.) He was a Regent of the University of California from 1982 to 1988. Family photos.

Noyce grins outside his Intel cubicle, 1983. Photo by Carolyn Caddes. Courtesy Carolyn Caddes and the Department of Special Collections, Stanford University Libraries.

Noyce shows off his Volant skis. He was a founding investor in the company. Family photos.

Noyce and his wife Ann Bowers enjoyed skiing together. Note Noyce's Intel ski cap. Family photos.

Noyce in the cockpit of his World War Two era Seabee airplane. Family photos.

To Ann Bowers and Robert Noyce
with best wishes,
Geo Bush

President George H. W. Bush congratulates Ann Bowers and Bob Noyce on Noyce's Draper Award. Family photos.

Noyce speaks at the official opening of SEMATECH, a joint government-industry manufacturing research consortium. From 1988 until his death in 1990, Noyce served as SEMATECH's founding CEO. Courtesy SEMATECH.

Noyce prepares to fly the RF-4C at Bergstrom Air Force Base near Austin, Texas, in September 1989. SEMATECH employees secretly arranged the flight as a surprise for Noyce. Family photos.

Noyce and his co-inventor Jack Kilby share the first Charles Stark Draper Award—the so-called "Nobel Prize of Engineering"—for their work on the integrated circuit. Family photos.

Two days before he died, Noyce was surprised to be greeted by dozens of SEMATECH employees wearing t-shirts emblazoned with the phrase "Bob Noyce, Teen Idol" and captioned with a quote from an admirer. Courtesy Intel Corp.

began investing with Arthur Rock after the Callanish Fund (Noyce's private investment partnership with Paul Hwoschinsky) was amicably dissolved in 1979. Noyce and Rock did not have a formal investment partnership, but as Rock puts it, "We'd rope each other in."[55]

The two men together funded several small companies: General Signal, Mohawk Data Sciences, and, at the urging of Mike Markkula, Volant, a manufacturer of a novel steel ski that Noyce, who tried a prototype, was convinced instantly improved his skiing. It was never clear to Volant's founders, Bucky Kashiwa and his brother Hank, that Noyce particularly cared about making money from the company. His primary concern was to get this fantastic new ski on the market—or at the very least, onto his own boot.[56]

Noyce and Rock also invested in Diasonics, a company that developed and built medical imaging systems, such as digital X-rays and computer-driven ultrasound equipment. The intersection of technology and medicine had long interested Noyce, and he had made a few small investments in the area in the past. But the nearly $800,000 that Noyce invested in Diasonics was by far the largest he had directed into any single business. In exchange, Noyce received 3.3 million shares of stock. (Rock, who chaired the board and invested slightly more than Noyce, held 3.9 million shares.) When Diasonics went public in 1983, it raised $123 million, more money than any company since the Adolph Coors Co. offering in 1975. Within weeks, Noyce's stake was worth almost $100 million. But Diasonics misjudged the market and less than a year after the IPO, the company was barely breaking even. The stock, which traded at almost $30 a share shortly after the IPO, was down to 7½ by 1985. Soon the SEC was investigating a Diasonics executive for alleged insider trading, and a group of shareholders filed suit, alleging the company misled investors about its prospects. By 1988, Rock's and Noyce's holdings were worth only $2.80 a share, less than what they had paid for them.[57]

NOYCE CONTINUED TO TRAIN most of his entrepreneurial attention on Caere, the barcode-scanner company for which he had written the blank check several years before. In 1985, Bob Teresi, Caere's longtime CFO who had recently been named the company's president, proposed that the firm take its small profits, repay its investors, and close up shop. Caere was clearly never going to make it big in the barcode-reader business.

Noyce thought the solution was to change the business model. "Bob had the idea [that a person should be able to] stick a magazine page in a scanner that would be able to recognize it and convert it into a format that could be edited," recalls Teresi. "I thought Bob's idea was just not reasonable—it would take a supercomputer to be able to process something as complex as what he was proposing.

"But Bob knew what was coming down the pipe in so many ways," Teresi continues. A few days after Noyce offered his rather outrageous suggestion for Caere's next product, Teresi met a pair of young men—a pianist and a computer programmer—who gave him a business plan proposing something very similar to Noyce's vision. Noyce thought their approach seemed plausible. Caere gave the pair and two other engineers a contract to develop the product and, in Teresi's words, "set them up in a space over a garage in Berkeley with a stipend and espresso machine."

In the names of these four employees—Vijayakumar Rangarajan, William W. Allen, James Chen, and Tong Chen—one can discern evidence of the wave of highly educated immigrants from India and China who helped to double the size of the foreign-born population of Santa Clara County between 1975 and 1990. By 1990, one-quarter of the engineers and scientists employed in California high-technology companies were born outside the United States. The young engineers' names now came from around the world, but the spirit of the quest was familiar to Noyce.[58]

Roughly once a month, Noyce and Teresi would drive across the Bay Bridge to Berkeley so Noyce could review the technical progress at the "skunk works." Within a year, the garage team had created a usable product, named OmniPage, that could scan text and convert it to a format that could be edited. At a board meeting shortly after OmniPage was developed, Teresi told Noyce that he planned to hardwire the product into a scanner that would sell for between $20,000 and $30,000. Teresi expected Caere would sell two of these scanners every month.

Noyce did not think this was the best way to go, but he never explicitly said as much to Teresi. Instead, he told Teresi that he would introduce him to Mike Markkula, now chairman of Apple Computer, who might have some other ideas for OmniPage. This redirection is vintage Noyce. "Even if he was blasting you," recalls Kenneth Oshman, CEO and founder of ROLM, the business communications and military computer systems firm on whose board Noyce served for two years, "you just felt good about it." The people on the receiving end of this "blasting" rarely believed that Noyce thought their work was inadequate or their ideas poorly considered. Instead, he seemed to be telling them that their already-excellent work could be taken even farther. One of his favorite lines was "Your ideas have made me wonder if . . ." Bob Teresi, for example, did not translate Noyce's suggestion to talk to Markkula to mean that his plan to build hardware was ill conceived. He read it as a compliment: this OmniPage product is so exciting that it deserves the attention of many people, Noyce seemed to be saying. So don't stop thinking yet.[59]

When Mike Markkula met with Teresi, he suggested that OmniPage should be sold as software, not hardware. He also thought that Apple might want to license the software for use in a scanner the company planned to introduce soon. In the end, Apple promoted OmniPage so heavily—President John Sculley personally introduced it at MacWorld 1988—that Caere had to do very little publicity itself. "The Apple endorsement gave the product immediate credibility and put a rocket under [Caere]," explained one computer sales executive. Sales of OmniPage were $10 million in the year following MacWorld 1988.[60]

The successful launch of OmniPage enabled Caere to go public in June 1989, with an offering that was one of the most successful of the year. By December, Noyce's nearly 400,000 shares were worth almost $9 million. The returns went a long way towards silencing the friends who for years had teased Noyce about his devotion to his "teenage startup."[61]

In his work with educational institutions and startup companies, in his speeches before Congress and industry groups about the importance of saving and learning, Noyce was doing his part, as he put it, to ensure American remained "the land of opportunity for all of those who will be the achievers of the future."[62]

ALL IN ALL, NOYCE WAS CONTENT. He enjoyed the SIA work. His children were grown and for the most part doing well. He and Ann Bowers were happy together. They remodeled the house on Loyola Drive. From the street it appeared as unassuming as ever, but inside, it "became a resort," as one friend put it, "something you would see on a house tour, and definitely a happening." In the backyard, Noyce and Bowers installed a large pond, a sauna, and a free-form pool with waterfalls and artificial rocks to hide the controls. Noyces' brothers privately called the remodeled property "Disneyland North."

Over the course of just a few years, Noyce and Bowers traveled with friends to Australia, Bora Bora, the Carribbean, Tahiti, the Great Barrier Reef, Bali, the Virgin Islands, Mexico, New Guinea, Korea, and Japan. They also spent several weeks each year in Aspen, where they had bought a home.[63]

In 1984, Noyce and Bowers joined an Intel delegation visiting China, where Noyce met with Chinese premier Zhao Ziyang—who asked his opinions on developing microcomputers and semiconductors in China—and was named "Honourable Professor" by the Beijing Institute of Aeronautics and Astronautics. The Intel representatives met with members of a "microcomputers users group" and spoke on trends in manufacturing and technology direction. By the trip's end, the Intel contingent was so tired of elaborate formal meals that for one night's dinner they decided to pool their private stashes from their suitcases. The stale potato chips and airplane-issued mini bottles of scotch they shared that night on the floor of Noyce and Bowers's hotel room tasted better than anything they could have imagined.[64]

Noyce discovered scuba diving and after a bit of practice in his Disneyland pool, he was certified to dive. He enjoyed taking photos deep beneath the surface and spent hours in his basement warming and shaping large pieces of plastic to work as waterproof casings for his cameras. He could have bought a waterproof camera, of course, but he always wanted the latest accessories, and they were rarely water resistant. During the many diving vacations he and Bowers took together, his cameras intermittently worked, leaked, and floated.

Every once in a while, Noyce would be struck with an idea—usually for an improvement to a camera—and he would jot down his thoughts on the nearest available sheet of paper: a random legal pad, hotel stationery, tiny memo sheets, the backs of computer printouts, the reverse side of a price list for photovoltaic modules. His "doodles," as he called them, are filled with graphs, equations, drawings, and electrical diagrams covering everything from focal length calculations, to strobe connector troubleshooting, to unidentified calculations that continue for the length of the page. Noyce clearly adored this sort of thinking. His doodles are punctuated with exclamation points and underlines that bring his excitement off the page.[65]

By the middle of the 1980s, Noyce had managed to design a nearly ideal jam-packed version of retirement for himself. He had time to travel and tinker and mentor young entrepreneurs, but at the same time, the SIA's efforts provided him meaningful work that returned him to the stage he had found so hard to leave.

When he wanted to escape his lobbying and investment work completely, Noyce could find peace in two places—at the 6,500-acre ranch in Carmel Valley that he and Bowers purchased in 1982, and in the air. The ranch was two hours from Silicon Valley, in an isolated spot that only people who had been told how to get there could have found. Away from the demands of the valley and Washington, Noyce and Bowers could ride horses and occasionally even read a cheap paperback together in a most unusual fashion. When Bowers finished a section, she would rip it out of the binding and hand it to Noyce to read.[66]

His planes offered even more release. Noyce liked to fly for practical reasons, of course. It saved him time. He estimated that he flew roughly 100 hours per year, 40 of those on business. He regularly flew himself to Washington and to business meetings until Bowers, worried he might fly himself home exhausted, asked him to hire a pilot. He also liked the physical challenge of controlling a plane—he once barreled right through a baby thunderhead cloud just to see if he could do it—and he resorted to cliché when he told a television reporter that what he enjoyed about flying was that "it's man over nature," with "technology allow[ing] man to do something that he could not earlier do." (As an aside, Noyce mentioned that the personal computer was similar to the airplane in this way: the PC was a technical advance that enabled people "to explore intellectual activities" that might otherwise have been beyond their grasp.)[67]

But people who flew with Noyce felt that he also took to the skies to escape his life on the ground. Jim Lafferty, Noyce's friend and sometime flight instructor, said, "He liked the aloneness. He loved to be disconnected, up there, by himself. You can do whatever you want to do, go wherever you want to go." Lafferty recalls flying with Noyce for an hour or more in complete silence. But it was not unusual for Noyce to want to "talk about space, about infinity, or eternity." One night in particular stands out: "I remember him talking about Boyle's Law. [Seventeenth-century scientist Robert Boyle's equation describing the relationship between the pressure and volume of a confined gas is an important part of the physics behind aircraft engines.] It was a dissertation, really. Bob took off into equations and calculations out of his head that were so far beyond what I could comprehend. . . . There he was at 39,000, 41,000 feet, with the airplane on auto pilot, the lights all turned down, and he's taking off on his own. I might as well have switched off and gone to the back of the airplane and let him talk to himself."[68]

In 1984, Noyce decided to buy a Cessna Citation, a light jet that required more sophisticated piloting skills than he had needed for any of his other aircraft. His plane would be delivered to the site of Cessna's flight school in Wichita, Kansas. After he graduated from a two-week training course with the type rating he needed for the Citation, he would be able to fly his plane home.[69]

Noyce paid for Jim Lafferty to attend the flight school with him, and both men found the program grueling. A typical day consisted of eight hours of direct instruction in classrooms and simulators, plus a few evening hours spent reviewing videos. Noyce had never flown such a fast or complex aircraft. He found it frustrating to grope his way around the new instrument panel. In the simulator, he had problems controlling the plane's speed and thought he flubbed his attempts at landing using instruments. His instructors, who saw students with these troubles all the time, assured Noyce that it would get easier with practice, but he did not enjoy thinking of himself as anything less than a highly competent pilot. A few days into classes, he told Lafferty, "I can't do this; I'm not ready right now." He wanted Lafferty, who was having a less difficult time, to finish the program and fly Noyce's jet back to California. Noyce would hone his skills by flying the plane with Lafferty and would return to flight school only when he was confident he could perform exceptionally well there.

After a few weeks training with Lafferty (who said Noyce "just wouldn't give up"), Noyce decided his skills met his own standards and returned to the Cessna school to complete his formal instruction. This time he easily obtained the type rating he needed.

In 1985, in yet another of his why-not-make-it-better moves, Noyce, along with Jim Lafferty and Mike Markkula, decided that Silicon Valley needed a top-of-the-line facility for private aircraft. The city-owned hangars had ten-year waiting lists. The trio joined forces with a group of 14 investors who bought a 15-acre property west of the San Jose airport and began building on it. The San Jose Jet Center opened in 1986 with 200,000 square feet of hangar and office space. Noyce served on the board of the Jet Center for several years, and the center's founders can tell a story, very similar to the one at Caere, about his refusing to let the project fail. His message, recalls Lafferty, was always the same: "Go ahead and do it. It'll be okay. And if it's not okay, I'll make it okay."[70]

12

Public Startup

I n the summer of 1988, Noyce decided to leave his satisfyingly busy retirement and his beloved California to run SEMATECH, a semiconductor
manufacturing consortium supported by the SIA and based in Austin, Texas.
Noyce's decision was curious, to say the least. Almost nothing about
SEMATECH, which was jointly staffed and funded by 14 semiconductor
companies, and that received $100 million annually from the Department
of Defense, jibed with Noyce's strengths or interests. He had spent his
career refusing to take on Defense Department-sponsored research projects
at his companies, but SEMATECH was its own sort of government research project. He was suspicious of all forms of bureaucracy, but it is hard
to imagine a more bureaucratic arrangement than a consortium operated
by more than a dozen companies and a hulking government agency. He
took great joy in building enduring teams and cultures, but SEMATECH
was designed to function with a revolving team of "assignees" who would
be paid by individual corporations and work at SEMATECH for a period
of only two years. In 1980, Noyce had testified before Congress that he
had doubted whether semiconductor companies could ever cooperate on
research—and cooperative research was the driving vision behind SEMA-
TECH. "Innovation is not fostered by committee decisions," he had said.
"Pluralism is not an American tradition. . . . individualism is, and most [Ameri-
can semiconductor] companies have . . . an entrepreneurial history, and they
believe they can do anything better than anybody else." How did a man with
such beliefs, at a stage in his life where he could have done anything, end up
running a defense-sponsored behemoth like SEMATECH?[1]

SEMATECH was conceived by the Semiconductor Research Corporation, an industry consortium that supports university research. Charlie Sporck
championed the project and personally visited dozens of executives at SIA-
member companies to argue that no matter how much legislation they pushed
through Congress, United States firms would never be able to compete with
the Japanese over the long-term unless American manufacturing processes

were improved. Sporck originally envisioned SEMATECH as a multi-firm operation, funded to a significant degree by the Department of Defense, that would manufacture memory devices in such volume and with such efficiency as to "destroy the prices," said Sporck, "really give the Japanese a hard time."[2]

This plan, largely modeled on Japan's highly successful consortium efforts of the late 1970s, was short-lived. Such an arrangement would almost certainly violate antitrust laws; and even if it did not, SIA-member companies Texas Instruments and IBM continued to sell large volumes of memory devices throughout the 1980s, and they would not appreciate "destroyed prices" for their products.

Replacing this mission for SEMATECH proved difficult. A series of SIA-sponsored meetings in Santa Clara in the summer 1987 made it clear that while everyone involved with the SIA wanted a SEMATECH-type organization to do *something* to improve American semiconductor manufacturing, no one knew precisely what that something should be.[3]

In the simplest terms, three different constituencies wanted three different missions for the consortium. Eight of the ten major military contractors were likely SEMATECH members, and they believed SEMATECH should focus on developing "flexible" manufacturing lines that could produce a small batch of specialized chips for one military specification and then be quickly re-tooled via computers to produce a completely different chip to meet another military requirement.[4]

At the other end of the spectrum were the large merchant semiconductor firms who eschewed a focus on flexible, specialized batch production in favor of honing the industry's ability to mass produce large volumes of next-generation chips. To achieve this goal, companies such as Intel, Texas Instruments, and Motorola wanted to improve the equipment and materials that went into their fabs. These companies were each accustomed to spending more than a year and several hundred million dollars evaluating and qualifying the tools they used to build chips. They wanted SEMATECH to do this de-bugging.

Yet a third group, made up of firms with smaller semiconductor operations (Hewlett-Packard, LSI Logic, and Micron, for example) wanted SEMATECH to focus not on the equipment used in the manufacturing process, but on the process itself. These companies usually lagged behind the big ones by a good year, so by the time they bought the equipment, the larger firms had effectively fine-tuned it for them. What these smaller companies wanted was a forum for sharing "black magic" manufacturing know-how, a place to learn how other companies had made the process work best for them, and ideally, a "recipe" book they could take back to their own firms telling them exactly how to do it themselves.

Each group worried that the other two were trying to get more out of SEMATECH than they put into it. Big operations said small ones were trying to avoid doing their own work. Small ones said big ones wanted to focus on advanced equipment improvements that would benefit only the big companies. Firms not centered around military contracts wondered aloud if the flexible manufacturing option was designed to benefit the Department of Defense more than the semiconductor industry. Everyone was concerned that their company's sizable contribution—membership dues were set at a one-time $1 million entry fee, plus annual dues equal to either 1 percent of a company's sales or $1 million, whichever was less—not be used to further a competitor's agenda.

The three competing visions for SEMATECH were never reconciled. Instead of a single unifying plan for the consortium, the brainstorming group produced a four-inch-thick "black book" that one person described as "a grandiose scheme to do everything that the member companies couldn't do—but with a total investment of only $100 million per year." The annual R&D budget at Intel, Motorola, or Texas Instruments was roughly $400 million—and yet none of these companies had accomplished even a portion of the ambitious agenda outlined in the black book.[5]

The black book also established a three-phased technical plan for SEMATECH. Each phase was defined by the width of the electrical paths on the semiconductor circuits. The number of circuits that can be traced on the surface of a semiconductor chip depends, in part, on the width of the circuit paths, which are measured in microns, one-millionths of a meter. (A human hair is about 75 microns in diameter.) The narrower the path, the greater the number of traceable circuits. The Phase I objective for the American chip industry was to build chips with 0.80-micron paths within three years, an easily attainable goal. The Phase II objective was to reduce this size to .50-micron lines by the second quarter of 1992. In Phase III, to be complete by the end of 1993, the geometries would be .35-micron—an ambitious target, since most projections held that companies working on their own would not be able to produce .35 micron chips (such as 64Mb DRAMs) before 1996. SEMATECH claimed that the three stages roughly corresponded to recovering global competitiveness, maintaining parity, and regaining global leadership for the United States semiconductor industry—but how SEMATECH would aid in the achievement of this neatly phased agenda was left unspecified.[6]

The black book was crowned with a mission statement so vaguely worded that no one could object to it. "To provide the U.S. semiconductor industry the capability for world leadership in manufacturing."[7]

Meanwhile, the SIA's platoon of lobbying executives began to push for federal government funding for SEMATECH, emphasizing that the ten companies already committed as members of the would-be consortium together accounted for some 80 percent of the American industry's manufacturing base. SEMATECH would be a one-shot way to help an entire industry that would also be helping itself by providing half the money for the consortium. SEMATECH's proponents, in fact, enjoyed describing the effort as "a high-tech barn raising." As one of them explained, "You know, the farmer's out there, and lightning hits the barn, and the neighbors from miles around come out and help him build a new one. And yet, then they turn right around and compete very heavily with each other as to who's going to raise the best cotton crop or whatnot." So it would be with SEMATECH, they promised.[8]

Noyce did his part to promote the consortium, speaking to both the House and the Senate on the need for a vehicle through which "the industry will develop and test advanced manufacturing technology under realistic production conditions." He pointed out that while the semiconductor industry already shared scientific and engineering knowledge—through published papers and technical conferences—no mechanism existed to share manufacturing knowledge. SEMATECH could fill that void.[9]

A report issued by a Defense Science Board Task Force on Semiconductor Dependency in February 1987 boosted the SIA's lobbying for SEMATECH. "The implications of the loss of semiconductor technology and manufacturing expertise, for our country in general and our national security in particular, are awesome indeed," proclaimed the report. Task force members recommended that "cooperative government, industry, and university action" be taken immediately to ensure such a loss never occurred.[10]

The contemporaneous and complementary efforts of the SIA and the Defense task force were no coincidence. Noyce served on the Defense task force advisory board, along with several senior executives from Texas Instruments and Motorola. Among the eight nongovernment members of the task force were the top two men from the SIA's Semiconductor Research Corporation, as well as Jack Kilby. To be sure, these men possessed the expertise one would hope to see involved with a high-level government task force. Many of them also knew the SIA's thoughts on the best solution for the industry's ills, and these thoughts undoubtedly influenced the task force's recommendations. On May 12, the Defense Department and representatives of the industry signed a memorandum of understanding that cleared the way for the funding process for SEMATECH to begin.[11]

The Defense Department imprimatur meant a good deal in Reagan-era Washington, but the SEMATECH proposal nonetheless faced strong opposition. A principal researcher for an interagency survey on the chip industry led by the National Science Foundation said that the semiconductor industry had "wildly overstated" its problems. The White House Science Council, chaired by the president's science adviser, William Graham, received the SEMATECH proposal skeptically and ultimately recommended funding by only a one-vote margin. The Department of Commerce, in a generally favorable review of the "Benefits and Risks of Funding for SEMATECH," raised questions about how the consortium's results would be distributed and whether the operation ran the risk of collusion or of detrimentally centralizing the nation's previously diverse research in semiconductors.[12]

One angry member of the House Science and Technology Committee, who had recently seen California's last major steel mill close in his district, all but accused the semiconductor industry of hypocrisy in his objections to SEMATECH. "Most of them are right-wing Republicans . . . basically against any government intrusion," he said. "But when they get into trouble because they've been damn fools, then they come to us for bailout." Certainly Noyce's testimony before Congress to urge support for the consortium raised a few eyebrows. "His latest mission hardly evokes the industry's history of rugged independence," said a skeptical *Washington Post* of Noyce. "He's in Washington pleading for a handout."[13]

Momentum was on the side of the SIA and SEMATECH, however. In its lobbying for the 1986 trade agreement with Japan, the SIA had made semiconductors a *cause celebre* in Washington. "The semiconductor industry has garnered enormous congressional support in the past few years," explained Republican senator John McCain from Arizona in 1987. "There is a perception that they [sic] represent the high technology edge of America's industrial competitiveness." The SIA's efforts were also aided by the organization's refusal to commit to a specific location for the consortium before the funding vote in Congress.[14]

In June of 1987, the House approved $500 million for SEMATECH in an omnibus trade bill. Four months later, the Senate unanimously approved an amendment to the 1988 Defense authorization bill in order to provide $100 million to SEMATECH in fiscal 1988 and 1989. With this authorization, funding for SEMATECH emerged very much along the lines that the SIA had imagined: a $250 million annual budget, with $100 million from the federal government, an equal amount provided by member companies, and the remaining $50 million from the local and state governments of the community in which the facility would be located. Incredible as it may seem, these sums were approved for an organization that still lacked a cohesive vision. Noyce nonetheless proclaimed SEMATECH a "bargain" for the American people—taken together, he pointed out, the consortium's total annual federal funding would buy only half a B-1 bomber.[15]

SEMATECH established temporary headquarters in Santa Clara and soon a site-selection committee issued a request for proposals for a permanent site. They expected perhaps a dozen responses but received proposals from some 135 locations in 34 states, all of them lured by SEMATECH's plan to employ nearly 800 high-tech workers who would collaborate on research and work in the brand new, multimillion-dollar, state-of-the-art fab that SEMATECH planned to build in order to simulate the "realistic production conditions" to which Noyce referred in his Senate testimony.[16]

The prospect of such a high-profile, high-tech anchor offered a singular appeal to the regions vying for the SEMATECH site. Almost from the birth of the transistor, cities and suburbs had tried to attract the glamorous electronics industry. In the 1960s, Frederick Terman, the Stanford provost who had offered to help William Shockley find suitable home for his company, consulted with interested regional developers in Texas and New Jersey eager to build electronics zones of their own. Charles Degaulle and members of the Japanese Diet had visited the Stanford Industrial Park. In the United States, the recession of the 1970s brought renewed interest in regional revitalization through high technology, and by 1981, the National Governors Association had formed a "Task Force on Technological Innovation" to seek "improvements in the national tax code which would encourage industrial innovation" and to help states "fulfill their federalist role as supporters of economic development in their states." One year later, the Congressional Joint Economic Committee issued a study that concluded, "High technology companies offer a brighter future for America but they [also] offer salvation for those regions of America that have borne the brunt of our economic decline."[17]

In the mid-1980s, regions across the country and around the world began trumpeting their high quality of life and low cost of living to traffic- and mortgage-weary technologists in Silicon Valley. "Remember the Silicon Valley as it was 20 Years Ago? That's Albuquerque Today!" promised one representative advertisement in the *San Jose Business Journal*. By 1989, the United States boasted regions calling themselves Silicon Forest (Portland, Oregon), Silicon Gulch (Phoenix, Arizona), Bionic Valley (Salt Lake City), Silicon Valley East (Troy-Albany, New York), Silicon Prairie (Dallas, Austin), and Silicon Mountain (Colorado Springs). Several European and Asian countries also possessed technology regions named in homage to Silicon Valley.[18]

Arguably the most successful of the American "Silicon Elsewheres," as they were derisively called on the San Francisco Peninsula, was Austin, Texas. The high-technology economy in the Lone Star State's capital emerged from the ashes of the domestic oil industry. Between 1982 and 1985, Austin added 10,000 manufacturing jobs to its economy—two-thirds of them in high-tech businesses. In this sun-drenched city, reported a somewhat concerned *San Jose Mercury News* in 1985, high-tech talk was becoming "as common as a tall Lone Star beer on a hot day." Within a few years, several prominent Silicon Valley companies—Intel, ROLM, Tandem Computers, Advanced Micro Devices, National Semiconductor—had sites in or near Austin. Motorola and Data General had facilities in the area, too, as did both IBM (which owned a 3.8-million-square-foot plant in Austin) and Microelectronics and Computer Technology Corp. (MCC), one of the earliest electronics research consortiums. Austin could thus offer

SEMATECH an established high-tech infrastructure as well as the attractions of the University of Texas and Texas A&M, low housing and labor
costs, a vibrant cultural life, and no corporate or personal income taxes.[19]

Austin's proposal for the SEMATECH site included a coordinated
effort among universities, companies, and state and local governments who
had decided in advance that Austin would be the only city the state would
offer for consideration. The University of Texas offered to buy a former
Data General plant for $50 million and then allow SEMATECH to use it
at no charge. The Austin city council supplemented this with $250,000
and a promise to "cut through any red tape hindering the project." The
Texas congressional delegation, under the leadership of House Speaker
Jim Wright and Representative J. J. Pickle (a member of the powerful House
Ways and Means Committee), actively assisted the SIA in its federal lobbying efforts to secure funding for SEMATECH. The state of California's
proposal efforts, meanwhile, were so fractured that Governor Deukmejian
bypassed the state legislature, which was drawing up its own plan, to submit San Jose's bid for SEMATECH.[20]

In January 1988, the site-selection committee announced that Austin,
not Silicon Valley, would house SEMATECH. Within months, construction on the fab was underway. Along with many others, San Jose mayor
Tom McEnery worried that the SEMATECH decision meant the state of
California was "in danger of losing our leadership position with the high-
technology industries."[21]

BY THIS POINT, SEMATECH had successfully assembled its "black book,"
consulted with the Department of Defense, lobbied Congress, chosen a
location, broken ground for a fab, determined a dues structure, and assembled a membership base of 14 companies and DARPA (the Defense
Advanced Research Projects Agency)—all without anyone having a clear
sense of what the consortium would actually do. There was a general agreement that a worthwhile first task would be for SEMATECH to try to manufacture a huge run of chips, not to sell, but as a research project. Engineers
at SEMATECH—half of them employed by the consortium, half of them
assignees from member companies – would implement and optimize the
production processes for these chips, learning from each other and sharing
their insights along the way. When the most efficient approach had been
determined for every step, SEMATECH would disseminate this information to its member companies.

But what chips would they build? In January, SEMATECH issued a
proud press release announcing that IBM and AT&T had both contributed "Manufacturing Demonstration Vehicles"—soup-to-nuts guidelines
to the several-hundred-step process needed to build advanced chips—to
SEMATECH. The chip that AT&T offered was brand new and had not

been produced in volume, so its value as a vehicle for demonstrating mass-production techniques was questionable. IBM's contribution was an established chip already in production, but the company, concerned about intellectual property, refused to release to SEMATECH details on a specific process step and further stipulated that only IBM assignees or SEMATECH direct hires could work with the technology. Upon hearing of IBM's proprietary restrictions, AT&T summarily imposed similar ones. Such limitations thoroughly undermined the very industry-wide sharing and cross-company interactions that SEMATECH was supposed to foster.[22]

Moreover, the AT&T and IBM devices were so different that SEMA-TECH's decision to accept both signalled the consortium's overall lack of direction. IBM's chip was a DRAM, the quintessential commodity chip that had served as a technology driver since the late 1960s, and the first chips that the Japanese built more successfully than the Americans. By contrast, AT&T's chip was an SRAM, a device built with the same process technology used to manufacture more specialized circuits, including small lots of special-application chips. Accepting both the IBM and AT&T demonstration vehicles enabled SEMATECH to postpone a decision on whether it would focus on commodity chips or more specialized devices.

The consortium's efforts were so diffuse, in part, because it had no leader. Three men, each of whom held a full-time, high-level management job at his own company, and none of whom was empowered to decide the direction SEMATECH should take, ran the consortium as an interim management team while a search committee vetted permanent CEO candidates. Meanwhile, almost 300 people (including the assignees from member companies) worked at SEMATECH, but there was no Human Resources department. One consultant called in to work with the consortium described the situation thus: "They stacked five hundred people out there all at once in what seemed to be a two week period, and there was no structure. Literally, there was no management structure to speak of. I'd never seen anything like it before." Nor was there any formal method to determine how money was spent, or how contracts for research and development were to be awarded.[23]

A search committee comprised of Sporck, Noyce, and Jerry Sanders of Advanced Micro Devices spent weeks sifting through some 200 names of potential CEO candidates. They found it nearly impossible to come up with a name acceptable to all 14 member companies and the Department of Defense, and often the names that came up—including Noyce's—belonged to men who were not interested in the job. The choices were further limited by the requirement, adopted at SEMATECH's founding, that none of the top officers at the consortium could work for a member company after their tenure at SEMATECH ended. This restriction was adopted in an effort to assure objectivity and reduce the risk of raiding, but it was quite a bit to ask, given that most viable candidates would likely be found in very senior management positions at member companies to which they would like to return. On the rare occasions that a promising candidate seemed interested in the SEMATECH job, his employer had offered him a raise and a promotion. "I got more damn guys promoted," Charlie Sporck mused a decade later.[24]

In April, 1988—ten months after Congress approved funding for SEMATECH—DARPA, citing the lack of "specific details on [the consortium's] operating plan," as well as the failure to find a CEO, announced that it was delaying the release of the federal portion of the consortium's funding. Funding was released one month later, but then a frustrated United States Senate threatened to trim SEMATECH's expected $100 million allotment for 1989 to $45 million on the grounds that without a chief executive, SEMATECH was falling behind schedule. These moves created even more problems for the CEO search committee. "No right-minded executive would interrupt a promising and lucrative career to commit to a project that might disintegrate beneath future legislative budget debates," opined *Electronic News*.[25]

NOYCE FOUND THE ENTIRE SITUATION appallingly embarrassing. One day in July, he called Richard Hodgson, his mentor since the earliest days at Fairchild. "I'd like your advice," Noyce said. He was considering volunteering for the job as SEMATECH CEO. Several people had urged him to take the position in the past, but he did not want to leave California and frankly thought he was too old to run another startup effort. In a comment reminiscent of his youthful reluctance to accept the general manager's job at Fairchild, Noyce had urged the SEMATECH search committee to "find someone better than me." But with SEMATECH's federal funding under threat, Noyce had begun to reconsider. He still did not want the job, he said, but "I prefer not to see all of [my] life's work go down in flames." He told Hodgson, "I wouldn't go down there, but I'm embarrassed by what's going on and it's just—it's ridiculous. [SEMATECH] is a good effort." He had told Ann Bowers the same thing.[26]

Hodgson advised Noyce not to take the job for two reasons: "You got married and you love to fly airplanes." There would not be much time to travel with his wife or muse on infinity if Noyce became SEMATECH's CEO. Noyce seemed to think his mentor had a point. Hodgson hung up the phone believing he had talked Noyce out of volunteering.[27]

The next day, Noyce flew to Austin, where the SIA board was meeting to discuss SEMATECH. On the flight back, Noyce sat next to his friend Charlie Sporck. The two were griping about the search problems over a few Beefeaters on the rocks when Noyce suddenly said, "You know, Charlie, I think *I* ought to probably be the CEO there."

Sporck was surprised but recovered immediately. "Bob," he said, "the job is yours."[28]

Sporck thinks that "the idea of bringing all of these companies together and making them play beautiful music was appealing to Bob. . . . He saw himself as good at that." But in a private Intel interview conducted shortly after Noyce was named SEMATECH CEO, Noyce said that he did not expect the position to offer much in the way of excitement or fun. He certainly never pretended he wanted to leave his life in California, and with a net worth in excess of $100 million, there was no reason he needed to.[29]

At the press conference announcing his new position, Noyce said, "SEMATECH is just too important for the industry and the country to ignore the call to leadership." For generations, Noyce men had heeded the call to service through leadership in its explicitly Christian guise. In his own career, Bob Noyce had tuned his ear to an entrepreneurial version of the same summons. To be sure, the desire to secure his own financial and professional success had driven the earliest stage of Noyce's career, but once he had accomplished this, he had turned to young startup companies precisely because this was how he believed he could be of best service. Not one of the entrepreneurs with whom Noyce worked ever thought he had been drawn in for the money—though Noyce welcomed that, too. Instead, he had wanted to help, to mentor, to nurture, and to give back. As one of Noyce's friends put it, "Bob spent his life walking along the edges of his Christianity."[30]

Perhaps Noyce was consoling himself or moving his decision into a realm from which he had drawn such pleasure in the past when he coined a new phrase to describe the consortium. SEMATECH, he said, was a "public start-up," an experiment in "national entrepreneurialism, with industry and government teaming up as venture partners." But if Noyce really did consider SEMATECH to be a novel sort of startup, then his decision to lead the effort in its time of crisis fits another pattern he had established long before. In the three decades he had worked in high-technology industry, Bob Noyce had never willingly allowed one of his startups to die.[31]

THE NEWS THAT NOYCE would head SEMATECH was greeted with praise and relief when it was announced on July 27, 1988. Sporck publicly rejoiced, calling Noyce, "the ideal guy with the greatest stature in the industry." Almost immediately upon receiving the news, congressional leaders assured Noyce that SEMATECH would receive the full $100 million it had expected. Even SEMATECH's most vocal critic was impressed. "I was afraid [SEMATECH] was going to turn into a turkey farm," said T. J. Rogers of Cypress Semiconductor, who had repeatedly predicted that the consortium would benefit only the largest firms in the industry. "But with a guy of Noyce's stature, that won't happen." One editorial said simply,

"When an infant business needs credibility, there's nothing like hiring a legend."[32]

Only Noyce's closest confidants expressed anything less than enthusiasm for his decision—not because they thought he would not be good at the job, but because they thought it would not be good for him. Before hearing that Noyce would run the consortium, several of his friends had believed SEMATECH was such a hodgepodge of strange bedfellows that it was doomed to fail. One letter from a colleague Noyce had known since Fairchild begins, "Condolences and congratulations on your new job." The entirety of Arthur Rock's comment to Noyce—"I think taking the Sematech chairmanship was a class act"—was not an unqualified endorsement of it. Nor was Andy Grove's note calling him a "mensch" for accepting the position. "The U.S. government, the U.S. semiconductor industry, and Sematech are damned lucky that you are a glutton for punishment," wrote Ken Oshman, founder of ROLM. "With you at the helm, a possibility I never contemplated, all my objections [to SEMATECH] evaporate." Gordon Moore summarized the feelings of many of Noyce's friends when he said the SEMATECH job was "a huge sacrifice" for Noyce. "I didn't think Bob wanted to take on a terribly difficult job, a job with a strong political content as well as a major managerial task at the time," Moore says. "But Bob did it, he went down there."[33]

Two weeks after Noyce was named CEO, Japanese semiconductor manufacturer NEC asked to join SEMATECH. The consortium refused the application with no public comment beyond the statement that it had "reaffirmed [its] intent to keep the consortium limited to U.S. companies."[34]

To have admitted a Japanese firm would have undermined the patriotic fervor that at times seemed the only thing uniting the 14 member companies and the Department of Defense. In its earliest incarnation, SEMATECH was so "tightly wrapped in the United States flag" (as one person put it) that management considered reserving its best parking spaces for American-made cars. The house banner, "The American Enterprise Flag," reproduced the famous colonial banner of a rattlesnake (but with 14 rattles) coiled above the phrase, "Don't Tread on Me." There had been talk of making this flag the focal point of SEMATECH's first annual report—the cover shot would have shown men in bunny suits raising the flag Iwo Jima-style—but Noyce, who approved of the sentiment, nonetheless squelched the idea as "too over the top."[35]

Noyce had originally planned to live in California and commute to Texas—he looked forward to the flying—but the sense that he needed to "lead by example" and commit himself fully to the job, coupled with the lack of a personal income tax in Texas, swung him to declare official residency in Austin. He and Bowers moved into a nice, but not extravagant, split-level home in August. After taking a previously scheduled trip to Tibet, Noyce assumed the helm of SEMATECH in September. The official opening of the SEMATECH facility two months later was a lavish affair. After a brief performance by the Austin Symphony and a fly-over by a pair of jets from a nearby Air Force base, Noyce took the stage beneath an enormous American flag. Arrayed on either side of him were members of Congress, officials of the Reagan and Texas gubernatorial administrations, the mayor of Austin, representatives of each of SEMATECH's 14 member companies, and various leaders of the University of Texas system—69 people in all. "Throughout the history of our nation, Americans have stepped up and met challenges," Noyce said. "SEMATECH is the American answer to a most modern challenge."[36]

NOYCE EXPECTED HIS JOB at SEMATECH to resemble the work he had done at Intel. He said that he would be "Mr. Outside," offering testimony in Washington and speaking around the country about the importance of SEMATECH and its mission. As far as internal affairs were concerned, he said, he would be "an observer and a counselor. . . . When I'm here I will sit in on the staff meetings and that sort of thing. Try to contribute what I can." He added, "I hope to be able to be a sounding board . . . and perhaps to be able to see some things about the organization just because I'm standing a little bit farther away from the force there [in Austin]."[37]

Playing "Mr. Inside" to Noyce's "Mr. Outside" would be Paul Castrucci, a 32-year veteran of IBM, who would serve as chief operating officer. Noyce and Castrucci had never met, but industry insiders pictured the arrangement as something akin to a Noyce-Grove partnership, with Noyce providing SEMATECH's public image, esprit de corps, and long-range vision; and Carstrucci serving as the get-things-done operations man. Noyce named his own chief administrative officer, Peter Mills, and then made the unexpected announcement that the three men would serve together in an Intel-style "Office of the Chief Executive," rather than Noyce serving as the sole chief.[38]

But Noyce soon found there were too many problems within the organization for him to focus exclusively on outside relations. The assignees at SEMATECH were paid by the member companies who sent them to the consortium. It took Noyce only a few weeks on the job to realize that most people at SEMATECH "have split loyalty. Is their cause [the company that pays them and to which they will return after their stint at SEMATECH], or is their cause SEMATECH? That's an interesting one to work around. How do we get that all pulled together?" he wondered.[39]

Miller Bonner, head of communications for SEMATECH, recalled that the member companies did not help the consortium's cause. Some of them saw SEMATECH as a place to dump low-performing employees.

Most of them sent their legal counsel to chat with assignees before they left for Austin. "Whatever you do, don't open your mouth. But take a lot of notes," the attorneys would advise. "And remember, we're suing companies B and C over here, so watch what you say." Concerns about intellectual property were so great that an early SEMATECH planning meeting had attracted 32 intellectual property lawyers from potential member companies and the Department of Defense. As Noyce put it, rather resignedly, "Everyone comes here to extract something from SEMATECH and nobody comes here to contribute something to SEMATECH." It was a classic tragedy-of-the-commons situation. If everyone did only what was best for his or her individual company, Noyce explained, "there isn't going to be anything to extract [from]."[40]

These troubles kept Noyce from performing the "Mr. Outside" job he had loved at Intel, and instead forced him to play a role similar to the general manager's function he had grown to detest at Fairchild. SEMATECH lacked much of the interdivisional tension that had hobbled Fairchild, but the wrangling among member companies produced the same effect. The lawyers' don't-tell counseling proved extremely effective, and Noyce found himself pulled into the very sorts of meetings he thought he would avoid at SEMATECH. He would have to go around a conference table, individually asking each engineer present how she or he thought whatever given problem at hand could best be solved. Bonner, the communications expert, claimed that Noyce's approach was effective. "When you've got somebody of that kind of stature looking you in the eye and asking for your opinion, you're not going to say, 'I'm not going to tell you.' In a very short time, it became very apparent that everybody was holding back the same kind of information."[41]

But it was effective only to a degree. To cut through the interfirm suspicion and find a compromise among the three competing agendas, Noyce brought in a consultant who had worked closely with Intel. Noyce also implemented a mandatory communications training session based on a model called "Constructive Confrontation" that Andy Grove had developed at Intel.

Noyce leaned heavily on his own personal magnetism. The first time he met with a large group of SEMATECH employees, he started the meeting by removing his tie. When SEMATECH's spending threatened to outpace its budget and Noyce approved the installation of a Budget Committee that nearly everyone at SEMATECH detested, he and his communications staff mapped out a plan to ease the tension. When Noyce mounted the stage at the next quarterly all-hands meeting, they plotted, the lights would go out. Noyce would then reach under the lectern, pull out a candle, light it, and ask his audience, all sitting in pitch darkness, "Did anyone clear this meeting with the Budget Committee?"[42]

They thought it would bring down the house. It did. But Noyce none-theless devoted most of the meeting to fielding irate questions from engineers who wanted their requests approved *now*. His response in this situation was always a variation on the same theme. "Well, I understand why this would be frustrating," he would say, "but we're not going to change the policy. And here is why you should be glad we're watching expenses." Noyce's sympathetic approach usually left the complainers happier than before they had vented their frustrations, but serving as a roadblock slowing the pace of work must have frustrated Noyce as much as it irritated the engineers. Noyce, however, had no choice. If SEMATECH overran its budget in a given quarter, it would look bad enough in Washington to jeopardize future appropriations.[43]

At the end of this meeting, in response to a question from an employee complaining that his job title did not accurately describe the high level of his responsibilities at SEMATECH, Noyce said that he had never put much stock in titles himself, but if the questioner—or anyone else—wanted to give himself a new job title, that was fine with Noyce. Within days, several employees had filed requests for business cards—which they promptly received. In much the same vein was Noyce's insistence, throughout his tenure at SEMATECH, that the consortium did not need an organization chart. He thought such documents did little more than encourage undue attention to hierarchy. His COO, who believed otherwise, secretly drew up an organization chart for his own reference.[44]

But neither Noyce's charisma nor his attempts at organizational innovation could lead the member companies to "make beautiful music together." The firms were willing to concede that they had similar problems in their manufacturing processes, but they did not want to go beyond that. This meant that SEMATECH's mission would not involve sharing black magic (as the smallest companies had hoped) or developing flexible production methods (as the defense interests had desired).

Instead, SEMATECH narrowed its agenda to focus on issues of greatest concern to the consortium's largest member companies: improving the equipment and materials that they used in their fabs. SEMATECH would identify the areas most critical for next-generation progress and fund contracts for suppliers to develop new tools and materials. The consortium would also work with suppliers to improve existing tools and equipment. Or as Noyce put it, "From our base of shared knowledge, we will define the needs and specifications for the advanced tool set and then . . . invest in joint R&D projects with U.S. equipment and materials suppliers to develop the advanced tool set." Once the new equipment was developed, Noyce said, SEMATECH would test, characterize, and demonstrate it to member companies so they could incorporate it into their own fabs.[45]

Forcing the consortium to pinpoint a mission—even a mission born more of a process of elimination than universal acclamation—was Noyce's single most important contribution to internal affairs at SEMATECH. Before he arrived, no one at SEMATECH could agree on what the consortium would do. A few months into Noyce's tenure, the mission was defined.

A focus on improving fab materials and equipment meant that SEMATECH would need to transform itself from a "horizontal" research collaboration among peers to what Noyce called a "'virtual' vertical integration" between its members and the suppliers from whom they bought equipment and materials. In many ways this made SEMATECH even more like a Japanese research consortium—roughly 80 percent of which were vertically integrated—than had originally been imagined.[46]

Once the mission was defined, Noyce began speaking of SEMATECH as an effort to "strengthen the infrastructure" that supported the semiconductor manufacturing business. In this sense, the move to reach out to suppliers can also be understood as a $250 million attempt to reproduce the close relationships that had nurtured the earliest silicon companies in Silicon Valley. SEMATECH's new mission hearkened back to the days when asking for advice felt like borrowing a cup of sugar and the guy who ran the company that built your furnace used to work for you.

But those harmonious relationships had long since disappeared. The supplier and manufacturing businesses had grown in very different directions. The supplier industry was only one-quarter the size of its manufacturing counterpart. Revenues for 1989, for example, were $5 billion and $20 billion, respectively. And in contrast to the manufacturing side, which was dominated by a few large companies such as Intel and Texas Instruments, 88 percent of the more than 800 American supplier companies were small businesses with annual sales of less than $25 million.[47]

By the time the manufacturing firms that belonged to SEMATECH decided to focus the consortium's attention on shoring up relations with suppliers, it seemed that most communications between the two industries were being conducted by lawyers. Suppliers believed that manufacturers said they wanted quality but really made decisions based on short-term costs. The suppliers also felt handicapped by the manufacturers' acute concern for intellectual property, which made it impossible to develop industry-wide equipment standards. Moreover, because most supplier companies were too small to build state-of-the-art fabs to test their equipment in a realistic mass-production environment, they had to de-bug on a customer's line—and then suffer castigation for "poor quality products" from manufacturers who thought the equipment should have been perfected earlier and who at the same time refused to share data on how the equipment performed.[48]

Manufacturers, of course, felt differently. As one long-time IBM employee explained, "Much of the very expensive equipment purchased by the chipmakers didn't work according to specifications when it got to their factories. This was particularly true with the latest models that were purchased for a new factory. The chip maker could have upwards of a billion dollars tied up in a factory that didn't work. It frequently took eighteen to twenty months to get up and running, [during which] time the chipmaker was losing his proverbial rear end and was also losing market share. Naturally all of the manufacturing middle management was shifting all the blame to the equipment makers [and] top management accepted this input."[49]

One person who attended the early talks between SEMATECH and the suppliers' trade organization SEMI said that he had attended friendlier lawsuits. Another participant recalls a representative from one organization referring to the other group's members as "thieves"—and then receiving an ovation for his candor.[50]

THE MOVE TO FOCUS on suppliers irritated the Department of Defense. Improved basic manufacturing—SEMATECH's original stated mission— offered a direct benefit to Defense efforts, because it increased the likelihood that American weapons could be built with American electronics. But bolstering suppliers seemed to many in Washington to be more clearly beneficial to industry than to the national defense. In late 1990, the head of DARPA came to SEMATECH, and during a meeting with the CEO, slowly and deliberately wrote D-A-R-P-A on the white board. Then he announced, "This stands for 'Defense Advanced Research Projects Agency.' SEMATECH is none of these things. It's not defense-related, it isn't advanced research, and it's not being run as a project. You don't fit in our program."[51]

By early 1989, Noyce was already feeling the Defense Department's disapproval of the new mission. He was also finding it increasingly difficult to work with Paul Castrucci, his COO. Castrucci had done an unassailable job overseeing the construction of SEMATECH's fab, which at $75 million and 32 weeks' building time, had set records in an industry that spent, on average, $200 million and 18 to 24 months to build a state-of-the-art fab. Shortly after the fab's completion, SEMATECH provided detailed engineering, business, and manufacturing design plans to member companies and the government—the first "technology transfer" at the consortium and an auspicious beginning in the eyes of several member companies.[52]

But as time progressed, Castrucci's top-down managerial style proved incompatible with Noyce's approach and SEMATECH's new mission. In March 1989, after several weeks of agonizing indecision, Noyce asked for Castrucci's resignation. He named Turner Hasty, who had served as interim operations chief prior to Noyce's arrival, as COO. Noyce and

Castrucci agreed to keep their counsel and say nothing more about the resignation after the initial announcement, but a few months thereafter Noyce, in a move that won him a plush muzzled eagle doll (representing himself) to keep on his desk, added a few details. The problems arose not over policy, but over what Noyce saw as "drifting" within the organization. He came within a breath of calling internal operations at SEMATECH the organization's "weak link." Noyce was spending nearly 40 hours per week on these internal operations and finding them so frustrating that he told several people that he suspected the consortium might run more smoothly with fewer member companies and interested government parties.[53]

Meanwhile, Noyce continued to serve on the Intel board—he tried not to miss a meeting—and to deliver occasional speeches as a representative of the company. He also had to fulfill the ongoing requirements of the full-time "Mr. Outside" work for which he had been hired. He spoke to at least one group nearly every week; in his first ten months at SEMATECH, he gave a speech or testified 58 times.[54]

Noyce was himself somewhat to blame for his packed speaking schedule. The communications team would decline an interview request, recalled Miller Bonner, but "whoever we declined would go in the back door and get Noyce on the phone. And he'd say, 'Well, okay. We can make that happen'—because he didn't want to disappoint people." The problem abated somewhat after Bonner took Noyce aside and said, "Bob, we've really got to focus this. I mean, you just can't say yes to everybody."[55]

Noyce was not simply being nice when he agreed to speak. He believed, as did Bonner, that "we [SEMATECH] need publicity; we need support of many, many masters. You've got the local, state, and federal governments. You've got the supplier industry. You've got the downstream [users of semiconductors]. You've got the members [of SEMATECH]. And you've got the non-members."[56]

Noyce added, "We've got to have someone very obviously, very soundly behind anything we say. I think that we need to try to express the objectives and the philosophy of why we are doing this. We need to try to articulate that pretty clearly so people can subscribe to it." Noyce, of course, was the "someone" who needed to ensure the support of SEMATECH's "many masters," particularly in the nation's capital. Between September 1989 and March of 1990, he flew to Washington, D.C. almost every month for two- or three-day visits that usually included congressional testimony, visits to policymakers and staffers, strategy sessions with the Dewey, Ballantine attorneys who had also worked with the SIA, interviews with the press, and working breakfasts, lunches, and dinners. It was not unusual for him to have a dozen different meetings on his agenda each day he was in Washington. In the regular returns to the East Coast and the need to garner support from outsiders mostly unfamiliar with semiconductors,

Noyce was re-living some of his least favorite aspects of the general manager's job at Fairchild.

Although Miller Bonner, like everyone else who knew Noyce well and watched him speak, thought Noyce seemed a little nervous at the podium, by this point Noyce possessed an extremely savvy public presence. A rare full-text transcription of a lengthy television interview that Noyce knew would be edited shows him interrupting himself midsentence—"that wasn't very good," he says—and then rephrasing the comment in a more pithy way. Noyce similarly edited himself early in his tenure at SEMATECH when he told the Intel employee interviewing him that the CEO's job was more enjoyable than he had imagined it would be. Almost immediately, he added, "I suppose I shouldn't be quoted that way."

Miller Bonner served as Noyce's speechwriter for much of his SEMATECH tenure. They used the same modular speech-building structure that had worked well for Noyce at Intel. Often the pair would assemble Noyce's presentations in the air en route from Austin to the location where he would speak, Noyce sitting in the cockpit with his pilot, shouting comments and ideas back to Bonner, who would key them into his portable computer.

Noyce always arrived at the podium with every word of his speech written out, but the text served more as a starting point than a script. Indeed, Noyce extemporized so much that Bonner, who regularly received requests from journalists for copies of Noyce's talks, had the following statement printed across the cover page of his speeches: "Dr. Noyce may deviate from the attached text, but he stands by the text as written."

NOYCE DID MANAGE to work in a bit of fun. He came to a SEMATECH Halloween party dressed as Bruce Springsteen, complete with a jet-black wig, a red bandana, and a t-shirt that read THE BOSS. He installed a "remote car starter" in the Mustang convertible he had bought when he moved to Texas. Whenever he spied from his office window someone near his car in the parking lot, he loved to push a button on his key-chain transmitter and watch the reaction when his empty car seemed to start itself. He also took a break from SEMATECH to return to Grinnell for his fortieth college reunion.[57]

Another enjoyable diversion came in September 1989, when Noyce was surprised to learn that the afternoon-long meeting on his calendar was really a trip to nearby Bergstrom Air Force Base, where members of the 67th Tactical Reconnaissance Wing helped him to suit up and then took him to fly an RF-4C jet. A photo of Noyce in the rear cockpit of the plane shows him giving an enthusiastic thumbs-up before take off. "He was like a kid in a candy store," recalled one person who accompanied him to the base.[58]

Jim Lafferty, now running the San Jose Jet Center, provided Noyce his favorite distraction when he put him in touch with an entrepreneur named Wayne Higashi who, along with inventor Paul Pires, had developed a mechanical transmission that they believed could reduce fuel consumption in many cars by as much as 20 percent. Noyce invited Higashi to Austin to demonstrate a prototype of the transmission, which was about the size of a shoe box and powered by a half-horsepower motor.

After about two hours with Higashi, Noyce said, "I don't think it has a uniform output." Without a uniform output, the speed of whatever device the transmission turned—automobile wheels, for example—could not be constant. They would rotate faster at some times and slower at others.

Higashi explained that he and Pires had developed a mathematical model of the transmission that proved its output was uniform. Any variation Noyce thought he saw must be the result of non-uniform input from the motor.

Noyce remained unconvinced. "I don't think it works," he said. He then made the move that had endeared him to so many people who worked with him. "It doesn't work, but it looks like a great idea," he said. "Leave your drawings and business plan with me, and I'll think about it." He then proceeded to spend every available minute of the next several weeks in his workshop, musing on the transmission—often until well past midnight. "With the two opposing shafts geared together, the system is equivalent to a simple crank arm system," he wrote, sketching as we went along. "This still gives basically a sinusoidal output, *slightly* modified by arm length, etc. The basic case is d/a>>1, l>>a. . . . But try as you may, this won't give a linear output (i.e. constant angular velocity)!" He then proceeded to fill several pages with equations, graphs, and line drawings, jotting notes all the while—"must have clutches [sic] efficiency!"—and clearly having what he told Ann Bowers was "the most fun he'd had since he had been in college working on physics."[59]

In short order Noyce proved mathematically that the transmission's output could not be uniform. When he showed this proof to Higashi on his next trip to Silicon Valley (where Highashi worked), the entrepreneur was skeptical. Noyce suggested, very pleasantly, that Higashi start the transmission. Noyce then reached into his pocket, extracted a credit card from his wallet, and held the card against the output drive gear on the transmission. The frequency oscillation of the clickety-clack of the card hitting the gear tooth was clearly not uniform. Instead of hearing a regular k-k-k-k-k-k-k-k-k sound, the men heard something like k-k-kkk-k-k-kkk. It was not random, but it was variable. "It amazed me," Higashi recalls. "Noyce developed his own complex mathematical model—and proved us wrong—just by looking at our drawings and observing our model."[60]

Noyce showed Higashi a second set of calculations from his basement research. He had mathematically modeled the non-uniformity of the transmission and had some ideas about how the entrepreneurs could use it to their advantage. It might work in a diesel vehicle, which has an engine with an output even more variable than that of the transmission. Or how about installing the transmission on a bicycle to make it easier to pedal more efficiently?

Noyce's calculations led Higashi and Pires to redesign one part of the transmission, a change that made the output more uniform by a factor of two. The pair eventually licensed the transmission to a manufacturer who wanted to use it for diesel truck transmissions.

Higashi offered Noyce stock in the startup in exchange for his help. But Noyce declined, saying he didn't need any more money and he had not messed around with the math because he had planned to make an investment or take stock in the company. (Higashi thinks Noyce's motivation was the desire for a very cool bicycle.) Noyce was also concerned that if other people knew he was making an investment, they would assume he believed the company was likely to make money. But Noyce had not looked into the market for the device or conducted any formal due diligence on its prospects. Noyce did, however, tell Higashi, "I'm here to support you if you ever get in trouble. If you need a helping hand [an emergency infusion of money], be sure to call me."

"It gave me a great deal of confidence to know that I had an angel back there that I could count on," Higashi says. "It was easier to move forward knowing that he wasn't going to let us fail. He would help me out if we needed it."[61]

BUT THE PLEASANT HOURS Noyce spent in his basement or at his college reunion were stolen from his extremely demanding job at SEMATECH. His life had changed dramatically. Before he moved to Austin, Noyce's days had been filled with a busy-ness of his own choosing, anchored by work he enjoyed and punctuated with evenings with friends of long standing. Now he was working 60- or 70-hour weeks and often did not pause for a weekend. His calendars from his tenure at SEMATECH are so crammed with activity that they are nearly illegible. In a private letter to Grant Gale, Ann Bowers said that Noyce was finding the SEMATECH job a "challenge"—and not a welcome one. "It's a real kick in the side of the head [for Bob] to go back to managing," she wrote. Pictures taken during his SEMATECH tenure show him looking more exhausted than at any other point in his life.[62]

His marriage sustained him, but other pressures outside SEMATECH drained Noyce. He had made an investment in an oil and gas outfit that was not doing well. The increasingly desperate owner was calling him multiple times a day to ask for advice and more money. His youngest daughter had moved to Austin, and after rejecting Bowers's attempts to help her find an apartment, she had joined a religious community with her young son. The community's leader was a charismatic, heavily tattooed former motorcycle gang leader who called himself "Brother Joseph." When Noyce and Bowers visited, Brother Joseph insisted on being present at all times to monitor their conversations.

AND YET, as was so often the case with Noyce, the parts of his life that were not difficult were fantastic. He continued to be showered with recognition. President Reagan awarded him the National Medal of Technology in 1987. Two years later, George H.W. Bush inducted him into the Business Hall of Fame.

The singular honor came in February 1990, when Noyce and Jack Kilby shared the first Charles Stark Draper Award—the so-called Nobel Prize of Engineering—for their work on the integrated circuit. President George H. W. Bush presented the award, sponsored by the National Academy of Engineering, in a black-tie ceremony held at the State Department. Paraphrasing Churchill, the president said of the integrated circuit, "Never has something so small done so much for so many." General Electric chairman and CEO Jack Welch, who chaired the National Academy of Engineering, asked, "How far do you have to reach to find a more profoundly transformational breakthrough? Electricity? Steam power? The wheel? . . . The limits of the invention to which they gave birth are literally the limits of the human imagination." Noyce, who believed the purpose of the award was "to inspire others to make their contributions to society," invited Grant Gale to attend the ceremony as his guest and thanked him for his "inspiration" in his speech. Gale later wrote to Noyce wishing for "a better way in the English language to convey appreciation and affection than a mere 'thank you.'"[63]

By the time Noyce returned from the Draper Award ceremonies, SEMATECH's focus on supplier relations had begun to show some results. The consortium increased its funding for outside research from $84 million to almost $140 million, mainly for projects to improve existing equipment and develop next-generation equipment. SEMATECH also developed technology "road maps" that detailed member companies' goals and timetables for developing next-generation technology. By June, executives from 63 equipment suppliers had attended one-on-one management meetings with manufacturing executives. SEMATECH had awarded 22 joint-development contracts to develop next-generation tools and materials and 13 equipment-improvement program contracts to improve existing equipment. One year earlier, only three contracts, total, had been awarded.[64]

The new focus had generated some opposition, as well. Two companies were unhappy enough with the decision to begin planning to withdraw from SEMATECH. And several suppliers alleged that SEMATECH was playing favorites with its research contracts. The consortium's decision to grant its member companies first dibs on any equipment or materials supported by a SEMATECH contract enraged manufacturers who were not members. After all, these manufacturers paid taxes and thus supported SEMATECH via the federal government's contribution. Why should they be discriminated against?

But even with these problems, SEMATECH was far better off with a clear mission than it had been before Noyce arrived. Noyce himself seemed pleased with his work, at one point proudly telling a meeting of supplier company executives, "We're all customers and we're all suppliers." He had taken the "public startup" beyond the startup phase and past the immediate dangers that had threatened its very existence. It was time for SEMATECH to focus on implementation, and Noyce knew he was not the man to lead it through this effort. In April 1990 Noyce began planning to leave SEMATECH at the end of the year. He confidentially asked the consortium's board to begin a search for his replacement.[65]

He had no immediate plans for the future. He was looking forward to spending a few months recuperating from the SEMATECH frenzy at a ranch he and Bowers had decided to buy on the California coast near Gordon Moore's hometown of Pescadero. (They had sold the Carmel Valley ranch before moving to Texas.) As Bowers put it, "Bob was up for hanging out for a while. He was so busy, so pushed, that he hadn't had a lot of time to think about what was coming next."[66]

ON MAY 10, Noyce—along with Jack Kilby, transistor inventor John Bardeen, composer Leonard Bernstein, medical researchers Lloyd Conover (who discovered tetracycline) and Gertrude Elion (who synthesized several key leukemia and herpes drugs), Polaroid founder Edwin Land, author James A. Michener, director Steven Spielberg, and songwriters Steven Sondheim and Stevie Wonder—received a "Lifetime Achievement Medal" during the bicentennial celebration of the Patent Act.

Perhaps two weeks later, Noyce drove to the religious community where his youngest daughter lived. It was his first trip to the community alone, and when he met with his daughter—and Brother Joseph, of course— she mentioned that she planned to educate her son not at a traditional school, but within the community. When Noyce said that he did not think this was a good idea, Brother Joseph cut him off. "Who do you think you are, giving advice on parenting?" he asked. He told Noyce that a man who was never home for his children and had been unfaithful to his wife had no right to tell his daughter anything about raising children. Then he announced that the meeting was over.[67]

The accusations left Noyce profoundly shaken. He did not like to think about his marriage to Betty Noyce and its effects on their children. As soon as Noyce arrived home, Ann Bowers could see something was wrong. He was so upset that he could barely tell her what had happened. Bowers was furious, not only at what had been said, but at herself for not accompanying Noyce.

A few days later, Noyce picked up the phone and called Paul Hwoschinsky, his Callanish Fund partner who had helped him through the divorce and administered his children's trusts. Hwoschinsky had known Noyce for more than 25 years. He had worked as Noyce's assistant at Fairchild and spent many days with the family on the ski slopes and at the house on Loyola Drive. He was perhaps the only person apart from Ann Bowers who bridged the private and public sides of Noyce's life.

"Well, hi," Noyce said.

"My God, where are you?" asked Hwoschinsky. It was midnight on the West Coast.

"Oh, I'm in Austin." It was two in the morning in Texas.

"What are you doing?"

"Well, I just thought I'd call you up."

"Bob, you didn't just call me up. There's a reason you called me, and what is the reason, because if I can be present to you, I will."

Noyce did not answer. Instead, he laughed a hoarse little laugh. Hwoschinsky knew that nervous chuckle, knew "there was something behind it."

Both men sat quiet for a moment. Then Hwoschinsky said, "Okay, I will choose a subject for our conversation."

"Fine."

"The issue is smoking and you've got to give it up or you're going to die," Hwoschinsky said. "I'm not going to lecture you . . . but what is it that any of your friends can do to be present to you? Any of us, myself included."

Noyce did not have much to say. "It was such a strange conversation," Hwoschinsky recalls more than a dozen years later. "I don't know to this day [why he called]. Honest to God, I don't know. I don't know as he knows. I don't really know. It was a real mystery. I could get to a feeling level. . . . I knew there was something really important happening, and I couldn't get it out of him."[68]

Why did Noyce call Hwoschinsky, with whom he had not had contact for several years? Was he upset about the conversation with Brother Joseph? Did he sense, as Hwoschinsky later suspected, some premonition of his death, which would come in less than two weeks? Certainly Noyce's actions were not those of a man who thought he would die soon. His calendar was full well into the summer. He had plans to trade in his Citation for a new, even higher performance jet in just a few days. And in connection with that purchase, he had undergone a battery of medical tests, administered as part of a full physical, all of which he passed. But the stress Noyce faced at SEMATECH was so great that many people who worked with him there think it contributed to his death. So perhaps he did sense something.

At the end of May, Noyce delivered a speech on SEMATECH in Silicon Valley. It would be his last visit. When he learned Noyce was coming to town, Steve Jobs, who wanted his fiancée to meet Noyce, invited him to his home for dinner. The three stayed up talking until early the next morning. Then Noyce flew back to Austin.[69]

Upon his return, Noyce was surprised to learn that SEMATECH had declared June 1, 1990, "Bob Noyce Day." It was not a good-bye party—almost no one at the consortium knew that he was planning to leave. Instead, the celebration was inspired by a comment that an equipment supplier had made to the *San Jose Mercury News*. Americans need to "change their idols," he said. He nominated Bob Noyce "for the pedestal." SEMATECH made up t-shirts printed with the quote, Noyce's picture, and the phrase "Bob Noyce, teen idol." A photo from the event shows Noyce on the SEMATECH lawn, grinning ear-to-ear, surrounded by women wearing the t-shirts.[70]

This is the last image of Noyce. Two days after photo was taken, he lay down for a rest after his regular morning swim. As he slept, he suffered a massive heart attack that took his life. The oil field owner who had been hounding Noyce for months called while the paramedics were in his bedroom vainly trying to revive him. The date was June 3, 1990. Noyce was 62 years old.

Conclusion

More than 1,000 people attended memorial services for Noyce in Austin. In Japan, hundreds came to a service honoring his memory. Another 2,000 attended ceremonies in San Jose, officiated by Noyce's brother Gaylord. At the end of that June afternoon in Silicon Valley, which the city officially declared "Bob Noyce Day," hundreds of red and white balloons were released into the clear sky. Then the roar of an airplane grew audible. Moments later, Noyce's newest Cessna Citation jet—the one that he had never had a chance to fly—soared past, a mere ten stories off the ground.

President George H. W. Bush phoned Ann Bowers to offer his personal condolences. Roughly two dozen members of Congress, from both sides of the aisle, entered their thoughts on Noyce into the Congressional Record. Defense Secretary Dick Cheney called him "a national treasure." White House science advisor D. Allan Bromley said he "was one of the very few in his generation, worldwide, who truly deserved the appellation of 'genius.'" Obituaries from newspapers around the world remembered Noyce as "the most powerful personal force in the electronics industry," who helped to "create an industrial revolution" and "transform the twentieth century." The *San Jose Mercury News* ran a special four-page tribute, filled with dozens of reminiscences from readers who ranged from a bank teller who had handled his check to buy a plane to those closest to him—Ann Bowers, Gordon Moore, and Grant Gale. Apple Computer's tribute to Noyce read, in part, "He was one of the giants in this valley who provided the model and inspiration for everything we wanted to become. He was the ultimate inventor. The ultimate rebel. The ultimate entrepreneur."[1]

Many people who knew Noyce described him as a "Renaissance man." How else to define someone who was an inventor, a scientist, an industrialist, a singer, and an explorer—all at the same time? Yet Noyce's life was rooted not in fifteenth-century Italy; but in a distinctively American exuberance. "Allons! Whoever you are come travel with me," wrote Walt Whitman in *Leaves of Grass*.

> From this hour I ordain myself loos'd of limits and imaginary lines.
> Going where I list, my own master total and absolute,
> Listening to others, considering well what they say,
> Pausing, searching, receiving, contemplating,
> Gently, but with undeniable will, divesting myself of the holds that
>   would hold me.

In the last interview he granted, Noyce was asked what he would do if he were "emperor" of the United States. He said that he would, among other things, "make sure we are preparing our next generation to flourish in a high-tech age. And that means education of the lowest and the poorest, as well as at the graduate school level." In keeping with these beliefs, most of Noyce's estate was channeled into a foundation, chaired by Ann Bowers, to provide grants to support "initiatives designed to produce significant improvement in the academic achievement of public school students in math, science, and early literacy in grades K–12." To date, Noyce Foundation grants have totaled more than $65 million.[2]

Many of the companies, organizations, and causes with which Noyce involved himself flourish today. In 2004, roughly $30 billion worth of microprocessors—the little chips Noyce once promoted with missionary zeal before incredulous audiences—were sold around the world. The largest company in this market is Intel, whose microprocessors drive more than 80 percent of the personal computers on the market today. Caere, Noyce's teenage startup, was sold to Scansoft in early 2000 for roughly $140 million.

The electronics industry, today the largest industry in the United States, is built upon integrated circuits of a complexity that Noyce never could have imagined in 1959, when he sketched out his ideas for the device. At that point he thought that maybe, someday, 100 components might be printed together as a circuit. The current generation of microprocessors contains 100 million components. In 2003, the semiconductor industry manufactured roughly 90 million transistors for every human on the planet; by 2010, this number should be 1 billion transistors.[3]

The Semiconductor Industry Association, the trade association that Noyce helped to found, today has some 90 member companies and a long record of legislative successes. The organization named its most prestigious award—"the industry's highest honor for leadership"—after Noyce. His great concern that Japan might permanently supplant the United States as home to the world's dominant semiconductor industry has not materialized. Today American firms account for 48 percent of the $166 billion world market for semiconductors; the Japanese account for 27 percent. (A rising industry in China and small East Asian countries accounts for the balance of the market.) Indeed, the perceived threat has diminished so dramatically that SEMATECH, founded in a flush of nationalistic save-our-industry fervor, now has member companies from five countries, including Japan.

Grinnell College named both its science center and its prize in computer science for Noyce. Intel's headquarters is today called the Robert Noyce Building, and the company sponsors three university fellowships in his honor. The IEEE has a Robert N. Noyce medal for exceptional contributions to the microelectronics industry. The Tech Museum of Innovation in San Jose has a Noyce building. The National Science Foundation dedicated its fortieth anniversary symposium to him and in 2002 established a Robert Noyce Scholarship Program to "encourage talented science, technology, engineering, and mathematics majors and professionals to become K–12 mathematics and science teachers." To date NSF has awarded more than $19 million to support approximately 1,700 new teachers under this program.[4]

But Noyce's most enduring legacy cannot be measured in buildings, accolades, awards, or honors, not in dollars earned or given away, nor in stock price or market share. It cannot be etched in silicon or printed on microchips. There is an informal sort of generational succession in Silicon Valley that places Noyce near the top of the family tree. A few years ago, for example, the founders of Google asked Steve Jobs for advice and mentorship in the same way Jobs had come to Noyce when Apple was young. And even when there is no such explicit tie back to Noyce—even if the latest generation of entrepreneurs do not know his name—his influence endures in a set of ideals that have become an indelible part of American high-tech culture: knowledge trumps hierarchy, every idea can be taken farther, new and interesting is better than established and safe, go for broke or don't go at all. There are countless other influences of course, but Noyce's vision is embedded deep in the eye of the swirling energy that is Silicon Valley, his spirit quietly urging anyone who might listen to "go off and do something wonderful."

Notes

Abbreviations for Sources of Material

Abbreviation	Full Name
AIP	Center for History of Physics, American Institute for Physics, College Park, Md.
Anon.	Source requested anonymity
ASB	Ann Bowers
CHC	California History Center, De Anza College, Cupertino, Calif.
DA	Dietz and Associates, Kennebunk, Maine
DSN	Donald S. Noyce
ELEC	Electrochemical Society, Pennington, N.J.
FMCA	Ford Motor Company archives, Ford Motor Company
GCA	Grinnell College archives, Grinnell College, Grinnell, Iowa
GRSPL	Grinnell Room, Stewart Public Library, Grinnell, Iowa
HPA	Hewlett-Packard archives, Hewlett-Packard Corporation
IA	Intel archives, Intel Corporation
IEEE	IEEE History Center Oral History Collection, Rutgers, New Brunswick, N.J.
LF	Libra Foundation, Portland, Maine
MIT	Institute Archives and Special Collections, MIT Libraries, Cambridge, Mass.
MITP	MIT University Physics Department
PSC	Pacific Studies Center, Mountain View, Calif.
SIA	Semiconductor Industry Association reading room
SSC	Stanford Special Collections, Stanford University, Stanford, Calif.
ST	SEMATECH archives

Introduction

1. **Bob Noyce took me under his wing:** Steve Jobs, interview by author.
2. **Big is bad, small cooperates more:** Noyce, "The Fruit of Success," *Chemtech*, Dec. 1979. **Restock the stream:** Noyce quoted in Susan J. Grodsky, "From the Covered Wagon to the Silicon Chip: Robert Noyce, Pioneer," *The Grinnell Magazine*, April–May 1983.
3. **Let's see if you can top:** Noyce in "Living Legends, Profiles from the National Business Hall of Fame," [video], ST. **He tried to excel:** Penny Noyce speaking at the SEMATECH memorial service for Bob Noyce, 9 June 1990 [video], ASB.
4. **Had never jumped:** Bill Davidow, interview by author. **Go out and do something:** Noyce in Bill Davidow, Gene Flath, and Robert Noyce oral history [1983], IA. **Like the pied piper:** Roger Borovoy, interview by author.
5. **Aloof and charming:** Andy Grove, interview by author.
6. **Everybody liked Bob:** Warren Buffett, interview by author.
7. **Portable telephones:** Noyce, interview by Herbert S. Kleiman, 1965, audiotape, SSC. **Butterfly hopping:** Andy Grove, interview by author.
8. **If you weren't intimidated by Noyce:** Jim Lafferty, interview by author.
9. **Thomas Edison and Henry Ford:** "Remembering Bob Noyce: A Special Tribute," four-page insert to *San Jose Mercury News*, 17 June 1990. **Man who changed the world:** "Osgood Files" [video], ASB. Tom Wolfe wrote about Noyce: Tom Wolfe, "The Tinkerings of Robert Noyce: How the Sun Rose on Silicon Valley," *Esquire*, Dec. 1983, 346–74. **Most important American:** George Gilder quoted in the internal Intel publication *Inteleads*, July 1990, IA. **Most important moment:** Isaac Asmiov quoted in Miller Bonner, W. Lane Boyd, and Janet A. Allen, "Robert N. Noyce, 1927–1990," commemorative brochure internally published by SEMATECH, ST.
10. **Roots are important:** Noyce's contribution to the Grinnell High School Class of 1945's fortieth reunion booklet, courtesy Robert Kaloupek. **My hobby is handicraft:** 1939 scrapbook labeled "My Hobby," ASB.

Chapter 1: Adrenaline and Gasoline

1. **All time high:** Noyce, Grinnell College application, courtesy Grinnell College. Scrapbook: "My Hobby," 1939, ASB.
2. **Paper balloons, lighting models afire:** Gaylord Noyce, eulogy at the San Jose service for Bob Noyce; Wilfred George, "'The Rest of the Story' about Dr. Robert Noyce," 4 Nov. 2001 [unpublished reminiscence], courtesy Wilfred George.
3. **Barnstormer plane ride:** Don Gregson, interview by author.
4. **Matthews and Smith contributions:** Bob Smith, interview by author; Charlotte Matthews, interview by author; Gaylord Noyce to author, 8 Sept. 2002. **Description of glider:** Gaylord Noyce to author, 8 Sept. 2002.
5. **We succeeded in running:** Gaylord Noyce to author, 8 Sept. 2002.
6. **Jump off the roof and live:** Noyce, Grinnell College application, courtesy Grinnell College.
7. **I made the paste:** Harriet Noyce, "I Remember" [unpublished memoir], 1988, DSN.
8. **Do a lot and do it well:** Gaylord Noyce, interview by author.
9. **To be Christian leaders:** Harriet Noyce, "I Remember."

10. **Denmark church:** Donald S. Noyce, "Candles to Computers" [unpublished family history], 133–150.

11. **Ralph Noyce's salary and expenses:** D. S. Noyce, "Candles to Computers," 133–148.

12. **Too bad he was a he:** undated letter, ASB.

13. **Ping Pong story:** Nilo Lindgren, "Building a Rational Two-Headed Monster," *Innovation*, 1970.

14. **Depression in Atlantic and Webster City:** D. S. Noyce, "Candles to Computers," 157–187. For reasons no one quite understood, the money from Reverend Noyce's account in the closed bank was restored a few weeks later.

15. **Someone to tell things to:** Ralph Brewster Noyce to Harriet Norton, 27 March 1921.

16. **Ralph Noyce's travel:** D. S. Noyce, "Candles to Computers."

17. **Mothering with a daddy on the road, I felt the sense of belonging:** Harriet Noyce, "I Remember," 34.

18. **Population of Grinnell:** "Report on Population, Grinnell Comprehensive Plan 2001," http://web.grinnell.edu/individuals/martzahn/Population.pdf Accessed Sept. 2002. **Church count:** "Grinnell During World War II" file, Collection #37, Stewart Library, Grinnell Room.

19. **Less than 2 percent:** *Historical Statistics of the United States*, Bicentennial ed. (Washington: U.S. Dept. of Commerce, Bureau of the Census, 1975): Series H 700–15. **Boys' great-great-grandfather:** "Robert Norton Noyce: in Admiration and Gratitude. A Resolution of the Grinnell College Board of Trustees, October 26, 1990," file labeled "Noyce Death," GCA.

20. **Rhodes scholarship:** Ralph B. Noyce to his mother, 9 Aug. 1949, DSN. **Noyce childhood grades:** report cards, ASB and DSN.

21. **D-Day in Grinnell:** Noyce refers to this in his valedictory speech (delivered 17 May 1945), courtesy Evan Ramstad.

22. **Nearly 2,000 men:** Alan Jones, *Pioneering: A Photographic and Documentary History of Grinnell College* (Grinnell College, 1996): 117. **Details on Grinnell's contributions to the war effort:** untitled scrapbook in "Grinnell During World War II," Collection #37, GRSPL.

23. **Harriet had her hands full:** Robert Smith, David Hamilton, and Charles Manly, interview by author. **Trying to build electrical arc:** Charlotte Matthews Keating, interview by author; Noyce's clipping of the *Popular Science* article is in his "My Hobby" scrapbook, ASB. **Noyce's high school antics:** author's interviews with Grinnell residents.

24. **Always in a hurry to get somewhere:** Robert Kaloupek, interview by author.

25. **All the girls were crazy about Bob:** Charlotte Matthews Keating, interview by author. **Most physically graceful:** Marianne Standing Woolfe, interview by Evan Ramstad, April 1995, courtesy Evan Ramstad. **Gift for trouble:** Harriet Noyce, "I Remember," 42.

26. **Very fine boy:** T. T. Cranny, letter recommending Bob's admission to Grinnell College, 26 April 1945, courtesy Grinnell College. **Quiz Kid of our class:** Grinnell High School year book, 1945, GRSPL. **Dismantling and rebuilding a watch:** Robert Smith, David Hamilton, and Charles Manly, interview by author.

27. **Noyce bereft at Gaylord's departure:** Harriet Noyce, "I Remember," 37.

28. **Relations between Noyces and Gales:** Grant Gale, "Remembering Bob Noyce as a Student," 4 Sept. 1990, DSN.

29. **Gale's teaching methods and homilies:** Keith Olsen, interview by author, 30 July 2002.
30. **Interest was infectious:** Noyce quoted in Ken Fuson, "The Man Who Shaped a Genius," *Des Moines Register*, 10 June 1990, GCA. **Noyce's behavior in Gale's class:** Bettie Noyce, interview by author. Bettie was a student in this course before she married Don Noyce.
31. **Almost a family tradition:** Noyce's college admissions essay, courtesy Grinnell College. **Bright but common:** Robert Smith, David Hamilton, and Charles Manly, interview by author.
32. **Getting a nice bit of review:** Bob Noyce to folks, "before July 1 [1945]," reprinted in D. S. Noyce, "Candles to Computers," 228.
33. **So Gay has seen the Statue of Liberty:** Bob Noyce to folks, "before July 1 [1945]," ibid.
34. **Whoopee!:** Undated fragment of a letter from the summer at Miami of Ohio, reprinted in D. S. Noyce, "Candles to Computers," 229.
35. **My front teeth almost fell out:** Bob Noyce to Home, 13 Aug. 1945, reprinted in D. S. Noyce, "Candles to Computers," 231.
36. **Another insignificant student:** letter fragment, 16 July [1945], reprinted in D. S. Noyce, "Candles to Computeres," 230. **We expect great things from you:** Samuel Stevens to Robert Noyce, 7 May 1945, courtesy Grinnell College.
37. **Interest in Smythe report:** Bob Noyce to Family, 22 Jan. [1946], ASB.
38. **He never pushed himself forward:** Scott Crom, interview by Evan Ramstad, April 1995, courtesy Evan Ramstad.
39. **Adrenaline and gasoline:** Ralph Noyce to Bob Noyce, 29 Oct. 1945, DSN.
40. **Noyce's academic work:** various letters, especially Bob Noyce to Home, undated but probably spring 1946, DSN. **You won't know:** Ralph Noyce to Bob Noyce, 29 Oct. 1945, DSN.
41. **I'm just sorry I've got such brothers:** Bob Noyce to Home, Wednesday night [no date, but probably 1947], ASB.
42. **$5 in the bank, $4 in my pocket:** Bob Noyce to Folks, 23 Sept. [1945], DSN. **$19 to buy shoes, not war bond:** Harriet Noyce, "I Remember," 36. **Check to the bank clerk:** letter fragment, 16 July [1945], reprinted in D. Noyce, "Candles to Computers," 230.
43. **Noyce's motivation for joining the diving team:** Bob Noyce to Folks, 23 Sept. [1945]. **Grinnell pool description:** George Drake, interview by author, 15 Aug. 2002.
44. **Envisioning myself at the next level:** Ann Bowers, interview by author, 22 June 2002.
45. **Noyce's diving championship:** "Midwest Conference Swimming and Diving Championships" (brochure) and accompanying newspaper articles, all ASB. **Noyce's concern that his parents might be disappointed:** Noyce to Folks, 7 March [1949], courtesy Penny Noyce.
46. **Description of the pig event and aftermath:** letters exchanged between Ralph Noyce and Grinnell College administration; Grant Gale, "Remarks Made at the Dedication Dinner of the Robert N. Noyce Science Center," 26 Sept. 1997, Gale Papers, GCA; and Ruth Greenwald, interview by author, 23 July 2002.
47. **Abortion:** mentioned in Rowland Cross, interview by Evan Ramstad, Feb. 1996, and confirmed by Penny Noyce, interview by author. **Coincidence with the pig incident:** based on Harriet Noyce's comment, in "I Remem-

ber" that Bob said he stole the pig because "I was in a lousy mood. I had a fight with [the girlfriend]" and on the author's knowledge of the rough dates during which the girlfriend and Bob dated.

48. **Mayor's motivation through intimidation:** "If you do not understand the necessity of getting in the scrap, of searching every corner of your property— well, you certainly can't read English." Clippings from "Grinnell During WWII," collection 37, GRSPL. **Dean would expel:** Grant Gale to George Drake, 6 June 1984, courtesy Evan Ramstad.

49. **In the agricultural state of Iowa:** Karl Dearborn (dean of Grinnell College Personnel Administration) to Ralph Noyce, 29 May 1948. A prize pig sold for $925 a month before Bob's pig heist according to the *Grinnell Herald-Register*, 26 April 1948).

50. **More concerned with hogs, have to be ready to accept youth's offer of repentance:** Ralph Noyce to Karl Dearborn, 2 June 1948, ASB.

51. **Annuitant table quite outdated:** Bob Noyce to Dad, July 1948, DSN. **Loneliness:** Bob Noyce to Dad, July 1948, DSN.

52. **Congratulations high dive brain child:** Western Union telegram from Mary Alice, 24 Feb. 1949, ASB. **Equitable job offer:** Noyce to Family Everywhere, 4 May 1949, courtesy Penny Noyce.

53. **Struck like an atom bomb:** "Living Legends" [video], ASB. **I couldn't grasp:** Bob Noyce, interview by T. R. Reid, 31 March 1982, courtesy T .R. Reid (henceforth Noyce, 1982 Reid interview).

54. **On the transistor and vacuum tubes:** Transistorized! (web page, http://www.pbs.org/transistor/); Riordan and Hoddeson, *Crystal Fire*.

55. **It was rather astonishing:** Noyce, 1982 Reid interview. **Phenomenally new:** "Living Legends" [video], ASB.

56. **They hooked up a microphone, in the tradition of Alexander Graham Bell:** Reid, *The Chip*, 50.

57. **Automatic transmissions, frozen foods coming on the market:** James T. Patterson, *Grand Expectations: The United States, 1945–1974* (New York: Oxford University Press, 1996): 70. *New York Times* **transistor story:** Ernest Braun and Stuart Macdonald, *Revolution in Miniature* (Cambridge: Cambridge University Press, 1982): cover image; Riordan and Hoddeson, *Crystal Fire*, 165.

58. **A load off a soldier's back, historians estimate:** army press release quoted in Riordan and Hoddeson, *Crystal Fire*, 169.

59. **Gale posting the clipping and his connections to the transistor:** Grant Gale to Dave Jordan, 22 March 1984, courtesy Evan Ramstad.

60. **Bell Labs monographs and Gale not receiving a transistor until after Noyce graduated:** In Gale to Jordan, 22 March 1984, Gale mentions an "attached original shipping invoice [for the transistors, sent from Bardeen to Gale] dated March 6, 1950" (now lost). Monograph titles are from a list in the Grant Gale papers, GCA.

61. **In electrical terms:** thanks to Ross Bassett for his edits on this and the following paragraph.

62. **Wriggled them just right:** Reid, *The Chip*, 50.

63. **A gross overstatement:** Grant Gale, untitled recollections of Bob Noyce, n.d., Gale Papers, GCA.

64. **MIT tuition scholarship:** Philip M. Morse to Bob Noyce, 25 March 1949, MITP.

65. **Best returns on the time spent studying:** Bob Noyce to Family Everywhere, 4 May 1949.

Chapter 2: Rapid Robert

1. **Noyce's scholarship:** Noyce's graduate school record, MITP. **Cost of a year at MIT:** *MIT Bulletin, June 1949, Catalogue Issue, 1949–1950.* **Construction site injury:** Ralph Noyce to Mother, 9 Aug. 1949, ASB. **Noyce shocked by country club extravagance:** Bob Noyce to Folks, 7 March [1947], ASB.
2. **Determination to secure a research fellowship:** Bob Noyce to Dear Family, 20 April [1950].
3. **MIT as a giant basement:** Penny Noyce, interview by author.
4. **Remote and austere:** Bud Wheelon , interview by author, 8 Oct. 2002.
5. **Incredibly difficult:** John Bailey, interview by author, 10 Oct. 2002. **Gale's request for an update on Noyce's progress** is referenced in Nathaniel Frank to Grant Gale, 24 May 1950, Grant Gale Papers, GCA.
6. **Asked girlfriend to stay away:** Bob Noyce to family, 25 Oct. 1949.
7. **Noyce's deficiencies:** Noyce graduate record, MITP. **Everyone did badly:** Noyce to family, 25 Oct. 1949.
8. **Bud Wheelon background:** Bud Wheelon, interview by author.
9. **Life looks unpleasant:** Bob Noyce to family, 25 Oct. 1949.
10. **How misdirected I am:** Bob Noyce to Folks, "Friday Evening," [clearly early in his time at MIT], courtesy Penny Noyce.
11. **29 out of 100, Slaughter and Flunk:** John Bailey, interview by author. **Noyce's course schedule:** MITP.
12. **John Slater's lectures:** David Jeffries, interview by author; Hugh Watson, interview by author.
13. **Physical Electronics seminar:** "Tenth Annual MIT Conference on Physical Electronics," [purple mimeographed program, 1949], Wayne Nottingham papers, MC 241, Box 1, Folder 30, MIT; "Dr. Nottingham of MIT Feted by Colleagues," *Boston Herald*, 27 March 1964, Wayne Nottingham Collection, MC 241, Box 1, Folder 3, MIT.
14. **Nottingham's course contents:** "Notes for Course 8.21 on Physical Electronics," [undated, probably 1949], "8.21 Notes, 1950," both in Wayne Nottingham Collection, MC 241, Box 1, Folder 21, MIT. By 1951, Nottingham was asking a few questions about semiconductors in his exams.
15. **Path of least resistance:** Noyce, 1982 Reid interview. **You had to study:** Noyce quoted in "Silicon Valley 'Father' Returns to Grinnell," *Times Republican* [Marshalltown, IA], 3 June 1989, ASB.
16. **Passed every course with honors:** MIT official transcript, ASB.
17. **Verbal shortcuts, dee x:** Maurice Newstein, interview by author.
18. **Wheelon-Slater conversation:** Bud Wheelon, interview by author.
19. **Teaching fellowship and staff award:** Noyce's graduate school record, MITP.
20. **He thought he should have stood up:** Maurice Newstein, interview by author. **Nothing good ever came from being angry:** Penny Noyce, interview by author. **Pass himself off as an expert:** Gaylord Noyce, interview by author.
21. **Raining beer party:** Jim Angell, interview by author, 6 June 2002; David Jeffries, interview by author.
22. **Chorus Pro Musica:** John Andres, interview by author; Henry Stroke, interview by author. **Smooth as silk:** John Andres, interview by author.
23. **Physical specimen:** Maurice Newstein, interview by author.
24. **Friends a challenge:** John Andres, interview with author; John Bailey, interview with author; Henry Stroke, interview with author.

25. **Noyce's building a telescope:** George Clark to author, 11 Feb. 2003. **Noyce's automatic mirror grinder:** Maurice Newstein, interview by author.
26. **Noyce's painting effort:** Maurice Newstein, interview by author.
27. **Noyce applying for Fulbright:** Noyce to Family, 22 Oct. 1950. **Noyce's rejecting Fulbright:** Harriet Noyce to Grant Gale, 20 Sept. 1951, Grant Gale Papers, GCA. **Faculty recommendations glowed:** "Noyce is one of our best graduate students, making a very fine record both as a student and on account of his general ability and character." "Noyce has displayed superior intellectual qualifications, and in addition to being an outstanding student is a very stable and pleasing person."
28. **Mr. Noyce has been an outstanding student:** Nathaniel Frank to Grant Gale, 24 May 1950, Grant Gale Papers, GCA.
29. **I was hoping something like this:** Bob Noyce to Dear Family, 20 April [1950].
30. **Noyce auditing at Harvard:** Graduate Record, MITP; Philip Morse to H. L. Hazen, 23 Sept. 1952, MITP.
31. **No thesis, no ski:** Bob Noyce to Family, no date, but Ralph responded 24 Nov. 1952, DSN.
32. **Professor's mind perverted:** Bob Noyce to Folks, 23 Sept. [1945], DSN. **Nottingham knew no theory:** Noyce to Family, 22 Oct. 1950, DSN.
33. **Atoms as houses:** many thanks to Jose Arreola for his cogent explanation of surface states.
34. **Noyce chose to study insulators:** Nottingham may have suggested insulators. One of his students, David Jeffries, had recently completed a master's thesis indicating that quartz would lend itself well to photoelectric investigations.
35. **Noyce had a hell of a time:** Jose Arreola, telephone conversation with author. **Noyce's dissertation work:** Robert Norton Noyce, "A Photoelectric Investigation of Surface States on Insulators," (unpublished MIT doctoral dissertation, September, 1953).
36. **Noyce's accident and visitors:** Bob Noyce to Folks, 13 Jan. 1953.
37. **Philco needed me:** Noyce quoted in Tekla Perry, "Famous First Jobs," *IEEE Spectrum*, July 1967: 48. **Noyce felt he would make a better name for himself:** Noyce had clearly mentioned this motivation in his interview for the Perry, "Famous First Jobs" article, but he deleted the reference to this ambition when he edited Perry's draft. Typescript of the "Famous First Jobs" article, IA.
38. **Brief conversation:** Harriet Noyce, "I Remember," 46. Reverend Noyce's notes from the time read, "Robert phoned about 3 o'clock Thursday afternoon August 20. **'Would you marry us?'** I had to ask the girl's name." Reprinted in Don Noyce, "Candles to Computers," 252. Bold in the original.
39. **Tongue as sharp as a razor:** Bob Noyce to Family, 21 May [1946?]. **Sharpen our wits:** Helen Bottomley quoted in Harriet Noyce to Dearest Mother, 27 Aug. 1953.
40. **Little human dynamo:** Helen Bottomley quoted in Harriet Noyce to Dearest Mother, 27 Aug. 1953.
41. **Production lines for entertainment:** Helen Bottomley quoted in Harriet Noyce to Dearest Mother, 27 Aug. 1953.
42. **All one could ask for, made her own decisions:** Harriet Noyce to Dearest Mother, 27 Aug. 1953.
43. **Noyce wanted to be free:** Harriet Noyce, "I Remember," 36.

44. **Old friends and family can slow you down:** Gaylord Noyce, interview by author.

45. **Feared Betty was pregnant:** Penny Noyce, interview by author.

46. **I felt it simply could not be:** Harriet Noyce, "I Remember." **Wedding description and preparations:** Don Noyce, "Candles to Computers," 252–253; Harriet Noyce, "I Remember," 46–47; Harriet Noyce to "Dearest Mother," 27 August 1953; Gaylord and Dotey Noyce, personal communications, 25 Nov. 2002 and 28 Nov. 2002; and George Clark, interview by author, 23 Oct. 2002.

47. **Darn:** Dotey Noyce, interview by author, 24 Oct. 2002.

48. **Harriet's comments:** Harriet Noyce to "Dearest Mother," 27 Aug. 1953; Ralph Noyce quoted in Don Noyce, "Candles to Computers," 252–253.

49. **It wouldn't have happened so soon:** Harriet Noyce to Dearest Mother, 27 Aug. 1953.

50. **They really say:** Harriet Noyce to Dearest Mother, 27 Aug. 1953.

51. **On Philco's military work:** John Paul Wolkonowicz, "The Philco Corporation: Historical Review and Strategic Analysis, 1892–1961," unpublished master's thesis (MIT, Management), 1981: 56; AR-82-34052, FMCA. **Navy line of credit:** "Philco Arranges $40,000,000 Three-Year V-Loan Credit for Defense Production," press release, 9 Jan. 1952, AR-84-56520, Box 1, FMCA.

52. **Useful member of society:** David B. Smith, Philco vice president of research, quoted in "Philco Research Develops First 'Surface-Barrier' Transistor for Military and Civilan Uses," Philco press release, AR-84-56520, Box 1, FMCA.

53. **IRE interest in surface-barrier transistor:** W. E. Bradley et al., "The Surface-Barrier Transistor, Part I–V," *Proceedings of the IRE* (Dec. 1953): 1702–1753.

54. **Noyce could contribute immediately:** Jim Angell, interview by author; George Messenger, interview by author; Frank Keiper, interview by author.

55. **Philco production innovation:** J. W. Tiley, "Part II—Electrochemical Techniques for Fabrication of Surface-Barrier Transistors," in "The Surface-Barrier Transistor, Part I–V," *Proceedings of the IRE* (Dec. 1953): 1706–1708. John Tiley, who developed the process, had no formal semiconductor education. Like many of his co-workers, he was a skill engineer who learned on the job. **Noyce's first patent:** #2,875,141, issued 24 Feb. 1959, filed 12 Aug. 1954. **Noyce's basic surface barrier paper:** R. N. Noyce and G. C. Messenger, "Surface Barrier Transistor Theory," 14 June 1955, courtesy George Messenger.

56. **Bocciarelli description:** Jim Angell, interview by author 6 June 2002. **When I talked in my sleep:** Noyce quoted in Tekla Perry, "Famous First Jobs."

57. **Bill Bradley description:** Albert Bradley to author, 4 April 2003. **White noise source:** Noyce quoted in Tekla Perry, "Famous First Jobs."

58. **Very easy to talk to:** George Messenger, interview by author. **Difficulty dealing with slow people:** Jim Angell, interview by author; George Messenger, interview by author; Frank Keiper, interview by author. **Image of cartoon bubble:** John Joss, interview by author.

59. **Highest mechanical precision:** "Philco Research Develops First 'Surface-Barrier' Transistor for Military and Civilian Uses," Philco press release, AR-84-56520, Box 1, FMCA. **Problems with transistor and Noyce's work to**

correct them: George Messenger, interview with author, 20 May 2002; Tekla Perry, "Famous First Jobs"; Frank Keiper, interview by author.

60. **Philco's problems:** *Philco Annual Report*, 1953–1956. By 1956, earnings were only $250,000. **Philco not convinced research pays:** Bob Noyce to Family, 9 March 1955.

61. **Bullshit, waste and good science:** Robert Noyce, interview by Herbert Kleiman, 1965, M827, SSC. **Noyce's procrastination on military compliance:** Joe Chapline, communication with author, 23 March 2002.

62. **Lousy job, took time away:** from Perry, "Famous First Jobs."

63. **Noyce taking car:** Betty Noyce to Family, Mon. [probably Spring 1955]. **Bob has got to go, Billy crying at sight of suitcase:** Betty Noyce to Grandmother and Mama H., Monday 22nd [1955], Adam Noyce papers, GCA. **What will they think of next:** Jim Angell, interview with author, 6 June 2002.

64. **Noyce never talked about his wife:** George Messenger, interview by author. **Kept her in the back:** Frank Keiper, interview by author.

65. **Betty wanted a house:** Betty Noyce to Family, Tuesday [probably August 1955], DSN. **Too snobbish:** Bob and Betty Noyce to Family, 9 March 1955, Adam Noyce papers, GCA.

66. **Westinghouse offer:** Betty Noyce to Folks, Nov. 1955 and Mon. AM, Adam Noyce Papers, GCA. **Start thinking of a permanent site:** Betty Noyce to Folks, 6 July 1955 and Monday eve [probably Aug. 1955], DSN.

67. **Noyce's statement of assets:** Noyce to Col. Paul G. Armstrong, Director of Illinois Selective Service System, 26 Aug. 1955, ASB.

68. **Indefinite postponement of induction:** Selective Service System Postponement of Induction, 12 Dec. 1955, ASB. **House decorated for Christmas:** Noyce to his parents, 20 Dec. 1955. This letter was written on the train home after a visit to Wright Field to visit with the Air Force's "transistor personnel." **Walk away:** Noyce quoted in Perry, "Famous First Jobs."

69. **Shockley's call:** date is from entry labeled "Noyce," in Record Book labeled "Jn-Fe 1956," (also in unmarked hardbound book, page 53), Shockley Papers, 95–153, Box B2, SSC. Shockley called Noyce again on Monday 30 January. **Shockley here:** Gordon Moore, interview by author. **Like talking to God:** Noyce quoted in Reid, *The Chip*, 73.

Chapter 3: Apprenticeship

1. **Half the worthwhile ideas:** Raymond M. Warner, Jr., "Microelectronics: Its Unusual Origin and Personality," *IEEE Transactions on Electron Devices* 48 (Nov. 2001): 2457–2467. Warner worked in transistor development at Bell Labs through most of the 1950s. **Shockley's efforts on behalf of his wife:** folder marked "JBS," Shockley Papers, 95-153, Box B2, SSC.

2. **Whole damn thing, Oh hell, Shockley, patent attorney's findings:** Michael Riordan and Lillian Hoddeson, *Crystal Fire: The Birth of the Information Age* (New York: W. W. Norton and Company, 1997): 145. Unless otherwise noted, sources for the description of Shockley and his work before starting his company are Riordan and Hoddeson, *Crystal Fire*; "Transistorized!" www.pbs.org/transistor/background1/events/nobelprize.html; and James M. Early, "Out to Murray Hill to Play: An Early History of Transistors," *IEEE Transactions on Electron Devices* 48 (Nov. 2001): 2468–72.

3. **Divorce from Jean Shockley:** Jean Shockley to Bill Shockley, 4 March 1946, in a folder marked "JBS," Shockley Papers, 95–153, Box B2, SSC.
4. **Shockley's fundraising attempts:** Riordan and Hoddeson, *Crystal Fire*, 232–233.
5. **Beckman 1955 performance:** *Beckman Instruments Annual Report*, 1954, 1955.
6. **Insurance against obsolescence:** *Beckman Instruments Annual Report*, 1955, 1956.
7. **Engage promptly and vigorously:** Arnold Beckman to William Shockley, 3 Sept. 1955, Shockley Papers, Accession #95–153, Box 4B, SSC. **Projected sales:** Terman Papers, Series III, Box 48, SSC. **Payment to Bell Labs:** Riordan and Hoddeson, *Crystal Fire*, 240.
8. **Information on Palo Alto:** Ward Winslow and the Palo Alto Historical Association, *Palo Alto: A Centennial History* (Palo Alto: Palo Alto Historical Association, 1993).
9. **Bearing fruit trees:** "Veterans—here's your 'Home among the Trees'" (advertisement), reprinted in Winslow, *Palo Alto*, 116.
10. **Community of technical scholars:** Terman quoted in Henry Lowood, "From Steeples of Excellence to Silicon Valley," (Varian Associates, 1987). **For more on Stanford's and Terman's efforts to attract industry:** Rebecca Lowen, *Creating the Cold War University: The Transformation of Stanford* (Berkeley: University of California Press, 1997); Margaret Pugh O'Mara, *Cities of Knowledge: Cold War Science and the Search for the Next Silicon Valley* (Princeton, New Jersey: Princeton University Press, 2004), chap. 3
11. **Stanford would heartily welcome, an exciting business:** Frederick Terman to William Shockley, 20 Sept. 1955; Terman Papers, Series III, Box 48, SSC.
12. **Playing for big stakes:** Note scrawled on yellow piece of paper, Terman Papers, Series III, Box 48, SSC.
13. **Mental temperature:** "Secrets of the Mind," *Newsweek*, 6 Dec. 1954, 72–73.
14. **No substitute for superiority:** *Beckman Instruments Annual Report*, 1955.
15. **Semiconductor symposium:** J. W. Faust [program chair of Semiconductor Symposium] to Shockley, no date, in folder marked "Meetings 1956," Shockley papers, Accession 95–153, Box B2. **Description of the conference:** program of the Electrochemical Society's 108th meeting, courtesy Electrochemical Society.
16. **Noyce only scientist:** entry dated October 10, 1955 in green memoranda notebook, Shockley Papers, Accession number 95–153, box 2B. This entry includes the comment "no other good man at Philco." Many thanks to Ross Bassett for his technical assistance on the "punch-through" problem.
17. **Is your future brighter?** Entry at page 67 in unmarked hardbound book, Shockley papers, 95–153, B2.
18. **All Iowans think:** "Quick Thinking for Chips," *The Economist*, 27 Dec. 1983. In Perry, "Famous First Jobs," Noyce recalled that someone in his hometown once put up a sign that read "California does not exist!" in a novel effort to keep young people from moving away. **Wanted to return to research:** Shockley's notes read, "Would like to live in WC [West Coast] . . . Leaving Philco?—management not R. [research] minded." Entry labeled "Noyce," in Record Book labeled "Jn–Fe 1956," Shockley Papers, SSC. **Getting that job:** Noyce quoted in Reid, *The Chip*, 73. **Wanted to see if I could stand up:** Noyce, 1982 Reid interview.

19. **Two-year agreement:** Penny Noyce, interview by author; Phyllis Kefauver, interview by author.
20. **Tennis problem:** James F. Gibbons, interview with author. Throughout his life, Shockley posed this question to people.
21. **Too much time on whether I liked my mother:** Fairchild Founder B, interviewed by author. **Line-drawing question:** Harry Sello, interview with author.
22. **First things first:** Noyce quoted in "Quick Thinking for Chips," *The Economist*, 27 Dec. 1980. **Date of Noyce's arrival:** entry labeled "Noyce," Record Book labeled Jn–Fe 1956, Shockley papers.
23. **Damn steady hands:** Jay Last, interview by Charlie Sporck.
24. **Descriptions of Shockley scientists:** author's interviews of the subjects and Charlie Sporck's interviews of the subjects, some of which have been excerpted in his book, Charlie Sporck, *Spinoff: A Personal History of the Industry that Changed the World* (Sarnac Lake Publishing, 2001).
25. **Only a handful over 30:** "Present Employees," May 21, 1956, unmarked hardback book, Shockley Papers 95–153, page 81, SSC. **Actually making a product:** Gordon Moore, interview by Allen Chen, 9 July 1992, IA.
26. **You'd do it his way:** James F. Gibbons, interview by author. Gibbons recalls receiving a letter in which Shockley spelled out his ideas quite explicitly.
27. **Salaries:** "Payroll Projected to July 1, 1956," unmarked hardback book, page 82, Shockley Papers, Accession #95–153, B2, SSC. **Icicles:** Fairchild Founder A, interview by author.
28. **He hadn't shaved:** Julius Blank, interview by Charlie Sporck. Blank tells a censored version of this story in Bob Ristelhueber, "Noyce Remembered: Unusual Ideas, Unusual Approaches," *Electronic News*, 11 June 1990.
29. **Rose in his teeth:** Riordan and Hoddeson, *Crystal Fire*.
30. **Shockley's early advocacy of silicon:** Letter excerpted in Riordan and Hoddeson, *Crystal Fire*, 230.
31. **Barbecue analogy:** Reid, *The Chip*, 73–74. Before the invention of the diffusion method, silicon devices had been built using either grown junction techniques or alloy techniques. **Shockley sent Noyce and Moore to Bell Labs seminar:** Noyce, 1982 Reid interview.
32. **Concern about outfitting lab:** Fairchild Founder A, interview by author. **Auto-parts warehouse:** Riordan and Hoddeson, *Crystal Fire*, 237.
33. **Description of lab space:** Harry Sello, interview by author.
34. **Clean vacuum-pump story:** Fairchild Founder B, interview by author. **In his mind:** Fairchild Founder A, interview by Christophe Lecuyer on 6 July 1996. Personal communication from Lecuyer to author, 11 Nov.1999.
35. **Noyce's contributions at Shockley:** Unmarked hardback book, pages 68, 71, and 81; entry dated 5 Jun 57, Empire Notebook, both in Shockley Papers, Accession #95–153, B2, SSC.
36. **Quiet leadership style:** R. Victor Jones, interview by author. **Felt they learned more from Noyce:** Fairchild Founder A, interview by author; Harry Sello, interview by author; "Dr. Moore, Tape 2, 6/8/94," IA.
37. **Noyce's only opinion that mattered:** Fairchild Founder A, interview by author; Harry Sello, interview by author.
38. **Noyce's tunnel diode:** Lab book entry dated 14 Aug. 1956, inserted at the front of his Fairchild lab book. How he managed to copy these pages is unclear—photocopy technology was in its infancy in the late-1950s, and Noyce

makes no note of going back to his Shockley notebooks later in his life—but that the pages are legitimate are indisputable. The only surviving notebook from Shockley Labs belonged to William Shockley and resides in the Special Collections of Stanford University. The pages on which Noyce's ideas are written are clearly from the same type of lab book that William Shockley issued to his staff, and this fact, along with the date of Noyce's work (which correlates with his 1979 comments about it), and Moore's recollections of the event further validate their authenticity.

39. **Balls tunneling through the wall:** Professor Stig Lundqvist of the Royal Academy of Sciences used this analogy in his speech presenting the 1973 Nobel Prize to Leo Esaki, Ivar Giaever, and Brian David Josephson.

40. **Boss showed no interest, powerful demotivator:** Noyce, "Innovation: The Fruit of Success," *Technology Review*, Feb. 1978: 24–27.

41. **Esaki's seminal paper:** Leo Esaki, "New Phenomenon in Narrow Germanium P-N Junctions, *Physical Review*, 1958, 109: 603. Esaki conducted his research in 1957, at roughly the same time Noyce noted his ideas. **On the response to this paper:** Leo Esaki, "The Global Reach of Japanese Science," http://www.jspsusa.org/FORUM1996/esaki.html, accessed 1 Nov. 2004.

42. **Similarities in Noyce and Esaki's work:** Both men used an energy-band diagram that represents the allowed energies on the y axis for electrons and holes versus their position in the P-N junction on the x axis. It shows where the electrons and holes are located. At small voltages, there are holes at the same energy as electrons, so tunneling current can flow, but at somewhat higher voltages, the electrons and holes are no longer at the same energy and the tunneling current ceases. Esaki and Noyce both also drew very similar current-versus-voltage graphs illustrating the unexpected drop in current in the region of negative resistance. **If I had gone one step further:** Gordon Moore, interview by author, 1 July 2004.

43. **Equivalent amount of knowledge:** Gordon Moore, interview by author, 1 July 2004. **When Shockley asked:** Michael F. Wolff, "The Genesis of the Integrated Circuit: How a Pair of U.S. Innovators Brought Into Reality a Concept that was on the Minds of Many," *IEEE Spectrum*, Aug. 1976, 49. Various versions of this story exist, including an official straw poll, but Wolff writes that Noyce confirmed this version of the story, albeit "with some embarrassment."

44. **Redesign bolts:** Eugene Kleiner, interview by Charlie Sporck; Jay Last quoted in Raymond M. Warner, "Microelectronics: Its Unusual Origin and Personality," *IEEE Transactions on Electron Devices* (Nov. 2001): 2457–2467, at 2461. **Hoerni's "banishment":** Jean Hoerni, interview by Charlie Sporck; Jay Last, interview by Charlie Sporck; Fairchild Founders A and B, interview by author.

45. **Blind leading blind:** Julius Blank, interview by Charlie Sporck, 15 July 1994.

46. **Would have taken six months:** Julius Blank, interview by Charlie Sporck.

47. **Shockley had a marvelous ability:** Noyce, 1982 Reid interview. **Electrons like cars in parking lot:** William Shockley, *Electrons and Holes in Semiconductors* (New York: D. Van Nostrand: 1950).

48. **Shockley's car and favorite restaurant:** Gordon Moore, interview by author.

49. **Champagne celebration:** "Oh, I certainly remember the day Bill got the Nobel Prize! I never [before had] adjourned to start drinking champagne at 9:00 in the morning!" Gordon Moore, quoted in "Transistorized!" www.pbs.org/transistor/background1/events/nobelprize.html

50. **Bardeen dropped:** "Transistorized!" www.pbs.org/transistor/background1/events/nobelprize.html

51. **Papers given by Bardeen, Brattain, and Shockley:** Nobel Prize Web site: www.nobel.se/physics/laureates/1956

52. **Invited him to join:** Riordan and Hoddeson, *Crystal Fire.*

53. **About time:** Vic Grinich, interview by Charlie Sporck.

54. **That will teach you:** Jay Last, interview by Charlie Sporck. **Salary figure:** "Payroll Projected to July 1, 1956," from unmarked hardback book in Shockley papers, accession 95–153, B2. **Am I really needed:** Noyce, "Innovation: The Fruit of Success," *Technology Review.*

55. **Only one light bulb:** Harry Sello, interview by author.

56. **Reduce almost to tears:** Harry Sello, interview by author. **Ritual humiliation:** Bob White, interview by author. White taught with Shockley at Stanford.

57. **Big psychiatric institute and quoting Eliot:** Jay Last, interview by Charlie Sporck. **Thumbtack in the door:** every Shockley employee interviewed gave a consistent account of this affair.

58. **Last confiding in Noyce:** Jay Last, interview by author; Jay Last, interview by Charlie Sporck.

59. **Data-processing group:** *Beckman Instruments Annual Report 1956.*

60. **Ran for benefit of his personality:** Shockley Employee A, interview by author.

61. **Four-layer diode:** "Inventor Cites Use in Computer," *Electronic News,* 24 Feb. 1958.

62. **Appeal of four-layer diode:** Fairchild Founder A, interview by author. For more on the difficulties of manufacturing the four-layer diode, see Riordan and Hoddeson, *Crystal Fire,* 267.

63. **Focus on transistor:** Gordon Moore, interview by author; Noyce, "Innovation: the Fruit of Success"; Fairchild Founder A recalls Noyce as the first member of the group to see the great potential in the transistor. Fairchild Founder A, interview by author. See also Riordan and Hoddeson, *Crystal Fire,* 250. **Plenty of market:** "Dr. Moore, Tape 2, 6/8/94." **Noyce's work with data systems operation:** Noyce to Bill Gunning [Data and Control Systems group], 17 April 1957, folder labeled "BECKMAN -Scien Instr Div"; Taylor C. Fletcher [head of the Data and Control Systems Group] to Shockley, 2 Nov. 1956, File labeled "BECKMAN-Fullerton 55–56," Shockley Papers, 90–117, Box 14, SSC.

64. **Offer to IBM:** Shockley to Bishop, 2 May 1957, Shockley papers, 90–117, Box 14.

65. **Mesa transistors:** K. J. Dean and G. White, "The Semiconductor Story: Search for the Best Transistor" (Part 2 of a four-part series), *Wireless World,* Feb. 1973, 67. This series of papers is a technical-but-readable introduction to semiconductor research and manufacturing.

66. **Bob you could talk to:** R. Victor Jones, interview by author.

67. **Certainly they knew:** patent in question is Shockley and Noyce, #2,967,985, filed 11 April 1957, granted 10 Jan. 1961. Though it is unclear how he did it, Shockley later had ownership of this patent assigned entirely to himself as an individual—a highly unusual situation, since most ownership assignments are to corporations.

68. **Certain inadequacies:** *Beckman Instruments Annual Report,* 1957.

69. **May 1957 meeting:** "Minutes of Interdivisional Research and Engineering Conference," folder marked "Beckman—1957," 16 May 1957, Shockley Papers 90–117, Box 14, SSC.

70. **Description of the meetings among Shockley, Beckman, and the scientists**: Gordon Moore, interview by author, and Riordan and Hoddeson, *Crystal Fire*, 247–251.
71. **Doing awful things, Vic Jones's departure**: R. Victor Jones, interview by author. Shockley was disappointed by Jones's decision but nonetheless gave him a glowing recommendation—a recommendation Shockley later turned to his own advantage by reading it aloud at an employee meeting. **Some drastic action**: Bob to "Everybody," 28 May 1957, courtesy Polly Noyce. **Look, goddammit**: Jay Last, interview by author.
72. **Voice quaking with anxiety**: Jay Last, interview by Charlie Sporck.
73. **First meeting with Beckman:** Somehow Shockley got enough information about this meeting to sketch out a diagram showing the seating arrangements of Beckman and the group. The sketch shows Beckman at one end of the table, with Noyce immediately to his right, followed by Kleiner, Hoerni, Grinich, Roberts, Moore, Last, and Knapic. Empire Notebook, Shockley Papers, Accession #95-153. **All Noyce quotes in this paragraph:** Noyce to Everyone, 28 May 1957, courtesy Polly Noyce.
74. **Shockley's reaction:** Harry Sello, interview by author; James F. Gibbons, interview by author; Riordan and Hoddeson, *Crystal Fire*, 249. **Drill sergeant analogy**: James F. Gibbons, interview by author.
75. **All quotes in discussion between Noyce and Shockley:** Entry dated 3 June 1957, Empire Notebook, Shockley Papers, Accession #95-153.
76. **Analyze staff from afar:** Noyce to Everyone, 28 May 1957. **Noyce's divided loyalties:** Several of the scientists thought that Noyce's relationship with Shockley was "cool" during the period of greatest tension. During this period, however, Shockley's notebook is full of entries like these: "Call to Noyce," "Noyce has only one suggestion," "Talk with Noyce." He recorded few conversations with any other lab employee, with the exception of Smoot Horsley.
77. **New organizational structure:** Entry labeled 6 Jun, Empire Notebook. Horsley, Knapic, and "S" [probably Sah] would report to Noyce. **Noyce lacked push:** "Impressions from AOB, call Thurs PM 6 Jun," Shockley Papers, Accession #95-153, SSC.
78. **Managing committee:** the other two members were Dean Knapic (production head), and E. L. Peterson (administration).
79. **Beckman's decision to support Shockley:** For more on this, see Riordan and Hoddeson, *Crystal Fire*, 250; Gordon Moore, interview by author.
80. **A very good man:** Bob and Betty Noyce to Family, 11 July 1957, courtesy Polly Noyce.
81. **More confident of eventual success:** Bob and Betty Noyce to Everybody, 28 May 1957.
82. **Atmosphere turned ugly:** "To say the least," administrative head Peterson wrote to Shockley, "the reaction was not favorable" E. L. Peterson to Shockley, dated August 7, 1957, Shockley Papers, Accession #95-153, SSC.
83. **Back where they were:** Letter to M. C. Hanafin from E. I. Peterson. Subject is Payroll Detail, Senior Staff, as of July 31, 1957, Shockley Papers, Accession #95-153. **Grossly overestimated our power:** Gordon Moore, "William Shockley," http://www.time.com/time/time100/scientist/profile/Shockley.html
84. **Last had another offer:** Jay Last, interview by author; Jay Last, interview by Charlie Sporck.

85. **He had joined Shockley:** Noyce's handwritten corrections to a draft of the article later published as Perry, "Famous First Jobs." **Son of a minister:** Fairchild Founder B, interview by author. Arthur Rock made similar comments about Noyce's sense of loyalty. Arthur Rock, interview by author, 25 Feb. 1999.

86. **The initial product:** Prospectus sent to Hayden, Stone, courtesy Jay Last.

87. **Horizontal ties are strong:** Prospectus sent to Hayden, Stone, courtesy Jay Last. **Concerns:** Julius Blank to author, 17 June 2003.

88. **Strongest selling point:** Arthur Rock, interview by author.

89. **Visit the seven:** Arthur Rock, interview by author; "Done Deals" excerpt by Arthur Rock, reprinted in *Upside Magazine*, Nov. 2000.

90. **Pretty good guys, need $1 million:** Arthur Rock, interview by author.

91. **Attachment to Bay Area:** Kleiner's original letter to Hayden, Stone, and Co. explicitly refers to the group's "attachment to this lower San Francisco peninsula area." Gordon Moore has jokingly called the desire not to move "the entrepreneurial spirit that drove the formation of Fairchild Semiconductor." Gordon Moore interview by Alan Chen.

92. **Not going to give away the store:** Fairchild Founder A, interview by Christophe Lécuyer.

93. **Chickening out:** Gordon Moore, interview by Alan Chen, IA. **Noyce's concerns:** John W. Wilson, *The New Venturers: Inside the High-Stakes World of Venture Capital*, (Menlo Park, Calif.: Addison-Wesley, 1985): 32.

94. **Two primary reasons:** Betty and Bob Noyce to Family, 11 July 1957.

95. **Nice to have you here:** Julius Blank, interview by author.

96. **Some kind of leader:** Arthur Rock, interview by author. **Big talker:** Fairchild Founder A, interview by author.

97. **Dollar bill ceremony:** Fairchild Founder A, interview by author.

Chapter 4: Breakaway

1. **Companies approached by group:** List reprinted in "Founding Documents."

2. **Noyce soaked his trees:** Betty and Gordon Moore, interview by Evan Ramstad, 18 May 1997. Courtesy Evan Ramstad.

3. **Transistor sales:** Statistics are for Oct. 1957. "1958: Everybody's Doin' It," and "The Transistor Emerges," *EN 25th Anniversary Issue*, 25 Jan. 1982, Section 2, pages 6, 23. Alfred Cook and Bob Shephard, "Heavy Commercial Push Top Feature at Wescon," *Electronic News*, 26 Aug. 1957, 1. **Dozen new transistor firms:** Richard Levin, "The Semiconductor Industry," in *Government and Technical Progress: A Cross-Industry Analysis*, ed. Richard R. Nelson (New York, 1982): 29.

4. **Every company turned them down:** Gordon Moore, interview by Alan Chen, IA. **Ethos of conformity:** Arthur Rock, interview by author.

5. **Wore a fresh pretty girl:** Multifarious Sherman Fairchild, *Fortune*, May 1960, 170; "Sherman Fairchild, Man of Few Miscalculations," *Electronic News*, 13 Sept. 1965, 8. Fairchild had studied at Cordon Bleu and thanks to a stint in the music-publishing business, he was on genial terms with the likes of George Gershwin and Jerome Kearn, whom he may have entertained at the French chateau he built for himself on Long Island. Yet at other times, Fairchild could be surprisingly thrifty. In his interview with the author, Richard Hodgson

said that after the starlet- and celebrity-filled weekend parties at his Long Island estate, Fairchild would have his cook drive the leftovers to the Manhattan townhouse.

6. **Acquisitions were easiest entrée:** Fairchild Camera and Instrument Board of Directors meeting minutes (henceforth FCI board minutes) for 21 Nov. 1957. Owner has requested anonymity.

7. **1957 uses of semiconductors:** Ken Stein, "Experience in Field is Opening Markets," *Electronic News*, 17 Feb. 1958, 1. **Had considered six months before:** *Fairchild Camera and Instrument Annual Report 1957.* **Fairchild primed and eager:** Noyce quoted in "Fairchild Semiconductor Corporation: Company Profile," *Solid State Journal*, Sept./Oct. 1960, 1.

8. **Get the company into electronics:** Richard Hodgson, interview by author. **Just right personality:** Fairchild Founder B, interview by author.

9. **Never going to be a problem:** Richard Hodgson, interview by author. Arnold Beckman later apparently rued his largesse. In 1962, after Shockley Transistor had been sold for underperformance, and the fortunes of Fairchild Semiconductor continued to soar, he said of "labor pirating": "Employer and employee alike should re-examine the moral precepts involved to determine what constitutes good ethical behavior. . . . If voluntary action should prove inadequate to maintain fair business practices, then it may be necessary to amplify legal controls." Robert R. Dockson, "A Comprehensive Study of the Electronics Industry," *Western Electronic News*, Nov. 1962, 17.

10. **Selling the group:** Bob Noyce to Mother and Dad, 4 Sept. 1957, courtesy Polly Noyce.

11. **Formal negotiations:** The negotiations were technically between the group of eight and Fairchild Controls, a subsidiary of Camera and Instrument. **Rock and Coyle ensured:** "Scientists meet with Coyle, Hodgkins [sic], and Somerwine," courtesy Jay Last. This document outlines an offer made by Fairchild and immediately rejected by Coyle.

12. **Works every time:** This story is from Julius Blank, interview by author.

13. **All quotes in this paragraph:** Bob Noyce to Mother and Dad, 4 Sept. 1957, courtesy Polly Noyce.

14. **Moore saddened:** Gordon Moore, interview by author.

15. **PhD production line:** Fairchild Founder A, interview by author.

16. **No real effect:** "8 Leave Shockley to Form Coast Semiconductor Firm," *Electronic News*, 20 Oct. 1957. **German scientists used to hierarchy:** James F. Gibbons, interview by author.

17. **Shockley hired an informant:** L. N. Duryea to Erickson, Wright, Hanafin, and Steinmeyer, Shockley papers, Accession # 95–153, SSC. **Patents filed by Shockley after Noyce left:** Noyce patent 2,869,055, filed 20 Sept. 1957, issued 13 Jan. 1959; Noyce patent 3,010,033, filed 2 Jan. 1958, issued 21 Nov. 1961; Noyce patent 3,111,590, filed 5 June 1958, issued 19 Nov. 1963; Noyce patent 3,098,160, filed 24 Feb. 1958, issued 26 Dec. 1961.

18. **Moses of Silicon Valley:** F. Seitz quoted in Riordan and Hoddeson, *Crystal Fire*, 275.

19. **Beckman feels:** Summary of Remarks, A. O. Beckman, 22 Sept. 1957, courtesy Jay Last.

20. **Betty in tears and Mrs. Shockley's last visit:** Polly Noyce, interview by author.

21. **Hello, Bob, How could you do this:** Malone, *Big Score*, 80.
22. **300 shares held in reserve:** Minutes of the First Meeting of Board of Directors of Fairchild Semiconductor Corporation (henceforth FSC board minutes), 16 Oct. 1957, Anon. **Voting trust:** There were seven voting trustees—Noyce and Kleiner; Carter, Hodgson, and two other Camera and Instrument senior managers; and Bud Coyle from Hayden, Stone. **Details of contract:** Contract between "the California Group" and "Fairchild Controls," 19 Sept. 1957, Shockley Papers, Accession # 95–153, SSC. See also letter from Bob Noyce to employees, "Fairchild Semiconductor, 1957–1977" (booklet of reproduced items pertaining to the first 20 years of Fairchild Semiconductor's existence), SSC. **A very good deal for both:** Fairchild Founder A, interview by author.
23. **I hope to hell:** Jay Last, interview by author.
24. **Refrigerator salesman story:** Penny Noyce, interview with author, 9 April 2002.
25. **To cover necessary expenditures:** Richard Hodgson to Bob Noyce, 2 Oct. 1957, Misc 581, SSC. **Noyce earned more:** Salaries for Blank, Grinich, Hoerni, Last, and Moore were $13,800. Kleiner and Roberts were paid $14,700 per year. Noyce received $15,600. FSC board minutes, Anon.
26. **Other founders "associated with Dr. Noyce":** "8 Leave Shockley to Form Coast Semiconductor Firm," *Electronic News*, 20 Oct. 1957. **More of a politician:** Jean Hoerni, interview by Charlie Sporck. **Always be captain:** Fairchild Founder A, interview by author.
27. **Sputnik launch:** Vic Grinich, interview by Charlie Sporck.
28. **Carefully moving:** Nelson Stone, interview by author.
29. **Didn't know bupkis:** Tom Bay, interview by author.
30. **Photo reconnaissance systems:** FCI board minutes, 20 March 1958, Anon.
31. **Air Force required:** Lecuyer, "Fairchild Semiconductor," 167–168.
32. **Bob is so articulate, never a doubt in his mind:** Tom Bay, interview by author.
33. **Private meeting:** Richard Hodgson, interview by author, 19 May 1999; "Fairchild Semiconductor Corporation: Company Profile," *Solid State Journal*, Sept./Oct. 1960, 1.
34. **IBM left little to chance:** Lecuyer, "Making Silicon Valley," 166.
35. **Develop own equipment, order elements from Sweden:** Gordon Moore, interview by Alan Chen. **Wafers the size of a dime**: Noyce speaks of "5/8-inch wafers" in 1963 in Noyce, "The Integrated Circuit: Origins and Impacts," *Core 1.3* [Magazine of the Computer Museum History Center], Sept. 2000, originally printed in The Computer Museum Reports, Vol. 11, Winter 1984–1985. Thanks to Ross Bassett for pointing me to this article.
36. **Noyce went to a photography store:** Gordon Moore, interview by Alan Chen.
37. **Work with Eastman Kodak:** Lecuyer, "Making Silicon Valley," 170.
38. **Low transistor yields:** At Fairchild Semiconductor in 1960, for example, Gordon Moore reported that yields were 85 percent at wafer test—and of this percentage, on 54 percent were fully operational at the end of processing. He called such results "a rather substantial improvement." "Progress Report—Physics Section, 1 April 1960," Fairchild R&D Division, Technical Reports and Progress Reports, M1055, SSC.
39. **Breakdown of job responsibilities:** L. N. Duryea to Erickson, Wright, Hanafin, and Steinmeyer.

40. **Noyce was the technical head:** Julius Blank, interview by Charlie Sporck.
41. **Everything but our names:** David Diffenderfer, interview by author, 1 May 2003.
42. **Baldwin never put in the cursory $500:** Gordon Moore, interview by Rob Walker, 18 Sept. 1995. Video, Silicon Genesis Collection, SSC. **Baldwin pressing for more stock:** Richard Hodgson, interview by author.
43. **An allowance:** Richard Hodgson, interview by author.
44. **Shoot ten times that high:** Bay quoted in Don Hoefler, "I Didn't Raise My Boy to be a Manager," *Electronic News*, 17 Oct. 1966. **Do one thing well:** Noyce, 1982 Reid interview.
45. **Group in circle:** Julius Blank, interview by author.
46. **We scooped the industry:** Last "meeting notes" notebook, courtesy Jay Last. **Details on Wescon and introduction of the Fairchild transistor:** Lecuyer, "Fairchild Semiconductor," 171.

Chapter 5: Invention

1. **All Fairchild notebooks:** Anon.
2. **On Shockley's research method:** Sheldon Roberts, interview by Christophe Lecuyer, 6 July 1996.
3. **Know the science, find not seek:** Noyce's comments recalled by Kathy Cohen, interview by author.
4. **Think about the fundamentals:** Sheldon Roberts interview by Lecuyer. **Ask himself why won't this work:** "Quick Thinking for Chips," *Economist*, 27 Dec. 1980.
5. **Many ideas, some of them good:** Gordon Moore, interview by author.
6. **Exchange between Noyce and Moore on aluminum contacts:** Gordon Moore, interview by author.
7. **All the conventional wisdom:** Gordon Moore, interview by author.
8. **Serve in many of the same applications:** Noyce notebook #8, entry dated 12 Jan. 1959. Patent for this device is Robert N. Noyce, "Semiconductor Scanning Device," U.S. Patent 2,959,681, filed 18 June 1959, patented 8 Nov. 1960. He also patented the switching device as Robert N. Noyce, "Semiconductor Switching Device," U.S. Patent #2,971,139, filed 16 June 1959, patented 7 Feb. 1961.
9. **Problems with aluminum contacts:** Gordon Moore notebook #6, entry dated 5 April 1958. **Noyce's suggestions:** Pulling-away ideas—Noyce notebook #8, entry dated 10 March 1958. **Nickel plating:** Noyce notebook #8, entry dated 25 Feb. 1958.
10. **Pure aluminum works:** Gordon Moore notebook #6, entry dated 2 May 1958. **Aluminum contact patent:** Gordon E. Moore and Robert N. Noyce, "Method for Fabricating Transistors," U.S. Patent 3,108,359, filed 30 June 1959, granted 29 Oct. 1963.
11. **Refer to IBM specifications:** Noyce lab notebook #8, 7; Moore lab notebook #6, 27. **The only thing that's technologically exciting:** Noyce quoted in Woolf, "Genesis of the Integrated Circuit," 53.
12. **Important as the wheel:** John Bardeen, quoted in "Passages," *Time*, 18 June 1990, 103.
13. **Failure within first two minutes:** Siekman, "In Electronics, the Big Stakes Ride on Tiny Chips," 122.

14. **Military efforts:** For more on the "Tinkertoy," "Micromodule," and "Molecular Electronics" projects, see Braun and MacDonald, *Revolution in Miniature*, 88–98; Reid, *The Chip*, 19–20; Wolff, "The Genesis of the Integrated Circuit," 49. The discussion of the tyranny of numbers in this book relies heavily on these sources, particularly Reid. **At least 20 companies:** Herbert S. Kleiman "The Integrated Circuit: A Case Study of Product Innovation in the Electronics Industry," (PhD diss., New York University, 1966): 114.
15. **Building up of an oxide layer:** Jean Hoerni, lab notebook #3, 3.
16. **Quotes and descriptions of tap testing:** Moore notebook #6, entry dated 3 July 1959. **Attended a conference:** Lecuyer, "Fairchild Semiconductor," 175.
17. **Hoerni's patent disclosures:** Hoerni, "Method of Protecting Exposed p-n Junctions at the Surface of Silicon Transistors by Oxide Masking Techniques," 14 Jan. 1959; "Selective Control of Electron and Hole Lifetimes in Semiconductor Devices," 20 Jan. 1959, courtesy Jay Last.
18. **Noyce's integrated circuit notebook entry:** Noyce notebook #8: 70–74.
19. **Noyce was imagining:** Noyce, "Machine that Changed the World" interview, video, IA.
20. **No recollection of light bulb going off:** Noyce, 1982 Reid interview.
21. **We were still a brand new company:** Noyce quoted in Reid, *The Chip*, 88.
22. **The idea was too obvious to bother mentioning:** Wolff, "Genesis of the Integrated Circuit," 51. (Last called the interconnection plan "an idea that was around"; Grinich said it was "one of those tings that just happened—one of those obvious things.")
23. **I wish you luck:** Julius Blank, interview by author. Richard Hodgson, interview by author. Rheem's president had been Hodgson's classmate at Stanford. **On departure of Baldwin from Fairchild:** R. Dale Painter, "Seek to Settle Suit on Rheem Semiconductor," *Electronic News*, 14 March 1960; Ed Woods, "Rheem Semiconductor Named in $1 Million Suit," *Electronic News*, 27 July 1959; Don Hoefler, "Silicon Valley, USA" (Part 1), *Electronic News*, 11 Jan. 1970. **Baldwin met with a representative:** L. N. Duryea to Eirckson, Wright, Hanafin, and Steinmeyer, Shockley papers, SSC.
24. **A disaster:** Fairchild Founder B, interview by author, 19 March 1999.
25. **Head and shoulders above:** Tom Bay, interview by author. **Everybody had still reported:** Tom Bay, interview by Charlie Sporck.
26. **Sure of [him]self:** Don Hoefler, "I Didn't Raise my Boy to be a Manager," *Electronic News*, 17 Oct. 1966.
27. **People doing research best to evaluate it:** transcript of interview with Dr. Robert Noyce, [by Nilo Lindgren], no date but probably 1965, courtesy Patricia Lindgren (henceforth: Noyce 1965, Lindgren interview). **Those with most insurance die soonest:** Penny Noyce, interview by author.
28. **Very good supervisor, casual, not interfere:** Hoerni quoted in Bob Ristelhueber, "Noyce Remembered: Unusual Ideas, Unusual Approaches," *Electronic News*, 11 June 1990, 4.
29. **I could direct the work:** Noyce, 1965 Lindgren interview.
30. **Fairchild Semiconductor growth:** *Fairchild Camera and Instrument Annual Report* 1959. **Fairchild-Rheem lawsuits:** suit filed on 15 July 1959 in the Supreme court of California and for the city and county of San Francisco entitled "Fairchild Semiconductor Corporation, A Corporation (plaintiff) vs. E. M. Baldwin et al.," #491279.

31. **Met with representatives:** "Top Scientist from Japan Visits Fairchild," *Leadwire*, Feb. 1960. **Good for [his] ego:** Hoefler, "I Didn't Raise my Boy to be a Manager."

32. **Electronically active regions:** Seidenberg, "From Germanium to Silicon."

33. **Cocoon of silicon dioxide:** Noyce quoted in Reid, *The Chip*, 76. **Noyce and Moore's reactions to the planar demonstration:** Jean Hoerni, interview by Charlie Sporck.

34. **Hoerni planar patents:** Hoerni, "Method of Manufacturing Semiconductor Devices," U.S. Patent #3,025,589, filed 1 May 1959, patented 20 March 1962; Hoerni, "Semiconductor Devices," U.S. Patent #3,064,167, filed 1 May 1959, patented 23 Nov. 1962. **Copyright name 'planar':** Richard Hodgson, interview by author. Dumont manufactured a vacuum tube that it called a "Planar Triode," but I have found no connection between this tube and the planar transistor. "Planar Triode in Production at Du Mont," *Electronic News*, 23 Feb. 1959, 15.

35. **Not aesthetic:** Noyce, interview by Kleiman. **Gordon Moore remembers:** Wolff, "Genesis of the Integrated Circuit," 51.

36. **I was trying to solve:** Noyce, "Machine that Changed the World," video. **They don't give Nobel Prizes:** Bill Noyce, interview by author.

37. **To provide improved:** Noyce, "Semiconductor Device-and-Lead Structure," U.S. patent #2,981,877, filed 30 July 1959, patented 25 April 1961. **Did not want to go through all that work:** Noyce, "Machine that Changed the World." He makes a similar point in "Silicon Valley," written, produced, and directed by Julio Moline, video, SSC.

38. **Idea whose time had come:** Wolff, "Genesis of the Integrated Circuit," 51.

39. **Both are necessary:** Noyce, 1965 Lindgren interview.

40. **Recall very vividly:** Noyce, 1965 Lindgren interview.

41. **Description of the flip-flop:** Jay Last, "Development of the Integrated Circuit, August 1959–January 1961," courtesy Jay Last.

42. **Noyce was instrumental:** Letter from Donald E. Farina, "Gut Feeling Launched Revolution," *San Jose Mercury News*, 17 June 1990; Isy Haas, interview by author, 26 July 2001. **Abysmal yields:** The math is roughly as follows. If only half of the transistors on a given wafer are good, that means that putting together any two transistors yields chances of only one in four that the combination works; put together four transistors, and only one-sixteenth of them are good. There was talk that with 20 or 30 transistors in a given circuit, yields would be so abysmally low that each circuit that actually worked would have to cost a fortune. (Even a best-case scenario of 90 percent of transistors being functional resulted in 12 percent overall yields of 20-transistor circuits.) For more on this point, see Noyce, "Machine that Changed the World"; Kilby, "Invention of the Integrated Circuit," 652.

    As late as July 1964, a 30 percent yield for an integrated circuit containing 30 transistors was considered very good, or perhaps even "on the optimistic side," according to Noyce. "Integrated Circuits in Consumer and Industrial Electronics," *Electronic Procurement* (July 1964).

43. **A simple gate:** Marshall Cox interviewed in "Silicon Valley," written, produced, and directed by Julio Moline, video, SSC. **Every pound of payload required a ton of fuel:** Robert Noyce, "Integrated Circuits in Military Equipment," *IEEE Spectrum*, June 1964, 71.

44. **Interesting and exciting:** Moore quoted in Wolff, "Genesis of the Integrated Circuit." **Go ahead and pursue [ideas]:** Noyce, 1965 Lindgren interview.

45. **87 percent profit margin:** Arthur Rock to partners at Hayden, Stone, and Co., "Founding Documents." **Estimated revenues would triple:** FCI board minutes, 22 Jan. 1959, Anon.

46. **Western Union telegram:** ASB

47. **Ruins the look of the building:** Noyce, 1965 Lindgren interview. **Paid for Noyce's parents:** D. S. Noyce, "Candles to Computers," 269.

48. **Our motivation:** Jay Last to folks, undated but clearly immediately after the deal with Fairchild Camera and Instrument was signed, courtesy Jay Last. **Tiny area of disquiet, the reward seemed too much:** Noyce, 1965 Lindgren interview.

49. **Answered questions with ease:** *Leadwire* (Fairchild Semiconductor internal newsletter), Nov. 1959. **People used to do things:** Richard Hodgson, interview by author. **It's a very satisfying thing:** Noyce quoted in Reid, *The Chip*, 186.

50. **We're not ever going to screw a customer:** Bob Graham, interview by Charlie Sporck. **Noyce's yield-based system prevailed:** Bob Graham, interview by Charlie Sporck. Sporck confirms the excess inventory of the low-performance device.

51. **Noyce's conversation with Yelverton:** Jack Yelverton, interview by author.

52. **5,000 wires:** "Off the Leadwire," *Leadwire*, May 1960. **An experienced workforce:** Jack Yelverton, interview by author.

53. **We could not wear pants:** Barbara Eiler, interview by author.

54. **Breakfast meetings, foremen offered management training:** *Leadwire*, March 1963. **Coffee-conversation meetings:** *Leadwire*, Oct. 1963.

55. **Introduced as Gaylord's brother:** Gaylord Noyce, interview by author.

56. **Noyce comments on trip to Japan:** "Dr. Robert Noyce Gives Comments on Visit to Japan," *Leadwire*, June 1960

57. **Noyce felt a little guilty, financially outperformed parents:** Noyce, 1965 Lindgren interview.

58. **Noyce share in plane:** Tom Bay, interview by author. **Betty did not want to be left:** Penny Noyce to author, 5 April 2004.

59. **Not the truth, thought religion kept people from achieving:** Penny Noyce, interview by author. **One event, or one man:** *Leadwire*, Jan. 1960.

60. **Immigration statistics:** U.S. census data. **Youth and education of new arrivals:** in Palo Alto, for example, median age decreased by three years and median family income increased by 50 percent between 1950 and 1960, Findlay, *Magic Lands*, 147.

61. **IBM Building 25:** Alan Hess, "A 45-Year-Old Building Worth Saving," *San Jose Mercury News*, 16 Nov. 2003.

62. **Electronics sales surpassed $500 million, nearly two-thirds:** Western Electronics Manufacturers Association 1961 report, reprinted in *Leadwire*, Oct. 1961. **New startups:** "Printed Circuits Firm Formed in Menlo Park," *Electronic News*, Oct. 1960; "Diotran Pacific Formed by Four In Palo Alto, Cal," *Electronic News*, 6 March 1961; "Firm Established in Palo Alto to Service Producers," 18 Sept. 1961. **Stanford Industrial Park tenants:** Findlay, *Magic Lands*, 140.

63. **Resources available to Fairchild Semiconductor:** "Progress Report, Chemistry Section, 1 Feb. 1960," Box 5, File 1, Fairchild R&D Reports, M1055, SSC; "Progress Report, Micrologic Section, 1 July 1960," Box 5, File 2, ibid.; Box 6, File 1, ibid.

64. **Mechanization of agriculture:** Saxenian, "Silicon Chips and Spatial Structure," 60. For a wide-ranging discussion of the experience of Latino workers in Silicon Valley, see Stephen J. Pitti, *The Devil in Silicon Valley: Northern California, Race, and Mexican Americans* (Princeton, N.J.: Princeton University Press, 2002). **Infrastructure development:** Findlay, *Magic Lands,* 21–22. **Consolidated educational system:** Preer, *Emergence of Technopolis,* 140.

65. **World was [his] oyster, could do anything:** Robert Noyce, "The Machine that Changed the World," IA.

66. **Just another employee:** Jay Last interview by Charlie Sporck; Last made a similar comment in his interview with author; Jean Hoerni, in his interview with Charlie Sporck, echoed the sentiment.

67. **Noyce wanted stock options and "creeping socialism":** Richard Hodgson, interview by author.

68. **Camera and Instrument expanded:** "The Micro-Renaissance at Fairchild Camera." Carter claimed that all the acquisitions made sense, fitting in one way or another into the company's core business strategy. "I didn't go out and buy a brassiere company just because it was making money," he said in defense of his buying spree.

69. **Stock holdings of Carter and Fairchild:** Carter owned 77,000 shares of Camera and Instrument stock to the founders' roughly 5,000 shares apiece. The acquisition of Fairchild Semiconductor increased Sherman Fairchild's personal net worth by $20 to $30 million, since the exchange of stock had immediately quadrupled Camera and Instrument's net profits *Fairchild Camera and Instrument Annual Report,* 1959. **Boost to Sherman Fairchild's personal fortune:** "Multifarious Sherman Fairchild," 171.

70. **Quotes for planned IBM meeting:** "IBM Strategy, Mar 15 [1961]," Noyce 1961 datebook, ASB.

71. **Semiconductor joined SGS:** Richard Hodgson, interview by author. Other information on Fairchild's arrangement with SGS is from "Fairchild 1961," *Leadwire,* Jan. 1961, and Tom Bay, interview by author.

72. **Minuteman contract:** "Minuteman!" *Leadwire,* Feb. 1961; "FSC Signs Two Autonetics Contracts," *Leadwire,* June 1960; "Autonetics Contracts: Now Total 8 Million," *Leadwire,* Dec. 1960.

73. **Personnel reductions in microcircuitry:** Gordon Moore, "Approximate Distribution of Effort as Defined in 10/4/60 Personnel Forecast," 18 Jan. 1961, courtesy Jay Last. **OK, we've done integrated circuits:** Gordon Moore, interview by author.

74. **Last has already:** Jay Last, interview by author. Tom Bay, in his interview by author, says, "I'm sure I made some comment along the lines that Jay remembers—we were spending a lot of money and not getting anything in terms of sales or fundamental interest—but I don't ever remember feeling like we should scrub integrated circuits. I felt that [the integrated circuit] was the future for the business, but at the same time, we could not afford to spend all our energy on five-year-away projects. We had a business to run."

75. **Noyce and Moore prevented from investing:** Gordon Moore, interview by author. **Davis and Rock history:** Harvard Business School, *Working Knowl-*

edge (newsletter), 4 Dec. 2000. http://hbswk.hbs.edu/pubitem.jhtml?
id=1821&t=special_reports_donedeals

76. **Teledyne deal**: Jay Last, interview by author.
77. **Signetics funding information:** Jack Yelverton, interview by author. **If personnel expansion rate:** Moore and Grinich to Noyce, 8 Feb., 1961; R&D Progress Report from Moore and Grinich to Noyce, 8 March 1961, Box 6, File 2. Fairchild R&D Reports, M1055, SSC.
78. **On the issue with the IRS:** Jay Last, interview by author; Fairchild Founder A, interview by author; Form 870, "Waiver of Restrictions on Assessment and Collection of Deficiency in Tax and Acceptance of Overassessment," 23 Dec. 1963, addressed to Jay Last and courtesy Jay Last.
79. **Just a job, a taste of blood:** Fairchild Founder B, interview by author.
80. **Growth of electronics stocks:** 60 percent vs. 30 percent growth in 1958; 50 percent vs. 38 percent growth in 1959, Stuart Gellman, "Industry Still Flying High in the Market," *Electronic News*, 28 Dec 1959, 1. **On spinouts:** "Ex-Employe[e]s File $700,000 Counter Claim," *Electronic News*, 30 Jan. 1961; "Silicon Transistor Sues Ex-Employe[e]s, Seeks $1 Million," *Electronic News*, 23 Jan. 1961; "Diotran Pacific Formed by Four In Palo Alto, Cal," *Electronic News*, 6 March 1961; "Melapar Sues Scope, Others for $500,000," *Electronic News*, 27 July 1961, 1. See also, reports on Maryland-based Computer Dynamics Corporation: "5 Man Firm Grows to 100 in First Year," *Electronic News*, 7 Jan. 1963. **At the end of 1961, 150–200 companies**: "The Semiconductor Industry: Mayhem and Millionaires," *Electronic News*, 25 Jan. 1982, Section 2, 16.
81. **Improper practices and brokers' willingness to float issues:** Alfred D. Cook, "Letter from the Editor," *Electronic News*, 15 Feb. 1960. **Ease of raising capital:** Kraus, "An Economic Study of the Semiconductor Industry," 110. See also, "Transitron Offer Sparks Broker Deluge," *Electronic News 25th Anniversary Edition*, 25 Jan. 1982, Section 2, 28.
82. **On problems from development to manufacturing:** R&D Progress Report from Moore and Grinich to Noyce, 11 April 1961, Box 6, File 3, Fairchild R&D Reports, M1055, SSC. References to the problems moving from development to manufacturing are rife in the R&D reports.
83. **Transfer procedure is plagued:** R&D Progress Report from Moore and Grinich to Noyce, 11 April 1961, Box 6, File 3, Fairchild R&D Reports, M1055, SSC. **Manufacturing complained:** R&D Progress Report from Moore and Grinich to Noyce, 14 June 1961, Box 6, File 5, Fairchild R&D Reports, M1055, SSC. See also, "R&D Progress Report from Moore and Grinich to Noyce, 11 August 1961," Box 6, File 7, ibid.
84. **Communication lines and rest of agenda:** Noyce, 1962 datebook, undated but clearly the first weekend of 1963, ASB.
85. **Noyce had occasionally joined Hoerni**: Jay Last, interview by author. **Noyce's reactions to departures:** Jack Yelverton to author, 18 Dec. 2003; Jerry Levine, interview by author; "Drs. Hoerni, Last Resign Posts at Fairchild to Join Teledyne," *Electronic News*, 13 Feb. 1961.
86. **Semiconductor doubled its share:** "Strong Position of Firm Cited by Fairchild Semiconductor VP," *Electronic News*, 20 March 1961, 16. **Record profits and sales:** *Fairchild Camera and Instrument Annual Report* 1961. **1962 figures:** *Fairchild Camera and Instrument Annual Report* 1962.

Chapter 6: A Strange Little Upstart

1. **Job of the manager:** Noyce quoted in Walter Guzzardi, "Wisdom from the Giants of Business," *Fortune* (3 July 1989): 78–91. **Hundred percent raise:** Paul Hwoschinsky, interview by author. Andy Grove shared a similar memory in his interview with the author.

2. **Staff met over cocktails:** Charlie Sporck, interview by author. **Camera and Instrument meetings:** Nelson Stone, interview by author.

3. **Executive expressions:** "All around the Plant," *Leadwire*, Sept. 1962. **Noyce imagining portable telephones:** Noyce, 1965 Kleiman interview, audiotape, SSC. **Every industry will have electronics shop:** Noyce, 1965 Lindgren interview. **Erased own interviews:** miscellaneous videos, ASB.

4. **Strange little upstart:** Grove quoted in Perry, "Famous First Jobs," 50. **PhDs play:** Frank Wanlass quoted in George Rostky, "Thirty Years." **16 percent of major innovations:** Levin, "The Semiconductor Industry," 54.

5. **Marketing divisions:** Walter Matthews, "Shift Semicon Sales Setup at Fairchild," *Electronic News*, 6 April 1964. **Stocking representatives:** "FCS Sets up 'Stocking Rep' Plan," *Electronic News*, 12 June 1961. For more on electronics distributors and Fairchild's relations with its distributors, see Robert Noyce, "integrated circuit Producers to Complement OEM Circuit Role," *Electronic News*, 10 May 1965. **First infomercial:** "A Briefing on Integrated Circuits," courtesy Harry Sello. "Fairchild 'Special' Aimed at Select Group," *Broadcasting* (2 Oct. 1967): 35. The article calls the special "a landmark event in television ... the first of its kind in TV history." The Fairchild annual report for 1967 notes that the show was carried by 32 stations and "viewed by an estimated 2 million persons. This is [the] first known use of commercial TV to teach a technical subject."

6. **Direct government purchases 35 percent of sales:** "Fairchild: Tiny Semiconductors, Big Business," *Palo Alto Times*, 10 Aug. 1960. **Fairchild worked closely with the government:** Charlie Sporck, interview by author; Jay Last, interview by author; Lecuyer, "Making Silicon Valley," chaps. 3 and 4.

7. **Government contracts unethical, have confidence in yourself:** Noyce, 1965 Kleiman interview.

8. **Written as if bidders were crooks:** Bill Noyce, interview by author. **Interesting slop; hard, young, hungry group**: Noyce, 1965 Kleiman interview. **Gordon Moore shared:** R&D Progress Report from Moore and Grinich to Noyce, 15 Feb. 1962, Box 7, File 2, Fairchild R&D Reports, SSC. **We like it that way:** "Man Behind the News," *Electronic News*, 3 Dec. 1962.

9. **Space in Hong Kong:** Noyce 1961 datebook (but entry from 21 May 1962).

10. **Automation in semiconductor industry:** "Semiconductor Field Mechanizing Fast," *Electronic News*, 21 March, 1960, 110. At this point, Semiconductor's automation was limited to testing, the area that was eventually spun into Fairchild Instrumentation. **Move to Hong Kong:** Jerry Levine, interview by author; Charlie Sporck, interview by author.

11. **Practically thrown out of the board room:** Richard Hodgson, interview by author; date is from minutes of the meeting of the Executive Committee of the Board of Directors of Fairchild Camera and Instrument, 22 Jan. 1964.

12. **Hong Kong wages:** Jerry Levine, interview by author. **Fairchild wages**: Eugene Kleiner to Gordon Moore, 1 Dec. 1960, Fairchild R&D Reports, SSC. **Korean plant and wages:** "FCS Plans Korea Plant," *Electronic News*.

13. **1968 overseas data:** *Fairchild Camera and Instrument Annual Report* 1968.

14. **Other firms imitated the move:** these include Continental Device Corp., General Electric, and ITT Semiconductor. Don Hoefler, "Hit 'Em Where They Ain't," *Electronic News*, 15 Jan. 1968, 1. **In 1974, 69 assembly plants:** Braun and McDonald, *Revolution in Miniature*.

15. **We lost the process:** Paul Hwoschinsky, interview by author. **We are going to bury:** James F. Gibbons, interview by author.

16. **Noyce's 1965 schedule:** Sept. and Oct. entries, 1965 datebook, ASB.

17. **Ask for 10 percent:** Noyce, 1961 datebook, undated entry. **Could get much more, Noyce is God in Japan:** Roger Borovoy, interview by author. **Excess of $100 million:** Borovoy, "The T.I. Integrated circuit Patents in Japan: What Really Happened?" unpublished memo, 27 Nov. 1989, courtesy Roger Borovoy.

18. **I'm concerned:** Noyce, 1965 Kleiman interview.

19. **An air force experiment:** Siekman, "In Electronics, the Big Stakes Ride on Tiny Chips."

20. **First commercial integrated circuit:** "Progress Report, Applications Engineering Section, 1 June 1961," Box 6, File 5, Fairchild R&D Division, Technical Reports and Progress Reports, SSC. **St. Moritz seminars:** Don Hoefler, "Integrated Circuit Billion $ Baby," *Electronic News*, 18 Oct. 1971.

21. **Computer in 1952 election:** Martin Campbell-Kelly and William Aspray, *Computer: A History of the Information Age* (New York: Basic Books, 1996), 121–123. **Only 100 corporations would need computers:** James W. Cortada, *The Computer in the United States: From Laboratory to Market* (Armonk, N.Y.: M. E. Sharpe, 1993). **Federal government statistics:** Martha Smith Parks, *Microelectronics in the 1970s*, (Rockwell International Corporation, 1974), 59.

22. **Interest in Micrologic devices:** *Leadwire*, April 1961. **Noyce tells Philco tough:** Noyce 1961 datebook, 29 June entry.

23. **By the end of 1961:** Bob Graham [Micrologic sales manager] to All Field Sales, 1 Dec. 1961, courtesy Jay Last. Graham letter is also the source of the Texas Instruments pricing information.

24. **Now Noyce wanted:** Noyce wrote "µckts group → systems" in his 1961 datebook. **Resistance to integrated circuits by design engineers:** For more on this point, see Bassett, "New Technology," 229.

25. **Would remain on R&D level:** Richard Gessell, "Integrated Circuitry Held Far From Payoff," *Electronic News*, 27 March 1963.

26. **Most important Fairchild First:** *Leadwire*, Oct. 1961. **Noyce's notes on microcircuits:** Noyce's 1961 and 1962 notebooks. In roughly February or March of that year, he has noted on his to-do list: "Cease and desist to Signetics, Amelco." **Find evidence of Signetics infringement:** 20 June 1962 entry in Noyce's 1961 notebook, ASB.

27. **Less than 10 percent effect:** "The Impact of Microelectronics."

28. **Advertised integrated circuit benefits:** "From Fairchild: Two Approaches to Multiple Devices" (advertisement), *Electronic News*, 8 May 1961. The company promoted similar qualities in its technical presentations.

29. **Percent of integrated circuits bought by military:** Michael G. Borrus, *Competing for Control: America's Stake in Microelectronics* (Cambridge, Mass.: Ballinger, 1988): 159. For more on the changes in military purchasing in the early 1960s, see Lecuyer, "Making Silicon Valley," 220–225.

30. **Selling ideas is engineering problem:** Noyce, "A Changing World: Key-note Speech Delivered Before Bendix Microprocessor Conference," 26 Oct. 1977: 1, IA. **Technical sophistication of customers:** Freund, "Competition and Innovation," 30; E. Floyd Kvamme, "Life in Silicon Valley: A First-Hand View of the Region's Growth," in *The Silicon Valley Edge: A Habitat for Innovation and Entrepreneurship*, ed. Chong-Moon Lee, William F. Miller, Marguerite Gong Hancock, and Henry S. Rowen (Stanford, Ca.: Stanford University Press, 2000).

31. **Sell for less than cost of device:** it is unclear whether the precise month in which the cost cutting occurred was March or May. Philip Siekman, "In Electronics, the Big Stakes Rides on Tiny Chips," 122; "Tiny Chip Brings a Big Payoff; Integrated Circuits Find More Commercial Applications," *Business Week* 17 April 1965: 85–88. See also, "Below $1 integrated circuit Price Nears," reprinted in *Electronic News* 25th Anniversary Issue, Section 2, 25 Jan. 1982. 76. **Bob's unheralded contribution:** Moore quoted in "A Macro View of Microelectronics: Gordon E. Moore of Intel," *IEEE Design and Test* (Nov., 1984), 17. The price slashing, while surprising, was not unprecedented. Fairchild had done something similar with its silicon transistors the year before. **Noyce smiled:** Rostky, "Thirty Years That Made A Difference," 64.

32. **Profit on low prices:** Events in Fairchild's recent history may well have given Noyce reason to be optimistic about his chances of success. Between 1959 and 1962, for example, Fairchild's production of its LPHF transistor line increased 660-fold, with costs only quintupling. The cost of the transistor fell by 90 percent, while at the same time, revenue grew ten-fold and profits tripled. Freund, "Competition and Innovation," Table XI, 70. **When there's a problem, lower the price:** Gordon Moore speaking at the Intel memorial service for Noyce, 18 June 1990.

33. **Book-printing analogy:** Noyce, "Machine that Changed the World"; letter from Bill Ford in "Robert Noyce, Special Tribute," *San Jose Mercury News*, 17 June 1990.

34. **I doubt if Noyce:** "Dr. Moore, Tape 2, 6/8/94." **Prices already falling:** The average price of an integrated circuit fell 41 percent between 1963 and 1964. Braun and Macdonald, *Revolution in Miniature*, 98. **Prices fell but profits tripled:** Freund, "Competition and Innovation," 70.

35. **Fairchild in top position:** Philip Siekman, "In Electronics, the Big Stakes Ride on Tiny Chips," 122. **1966 sales figures:** Bob Tamarkin, "Tiny Circuitry's Big World," *Chicago Daily News*, 3 Nov. 1966. Lecuyer points to several reasons for this explosive growth in the commercial market, including growth in the early computer industry, as well as the FCC's decision to require all television monitors to be able to receive UHF signals. Lecuyer, "Making Silicon Valley," 226–229.

36. **A single order:** The order was probably for Loran Systems. "Fairchild Semicon Gets Sperry Order," *Electronic News*, 5 April 1965. **1966 Burroughs order:** *Leadwire*, Dec. 1966. **Uses for integrated circuits:** "A Briefing on Integrated Circuits"; "Engineers Eye Integrated Consumer Products," *Television Digest*, 30 March 1964, 7–8; Michael F. Wolff, "When Will Integrated Circuits Go Civilian? Good Guess: 1965," *Electronics*, 10 May 1963, 20–24.

37. **Cost of IBM System/360:** Campbell-Kelly and Aspray, *Computer*, 140. **Only computers anyone would need:** Don Palfreman and Doron Swade, *The Dream Machine: Exploring the Computer Age* (London: BBC Books, 1993), 78–

80. For a contemporary description of the IBM System/360 series, see International Business Machines, *Introduction to IBM Data Processing Systems* (White Plains, N.Y.: 1969). Electronic Girl Fridays: Martha Smith Parks, *Microelectronics in the 1970s* (Rockwell International Corporation: 1974), 59. **95 percent of banks:** Palfreman and Swade, *Dream Machine*, 78.

38. **In 1966, 3,600 minicomputers:** Campbell-Kelly and Aspray, *Computer*, 229.

39. **Significant and essential contributions:** "Medal Days," *The [Franklin] Institute News*, Oct. 1966. **Full extent of revolution:** Report No. 3467 of the Franklin Institute, Investigating the Work of Jack S. Kilby, of Dallas, Texas, and Robert N. Noyce, of Los Altos, California [issued 15 June 1966], IA.

40. **No huge lightbulb:** Wolff, "Genesis of the Integrated Circuit," 51.

41. **Camera and Instrument share price:** "What Made a High Flier Take Off at Top Speed," *Business Week*, 30 Oct. 1965, 118–22; "Exchange Calls FC&I Pacer," *Electronic News*, 7 Feb. 1966. **IBM cross licensing deal:** *Leadwire*, Dec. 1965; "Fairchild Camera, IBM in Cross Deal," *Electronic News*, 29 Sept. 1965; Noyce's notes are in his 1965 datebook, 16 March entry, ASB. **Salesmen were encouraged:** Robert Graham, interview by Charlie Sporck.

42. **Riding a fast horse:** Paul Hwoschinsky, interview by author.

43. **Quantities of half million:** *Fairchild Camera and Instrument Annual Report* 1965.

44. **Fairchild reporting structure:** Charlie Sporck, interview by author, 28 Dec. 2000.

45. **Noyce split his time:** 1965 datebook.

46. **Spend two hours:** Moore quoted in Lindgren, "Two-Headed Monster." **Bob at party:** Betty Noyce to Bill Noyce, 22 July 1963.

47. **Tom Swifties:** Betty Noyce to Bill Noyce, 22 July 1963. **Sock puppets:** Phyllis Kefauver, interview by author. In 1972, Betty Noyce wrote a slightly fictionalized account of the sock escapade, "Sock-Dol-O-Gy" under the pen name E. N. Barry.

48. **Helped Charlie Sporck:** Charlie Sporck, interview by author. **Took Billy to tune:** Jim Angell, interview by author. **Scheduled weekend meetings:** Noyce, 1962 datebook. **Cottage at Lake Tahoe:** Bob and Phyllis White, interview by author; Bob and Phyllis Kefauver, interview by author. **A thousand times:** Penny Noyce, speaking at the SEMATECH memorial service for Bob Noyce.

49. **Relaxing to work on something:** Bill Noyce, interview by author.

50. **Worried she was damaging:** interview with family friend requesting anonymity. Several of Noyce's children confirmed their mother's childrearing tactics. **Story of the skydiver:** Penny Noyce speaking at the Intel memorial service for her father.

51. **He wanted children:** Polly Noyce, interview by author.

52. **Did not want a man:** Shockley notebook marked "Trip 25 Nov to 5 Dec 1955," Shockley papers, 95–153, SSC. **Description of ideal wife:** "Executive Wives," *Electronic News*, 6 June 1966.

53. **I fear I neglect:** Betty Noyce quoted in *Melbourne [Australia]Sun*, 12 May 1966. Courtesy Polly Noyce.

54. **Meals should not take longer:** Penny Noyce, interview by author. **Why is it:** Richard Hodgson, interview by author.

55. **Miss the beautiful young girls:** *Leadwire*, Nov. 1959.

56. **Stranger to his own family, you're nothing:** Nilo Lindgren, "Two-Headed Monster."
57. **Reorganization:** Charlie Sporck, interview by author, 28 Dec. 2000.
58. **Meeting one-third of commitments:** Hoefler, "FC&I Profit Dip on integrated circuits," *Electronic News*, 21 Nov. 1966. **Devices never manufactured:** Don Hoefler, "FC&I Profit Dip on integrated circuits"; Walter Matthews, "Geographic Expansion Set by Fairchild," *Electronic News*, 19 July 1965. **First parts from R&D:** Roger Borovoy, interview by author, 27 Jan. 1999.
59. **If I could just buy:** "What Made a High Flier Take Off at Top Speed."
60. **FAIRCHILD 71:** *Fairchild Camera and Instrument Annual Report* 1966. **Division more profitable:** Robert Noyce to Sherman Fairchild, 25 June 1968. Camera and Instrument did not break down earnings by division, but *Time* estimated that Semiconductor was responsible for 98 percent of the parent company's profits. "Mighty Miniatures," *Time*, 4 March 1965, 93–94. **Noyce not director:** *Fairchild Camera and Instrument Annual Report* 1966.
61. **Sporck and others to National:** "Nat'l Semiconductor Moving, Realigning Top Management," *Electronic News*, 6 March 1967. Among those who left with Sporck, or shortly thereafter to join him, were Floyd Kvamme, marketing manager for integrated circuits, Pierre Lamond, integrated circuit production manager; Roger Smuller, manufacturing manager for integrated circuits; Fred Bialek, overseas operations manager for microcircuits; and Don Valentine, director of marketing. **Throwing away, why don't I do that:** Charlie Sporck, interview by author.
62. **I essentially cried:** Noyce quoted in Malone, *Big Score*, 108. **Technical reports:** owner requested anonymity.
63. **Company was a mess:** Gordon Moore, interview by author, 2 July 2004.
64. **Our scheme had worked:** Communication from Brenda Borovoy to the author, 11 May 1998.
65. **Felt things were falling apart:** Robert Noyce, "Machine that Changed the World."
66. **Administrative details:** Noyce notebooks for 1961, 1962, 1965, all ASB. **Try to get East Coast out:** Noyce 1962 notebook, entry around 2 Jan. 1963.
67. **Going to the lab:** "Parent and Child," *Electronics* (8 July 1968): 54. **After growing up:** "Turning a Science into an Industry," *IEEE Spectrum*, Jan. 1966, 101.
68. **Democratization of stock options:** This figure takes into account a three-for-two stock split during 1967. The additional shares followed on the granting of 215,525 new options—an enormous increase (even taking into account the stock split) over the previous year's 73,400, and the 1965 grant of 5,300. *Fairchild Camera and Instrument Annual Report* 1965, 1966, 1967. **Stock option details:** Minutes of the FCI Stock Option Committee, 1 March 1967, 16 March 1967, 18 May 1967, 21 Sept. 1967, Anon.
69. **35 people joined Sporck, every semiconductor company:** "The Fight That Fairchild Won," 100.
70. **Difficulties overcome:** "Coast Firm Unplugs Jam in Output," *Electronic News*, 20 March 1967. **Drop in demand:** "Paying the Piper," *Forbes*, 15 Nov. 1967; "FC&I Head Resigns; Earnings Plummet," *Electronic News*, 27 Oct. 1967. **Fairchild reported losses:** Don Hoefler, "FC&I, Mountain View, Breathes Easier," *Electronic News*, 30 Oct. 1967.

71. **Third-quarter performance:** "Paying the Piper"; "Carter Resigns; Earnings Plummet," *Electronic News*, 23 Oct. 1967. **Stock price slid:** Alfred D. Cook, "Sherman Fairchild's July 4th Fizzles," *Electronic News*, 8 July 1968.

72. **Carter out, Hodgson in:** Carter attempted to rally a small group of directors to defend his acquisitions strategy when the rest of the board wanted to divest themselves of the losing operations. When Carter's rally failed, he quit before he could be fired. FCI board minutes. **When you kill the king:** Noyce quoted in Don C. Hoefler, "Captains Outrageous," *California Today*, 28 June 1981, 42.

73. **$7.7 million loss:** *Fairchild Camera and Instrument Annual Report* 1967. The report notes that "the Semiconductor Division accounts for well over half of the Corporation's sales." **Group all losses:** Cook, "Sherman Fairchild's July 4th Fizzles," 1.

74. **I'm thinking of leaving Fairchild:** Gordon Moore, interview by author, 2 July 2004.

75. **Number of minicomputers:** Campbell-Kelly and Aspray, *Computer*, 229. **Fairchild held 80 percent:** Lecuyer, "Making Silicon Valley," 22. **Fairchild itself:** Gordon Moore, interview by author. **IBM had been researching:** Basset, "New Technology," 332.

76. **Everyone expected:** *Electronic News*, 27 May 1968; Charlie Sporck, interview by author; Gordon Moore, interview by author; Roger Borovoy, interview by author. **Presidential material someday:** Robert Noyce to Sherman Fairchild, 25 June 1968, Anon. **Kind of ticked off:** Gordon Moore, interview by Rob Walker, SSC. **Tail wagging the corporate dog:** "Semiconductor was the company," Noyce said, "but they [Camera and Instrument] insisted on treating it as just another division." Don Hoefler, "Dr. Noyce Happy Doing His Thing," *Electronic News*, 28 Oct. 1968.

77. **Noyce verbally resigned:** "The Fight That Fairchild Won," 112. This version of events is supported by details in "Musical Chairs," *Electronics*, 19 July 1968. **Noyce's negotiations with Hogan:** C. Lester Hogan, interview by Rob Walker, SSC.

78. **The Hogan:** "Where the Action is in Electronics," *Business Week*, 4 Oct. 1969; Malone, *Big Score*, 124. **Brought every manager:** The one exception was marketing VP Tom Connors. In two years, some 60 former Motorola employees caught what one wag called "the Motorola-to-Fairchild Express" to California. **Move headquarters:** "Fairchild Camera Formalizes Base Location to California," *Electronic News*, 30 Sept. 1968. **I wouldn't have gone:** Lester Hogan, interview by Rob Walker, 22 Aug. 1995, SSC.

79. **As the company has grown, twice the population:** Robert Noyce to Sherman Fairchild, 25 June 1968.

80. **All quotes in this paragraph:** Robert Noyce to Sherman Fairchild, 25 June 1968.

81. **All quotes in this paragraph:** Robert Noyce to Sherman Fairchild, 25 June 1968.

82. **Bob really thought:** Moore quoted in Bob Ristleheuber [sic], "Noyce Remembered: Unusual Ideas, Unusual Approaches," *Electronic News*, 11 June 1990, 4. **Too nice to too many people:** Harry Sello, interview by author. **You could get him to say yes:** Charlie Sporck, interview by author.

83. **Produced entrepreneurs, not products:** Alfred D. Chandler, Jr., "The Information Age in Historical Perspective," introduction to Alfred D. Chandler,

Jr. and James W. Cortada, eds., *A Nation Transformed by Information: How Information Has Shaped the United States from Colonial Times to the Present* (New York: Oxford University Press, 2000): 31. By the end of Noyce's tenure at Fairchild, one reporter could write that the company "seemed dedicated to technology for its own sake. . . . At Fairchild, it almost seemed that no engineer wanted to be in production." (Erickson, "How Hogan Rescued Fairchild," 22.)

84. **Gave up and tried again:** Noyce quoted in McIlheny, "Dissatisfaction as a Spur to Career," 15 Dec. 1976. **One thing I learned:** Robert Noyce, interview by Mary Burt Baldwin, transcript, IA.

Chapter 7: Startup

1. **On rumors:** *Electronic News* throughout July 1968. **The industry has devoured:** Advertisement in *Electronic News*, 3 Oct. 1968.

2. **Bob is having a harrowing time:** Betty Noyce quoted in Harriet Noyce to Bob Noyce, undated (but clearly summer, 1968), IA. **Startled Noyce out of bed:** Noyce in Bill Davidow, Eugene Flath, and Robert Noyce, Oral History, 13 Aug. 1983, IA (henceforth Davidow, Flath, and Noyce oral history). **Back you financially:** Dot [Noyce's assistant] to Noyce, 1 July 1968, ASB.

3. **Noyce did little:** See, for example, Hoefler, "Dr. Noyce Happy Doing His Thing," *Electronic News*, 28 Oct. 1968. **Pushing more and more paper:** "Resignations Shake Up Fairchild," *San Jose Mercury*, 4 July 1968. **When asked why:** Cook, "Sherman Fairchild's July 4th Fizzles," *Electronic News*.

4. **Practically unobserved:** Interview with Dr. Gordon Moore, 6/29/94, IA. **Wouldn't have any trouble:** Noyce in Davidow, Flath, and Noyce oral history, IA. **It's about time:** Arthur Rock speaking at Computer History Museum's venture capital panel, 30 Sept. 2002.

5. **Weekends spent painting the windows:** Bob White, interview by author.

6. **Does it for the fish:** Paul Hwoschinsky, interview by author.

7. **Whatever you're planning to do:** Andy Grove, interview by author. **Human resources manager:** Les Vadasz, interview by Evan Ramstad.

8. **Instead of drawing the people closer together:** Noyce quoted in "Industry Leaders Join in Kennedy Tributes," *Electronic News*, 10 June 1968. **On Kennedy assassination:** Bob Graham, interview by Charlie Sporck.

9. **Let people bite into each other, did not argue:** Andy Grove, interview by author. **On Grove's life:** Andy Grove, *Swimming Across: A Memoir*, (New York: Warner Books, 2002). **Graduated first in his class:** Nilo Lindgren, "Building a Rational Two-Headed Monster: The Management Style of Robert Noyce and Gordon Moore," *Innovation* (no date, but clearly 1970).

10. **We don't care:** Bill Noyce, interview by author. **It's very comfortable:** "Interview with Dr. Gordon Moore," 29 June 1994, IA. **Pay cut:** Robert Noyce, "Innovation: Nothing to Fear but Fear" [summary of his presentation at the MIT symposium on the management of innovation], *Technology Review*, Feb. 1977.

11. **Represented a sizable portion:** Arthur Rock, interview by author. **Concentrated in Fairchild stock:** Noyce to Sherman Fairchild.

12. **Breakdown of startup expenses:** "Proposed Use of Proceeds," IA. **Noyce could not resist:** Gaylord Noyce, interview by author.

13. **Silicon suppliers reported:** "Silicon Usage Pushes Suppliers; Deliveries Stretch to 4 Months," *Electronic News*, 4 Aug. 1969.
14. **Cartoon:** "Where the Action is in Electronics," *Business Week*, 4 Oct. 1969, 86–87. A closer look at the cartoon reveals that this activity is actually being witnessed by a man peering through a microscope at the inner workings of an integrated circuit. Rather than magnifying a cluster of transistors and other circuit components, the microscope reveals this frenzied world.
15. **Attendance at a session:** Don Hoefler, "Engineers Jam Business Panel," *Electronic News*, 25 Aug. 1969; "Wescon Session to Spotlight Financial Needs of Start-Ups," *Electronic News*, 18 Aug. 1969.
16. **Moore's Law:** Gordon Moore, "Cramming More Components onto Integrated Circuits," *Electronics*, 19 April 1965: 114–117. **Already Moore's own R&D group:** Reid, *The Chip*, 128.
17. **Noyce predicted:** Noyce quoted in "Turning a Science into an Industry," *IEEE Spectrum*, Jan. 1966, 102.
18. **Technology looking for applications:** Moore in Moore, Vadasz, Parker oral history.
19. **We have no idea:** Harriet Noyce to Bob Noyce, undated (but clearly summer, 1968), IA.
20. **On Noyce's activities at the start of Intel:** Noyce 1968 datebook, ASB; Noyce to Frank Roberts [attorney], 20 July 1968.
21. **Jay Last's Teledyne rented:** "Antenna—Can't Keep a Good Man Down," *Electronic News*, 17 Nov. 1969. Carter's firm was called "Carter Semiconductor of Hong Kong." It received somewhere around 100 million transistor dice in 1969 from Raytheon. **Schools weren't turning out:** Noyce, "Machine that Changed the World," transcript, IA.
22. **We are only going to hire perfect people:** Bill Noyce, interview by author. **Fairchild circus:** Noyce 1968 datebook.
23. **Noyce on East Coast:** Scandling, "2 of Founders Leave Fairchild." **Like Pied Piper:** Roger Borovoy, interview by author. **Please drop a note with qualifications:** "Every Pinhole Counts!" Undated advertisement (but obviously from 1968), IA.
24. **Gordon and I have left:** Jim Angell, interview by author. **Could tell whether a computer program:** Jim Angell, interview by author.
25. **If you're in academia:** Ted Hoff, interview by author.
26. **Noyce-Hoff interview:** Ted Hoff, interview by author.
27. **Get close to advanced technology:** Robert Noyce to Sherman Fairchild, 25 June 1968. **No one knew the business better, could sell Intel to a computer company:** Noyce in Davidow, Flath, and Noyce oral history, IA.
28. **Do quite well, I felt I was young:** Ted Hoff, interview by author.
29. **Would wander through the neighborhood:** Bob White, interview by author.
30. **Sort of sexy, four had been taken:** Noyce in Davidow, Flath, and Noyce oral history. **Names under consideration:** paper headed "Titles," IA.
31. **Implied other things:** Robert Noyce in Davidow, Flath, and Noyce oral history, IA.
32. **Man has to have killer instinct:** Rock quoted in "Venture Capitalist with a Solid Intuition," *Business Week*, 30 May 1970. **The main thing is:** Noyce quoted in Pete Carey, "The Hero of Venture Capitalists," *San Jose Mercury News*, 19 Feb. 1978.

33. **More detail on the Intel debentures**: they had a ten-year term, paid 6 percent interest (waived for three years), and were convertible at $5 per share. "Fully subordinated to all indebtedness; non-callable for one year; sinking fund beginning in the fifth year to retire one-half of the outstanding debentures; anti-dilution protection against stock splits . . .; negative restriction against payment of dividends on common stock." "Intel Corp $2,500,000 Convertible Debentures," 1–2, IA.

34. **Intended to fund**: "Intel Corp $2,500,000 Convertible Debentures," IA. Directors of the company did not participate in the plan.

35. **Noyce had begun outlining**: Jerome Dougherty [attorney] to Noyce, 18 July 1968, IA. **Scientific Data Systems had given options**: Arthur Rock, interview by author.

36. **There are too many millionaires**: Art Rock to Frank Roberts, 27 Aug. 1968, IA.

37. **Every eligible employee**: Noyce to shareholders, 25 April 1969, IA. **Options on 64,700 shares**: Intel Corporation Balance Sheet, 31 December 1968, IA.

38. **Prudent man rule**: The "prudent man" rule sharply limited pensions funds' ability to invest in high-risk ventures. Beginning in 1979, with changes to the Employee Retirement Income Security Act, pension funds were allowed to allocate up to 10 percent of assets in high-risk venture funds. Paul A. Gompers, "The Rise and Fall of Venture Capital," *Business and Economic History*, Vol. 23, No. 2, 1992: 1. See also Bygrave and Timons, *Venture Capital at the Cross-roads* (Boston: Harvard Business School Press, 1992). **Offers of financial assistance**: Charles J. Coronella to Noyce, 10 July 1968; Robert R. Barker to Noyce, 24 July 1968; John K. Koeneman to Noyce, 18 July 1968; Sterling Grumman to Noyce, 7 Aug. 1968; Elmor Howard to Noyce, 25 July 1968; Dick Hand to Noyce, 4 Dec. 1968. All ASB. **Cook had recently offered Noyce and Moore the opportunity**: Paul Cook, interview by author, 2 Feb. 1999; Gordon Moore, interview by author. **Noyce proposed Sherman Fairchild**: untitled page (clearly a list of potential investors) in Investors file, ASB.

39. **Hoped the investment would generate $10 million**: Joe Rosenfield to Sam Rosenthal, Don Wilson, and Warren Buffett, 17 April 1973, courtesy Warren Buffett. **Betting on the jockey**: Warren Buffett, interview by author, 28 Aug. 2002.

40. **Business plan**: "Intel Corp $2,500,000 Convertible Debentures," IA. **Didn't want people to know**: Noyce in Davidow, Flath, and Noyce oral history, IA.

41. **Kind of lined up**: Rock quoted in Gene Bylinsky, "How Intel Won Its Bet on Memory Chips," *Fortune*, Nov. 1973, 144. **People had to return calls**: Arthur Rock, interview by author.

42. **Betty Moore received several calls**: "Interview with Dr. Gordon Moore, 6/29/94," IA. **Keenly disappointed**: Robert B. Barker to Bob Noyce, 24 July 1968. **He told them Rock was in charge**: Robert Noyce in Davidow, Flath, and Noyce oral history, IA.

43. **Intel is probably the only company**: Arthur Rock quoted in Udayan Gupta, ed., *Done Deals: Venture Capitalists Tell Their Stories* (Boston: Harvard Business School Press, 2000).

44. **Failures of companies**: "Electronics Industry Failures Fall to Lowest Level Ever," *Electronic News*, 10 June 1968. **Age of Electro-Aquarius**: "The Splintering of the Solid-State Electronics Industry."

45. **The last year**: "Where the Action is in Electronics," *Business Week*, Oct. 1969, 86. **Market fully saturated**: Jackson, *Inside Intel*, 47.

46. **Participation in War on Poverty**: Neil Kelly, "Coast Firms Eager in Poverty Fight," *Electronic News*, 22 July 1968. **Army's computerized facility**: Heather M. David, "Army Opens Riot Control Center," *Electronic News*, 14 July 1969.

47. **Knew Intel would lose money**: "Intel Corp $2,500,000 Convertible Debentures," IA. **More aggressive**: Gordon Moore, interview by author.

48. **In early August, Noyce left**: Noyce 1968 datebook, ASB **Description of Maine house**: author's visit.

49. **On Route 128**: Saxenian, *Regional Advantage*. **The whole concept of Intel**: Dick Hodgson, interview by author.

50. **So Betty's home**: Harriet Noyce to Bob Noyce, undated (but clearly summer, 1968), IA. **Harriet thought Betty had made Bob overly interested in money**: Penny Noyce, interview by author.

51. **High muckety-mucks**: Noyce in Davidow, Flath, and Noyce oral history, IA. **Professionally decorated**: Jean Jones, interview by author. **On arrangement of offices**: Andy Grove, interview by author.

52. **Cafeteria and communications center**: Jean Jones to Dinah Lee, Subject: Admin SLRP, 9 April 1992, IA.

53. **Sewer pipe running out to the street**: Gordon Moore oral history, 17 Oct. 1983, IA.

54. **Equivalent of a checkbook, I'll have one of those**: Gene Flath in Davidow, Flath, and Noyce oral history, IA

55. **Betty Noyce had already announced**: Ted Hoff, interview by author.

56. **Gods of the industry**: Tom Innes in Tom Innes and Tom Rowe oral history, IA.

57. **$1,000 per month**: Andy Grove in Ed Gelbach, Andy Grove, and Ted Jenkins oral history, 24 Oct. 1983, IA (henceforth Gelbach, Grove, Jenkins oral history). **A lot of sex appeal, steering the future**: John Reed, interview by author.

58. **Two-headed monster**: Lindgren, "Building a Rational Two-Headed Monster." **Senior executives from computer companies**: Max Palevsky, who ran Scientific Data Systems, and Gerard Currie, who ran Data Technology.

59. **On Intel's strategy**: Marian Jelinek and Claudia Bird Schoonhover, *The Innovation Marathon: Lessons from High Technology Firms* (Oxford:, OX, UK; Cambridge, Mass., USA: B. Blackwell, 1990) discuss this strategy at length.

60. **Group think, a single yes**: Noyce, "The Fruit of Success," *Chemtech*, Dec. 1979.

61. **Use money to buy time**: Gene Flath, interview by author. **A rifleman who shoots**: Gordon Moore, "Intel—Memories and the Microprocessor," *Daedalus* 125, Spring 1966: 55–80. In this article, Moore offers the following example of first-mover advantage: the 1101, Intel's first MOS memory device, was initially designed to operate at standard power supply voltages of +5 and +12v. Intel soon discovered, however, that "12 volts was more than the device structure could handle." Since no system had yet been built to use semiconductor memories, Intel was free to adjust the voltage, effectively decreeing that semiconductor memories would run at +5 and +9v—specifications that eventually became industry standards.

62. **All we have to do**: Noyce in Noyce, Davidow, Flath oral history, IA. **Sold for about 4 percent**: "Interview Robert Noyce—1973," IA.

63. **Core memories had netted**: Campbell-Kelly and Aspray, *Computer,* 167. In much the same way that Noyce at Fairchild and Kilby at Texas Instruments independently conceived and developed the integrated circuit, magnetic core (or ferrite) memories had been almost simultaneously developed by researchers at MIT, Harvard, and RCA in 1951. MIT was eventually awarded the patent.

64. **Travel along ten square feet**: Reid, *The Chip,* 128. In 1999, Arthur Rock jokingly estimated that it would take "the entire world's population to string cores" for the number of computers in use at the turn of the twenty-first century. Arthur Rock, interview by author.

65. **Formal product plans**: Noyce 1968 datebook.

66. **MOS:** As historian Ross Bassett puts it, "If the classic definition of the bipolar transistor is a 'sandwich,' with the main effects happening at the intersection of the bread and the filling, the MOS transistor is more like a pizza, with the main effects happening at the surface."

67. **On the flip chip**: Gordon Moore, interview by author; Barbara Eiler, interview by author. Eiler explains that the flip chip group was trying to eliminate the traditional bonding process, in which very small wires are attached from the package leads to special bonding pads on the chip. Barbara Eiler to author, 26 July 2004.

68. **Why three-pronged approach**: Gordon Moore, interview by author.

69. **Using blown diodes**: Ted Hoff, interview by author.

70. **His questions were so perceptive**: Ted Hoff, interview by author. **He challenged you all the time**: Les Vadasz, interview by Evan Ramstad.

71. **Donald S. Noyce to Adam Noyce**, 1 May 2002, GCA.

72. **Noyce principle of minimum information**: Gordon Moore, "Some Personal Perspectives on Research in the Semiconductor Industry," in Rosenbloom and William J. Spencer, *Engines of Innovation: U.S. Industrial Research at the End of an Era* (Boston, Mass.: Harvard Business School Press, 1996), 165–174. **Five or six man years to design a circuit**: Davidow, Flath, Noyce oral history.

73. **Noyce calling Grove the whip**: Noyce in Davidow, Flath, and Noyce oral history, IA. **It is tough for me to do the hard things**: Kathy Cohen, interview by author. **You had to do something**: Rowe in Rowe and Innes oral history.

74. **Best thing since the Pill**: Tom Innes in Tom Innes and Tom Rowe oral history.

75. **I don't think I talked to Bob for months**: Ann Bowers, interview by author, 5 Aug. 2004. **I guess I officially reported to Bob**: Roger Borovoy, interview by author. **Nobody actually reported to Bob**: Ann Bowers, interview by author, 16 Aug. 2004.

76. **On Noyce-Moore-Grove relationship:** Regis McKenna, interview by author.

77. **Plain dumb luck**: Noyce in "Machine That Changed the World," IA. **Self doubts, Faking It**: Andy Grove in Gelbach, Grove, Jenkins oral history, IA.

78. **Grove's problems with Graham**: Andy Grove, interview by author.

79. **Graham's problems with Grove**: Bob Graham, interview by Charlie Sporck.

80. **Enmity began to poison**: Mike Markkula, interview by author.

Chapter 8: Takeoff

1. **Noyce's activities:** 1968 and 1969 datebooks, ASB. An entry from 3 Oct. 1968 reads "Disclosure of plans to customers."
2. **Nobody in the industry:** Andy Grove, interview by author.
3. **Family cutting rubylith:** Bill Noyce, interview by author. **They made one, they made one:** Roger Borovoy, interview by author.
4. **Began to talk of taking Intel public:** Gordon Moore, interview by author. **On Noyce's concerns about stock options:** Lindgren, "Building a Rational Two-Headed Monster."
5. **At prices that rivaled:** Noyce to employees, 20 Oct. 1969, courtesy Ted Hoff.
6. **Interesting transformation:** Gordon Moore, interview by Adam Noyce, GCA.
7. **Isn't management, drastic effect, and I don't get my kicks:** Lindgren, "Building a Rational Two-Headed Monster."
8. **Revenue trickle:** Gene Flath, interview by author.
9. **Problems with the multichip:** Tom Innes in Innes, Rowe oral history. **Moore's shock resistance test:** Gordon Moore in Moore, Vadasz oral history, IA.
10. **On the deposition:** notation in Noyce datebook, 14 March 1969: "FCI Depositions"; Roger Borovoy, personal communication to author, 2 Apr. 2004. **Evolutionary improvements:** Noyce in Davidow, Flath, and Noyce oral history, IA.
11. **There was no way:** Roger Borovoy, interview by author.
12. **Off and limping:** the progress report is quoted in Davidow, Flath, Noyce oral history. **Like peeling an onion:** Tom Rowe quoted in *Revolution in Progress* (1983, internal Intel publication): 10. **One day ho:** 4 Nov. 1968 report quoted in Innes, Rowe oral history, IA.
13. **Best news I've ever gotten, swamped with guilt:** Noyce in Davidow, Flath, Noyce oral history.
14. **Need is not for drill bits:** Noyce, 1965 Kleiman interview.
15. **Invention and development of the microprocessor:** see, for example, Robert Noyce and Marcian E. Hoff, Jr. [Ted Hoff], "A History of Microprocessor Development at Intel," *IEEE Micro* (Feb. 1981): 9; Frederico Faggin, "The Birth of the Microprocessor," reprinted in Jay Ranade, Alan Nash, eds., *Best of Byte* (N.Y.: McGraw-Hill, 1994), 355; Aspray, "Social Construction of the Microprocessor."
16. **500 inventors:** Bill Davidow, interview by author. Intel patent issued to Hoff et al., patent #3,821,715, filed 22 Jan. 1973, granted 28 June 1974; Micro Computer patent issued to Gilbert Hyatt, patent #4,942,156, filed 28 Dec. 1970, granted 17 July 1990; Texas Instruments patent issued to Gary W. Boone, patent #3,757,306, filed 31 Aug. 1971, granted 4 Sept. 1973.
17. **Funny deal with the microprocessor:** Gordon Moore, interview by author, 1 July 2004.
18. **Microprocessor would not have happened:** Andy Grove, interview by author.
19. **Intel nearly only manufacturer without partner:** Noyce in Davidow, Flath, Noyce oral history.
20. **On Sasaki and Sharp:** Dr. Tadashi Sasaki to author, 9 Oct. 2004. Willliam Aspray, "The Social Construction of the Microprocessor: A Japanese and

American Story," in Andrew Goldstein and William Aspray, eds. *Facets: New Perspectives on the Hsitory of Semicondcutors* (New Brunswick, N.J.: IEEE Center for the History of Electrical Engineering, 1977): 216–267.

21. **A god**: Roger Borovoy, interview by author. **We designed this because of you**: Ed Gelbach, interview by author. **Busicom appeared**: Gordon Moore, interview by author, 1 July 2004.

22. **Specifics of the Busicom/Intel agreement:** Provisional Agreement between Intel and Nippon Calculating Machine [parent company of Busicom], 28 April 1969, courtesy Ted Hoff.

23. **I had no design responsibilities:** Ted Hoff, interview by author.

24. **Kind of shocked:** Ted Hoff, interview by author.

25. **One chip performed:** James F. Donohoe, "The Microprocessor's First Decades: The Way It Was," *EDN Microprocessor Issue*, 27 Oct. 1988.

26. **Detail was not so good:** Shima quoted in Willliam Aspray, "The Social Construction of the Microprocessor: A Japanese and American Story," in Andrew Goldstein and William Aspray, eds. *Facets: New Perspectives on the History of Semicondcutors* (New Brunswick, N.J.: IEEE Center for the History of Electrical Engineering, 1977): 216–267.

27. **Exchange between Noyce and Hoff:** Ted Hoff, interview by author. **Argued yourself into some smart things**: Les Vadasz, interview by author.

28. **Why don't you go ahead**: Ted Hoff, interview by author.

29. **Made an announcement**: Gordon Moore in Moore, Vadasz, Parker oral history, 17 Oct. 1983, IA. **Reverse engineered a competing chip**: Tom Rowe in Innes, Rowe oral history, IA.

30. **Les was so excited**: Tom Rowe quoted in *Revolution in Progress* (1983, internal Intel publication): 10.

31. **Twenty to sixty cents per bit**: Bassett, *To the Digital Age*, 191. **Sales were sluggish**: "Intel Slices 2 Circuit Prices," *Electronic News*, 26 Jan. 1970.

32. **Always very helpful**: Ted Hoff, interview by author. **Enthusiasm not so obvious**: Gordon Moore, interview by author, 1 July 2004.

33. **All quotes from the letter:** Noyce to Mr. Y. Kojima, 21 Aug. 1969, courtesy Ted Hoff. **Bob Graham followed up with a letter:** Robert Graham to Mr. Y. Kojima, 16 Sept. 1969, courtesy Ted Hoff.

34. **Bit of a coup:** Hoff quoted in Aspray, "Social Construction of the Microprocessor."

35. **Agreement between the two companies:** agreement between Intel and Nippon Calculating Machine, 6 Feb. 1970, courtesy Ted Hoff. **Busicom executive sent a gently worded letter:** Saburo Yamada to Noyce, 20 March 1970, courtesy Ted Hoff.

36. **We're starting another project; go away, go away:** Andy Grove, interview by author.

37. **Management near panic:** this chart is referenced in Innes, Rowe oral history, IA. **More painful for Noyce than Moore**: Lindgren, "Two-Headed Monster."

38. **Headlines:** *Electronic News*, 27 July 1990.

39. **Rock was quite comfortable**: Gerard Currie, interview by author, 12 April 2004.

40. **The thing just couldn't remember**: Grove in Gelbach, Grove, Jenkins oral history, IA. **Hoff's 28-page memo:** "The Intel 1103: The MOS memory that defied cores," *Electronics*, 23 April 1973.

41. **1103 more challenging:** Gordon Moore, interview by author, 1 July 2004.
42. **When the light bulb was invented:** Steve Jobs quoted in Regis McKenna, *Real Time: Preparing for the Age of the Never Satisfied Customer* (Boston: Harvard Business School Press, 1997): 165.
43. **All you had to do:** Noyce in Davidow, Flath, Noyce oral history, IA. **Details on MIL agreement:** Securities and Exchange Commission, Intel Corporation Capital Stock Preliminary Prospectus, 20 July 1971. **Noyce told Intel's investors:** Noyce to Shareholders, 16 July 1970, courtesy Ted Hoff. **It's not every day:** Andy Grove, interview by author.
44. **As aggressively as I was capable, this will be the death of Intel:** Andy Grove, interview by author.
45. **We have decided to do this:** Andy Grove, interview by author. **MIL payment lowered losses:** Intel Corporation Consolidated Financial Statements, 31 Dec. 1971 and 1970, IA.
46. **Noyce at MIL party:** Stan Mazor in Mazor, Thompson, Whittier oral history.
47. **Your part depends:** "Noyce's Medieval Moonlighting," *Peninsula Electronics News*, 27 March 1972. **Hierarchy power and knowledge power:** Les Vadasz, interview by author. **Operations managers presenting to board:** Richard Hodgson, interview by author; Mike Markkula, interview by author.
48. **Wheel-type organization chart:** This anecdote is from Jackson, *Inside Intel*, 36.
49. **We, not I, did this:** Judy Vadasz, interview by author.
50. **One of the reasons:** Lindgren, "Building a Rational Two-Headed Monster." **On Cybercom:** Julius Blank to author, 17 May 2004.
51. **On Coherent Radiation:** Jim Hobart, interview by author; Coherent Radiation Annual Reports, 1970–1983; Coherent Radiation Initial Public Offering Prospectus, 19 May 1970.
52. **On Four-Phase:** Lee Boysel, interview with author. For a discussion of why Boysel did not trumpet the news of Four-Phase's microprocessor, see Bassett, *To the Digital Age*, 256–261.
53. **Somehow they usually reached:** Glenn Leggett, interview by author.
54. **This College:** FBI report quoted in Alan Jones, *Pioneering*, 176. **Playboy is a money changer:** Alan Jones, *Pioneering*, 173. **Outside agitators:** Penny Noyce to author, 27 April 2004.
55. **Big city kids:** Glenn Leggett, interview by author. **Violent action:** Glenn Leggett to Grinnell parents, reprinted in *Grinnell Scarlet & Black*, 15 May 1970. **Act of official repression:** resolution quoted in Alan Jones, *Pioneering*, 177. For protests and tensions at Grinnell in April and May 1970, the best source is the student newspaper, *Grinnell Scarlet & Black*. **Temperature at that campus was rising:** Glenn Leggett, interview by author.
56. **We [trustees] don't know anything:** Glenn Leggett, interview by author.
57. **Events at Kent State predictable:** Penny Noyce to author, 28 April 2004. **A pioneering adventure:** Alan Jones, *Pioneering*, 177. **Student athletes refusing to compete, Noyce worried that the college was pandering:** George Drake, interview by author. **We are the revolutionaries:** Moore quoted in Gene Bylinsky, "How Intel Won Its Bet on Memory Chips," *Fortune*, Nov. 1973, 143.
58. **It helped, Andy couldn't have done that:** Ed Gelbach, interview by author.
59. **Japan's percentage of Intel's sales:** Intel SEC filing, March 1972. **Kojima wanted Intel:** My choice of the February date for this conversation is based

on notations in Noyce's 1971 datebook, which indicate the two men met on February 8 in Japan. Mr. Kojima does not appear again in Noyce's notes until September 21.

60. **Standard 2-by-4 or 6-penny nail**: Noyce quoted in "The past, present and future of microprocessors," *San Jose Mercury News*, 19 Oct. 1981.

61. **On Noyce's private market research**: Noyce in Davidow, Flath, Noyce oral history; Bill Davidow recalls being buttonholed by Noyce in early 1970 (when Davidow was at Intel competitor Signetics), who asked him about his thoughts on "a general purpose way of programming logic." Noyce's datebooks show conversations with Davidow in November and December 1969.

62. **Noyce was almost alone among senior management**: Ted Hoff, interview by author; Les Vadasz, interview by author. **Hoff thinks**: Gordon Moore, interview by author. **2,000 units per year**: Noyce and Hoff, "A History of Microprocessor Development at Intel," *IEEE Micro*, Feb. 1981.

63. **On office building**: "Intel Corp. Breaks Ground for New Headquarters," *Palo Alto Times*, 21 April 1970.

64. **When I came down for breakfast**: Ted Hoff, interview by author.

65. **Every major computer manufacturer**: "Markkula Takes Intel Market Post," *Electronic News*, 8 Feb. 1971. **Noyce and Rock felt**: Arthur Rock, interview by author. **One robin doesn't make a spring**: Noyce to All Employees, undated but clearly Sept. 1971, courtesy Ted Hoff.

66. **Noyce's IPO-related activities**: Noyce 1971 datebook.

67. **Options to every employee, including janitors**: Mike Markkula, interview by author. **Details of stock purchase plan**: Noyce to All Employees, 25 Jan. 1972, courtesy Ted Hoff.

68. **It was far too painful, Grove conversation with Moore**: Andy Grove, interview by author.

69. **Noyce began interviewing**: Noyce 1971 datebook. **Grove interviewed Gelbach**: Ed Gelbach, interview by author. **Mustache impressed Grove**: Grove, Gelbach, Jenkins oral history, IA.

70. **Made it a lot easier for me**: Gordon Moore, interview by author. **Noyce interaction with Graham, Graham conversation with his wife**: Bob Graham, interview by Charlie Sporck.

71. **Like cutting out his liver**: Andy Grove, interview by author.

72. **All quotes on microprocessor**: Noyce 1971–1973 record book.

73. **Exclusivity**: 31 Aug. 1971 entry in 1971-73 record book **Negotiations finalized September 21**: Noyce's meeting with Busicom is from his datebook. In a 1983 interview, Noyce said that the negotiations were conducted in Japan, and that he attended them. Moreover, materials Intel filed with the SEC, dated 20 July 1971, make no mention of a microprocessor or logic-circuit business, which leads me to believe the rights were negotiated back to Intel after this date. **Japanese don't use lawyers**: Noyce in Davidow, Flath, Noyce oral history, IA.

74. **Tiger by the tail**: Ted Hoff, interview by author. **Should we wait to get something better**: Noyce in Davidow, Flath, Noyce oral history, IA. **On board fears of microprocessor**: Gelbach, Grove, and Jenkins oral history; Noyce and Hoff, "History of Microprocessor Development at Intel," 13.

75. **Every time you delay**: Ted Hoff, interview by author.

76. **Microprocessors meant nothing**: Andy Grove, interview by author.

77. **On Intel IPO:** Securities and Exchange Commission, *Intel Corporation Capital Stock Preliminary Prospectus*, 20 July 1971.
78. **All biographical details about Barbara Maness and details about her relationship with Noyce:** Barbara Eiler (the former Barbara Maness), interview by author.
79. **An open invitation for Bob to find another woman:** Intel executive requesting anonymity.
80. **I was very protective:** Barbara Eiler, interview by author.
81. **A millionaire ten times over:** Securities and Exchange Commission, *Intel Corporation Capital Stock Preliminary Prospectus*, 20 July 1971.
82. **Tough to teach values, easier to be raised by a poor father:** Kathy Cohen, interview by author.
83. **A new era:** "Announcing a New Era of Integrated Electronics," (advertisement), *Electronic News*, 15 Nov. 1971. **More than 5,000 people, reference to the suite:** Aspray, "Social History of the Microprocessor," 243.
84. **Changes not by moving objects:** Noyce and Hoff, "A History of Microprocessor Development at Intel," 13.
85. **Couldn't promote:** Regis McKenna, interview by Rob Walker, Silicon Genesis collection, SSC. **Independent microprocessor marketing:** "We absolutely had a small company going for practical purposes." Ed Gelbach in Gelbach, Grove, Jenkins oral history. **Owners' manual ran over 100 pages:** Frederico Faggin, "The Birth of the Microprocessor," 356. **Lots of people who wanted to read:** Bill Davidow in Davidow, Flath, and Noyce oral history.
86. **Lower confrontation level:** Bill Davidow in Davidow, Flath, Noyce oral history. **Intel seminars:** "Intel's Second Computer On a Chip!" advertisement, *Electronic News*, 24 April 1972.
87. **Uses of microprocessors:** Regis McKenna, interview by author. **Customers to be proud of:** Gelbach, Grove, Jenkins oral history.
88. **How Noyce defused problems:** Mike Markkula, interview by author; Roger Borovoy, interview by author.
89. **Missionary work:** Noyce and Hoff, "A History of Microprocessor Development at Intel," *IEEE Micro*, Feb. 1981. **Noyce's speech during family bus ride:** Linda Vognar and Bob Noyce [Don Noyce's son], interview by author.
90. **Microprocessor was just a toy:** Bill Davidow, interview by author.
91. **Microprocessor falling through the floor:** Regis McKenna, interview by author; Ted Hoff, interview by author; Lindgren, "Building a Rational Two-Headed Monster." **On microprocessor repairs:** Ted Hoff, interview by author.
92. **Battle of opinion:** Noyce quoted in Donohue, " Microprocessor's First Two Decades: The Way it Was."
93. **Noyce visit to General Motors:** Davidow, Flath, and Noyce oral history, IA.
94. **4004 slow and rudimentary:** "The Chip—Twentieth-Century Revolutionary," [roughly 1983], IA.
95. **Noyce taking concept car for a spin:** Noyce in Davidow, Flath, Noyce oral history.

Chapter 9: The Edge of What's Barely Possible

1. **We are not doing well at all:** Grove's ESM [Executive Staff Meeting] notes 10 Jan. 1972, IA. **Brief, between long periods of silence and sighs:** Grove's ESM notes, 4 Dec. 1972, IA.

2. **One hundred thousand 1103s each year:** Noyce quoted in "Viewpoint," *New Electronics*, 25 April 1972. **No competitors:** "Gelbach Maps Intel Goals," *Electronic News*, 23 Aug. 1971. **Effectively all of Intel's revenue was dependent on the 1103:** Ed Gelbach quoted in Gelbach, Grove, and Jenkins oral history, IA. An academic who team-teaches a course at Stanford with Andy Grove estimates that the 1103 accounted for fully 90 percent of Intel's 1972 revenue. Robert A. Burgelman, "Fading Memories: A Process Study of Strategic Business Exit in Dynamic Environments." *Administrative Science Quarterly* 39 (1994): 24–56.

3. **Noyce's interest in daycare center:** "Day care center—get involved," note from 31 Jan. 1972, record book; conversation with Jean Jones.

4. **$2 million for Microma:** Minutes of Board of Directors meeting, 13 April 1972, IA. **$20 million expected Microma sales:** Sam Rosenthal to Joe Rosenfield, 27 Nov. 1972, courtesy Warren Buffett.

5. **Boy Noyce showed us:** Sam Rosenthal to Joe Rosenfield, 27 Nov. 1972, courtesy Warren Buffett.

6. **Forty percent pretax margin:** Joe Rosenfield to Sam Rosenthal, Don Wilson, and Warren Buffett, 17 April 1973, courtesy Warren Buffett.

7. **Moved 1974 research to 1973, Bob is very anxious:** Joe Rosenfield to Sam Rosenthal, Don Wilson, and Warren Buffett, 17 April 1973, courtesy Warren Buffett.

8. **Intel is the best vehicle we have:** Warren Buffett to Joe Rosenfield, 20 April, 1973. Courtesy Warren Buffett.

9. **Just to put your minds at rest:** Noyce to Optionees, 3 March 1973, IA. **Only thing limiting its growth:** Noyce quoted in Lloyd Watson, "A Classic Case of Growth," *San Francisco Chronicle*, no date, but clearly 1973.

10. **Assumed petrochemicals and power were free and available:** "Coast Semicon firms Gird for Worst in Energy Crisis," *Electronic News*, 3 Dec. 1973. **Power consumption of fabs:** "Electronics Industry's Power Plea," *San Francisco Chronicle*, 4 Dec. 1973.

11. **After a third blackout:** Noyce quoted in "Electronics Industry's Power Plea," *San Francisco Chronicle*, 4 Dec. 1973. **Pushed for bill:** "Semicon Firms Hit Power Cut Plans," *Electronic News*, 10 Dec. 1973; "Bay Area Energy Crisis Spreads Throughout California, *Electronic News*, 24 Nov. 1973; "Energy Fight in 2d Phase," *Electronic News*, 17 December 1973; "Utilities Commission Holds Bay Area Fate," *Electronic News*, 3 Dec. 1973; "Electronics Industry's Power Plea," *San Francisco Chronicle*, 4 Dec. 1973; "Bill to Prohibit Blackouts in Calif. 'Watered Down,'" *Electronic News*, 4 Feb. 1974.

12. **This really is a controlled society:** Noyce quoted in Lindgren, "Building a Rational Two-Headed Monster."

13. **Government affecting our lives more and more:** Noyce quoted in Ron Iscoff, "No Slowdown in Demand for Semicons: Noyce," *Electronic News*, 31 Dec. 1973.

14. **Teetering on the edge of what's barely possible, electronic applications appear to be unlimited:** Noyce in *Peninsula, Electronics News*, 31 Dec. 1973.

15. **Value of Noyce's stock:** calculated by multiplying the number of his shares by the appropriate market price of Intel's stock as recorded in a historical chart included in Form S-8 filed with the Securities and Exchange Commission, 21 June 1976.

16. **Do you think I could do:** Penny Noyce, interview by author. **Get the barriers out of the way:** Noyce quoted in Walter Guzzardi, "Wisdom from the Giants of Business," *Fortune* 3 July 1989, 78–91.

17. **Noyce's work with the puffins:** Steve Kress (director of the Puffin Project), interview by author.

18. **You do a little work for a little money:** Penny Noyce, interview by author.

19. **Money can do lots of things:** Polly Noyce, interview by author.

20. **On the first use of the term "Silicon Valley":** Don Hoefler, "Silicon Valley—USA," *Electronic News* (11, 18, and 25 Jan. 1971); and Hoefler, "Captains Outrageous" and "Taking Blame for the Name," *California Today* (supplement to the *San Jose Mercury News*), 28 June 1981, 42–45. Sources for other names for the region are Charles Petit, "Wizard of Silicon Gulch," *Peninsula Times Tribune*, 21 Sept. 1977; Bill Densmore, "The Santa Clara Valley electronics industry comes of age during the 'me' generation decade," *Peninsula Times Tribune*, 28 Dec. 1979, "The Splintering of the Solid-State Electronics Industry," *Innovation* 8, 1969. **Articles on Noyce and Moore:** "Why cores could become just a memory," *Business Week*, 26 Dec. 1970—ostensibly about the memory business, but contains exactly one photo—of Noyce. *Fortune* **article:** Gene Bylinsky, "How Intel won its bet on memory chips," *Fortune*, Nov. 1973.

21. **Extension of the microcomputer into just about everything:** "Interview Robert Noyce—1973," IA. **Control gadgetry will permit:** Lindsay Arthur, "The Computer Miracle for the Home and Car," no date, but clearly 1973, IA. **Noyce's speech:** Bill Noyce to family, 14 April [1973].

22. **Dr. Noyce finds time for skiing:** "Bob Noyce of Intel Speaks Out on the Integrated Circuit Industry," *EDN/EEE*, 15 Sept. 1971. **Just what every parent hopes:** "Noyce's New Winner: Intel," *Electronic Engineering Times*, 11 Sept. 1972.

23. **Uncle Bob's new watch:** Don Noyce to Nancy and Don Noyce, 29 Sept. 1972, DSN.

24. **If I made the simplest request:** Penny to Mummy, Polly, and Bill, 11 Aug. [1972], courtesy Penny Noyce. **Crash of the charter plane:** Penny Noyce, interview by author; Bill Cohen, interview by author; note dated 3/12[/74], courtesy Penny Noyce, reading, "Your 414 is down. Mr. _ and three other people are aboard. They have a report of a radio beacon in the Carson City area. Please call for more details."

25. **Society's negative attitude towards technology:** Noyce, 1982 Reid interview.

26. **Didn't like myself, tried to switch:** Noyce in Davidow, Flath, Noyce oral history, IA.

27. **Only bad mothers weren't home for their children:** Penny Noyce, interview by author.

28. **Intel like the war effort:** Judy Vadasz, interview by author.

29. **Too much executive ability:** Penny Noyce, interview by author. **Just another husband carrying a briefcase:** Phyllis and Bob Kefauver, interview by author. **Betty Noyce yelling or crying:** multiple interviews, all requesting anonymity on this detail.

30. **Smoking a pack of cigarettes each:** Jim Angell, interview by author.

31. **Simpler to get on a plane to New York:** Glenn Leggett, interview by author.

32. **I'm not afraid of the responsibility:** Bill to Da, 18 Oct. 1973, courtesy Penny Noyce. Noyce's letter to Bill is lost, but this reply directly references Noyce's objections.

33. **I am overwhelmed, awed:** Penny Noyce to Bob Noyce, 6 Nov. 1974.

34. **Betty's unsent letter to her mother:** Betty Noyce to Mimi [her mother], 25 April 1974, courtesy Penny Noyce. All quotes from Betty regarding the divorce come from this letter.

35. **Divorce was wrong:** Gaylord Noyce, interview by author.

36. **Profit margin and net income statements:** 1974 Intel annual report. **60 percent of plant space, 70 percent of employees:** Andy Grove quoted in William Doyle, "Intel Out to Prove Drucker Wrong," *Oakland Tribune*, 27 Feb. 1974. **Could be bought for less than one-tenth of a penny:** "Boom Times Again for Semiconductors," *Business Week*, 20 April 1974, 66.

37. **A billion bits per month:** "Intel Sees New Products Cutting Into Profit Margins," *Electronic News*, 4 March 1974. **Eighteen competing microprocessors:** Noyce, "Microprocessors," *Electronic Engineering Times Anniversary Issue* (Nov. 1987): A15–A20, IA.

38. **Skipped the adventures:** Steve Kress, interview by author.

39. **It was outright warfare:** Anonymous interview by author.

40. **Money is just one part:** Paul Hwoschinsky, *True Wealth* (Berkeley, Ca.: Ten Speed Press, 1990): 2.

41. **If you walk off a cliff:** Paul Hwoschinsky, interview by author, 3 June 2003.

42. **The bulk was Intel stock:** Paul Hwoschinsky, interview by author, 3 June 2003.

43. **What's this?:** All quotes in the discussion of the shoebox startups are from Paul Hwoschinsky, interview by author, 3 June 2003.

44. **Well, so what?:** Les Vadasz, interview by Evan Ramstad.

45. **Page Mill Partners drinking group:** Jack Melchor, interview by author.

46. **Da is a little sad:** Penny Noyce to Betty Noyce, 4 Sept. 1974, courtesy Penny Noyce. **Choose parent for parents' weekend:** Margaret Noyce to Betty Noyce, 5 Oct. 1974, courtesy Penny Noyce. **Nothing else I've done matters:** interview with a person at the dinner who requested anonymity.

47. **Precipitous drop in Intel's share:** this stemmed from a bizarre coincidence of events. After the market closed on Wednesday, July 3, Intel announced that its second-quarter revenues were lower than expected. The traders familiar with Intel stock were not at their desks to hear the news, however. Their annual convention was being held the following week, and most of them had decided to spend a long Independence Day holiday near the convention site in Florida. When the stock market reopened on Friday, July 5, the reserve traders, having read the reports of Intel's lower-than-expected sales, began furiously selling Intel stock. The price of an Intel share plummeted from 63½ to 44½ **Details of the same-day stock-sale program:** Bob Harrington, interview by author.

48. **Virtually all:** Larry Hootnick [vice president, finance] to Andy Grove, 2 April 1975, IA.

49. **Seed came from:** Bob Harrington, interview by author.

50. **1974 layoffs in the semiconductor industry:** "Intel Shuts Down for Week; AMI Cuts 230; Cite Flatness," *Electronic News*, 6 Sept. 1974; "Intel, Intersil Trim Payroll," *Electronic News*, 12 Aug. 1974, 16.

51. **Microma pretax loss in Dec. 1974:** Larry Hootnick to Board of Directors, "Subject: Microma—December, 1974 Actual vs. Plan 75.0," 15 Jan. 1975, IA. **Intel second-sourcing Mostek:** *Electronic News,* 30 Dec. 1974. **AMD, Signetics, and Mostek performance:** AMD 1975 annual report, Signetics 1974 annual report, Mostek 1975 annual report.

52. **Necessary to have a reduction in our work force:** Noyce to all employees, 7 Oct. 1974, IA.

53. **Layoff data:** Real, *Revolution in Progress,* 47. **For a few goddamned points:** Regis McKenna, interview by author.

54. **Did not anticipate changes, tremendous price attrition:** Martin Gold, "Intel's Noyce: No Semicon Upturn in Next 6 Months," *Electronic News,* 14 Oct. 1974. Paul Plansky," Protests Mark Wema Meeting," *Electronic News,* 2 Dec. 1974.

55. **Nearly 20 percent laid off:** Ramon C. Sevilla, "Employment practices and industrial restructuring: A case study of the semiconductor industry in Silicon Valley, 1955–1991," (PhD dissertation, UCLA, 1992), Table 3.10, 179. **Noyce a dominant force:** "WEMA Medal of Achievement to Intel's Dr. Robert Noyce" [WEMA Press Release], 27 Sept. 1974, ASB. **Slogans on signs:** Paul Plansky," Protests Mark Wema Meeting."

56. **Rock conjectures:** Arthur Rock speaking at the San Jose memorial service, 18 June 1990. **It was not unusual:** Gordon Moore, interview by author, 1 July 2004.

57. **Grove wanted more and more:** Richard Hodgson, interview by author. **Andy had gotten over his PhD:** Gordon Moore, interview by author, 1 July 2004.

58. **Five-week cycle for staff meetings:** Noyce record book, 3 Jan. 1972.

59. **From outside Bob running:** Intel employee who requested not to be attributed on this point.

60. **How can we get you ready/give me the job:** Andy Grove, interview by author.

61. **Noyce and Grove planned:** Noyce's 1975 datebook.

62. **Wild expansionist:** Moore quoted in Lindgren, "Two-Headed Monster." **Walking the thin line next to the cliff:** Noyce quoted in Lloyd Watson, "A Classic Case of Growth," *San Francisco Chronicle,* no date, but clearly 1973.

63. **Our five year goal:** Noyce in Davidow, Flath, Noyce oral history, IA.

64. **Let's take the hill:** Roger Borovoy, interview by author.

65. **Fully functional $300 computer:** Gelbach, Grove, Jenkins oral history.

66. **Bill Noyce's comments to his grandmother:** a photo of the computer screen in a family photo album, courtesy Polly Noyce. Computer/motor analogy: Bill Noyce, interview by author.

67. **Thought he would either faint or hit me:** Gelbach in Gelbach, Grove, Jenkins oral history. **Ours is not a general purpose microcomputer:** Andy Grove, interview by author. It is interesting to note that in an interview from the mid-1980s ("Machine that Changed the World" interview, IA), Noyce says that he "missed the personal computer"—that he did not appreciate the potential size of the market nor the probable impact of the device. This comment may mean that Noyce envisioned the Intel machine for business use, or that he simply underestimated the size of the market—or that he was being characteristically self-effacing. In any case, Gelbach, Grove, and Moore all independently told very similar stories about Noyce's push for an Intel computer. Documentary evidence has yet to emerge.

68. **World's largest computer manufacturer:** Noyce quoted in Gene Bylinsky, "Here Comes the Second Computer Revolution," *Fortune*, Nov. 1975.
69. **Emphasis shifting to control:** "Intel's Robert Noyce Kicks Himself Upstairs," *Business Week*, 14 Dec. 1974.
70. **Leadership by personal contact:** "Intel's Robert Noyce Kicks Himself Upstairs," *Business Week*, 14 Dec. 1974. McIntel and high-technology jelly beans: Victor K. McElheny, "High Technology Jelly Bean Ace," *New York Times*, 5 June 1977. Grove originally made these comments to a meeting of security analysts in 1974.
71. **Bob practically disappeared:** Andy Grove, interview by author.
72. **Population of Crete:** approximation based on census data . **$50,000 donation:** Philip Heckman to Bob Noyce, 21 June 1975, ASB.
73. **Dedication of the Noyce Chapel at Doane College:** Unless otherwise noted, the description and quotes are from a booklet of recollections Harriet Noyce assembled, "The Noyce Chapel, A Service of Tribute and Dedication," ASB.
74. **How deeply it moves me:** Ralph Noyce to Bob Noyce, 21 May 1975.

Chapter 10: Renewal

1. **Ann Bowers biography:** Ann Bowers, interview by author, 5 Aug. 2004 and 16 Aug. 2004.
2. **He could recall slogan:** In his 1982 interview with T. R. Reid, Noyce recited this slogan without any prompting from Reid.
3. **Largest single stockholder:** Betty Noyce quoted in "Betty Noyce Starts a Bank of Her Own," *Maine Times*, 4 Oct. 1991. **Rumors that Betty Noyce:** "Intel Founder's Ex-Wife Reported Selling Shares," *San Francisco Examiner*, 25 June 1976.
4. **On Betty Noyce's philanthropy:** Ellen Goodman, "Making a Difference," *San Francisco Chronicle*, 26 Sept. 1996); "Betty Noyce Starts a Bank of Her Own," *Maine Times*, 4 Oct. 1991; obituaries in *Portland Press Herald* (23 Sept. 1996) and *Bangor Daily News* (19 Sept. 1996); articles on the opening of the public market and an L.L. Bean store from June and July, 1996 in *Portland Press Herald* and *Maine Sunday Telegram*. An excellent profile of Betty Noyce is Kim Strosnider, "Noyce shuns limelight while showing the way," *Maine Sunday Telegram*, 3 Dec. 1995. All articles courtesy Libra Foundation and Owen Wells.
5. **Bowers conversation with Grove:** Ann Bowers, interview by author, 5 Aug. 2004.
6. **All quotes this paragraph:** Gordon Moore to employees, 4 June 1976, IA.
7. **Non-union and wish to remain so:** "Non-Union Seminar Slated," *Palo Alto Times*, 26 Dec. 1973. The seminar was conducted in January 1974, PSC. **A copy of the leaflet on every desk:** Mike Eisenscher quoted in Sevilla, "Employment Practices and Industrial Restructuring," 295.
8. **25 percent more:** Charles Goldstein quoted in Ron Iscoff, "Wages Not Key Factor in Employee Unionization," *West Coast Electronic News*, 18 April 1977, PSC. **5,000 workers struck:** "3 Electronics Firms Hit By Strikes in Bay Area," *Electronic News*, 8 April 1968; Sevilla, 156.
9. **Intel bonus meetings:** Sevilla 296. **If you believe:** Charles Goldstein quoted in Ron Iscoff, "Wages Not Key Factor in Employee Unionization," *West Coast Electronic News*, 18 April 1977, PSC.

10. **Scary places to work:** Gene Flath in Davidow, Flath, and Noyce oral history, IA. **Big 1103 machine:** Real, "Revolution in Progress," 41, IA.
11. **We were petrified:** Linda Erlich, interview by Rachel Stewart, IA.
12. **They were just so nervous:** Gene Flath in Davidow, Flath, and Noyce oral history, IA.
13. **36 percent to 27 percent:** Statistical Abstract of the United States, 1990, Chart 728; Statistical Abstract of the United States, 1984, Chart 698. **Demographics of production workers:** Sevilla, "Employment Practices and Industrial Restructuring," 172, 292. **1979 turnover rates:** Sevilla, "Employment Practices and Industrial Restructuring," 299.
14. **Our non-union status:** Gordon Moore to all employees, 6 July 1976, IA.
15. **Too strong:** Gordon Moore, interview by author, 1 July 2004. **Noyce speaking on automotive electronics:** See, for example, Noyce, "Power Train Control: A Convergence of LSI Technologies," *Automotive Electronics*, 1978, IA; Noyce and Craig R. Barrett, "The Automobile and the Microcomputer Revolution—Solving the Reliability Problem," [1984?], IA. **Noyce analyst presentation:** Noyce, "Intel Corporation Presentation to the New York Society of Security Analysts," 31 Jan. 1978, ASB.
16. **I ran into Noyce:** Tom Rowe in Innes, Rowe oral history, IA.
17. **I've been doing a lot of venture stuff:** Paul Hwoschinsky, interview by author.
18. **Noyce most likely among them:** in his interview with the author, Eugene Kleiner stressed that it had been very difficult to find limited partners for the first Kleiner Perkins fund. Kleiner and Noyce had already invested in each other's companies once (Kleiner in Intel and Noyce in Kleiner's peripherals company Cybercom). It is thus almost certain that Kleiner would have offered Noyce an opportunity to invest in his venture fund. Noyce almost certainly would have taken him up on this offer, but a firm's list of limited partners is, of course, proprietary. It should be noted, however, that Ann Bowers says that after their 1975 marriage, Noyce was not a limited partner in any Kleiner Perkins fund.
19. **Invest and hope:** Eugene Kleiner, interview by author.
20. **First fund returned 40 times:** Eugene Kleiner, interview by Charlie Sporck.
21. **Can only lose 100 percent:** Paul Hwoschinsky, interview by author, 3 June 2003.
22. **Callanish Fund:** Unless otherwise noted, information is from Paul Hwoschinsky, interview by author, 3 June 2003. The names of many Callanish companies appear throughout Noyce's datebooks.
23. **Noyce's other company:** Jay Palmer, "Achieving Recognition—Caere, the *Other* Noyce Company, is Coming into Its Own," *Barron's*, 5 Aug. 1991.
24. **Helped convince his friends:** Among the investors in Caere were Grinnell College, Venrock Associates (with whom Noyce had invested at Intel and Coherent Radiation), and Asset Management Partners (whose principal Pitch Johnson was a major investor in Coherent Radiation). Caere IPO Prospectus, 19 Oct. 1989, courtesy Bob Teresi.
25. **Caere:** Unless otherwise indicated, information is from Bob Teresi, interview by author.
26. **Paying back the system:** Jim Dutton, interview by author.
27. **Probably $250,000:** Neither Dutton nor Teresi recalls the precise amount. Since the company was privately held at the time, no record of the transaction was filed with the Securities and Exchange Commission.

28. **Electronics company of the year:** unidentified clipping, IA.
29. **I propose:** Gordon Moore to Ricard Gottier (Control Data Corporation), 4 Apr. 1975. **Will you two please look:** Moore to R. S. Borovoy and L. R. Hootnick, 18 July 1975. **You should concentrate:** Moore to W. F. Jordan, 20 Jan. 1975. **Ann Bowers has announced:** Moore to employees, 20 May 1976. **Grove amplifying Moore:** Gordon Moore, interview by Rachel Stewart, no date. All items, IA.
30. **Noyce's personality was so outstanding:** Gordon Moore, interview by Adam Noyce, no date [probably 2000], GCA.
31. **What really differentiates:** Regis McKenna, interview by author.
32. **I was just born:** Bob Harrington, interview by author.
33. *Business Week* **cover:** "New Leaders in Semiconductors," *Business Week*, 1 March 1976. *New York Times* **profile:** Viktor K. McElheny, "Dissatisfaction as a Spur to Career," *New York Times*, 15 Dec. 1976.
34. **It is rare:** James M. Early to Noyce, 9 Dec. 1977, ASB.
35. **Model of entrepreneurial endeavor:** general Christmas letter from Ann Bowers and Bob Noyce, 7 Dec. 1978, Grant Gale Papers, GCA. **Only risk:** Viktor K. McElheny, "An Industrial 'Innovation Crisis' is Decried at MIT Symposium," *New York Times*, 10 Dec. 1976. **Entrepreneur not John Wayne:** Noyce, "Speech Outline: Entrepreneurship, MIT," [no date, but clearly delivered at the MIT symposium], IA. **Be confident of success:** Robert Noyce, "Innovation: Nothing to Fear but Fear" [summary of MIT Symposium on the management of Innovation], *Technology Review*, Feb. 1977.
36. **A little humble, a little proud:** clip from an unidentified interview included in "Remembrance of a Life Well Lived," video, IA.
37. **Several people hasten to tell me:** Herb Caen, "Update," *San Francisco Chronicle*, 5 Feb. 1980.
38. **My father was good at everything:** Penny Noyce, interview by author, 9 Apr. 2002.
39. **You've got a nice family:** interview subject requested anonymity.
40. **Make Andy more visible:** Regis McKenna, interview by author. **Feature article on Grove:** Viktor K. McElheny, "Spotlight: High-Technology Jelly Bean Ace," *New York Times*, 5 June 1977.
41. **Showoff side to Bob:** Ann Bowers, interview by author, 22 Jun. 2002. **Hell of a diving show:** Charlie Sporck, interview by author. **K2 jacket story:** Richard Hodgson speaking at the Intel memorial service for Noyce, video, ASB. **Liked being special:** Jim Lafferty, interview by author.
42. **Noyce stepped in front of me:** Harry Sello, interview by author.
43. **Jackie Onassis:** Harriet Noyce to Girls, 8 Feb. 1984, DSN. **Pictorial salute to Noyce:** much-altered *Playgirl*, Jan. 1984, ASB.
44. **Sales of $500 billion:** Wells Fargo Bank, N.A., "Economic Forecast—Santa Clara County: Growth Prospects to 1990," April 1982, 9, IA. **18 percent annual growth:** Wells Fargo Bank, "Economic Forecast," 9. **1.5 million manufacturing workers:** Susan Benner, "Storm Clouds Over Silicon Valley," *Inc.*, Sept. 1982, 84. **High-technology employment grew:** Association of Bay Area Governments, "Silicon Valley and Beyond: High Technology Growth for the San Francisco Bay Area," (Working Papers on the Region's Economy, No. 2), 1; "The Silicon Valley Economy," *FRBSF [Federal Reserve Bank of San Francisco] Weekly Newsletter*, Number 92–22, 29 May 29 1992. (Jobs increased from 380,000 to 665,000.) **Sixty pages of advertisements:**

Sevilla, "Employment Practices and Industrial Restructuring," 238. **Per capita personal income growth:** Wells Fargo Bank, "Economic Forecast," 17.

45. **More millionaires:** Kindel and Teitelman, "Go East, Young Man," 132. **More than 1,000 companies:** "A U.S. Revolution: Instant Tycoons in Silicon Valley," *San Francisco Chronicle*, 23 Sept. 1980. **If there is any hope:** Arthur Levitt, Jr., quoted in Alexander L. Taylor III, "Striking It Rich," *Time*, 15 Feb. 1982.

46. **Small entrepreneurs depend totally:** Robert Noyce, Testimony before Congress, Telecommunications and Finance Subcommittee of the House Energy and Commerce Committee, *High Definition Television: Hearing Before the House Telecommunications and Finance Subcommittee of the House Energy and Commerce Committee*, 13 Sept., 1989.

47. **Apple founding:** Mike Markkula, interview by author; Steve Jobs, interview by author; Michael Moritz, *The Little Kingdom: The Private Story of Apple Computer* (New York: William Morrow and Co., 1984).

48. **Nothing else was in Intel's interest:** Mike Markkula, interview by author. Even a supplier-customer relationship between Intel and Apple failed to materialize. Wozniak had originally chosen a Motorola processor for Apple machines, and even though Markkula says he and Grove met several times to discuss whether a switch to an Intel chip was warranted, "the timing was never right," and so Apple stayed with Motorola.

49. **Jobs at McKenna dinner:** Ann Bowers, interview by author.

50. **Not very appealing:** Arthur Rock quoted in "HBS [Harvard Business School] Working Knowledge," http://hbswk.hbs.edu/pubitem.jhtml?id=1821&t=special_reports_donedeals

51. **Noyce and Jobs Seabee accident:** Steve Jobs, interview by author.

52. **Remember personal things:** Steve Jobs, interview by author.

53. **Apple Computer IPO:** Apple Computer prospectus, 12 Dec. 1980.

54. **On Tandem:** Smith, "Silicon Valley Spirit"; "The fall of an American Icon," *Business Week*, 5 Feb. 1996. **Compaq acquisition of Tandem:** David Lazarus, "Compaq Boosts High End with Tandem Deal," *Inc.*, 23 June 1997.

55. **On Atari:** http://www.campusprogram.com/reference/en/wikipedia/n/no/nolan_bushnell.html

56. **On Genentech:** Timeline and Investors Fact Sheet at http://www.gene.com, accessed 24 Aug. 2004.

57. **More than 3,000 small firms:** Lenny Siegel, Testimony Prepared for the Subcommittee on Science, Research, and Technology of the House Committee on Science and Technology and the Task Force on Education and Employment of the House Budget Committee, 16 June 1983, PSC. **Supply chain:** James F. Gibbons, "The Relationship Between Stanford and Silicon Valley," unpublished speech manuscript, 11, courtesy James Gibbons.

58. **Noyce joined drinking club:** Jack Melchor, interview by author.

59. **Educational offerings:** This paragraph relies heavily on Saxenian, *Regional Advantage*, 42.

60. **Prestige and clean image:** Wells Fargo, "Economic Forecast," IA. **Business machine:** Andy Grove, handwritten notes titled "Stanford talk—Si Valley," IA.

61. **Look around Silicon Valley:** Noyce quoted in "Bob Noyce talks to *Upside*," *Upside*, July 1990 [interview date is 23 May 1990]. Former Stanford Dean of Engineering James Gibbons, a long-time participant in and observer of Silicon

Valley, makes the identical point—"the heroes in Silicon Valley are the entrepreneurs" in James F. Gibbons, "The Role of Stanford University: A Dean's Reflections," in *The Silicon Valley Edge: A Habitat for Innovation and Entrepreneurship*, ed. Chong-Moon Lee, William F. Miller, Marguerite Gong Hancock, and Henry S. Rowen (Stanford: Stanford University Press), 200–217.

62. **Why do we love:** Martin Meeker, "Silicon Valley's Silver Lining," (Letter to the Editor), *Inc.*, Dec. 1982, 11.

63. **Violation of Murphy's Law:** Noyce, "Big Bang Paris—RNN Talking Points," [speech outline] 12 Apr. 1988, IA. **Established companies flourished:** Only one semiconductor company was launched in the 1973–1978 period, when the prohibitively high fixed costs of building a fab—roughly six times what Noyce and Moore paid in 1968—discouraged most new entrants to the industry. **Top twelve American firms:** *Electronic Market Data Book: 1981 Edition* (Electronic Industries Association: 1981), 92.

64. **Intel tenth anniversary celebration:** "Intel Celebrates," *San Jose Mercury News*, 23 Aug. 1978.

65. **Birthplace of freedom:** Such ideas can be traced to the writings of historian Frederick Jackson Turner. The "free lands" of the West, Turner wrote, served as a "gate of escape" and reinvigorated the country by promoting "individualism, economic equality, freedom to rise, [and] democracy." Frederick Jackson Turner, "Contributions of the West to American Democracy," *Atlantic Monthly*, 91, Jan. 1903, 91. **Broad and fertile plain:** Noyce, "Competition and Cooperation—A Prescription for the Eighties," *Research Management*, March 1982, 14, IA. **Thanks, in part, to Noyce:** Jacobson, *Passing Farms, Enduring Values: California's Santa Clara Valley*, (Los Altos, Ca.: William Kaufmann, Inc., 1984), 237.

66. **Surely as America:** Ronald Reagan, "Address Before a Joint Session of the Congress on the State of the Union: January 25, 1983," *Papers of the Presidents: Administration of Ronald* Reagan, 107. **I wish I'd said:** Noyce "High Technology Industries: Pulbic Policies for the 1980s," 1–2 Feb. 1983, IA.

Chapter 11: Political Entrepreneurship

1. **Political entrepreneurship:** Philip A. Mundo uses the term "political entrepreneurs" to describe executives working with the Semiconductor Industry Association. Philip A. Mundo, "The Semiconductor Industry Association," *Interest Groups: Cases and Characteristics* (Chicago: Nelson-Hall, 1992): 41–66.

2. **Close deals:** In June 1985, Noyce submitted an expense report for his having traveled to present on the Intel microprocessor to IBM. Noyce's expense reports from this period also list a meeting with Burroughs in April 1983 and an LME Customer Meeting in January 1984 (expense reports, ASB). **Access important accounts:** Intel marketing executive William H. Davidow discusses Noyce's help in closing deals and accessing executives in *Marketing High-Technology, An Insider's View* (New York: The Free Press, 1986): 130, 152. **Watch the store:** Noyce, "Creativity by the Numbers," *Harvard Business Review*, May–June 1980.

3. **Rare Bob Noyce Sighting:** *Inteleads*, 1 Apr. 1983, IA. **Twentieth anniversary celebration:** video, IA. **Hard to get off the stage:** Mar Dell Casto, interview by author.

4. **Noyce's poem:** courtesy Maryles Casto. The poem is signed, "1980, Bob Noyce."

5. **Friendship, friendship:** Oh Say, Can IC? (script excerpt), First Annual Industry Banquet, Semiconductor Equipment and Materials Institute, 26 May 1971, IA.

6. **Japanese vs. American share of market:** Leonard Hills [Intel employee] to List, 15 Oct. 1986, IA. Hills includes figures from Dataquest that he describes as "'Doom & Gloom' graphs" in his letter. Figures based on world market revenues.

7. **Like taking a hilltop:** Jeffrey Beeler, "Semi Industry Reps Raise Alarm on Japanese," *Computerworld*, 25 June 1979, 64.

8. **1985 trade deficit:** McCraw, *From Partners to Competitors*, 4. **Nippon Steel, Japan number one threat**: Richards, "How America Lost the Edge"; Lou Harris and Associates poll results cited in Robert Noyce, "SIA Industry Conference," 3 Sept. 1989, SIA.

9. **Originating and nurturing:** Robert Noyce, World Trade and the Challenges Facing the U.S. Semiconductor Industry: Semiconductor Industry Association Annual Forecast Dinner, 28 Sept. 1978, SIA. **Nineteen firms purchased:** Noyce, Testimony Before the United States International Trade Commission on Behalf of the Semiconductor Industry Association, 30 May 1979, SIA.

10. **Brilliant minds:** Noyce, "Keeping California Competitive in R&D," 10 Oct. 1986, IA. **Slit our throats:** Noyce quoted in Gene Bylinsky, "The Japanese Spies in Silicon Valley," *Fortune*, 27 Feb. 1978; **Almost thrown out of Japan:** Rich Karlgaard, "Bob Noyce Talks to *Upside*," *Upside*, July 1990 (interview 23 May 1990). **Karate chop:** Noyce, World Trade and the Challenges Facing the U.S. Semiconductor Industry [speech before the SIA Annual Forecast Dinner], 28 Sept. 1978. **1981 meeting with Japanese:** Charlie Sporck, *Spinoff: A Personal History of the Industry that Changed the World* (Sarnac Lake, N.Y.: Sarnac Lake Publishing, 2001): 247. **Noyce burning paper flags on cake:** sources requested anonymity.

11. **Slow down Japanese government:** Minutes of SIA Board of Directors meeting 16 June 1977, SIA.

12. **Seven percent of revenues:** Joel Stern, "International Structural Differences in Financing," (Study undertaken by Chase Financial Policy at the request of the SIA), IA.

13. **Government-conferred benefits:** Okimoto, Sugano, and Weinstein, *Competitive Edge*, 6. **Japanese banking:** Stern, "International Structural Differences in Financing," 134–135. Stern estimates, "Many Japanese semiconductor companies maintain debt-to-capital ratios as high as 60 to 70 percent. . . . During the past three years [1978–1980], the median debt-to-capital ratios of the nine US companies reviewed were between 16 and 18 percent." In part, the willingness of Japanese banks to lend to such highly leveraged firms also stemmed from the "keiretsu" structure of Japanese industry. Each of the major Japanese semiconductor firms was a longstanding member of one or two "keiretsu," cross-industry corporate groups—usually headed by a major commercial bank—joined together through equity and cross-shareholdings, management and interlocking directorates, financing, and buying/selling relationships.

14. **On the capital gains tax:** Ed Zschau, interview by author; J. Andrew Hoerner, ed., *The Capital Gains Controversy: A Tax Analysts Reader* (Arlington, Va.: Tax Analysts, 1992).

15. **American share of market:** Douglas A. Irwin, "Trade Politics and the Semi-conductor Industry," *NBER Working Paper 4745*. **16K EPROM price cuts:** Noyce, Sacto Speech, 28 Sept. 1983, IA. **Lead the group in prayer:** Noyce, SIA Speech, 1 Oct. 1981, SIA.

16. **Japanese share surpassed American:** SIA, "The Semiconductor Industry Association, Key Facts and Issues," 4.

17. **$2 billion, 27,000 jobs:** Noyce, "Testimony on National Technology Development and Utilization Provided to the Technology Policy Task Force Committee on Science, Space, and Technology, U.S. House of Representatives," 25 Sept. 1987. **How far we've fallen:** "Fairchild Sale Touches Us All," *San Jose Mercury News*, 26 Oct. 1986. **Industry considered united opposition:** Evelyn Richards, "Bottom Line Indicated Who Would Buy Fairchild," *San Jose Mercury News*, 7 Sept. 1987. **World turned upside down:** Christopher H. Schmitt, "Japanese to Buy Most of Fairchild: Fujitsu Ltd would Take Over 80 Percent of Chip Pioneer," *San Jose Mercury News*, 24 Oct. 1986.

18. **Go through the revolving door:** Andy Grove quoted in Robert A. Burgelman, "Fading Memories: A Process Study of Strategic Business Exit in Dynamic Environments," *Administrative Science Quarterly*, Vol. 39 (1994), 24–56.

19. **Most gut-wrenching decision:** Arthur Rock, speaking at a "Legends of Venture Capital" panel, Computer History Museum, Mountain View, Calif., 30 Sept. 2002. **Japanese beating the heck:** Ann Bowers, interview by author, 16 Aug. 2004.

20. **7,200 jobs, annual losses:** Noyce, "Testimony on National Technology Development and Utilization Provided to the Technology Policy Task Force Committee on Science, Space, and Technology, U.S. House of Representatives," 25 Sept. 1987. **How to shut down Intel:** Ann Bowers, interview by author, 16 Aug. 2004. **Japanese Buy Intel:** *Inteleads*, 1 April 1987, IA. **It's hard for someone:** Daryl Hatano to author, 2 Feb. 1998.

21. **Decline of empire:** Noyce, Competing in an Open Economy, Keynote Address UCB [University of California at Berkeley], 22 Jan. 1987, IA. **Death spiral:** Noyce quoted in Evelyn Richards. "How America Lost the Edge on the World Trade Battlefield," *San Jose Mercury News*, 20 April 1986. **What would you call Detroit:** Noyce quoted in Evelyn Richards, "Two Valley Visionaries Don't See Same Horizon," *San Jose Mercury News*, 20 Jan. 1986. **Job loss figure:** David Sylvester, "2017, A Silicon Valley Odyssey," *West Magazine* (Sunday supplement to the *San Jose Mercury News*), 7 June 1987, 18. **Optimism is essential:** Robert Noyce, "Innovation for Prosperity: The Coming Decade," delivered to the National Governor's Association 21 Feb. 81 and to SIA's conference on the "International Microelectronics Challenge: A Response by the Industry, the Universities and the Government," Washington D.C. 10–11 March 1981, IA.

22. **Target entrepreneurs:** Noyce, "High Technology Industries: Public Policies for the 1980s," [speech], 2 Feb. 1983, IA.

23. **Democratic argument:** Lazarus and Litan, "Democrats' Coming Civil War," 95.

24. **Time for more attention to micro requirements:** Senator Adlai Stevenson II quoted in U.S. Senate Democratic Task Force on the Economy, "Report of the Subcommitteee on Industrial Policy and Productivity," 4 Aug. 1980, 3–4. **Make and guarantee loans:** Lazarus and Litan, "Democrats' Coming Civil War," 93.

25. **Supporters cannot demonstrate best and brightest in Washington:** Congressman Dan Lundgren quoted in Congress of the United States Joint Economic Committee, "Press Release: JEC Study Finds Industrial Policy Deficient," 28 June 1984, SIA.

26. **Federal government purchasing statistics:** Robert B. Reich, "Why the U.S. Needs an Industrial Policy," *Harvard Business Review*, January–February 1982: 75. Of course, as the contours of Noyce's own career make abundantly clear, in Silicon Valley high-tech entrepreneurship and federal government support were far from mutually exclusive. Nearly all of Fairchild's early products went to government—primarily military—uses. The Defense Department invested over $1 billion in semiconductor R&D between 1958 and 1974, and as late as 1965, the Pentagon purchased 70 percent of the nation's integrated circuit output. Even after the rapid growth of the consumer electronics market in the 1970s reduced semiconductor companies' dependence on government customers—by 1978, the Pentagon's integrated circuit purchases accounted for only 7 percent of sales—the military maintained a strong presence in Silicon Valley. By one estimate, in 1980, Santa Clara County, with 0.6 percent of the American population, captured 3 percent of all Department of Defense prime contracts. (Defense department invested: Saxenian, *Regional Advantage*, 42.) **Three percent of prime contracts:** Findlay, *Magic Lands*, 144–145, citing SRI International, *The Role of Defense in Santa Clara County's Economy* [Washington, D.C., 1980], v–vii.) **American industrial policy implemented by Defense Department:** Johnson, "Introduction: The Idea of Industrial Policy," 4.

27. **Commission on Industrial Competitiveness:** "Global Competition: The New Reality," Report of the President's Commission on Industrial Competitiveness, Jan. 1985, SIA.

28. **Brown commission comments:** *Winning Technologies: A New Industrial Strategy for California and the Nation, Executive Summary.* Report of the California Commission on Industrial Innovation, Sept. 1982, 10.

29. **We are attempting to influence:** Robert Noyce, "Introduction and Conference Theme," in SIA, "Public Policies and Strategies for U.S. High Technology Industry: Proceedings of the SIA Long Range Planning Conference," 22 Nov. 1982, SIA.

30. **One is a nation of immigrants:** Richards, "How America Lost the Edge."

31. **Chip dumping:** Douglas A. Irwin challenges the SIA's allegations that the Japanese were dumping chips. Douglas A. Irwin, "Trade Politics and the Semiconductor Industry," *NBER Working Paper 4745*. **EPROM antidumping case:** Christopher R. Schmitt, "New Dumping Charges Leveled at Japanese," *San Jose Mercury News*, 25 July 1986, 15E. In June, Micron Technology had filed an antidumping complaint about 64K DRAMs. SIA, "Events Leading to the Negotiation of the Agreement: Appendix A," *One and One-Half Years of Experience under the U.S.-Japan Semiconductor Agreement: Semi-Annual Report to the President by the Semiconductor Industry Association*, 43. SIA had considered filing the petition: Daryl G. Hatano, "Why SIA Filed the 301 Trade Action," *Japan Economic Journal*, 12 October 1985.

32. **Semiconductor PACs donated:** Irwin, "Trade Politics," 14. **SIA image meeting:** entry dated 23 Sept. 1984, Noyce 1984 datebook.

33. **Congressional semiconductor support group:** this description relies heavily on Yoffie, "How an Industry Builds Political Advantage," 87; see also Tom

Redburn and Robert Magnuson, "Stung by Tax Bill, Electronics Firms Seek Broader Political Base," *Los Angeles Times*, 15 Nov. 1981. **California Senators supported:** Irwin, "Trade Politics and the Semiconductor Industry," 8.

34. **Permanent fixtures in Washington:** Clayton Yeutter, "Speech to SIA Annual Forecast Dinner: September 23, 1986," in *Japan Semiconductor Market Access: Background and Source Book*, 46. **Direct lobbying is most effective:** Mundo, "Semiconductor Industry Association," 56. **The secret to the SIA's success:** Charlie Sporck, interview by author.

35. **Appealing to Washington was not easy:** Clyde Prestowitz, *Trading Places: How We Allowed Japan to Take the Lead* (New York: Basic Books, 1988), 149.

36. **He is something of a legend:** Yoffie, "How an Industry Builds Political Advantage," 88.

37. **Money gave you power:** Noyce, transcript of "Machine that Changed the World," Tape F8, IA.

38. **American firms money hungry and overconfident:** a more sympathetic explanation would note that because most Japanese markets were closed to U.S. firms, when the firms received offers (quite generous ones at that) to import their technology into Japan, they jumped. As one scholar put it, the Americans knew that the Japanese "would simply have gone to other sources—namely European high-technology companies such as Siemens, AEG and Philips—to get what was needed in Japan." Thomas K. McCraw, *From Partners to Competitors: An Overview of the Period Since World War II* (Cambridge, Mass.: Harvard University Press, 1986), 17–18.

39. **Bob was a very trusting person:** Ann Bowers, interview by author, 16 Aug. 2002.

40. **Noyce informal meetings:** 1985 and 1986 datebooks and Intel expense reports dated 6 Nov. 1984, 30 Nov. 1984, 26 Feb. 1985, 10 March 1985, 10 June 1985, 29 July 1985, 3 Oct. 1985, and 2 Dec. 1985, all ASB. **He really helped me to see:** Tom Campbell, interview by author.

41. **Representative of all high tech:** Noyce, Statement before the Committee on Ways and Means, United States House of Representatives, on behalf of Electronic Industries Association, Scientific Apparatus Makers Association, Computer and Business Equipment Manufacturers Association, American Electronics Association, and Semiconductor Industry Association, 2 Apr. 1981, IA.

42. **All quotes from Jim Jarrett:** Jim Jarrett, interview by author.

43. **Intel paid over $245 million:** Noyce, "Innovation for Prosperity." **Crude oil of electronics industry:** Robert Noyce, "Statement Before the Committee on Ways and Means, United States House of Representatives," 2 April 1981, IA. **Semiconductors are in everything:** Paul Richter, "Silicon Valley Wrestles with Hard Times," *Los Angeles Times*, 15 Nov. 1981.

44. **Social surplus:** Robert Noyce, "Innovation for Prosperity: The Coming Decade," speech before the National Governors' Association, 1 Feb. 1981, IA.

45. **Half of the country's work force dealing with information:** Robert Noyce, "Overview of the Semiconductor Industry," Testimony before the International Trade Administration, Department of Commerce, April 1983. In *High Technology Industries: Profiles and Outlooks—The Semiconductor Industry* (Government Printing Office, 1983), 16.

46. **America has a concern:** Noyce, International Competition in Electronics— An American View [speech to the Financial Times Conference on World Electronics], 11 May 1981, IA.

47. **National security argument:** SIA, "Trade and National Security," in *The International Microelectronics Challenge: An American Response by the Industry, the Universities, and the Government.* Proceedings from a conference held 10–11 March 1981, in Washington D.C., G2, SIA.

48. **Preliminary determination:** International Trade Administration [A-588-504], "Erasable Programmable Read Only Memory Semiconductors From Japan; Suspension of Investigation," *Federal Register*, Vol. 51, No. 151. 6 Aug. 1986, 28253. Gordon Moore recalls that the price of the leading EPROM chip dropped 90 percent—from $30 to $3 in the nine months before the preliminary findings were issued. Fair market value was defined as a company's cost of production, plus an 8 percent profit.

49. **SIA most effective:** Pollack, "Small Lobby's Large Voice."

50. **Outcome of proposed Fairchild sale:** Richards, "Bottom Line Indicated Who Would Buy Fairchild." Charlie Sporck says, "We bought Fairchild Semiconductor, with all of that company's properties, for $122 million. . . . [W]e gradually sold off parts of Fairchild for more than $150 million, and then we sold the remains of the company to new owners for $500 million!" Sporck, *Spinoff*, 238.

51. **Cessation of dumping has helped:** Michael Feibus, "Is the Chip Pact Working? U.S Chip Makers' Profits are Up, but Agreement May Not Deserve Credit," *San Jose Mercury News*, 24 August 1987.

52. **Economies and societies are the laboratories:** Noyce, "False Hopes and High-Tech Fiction," *Harvard Business Review*, Jan.–Feb. 1990.

53. **I am spending more time:** Noyce to Grant Gale, 17 Dec. 1985, Grant Gale Papers, GCA. **National saving rate:** Noyce, Remarks to the Central Iowa Junior Achievement Business Hall of Achievement Annual Banquet, 29 March 1990.

54. **Microelectronics is giving us:** Noyce, Microelectronics and the Information Society [speech to various universities], 31 March 1983. **First principles:** Noyce, Remarks to the Central Iowa Junior Achievement Business Hall of Achievement Annual Banquet, 29 March 1990.

55. **On Censtor:** Ed Zschau, interview by author; Kip Hagopian, interview by author. **Collective individualism:** Noyce, International Competition in Electronics—An American View [speech delivered at *Financial Times* Conference on World Electronics, London, England], 11–12 May 1981 **Rope each other in:** Arthur Rock, interview by Evan Ramstad, 19 May 1997, courtesy Evan Ramstad.

56. **On Volant:** Hank Kashiwa, interview by author; Bucky Kashiwa, interview by author.

57. **Other small investments:** Rock to Noyce, stamped "rec'd 3 Dec. 1980," ASB. **On Diasonics:** Noyce and Rock holdings: Diasonics IPO Prospectus, 23 Feb. 1983; **Largest offering since Coors:** Gary Putka, "Diasonics Debut On Wall Street Cheered by Investors," *Wall Street Journal*, 24 Feb. 1983; **Problems:** "Diasonics' Waxman Quits Two Leading Posts at Firm," *WSJ*, 20 Nov. 1987; Diasonics Inc. Agrees to Settle Litigation by Paying $12 Million," *WSJ*, 4 June 1987; Fred R. Bleakley, "The Volatile World of Medical Imaging," *New York Times*, 27 Nov. 1983; Nathaniel C. Nash, "2 Charged In Insider Trading," *NYT*, 31 Dec. 1986.

58. **Development team members:** Peter H. Lewis, "Heroes of Information Revolution," *New York Times*, 14 Nov. 1989. **Foreign-born population doubled:**

Analee Saxenian, Silicon Valley's New Immigrant Entrepreneurs (San Francisco : Public Policy Institute of California, 1999): 11. **75 percent Asian:** Sevilla, 278. **One-quarter of engineers:** Analee Saxenian, "Networks of Immigrant Entrepreneurs," in Chong Moon Lee et al., *The Silicon Valley Edge: A Habitat for Innovation and Entrepreneurship* (Stanford, Calif.: Stanford University Press, 2000): 249. Unless otherwise noted, Teresi is also the source for information on Caere.

59. **Even if he was blasting you:** Ken Oshman, interview by author.
60. **The Apple endorsement:** Martin Mazner, executive vice president for ComputerWare, quoted in Ken Siegmann, "Caere Plans Initial Stock Offering," *Macintosh News*, 18 Sept. 1989. **$10 million sales:** Bob Teresi to author, 18 Oct. 2004, citing 1989 annual report and IPO prospectus.
61. **Year's five most successful:** Clipping, probably from the *San Francisco Examiner*, undated, Caere scrapbook, courtesy Donna Teresi. **Noyce's nearly 400,000 shares:** Caere IPO Prospectus, 19 Oct. 1989, courtesy Bob Teresi.
62. **Land of opportunity:** unidentified clip of Noyce speaking [probably when he received the National Medal of Technology in 1990] included in "Remembrance of a Life Well Lived," video, ASB.
63. **Noyce travels:** Mar Dell Casto, Maryles Casto, Kathy Cohen, Bill Cohen, Judy Vadasz, interviews by author. **Balloon tours:** Copy of form and check from Noyce ordering a video cassette "Ballooning in Europe," 22 Nov. 1985, ASB.
64. **May 1984 China trip:** "Intel Corporation Delegation Visit May 21–May 31 [1984] to People's Republic of China," [detailed itinerary], ASB; "Zhao Ziyang Meets US Scientist," *China Daily*, 26 May 1984, ASB. **Potato chips and scotch:** Ann Bowers, interview by author, 22 June 2002.
65. **Doodles:** file marked "RNN—Doodles!" none of the contents dated but apparently from the mid- to late 1980s, ASB.
66. **6,500-acre ranch:** Sean Flavin to Noyce, 29 Nov. 1982, ASB.
67. **Estimates of Noyce flying time:** Noyce to Diane Labrador [Intel], 24 Feb. 1984, ASB. **Noyce quotes on flying and the personal computer:** Noyce, transcript of "The Machine that Changed the World," IA.
68. **All Jim Lafferty quotes:** Jim Lafferty, interview by author.
69. **Noyce's flight-school experience:** Jim Lafferty, interview by author.
70. **Ten-year waiting lists:** Kristin Downey, "Getting Off the Ground, Investors are Determined to Build a Private Air Terminal at S.J. Airport," *San Jose Mercury News*, 23 Jan. 1986. **Go ahead and do it:** Jim Lafferty, interview by author.

Chapter 12: Public Startup

1. **Innovation not fostered by committee:** Noyce quoted in United States Senate, "Uncorrected Transcript of Proceedings, Committee on Banking, Housing, and Urban Affairs: Subcommittee on International Finance, Oversight Hearing on Trade and Technology in the Electronics Industry," (Washington, D.C.: 15 Jan. 1980) 113–115, SIA.
2. **Destroy the prices:** Charlie Sporck, interview by author.
3. **Working group participants**: Advanced Micro Devices, AT&T, Digital Equipment Corporation, Hewlett-Packard, Intel, IBM, LSI Logic, Micron

Technology, Motorola, National Semiconductor, NCR, Rockwell International, and Texas Instruments. These companies, plus Harris Corporation, were the founding members of SEMATECH.

4. **Three competing agendas:** this discussion relies heavily on Browning and Shetler, *SEMATECH*, 60–62.

5. **Grandiose scheme:** Craig Barrett quoted in Browning and Shetler, *SEMATECH*, 55. **Annual R&D budget:** Robert Noyce, "Remarks to the DARPA Lab Directors Dinner Meeting," 14 March 1990, ST.

6. **Three-phase goal:** Advisory Council on Federal Participation in Sematech, *SEMATECH: Progress and Prospects 1989*, ES-2, ST; *SEMATECH Strategic Overview, December 1991*, D-2, ST; *1989 SEMATECH Operating Plan*, 3, ST.

7. **To provide:** SEMATECH Web site: http://www.sematech.org/public/corporate/history

8. **High-tech barn raising:** Miller Bonner, interview by author.

9. **Noyce spoke to House and Senate:** Noyce, "Testimony on National Technology Development and Utilization Provided to the Technology Policy Task Force Committee on Science, Space, and Technology, 25 Sept. 1987, IA; Noyce, "Testimony Before the Senate Committee on Government Affairs Regarding Senate Bill 1233, 'The Economic Competitiveness, International Trade, & Technology Development Act of 1987,'" 9 June 1987, IA.

10. **Implications are awesome:** "Memorandum for the Secretary of Defense," United States Defense Science Board Task Force on Defense Semiconductor Dependency, *Report of Defense Science Board Task Force on Semiconductor Dependency* (Feb. 1987).

11. **Bias in defense science boards:** See, for example, *Favoritism and Bias Within the Defense Science Board and Other Military Advisory Panels* (Hearing Before a Subcommittee of the Committee on Government Operations, U.S. House of Representatives, 98th Congress, September 22, 1983). There was a disagreement in Congress as to whether the Department of Commerce (favored by the House of Representatives, as well as several industry leaders who had worked with Secretary Malcom Baldridge) or Department of Defense (favored by the Senate) would be the appropriate government agency to fund and work with SEMATECH. The House had put together a Trade Resolution in support of SEMATECH, and the Senate had passed a Defense Appropriations Bill. Ultimately, the president's Economic Policy Council, which had expressed dislike of industrial policy (and thus of Commerce's involvement) recommended that Defense participate in Sematech in the interest of national security. This recommendation, coupled with the practical reality that the Defense Department already had funding mechanisms in place for high-technology grants, swung the decision in the Defense Department's favor. Browning and Shetler, *SEMATECH*, 29, 51; Miller Bonner, interview by author, 4 Feb. 1999.

12. **Wildly overstated:** Peter Waldman, "Chip Makers' SEMATECH Venture Rushes to Vanquish Foe, but Path is Questioned," *Wall Street Journal*, 8 Jan. 1988. **Department of Commerce raised questions:** Congressional Budget Office, *The Benefits and Risks of Federal Funding for SEMATECH*, Sept. 1987, 46.

13. **Most are right-wing Republicans:** Willman, "Congress Cool to Chips Aid." **Pleading for a handout:** Robert J. Samuelson, "Chip Industry's Plea," *Washington Post*, 24 June 1987.

14. **Perception they represent:** Senator John McCain quoted in Louise Kehoe, "Chip Makers Ask Congress for Help," *Financial Times of London*, 5 March 1987. **SIA refused to commit to location:** Charlie Sporck, interview by author. To sidestep anticompetitive issues, the SIA designed SEMATECH to fit within the parameters of the National Cooperative Research Act of 1984 (an act the SIA had championed).

15. **SEMATECH is a bargain:** Noyce, "RNN SIA Speech 12/7/88," ST.

16. **Site-selection process:** Miller Bonner, interview by author; Charlie Sporck, interview by author. Committee's expectations are from Browning and Shetler, *SEMATECH*, 43.

17. **National Governor's Association task force:** *State Activities to Encourage Technological Innovation: An Update* (Feb. 1982). "Prepared for the National Governors Association Task Force on Technological Innovation," iv, ST. **High-tech companies offer salvation:** *Location of High Technology Firms and Regional Economic Development* (1 June 1982). "A staff study prepared for the use of the Subcommittee on Monetary and Fiscal Policy of the Joint Economic Committee, Congress of the United States," v. Thanks to Margaret O'Mara for pointing me to international visitors to the Stanford Industrial Park. Excellent discussions of early technology regions include Margaret O'Mara, *Cities of Knowledge: Cold War Science and the Search for the Next Silicon Valley*, (Princeton, N.J., Princeton University Press, 2004) and Stuart W. Leslie and Robert H. Kargon, "Electronics and the Geography of Innovation in Post-War America," *History and Technology*, Vol. 11, 1994, 217–231. For an international discussion, see Rolf Sternberg, "Technology Policies and the Growth of Regions: Evidence from Four Countries," *Small Business Economics* 8 (1996), 75–86.

18. **Advertisement for Albuquerque:** *San Jose Business Journal*, 25 Sept. 1989. In a bid to attract entrepreneurs, the advertisement stressed the relatively low cost of labor in Albuquerque—average weekly earnings of $347 versus $451 in San Jose. For an excellent sample of a variety of regional advertisements, see "Special Report: Industrial Development/Site Selection," *Electronic Engineering Times*, 9 Nov. 1981.

19. **Austin added 10,000 jobs:** Thomas C. Hayes, "Is Austin the Next Silicon Valley?" *New York Times*, 13 Jan. 1988, 6. **Common as a Lone Star beer:** Mary A. C. Fallon, "Roping High Technology—Texas Cities Trying to Tie Up Silicon Valley Business," *San Jose Mercury News*, 1 July 1985.

20. **Austin's offer:** "Texas City's Persistence Pays in Battle to Snare SEMA-TECH," *Boston Globe*, 27 Jan. 1988. **California's fractured bid:** Douglas Shuit, "Deukmejian Quietly Bids for High-Tech Study Center," *Los Angeles Times*, 5 Sept. 1987.

21. **California in danger:** Tom McEnery quoted in Louise Kehoe, "SEMATECH Blow to Silicon Valley," *Financial Times of London*, 8 Jan. 1988.

22. **AT&T and IBM Manufacturing Demonstration Vehicles:** Browning and Shetler, *SEMATECH*, 58–59. For more on the public announcement of the MDVs, see SEMATECH Web site: http://www.sematech.org/public/corporate/history and "IBM, AT&T Contributing Technology to SEMATECH," *Los Angeles Times*, 27 Jan. 1988.

23. **Three leaders:** Jim Peterman (Texas Instruments), Sandy Kane (IBM), and George Schneer (Intel). **They stacked 500 people:** Bill Daniels quoted in Browning and Shetler, *SEMATECH*, 93.

24. **More damn guys promoted:** Charlie Sporck, interview by author.

25. **DARPA delayed funding:** Jack Robertson, "Report DARPA Presses Sematech," *Electronic News*, 25 April 1988; Robert Ristelhueber, "Sematech Chairman: We'll Decide R&D," Ibid.; Jack Robertson, "DARPA Gets Sematech Voice," Ibid., 16 May 1988. **Senate threatening to trim:** "Bob Noyce Created Silicon Valley and Now He's Asked to Save It," *Physics Today*, Sept. 1988, 50; Andrew Pollack, "SEMATECH's Weary Hunt for a Chief," *New York Times*, 1 April 1988, 1. **No right-minded executive:** Richard Bambrick and Robert Ristelhueber, "Sematech CEO: Why No Takers?" *Electronic News*, 23 May 1988.

26. **Find someone better:** Robert N. Noyce, "SEMATECH Presentation, Washington Press Conference, July 27, 1988," IA; Otis Port, "Bob Noyce Created Silicon Valley. Can He Save It?" *Business Week*, 15 Aug. 1988, 76. **Prefer not to see life's work:** Noyce quoted in "Living Legends, Profiles from the National Business Hall of Fame [1989]," ST.

27. **Noyce-Hodgson conversation:** Richard Hodgson, interview by author.

28. **Noyce-Sporck conversation:** Charlie Sporck, interview by author.

29. **Beautiful music together:** Charlie Sporck, interview by author. **Not expecting fun:** Interview, Robert Noyce, Regarding his Work at SEMATECH, IA. **Net worth:** calculation based on number of Noyce's shares times share price in June of 1988.

30. **Too important to ignore call:** Noyce, SEMATECH Presentation, Washington Press Conference, 27 July 1988. **Noyce walking the edges of his Christianity:** Mar Dell Casto, interview by author.

31. **Public startup:** Robert N. Noyce, "SEMATECH Presentation, Washington Press Conference, July 27, 1988," ST.

32. **Ideal guy:** Sporck quoted in Carrie Dolan and Eduardo Lachica, "SEMATECH Names Intel's Noyce to Head Semiconductor Industry Research Group," *Wall Street Journal*, 28 July 1988. **Congressional reaction:** "Bob Noyce Created Silicon Valley and Now He's Asked to Save It." **Turkey farm:** Dolan and Lachica, "SEMATECH Names Intel's Noyce." **Nothing like hiring a legend:** "Chipping In To SEMATECH," *San Jose Mercury News*, 29 July 1988.

33. **Reactions to Noyce's decision:** Richard Steinheimer to Noyce, 30 July 1988; Arthur Rock to Noyce, undated; M. Kenneth Oshman to Noyce, undated; Bill Davidow to Noyce, 29 July 1988; Andy Grove to Noyce, undated; all ASB. "Gordon Moore Interview, 8/17/94," IA.

34. **Limit consortium to American firms:** http://www.sematech.org/public/corporate/history

35. **Wrapped in the flag, Iwo Jima image over the top:** Miller Bonner, interview by author.

36. **Sixty-nine people:** list of VIP section for November 15 dedication, ASB. **Throughout the history:** Noyce, "RNN/Dedication," 10 Nov. 1988, ASB.

37. **Mr. Outside:** Interview, Robert Noyce, regarding his work at SEMATECH, IA.

38. **Office of chief executive:** *SEMATECH Operating Plan 1989*, 6, ST.

39. **Split loyalty:** Interview, Robert Noyce, regarding his work at SEMATECH, IA.

40. **Don't open your mouth:** Miller Bonner, interview by author. **Meeting drew 32 lawyers:** Browning and Shetler, *SEMATECH*, 32. **Nothing to extract from:** Interview, Robert Noyce, Regarding his Work at SEMATECH, IA.

41. **Noyce going around conference table:** Miller Bonner, interview by author.
42. **Noyce removed his tie:** Browning and Shetler, *SEMATECH*, 82–83.
43. **Budget meeting story:** Miller Bonner, interview by author.
44. **Business cards:** Miller Bonner, interview by author; Dan Seligson, interview by author. **Organization chart:** Turner Hasty, interview by author.
45. **From our base of shared knowledge:** Noyce, "National Advisory Council on Semiconductors, Remarks by Dr. Robert N. Noyce," 8 Mar. 1989, ST.
46. **Virtual vertical integration:** Noyce quoted in "Partnering for Total Quality," ("Prepared by SEMATECH for the U.S. Semiconductor Industry"), vol. 1, 15 Jun. 1990, 1, ST. **Vertical integration of 80 percent of Japanese consortiums:** Grindley, Mowery, and Silverman, *SEMATECH and Cooperative Research*, footnote 15.
47. **88 percent small businesses:** *A Strategic Industry at Risk*, 12.
48. **Supplier-manufacturer relations:** An excellent survey from the late 1980s is Government Accounting Office, *SEMATECH's Efforts to Strengthen the U.S. Semiconductor Industry*.
49. **Manufacturer's perspective:** Turner Hasty to author, 11 August 2000.
50. **Friendlier lawsuits:** Turner Hasty to author, 11 August 2000. **Ovation:** Browning and Shetler, *SEMATECH*, 37.
51. **D-A-R-P-A:** William Spencer, interview by author.
52. **Fab construction records:** *SEMATECH Operating Plan 1989*, 15. SEMATECH and industry standard fab costs are from Browning and Shetler, *SEMATECH*, 86.
53. **Agonizing indecision:** Ann Bowers, interview by author, 16 Aug. 2004. **Weak link:** Noyce quoted in Darrell Dunn, "SEMATECH Chief Details Exec Rift," *Electronic News*, 3 April 1989. Under the terms of a three-year employment agreement, SEMATECH continued making salary payments to Castrucci. **Might run more smoothly:** Noyce quoted in Kirk Ladendorf, "SEMATECH Could Grow With Fewer Members: Downsizing May Help Consortium Function Smoother," *Austin American-Statesman*, 19 Jan. 1992.
54. **Deliver occasional speeches:** "Big Bang, Paris, RNN Talking Points," 12 April 1988, IA; "RNN Talking Points, Cowen Investment Group," 22 June 1988, IA; "RNN, Intel: Preparing for the Challenges of the 1980s," CIS Summit Talk, 19 July 1988. **58 speeches:** Miller Bonner, interview by author.
55. **Noyce-Bonner conversation:** Miller Bonner, interview by author.
56. **Many masters:** Interview, Robert Noyce, regarding his work at SEMATECH, IA.
57. **Noyce as Springsteen:** family photo, ASB. **Remote car starter:** Miller Bonner, interview by author; "AutoCommand &AutoCommand PLUS Remote Car Starter Installation Manual," ASB.
58. **Noyce flying fighter jet:** "Robert Noyce Flies the RF-4C, 7 September 1989, Bergstrom AFB, TX" [photo album], ASB. **Kid in a candy store:** Miller Bonner, interview by author.
59. **Noyce's jottings:** unlabeled pages appearing in file marked "RNN-Doodles!" ASB. **Most fun he'd had since college:** Jim Lafferty, interview by author.
60. **It amazed me:** Wayne Higashi, interview by author. Higashi and Jim Lafferty, in their interviews with the author, are the sources for the mechanical transmission story.
61. **It gave me a great deal of confidence:** Wayne Higashi, interview by author. A variant of the transmission with which Noyce helped is described in

Frank A. Fritz and Paul B. Pires, "A Geared Infinitely Variable Transmission for Automotive Applications," *SAE [Society of Automotive Engineers] Technical Paper Series* 910407, courtesy Wayne Higashi.

62. **Impacted calendar:** Noyce 1989 datebook, ASB. **Kick in the side of the head:** Ann Bowers to Grant Gale, no date but envelope postmarked 14 Dec. 1988, GCA.

63. **How far do you have to reach:** J .F. Welch, "Draper Prize," [speech typescript], ASB. **Noyce's Draper comments:** Noyce, notes for Draper speech, ASB. **Gale thanking Noyce:** Gale to Noyce, 2 March 1990, ASB.

64. **Increased funding:** *SEMATECH's Efforts*, 5, 26; Grindley, Mowery, and Silverman, *SEMATECH and Collaborative Research*, 16. **SEMATECH contracts awarded:** United States Government Accounting Office *SEMATECH's Efforts*, 26. **Previous year's contracts:** Advisory Council on Federal Participation in Sematech, *SEMATECH 1990: Report to Congress*, ES-4.

65. **We're all customers:** Robert Noyce, "SEMATECH and the National Agenda: Remarks Before SEMI/SEMATECH Members," 24 May 1990, ST.

66. **He was up for hanging out:** Ann Bowers, interview by author, 16 Aug. 2004.

67. **Description of the conversation with Brother Joseph:** Ann Bowers, interview by author; Penny Noyce, interview by author.

68. **Conversation with Hwoschinsky:** Paul Hwoschinsky, interview by author.

69. **Evening with Jobs:** Steve Jobs, interview with author. Jobs recalls this evening taking place "about a week" before Noyce's death. Noyce delivered a speech to members of SEMI-SEMATECH in San Mateo on 24 May 1990.

70. **Change their idols:** Miller Bonner et al., "Robert N. Noyce, 1927–1990," memorial brochure internally published by SEMATECH, ST.

Conclusion

1. **Entered their memories of Noyce into the Congressional Record:** these include Albert Gore, Joseph Lieberman, Alan Cranston, Norman Mineta, Richard Gephardt, Lloyd Bentsen, Don Edwards, Melvin Levine, Leon Panetta, Jake Pickle. (Congressional Record, House, 5 June and 6 June 1990; Congressional Record, Senate, 5 June 1990, 6 June 1990, 13 June 1990, 14 Sept. 1990; Congressional Record, Extension of Remarks, 6 June 1990, 11 June 1990, 13 June 1990, 14 June 1990.) **National treasure:** Dick Cheney to Ann Bowers, 14 June 1990 [stamped as received on that date], ASB. **One of the few:** D. Allan Bromley to Ann Bowers, 7 June 1990, ASB. **Most powerful personal force:** Stan Baker, "Industry Mourns Loss of a Leader," *Electronic Engineering Times*, 11 June 1990. **Create industrial revolution:** Evelyn Richards, "In Noyce's Passing, An Era Also Ends," *Washington Post*, 5 June 1990. **Transform twentieth century:** Judy Mann, "The Best Role Models are Those Without Fame," *Washington Post*, 8 June 1990. **Apple tribute:** ASB.

2. **Make sure we're preparing:** Noyce quoted in Karlgaard, "Bob Noyce Talks to *Upside*."

3. **Maybe 100 components:** Turner Hasty, interview by Evan Ramstad, 25 April 1997, courtesy Evan Ramstad. **90 million transistors per person:** SIA Web site: http://sia-online.org/pre_facts.cfm

4. **NSF Robert Noyce Scholarship Program:** Joan T. Prival to author, 25 Jan. 2005.

Bibliography

Arthur D. Little, Inc. "The Semiconductor Industry." In Arthur D. Little, "Patterns and Problems of Technical Innovation in American Industry: Report to the National Science Foundation, September 1963.

Aspray, William. "The Social Construction of the Microprocessor: A Japanese and American Story," In *Facets: New Perspectives on the History of Semiconductors*, eds. Andrew Goldstein and William Aspray, 215–267. New Brunswick: IEEE Press, 1997.

Association of Bay Area Governments. "Silicon Valley and Beyond: High Technology Growth for the San Francisco Bay Area." Working Papers on the Region's Economy, No. 2.

Bassett, Ross Knox. *To the Digital Age: Research Labs, Start-Up Companies, and the Rise of MOS Technology*. Baltimore: The Johns Hopkins University Press, 2002.

Beyer, Janice M., and Larry D. Browning "Transforming an Industry in Crisis: Charisma, Routinization, and Supportive Cultural Leadership," *Leadership Quarterly* 10 (Spring 1999): 483–520.

Borrus, Michael, James Millstein, and John Zysman. *U.S.-Japanese Competition in the Semiconductor Industry: A Study in International Trade and Technological Development*. Berkeley: Institute of International Studies, 1982.

Borrus, Michael. *Competing for Control: America's Stake in Microelectronics*. Cambridge, Mass.: Ballinger, 1988.

Braun, Ernest, and Stuart Macdonald, *Revolution in Miniature*. Cambridge: Cambridge University Press, 1982.

Browning, Larry D., and Judy C. Shetler. *SEMATECH: Saving the U.S. Semiconductor Industry*. College Station, Tex.: Texas A&M University Press, 2000.

Burgelman, Robert A. "Fading Memories: A Process Study of strategic Business Exit in Dynamic Environments." *Administrative Science Quarterly* 39 (1994): 24–56.

Burgelman, Robert A., Dennis L. Carter, and Raymond S. Bamford. "Intel Corporation: The Evolution of an Adaptive Organization." Stanford Graduate School of Business Case SM65. Stanford University, 1999.

Bygrave, William D., and Jeffry A. Timmons. *Venture Capital at the Crossroads*. Boston: Harvard Business School Press, 1992.

Bylinsky, Gene. *The Innovation Millionaires: How they Succeed*. New York: Charles Scribner's Sons, 1976.

369

Caddes, Carolyn. *Portraits of Success: Impressions of Silicon Valley Pioneers.* Palo Alto: Tioga Publishing, 1986.

Campbell-Kelly, Martin, and William Aspray, *Computer: A History of the Information Age.* New York: Basic Books, 1996.

Cannon, Lou. *Reagan.* New York: G. P. Putnam's Sons, 1982.

Chandler, Alfred D., Jr. "The Information Age in Historical Perspective." Introduction to Alfred D. Chandler, Jr. and James W. Cortada, eds. *A Nation Transformed by Information: How Information Has Shaped the United States from Colonial Times to the Present,* 3–38, Oxford: Oxford University Press, 2000.

Cheape, Charles W. *Strictly Business: Walter Carpenter at Du Pont and General Motors.* Baltimore: The Johns Hopkins University Press, 1995.

Chemers, Martin M., and Roya Ayman, eds. *Leadership Theory and Research: Perspectives and Directions.* New York: Harcourt Brace Jovanovich, 1993.

Cortada, James W. *The Computer in the United States: From Laboratory to Market.* Armonk, N.Y.: M. E. Sharpe, 1993.

Cringley, Robert. *Accidental Empires: How the Boys of Silicon Valley Make Their Millions, Battle Foreign Competition, and Still Can't Get a Date.* New York: Addison Wesley, 1992.

Davidow, William H. *Marketing High Technology: An Insider's View.* New York: The Free Press, 1986.

Davis, Gordon B. *Introduction to Electronic Computers.* 2nd Edition. New York: McGraw-Hill, 1972.

Doerflinger, Thomas M., and Jack L. Rivkin. *Risk and Reward.* New York: Random House, 1987.

Drucker, Peter. *Innovation and Entrepreneurship: Practice and Principles.* London: William Heinemann, 1985.

Electronic Market Data Book: 1981 Edition. Electronic Industries Association: 1981.

Findlay, John. *Magic Lands: Western Cityscapes and American Culture after 1945.* Berkeley: University of California Press, 1992.

Florida, Richard L., and Martin Kenney, "Venture capital-financed innovation and technological change in the USA." *Research Policy* 17 (1988), 119–137.

Freear, John, Jeffrey E. Sohl, and William E. Wetzel. "Angels: Personal Investors in the Venture Capital Market." *Entrepreneurship and Regional Development* 7 (1995), 85–94.

Gompers, Paul A. "The Rise and Fall of Venture Capital." *Business and Economic History* (Vol. 23, No. 2, 1992): 1.

Greenwood, Ronald G. "Management by Objectives: As Developed by Peter Drucker, Assisted by Harold Smiddy." *The Academy of Management Review,* April 1981, 225–230.

Grindley, Peter, David C. Mowery, and Brian Silverman. *SEMATECH and Collaborative Research: Lessons in the Design of High-Technology Consortia.* CCC Working Paper No. 93-21, January 1994. Consortium on Competitiveness and Cooperation, University of California at Berkeley Center for Research Management.

Hanson, Dirk. *The New Alchemists: Silicon Valley and the Microelectronics Revolution.* Boston: Little, Brown, and Company, 1982.

Hayes, Dennis. *Behind the Silicon Curtain: The Seductions of Work in a Lonely Era.* Boston: South End Press, 1989.

Heenan, David A., and Warren Bennis. *Co-Leaders: The Power of Great Partnerships.* New York: John Wiley and Sons, 1999.

Hersey, Paul. *The Situational Leader*. New York: Warner Books, 1984.

Hodges, David A. "Large-Capacity Semiconductor Memory." *Proceedings of the IEEE*, Vol. 56, No. 7, July 1968, 1148.

Hoerner, Andrew J., ed. *The Capital Gains Controversy: A Tax Analysts Reader*. Arlington, Va.: Tax Analysts, 1992.

Holbrook, Daniel. "Diversity, Complementarity, and Cooperation: Materials Innovation in the Semiconductor Industry." In *Facets: New Perspectives on the History of Semiconductors*, ed. Andrew Goldstein and William Aspray, 75–134. New Brunswick: IEEE Press, 1997.

Hughes, Thomas. *American Genesis: A Century of Invention and Technological Enthusiasm, 1870–1970*. New York: Viking, 1989.

Irwin, Douglas A. "Trade Politics and the Semiconductor Industry." NBER [National Bureau of Economic Research] Working Paper 4745.

Jackson, Peter. *The Chip*. New York: Warwick Press, 1985.

Jackson, Tim. *Inside Intel: Andy Grove and the Rise of the World's Most Powerful Chip Company*. New York: Dutton, 1997.

Jacobson, Yvonne. *Passing Farms, Enduring Values: California's Santa Clara Valley*. Los Altos: William Kaufmann, Inc., 1984.

Jelinek, Mariann, and Claudia Bird Schoonhoven. *The Innovation Marathon: Lessons From High Technology Firms*. San Francisco: Jossey-Bass Publishers, 1993.

Johnson, Chalmers. "Introduction: The Idea of Industrial Policy." In *The Industrial Policy Debate*, ed. Chalmers Johnson, 3–26. San Francisco: ICS Press, 1984.

Jones, Alan. *Pioneering: A Photographic and Documentary History of Grinnell College*. Grinnell, Iowa: Grinnell College, 1996.

Kennedy, David M. *Freedom from Fear: The American People in Depression and War, 1929–1945*. New York: Oxford University Press, 2001.

Langlois, Richard N., and W. Edward Steinmueller. "The Evolution of Competitive Advantage in the Semiconductor Industry, 1947–1996." In *Sources of Industrial Leadership, Studies of Seven Industries*, ed. David C. Mowery and Richard R. Nelson, 19–78. Cambridge: Cambridge University Press, 1999.

Lazonick, William, and Johnathan West. "Organizational Integration and Competitive Advantage: Explaining Strategy and Performance in American Industry." In *Technology, Organization, and Competitiveness: Perspectives on Industrial and Corporate Change*, ed. Giovanni Dosi, David J. Teece, and Josef Chytry, 247–288, Oxford: Oxford University Press, 1998.

Lee, Chong-Moon, William F. Miller, Marguerite Gong Hancock, and Henry S. Rowen, "The Silicon Valley Habitat." In *The Silicon Valley Edge: A Habitat for Innovation and Entrepreneurship*, ed. Chong-Moon Lee, William F. Miller, Marguerite Gong Hancock, and Henry S. Rowen, 1–15. Stanford: Stanford University Press, 2000.

Leslie, Stuart W. *The Cold War and American Science: The Military-Industrial-Academic Complex at MIT and Stanford*. New York: Columbia University Press, 1993.

———. "How the West Was Won: The Military and the Making of Silicon Valley." In William Aspray, ed., *Technological Competitiveness: Technological and Historical Perspectives on the Electrical, Electronics, and Computer Industries*. Piscataway, N.J.: IEEE Press, 1993.

Leslie, Stuart W., and Robert H. Kargon, "Electronics and the Geography of Innovation in Post-War America," *History and Technology*, Vol. 11, 1994, 217–231.

Levin, Richard. "The Semiconductor Industry." In *Government and Technical Progress: A Cross-Industry Analysis*, ed. Richard R. Nelson, 9–100. New York: Pergamon Press, 1982.

Livesay, Harold C. "Entrepreneurial Dominance in Businesses Large and Small, Past and Present." *Business History Review* 63. Spring 1989.

Lowen, Rebecca. *Creating the Cold War University: The Transformation of Stanford*. Berkeley: University of California Press, 1997): 130.

Malone, Michael S. *The Big Score: The Billion Dollar Story of Silicon Valley*. Garden City, N.Y.: Doubleday, 1985.

Malone, Michael. *The Microprocessor: A Biography*. Santa Clara, Calif.: TELOS, 1995.

Margaret B. W. Graham, *The Business of Research: RCA and the VideoDisc*. New York: Cambridge University Press, 1986.

Marksuen, Ann, Peter Hall, Scott Campbell, Sabina Deitrick. *The Rise of the Gunbelt: The Military Remapping of America*. New York: Oxford University Press, 1991.

Markusen, Ann, Peter Hall, and Amy Glasmeier. *High-Tech America: The What, How, Where, and Why of the Sunrise Industries*. Boston: Allen & Unwin, 1986.

McCraw, Thomas K. "Schumpeter Ascending." *American Scholar* 60. Summer 1991: 371–392.

———. *From Partners to Competitors: An Overview of the Period Since World War II*. Cambridge, Mass.: Harvard University Press, 1986.

McCraw, Thomas K., and Jeffrey L. Cruikshank. *The Intellectual Venture Capitalist: John H. McArthur and the Work of the Harvard Business School, 1980–1995*. Boston: Harvard Business School Press, 1999.

McKenna, Regis. *Relationship Marketing: Successful Strategies for the Age of the Customer*. New York: Addison-Wesley, 1991.

———. *Real Time: Preparing for the Age of the Never Satisfied Customer*. Boston: Harvard Business School Press, 1997.

———. *The Regis Touch: Million-Dollar Advice from America's Top Marketing Consultant*. Reading, Mass.: Addison-Wesley, 1985.

Moritz, Michael. *The Little Kingdom: The Private Story of Apple Computer*. New York: William Morrow and Company, 1984.

Mundo, Philip A. "The Semiconductor Industry Association." In *Interest Groups: Cases and Characteristics*, 41–66. Chicago: Nelson-Hall, 1992.

Nasar, Sylvia. *A Beautiful Mind: A Biography of John Forbes Nash*. New York: Touchstone, 1998.

O'Mara, Margaret. *Cities of Knowledge: Cold War Science and the Search for the Next Silicon Valley*. Princeton, N.J.: Princeton University Press, 2004.

Okimoto, Daniel I., Henry S. Rowen, and Michael J. Dahl. *The Semiconductor Competition and National Security: A Special Report of the Northeast Asia-United States Forum on International Policy*. Stanford: Stanford University Press, 1987.

Okimoto, Daniel I., Takuo Sugano, and Franklin B. Weinstein. *Competitive Edge: The Semiconductor Industry in the U.S. and Japan*. Stanford: Stanford University Press, 1984.

Ozaki, Robert S. "How Japanese Industrial Policy Works. In *The Industrial Policy Debate*, ed. Chalmers Johnson, 47–70. San Francisco: ICS Press, 1984.

Palfreman, Don, and Doron Swade. *The Dream Machine: Exploring the Computer Age*. London: BBC Books, 1993.

Parks, Martha Smith. *Microelectronics in the 1970s*. Rockwell International Corporation, 1974.

Patterson, James T. *Grand Expectations: The United States, 1945–1974*. New York: Oxford University Press, 1996.

Pitti, Stephen J. *The Devil in Silicon Valley : Northern California, Race, and Mexican Americans*. Princeton, N.J.: Princeton University Press, 2004.

Preer, Robert W. *The Emergence of Technopolis: Knowledge Intensive Technologies and Regional Development*. New York: Praeger, 1992.

Prestowitz, Clyde. *Trading Places: How We Allowed Japan to Take the Lead*. New York: Basic Books, 1988.

Real, Mimi. "A Revolution in Progress: A History of Intel To Date," 1984. Available from Intel.

Reid, T. R. *The Chip: How Two Americans Invented the Microchip and Launched a Revolution*. New York: Simon and Schuster, 1985.

Riordan, Michael, and Lillian Hoddeson. *Crystal Fire: The Birth of the Information Age*. New York: W. W. Norton and Company, 1997.

Rogers, Everett M., and Judith K. Larsen. *Silicon Valley Fever: Growth of High-Technology Culture*. New York: Basic Books, 1984.

Rostky, George. "Thirty Who Made A Difference," courtesy George Rostky.

Saxenian, Annalee. "Silicon Chips and Spatial Structure: The Industrial Basis of Urbanization in Santa Clara County, California," Berkeley Institute of Urban and Regional Development Working Paper 345.

———. "The Genesis of Silicon Valley," in *Silicon Landscapes*, ed. Peter Hall and Ann Markusen, 20–34. Boston: Allen and Unwin, 1985.

———. "Contrasting Patterns of Business Organization in Silicon Valley," *Environment and Planning D: Society and Space*, Vol. 10, 377–391.

———. "In Search of Power: The Organization of Business Interests in Silicon Valley and Route 128" *Economy and Society*, Vol. 18, February 1989, 25–70.

———. *Regional Advantage: Culture and Competition in Silicon Valley and Route 128*. Cambridge: Harvard University Press, 1994.

Schaeffer, Dorothy. "Management by Objectives." *Supervision*, July 1978, 4.

Schoonhoven, Claudia Bird. "High Technology Firms: Where Strategy Really Pays Off." *Columbia Journal of World Business*, Winter 1980, 5–16.

Schumpeter, Joseph. *The Theory of Economic Development: An Inquiry into Profits, Capital, Credit, Interest, and the Business Cycle*. Translated by Redvers Opie. New York: Oxford University Press, 1961.

Seidenberg, Philip. "From Germanium to Silicon: A History of Change in the Technology of the Semiconductors. " In *Facets: New Perspectives on the History of Semiconductors*, eds. Andrew Goldstein and William Aspray, 35–74. New Brunswick: IEEE Press, 1997.

Semiconductor Industry Association 1979 Yearbook and Directory. Cupertino, Calif.: SIA, 1979.

Sideris, George. "The Intel 1103: The MOS Memory that Defied Cores." *Electronics*, 26 April 1973, 108.

Siegel, Leonard M., and John Markoff. *The High Cost of High Tech*. New York: Harper and Rowe, 1985.

"The Silicon Valley Economy," *FRBSF [Federal Reserve Bank of San Francisco] Weekly Newsletter*, Number 92–22, 29 May 1992.

Slater, Robert. *Portraits in Silicon*. Cambridge: MIT Press, 1987.

Slotkin, Richard. *Gunfighter Nation: The Myth of the Frontier in Twentieth-Century America*. New York: Atheneum, 1992.

Spencer, William J., and Peter Gindley. "SEMATECH After Five Years: High-Technology Consortia and U.S. Competitiveness." *California Management Review* 35, Summer 1993, 16.

Sporck, Charles E. *Spinoff: A Personal History of the Industry that Changed the World.* Sarnac Lake, N.Y.: Sarnac Lake Publishing, 2001.

Sternberg, Rolf. "Technology Policies and the Growth of Regions: Evidence from Four Countries," *Small Business Economics* 8 (1996), 75–86.

Strauss, George. "Mangement by Objectives—A Critical View." *Training and Development Journal*, April 1972, 10.

Swedberg, Richard, ed. *Entrepreneurship: The Social Science View.* Oxford: Oxford University Press, 2000.

Taylor, William. "The Business of Innovation: An Interview with Paul Cook." *Harvard Business Review*, March–April 1990, 97–106.

Van Horne, James C. *Financial Management and Policy*, 10th Edition. Englewood Cliffs, N.J.: Prentice Hall, 1995.

Von Hippel, Eric. *The Sources of Innovation.* New York: Oxford University Press, 1988.

Warshofsky, Fred. *The Chip War: The Battle for the World of Tomorrow.* New York: Charles Scribner's Sons, 1989.

Weiss, Joseph W., and Andre Delbecq. "Regional Cultures and High-Technology Management: Route 128 and Silicon Valley." In *Regional Cultures, Managerial Behavior, and Entrepreneurship: An International Perspective*, ed. Joseph Weiss, 9–22. New York: Quorum Books, 1988.

———. "The Business Culture of Silicon Valley: Is it a Model for the Future?" In *Regional Cultures, Managerial Behavior, and Entrepreneurship: An International Perspective*, ed. Joseph Weiss, 23–42. New York: Quorum Books, 1988.

Whittington, Dale, ed. *High Hopes for High Tech: Microelectronics Policy in North Carolina.* Chapel Hill: University of North Carolina Press, 1985.

Wills, Garry. *John Wayne's America: The Politics of Celebrity.* New York: Simon and Schuster, 1997.

Yoffie, David B. "How an Industry Builds Political Advantage." *Harvard Business Review*, May–June 1988, 82–89.

Recollections, Presentations, and Memoirs

"A Macro View of Microelectronics: Gordon E. Moore of Intel," *IEEE Design and Test*, November 1984, 17.

"Art Rock on Faith and Luck," *Upside Preview Issue*, Summer 1989, 15.

Faggin, Frederico "The Birth of the Microprocessor." Reprinted in *Best of Byte*, ed. Jay Ranade and Alan Nash, 354–357. New York: McGraw-Hill, 1994.

Hogan, C. Lester. "It's Time for a Decision on Integrated Circuits." *Western Electronic News*, February 1963, 24.

———. "Reflections on the Past and Thoughts About the Future of Semiconductor Technology." *Interface Age*, March 1977, 19–36.

Kilby, Jack S. "Invention of the Integrated Circuit." *IEEE Transactions on Electron Devices* 33, No. 7 (July 1976).

Kvamme, E. Floyd. "Life in Silicon Valley: A First-Hand View of the Region's Growth." In *The Silicon Valley Edge: A Habitat for Innovation and Entrepreneurship*, ed. Chong-Moon Lee, William F. Miller, Marguerite Gong Hancock, and Henry S. Rowen, 59–80. Stanford: Stanford University Press, 2000.

Moore, Gordon. "Some Personal Perspectives on Research in the Semiconductor Industry." In *Engines of Innovation: U.S. Industrial Research at the End of an Era*, ed. Richard S. Rosenbloom and William J. Spencer, 167. Boston: Harvard Business School Press, 1996.

———. "Intel—Memories and the Microprocessor," *Daedalus* 125, Spring 1966: 55–80.

———. "Cramming More Components onto Integrated Circuits." *Electronics*, 19 April 1965, 114–117.

Noyce, Donald S. "From Candles to Computers: A Life of Ralph Brewster Noyce (1893–1984)." Unpublished family history, Nov. 1995. Courtesy Don Noyce.

Noyce, Harriet Norton. "I Remember." Unpublished family history, 1988. Courtesy Don Noyce.

Rock, Arthur. "Strategy vs. Tactics from a Venture Capitalist." *Harvard Business Review*, November–December 1987, 63–67.

———. Presentation at "Legends of Venture Capital" panel, Computer History Museum, Mountain View, Calif., 30 Sept. 2002.

Theses

Bassett, Ross Knox. "New Technology, New People, New Organizations: The Rise of the MOS Transistor, 1945–1975." PhD diss., Princeton University, 1998.

Conrad, Rebecca. "Slurbanizing the Valley of the Heart's Delight." University of California Santa Barbara thesis, 1983.

Freund, Robert E. "Competition and Innovation in the Transistor Industry." PhD diss., Duke University, 1971.

Kleiman Herbert S. "The Integrated Circuit: A Case Study of Product Innovation in the Electronics Industry." PhD diss., New York University, 1966.

Kraus, Jerome. "An Economic Study of the Semiconductor Industry." PhD diss., New School for Social Research, 1973.

Lécuyer, Christophe. "Making Silicon Valley: Engineering Culture, Innovation and Industrial Gowth, 1930–1970." PhD diss., Stanford University, 1999.

Lowen, Rebecca. "Exploiting a Wonderful Opportunity: Stanford University, Industry, and the Federal Government, 1937–1965." PhD diss., Stanford University, 1990.

Sevilla, Ramon C. "Employment Practices and Industrial Restructuring: A Case Study of the Semiconductor Industry in Silicon Valley, 1955–1991." PhD diss., UCLA, 1992.

Steinmueller, William Edward. "Microeconomics and Microelectronics: Economic Studies of Integrated Circuit Technology." PhD diss., Stanford University, 1987.

General articles from the popular press

Business Week. 26 March 1960, 30 October 1965, 5 October 1968, 4 October 1969, 20 April 1974, 14 December 1981, 5 February 1996.

Electronic News. August 1956–December 1980.

New York Times. 27 February 1983, 13 January 1984, 10 November 1984 , 9 March 1984, 8 March 1987, 13 January 1988, 1 April 1988, 7 September 1989.

San Francisco Chronicle. 22 September 1980, 23 September 1980, 30 September 1980.

San Jose Mercury News. January 1985–December 1987.

Standard and Poor's Industry Surveys. January 1980–December 1986.

Western Electronic News. January 1956–December 1962.

"Engineers Eye Integrated Consumer Products," *Television Digest*, 30 March 1964, 7–8.

"How the U.S. Can Compete Globally," *Fortune*, 5 June 1989, 248.

"IBM, AT&T Contributing Technology to SEMATECH," *Los Angeles Times*, 27 January 1988.

"Quick Thinking for Chips," *The Economist*, 27 December 1980: 65–66.

Smith, Adam. "Silicon Valley Spirit." *Esquire*, November 1981, 13.

"Special Report: Industrial Development/Site Selection." *Electronic Engineering Times*, 9 November 1981.

"Texas City's Persistence Pays in Battle to Snare SEMATECH." *Boston Globe*, 27 January, 1988.

"The Founding Documents," *Forbes ASAP*, 29 May 2000, unpaginated.

"The Microprocessor's 25th Birthday: An Industry Debate," *Upside*, 1 November 1994.

"The Splintering of the Solid-State Electronics Industry," *Innovation* 8, 1969.

"US Consortiums Mimic Japanese Organisation." *Far Eastern Economic Review*. 24 May 1990.

"Fairchild Camera—Portrait of a Growth Company." *Financial World*, 12 September 1962, 10.

"Fairchild Semiconductor Corporation: Company Profile." *Solid State Journal*, September/October 1960, 1.

"Fifty Years of Electronics," a special issue of *Electronics*, 17 April 1980, 326.

"Hottest Thing in Electronics." *Barron's*, 11 August 1958.

"Mighty Miniatures." *Time*, 4 March 1965, 93–94.

"Turning a Science into an Industry," *IEEE Spectrum*, January 1966, 102.

Appelbome, Peter. "The Chips Are Down." *Texas Monthly*, October, 1985.

Bagamery, Anne. "No Policy is Good Policy." *Forbes*, 18 June 1984.

Beeler, Jeffrey. "Semi Industry Reps Raise Alarm on Japanese." *Computerworld*, 25 June 1979.

Benner, Susan. "Storm Clouds Over Silicon Valley." *Inc.*, September 1982, 84.

Blumenthal, Karen. "Chip Consortium's Organizer Wants U.S. to Provide $125 Million Annually." *Wall Street Journal*, 13 May 1987.

Brody, Herb. "The High Tech Sweepstakes: States Vie for a Slice of the Pie." *High Technology*, January 1985.

Brooks, Nancy Rivera. "State Officials Lament Loss of SEMATECH to Texas." *Los Angeles Times*, 7 January 1988.

Burrows, Peter. "Bill Spencer Struggles to Reform SEMATECH." *Electronic Business*, 18 May 1992.

Bylinsky, Gene. "The Japanese Spies in Silicon Valley." *Fortune*, 27 February 1978.

———. "How Intel Won Its Bet on Memory Chips." *Fortune*, November 1973.

Caldo, J. T. "Semiconductors, Young Giant of the Electronics Industry." *Analysts Journal*, 15 August 1959, 71–72.

Churbuck, David. "Today's Companies Give Innovation a Chance." *PC Computing*, September 1989.

Coll, Steve. "When the Magic Goes." *Inc.*, October 1984, 83.

Dean, K. J., and G. White. "The Semiconductor Story: Search for the Best Transistor." Part 2 of a 4-part series. *Wireless World*, Februrary 1973, 67.

Densmore, Bill. "The Santa Clara Valley Electronics Industry Comes of Age During the 'Me' Generation decade." *Peninsula Times Tribune*, 28 December 1979.

Djean, David. "Westward Ha! A Visitor's Guide to Silicon Valley." *PC-Computing*, June 1989, 99.

Donohue, James F. "The Microprocessor's First Two Decades: The Way it Was." *EDN Microprocessor*, 27 October 1988, 22–23

Engstrom, Therese. "Little Silicon Valleys." *High Technology*, January 1987.

Erickson, Stanford. "How Hogan Rescued Fairchild." *International Management*, July 1970, 22.

Fallows, James. "American Industry: What Ails It, How to Save It." *The Atlantic*, September 1980, 35–50.

Gelman, Eric. "Showdown in Silicon Valley." *Newsweek*, 30 September 1985, 46.

Hatano, Daryl G. "Why SIA Filed the 301 Trade Action." *Japan Economic Journal*, 12 October 1985.

Johnston, Moira. "High Tech, High Risk, and High Life in Silicon Valley." *National Geographic*, October 1982, 459.

Kehoe, Louise. "Chip Makers Ask Congress for Help." *Financial Times of London*, 5 March 1987.

———. "SEMATECH Blow to Silicon Valley." *Financial Times of London*, 8 January 1988.

Kindel, Stephen and Robert Teitelman. "Go East, Young Man." *Forbes*, 20 June 1983, 132.

Ladendorf, Kirk. "SEMATECH Could Grow With Fewer Members: Downsizing May Help Consortium Function Smoother." *Austin American-Statesman*, 19 January 1992.

Lazarus, Simon, and Robert E. Litan. "The Democrats' Coming Civil War over Industrial Policy." *Atlantic Monthly*, September 1984.

Miller, Barry. "Microelectronics Causes Avionics Turmoil." *Aviation Week and Space Technology*, 19 March 1962, 55–73.

Miller, Jack. "Electronics is Hailed as Big Lusty Infant." *San Francisco News*, 24 August 1955.

Petit, Charles. "Wizard of Silicon Gulch," *Peninsula Times Tribune*, 21 September, 1977

Redburn, Tom, and Robert Magnuson. "Stung by Tax Bill, Electronics Firms Seek Broader Political Base." *Los Angeles Times*, 15 November 1981.

Reich, Robert B. "Why the U.S. Needs an Industrial Policy." *Harvard Business Review*, January–February 1982.

Reid, T. R. "Birth of a New Idea: Two Men Whose Names You Don't Know Whose Notions Changed Your World." *Washington Post*, 25 July 1982.

Richter, Paul. "Silicon Valley Wrestles with Hard Times." *Los Angeles Times*, 15 November 1981.

Salisbury, David F. "High-Tech Experts Describe What it Takes to Nurture their Industry." *Christian Science Monitor*, 31 August 1984.

Samuelson, Robert J. "Chip Industry's Plea." *Washington Post*, 24 June 1987.

Scandling, Marge. "2 of Founders Leave Fairchild, Form Own Electronics Firm." *Palo Alto Times*, 2 August 1968.

Shuit, Douglas. "Deukmejian Quietly Bids for High-Tech Study Center," *Los Angeles Times*, 5 September 1987.

Siekman, Philip. "In Electronics, the Big Stakes Ride on Tiny Chips." *Fortune*, June 1966, 120.

Smith, Lee. "Can Consortiums Defeat Japan?" *Fortune*, 5 June 1989, 245.

Tamarkin, Bob. "Tiny Circuitry's Big World." *Chicago Daily News*, 3 November 1966.

Turner, Frederick Jackson. "Contributions of the West to American Democracy" *Atlantic Monthly*, January 1903, 91.

Waldman, Peter, and Brenton R. Schlender, "Falling Chips: Is a Big Federal Role the Way to Revitalize Semiconductor Firms?" *Wall Street Journal*, 17 February 1987.

Waldman, Peter. "Chip Makers' SEMATECH Venture Rushes to Vanquish Foe, but Path is Questioned." *Wall Street Journal*, 8 January 1988.

Wolfe, Tom. "The Tinkerings of Robert Noyce: How the Sun Rose on Silicon Valley," *Esquire*, December 1983, 346–74.

Published Articles About or By Robert Noyce

"Bob Noyce Created Silicon Valley and Now He's Asked to Save It." *Physics Today*, September 1988, 50.

"Bob Noyce of Intel Speaks Out on the Integrated Circuit Industry." *EDN/EEE*. 15 September 1971.

"Creativity by the Numbers: An Interview with Robert Noyce." *Harvard Business Review*, May–June 1980, 122–132.

"Intel's Robert Noyce Kicks Himself Upstairs." *Business Week*, 14 December 1974, 32–33.

"New Leaders in Semiconductors." *Business Week*, 1 March 1976.

"Robert Noyce: Special Tribute," *San Jose Mercury News*, 17 June 1990.

Berlin, Leslie. "Robert Noyce and Fairchild Semiconductor, 1957–1968." *Business History Review* 75 (Spring 2001): 63–101.

Bonner, Miller, W. Lane Boyd, and Janet A. Allen. "Robert N. Noyce, 1927–1990," commemorative brochure internally published by SEMATECH.

Bradsher, Keith. "Noyce Named Head of SEMATECH Consortium," *Los Angeles Times*, 28 July 1988.

Caen, Herb. "Update." *San Francisco Chronicle*, 5 February 1980.

Dolan, Carrie, and Eduardo Lachica. "SEMATECH Names Intel's Noyce to Head Semiconductor Industry Research Group." *Wall Street Journal*, 28 July 1988.

Flanagan, James. "Robert Noyce or Ivan Boesky? The Choice is Really Ours," *Los Angeles Times*, 10 June 1990.

Karlgaard, Richard. "Bob Noyce Talks to Intel." *Upside*, July 1990, 54.

Lindgren, Nilo. "Building a Rational Two-Headed Monster: The Management Style of Robert Noyce and Gordon Moore," *Innovation* [1970].

Lowood, Henry. "Robert Norton Noyce (12 December 1927–3 June 1990)." *American National Biography*, ed. John A. Garraty and Marc C. Carves, 541–543. New York: Oxford University Press, 1999.

McElheny, Viktor K. "Dissatisfaction as a Spur to Career," *New York Times*, 15 December 1976.

Noyce, Robert N. "False Hopes and High-Tech Fiction." *Harvard Business Review*, January–February 1990, 31–34.
———. "Microelectronics." *Scientific American*, September 1977.
———. "Hardware Prospects and Limitations." In *The Computer Age: A Twenty-Year View*, ed. Michael Dertouzous and Joel Moses, 321–337. Cambridge: MIT Press, 1979.
———. "Competition and Cooperation—A Prescription for the Eighties." *Research Management*, March 1982, 13–17.
Noyce, Robert, and Marcian E. Hoff, Jr. [Ted Hoff]. "A History of Microprocessor Development at Intel," *IEEE Micro*, February 1981.
Perry, Tekla. "Famous First Jobs," *IEEE Spectrum*, July 1967, 48.
Petit, Charles. "Wizard of Silicon Gulch." *Peninsula Times Tribune*, 21 September 1977.
Port, Otis. "Bob Noyce Created Silicon Valley. Can He Save It?" *Business Week*, 15 August 1988, 76.
Richards, Evelyn. "In Noyce's Passing, an Era Also Ends: Electronics Pioneer Symbolized a Swashbuckling, Innovative Age." *Washington Post*, 5 June 1990.
Slater, Robert. "Robert Noyce: The Mayor of Silicon Valley." In Slater, *Portraits in Silicon*. Cambridge: MIT Press, 1987.
Stroud, Michael. "Intel's Noyce Tells Silicon Valley: Don't Blame Others for Our Mistakes." *Peninsula Times Tribune*, 13 November 1985.
Tedlow, Richard S. "Robert Noyce and Silicon Valley: Toward a New Business World." *Giants of Enterprise: Seven Business Innovators and the Empires they Built*. New York: Harper Collins, 2001.
Watson, Lloyd. "Chip Inventors to Share $350,000 Cash Prize." *San Francisco Chronicle*, 4 October 1989.
Wolff, Michael F. "The Genesis of the Integrated Circuit: How a Pair of U.S. Innovators Brought Into Reality a Concept that was on the Minds of Many." *IEEE Spectrum*, August 1976.

Congressional Testimony and Government Documents

"Favoritism and Bias Within the Defense Science Board and Other Military Advisory Panels." Hearing Before a Subcommittee of the Committee on Government Operations, U.S. House of Representatives, 98th Congress. 22 September 1983.
"Location of High Technology Firms and Regional Economic Development." Staff study prepared for the use of the Subcommittee on Monetary and Fiscal Policy of the Joint Economic Committee, Congress of the United States. 1 June 1982.
"Memorandum for the Secretary of Defense." In United States Defense Science Board Task Force on Defense Semiconductor Dependency, *Report of Defense Science Board Task Force on Semiconductor Dependency*. February 1987.
"Winning Technologies: A New Industrial Strategy for California and the Nation." Report of the California Commission on Industrial Innovation. September 1982.
A Strategic Industry at Risk. Report to the President and the Congress from the National Advisory Committee on Semiconductors, 1989.

Advisory Council on Federal Participation in Sematech. *SEMATECH 1990: A Report to Congress.* May 1990.

———. *SEMATECH: Progress and Prospects 1989.*

Congressional Budget Office. *The Benefits and Risks of Federal Funding for SEMATECH.* September 1987.

Department of Commerce. *Assessment of U.S. Competitiveness in High Technology Industries.* Government Printing Office, 1983.

International Trade Administration [A-588-504]. "Erasable Programmable Read Only Memory Semiconductors From Japan; Suspension of Investigation." *Federal Register,* Vol. 51, No. 151. 6 August 1986, 28253.

Noyce, Robert. "Overview of the Semiconductor Industry." Testimony before the International Trade Administration, Department of Commerce, April 1983. In *High Technology Industries: Profiles and Outlooks—The Semiconductor Industry.* Government Printing Office, 1983.

———. A Unique Approach Against Trade Violators." Testimony delivered before the Section 301 Committee of the U.S. International Trade Commission. 24 May 1989.

———. Statement Before the Committee on Ways and Means, United States House of Representatives." 2 April 1981.

———. Testimony Before Congress, Telecommunications and Finance Subcommittee of the House Energy and Commerce Committee, *High Definition Television: Hearing Before the House Telecommunications and Finance Subcommittee of the House Energy and Commerce Committee.* 13 September 1989.

Preserving the Vital Base: America's Semiconductor Materials and Equipment Industry. Working Paper of the National Advisory Committee on Semiconductors. July 1990.

Reagan, Ronald. "Address Before a Joint Session of the Congress on the State of the Union: 25 January 1983. *Papers of the Presidents: Administration of Ronald Reagan.*

Sanders, W. J. III, "International Trade Policy." Testimony before the International Trade Administration, Department of Commerce, April 1983. In *High Technology Industries: Profiles and Outlooks—The Semiconductor Industry.* Government Printing Office, 1983.

Siegel, Lenny. Testimony Before Congress, Subcommittee on Science, Research, and Technology of the House Committee on Science and Technology and the Task Force on Education and Employment of the House Budget Committee. 16 June 1983, 1100–1101.

Subcommittee on Trade of the Committee on Ways and Means, U.S. House of Representatives. *High Technology and Japanese Industrial Policy: A Strategy for Policymakers.* 1 October 1980, Washington: U.S. Government Printing Office, 1980.

U.S. Department of Commerce International Trade Administration. *High Technology Industries, Profiles and Outlooks: The Semiconductor Industry.* April, 1983.

U.S. General Accounting Office, *Lessons Learned from Sematech,* GAO/RCED-92-289, Washington, D.C., September 1992.

U.S. International Trade Commission. *Competitive Factors Influencing World Trade in Integrated Circuits.* Washington, D.C.: GPO, November 1979.

U.S. Senate Democratic Task Force on the Economy. "Report of the Subcommitteee on Industrial Policy and Productivity." 4 August 1980.

United States Defense Science Board Task Force on Defense Semiconductor Dependency. "Report of Defense Science Board Task Force on Semiconductor Dependency." February 1987.

United States Government Accounting Office. "International Trade: Observations on the U.S.-Japan Semiconductor Arrangement." Briefing Report to the Honorable Lloyd M. Bentsen, United States Senator. Government Printing Office, USIAD-87-134BR.

———. *Assessment of the Financial Audit for SEMATECH's Activities in 1989* April 1991.

———. *SEMATECH's Efforts to Strengthen the U.S. Semiconductor Industry* September 1990.

United States Senate. "Uncorrected Transcript of Proceedings, Committee on Banking, Housing, and Urban Affairs: Subcommittee on International Finance, Oversight Hearing on Trade and Technology in the Electronics Industry." Washington, D.C.: 15 January 1980.

Venture Capital and Innovation. Study prepared for the Joint Economic Committee Congress of the United States. 28 December 1984, S. Prt. 98–288.

Videos

"Living Legends, Profiles from the National Business Hall of Fame." No date [1988, 1989, or early 1990]. Video, SEMATECH archives.

"A Briefing on Integrated Circuits." Video distributed by Fairchild Semiconductor. 1966, courtesy Harry Sello.

Noyce interview for "The Machine that Changed the World." Video, Intel archives.

"Silicon Valley." Written, Produced, and Directed by Julio Moline. Video, SSC.

Memorial Service. 9 June 1990, Austin, Texas. Video, SEMATECH archives.

Memorial Service. 18 June 1990, San Jose, California. Video, Intel archives.

Interviews and Oral Histories

The author's interviews are listed in Appendix A, page 385.

Oral histories held in the Intel archives, all conducted by an interviewer identified as "Stein."

      Bill Davidow, Gene Flath, and Bob Noyce, 13 Aug. 1983

      Tom Rowe, 10 Oct. 1983 and 15 Feb. 1984

      Gordon Moore, Gerry Parker, and Les Vadasz, 17 Oct. 1983

      Ed Gelbach, Andy Grove, and Ted Jenkins, 24 Oct. 1983

      Stan Mazor, Keith Thomson, and Ron Whittier

Oral histories by Rob Walker, Video, Silicon Genesis Collection, Stanford Special Collections.

      Steve Allen, Lawrence Bender, and Richard Steinheimer, 25 May 1995

      Frederico Faggin, 22 April 1995

      Richard Hodgson, 19 Sept. 1995

      Lester Hogan, 22 Aug. 1995

      Ted Hoff, 3 March 1995

      Regis McKenna, 22 Aug. 1995

Gordon Moore, 18 Sept. 1995
Arthur Rock, 12 Nov. 2002
Jerry Sanders, 18 Oct. 2002
Harry Sello, 8 April 1995
Interviews by Evan Ramstad. Provided to the author courtesy Evan Ramstad
Scott Crom, April 1995
Rowland Cross, Feb. 1996
Grant Gale, Oct. 1994
Gordon and Bettie Moore, 18 May 1997
Arthur Rock, 19 May 1997
Marianne Standing Woolfe, April 1995
Les Vadasz, 18 May 1997

Interviews by Charlie Sporck, undated but conducted in the second half of the 1990s. Provided to the author courtesy Charlie Sporck.

David Allison
Tom Bay
Julius Blank
Bob Graham
Vic Grinich
Andy Grove
Daryl Hatano
Richard Hodgson
Jean Hoerni
Eugene Kleiner
Floyd Kvamme
Jay Last
Regis McKenna
Gordon Moore
Jerry Sanders
Don Valentine

Extended interviews of Robert Noyce

Robert N. Noyce and others, interviews by Herbert S. Kleiman. Interviews conducted for research on "The Integrated Circuit: A Case Study in Process Innovation in the Electronics Industry," 1965. Audio tape recordings, Stanford Special Collections.

Transcript of the "Machine that Changed the World" interview, Intel archives.

Noyce interview by Rich Karlgaard, 23 May 1990. Printed in "Bob Noyce Talks to *Upside*," *Upside*, July 1990.

"Interview Robert Noyce—1973," Intel Archives.

Interview, Robert Noyce, Regarding his Work at SEMATECH, Intel Archives.

Robert Noyce, interview by Nilo Lindgren. No date, but roughly 1965. Courtesy Patricia Lindgren.

Robert Noyce, interview by T. R. Reid, 31 Mar. 1982. Courtesy T. R. Reid.

Websites accessed

"A History of the Computer: Mini" Web site.
http://www.pbs.org/nerds/timeline/mini.html

AeA [American Electronics Association] home page.
http://www.aeanet.org Accessed 27 May 2001.

Leo Esaki, "The Global Reach of Japanese Science,"
http://www.jspsusa.org/FORUM1996/esaki.html Accessed 1 Nov. 2004.

Fullman Glossary of the Semiconductor Manufacturing Process
http://www.fullman.com/semiconductors/Semiglossary Accessed 20 Mar. 2001.

Genentech Web site.
http://www.gene.com Accessed 24 Aug. 2004.

Harvard Business School, *Working Knowledge* newsletter, 4 Dec. 2000.
http://hbswk.hbs.edu/pubitem.jhtml?id=1821&t=special_reports_donedeals

HP [Hewlett-Packard] History and Facts Web site.
http://www.hp.com/hpinfo/abouthp/histnfacts.htm

Intel museum.
http://www.intel.com/intel/museum/25anniv/html Accessed 17 Jan. 1999.

Intel Web site.
www.intel.com Accessed 28 Jan. 2001.

Intersil Lexicon of Semiconductor Terms
http://rel.semi.harris.com/docds/lexicon/preface.html Accessed 20 March 2001.

Microelectronics in Silicon Valley Web site.
http://www-sul.stanford.edu/edpts/hasrg/histsci/microel.html Accessed 18 June 2001.

MIT Research Laboratory of Electronics Web site:
http://webrle.mit.edu/groups/g-surhst.HTM Accessed 28 March 2001.

Nobel Prize Web site for Physics.
www.nobel.se/physics/laureates/1956 Now http://nobelprize.org/physics/

"Nolan Bushnell."
http://www.campusprogram.com/reference/en/wikipedia/n/no/
nolan_bushnell.html

PBS Web site for "Transistorized!"
http://www.pbs.org/transistor Accessed 20 March, 2001.

SEMATECH Web site.
http://www.sematech.org/public/corporate/history Accessed 15 March 2001.

Semiconductor Industry Association (SIA) Web site.
http://sia-online.org/home.cfm

William Shockley page at *Time* Web site.
http://www.time.com/time/time100/scientist/profile/Shockley.html

Appendix A
Author's Interviews and Correspondence

Unless otherwise indicated, all footnoted references to interviews refer to the author's first interview or communication with a subject

*indicates taped interview

Jim Angell	6/6/2002
Jose Arreola	2/23/2003
John Bailey*	10/10/2002
Tom Bay*	3/12/2004
Dave Beadling	4/7/2004
Jim Birkenstock	2/11/2004
Julius Blank*	8/29/2002
Miller Bonner	2/4/1999
Roger Borovoy	11/7/2003
Roger Borovoy	1/27/1999
Ann Bowers	8/16/2004
Ann Bowers	8/5/2004
Ann Bowers	6/22/2002
Ann Bowers	5/16/2000
Lee Boysel	8/9/2004
Albert Bradley	4/4/2003
Kay Bucksbaum	6/21/2002
Warren Buffett	8/28/2002
Tom Campbell	9/7/2004
Mar Dell Casto	9/3/2003
Maryles Casto*	6/9/2003
Joe Chapline	3/23/2002
George Clark*	10/23/2002
Kathy and Bill Cohen*	5/12/2003
Paul Cook	2/2/1999

Jeff Cotton*	6/25/2003
Gerard Currie	4/12/2004
Bill Davidow*	6/22/2004
David Diffenderfer	5/1/2003
George Drake	8/15/2002
Jim Dutton	8/20/2004
Barbara Eiler	6/10/2004
Bruce Everitt	2/6/2004
David Finkelstein	9/26/2002
Eugene Flath	11/13/2000
Edward Gelbach	3/27/2001
Wilfred George	8/26/2002
John Germer	7/1/2002
James F. Gibbons	6/2/1999
Ruth Greenwald	7/23/2002
Don Gregson	8/14/2002
Andy Grove*	8/19/2003
Isy Haas	7/26/2001
Kip Hagopian	8/27/2004
David Hamilton	7/24/2002
Bob Harrington*	5/7/2003
Daryl Hatano	10/26/2004
Turner Hasty	8/10/2000
Wayne Higashi	11/2/2004
Fred Hoar	3/6/2000
Jim Hobart	7/16/2004
Richard Hodgson	5/19/1999
Ted Hoff	9/25/2003
Paul Hwoschinsky*	6/3/2003
Paul Hwoschinsky	3/25/1999
David Jeffries	10/4/2002
Steve Jobs*	5/24/2003
Victor Jones	9/6/2002
Alan Jones	7/24/2002
Jean Jones	7/17/2003
Jean Jones	3/3/2000
John Joss	6/3/2002
Bucky Kashiwa	10/29/2004
Hank Kashiwa	9/26/2004
Bob Kaloupek	7/25/2002
Charlotte Matthews Keating	8/26/2002
Frank Keiper	8/2/2002
Frank Keiper	6/19/2002

Arthur Kerman	10/4/2002
Eugene Kleiner	3/19/1999
Don Kobrin	2/17/2000
Steve Kress	7/6/2004
Jim Lafferty*	6/2/2003
Jay Last	11/20/2003
Jay Last	2/9/2004
Jay Last*	2/10/2004
Glenn Leggett	7/23/2002
Jerry Levine*	11/6/2003
Patricia Lindgren	6/18/2002
Bruce Mackay	6/26/2000
Charles Manly	7/24/2002
Mike Markkula*	7/1/2003
Regis McKenna	4/11/2000
Charles and Anne McMurray	7/26/2002
Jack Melchor	8/12/2004
George Messenger	5/20/2002
Gordon Moore*	7/1/2004
Gordon Moore	3/30/1999
Donna Myers	e-mails in Sept. 2002
Ron Newburgh	6/26/2003
Maurice Newstein*	1/17/2003
Hester P. Newton	3/24/2003
Bob Norman	9/6/2000
Penny Noyce	4/9/2002
Bill Noyce	6/26/2003
Bob Noyce (son of Don Noyce)	5/11/2004
Don and Bettie Noyce*	6/25/2002
Gaylord and Dotey Noyce*	10/24/2002
Penny Noyce*	10/22/2004
Ralph Noyce*	5/8/2003
Polly Noyce*	6/24/2003
Keith Olson	7/30/2002
Ken Oshman	9/20/2004
Evan Ramstad	5/24/2002
John Reed	2/15/2000
Sheldon Roberts	1/2/2000
Arthur Rock	2/23/1999
Tadashi Sasaki	10/9/2004
Dan Seligson*	12/3/2003
Harry Sello	1/25/1999
Eugene Sharkoff	9/2/2002

Tom Skornia*	8/20/2004
Robert Smith	7/24/2002
William Spencer	9/1/2000
Nelson Stone	2/5/1999
Charlie Sporck	2/16/1999
Charlie Sporck	12/28/2000
Henry Stroke*	12/4/2002
Bob Teresi*	5/5/2003
Les and Judy Vadasz*	7/30/2002
Don Valentine	11/17/2004
Linda Vognar	5/11/2004
Hugh Watson	10/1/2002
Gene Weckler	5/23/2002
Alfred "Bud" Wheelon*	10/8/2002
Bob and Phyllis White*	11/4/2002
Marianne Woolfe	7/29/2002
Jack Yelverton*	10/3/2003
Ed Zschau	8/25/2004

Appendix B

Robert Noyce's Patents

Number	Title	Issue Date	File Date	Notes
2,875,141	Method and Apparatus for Use in Forming Semiconductive Structures	2/24/1959	8/12/1954	
2,968,750	Transistor Structure and Method of Making the Same	1/17/1961	3/20/1957	
2,929,753	Transistor Structure and Method	3/22/1960	4/11/1957	
3,140,206	Method of Making a Transistor Structure	7/7/1964	4/11/1957	Co-inventor with William Shockley
2,967,985	Transistor Structure	1/10/1961	4/11/1957	Co-inventor with William Shockley
2,869,055	Field Effect Transistor	1/13/1959	9/20/1957	
3,010,033	Field Effect Transistor	11/21/1961	1/2/1958	
3,111,590	Transistor Structure Controlled by an Avalanche Barrier	11/19/1963	6/5/1958	
3,098,160	Field Controlled Avalanche Semi-conductive Device	7/16/1963	2/24/1958	
3,015,048	Negative Resistance Transistor	12/26/1961	5/22/1959	

Number	Title	Issue Date	File Date	Notes
2,971,139	Semiconductor Switching Device	2/7/1961	6/16/1959	
2,959,681	Semiconductor Scanning Device	11/8/1960	6/18/1959	
3,108,359	Method for Fabricating Transistors	10/29/1963	6/30/1959	Co-inventor with Gordon Moore
2,981,877	Semiconductor Device-and-Lead Structure	4/25/1961	6/30/1959	
3,150,299	Semiconductor Circuit Complex Having Isolation Means	9/22/1964	9/11/1959	
3,117,260	Semiconductor Circuit Complexes	1/7/1964	9/11/1959	
3,325,787	Trainable System	6/13/1967	10/19/1964	Co-inventor with James B. Angell and Harley A. Perkins

Index